a History of Psychology

Second Edition

John G. Benjafield

OXFORD

UNIVERSITY PRESS

1904 ❦ 2004

100 YEARS OF
CANADIAN PUBLISHING

OXFORD
UNIVERSITY PRESS

70 Wynford Drive, Don Mills, Ontario M3C 1J9
www.oup.com/ca

Oxford University Press is a department of the University of Oxford.
It furthers the University's objective of excellence in research, scholarship,
and education by publishing worldwide in

Oxford New York

Auckland Bangkok Buenos Aires Cape Town Chennai
Dar es Salaam Delhi Hong Kong Istanbul Karachi Kolkata
Kuala Lumpur Madrid Melbourne Mexico City Mumbai Nairobi
São Paulo Taipei Tokyo Toronto

Oxford is a trade mark of Oxford University Press
in the UK and in certain other countries

Published in Canada by Oxford University Press

National Library of Canada Cataloguing in Publication
Benjafield, John G.
A history of psychology/John G. Benjafield.—2nd ed.
Includes bibliographical references and index.
ISBN 0-19-541820-4

1. Psychology—History. I. Title.

BF81.B3 2005   150'.9   C2004-903880-X

Cover and text design: Brett Miller
Text composition: Valentino Sanna, Ignition Design and Communications

1 2 3 4 - 08 07 06 05

This book is printed on permanent (acid-free) paper ∞.

Printed in Canada

CONTENTS

Chapter 3   The Nineteenth-Century Transformation of Psychology   51

Chapter 4   Wundt and His Contemporaries   71

Chapter 5   William James   84

Chapter 6   Freud and Jung   95

Chapter 7   Structure or Function?   120

Chapter 10   Research Methods   193

Chapter 11   Theories of Learning   207

Chapter 12   The Developmental Point of View   235

Chapter 13   Humanistic Psychology   265

Chapter 14   Cognitive Psychology   289

Chapter 15   The Future of Psychology   315

PREFACE
TO THE SECOND EDITION

Since the first edition of *A History of Psychology* was published in 1996, I have received a great deal of feedback from students that has proven invaluable in reworking this material. I have also benefited from published reviews by Ronald W. Mayer (1997), M. Brewster Smith (1998), and Nadine Weidman (1997), as well as informal advice from numerous colleagues. Participating in a year-long York Seminar for Advanced Research devoted to nineteenth-century psychology proved very informative and stimulating. I am extremely grateful to Chris Green, Marlene Shore, and Thomas Teo, who organized the seminar and edited the results (Green et al., 2001).

The influences I have just outlined provided a wealth of material that has informed this revision. Another important development for any historian of psychology is the appearance of a new journal, *History of Psychology*, which has provided an important forum for scholars in this area. The last few years have been especially fruitful for research in the history of psychology and I have tried to incorporate as much of this new material as I can while still preserving what continues to be relevant from the first edition.

While important changes have been made to each chapter, some of these changes are more notable than others. Chapter 1 now contains a comparison of the similarity of Aristotle's theory of intelligence to a modern version. At the suggestion of reviewers, more material on associationism, particularly in regard to the Mills, has been added to Chapter 2. As pointed out above, there has been a great deal of recent research on nineteenth-century psychology, enriching Chapters 3 (nineteenth-century pioneers), 4 (Wundt and his contemporaries), and 5 (James). Freud and Jung (Chapter 6) continue to be

controversial figures. For example, Freud's 'seduction theory' is the focus of continuing investigation. The contemporary relevance of functional psychology is more clearly brought out in Chapter 7. Intriguing new research has also been brought to bear on Bekhterev, Lashley, and Skinner (Chapter 8). We now have a much fuller understanding of their psychology and its relation to their character and cultural context. Our understanding of Gestalt psychology (Chapter 9) as a movement and its relation to German culture has also benefited from new scholarship. Fisher and the null hypothesis (Chapter 10) have in recent years become a very rich and controversial story. Chapter 11 (Theories of Learning) now contains material on Roger Sperry, whose work had unfortunately been omitted from the first edition. Chapter 12 (The Developmental Point of View) now considers the history of the developmental approach at the University of Toronto, including a discussion of the treatment of the Dionne quintuplets. After being a somewhat dormant force in psychology, the humanistic approach (Chapter 13) shows signs of being appreciated anew. Cognitive psychology (Chapter 14), still one of the dominant orientations in contemporary psychology, has been the focus of much attention from historians, allowing us to appreciate its origins more deeply. All of the topics in Chapter 15, including the nature of paradigms, social constructionism, feminism, and postmodernism, have been intensely investigated recently. Taken as a whole, the new research in the history of psychology demonstrates its continuing relevance to the psychology curriculum.

In addition to the foregoing, the following specific changes have been made to the new edition:

- The bibliography has been made more useful to students. For example, the first edition contained several references to conference papers, and these have been replaced with citations to published material where possible. In general, where multiple citations to the same work exist, that citation most likely to be available to students has been chosen.
- The index has been revised to ensure that students will more easily find topics and people of interest. Gaps in the previous index have been filled, and the student is now given a more sensible and relevant set of headings and sub-headings.
- Introductions have been written for each chapter, and annotated suggested readings and lists of important names, works, and concepts are included at the end of each chapter.

I would like to thank three anonymous reviewers whose comments made this a better book than it would otherwise have been. I would also like to thank Phyllis Wilson and Jesse Bundon for their excellent editorial work at Oxford University Press and Dr Richard Tallman for a splendid job of editing the manuscript.

Finally, I am extremely grateful to David Stover of Oxford University Press, who has been very helpful throughout the preparation of this book, and to Cliff Newman, whose interest in this project made it possible.

CHAPTER 1

TOUCHSTONES: THE ORIGINS OF PSYCHOLOGICAL THOUGHT

Introduction

This book is not like the texts you read in other psychology courses. Rather than being about a specific aspect of psychology, such as personality or learning, this book is about psychology as a whole. Just as we study the history of a life in order to understand why someone turned out as they did, so we study psychology's history to understand the forces that have shaped it and made it into what it is today.

In this chapter, we will examine the origins of psychological thought. People have been asking psychological questions for thousands of years. The questions they have asked are often quite sophisticated, even to the contemporary mind. Western psychology has its roots among the ancient Greeks, whose speculations about the nature of mathematics and its apparent ability to represent reality have been supremely important in the history of Western science. The Greeks also conjectured about such enduring issues as the relation between mind and body, between experience and reality, and the nature of memory. Of course, psychology is not purely a Western invention. For example, Lao-tzu was a Chinese sage whose psychological descriptions were extremely acute and are still relevant to us today. To understand properly the history of psychology, we need to guard against our own cultural biases while examining the development of psychological thought in the English-speaking world.

Touchstones

The word 'touchstone' originally referred to a stone used to test the quality of gold or silver because of the mark it left upon them. Subsequently, 'touchstone' came to mean any criterion by which the value of something is measured. In both this chapter and the next, we will examine some famous thinkers who have left their mark. Their works are touchstones for evaluating the theories that have descended from them. The ideas we will examine in the first two chapters have stood the test of time, and, as the saying goes, 'Time is the only true touchstone of merit.'

Important ideas in psychology or any other discipline do not come out of nowhere. This generation of psychologists draws on a rich store of ideas from previous generations. Throughout history, the contributions of each generation would have been impossible without the foundation laid by its predecessors. It is commonplace for the most profound thinkers to confess their indebtedness to those who have preceded them. A recurring phrase that expresses this indebtedness is that 'We stand on the shoulders of giants' (Manuel, 1965: 69). In these two chapters we will consider the work of some of the giants.

Pythagoras (570–495 BC)

Pythagoras, one of the most famous figures in the Western intellectual tradition, is often characterized as having had a peerless influence on the course of Western thought (e.g., Russell, 1945: 29). Very little can be said with certainty about his life, and so in dealing with Pythagoras we are dealing as much with a mythic as with a real person (e.g., Gorman, 1979). He was often described as having miraculous powers, and even referred to as the incarnation of Apollo, the Greek god most typically associated with otherworldly wisdom. He was thought to have studied in Egypt and to have been initiated into the mathematical and religious secrets of the priesthood there. The mythic aura surrounding Pythagoras is annoying because it prevents us from seeing the person clearly. Historically, however, the myth has captured the thought of many real people. It is the *myth* of Pythagoras that has had such a great influence on the way many people in the West think about the world.

One of the central features of the Pythagorean myth is that he founded a semi-secret society in Italy. The members of this society were supposed to have been able to attune themselves to the *harmony* that ordered the universe. The concept of harmony is a central one in Pythagorean thought. It is closely linked to the notion, which has been so influential in the history of science, that the structure of mathematics is the structure of reality. The story has often been told of how Pythagoras first understood that reality has an underlying mathematical order. It is said that upon hearing the

sounds from a blacksmith's hammers he realized that pitch and the hammer's weight were correlated—high sounds with light hammers, low sounds with heavy hammers. The same sort of correlation obtains between the length of plucked strings and the sound they produce. An example of this kind of relation is shown in Figure 1.1. As one goes up the scale on a piano, the piano strings get progressively shorter. These relations are not arbitrary. Rather, the notes one hears and the lengths of the corresponding strings bear exact relations to one another. There is nothing mythic about the relation between mathematics and music. A provocative contemporary account of this relationship, and its importance for psychology, is given by Leonard Bernstein (1976).

Pythagoras was astounded by his discovery of mathematical relationships in everyday experiences such as listening to music. He felt that he had an insight into the unity of the cosmos. While our experiences are many and varied, they are not chaotic. Rather, the phenomena of our experience are united mathematically.

According to Cornford (1967 [1950], 1974 [1922]), the view that phenomena are ordered mathematically is one way of resolving the puzzles of everyday experience. The Pythagoreans were convinced of the virtue of *unity* and all that this concept implies. Unity implies *wholeness* and *oneness*; a simplicity that is perfect. The opposite of unity is undesirable, leading to *chaos*. It is clear to all of us that everyday life is not a series of purely positive experiences. Rather, we can find all manner of opposing tendencies in our experience: *light* and *dark*; *good* and *evil*; *strong* and *weak*. Although unity and wholeness are what we value, our experience can only be described in terms of contradictory tendencies. A problem felt by every person is how to reconcile the discordant state of affairs we normally experience with the one that we value.

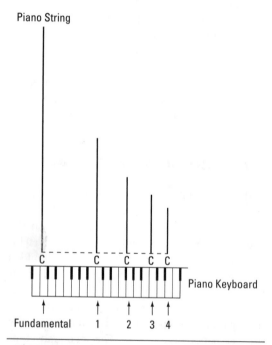

FIGURE 1.1

The relation between different pitches on a piano and the length of the corresponding strings. Source: Bernstein (1976: 23). Reprinted by permission of Harvard University Press. Copyright © 1976 by Leonard Bernstein.

Pythagorean Cosmology

The Pythagoreans responded to this puzzle in a way that is partly distinctive from and partly similar to answers given by thinkers in other, very diverse cultures (Cornford, 1974: 150). As we shall see, there are surprising similarities across ancient world views, ranging from the Pythagorean **cosmology** to the Yin/Yang philosophy of Chinese Taoism (Osgood and Richards, 1973). Many see the universe as initially a unity that becomes differentiated into pairs of opposites. These opposites are then reunited, or *harmonized*, to generate the various forms of life we witness. This conception of the process of creation—from unity to differentiation to integration—is by no means an ancient relic with no relevance to modern thought. In contemporary psychology, the process of *ontogeny* (individual development) is sometimes understood in a similar way, as we will discover in Chapter 12 on developmental psychology. While there are, of course, important differences between the ancient and modern conceptions, it is still correct to say that the basic frames of reference are similar. There are, however, several features of the Pythagorean world view that are elaborated in a distinctive way. The most important of these are their ideas concerning: (a) the nature of *opposites*; and (b) the importance of *number* in regulating phenomena.

The Pythagorean Opposites

The Pythagoreans believed that some pairs of opposites were particularly useful to describe our experience (Cornford, 1939: 6; Philip, 1966). The most important is *limit* versus *unlimited*. This distinction is regarded as crucially important to the process of creation. Opposites arise out of an original unity. The integration of opposites produces the *limited*. We do not experience things that are *unlimited*. Everything we experience has a *limit*. The union of the unlimited and limited produces the world we experience. While this all sounds mysterious, the phenomena the Pythagoreans had in mind are quite obvious. Consider a mundane phenomenon like snow. I know from my own experience that while I am shovelling it, snow seems to be limitless. However, as **Johann Kepler** (1571–1630) observed, if you carefully examine

particles of snow under a magnifying glass, you will see that all snowflakes have 'six corners' (Kepler, 1966 [1611]: 7). Each snow crystal demonstrates that snow, while appearing to be an unlimited substance, in fact has a precise mathematical structure. Similarly, if we examine *any* of our experiences, we will see that each one involves something that is potentially unlimited, like snow, being given a precise mathematical structure, or *limit*. Echoes of the Pythagorean view of phenomena may easily be found in contemporary thought. Thus, a book on natural forms by Stevens (1974) is full of examples of the ways in which natural phenomena take on definite configurations.

> the visual patterns and forms in the natural world . . . are peculiarly restricted . . . the immense variety that nature creates emerges from the working and reworking of only a few formal themes. Those *limitations* on nature bring harmony and beauty to the natural world. (Ibid., 3; emphasis added)

From the Pythagorean conception that the union of limit and unlimited produce all sensible phenomena, it is but a short step to the idea that there should be a proper balance between opposites. When the mixture of opposite tendencies is just right, the result is a *harmony*. Central to Pythagorean doctrine is the concept of *proportion*. When opposites are mixed in the right proportion, there is a harmonious outcome, a **union of opposites** that achieves the unity and integrity we value. The **psyche**, or soul, seeks precisely such a harmony. When it is properly 'tuned', when the opposing forces within the individual are properly blended, then the soul can resonate to other harmonious structures. Specifically, the soul can resonate to the mythic *music of the spheres* that surrounds us always. We seldom hear this 'music' because, as one of Pythagoras's commentators put it, we are like 'bronze smiths who become so accustomed to the noise of their forge that they grow oblivious of it.' We are able to experience harmonious structures around us only if we are organized ourselves to be sympathetic to them. Ordinarily, however, we overlook the beauty that surrounds us, not having reached the state where we can mimic that which would make us most happy. This doctrine is less arcane than it may sound. We have a saying, 'The fish is the last to discover water', which captures the flavour of the Pythagorean notion. Some twentieth-century psychologists (e.g., Köhler, 1960 [1940]: 5) have insisted that the most important phenomena were possessed of a simple, beautiful structure, but, like snowflakes, were often overlooked precisely because they were so simple. Along the same lines, the Russian poet Shkloversuskij (cited by Chomsky, 1968: 21) said:

> People living at the seashore grow so accustomed to the murmur of the waves that they never hear it. By the same token, we scarcely ever hear the words that we utter. We look at each other, but we do not see each other any more. Our perception of the world has withered away; what remains is mere recognition.

Thus, a particularly important task in psychology is to remind ourselves of things that are significant, but so commonplace that we may fail to see their significance. From a Pythagorean viewpoint, the things we overlook are those harmonies developing out of the interplay of opposites.

While *limit versus unlimited* was the most important of the Pythagorean opposites, there were also others such as *good versus evil, light versus dark, odd versus even, unity versus disunity,* and *square versus oblong*. In each case, the first member represents a 'positive' quality, while the second member refers to a 'negative' quality. This evaluation must be understood from within the Pythagorean system. While it seems intuitively obvious to us that, for example, *good* is positive and *evil* negative, it is perhaps less obvious that *limit* is positive and *unlimited* negative. However, the Pythagoreans used these terms in a very precise way. *Unlimited* as it is used here does not carry the positive connotations conveyed by such phrases as 'unlimited resources'.

Rather, that which is unlimited is regarded as being out of balance, as lacking proportion. It is only by putting limits on something that it attains its proper balance. Similarly, *light* is positive and *dark* negative because the former allows us to see things (limited phenomena) that cannot be seen in the limitless dark. The other members of the set of dimensions also are not haphazardly chosen, but are closely related to one another. To illustrate this, let us take the positive terms *odd, unity,* and *square,* and contrast them with their negative opposites *even, plurality,* and *oblong*. A consideration of these dimensions will not only shed light on the logic of Pythagoras's system but also serve to introduce us to Pythagorean mathematics.

Pythagorean Mathematics

In ancient times it was customary for mathematical discussions to make use of pebbles to stand for units and of figures drawn in the sand (Kirk and Raven, 1957: 243; Wheelwright, 1966: 204). Consider the topmost configuration in Figure 1.2 and imagine it as an arrangement of 16 pebbles. At this point it will be useful to introduce the concept of a *gnomon*. Concretely, this word refers to a carpenter's square, but abstractly it means the addition or subtraction of one figure from another figure of the same shape. This may sound confusing, but Figure 1.2 simplifies this. The right-angled line above and to the right of the first pebble in the lower left-hand corner is the first gnomon. It is a part of the total figure that has the same shape as the whole figure. We can add successive gnomons, as indicated by the lines above and to the right of the next three and five pebbles. Notice that as the area enclosed by the gnomons increases in size, it nonetheless retains several invariant features. We begin with *unity* (one pebble), and, as we add successive gnomons, *odd* numbers of pebbles—3, 5, 7, etc.—are enclosed. The figure is always a *square*. By way of contrast, consider the configuration at the bottom right of Figure 1.2. Here we begin not with unity (one pebble), but with two. The successive gnomons enclose *even* numbers—

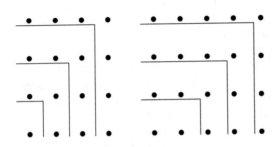

FIGURE 1.2
Pebbles in the sand.

4, 6, 8, etc.—and the figure tends to no definite shape, but rather becomes increasingly *oblong*. The basic contrast between the two figures is that the first has a definite *limit*, and thus the properties of *odd*, *square*, and *unity*, while the second is *unlimited*, being also *plural*, *oblong*, and *even*. These examples show that the Pythagorean opposites were intended to refer to specific occurrences. Moreover, they denote mathematically precise relationships, illustrating the Pythagorean belief that everything that occurs can be described in a mathematically exact way.

The Pythagoreans viewed numbers as underlying all phenomena. Numbers are responsible for uniting the opposites in a harmonious manner. For example, in the sequence of positive integers, *odd* and *even* numbers alternate. This sequence is a *union of opposites*, brought together through number itself. Thus, for the Pythagoreans, number was a property of everything. When we examine things and events, then we discover number *in* them. Cornford (1974: 152) put it this way: 'To him [Pythagoras] numbers and their relations were not only invested with a halo of divine and mysterious properties, but were also implicated in the sensible world, serving as the substructure of reality within that world and occupying space.' The harmony to which numbers gave rise can most clearly be seen in the proportions that parts of geometrical constructions bear to one another. The famous *theorem of Pythagoras* is a demonstration of invariant pro-

portion. The square on the hypotenuse of a right-angled triangle *always* equals the sum of the squares on the other two sides. Thus, consider a right-angled triangle with sides of lengths 3 and 4 units, and a hypotenuse of 5 units, as shown in Figure 1.3. It turns out that $3^2 + 4^2 = 5^2$.

More than one young initiate into the truths of geometry has found the Pythagorean theorem, and others like it, both beautiful and profound. For example, H.E. Huntley (1970: 5) wrote a lovely book on geometry in which he described the enthusiasm of one of his teachers, who had drawn a figure on the blackboard to demonstrate an important geometric relation.

> Striding rapidly up and down between the class and the blackboard, waving his arms about excitedly, with his tattered gown, green with age, billowing out behind him, he spoke in staccato phrases: 'Och, a truly beautiful theorem! Beautiful! . . . Beautiful! Look at it! *Look at it!* What simplicity! What economy!' . . . His voice rises in a crescendo. 'What elegance! . . . Its generality is *astonishing*.' Then, muttering to himself 'Beautiful! . . . beautiful! . . . ,' he stopped, slightly embarrassed . . . , and returned to earth.

If you are fortunate enough to have had such a teacher, then you may have gained an enthusiasm for mathematics yourself. Even if you do not have much of a feeling for mathematics, you should still

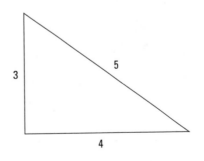

FIGURE 1.3
The theorem of Pythagoras.

appreciate how important such a feeling is in the history of all sciences, including psychology. As we will see, the mathematical analysis of phenomena is a central feature of many branches of psychology. However, the application of mathematics in psychology is sometimes controversial, and at several points we will consider debates about when and if its use is appropriate.

Plato (427–347 BC)

Pythagoras, Plato, and the Problem of the Irrational

We have already discussed the way that the Pythagorean theorem followed from a mathematical view of reality. Ironically, this theorem itself eventually led to a serious difficulty for the Pythagorean world view. For triangles of the right proportions, such as the triangle we considered above, the numbers describing the lengths of the sides were *rational*. For others, however, no rational solution was possible, in the sense that no *integers* could be found to express the lengths (Thompson, 1929). For example, consider a right-angle triangle with sides of 1 unit each, as shown in Figure 1.4; in this case, the sum of squares of the sides $1^2 + 1^2$ equals 2. This means that the square on the hypotenuse must equal 2, and that the

length of the hypotenuse is the square root of 2, or $\sqrt{2}$. The square root of 2 cannot be expressed as a single number; it is an irrational number. Thus, the Pythagoreans came upon the *irrational* as an unavoidable aspect of reality (Chakerian, 1972). The way the Greeks and subsequent thinkers tried to comprehend things that were irrational is an important part of our story.

The **problem of the irrational** became a preoccupation for Greek mathematicians. 'It was the irrational number . . . which was a constant object of search, whose nature as a number was continually in question, and whose genesis as a number cried aloud for explanation or justification' (Thompson, 1929: 44). Following Pythagoras, many attempts were made to solve the problem of the irrational. Thompson shows how this was done for the **Golden Section**, a famous proportion in the history of Western thought (Herz-Fischler, 1998). Rightly or wrongly, it has often been claimed to be a more beautiful proportion than any other, and has been used frequently by artists in their work (Benjafield, 1985; Green, 1995). Moreover, the Golden Section has intrigued many of the psychologists we will study later on (e.g., Fechner, 1871; Hilgard, 1987: 165; Thorndike, 1917; Witmer, 1894; Woodworth, 1938: 384–91).

The Golden Section can be obtained by dividing a line into two segments such that the smaller is to the larger as the larger is to the whole line. A line divided in its Golden Section is shown in Figure 1.5. In that figure, BC/AB = AB/AC. This means that AB is approximately 0.618 of the entire line AC.

The Golden Section is an irrational proportion. Its value can, however, be approximated by using the following series of numbers. Suppose you begin with the numbers 0 and 1, and then generate addi-

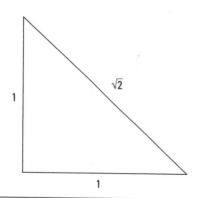

FIGURE 1.4
A root-two right-angle triangle.

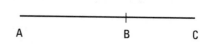

FIGURE 1.5
The Golden Section.

tional numbers such that each one is the sum of the two preceding numbers. Thus the series would go:

$$0, 1, 1, 2, 3, 5, 8, 13, 21, 34, 55, 89, \ldots$$

The series is called the *Fibonacci numbers* after the thirteenth-century mathematician who introduced the Arabic number system into Europe. According to D'Arcy Thompson (1929: p. 52), the ancient Greeks used the properties of the Fibonacci numbers to understand the nature of the irrational. In order to see how they did this, we need to note the close relationship between the Fibonacci numbers and the Golden Section. As the successive numbers in the Fibonacci series become larger and larger, the ratio of any two successive numbers gets closer and closer to the Golden Section, as shown below.

1/2 = 0.50	8/13 = 0.615
2/3 = 0.67	13/21 = 0.619
3/5 = 0.60	21/34 = 0.6176
5/8 = 0.625	34/55 = 0.6182

There are two things to note about the preceding list. The first is that the series very rapidly generates good approximations to the Golden Section. The second is that the successive approximations are alternately greater than and less than the value of the Golden Section, which is 0.6180 to four decimal places.

People often read a lot of meaning into simple facts. In this case, Thompson argued, the Greeks found the relationship between the Fibonacci numbers and the Golden Section full of meaning. The Golden Section is an ideal proportion. A series of numbers that alternately exceeds and falls short of such an ideal value can be used to represent the notion that each particular thing we experience is a more or less imperfect representation of something ideal. No matter how closely we may come to our ideals, we always seem to fall a little bit short or go a little bit too far. Thompson (1929: 55) draws the analogy between the way we try to reach ideals and the process of discovery in science. For example, consider the attempts of biologists to describe a particular species:

> Just as we study the rational forms of an irrational number, and through their narrowing vista draw nearer and nearer to the ideal thing, but always fail to reach it by the little more or the little less; so we may, as it were, survey the whole motley troop of feathered things, only to find each one of them falling short of perfection, deficient here, redundant there: all with their inevitable earthly faults and flaws. Then beyond them all we begin to see dimly a bird such as never was on sea or land, without blemish, whether of excess or defect: it is the ideal *Bird* . . . .

Thompson is presenting us with the notion that each bird we see will be an imperfect example of some ideal Bird. The same would be true of any creature. Each individual dog or cat, for example, only illustrates imperfectly the perfect specimen that would embody all the ideal features of the species. To generalize further, *any* event is only an imperfect illustration of some ideal event. Think of athletics here. Even though judges at the Olympics have occasionally given 'perfect 10s' to a gymnast, or a figure skater, or a diver, are not all athletic performances imperfect, if only slightly? Perhaps it is the *judges* whose performance is the most imperfect of all!

The Forms

The distinction between the way things *appear* and the way things *really are* is a very important distinction, not only in the history of Western thought generally, but in psychology in particular. **Plato** advanced the notion that there are perfect **forms** on the one hand and imperfect appearances on the other. The perfect forms are in an important sense more *real* than the imperfect appearances. Belief in an ideal world of perfect forms can arise as a result of confronting problems such as the nature of the irrational. Such problems can force us to give up seeking answers in the things we experience through our senses, because our senses give us imperfect information. Instead, imagine another world that underlies the one we typically experience, and that contains the perfect forms we seek. Our everyday world is flawed and incapable of satisfying us; perhaps there is another world that has what we are actually looking for. Such Platonic ideas have attracted thinkers for ages, and it is to a consideration of them we now turn.

It is a commonplace to refer to the history of Western thought as but a footnote to Plato. Box 1.1 illustrates the influence of Plato throughout Western history. His philosophy has been the benchmark against which all other subsequent systems of

---

BOX 1.1

THE RELATIVE IMPORTANCE OF PLATO AND OTHER THINKERS

There are many different ways to measure the impact in the English-speaking world of the seminal thinkers we are considering in the first two chapters. An imperfect, but interesting, way of measuring their relative importance is to count the number of times they are mentioned in the *Oxford English Dictionary* (OED). The OED is one of the standard reference works for the English language. The print version of the 1989 edition was 20 volumes, 22,000 pages, and defined over 500,000 words. The OED is one of the great scholarly achievements of the English-speaking world. A useful feature of the OED is that it not only provides such information as the part of speech, pronunciation, and etymology of each word, but also includes quotations to illustrate the various senses of a word. Thus, to take an arbitrary example, the word 'tufthunter' is defined as someone 'who meanly or obsequiously courts the acquaintance of persons of rank and title . . . at the universities'. It goes on to give several quotations containing this word, including one dated 1789 from a periodical titled the Loiterer, stating that tuft-hunting has a long history of occurrence at Oxford. There are nearly 2.5 million quotations like this in the OED.

Because the *Oxford English Dictionary* is available on CD-ROM (1992), it is possible to search the dictionary and discover how often a theorist such as Plato is mentioned. It turns out that there are 2,918 mentions of Plato occurring in entries for such words as 'academic', 'beauty', 'idea', 'mathematics', 'mind', and 'symposium'.

Below is a table giving the frequencies with which the theorists considered in the first two chapters are mentioned in the OED. This is only one possible measure of a theorist's impact, and obviously applies only to the English-speaking world. Notice that Plato outranks such native English speakers as Darwin, Newton, and Hume. This is a testament to the centrality of Plato in the history of Western thought. However, the point has often been made that Western intellectual history can be ethnocentric. To be ethnocentric is to regard the values of one's own culture as superior to those of any other culture. Ethnocentrism acts to reduce our ability to appreciate the virtues of different forms of thought in other cultures, as well as the thought of people in our own culture who do not share its typical values. For example, many of us in the English-speaking world may have emphasized the thought of English-speaking men and not paid enough attention to the thought of English speaking women, not to mention the thought of people from non-English-speaking cultures. Notice that the last three people in the table below are a woman, a Chinese sage, and a French philosopher.

Name	Frequency of mention
Plato	2,918
Darwin	2,408
Newton	1,929
Hume	1,634
Aristotle	806
Kant	393
Pythagoras	162
Descartes	109
Wollstonecraft	81
Lao-tzu	7

thought have been measured. In large part, his significance is the result of his ability to articulate the implications of the thought of his predecessors. Much of Platonic thought was an extension of the Pythagorean doctrines we considered earlier (Sambursky, 1956: 43). We have already seen how one possible outcome of the search for the irrational is a belief in perfect 'forms' that underlie the world of appearances. From a Platonic point of view, it is possible to gain knowledge of these forms, but we are usually not aware of them. The phenomena with which we interact are mere 'shadows' of their forms, or essences.

Plato advanced his theories by means of dialogues in which Socrates was the protagonist. **Socrates** (469–399) was one of the great figures of ancient Greece. It is difficult to separate Plato's ideas from those originating with Socrates. Much more was written about him than appeared in Plato's dialogues (Ferguson, 1970), but it is largely through Plato's dialogues that Socrates is familiar to us today. Following Weimer (1973), we will focus on one of these dialogues, the *Meno*.

The *Meno* developed a typical theme that runs throughout all the dialogues. Here is the beginning of the dialogue, spoken by Meno (Hamilton and Cairns, 1961: 354).

> Can you tell me, Socrates—is virtue something that can be taught? Or does it come by practice? Or is it neither teaching nor practice that gives it to a man but natural aptitude or something else?

Psychology students will recognize this as a type of question that still arises in practically all areas of psychology. Whether it is the nature of virtue (or morality), or any other psychological concept such as *intelligence* or *personality*, we can always ask whether or not it is something we learn or something we have innately. Are people innately virtuous (or immoral)? Is a person's intelligence innately determined, or is it acquired? Is temperament given innately, or is it learned?

Socrates makes the point that it is very difficult to define concepts such as *virtue*. Any definition

that is proposed includes either too much or too little, is either too narrow or too broad. While Meno is able to give examples of virtuous behaviour, he is unable to answer the question 'What is virtue?' by specifying what it is that all virtuous behaviours have in common (ibid., 355). Again, this is a recurrent problem with any psychological concept. As we shall see in Chapter 5, when psychologists in the twentieth century became fascinated with the concept of *intelligence*, they were able to come up with many different examples of intelligence, such as the ability to remember strings of numbers (digit span), the ability to give the meanings of words (vocabulary), and so on. Nevertheless, a great debate has raged over precisely what is meant by the term *intelligence* and whether or not intelligence is innate or acquired. It is just this kind of question Plato (through Socrates) was exploring in the *Meno*.

Socrates proposed to resolve the problem by suggesting that someone cannot 'know what a part of virtue is, without knowing the whole' (ibid., 362). That is, we would not be able to give examples of virtue unless we knew what virtue itself really was.

> Thus the soul, since it is immortal and has been born many times, and has seen all things both here and in the other world, has learned everything that is. So we need not be surprised if it can recall the knowledge of virtue or anything else which, as we see, it once possessed. All nature is akin, and the soul has learned everything, so that when a man has recalled a single piece of knowledge—*learned* it in ordinary language—there is no reason why he should not find out all the rest, if he keeps a stout heart and does not grow weary of the search, for seeking and learning are in fact nothing but recollection. (Ibid., 364)

A famous example of the process of awakening **innate knowledge** is given by Plato in the *Meno*, where he describes the ability of Socrates to elicit from a slave boy the solution to Pythagoras's theorem. The point of his interrogation of the boy is to demonstrate that the solution is already 'known' in the sense of being a deduction from what the boy knows innately. A more recent illustration of the same kind of point comes from the work of the German psychologist Max Wertheimer (1959). Wertheimer was a member of a group of psychologists called *Gestalt psychologists*. We will study them in detail in Chapter 9. For now all you need to know is that **gestalt** means 'form' or 'configuration', and the gestalt psychologists stressed the importance of innate tendencies towards 'good form'. Thus, for them, our experience is shaped by our innate tendencies towards 'good form'. An example of this notion is Wertheimer's so-called 'altar window problem', which is illustrated in Figure 1.6. Read the description of the problem given in the caption to Figure 1.6, and see if you can solve it without reading any further.

It is easy to find the area of the window itself, since it is just a circle. Similarly, it is easy to find the

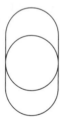

FIGURE 1.6

The altar window problem: Painters are at work, painting and decorating the inner walls of a church. Above the altar there is a circular window. For decoration, the painters have been asked to draw two vertical lines tangent to the circle, and of the same height as the circular window; they were then to add half circles above and below, closing the figure. This area between the lines and the window is to be covered with gold. For every square inch, so and so much gold is needed. How much gold will be needed to cover this space (given the diameter of the circle); or, what is the area between the circle and the lines?

Source: Wertheimer (1959: 266) Copyright © 1959 by Valentin Wertheimer; renewed © 1987 by Michael Wertheimer. Reprinted by permission of Harper-Collins Publishers, Inc.

area of the semi-circles at the top and the bottom of the figure. However, that leaves the problem of finding the area of 'the four funny remainders'.

Wertheimer gave this problem to a child with no mathematical training, whose first reaction to the problem was to say that, of course, he could not solve it. Immediately thereafter, however, he realized that the top and bottom semi-circles fit inside the window. Thus, the solution to the problem is simply to find the area of the square drawn with its sides tangent to the circle. If you cannot see this solution, ask a friend to help you with it.

Wertheimer's example is congruent with that of Socrates and the slave boy. In both cases, the solution to a problem *emerges* on the basis of what the child already knows. The child is capable of seeing certain necessary relationships, and this (apparently) innate ability is all that is required to enable him to derive the solution. The implication of both Plato's and Wertheimer's analysis is that we are all in possession of all we need to know to understand fully our experience. However, we must draw out the implications of what we already know.

From this point of view, then, the difficulties we experience in everyday life stem from an inability to perceive essential relationships. Since, from the Platonic viewpoint, the ability to perceive relationships is given innately, our difficulties are due to our inability to *remember* the basic ideas that allow us to organize our experiences in a meaningful way. Often we act as if we have forgotten what we most need to know, and behave as if we have lost touch with those ideas that could give our experience depth and meaning. 'All so-called learning is actually remembering . . . there is no real "learning" at all. This is the doctrine of *anamnesis* (recollections)' (Weimer, 1973: 16). A skilled, 'Socratic' teacher is one who can make the student aware of what she or he already knows, but does not know that she/he knows.

If our deepest and most important ideas are innate, then what is the origin of these innate ideas? This is one of the most recurrent issues in psychology, and many different reasons for the existence of innate ideas have been given. From the Platonic viewpoint, innate ideas exist because 'the human soul is immortal (divine) and is purified through a round of incarnations, from which, when completely purified, it may finally escape' (Cornford, 1960 [1935]: 2). Recall the quotation from the *Meno* given earlier: 'Thus the soul, since it is immortal and has been born many times, and has seen all things both here and in the other world, has learned everything that is' (Hamilton and Cairns, 1961: 364). This is a religious view of the origin of innate knowledge, and it has had several defenders over the millennia. However, we will come across several other interpretations of the nature of innate knowledge as we go along, so keep an eye out for them.

Lao-tzu (sixth century BC)

Lao-tzu is as much of a mythical figure as Pythagoras, there even being some debate about whether or not he actually existed (Kaltenmark, 1969; Lau, 1963). He was said to have lived a very long life, and one of the meanings of 'Lao-tzu' is old man. At that time in China old age and wisdom were thought to go together, an insight that seems to have been rediscovered (e.g., Baltes and Staudinger, 1993). Lao-tzu is an example of a *sage*. According to the *Oxford English Dictionary*, a *sage* is 'A person of profound wisdom; especially one of those persons of ancient history or legend who were traditionally famous as the wisest of mankind.' The wisdom of Lao-tzu is called **Taoism**.

The Tension between Confucianism and Taoism

Many people today are similar to people in ancient China in that they have the same desire for explicit guidelines for dealing with the problems that arise in everyday life. Just as there is no shortage today of advisers to tell us how to live (many of whom are psychologists), so it was in ancient China. We will come to Lao-tzu's advice presently, but first we should briefly consider the contrasting advice

given by another great Chinese sage, **Confucius**. The advice of Confucius affirmed the importance of developing one's intelligence through education and of following traditional values, such as loyalty to one's family and to one's government (Kaltenmark, 1969: 9).

Bond and Hwang (1986: 216) summarize the recommendations of **Confucianism** as follows. People 'exist through, and [are] defined by, [their] relationships to others; . . . these relationships are structured hierarchically; . . . social order is ensured through each party's honoring the requirements in the role relationship.' Important role relationships, such as being a father, a son, or a friend, provided a framework within which social behaviour was regulated.

A famous incident in the story of Lao-tzu's life was an encounter he had with Confucius. In descriptions of this meeting, it almost appears as if Lao-tzu is making fun of Confucian traditionalism. Here is a part of what Lao-tzu is supposed to have said to Confucius (from Kaltenmark, 1969: 8):

> The man who is intelligent and clear-sighted will soon die, for his criticisms of others are just; the man who is learned and discerning risks his life, for he exposes others' faults. The man who is a son no longer belongs to himself; the man who is a subject no longer belongs to himself.

Although Confucianism and Taoism share much in common, Taoism is typically regarded as less explicit and more mystical. Confucianism emphasized the social and moral order, to the exclusion of an interest in natural phenomena. By contrast, Taoism treated the natural and social orders as continuous (Ronan and Needham, 1978: 94). As the great scholar Joseph Needham (1962: 33) put it, Confucianism 'was masculine and managing: the Taoists condemned it and sought after a feminine and receptive knowledge which could arise only as the fruit of a passive and yielding attitude in the observation of Nature.' For the Taoist, both nature and society worked the same way. Everything illustrated the Tao.

What Is Tao?

The simplest translation of the word *Tao* is 'the Way', which referred to the 'way in which the Universe worked; in other words, the order of Nature . . . which brought all things into existence and governs their every action, not so much by force as by . . . controlling the orderly processes of change' (ibid., 36).

The writings attributed to Lao-tzu are called the **Tao Te Ching**. Here is an oft quoted passage from the *Tao Te Ching* that illustrates the Taoist preoccupation with the nature of change (Lau, 1963: 139).

Is not the way of heaven like the stretching
  of a bow?
The high it presses down,
The low it lifts up;
The excessive it takes from,
The deficient it gives to.

This passage expresses the belief that any situation is always in the process of changing into its opposite. This means that it is fruitless to search for something that does not change. Many scholars (e.g., Wilhelm, 1975: 15) have compared the Taoist view of change to that of the Greek philosopher Heraclitus (*c*. 540–*c*. 470 BC). The following quotation from Heraclitus (Wheelwright, 1966: 71) illustrates this similarity to Taoism: 'You cannot step into the same river twice, for other waters and yet others go ever flowing on.'

This emphasis on the pervasiveness of change should be contrasted with Plato's views (Lau, 1963: 20). While Plato believed that it was possible to discover a permanent world of forms behind the flow of everyday experience, for the Taoist such a hope is illusory. The Tao cannot be 'discovered' or 'named' (ibid., 91):

The way is forever nameless . . .
Only when it is cut are there names
As soon as there are names
One ought to know that it is time to stop.

What we can describe are individual phenomena. However, we cannot give a general description of the Tao that 'explains' all individual phenomena. The Tao resists description because any name that can be applied to it is misleading: 'Dimly visible, it cannot be named' (ibid., 93).

As was mentioned above, Taoism emphasizes the virtue of a passive observation of nature (Needham, 1962: 57). Such passivity does not impose itself upon nature but is open to observing what is actually there. In a way, this aspect of Taoism anticipates what has become a very important aspect of scientific observation. When properly conducted, science makes no assumptions about what nature *must* be; it is not founded on dogmatic principles. Rather, it begins with observations of what *actually* happens, regardless of what anyone's theory says *should* be happening.

The Book of Changes

Many of you will have come across the **I Ching**, or *Book of Changes* (1967). As an expression of ancient Chinese culture, it has an affinity with both Confucian and Taoist ideas. The *I Ching* has fascinated many Western scholars, from **G.W. Leibniz** (1646–1716) to **C.G. Jung** (1875–1961).

At its most superficial level, the *I Ching* is a fortune-telling device. Wanting to predict one's future is a pervasive wish today just as it was in ancient China. In order to make such predictions, one needs a system for codifying possible future outcomes. It is here that the *I Ching* is particularly prescient, because its codification scheme involves what later came to be known as a *binary* number system.

A binary system uses only two values, such as 1 and 0. In the *I Ching*, these two values are labelled **Yang and Yin**. Yang and Yin represent the fundamental cosmic forces. Yang and Yin may be characterized by opposing pairs of adjectives, with Yang representing that which is masculine, firm, and light, while Yin stands for that which is feminine, yielding, and dark (Osgood and Richards, 1973). In general, Yang and Yin are both equally important, although one or the other may predominate in a particular situation. As it says in the *I Ching* (1967: 297–8):

> That which lets now the dark, now the light appear is tao . . . . The primal powers never come to a standstill; the cycle of becoming continues uninterruptedly. The reason is that between the two primal powers there arises again and again a state of tension, a potential that keeps the powers in motion and causes them to unite, whereby they are constantly regenerated. Tao brings this about without ever becoming manifest. The power of tao to maintain the world by constant renewal of a state of tension between the polar forces, is designated as good.

Notice that change is conceptualized as cyclical. This sense of 'a movement that returns to its starting point . . . may have been derived from the orbits of the heavenly bodies or the course of the seasons. . . . The notion of progress . . . is alien to the ancient concept of change' (Wilhelm, 1975: 19–20). This conception of historical change as cyclical is a possibility we will need to take seriously. As we go along we consider further the question of whether or not the history of psychology involves more repetition than progress.

A simple and easily understood way of representing **cyclical change** is by means of a circle. In the *I Ching*, this is accomplished by using a circular diagram like that in Figure 1.7. This circular diagram is generated by combining trigrams, each of which is composed of three lines. Each line is either solid (Yang) or broken (Yin). There are eight unique trigrams. For example, a trigram of three unbroken (Yang) lines is called *Ch'ien: the Creative*, while its opposite is a trigram of three broken (Yin) lines, called *K'un: the Receptive*. The entire set of trigrams is given in Figure 1.8. Notice that each row of Figure 1.8 contains four Yang and four

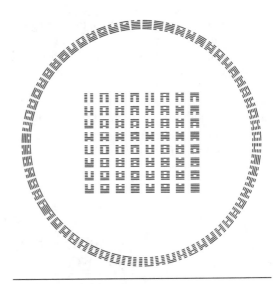

FIGURE 1.7
The circular structure of the *I Ching*.
Source: H. Wilhelm (1975: 84).
Reprinted by permission.

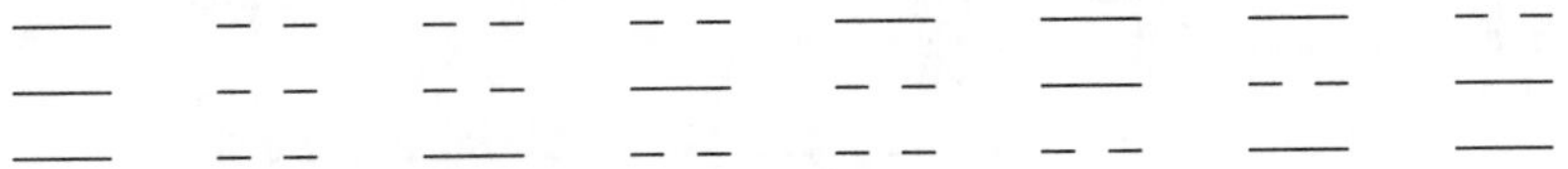

Yin lines, and that the eight trigrams represent all possible combinations of three solid/broken lines. The 64 hexagrams of Figure 1.7 are obtained by combining the eight trigrams in all possible ways. Each hexagram has a different name and represents a different possible state of affairs. For example, at the bottom of Figure 1.7, the hexagram containing all broken lines is called *K'un: the Receptive*, and represents 'the nature of the earth, strong in devotion; among the seasons it stands for late autumn, when all the forces of life are at rest' (Wilhelm, 1967: li). At the top of the circle is *Ch'ien: the Creative*, which has the opposite meaning to *K'un*. 'Ch'ien . . . whose symbol is heaven . . . is associated with the Chinese fourth month, approximately our May—that is, the time when growth and flowering is at a peak' (Wilhelm, 1975: 50).

FIGURE 1.8
The eight trigrams underlying the *I Ching*.

For our purposes, the fact that the *I Ching* has traditionally been used to tell fortunes is not its most important feature. What has intrigued scholars such as Leibniz is the fact that the *I Ching* begins with a simple binary arithmetic from which is constructed a model of all possible situations (Mungello, 1977; Wilhelm, 1975: 90–2). Moreover, the circular structure enables the representation of the way that phenomena may be transformed over time.

Circular models are quite common in the history of psychology, although they are typically models of much smaller scope than the *I Ching*. Such models, often called **circumplexes**, have been created for many domains in psychology. In Western psychology, the most pervasive circumplex model has been **Galen's typology** of temperaments. Galen (*c.* 130–*c.* 200) identified four temperaments, called *melancholic* (or pessimistic); *sanguine* (or sociable); *choleric* (or proud); and

---

BOX 1.2

WHERE ARE WE NOW?
A SUMMARY AND SOME IMPLICATIONS

So far we have considered the contrasting views of Pythagoras, Plato, and Lao-tzu. Now is a good time to take a breather, and try to spell out some of the major issues that emerge from a consideration of these three. The following issues can be traced back to the period we are considering, although they have been formulated in different ways at different times. Regardless of how they are put, these issues are still capable of generating debate in psychology, and we will have an opportunity of seeing different generations of psychological theorists deal with them.

1. *Nature versus culture.* Taoism treats human behaviour as a part of the natural order, and not as something different from other natural phenomena. An alternative approach would be to regard human behaviour as determined by principles unique to it. For example, culture might have so powerful an effect on behaviour as to make it impossible to understand as a purely natural phenomenon. The issue here is this: Can human behaviour be understood in the same way as we understand natural phenomena, or must it be understood in terms of its own culturally determined rules?

2. *Process versus structure.* Taoism treats change as the fundamental characteristic of experience. **Platonism** encourages us to seek a perfect world of unchanging forms. This issue can be phrased as follows: Is psychology best seen as the study of *processes* in continuous change, or is it best seen as the study of the underlying *structures* that determine behaviour? What is the relation between process and structure? As we will see, the great American psychologist William James (1890) compared consciousness to a stream, just as Heraclitus compared life to a stream. If consciousness is like a stream, then nothing recurs in it. If nothing recurs, then can it have any permanent structure?

3. *The individual case versus the general law.* If it turned out to be true that our experience has no an underlying structure, then there would appear to be nothing very general that can be said about human behaviour. Each person's life will be relatively unique, and it would be pointless to try to see his or her behaviour as the result of some general laws. However, if, as Pythagoras believed, everything has a mathematical structure, then everything will be an illustration of an underlying law.

4. *Pure observation versus theory-driven observation.* The Taoist approach to observation was to make no assumptions about what we will find in nature. Perhaps observation should be passive, and not determined by theoretical preconceptions. If our observations of behaviour are determined by a preconceived theory, then we may not be open to observing what people actually do. However, is it always wise to approach the study of behaviour without a theory? Does not a good theory provide direction to one's exploration of nature?

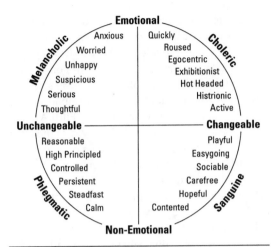

FIGURE 1.9
Galen's circumplex model of temperament.
Source: Eysenck & Eysenck (1985: 45).
Reprinted by permission of the author and Kluwer
Academic/Plenum Publishers.

phlegmatic (or controlled). These four temperaments can be arranged in a circle as in Figure 1.9.
This model has influenced many subsequent
psychologists (Martindale and Martindale, 1988;
Miller, 1988). Other areas in which circumplex
models have been applied in psychology include
colour (e.g., Goethe, 1970 [1840]: lvii), facial
expression (e.g., Schlosberg, 1952), interpersonal
characteristics (e.g., Kiesler, 1983), and emotion
(e.g., Russell, 1980). We will examine some of
these models later on. Box 1.2 summarizes the
major issues with which we have dealt thus far.

Aristotle (384–323 BC)

Aristotle's Differences with Plato

As a young man, **Aristotle** studied with Plato at the
Academy in Athens. After Plato's death, Aristotle
left Athens and subsequently became tutor to the
young man who was to become Alexander the
Great. Upon returning to Athens, he founded his
own school, called the Lyceum. Aristotle's mature

philosophy is among the most influential in the
history of Western culture. Let us begin a consideration of Aristotle's contributions to psychology by
sketching the way in which his views differed from
those of Plato.

In the first place, Aristotle rejected Plato's theory of forms. Recall that Plato believed there was a
world of ideal forms existing independently of the
world of ordinary experience. Aristotle argued
instead that form and matter were intertwined.
Matter does not exist without form, nor does
form exist without matter. Far from being arcane,
Aristotle's point is an expression of what has
become common sense in Western culture. In
order to see how intuitively obvious Aristotle's
point is, let us briefly consider an argument made
by the linguist Benjamin Lee Whorf (1897–1941).
Whorf (1956) suggested that all of us in the
Western world unconsciously construct our experience in a particular way, and observed that we
commonly 'carve up' reality into units defined by
the general formula *form-plus-substance*. Thus, we
say 'a *quart* of *milk*' and not just 'a *milk*'; 'a *kilogram*
of *meat*' and not 'a *meat*'; a '*snow crystal*' and not
just 'a *snow*'. This is close to Aristotle's view: we
ordinarily understand all substances as having
particular forms, and that forms cannot exist apart
from the substances they shape.

Aristotle observed that substances had the
potential to take on different forms. What a substance *actually* became depended on the form it
took. Baumrin (1975: 487) uses the following
example to illustrate how the distinction between
potentiality and actuality worked in the case of
living beings.

> By way of illustration, consider the stillborn
> fetus. It is a body that is both material and has
> form but not soul. Its body is the sort of body
> that could potentially live; moreover it actually
> had to have been alive for some time to have the
> form it has at birth. The soul is both the form of
> a living body in the sense that it is the organiza-
> tion of that body and in the sense that it is the
> life of that body when it is alive.

The distinction between a living and a dead body is that the former has what Baumrin calls a soul. However, different living things have different powers, and Aristotle compared the powers possessed by plants, animals, and human beings. Plants fulfill minimal conditions for being alive in that 'they grow up and down, and everything that grows increases its bulk alike in both directions or indeed in all, and continues to live so long as it can absorb nutriment' (McKeon, 1941: 557).

At the next level are creatures with 'the power of sensation'. What distinguishes animals from plants is that the former have senses, such as touch: 'The primary form of sense is touch, which belongs to all animals' (ibid.). Aristotle argued that human beings have five senses: vision, the sense of sound (audition), the sense of smell (olfaction), the sense of taste, and touch. This fivefold classification of the senses became 'common sense', and 'has upon it the sanction of the centuries' (Geldard, 1972: 258).

In addition to the powers of 'self-nutrition' and sensation, human beings also possess the power to think (McKeon, 1941: 559). To Aristotle, reasoning seemed like a peculiarly human attribute, and he delineated the forms of reasoning in great detail. Among these forms, Aristotle was particularly interested in the **syllogism**. A syllogism consists of two premises and a conclusion, and in a valid syllogism the conclusion follows necessarily from the premises. There are a great many forms of valid syllogism, but one of particular interest to Aristotle was the so-called *practical syllogism*. We use practical syllogisms when 'the conclusion drawn from the two premises becomes an action' (Henle, 1968 [1962]: 103). Here is an example of a practical syllogism.

Premise 1: It is necessary for me to understand psychology as a whole.

Premise 2: The only way to understand psychology as a whole is through the study of the history of psychology.

Conclusion: Therefore, it is necessary for me to study the history of psychology.

You may disagree with the premises, but if you accept them, then the conclusion necessarily follows. Henle has provided examples showing that the practical syllogism is a very common feature of everyday life. One of her examples is the following: 'It is too far to walk to the public library; I must take the subway or bus. The Fifth Avenue bus passes the Public Library. I must take the Fifth Avenue bus' (ibid., 103). Henle goes on to observe that 'it is difficult to see how the individual could cope with the ordinary tasks of life if the practical syllogism embodied techniques which are not . . . the common property of the unsophisticated subject' (ibid.). The practical syllogism is an illustration of the way our behaviour is regulated by our reason. Our ability to reason is what most distinguishes human beings from other forms of life.

Aristotle believed certain parts of the soul, particularly the power of reason, were indestructible. This meant that even though bodily functions decline throughout the process of normal aging, reason is left intact. However, it may *seem* as if reason declines, because the body declines, and the body is the only vehicle through which reason can express itself. In the following quotation, the word *impassible* means 'to be incapable of suffering or pain'. Thus, to say the mind is impassible means that it is not prone to the diseases and degeneration that may afflict an aging person.

The case of mind is different; it seems to be an independent substance implanted within the soul and to be incapable of being destroyed. If it could be destroyed at all, it would be under the influence of old age. What really happens in respect of mind in old age is, however, exactly parallel to what happens in the case of the sense organs; if the old man could recover the proper kind of eye, he could see just as well as the young man. The incapacity of old age is due to an affection not of the soul but of its vehicle, as occurs in drunkenness or disease. Thus it is that in old age the activity of mind or intellectual apprehension declines only through the decay of some other inward part; mind itself is impassible. (McKeon, 1941: 548)

The issue, then, is whether reason itself declines, or whether its full expression is prevented because of disease or decay in other parts of the body, such as the brain. Although this is an ancient question, its relevance has not diminished with the passage of time. Consider the cases depicted by the neurologist Oliver Sacks (1973). In his book *Awakenings*, which was subsequently made into a film, Sacks described patients with Parkinson's disease. People who have severe cases of Parkinsonism may deteriorate into 'a 'frozen' state of rigid immobility and unresponsiveness to external stimuli' (Flowers, 1973: 590) that may persist for several years. However, this does not mean that their mental life has irreversibly ceased. Sacks described several cases of people who, as a result of drug therapy, were 'awakened' for at least a while, and showed signs of reason and other mental powers where there had appeared to be none before. Aristotle would surely have seen such 'awakenings' as illustrations of his point that the mind is impassible, and able to recover with the appropriate therapy to the appropriate parts of the body (in this case, the brain). Although contemporary neurologists would, no doubt, offer other, and vastly more detailed, accounts of such phenomena, the view that people have souls, and that the soul is indestructible, is still very widely held in many cultures.

The Nature of Human Action

If we follow Aristotle and say that human behaviour can be regulated by reason, then we will expect people to be able to give reasons for their actions. These reasons are usually statements of what Aristotle called the *final cause*. Final causes are 'the end, i.e., that for the sake of which a thing is, e.g., health is the cause of walking. For "Why does one walk?" we say "that one may be healthy"; and in speaking thus we think we have given the cause' (McKeon, 1941: 752). Human behaviour appears to be *purposive*. We act with certain ends in mind, and those ends may explain our action. Thus, if you meet me when I am out walking and

ask me what I am doing, I may explain myself by saying that I am walking for my health. My health is the goal that determines my behaviour.

Hamlyn (1962 [1953]: 63) has shown how Aristotle's conception of human action requires us to distinguish **action versus motion**. Actions can be accomplished in a variety of ways. Thus, suppose I want to mail a letter. I may accomplish this through any number of bodily movements. For example, I may open the letter box with my right hand, or with my left hand. It is impossible to specify the particular movements required to accomplish an action. It follows that an explanation of bodily movements will not be a complete explanation of action. A complete explanation of actions will involve the actor's reasons for behaving in a particular way.

If someone pushes me off the edge of the Grand Canyon, then my fall is aptly described as motion. This simple motion can be given a completely mechanical explanation—someone applied a force to my back, and then gravity took over. Falling into the Grand Canyon is not something for which I can give an explanation in terms of my goals. However, if I am *walking* down a trail towards the floor of the Canyon, then it is reasonable to expect me to be able to give an explanation of my behaviour in terms of my goal. Thus, if I am asked why I am walking down the trail, I might answer that I want to be able to appreciate the canyon from that vantage point.

Psychology is often defined as the study of *behaviour*. As Hamlyn (ibid., 62) observed, the word 'behaviour' is often used in an ambiguous way. Sometimes 'behaviour' refers to the movements that organisms make; other times it refers to their actions. The explanation of behaviour may require more than an explanation of bodily movements; it may also require an explanation in terms of the person's goals or purposes. Explanations in terms of goals are called teleological. The role of **teleological explanations** of behaviour has often been problematic in the history of psychology, and we will return to this issue often as we go along.

Memory

Aristotle defined memory as the process whereby a person revives a previous experience. **Memory** involves the 'reinstatement in consciousness of something which was there before but had disappeared' (McKeon, 1941: 613). Aristotle is often called the originator of the notion that memory is governed by *associations* (e.g., Mandler and Mandler, 1964: 8). For an associationist, one idea will follow another in memory if they were previously experienced in relation to each other. The doctrine of associationism is very important in the history of psychology, and we will follow its development closely.

According to Aristotle, when we try to remember something we follow a chain of associated ideas until we succeed in recovering what it is we wanted to recall. We may not find what we want to remember right away. Rather, there may be a sequence of ideas that begins with 'something either similar, or contrary, to what we seek, or else from that which is contiguous with it' (McKeon, 1941: 612). The hypothesis that associations are produced by *similarity*, *contrast*, and *contiguity* is one of Aristotle's most important contributions.

1. *Association by similarity* means that we tend to be reminded of something to the extent that it resembles what we are currently experiencing. For example, upon thinking of Plato we may then think of Aristotle because they both share many common properties, such as being not only ancient and Greek, but also philosophers.
2. *Association by contrast* refers to the fact that we are sometimes reminded of something to the extent that it means the opposite of what we are currently experiencing. Thus, if I ask you to say the first thing that comes into your head when I say *black*, you are liable to respond with *white*.
3. *Association by contiguity* occurs whenever we are reminded of something because it had been previously experienced together with whatever we are currently experiencing. For example, if I ask you to say the first thing that comes into your head when I say *salt*, you are liable to respond with *pepper* because salt and pepper shakers tend to be side by side.

These three can be called the first **laws of association**. Over the years, there has been a great deal of debate about the relationships of these three laws and which of them is most important. We will develop the story of associationism in Chapter 2 when we come to the British empiricists. However, we should not leave Aristotle's account of memory without noting that it contained more than just the principles of association. For example, Aristotle noted that 'recollection is, as it were, a mode of inference. For he who endeavors to recollect *infers* that he formerly saw, or heard, or had some such experience, and the process . . . is, as it were, a sort of investigation' (ibid., 616). Here Aristotle is suggesting that recollection can be more like imagination than a literal rendition of the past.

Mnemonics

The central role of imagination in memory was well known to the ancients. Imagination played a crucial part in their elaborate **mnemonic techniques**. A mnemonic technique is a way of improving your memory, and we have probably all used mnemonic techniques at one time or another. For example, if I want to remember to buy eggs, cherries, lemons and margarine at the supermarket, I may take the first letters of each item, rearrange them, and make a name out of them, such as CLEM. Then all I have to do is remember the one word rather than the four items and properly decode the word when I am in the supermarket. Such simple mnemonics are feeble attempts when compared to the elaborate mnemonic techniques described by Aristotle and practised from ancient times throughout the Middle Ages and into the Renaissance (Carruthers, 1990).

Ancient memory systems were explored by Frances Yates in *The Art of Memory* (1966). She begins by presenting an outline of mnemonics given in an anonymous document called the *Ad Herennium*, written in the first century BC. Written for students, it describes an **artificial memory** that would enable someone who was properly trained to recall accurately a great many items. The system is called an 'artificial memory' to distinguish it from the memory we have naturally, without training. In order to develop an artificial memory, a student would have to invest a considerable amount of time and effort, as we shall see.

The artificial memory has two parts, places (loci) and images. 'A *locus* is a place easily grasped by the memory, such as house, an intercolumnar space, a corner, an arch, or the like. Images are forms, marks . . . of what we wish to remember. For example, if we wish to recall the genus of a horse, of a lion, of an eagle, we must place their images on definite *loci*' (ibid., 6). The 'art of memory' involves creating a memory that can be read like a book.

> The art of memory is like an inner writing. Those who know the letters of the alphabet can write down what is dictated to them and read out what they have written. Likewise those who have learned mnemonics can set in places what they have heard and deliver it from memory. For the places are very much like wax tablets or papyrus, the images like the letters, the arrangement and disposition of the images like the script, and the delivery is like the reading. (Ibid., 6–7)

Learning a set of *loci* is the would-be mnemonist's first task. It was necessary to learn a great many *loci* by following these rules:

- The *loci* must be learned in a particular serial order, and overlearned so that the student could imagine going in either direction from any particular *locus*. Aristotle was apparently referring to this ability when he described people who 'are supposed to recollect sometimes by starting from mnemonic *loci*' (McKeon, 1941: 614).
- *Loci* should be selected from 'a deserted and solitary place' such as a building when no one is around (Yates, 1966: 7).

- The *loci* should be as much unlike one another as possible.
- The *loci* should be a fair distance apart, and bright. The *Ad Herennium* suggests a distance of about 30 feet.
- Every fifth *locus* should be marked in a distinctive way. For example, one could 'mark the fifth locus with a golden hand' (ibid.). The hand has five fingers, and so is a good symbol for the fifth *locus*.

The *loci* could be reused again and again. Having constructed a series of *loci*, the student was ready to place the to-be-remembered material in them. This material was encoded in the form of *images*, a single image for each item to be remembered. Each image was stored in a *locus*. The student could then recall this material by mentally strolling through the *loci*, collecting the images stored there. The images should be as bizarre and distinctive as possible, 'of exceptional beauty or singular ugliness; . . . ornament some of them, as with crowns or purple cloaks . . . or . . . disfigure them, as by introducing one stained with blood or soiled with mud' (ibid., 10).

By using this method, the Ancients are reputed to have been able to recall astonishing numbers of items. For example, 'the elder Seneca . . . could repeat two thousand names in the order in which they had been given; and when a class of two hundred students or more spoke each in turn a line of poetry, he could recite all the lines in reverse order, beginning from the last one said and going right back to the first' (ibid., 16).

Aristotle discussed the artificial memory on several occasions. For example, he described people who dream that they are 'mentally arranging a given list of subjects according to the mnemonic rule' (McKeon, 1941: 619). Yates (1966: 31) notes that this is 'rather a warning, one would think, against doing too much in artificial memory', but goes on to show that the importance of imagination in Aristotle's theory of memory was consistent with the way that ancient mnemonists approached their task. For example, Aristotle argued that 'imagining lies within our own power whenever we wish (e.g., we can call up a picture, as in the practice of mnemonics by the use of mental images)' (McKeon, 1941: 587). Not only did Aristotle believe that imagery was an important mnemonic tool, but also he held that thinking was impossible without images. After all, the mind requires something to think about, and what else do we think with other than images? This is a claim that has been controversial throughout the history of psychology, as we shall see.

The elaborate mnemonic techniques of the Ancients faded away with the arrival of printing, which made it easy to store large amounts of information outside of one's memory. However, after Yates wrote her book there was renewed interest in mnemonics. A particularly important paper in this revival was written by Bower (1970), who showed that many of the ancient techniques had a sound psychological basis and are still useful. Another example of the way in which Aristotle's views are still relevant is given in Box 1.3.

The *Scala Naturae*

Recall that Aristotle had differentiated between forms of life in terms of the powers that they possessed. Thus, plants had only the power of self-nutrition, animals had both self-nutrition and sensation, while humans were also able to think in addition to the first two powers. Notice that this creates a *hierarchy* with humans at the top, followed by animals, and then plants. If all creatures 'could be ranked on a unitary, graded, continuous dimension' (Hodos and Campbell, 1969: 338), then one would have what has been called a *scala*

BOX 1.3

ARISTOTLE'S THEORY OF INTELLIGENCE

The contemporary relevance of Aristotle's theory of intelligence has been pointed out by Tigner and Tigner (2000). They observed that Aristotle recognized three kinds of intelligence. The first is *theoretical intelligence*, which corresponds to what most people now think of as 'intelligence'. It is the ability to understand subjects such as mathematics and science. Aristotle's second kind of intelligence is *practical intelligence*. Here the focus is on being able to choose a wise course of action. Finally, there is *productive intelligence*, which is concerned with being able to make things. It is perhaps best exemplified by the arts.

Why should we believe that Aristotle's classification of the kinds of intelligence has merit? As Tigner and Tigner point out, Aristotle's system has strong similarities to the highly respected *triarchic theory of intelligence* proposed by the contemporary psychologist Robert Sternberg (1988). Although Sternberg uses different labels for them (*analytical*, *prac-*

tical, and *creative*), his three kinds of intelligence are essentially the same as Aristotle's. Sternberg did not copy Aristotle's system, but arrived at it using the empirical methods of contemporary psychology. Thus, one reason for believing that Aristotle's system has merit is that it has been independently verified by another investigator using different methods and in a very different era.

Sternberg (2000: 178) makes the sage observation that the similarity between his theory and Aristotle's illustrates the importance of studying the history of psychology. 'If both philosophical [analysis] and psychological analysis support an idea, the idea gains credibility by virtue of the overlap in substantive findings across methods of analysis. . . . Tigner and Tigner's (2000) analysis shows how important it is to study the history and philosophy of psychology. There are many alternative paths to knowledge and understanding about the human mind.'

naturae. Aristotle conceived of this 'natural scale' as a measure of the 'degree of perfection' of each creature. 'It is based on the "powers of the soul" . . . from the nutritive, to which plants are limited, to the rational, characteristic of man . . . each higher order possessing all the powers of those below it in the scale, and an additional differentiating one of its own' (Lovejoy, 1971 [1936]: 58).

St Thomas Aquinas (1225–74) and the Medieval View of the Universe

Such a hierarchical order was greatly elaborated over the years following Aristotle, especially during the Middle Ages, which lasted from about AD 500 until roughly the fifteenth century. During this period Christianity became the dominant religion in Europe. One of Aristotle's most successful interpreters was the great Catholic theologian, **St Thomas Aquinas** (1225–74). Aquinas demonstrated that much of what Aristotle said was consistent with a Christian world view. For example, the idea of a *scala naturae*, or **great chain of being** (ibid., 73–7) was quite consistent with Catholic theology. According to Aquinas, 'the universe is hierarchically arranged' with beings ordered 'according to their internal perfection' (Wulf, 1959 [1922]: 62). In this system, 'reality mounts step by step from one specific nature to another, following a certain definite order. . . . Things evolve . . . in a certain order, the investigation of which is the work of the particular sciences, and calls for patient observation. If there are any leaps in nature, they are never capricious' (ibid., 72). The great chain of being illustrates God's plan, as described in the following quotation from Aquinas (Pegis, 1948: 260–1):

Hence we must say that the distinction and multitude of things is from the intention of the first cause, who is God. For he brought things into being in order that His goodness might be communicated to creatures, and be represented by them. And because His goodness could not

be adequately represented by one creature alone, He produced many and diverse creatures, so that what was wanting to one in the representation of the divine goodness might be supplied by another. For goodness, which in God is simple and uniform, in creatures is manifold and divided; and hence the whole universe together participates in the divine goodness more perfectly, and represents it better, than any given single creature. And because the divine wisdom is the cause of the distinction of things, therefore Moses said that things are made distinct by the Word of God, which is the conception of His wisdom; and this is what we read in *Genesis* (i.3, 4): *God said: Be light made. . . . And he divided the light from the darkness.*

It is impossible to overestimate the importance to Western culture of this religious conception of the evolutionary process. Some of its main features and tenets include the following:

- Creatures are hierarchically ordered, reflecting God's purpose.
- Nothing in this plan is 'capricious' (i.e., occurs merely by chance). Rather, everything and everyone has a place in a purposeful order that culminates in God.
- This view of nature is consistent with what we are told in the Bible, which is an irrefutable source of knowledge.

This view of the world as a hierarchically arranged and purposefully ordered system, with God at its apex and humans as the most God-like creatures, remained in place for hundreds of years in Western culture. It was not until Darwin presented his theory of evolution in the nineteenth century that the religious world view faced its most serious challenge. We will review the dispute between traditional theology and Darwinian evolutionary theory in Chapter 2. However, the stability of the medieval system was shaken well before the nineteenth century by the coming of the Renaissance, a topic also to be considered in the next chapter.

IMPORTANT NAMES, WORKS, AND CONCEPTS

Names and Works

Aristotle

Confucius

I Ching

Jung, Carl G.

Kepler, Johan

Lao-tzu

Leibniz, Gottfried Wilhelm

Plato

Pythagoras

St Thomas Aquinas

Socrates

Tao Te Ching

Concepts

action versus motion

artificial memory

circumplexes

Confucianism

cosmology

cyclical change

forms

Galen's typology

gestalt

Golden Section

great chain of being

innate knowledge

laws of association

memory

mnemonic techniques

Platonism

potentiality and actuality

problem of the irrational

psyche

Pythagorean opposites

scala naturae

syllogism

Taoism

teleological explanations

union of opposites

Yang and Yin

RECOMMENDED READINGS

History of Psychology

An excellent source for material dealing with all aspects of the history of psychology is the 'History and Philosophy of Psychology Web Resources' page maintained by Christopher Green at <http://www.psych.yorku.ca/orgs/resource.htm>. Another promising site is the 'Virtual Laboratory' at <http://vlp.mpiwg-berlin.mpg.de/>. On the latter, see H. Schmidgen and R.B. Evans, 'The virtual laboratory: A new on-line resource for the history of psychology', History of Psychology 6 (2003): 208–13.

Pythagoreanism

A fascinating collection of writings pertaining to Pythagoreanism is K.S. Guthrie, *The Pythagorean Sourcebook and Library* (Grand Rapids, Mich.: Phanes Press, 1987 [1920]). D.J. O'Meara presents a thorough review of the influence of Pythagorean mathematical ideas in *Pythagoras Revived: Mathematics and Philosophy in Late Antiquity* (Oxford: Clarendon Press, 1987). If you wish to explore the cultural context and influence of Pythagorean ideas, consult P. Kingsley, *Ancient Philosophy, Mystery, and Magic: Empedocles and Pythagorean Tradition* (Oxford: Clarendon Press, 1995).

Plato and Platonism

For additional examples of the ways in which Platonic ideas have been used by psychologists, see R.B. MacLeod, *The Persistent Problems of Psychology* (Pittsburgh: Duquesne University Press, 1975) and L. Stevenson, *Seven Theories of Human Nature* (New York: Oxford University Press, 1974), both of which contain accounts of Plato's psychology as well as reviews of many of the other figures we will consider in this book. More on the implications of the doctrine of the *Golden Mean* may be found in T.J. Tracy, *Physiological Theory and the Doctrine of the Mean in Plato and Aristotle* (The Hague: Mouton, 1969).

Taoism and Eastern Thinking

G. Murphy and L.B. Murphy, *Asian Psychology* (New York: Basic Books, 1968), is an edited compendium of sources on Asian psychology that provides a thorough introduction. An appreciation of Taoism is perhaps best gained through exposure to its art, and a good beginning source is P. Rawson and L. Legeza, *Tao: The Chinese Philosophy of Time and Change* (London: Thames & Hudson, 1973). Taoism as a contemporary religion is presented in J. Lagerwey, *Taoist Ritual in Chinese Society and History* (New York: Macmillan, 1987), and its centrality to Chinese culture is thoroughly considered in Z. Bokun, 'Daoist patterns of thought and the tradition of Chinese metaphysics', *Contemporary Chinese Thought* 29 (1998): 13–71.

An investigation of the enormous range of Eastern psychology is beyond the scope of this book. In particular, the teachings of Buddha (566–480 BC) have intrigued many psychological thinkers. There are different varieties of Buddhism, and D.T. Suzuki, *Zen Buddhism: Selected Writings of D.T. Suzuki*, ed. W. Barrett (Garden City, NY: Doubleday, 1956), offers a good introduction to one strand. Good examples of the way Buddhism has influenced psychology are provided by E.H. Rosch, 'Is wisdom in the brain?', *Psychological Science* 10 (1999): 222–4, and F.J. Varela, E. Thompson, and E. Rosch, *The Embodied Mind* (Cambridge, Mass.: MIT Press, 1991).

Aristotle and St Thomas Aquinas

A thorough outline of Aristotle's approach to psychology is in D.N. Robinson, *Aristotle's Psychology* (New York: Columbia University Press, 1989). Aristotle's role as an early predecessor of contemporary psychology is explored by C.D. Green, 'The thoroughly modern Aristotle: Was he really a functionalist?', *History of Psychology* 1 (1998): 8–20. A brief, readable introduction to the psychological implications of Aquinas's philosophy is F.J. Fitzpatrick, 'Aquinas', in R.L. Gregory, ed., *The Oxford Companion to the Mind* (Oxford: Oxford University Press, 1987), 36–8.

CHAPTER 2

TOUCHSTONES:
FROM DESCARTES TO DARWIN

Introduction

During the Renaissance people began to think for themselves on a scale that had not been seen since classical times. In France, René Descartes exemplified this theme, by doubting everything that he could not rationally demonstrate. His emphasis on reason led him to believe that the mind possessed innate ideas. In Britain, Isaac Newton introduced a powerful new approach to natural science that was widely emulated. John Locke, George Berkeley, and David Hume presented an empiricist approach that contrasted with that of Descartes by regarding ideas as the product of experience rather than being innate. Women's issues were brought to the fore by Mary Wollstonecraft, who argued forcefully for women's right to education. In Germany, Immanuel Kant argued that the mind was regulated by its own rules, and that as a result our experience was our own construction rather than something imposed on us by the external world. All of these developments culminated in Charles Darwin and his theory of evolution. This theory provided a framework within which a scientific psychology seemed like a real possibility.

As we shall see, many approaches to psychological questions have been proposed over the centuries. The history of these ideas is not a straightforward story of progress but involves many repetitions of old ideas, although often the older concepts have been rejuvenated at a more sophisticated level.

Renaissance means 'rebirth', and refers to the renewal of interest in classical antiquity that originated in Italy in the fourteenth century and spread throughout Europe in the fifteenth and sixteenth centuries. This renewed interest in classical sources also brought with it a questioning attitude towards the received wisdom of the medieval period, 'a spirit of criticism which first undermined, then finally destroyed the old beliefs, the old conceptions, the traditional truths. . . . Little by little, doubt stirs and awakens. If everything is possible, nothing is true. If nothing is assured, the only certainty is error' (Koyré, 1954). It was in this climate of doubt and uncertainty that Descartes took it upon himself to discover what, if anything, could be known for sure.

René Descartes (1596–1650)

Born in France, **René Descartes** travelled extensively and lived for most of the latter part of his life in Holland. In 1619, while serving in Germany as a soldier, Descartes found himself without the sort of companion with whom he could discuss philosophical issues and consequently spent time by himself, reflecting on what was worth believing. During one day of isolation, he had a clear vision of what was beyond doubt. To begin with, Descartes saw that our beliefs typically grow in the way that cities grow. 'Ancient cities which were originally mere boroughs, and have become large towns in the process of time, are as a rule badly laid out' (Anscombe and Geach, 1954: 15) because they were constructed over a very long period of time by many different people. Similarly, our beliefs are the result of a long process of development that lacks any clear plan. What is required is for *one person* to begin again. Just as 'buildings undertaken and carried out by a single architect are generally more seemly and better arranged than those several hands have sought to adapt', so Descartes felt that the best chance of finding truth was for him to start from the beginning and see what he could discover by himself. 'I was . . . forced to become my own guide' (ibid., 20–1).

In order to carry out this project, Descartes vowed to accept as true 'only what presented itself to my mind so clearly and distinctly that I had no occasion to doubt it' and to make inferences using 'long chains of perfectly simple and easy reasonings by means of which geometers are accustomed to carry out their most difficult demonstrations' (ibid.). Thus, Descartes's way of discovering the truth begins with *clear and distinct ideas* that cannot be doubted. These ideas are treated as premises from which conclusions can be drawn by 'simple and easy reasoning'. Such a procedure is the hallmark of **rationalism**: provided our premises are correct, our ability to use reason is sufficient to provide us with the truth.

Notice that rationalism requires us to begin with sound premises, and thus the discovery of a premise that is beyond doubt is of primary importance. Descartes began by deciding to act is if:

everything that had entered my mind hitherto was no more than the illusions of dreams. But immediately upon this I noticed that while I was trying to think everything false, it must needs be that I, who was thinking this (*qui le pensais*), was something. And observing that this truth 'I am thinking (*je pense*), therefore I exist' was so solid and secure that the most extravagant suppositions of the sceptics could not overthrow it, I judged that I need not scruple to accept it as the first principle . . . I was seeking. (Ibid., 31–2).

This passage is one of the most important in the history of Western thought. Descartes reasoned that he cannot doubt the fact of his own thought, and therefore there must be a thinker who is thinking those thoughts. The thinker is, of course, Descartes himself, and so the fact of his existence is beyond doubt. In Latin, the passage 'I am thinking, therefore I exist' is **Cogito, ergo sum**. This argument is traditionally 'known as Descartes's *Cogito*, and the process by which it is reached is called **Cartesian doubt** (Russell, 1945: 564).

For Descartes, several significant conclusions follow from the *Cogito*. Clear and distinct ideas must come from God, since Descartes himself was too imperfect to have generated them on his own. Such ideas include the truths derived through mathematical reasoning, such as that 'the idea of a sphere includes the equidistance of all parts (of its surface) from the center' (Anscombe and Geach, 1954: 35). There are things that people know without having to learn them, and such truths can be called **innate ideas**. As we have already seen, the question of whether or not people know things innately is a perennial issue in psychology. For Descartes and his followers, the existence of innate knowledge is beyond question.

Descartes went on to argue that the mind is quite separate from the body. Each of us is essentially a *conscious being* that is capable of mental acts such as doubt and imagination. While a mind may interact with the body in which it is housed, each is of a different nature than the other. The notion that mind and body are fundamentally different is called **dualism**. From Descartes's viewpoint, the mind comes from God and is immortal. By contrast, the body is mechanical, and operates in the same way as does a clock or any other machine. This way of seeing things naturally raises the question of where, exactly, the mind interacts with the body. Descartes suggested that the interaction took place via the *pineal gland*, a singular structure at the base of the brain, because:

all other parts of the brain are double, and . . . the organs of 'external sense' are also double—two eyes, two ears, and so on. . . . . The pineal gland is also termed the *common sense* . . . [and] may be regarded as the central agency which receives sensory impressions from various organs, coordinates them, and sends out other impressions so as to enable the adaptive functioning of the body. Descartes [regarded] many [of these] . . . coordinations . . . as purely *reflexive* or automatic. (Pastore, 1971: 20–1; emphasis added)

Although the hypothesis that the pineal gland is the seat of the soul is no longer taken seriously, Descartes's overall model of mind/body interaction has been enormously influential. In fact, his model of the mind-body relation, often called **interactionism**, became so widespread as to be almost 'common sense' itself. As one famous twentieth-century philosopher observed, Descartes's view is that the mind is in the body as if it was a **ghost in a machine** (Ryle, 1949).

> The official doctrine, which hails chiefly from Descartes, is something like this . . . every human being has both a body and a mind. . . . [B]ody and mind are ordinarily harnessed together, but after the death of the body [the] mind may continue to exist and function. Human bodies are in space and are subject to the mechanical laws which govern all other bodies in space. Bodily processes and states can be inspected by external observers. So a [person's] bodily life is as much a public affair as are the lives of animals. . . . But minds are not in space, nor are their operations subject to mechanical laws. The workings of one mind are not witnessable by other observers; its career is private. Only I can take direct cognisance of the states and processes of my own mind. A person therefore lives through two collateral histories, one consisting of what happens in and to his [or her] body, the other consisting of what happens in or to his [or her] mind. The first is public, the second private. (Ibid., 11)

Because the Cartesian model has been so central to Western psychology, it is important that we be absolutely clear about its most important features. Consider the following list carefully, which is derived from Ryle's description given above:

- Mind and body are separate.
- While the human body is subject to the same mechanical laws as any other physical body, the mind operates according to its own rules, which come from God.
- We know our own mind directly, through introspection. We cannot know other people's minds directly, since we cannot observe them. All we can observe about other people is the state of their bodies.

Introspection means 'the act of looking inward, the examination of one's mental experience' followed by 'the report of . . . the mental contents of one's consciousness' (Reber, 1985: 373). The Cartesian model suggests that introspection is the proper psychological method, and we will examine introspective psychologies later on. For now, all we need to be aware of is that Descartes leaves us with a picture of the mind as a private place in which thoughts and other mental events occur (Ryle, 1949: 27).

The Body as a Machine

Not only was Descartes's model of the mind influential, but so was his conception of the body as a machine. By comparing the body to a machine, Descartes was illustrating a well-known scientific strategy. Gigerenzer (1991) has pointed out that the history of science is replete with examples of machines that have been treated as models of human nature. Consider this remark from the British philosopher **Thomas Hobbes** (1588–1679), as cited by Mischel (1967: 5): 'What is the heart but a spring, the nerves strings, the joints wheels giving motion to the whole body?' Hobbes was using tools such as springs and wheels to provide models for the way that the body works. Although the heart is not really a spring, Hobbes found it useful to think about it that way. Although Hobbes and Descartes disagreed about many things, they both found such mechanical models to be extremely useful.

Another good example of the use of mechanical models may be found in the work of the eighteenth-century inventor Jacques de Vaucanson, who not only built a statue that played the flute, but also a duck that 'stretches out its neck to take corn out of your hand, it swallows it, and discharges it digested by the usual passage' (Fryer and Marshall, 1979: 267). These models were not merely entertainments, although they did intrigue the French aristocracy, but part of a serious attempt to construct machines capable of imitating organisms. If an organism is like a machine, then you should be able to build a machine that is indistinguishable from that organism. For generations, scientists have been so impressed with the similarity between people and machines that they often try to build machines to simulate people, believing that if they are successful they will have shown that they really understand something important about people. This is an idea that many people in the twentieth century had about computers, believing that computers would ultimately be able to mimic everything that people do.

Descartes himself did not believe that the attempt to mimic human behaviour by means of a machine could succeed. However, he did believe that 'if there were machines with the organs and appearance of a monkey, or some other irrational animal, we should have no means of telling that they were not altogether of the same nature as those animals' (Anscombe and Geach, 1954: 41). People, however, differ from both animals and machines in that they are much more flexible in response to changing circumstances. For example, we are able to speak in ways that are spontaneous and novel, something Descartes believed no animal or machine could be trained or made to do. It is the fact that humans possess minds that enables them to adjust so smoothly to changing situations.

While Descartes made a sharp distinction between people and animals, he made none whatsoever between animals and machines. Animals did not possess souls and so were indistinguishable from machines. Descartes's attitude towards animals is one that many people may find offensive today. 'Animals were . . . not conscious, not really living—machines without will or purpose or any feeling whatever. [Descartes] dissected them alive (anesthetics were far off in the nineteenth century) amused at their cries and yelps since these were

nothing but the hydraulic hisses and vibrations of machines' (Jaynes, 1973: 170). In the years since Descartes, animal research has become common practice. In most jurisdictions, there are now stringent regulations designed to prevent the mistreatment of animals used in research. However, precisely what constitutes the proper treatment of animals used in research remains a controversial issue, which will be considered in Chapter 8.

Our discussion of Descartes's views concerning the body points to three controversial issues to which we will return later on:

1. Can a machine be built that will simulate human behaviour in way that makes its actions indistinguishable from human behaviour?
2. Are there qualitative differences between humans and other organisms?
3. Should we be able to do whatever we want with animals in our research?

Among the areas to which Descartes made strong contributions was the study of *visual perception* (Pastore, 1971). The study of the laws of visual perception was an area of intense activity during the Renaissance, and some of the discoveries of Renaissance artists and scientists have shaped psychological theories ever since. An illustration of this is given in Box 2.1.

Isaac Newton (1642–1727)

Sir Isaac Newton has been called 'the greatest scientific genius the English-speaking peoples have produced' (Randall, 1953: ix). As J.M. Keynes (1956: 277) put it:

> He was the last of the magicians, the last of the Babylonians and Sumerians, the last great mind which looked out on the visible and intellectual world with the same eyes as those who began to build our intellectual heritage rather less than 10,000 years ago. Isaac Newton, a posthumous child born with no father on Christmas Day, 1642, was the last wonder-child to whom the Magi could do sincere and appropriate homage.

No less an authority than Albert Einstein (1952: lix) said of Newton that 'Nature to him was an open book, whose letters he could read without effort.' Newton's interests were extraordinarily broad, covering everything from **alchemy** (a mystical precursor to chemistry) to history. However, his fame rests largely on a work known as the *Principia*, published in 1687. While the *Principia* forms the foundation for classical physics, it also has important implications for psychology.

The Laws of Motion

A *law* is a basic rule or truth. Sciences that are older and simpler than psychology often lay claim to certain laws. Typical, and famous, examples are

---

BOX 2.1

THE CONCEPT OF PERSPECTIVE

One can learn a lot about the history of psychology by examining the history of art. Renaissance artists revived the classical use of *perspective* whereby a scene is depicted from a single *point of view* (Edgerton, 1975). The use of perspective relies on the notion that a picture is like a window. To see what this means, examine the figure below, which illustrates the *projective model of vision* (Sedgwick, 1980).

The projective model represents the eye as being located at the apex of a *visual pyramid*. What the artist represents on the *picture plane* is a *projection* of the surface of an object. The result is that objects depicted in a picture appear to lie behind the picture plane. The picture plane is like a window through which you are looking at objects in the distance. Notice that the eye can only be at one place when the picture is constructed. That position is called the *station point* (ibid., 40). The station point gives the spectator a *point of view*. Changing the station point changes what will be represented in the picture, just as moving in relation to a window changes what you see through it. 'As we approach a window we see more of the scene; as we move to the left, a portion of the scene on the left side becomes hidden by the window frame while more is revealed on the right, etc.' (ibid., 41).

A great deal of research and theory in the psychology of perception is based on the projective model, and we will explore it further as we go along. However, for now we will only note one other consequence of the projective model,

which is discussed by Edgerton (1975: ch. 11) and by Kubovy (1986: chs 9 and 10). Over time the projective model has become generalized far beyond its original context of painting. We now talk about individuals having different 'points of view' on a situation, and mean more than just that they have different station points. We use the concept of a 'point of view' to indicate that there are many different possible 'perspectives' on a situation. A great scientist, like a great artist, gives us a perspective that we might never have thought of taking ourselves. However, in most cases, no one person's viewpoint is more privileged than that of anyone else, and each person's viewpoint is worth taking seriously.

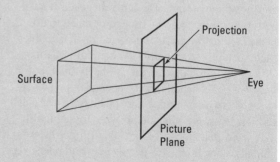

The visual pyramid and the picture plane.
Source: Hagen (1980: 36). Copyright © 1980, with permission from Elsevier.

Newton's **laws of motion**. Newton's First Law of Motion stated that 'Every body continues in a state of rest, or of uniform motion in a straight line, unless it is compelled to change that state by forces impressed upon it' (Sears and Zemansky, 1970: 15). His Second Law of Motion deals with *acceleration*, or the rate of change in velocity: 'Acceleration . . . is . . . the resultant of all the external forces exerted' (ibid., 13). In other words, the extent to which a body will move faster or slower depends on how many forces are acting on it and how intense those forces are.

Newton was able to express these laws in precise mathematical terms. His achievement can be seen as a triumph of the attempt, which began with Pythagoras, to give nature a precise mathematical description.

Can Newton's Laws Be Generalized to Psychology?

Consider the title of a paper by Kimble (1990): 'Mother Nature's bag of tricks is small', which suggests that the same laws will hold in all areas of inquiry, whether in the natural sciences, such as physics, or in the social sciences, such as psychology. Thus, Kimble is suggesting that Newton's laws apply in psychology just as they do in physics. This argument has been made in many forms over the years. Many psychologists have been impressed by the success of the physical sciences in explaining inanimate matter, and have sought to import concepts from the physical sciences in general, and physics in particular, to explain psychological events. Thus, instead of seeing psychology as having a unique subject matter, it is possible to see organisms as physical systems operating according to the same laws that regulate other physical systems. One can attempt to take physics and apply it to mental life, thereby trying to explain the mind in the same way as one would any other physical system. This endeavour has several important consequences for psychological research.

One consequence of taking physics as a model for psychology is that the *subject matter* of psychology is seen as essentially the same as physics. For example, in Newtonian physics the basic subject matter is the *motion* of objects. In physics, one seeks to discover the laws that regulate motion—how much force is required to move an object, how fast things move if a force is applied to them, and so on. Kimble argues that *motion* is also the subject matter of psychology, but it is the motion of organisms—*behaviour*—rather than the motion of inanimate objects that the psychologist tries to understand.

As we saw above, Newtonian physics tells us that an object will remain at rest unless some force is applied to it. If we transfer that idea to psychology, it means that the organism will not move unless some force is applied to it. However, the organism will not move if *just any* force is applied. That is the point of Newton's second law—the forces acting on the organism must be above a certain level before the organism will act. You can see this for inanimate objects easily enough. If you push lightly on a coffee cup or other small object, it does not move because of its *inertia*. Only if you apply enough force does it begin to slide across the table. Then, only if you increase or decrease the force you are applying will the speed of the object change. Similarly, the organism will remain at rest until the forces acting on it are sufficient to make it move. Once the organism begins to move, then it will only change its behaviour if the forces acting on it change. Box 2.2 gives some examples of the relationship between behaviour and the forces controlling it.

Many psychologists have searched for very abstract relationships, such as those proposed by Newton, that may also apply in psychology. As we observed earlier, perhaps it is possible to understand human behaviour in the same way as we understand other natural phenomena. Many psychologists have tried to use concepts that have been imported from outside of psychology, particularly from physics (Marks, 1984). This illustrates the persistent attempt to find 'underlying unity amidst apparent variety' (Arnheim, 1974).

The Nature of Colour

Newton (1952 [1730]) not only proposed laws of potentially great generality, but he also did experimental work on concrete phenomena such as *colour*. In fact, Newton's work on colour had far-reaching consequences for psychology.

One of Newton's best-known experimental procedures is illustrated in Figure 2.1. By passing white light through a prism, Newton discovered that it was decomposed into the colours of the spectrum. It appeared that white light yielded a mixture of the other colours. Newton was able to further demonstrate colour mixture by passing the colours of the spectrum through another prism. This procedure yielded white light.

Newton's experiment might appear to mean that some elementary colours (such as red, yellow, green, and blue) can be combined to give other colours (such as white). However, Newton did not

---

THE CONCEPT OF A THRESHOLD

When the forces acting on the organism are not strong enough to manifest themselves in behaviour, then we say that they are *below threshold*. The concept of a threshold, or *limen*, has a very distinguished history in psychology. It is an especially important notion in *psychophysics*, which we will consider in a later chapter. Kimble has shown that the threshold concept is very powerful. The accompanying figure shows how a threshold model can be applied to a wide variety of situations. In the figure, 'potential' refers to the readiness of a system to respond and 'instigation' refers to the amount of a stimulus that is applied to the system. The threshold curve shows that the greater the potential, the lower the instigation required to elicit a response from the system.

Kimble (1990: 37) gives several examples that illustrate this relationship:

- The more sensitive the observer, the more easily can a signal be picked up.
- If someone is racially biased, then he/she picks up even the slightest evidence as proof of that prejudice.
- If someone is prepared to learn, then you only have to suggest a direction for inquiry, and the student does the rest on his or her own.
- Some people can only take a small quantity of a drug before showing its effects; others seem to have a much higher tolerance.

- In certain situations, some people show the effects of stress before others. Everyone can tolerate a certain amount of stress, but as it accumulates, even those who are relatively invulnerable to it will show its effects.

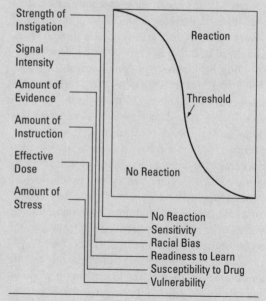

Kimble's threshold model.
Source: Kimble (1990). Reprinted with permission of Blackwell Publishing.

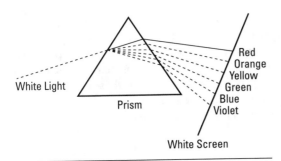

FIGURE 2.1
The use of a prism to disperse white light.

believe that light rays themselves were coloured. 'Indeed, rays, properly expressed, are not coloured. There is nothing else in them but a certain power or disposition . . . [to] produce in us the sensation of this or that colour' (Newton, 1952, cited by Judd, 1970: ix). Newton distinguished between the *stimulus* for colour and the *subjective experience* of colour. Light of different wavelengths constitutes the stimulus for colour. These stimuli produce the visual perception of different colours. However, a complete description of *light* as a physical stimulus will not be a complete description of the *subjective experience* of light. In addition to the description of the physical stimuli, one would also need a description of the resulting experiences or perceptions.

This last point was taken up with great enthusiasm by the German poet and naturalist **Johann Wolfgang von Goethe**. Goethe failed to give Newton credit for the subtlety of his understanding of colour phenomena and misinterpreted his analysis as meaning that colour itself could be understood as a physical property of light. Although Goethe misinterpreted Newton, he did make many significant descriptions of colour as a subjective experience. For example:

> Let a small piece of bright-colored paper . . . be held before a moderately lighted white surface; let the observer look steadfastly on the small colored object, and let it be taken away after a time

while his eyes remain unmoved; the spectrum of another color will then be visible on the white plane. (Goethe, 1970 [1840]: 20–1)

Goethe is describing the phenomenon known as *after-images*. For example, if you stare at a red patch displayed against a white background for about two minutes, and then gaze at a blank white background, you will see a green patch (e.g., Coren et al., 1984: 204). After-images are of great theoretical interest and historical importance, as we will see later on. Although he completely misunderstood Newton, Goethe was still capable of making interesting psychological observations. Descriptions of value to psychology need not (and sometimes are not) accompanied by any very good explanation of *why* the phenomena are as they are.

The British Empiricists: John Locke (1632–1704), George Berkeley (1685–1753), and David Hume (1711–76)

Perhaps no group has influenced the subsequent development of Western psychology as much as the **British empiricists**. Locke, Berkeley, and Hume invented concepts of far-reaching import for psychology. **Empiricism** is to be contrasted with the sort of *rationalism* that was characteristic of Descartes's approach. Rather than rely on reason to provide us with the truth, the empiricist only trusts the evidence provided by our senses.

John Locke

John Locke, an Englishman, was a physician and political activist whose political activities brought him into disfavour with King Charles II (Alexander, 1987). As a result, he fled to Holland in 1683, where he wrote much of what was to become his most influential work, *An Essay Concerning Human Understanding*, which was published upon his return to England (Locke, 1964 [1690]).

In his *Essay*, Locke argued that 'there are no innate principles in the mind', thus taking a position contradictory to Descartes. Locke's argument is partly that even if there were ideas in which everyone believed, that would not show them to be innate, since people could have arrived at this unanimity in some other way. In any case, one can always find people, such as 'children and idiots' (ibid., 68), who do not possess any idea you care to name.

By an *idea*, Locke meant 'whatsoever is the *object* of the understanding' when someone thinks (ibid., 66). The following are examples of ideas: '*whiteness, hardness, sweetness, thinking, motion, man, elephant, army, drunkenness*' (ibid., 89). Locke suggested that we get ideas from two different sources. The first is *sensory experience*, which furnishes us with the experiences we need to have ideas such as '*yellow, white, heat, cold soft, hard, bitter, sweet* and all those we call sensible qualities' (ibid., 90). The second source of our ideas is **reflection**, by which Locke meant the 'perception of the operations of our own mind within us' (ibid., 90). We can observe ourselves engaged in such operations as '*perception, thinking, doubting, believing, reasoning, knowing, willing*' (ibid.), and thus have some idea of these activities. If we follow Locke, self-observation will be the most important source of information about psychological concepts. Although introspection may have seemed to Locke to be an obvious source of psychological knowledge, many psychologists who came after Locke believed it to be a method prone to error. The role of introspection as a method in psychology has been a continuing source of controversy and will be an important part of our story in succeeding chapters.

For Locke, and for the British empiricists generally, our understanding is primarily the product of our experience, not of our reason. In fact, that is what it means to be an empiricist. 'Light and colours are busy at hand everywhere, when the eye is but open; . . . it will be easily granted that, if a child were to be kept in a place where he never saw any other but black and white till he were a man, he would have no more ideas of scarlet or green than he that from his childhood never tasted an oyster, or a pine-apple, has of those particular relishes' (ibid., 92). Locke is here suggesting that even basic concepts, such as those of colour, must be acquired, along with less common experiences, such as the taste of an oyster.

Locke attempted to demonstrate his empiricist orientation by means of a 'thought experiment' that had been proposed by his friend Molyneux. A thought experiment is a device often used in science that involves considering the results of an imaginary experiment, which, if it could be performed, would yield important conclusions. The thought experiment suggested by Molyneux went as follows:

> Suppose a man born blind, and now adult, and taught by his touch to distinguish between a cube and a sphere of the same metal, and nighly of the same bigness, so as to tell when he felt one and the other, which is the cube, which the sphere. Suppose then the cube and sphere placed on a table, and the blind man be made to see: query, whether by his sight before he touched them he could now distinguish and tell which is the globe, which the cube? (Pastore, 1971: 66)

That is, would a newly sighted adult be able to distinguish visually between two shapes without touching them? As far as Locke was concerned, the answer was clearly 'No', and the result of the Molyneux experiment was a foregone conclusion. While a formerly blind adult may have been able to tell that the two shapes were different, such a person could not reliably identify a globe, a cube, or, for that matter, any other shape. By no means did everyone regard Locke's answer to the Molyneux thought experiment as definitive. Indeed, the problem has generated a lot of controversy ever since Locke's day (ibid.), and a great deal of research has been devoted to exploring the perceptual experience of blind people (e.g., Kennedy, 1997; Warren, 1978).

Simple and Complex Ideas

Simple ideas, as the name suggests, cannot be reduced to anything more elementary, such as 'the coldness and hardness' felt 'in a piece of ice being as distinct ideas in the mind as the smell and whiteness of a lily' (Locke, 1964: 99). *Complex ideas* are compounded out of simple ones, and by this process of combination we may arrive at abstract ideas such as *army, constellation*, and, ultimately, *universe* (ibid., 199).

The existence of complex ideas points to the importance of the **association of ideas**, a process we considered earlier when we were discussing Aristotle. While people have many ideas in common, each of us may also have ideas that may strike others as unusual, because each of us will have had some idiosyncratic experiences. Moreover, each of us may have particular *sequences* of ideas that 'always keep in company, and the one no sooner at any time comes into the understanding but its associate appears with it; and if there are more than two which are thus united, the whole gang, always inseparable, show themselves together' (ibid., 251). An example Locke used is the way a familiar tune will play out in our minds after we have heard only a few notes.

Locke's view was that 'custom settles habits of thinking' (ibid.). The beliefs and attitudes we express are the result of the way in which our ideas have become *associated*. As we shall see, many psychologists have regarded the process of association as *the* basic psychological process.

Rewards, Punishments, and the Process of Education

Locke's view that ideas recur because they have been previously experienced together had important implications for education. For example, Locke reflected on the unfortunate consequences of punishment children receive at school.

> Many children, imputing the pain they endured at school to their books they were corrected for, so join those ideas together that a book becomes their aversion, and they are never reconciled to the study and use of them all their lives after;

and thus reading becomes a torment to them, which otherwise possibly they might have made the great pleasure of their lives. (Ibid., 254)

Locke (1965 [1699]: 61) held that **rewards and punishments** are the 'Spur and Reins whereby all Mankind is set on work, and guided'. To make children act reasonably, adults must apply rewards and punishments in the proper ways. For Locke it was essential to inculcate a sense of esteem when the child behaved properly and a sense of disgrace when it behaved badly. This was to be accomplished by making sure that agreeable things occurred when the child performed estimable acts, just as disagreeable things accompanied disgraceful acts. For example, children 'find a Pleasure in being esteemed, and valued . . . by . . . those they depend on' and can be influenced if these adults 'caress and commend them when they do well; shew a cold and neglectful Countenance to them upon doing ill' (ibid., 62). By acting consistently in this way, the adult can 'shame them out of their Faults, (for besides that, I would willingly have no Punishment,) and make them in love with the Pleasure of being well thought on' (ibid., 63). Locke's appreciation of the efficacy of reward and punishment presages a continuing interest in them throughout the history of psychology, particularly in the learning theories of twentieth-century psychologists, who believed reward and punishment to be of special importance.

Primary and Secondary Qualities

Objects have *qualities*, by which Locke meant 'the power to produce any idea in our mind . . . . Thus a snowball [has] the power to produce in us the ideas of white, cold and round' (Locke, 1964: 112). A *primary quality* is one that is in the object itself. For example, the fact that an object is *moving* is a primary quality, because motion is a property of the object itself. When we perceive motion, we are perceiving a primary quality. Other primary qualities include *size* and *number* (how many or how few objects there are). However, objects also have the power to produce experiences in us that are not the same as any property of the object. Locke gives '*colours, sounds* and *taste*' (ibid.) as examples. Recall our discussion of Newton's **colour theory**, in which we noted the importance of the distinction between the *stimulus* for colour and the *experience* of colour. Locke is making a similar point, by drawing our attention to *secondary qualities* that, unlike primary qualities, do not correspond to the experience to which they give rise. A feather can tickle you, but the tickle is not in the feather, it is only in you.

George Berkeley

Born in Ireland, **George Berkeley** was a precocious intellect who wrote his most important work before he was 30 years old (Warnock, 1987). In his first book, *A New Theory of Vision* (Berkeley, 1910 [1709]), he argued that there were no unambiguous visual cues to the spatial location of objects. Although Berkeley's argument is both complex and subtle, some inkling of his major point can be gained from an examination of Figure 2.2, which uses the same concepts as the 'visual pyramid' shown in Box 2.1 but introduces the possibility that surfaces at different distances could look as if they were at the same distance

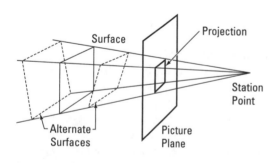

FIGURE 2.2
Three surfaces at three different distances from the eye that might look as if they were the same distance away.
Source: Sedgwick (1980: 48). Copyright © 1980, with permission from Elsevier.

from the observer. If you were an observer, how could you tell which object was closest to you, since they all yield the same projected surface? It seems as if the information available on your retina would not be enough to enable you to locate objects very precisely.

Berkeley resolved this problem by suggesting that the *sense of touch* provided the observer with an important source of information that supplemented the visual information available.

> Having of a long time experienced certain ideas, perceivable by touch . . . to have been connected with certain ideas of sight, I do upon perceiving these ideas of sight, forthwith conclude what tangible ideas are . . . like to follow. Looking at an object, I perceive a certain visible figure and colour . . . which from what I have formerly observed, determine me to think that if I advanced so many paces or miles, I shall be affected with such and such ideas of touch: so that in truth and strictness of speech, I neither see distance itself nor anything that I take to be at a distance. (Ibid., 32–3)

To better understand what Berkeley is talking about, consider why it is that you do not see an object as actually getting smaller as it recedes from you. After all, as an object (e.g., a car) gets further and further away, it will make a smaller and smaller image on the surface of your retina. However, rather than see the car as shrinking, we see it as staying the same size but getting further away. This phenomenon is called *size constancy*. Berkeley's explanation is that we remember how far we would have to travel to reach an object that yielded a visual image of the size we are currently experiencing. The visual image of an object is *associated* with a previous experience of moving a certain distance in order to touch the object. Perceiving distance is really a form of remembering, and is thus something we must learn. From an empiricist viewpoint like Berkeley's, very young children would not have size constancy, since they lack the requisite experiences.

Here is a concrete illustration from my own experience of the sort of phenomenon dear to the hearts of empiricists. I once wore a set of goggles fitted with a pair of *displacing prisms*. The use of such prismatic lenses has a long tradition in psychology, beginning with George Stratton (1964 [1897]), who wore lenses that made the world appear to be upside down. The goggles I wore had a less spectacular effect—they made everything appear to be displaced to the right. This meant, for example, that if you threw darts at a dartboard, then you would systematically throw the darts too far to the right. However, if you continued to throw darts at the dartboard for a few minutes, you would become more and more accurate. Your visual perception of the dartboard would be brought into line with feedback you were getting from throwing the darts. Your action corrects your vision. This illustrates one of Berkeley's points: the perceived location of objects is determined by what you do in relation to them.

If a tree falls in the forest, does anybody hear?

This question is the title of a song by Bruce Cockburn (1988). Although Cockburn intends the song to be an environmentalist's lament for our apparent inability to preserve our forests, the title is also reminiscent of one of Berkeley's most famous doctrines. In *A New Theory of Vision* (1910: 114), Berkeley argued that 'unthinking things' could not 'have any existence, out of the minds of thinking things which perceive them.' Berkeley's position is often put in terms of the following slogan: **To be is to be perceived**. Nothing exists apart from our experience of it.

Berkeley's doctrine is often treated as being so arcane as to not be worth taking seriously. However, there is an important psychological point behind it. If a tree falls in the forest and no one is there to hear it, then it is not psychologically real for anyone. An event must be in at least one person's experience to have an effect on anyone's behaviour. What is real for us is only what we experience.

David Hume

David Hume was a Scot whose ideas had a profound effect on many subsequent thinkers, including Kant, whom we will consider later in the chapter. Hume made incisive observations about such fundamental concepts as causality and the self.

Causality

Hume (1951 [1748]: 199) observed that 'it is a general maxim in philosophy that *whatever begins to exist, must have a cause of existence.*' The category of *causality* is a fundamentally important one. We use it to understand why things are the way they are. **Causality** is an idea that psychology can hardly do without. And yet, what does causality actually amount to? If we examine our experience, what do we find that corresponds to our idea of *causality*?

Let us examine a possible cause-effect relationship, adapted from a paper by the Nobel Prize-winning psychologist Herbert Simon (1954), whom we will encounter in Chapter 14. Suppose we do a study of employee absenteeism in a particular company. We discover that the average number of absences per week per employee is highly correlated with the average number of children per employee. We would then probably conclude that children make demands of one sort or another on parents' time, which in turn increases absenteeism. That is, we would believe that having children *causes* absenteeism, at least in part. However, notice that what we actually have is a *correlation* between number of children and absenteeism, and nothing more than a correlation. In fact, in any case we can imagine, our notion of causality always boils down to mere correlation.

Hume (1951: 71) argued that if we look closely at any cause-effect relationship, then we will 'immediately perceive that, even in the most familiar events, . . . we only learn by experience the frequent *conjunction* of objects, without ever being able to comprehend anything like *connexion* between them.' There is nothing in our experience corresponding to a 'cause', if by a cause we mean some 'necessary connection' between two events

(Pears, 1990: 75). When one billiard ball hits another, there is only the experience of one ball moving followed by the other moving. 'And experience only teaches us how one event constantly follows another; without instructing us in the secret connexion which binds them together, and renders them inseparable' (Hume, 1951: 67).

We do not perceive causality. The experience of causality is the result of an association built up between one event and another. After repeatedly experiencing one event (e.g., having many children) followed by another (e.g., absenteeism), we find it natural to think of the latter as the effect of the former. Thus, Hume's definition of cause both is simple and avoids implicating a necessary connection: 'an object followed by another, and whose appearance always conveys the thought to that other' (ibid., 78).

If correct, Hume's conclusion places sharp limits on what it is that we can ever hope to understand. We can never have a deep insight into the inner workings of nature. Our knowledge can never amount to more than a set of beliefs based only on our experience of what goes with what.

Hume is usually regarded as a *skeptic*, or someone who finds it difficult to believe that certain knowledge is possible. Hume (1927 [1757]: 283) expressed this skeptical attitude in the following manner:

> The whole is a riddle, an enigma, an inexplicable mystery. Doubt, uncertainty, suspense of judgment appear the only result of our most accurate scrutiny, concerning this subject.

The Self

Recall that Descartes had begun his inquiries by being certain of only one thing: that he existed. Indeed, it has seemed obvious to many people that, as Hume wrote, 'we are every moment intimately conscious of what we call our **self**; that we feel its existence and its continuance in existence; and are certain, beyond the evidence of a demonstration, both of its perfect identity and simplicity' (ibid., 226). Hume, however, was not convinced

that the self is so easily grasped. In order to see why Hume thought that it was not at all obvious that the self existed, we first need to introduce his distinction between *impressions* and *ideas*. By an *impression*, Hume meant 'all our more lively perceptions, when we hear, or see, or feel, or love, or hate, or desire, or will. And impressions are distinguished from ideas, which are the less lively perceptions, of which we are conscious, when we reflect on any of those sensations or movements above mentioned' (ibid., 16). All of our ideas are derived from impressions. We have an idea of ourselves, but, Hume wondered, 'from what impression could this idea be derived?'

> For my part, when I enter most intimately into what I call *myself*, I always stumble on some particular perception or other, of heat or cold, light or shade, love or hatred, pain or pleasure. I can never catch *myself* at any time without a perception, and can never observe anything but the perception. (Ibid., 227)

Since the *self* would appear to be a central concept in psychology, its status is particularly important. Hume is suggesting that there is nothing that uniquely corresponds to the concept of a self. Our belief that we possess a self is an illusion. If we honestly examine our experience, then we will discover that all we really possess is a series of impressions of one sort or another. Of course, many people have resisted Hume's stark conclusion, and later on we will see how they have tried to keep the self alive.

James Mill (1773–1836) and John Stuart Mill (1806–73)

In James and John Stuart Mill we have one of the most famous father-son combinations in the history of psychology. **James Mill** 'is usually said to represent the peak of associationism' (Dennis, 1948: 140). He distilled the British empiricist and associationist principles we have been discussing down to a simple, straightforward psychology. In the following passage, James Mill (1948 [1829]: 149) describes how **sensations** are the ultimate building blocks of the mind:

> In using the names, tree, horse, man, the names of what I call objects, I am referring, and can be referring, only to my sensations; in fact, therefore, only naming a certain number of sensations regarded as in a particular state of combination. . . . Particular sensations of sight, of touch, of the muscles, are the sensations, to the ideas of which, colour, extension, roughness, hardness, smoothness, taste, smell, so coalescing as to appear one idea, I give the name, idea of a tree.

This passage is important not only because it identifies sensations as the most basic elements of the mind, but also because it suggests that language refers, ultimately, to our sensations. Thus, when I describe a tree (or anything else for that matter) I am not referring directly to anything in the external world. Rather, I am describing the sensations that the tree has given rise to in me. This is consistent with the notion that a suitable way of discovering the elementary structure of the mind would involve the description and classification of sensations. As we shall see, this activity became an extremely important part of psychology in the late nineteenth and early twentieth centuries.

For James Mill, mental events combine following the laws of association to create ideas of increasing complexity. 'Brick is one complex idea, mortar is another complex idea; these ideas . . . compose my idea of a wall. . . . In the same manner my complex idea of glass, and wood . . . compose my . . . idea of a window; and these . . . ideas, united together, compose my idea of a house.' And so on and so on, until one reaches 'the idea called Every Thing' (ibid., 154). There is nothing more to any idea, no matter how complex, than the sum of its component parts.

James Mill educated his son John Stuart in a highly disciplined and rigorous manner, with the result that J.S. Mill mastered at a very young age what were then taken to be the elementary disciplines (e.g., Greek and mathematics). Widely regarded as a genius, **John Stuart Mill** made lasting contributions to a variety of disciplines, including logic, politics, and psychology.

J.S. Mill followed his father's approach to psychology in outline, but made it 'more sophisticated and more plausible' (Mandler and Mandler, 1964: 93). One of J.S. Mill's (1973 [1846]) best-known conceptual innovations was what he called **mental chemistry**, which treats complex ideas as the product of a process analogous to a chemical reaction. For example, the combination of hydrogen and oxygen produces water, but one cannot observe the components (hydrogen and oxygen) in the result (water). Similarly, when one observes a complex idea one typically cannot detect its components. While it is true, as we saw in our discussion of Newton, that the colours of the spectrum can produce the experience of white, there is nothing in our experience of white that allows us to detect the spectrum of colours. Thus, for J.S. Mill, a complex idea 'formed by the blending together of several simpler ones, when it really appears simple (that is, when the separate elements are not consciously distinguishable in it) [can] be said to *result from*, or be *generated by*, the simple ideas, not to *consist* of them (J.S. Mill, 1948 [1843]: 173). One of the consequences of the doctrine of mental chemistry, however, is to make more difficult the use of introspection as a method for the discovery of mental elements. How psychologists dealt with this difficulty will be discussed at length in Chapter 7.

As mentioned above, J.S. Mill's interests were extremely broad, and he wrote influential works about ethical, political, and social issues. His book *The Subjection of Women* is a famous argument against 'the legal subordination of one sex to the other' and in favour of the 'principle of perfect equality, admitting no power or privilege on the one side, nor disability on the other' (J.S. Mill, 1986 [1861]: 7). The assertion of the rights of women has been part of a long struggle in which the person we will consider next was a pioneer.

Mary Wollstonecraft
(1759–97)

In the National Portrait Gallery hangs a picture of Mary Wollstonecraft, a picture of her as she was a scant few months before her death. I remember the child I was when I saw it first, haunted by the terror of youth before experience. I wanted so desperately to know how other women had saved their souls alive. And the woman in the little frame arrested me, this woman with the auburn hair, and the sad steady brown eyes and the gallant poise of the head. She *had* saved her soul alive; it looked out from her eyes unafraid. (Benedict, 1959: 519)

Until now we have been discussing only the work of men, and mainly of European men at that. Until recently, there has been a tendency for history to be only the story of Dead White European Males, or DWEMs (e.g., Knox, 1993). This is particularly unfortunate in psychology, in which most of the students are women.

It is generally believed that women have had a lower status in North American and European society than have men. One reason for this conclusion is the fact that women typically found employment in occupations of a relatively low status (Archer and Lloyd, 1982: ch. 8). During the prehistoric era, women may have enjoyed a higher status relative to men than they did subsequently (Tanner, 1983), but masculine roles appear to have had a higher status than feminine ones throughout most of our recorded history (Hartmann, 1976). Generally speaking, this has been true for disciplines such as psychology, in which the high status roles have traditionally tended to be filled by men, with the rest being left for women. Furomoto (1987: 109) has shown that:

> historically women have been relegated to the bottom of the professional hierarchy, to 'the "dirtiest" areas of professional service . . . those involving the most human contact with all its attendant complexities' (Brunberg and Tomes,

1982: 287–8). More specifically, during the nineteenth century women assumed primary care of such problematic clienteles as the young, the poor, the immigrant, the intemperate and the sick. The best employment opportunities for women thus came to be found in the so-called helping professions, such as social work and public health. . . . The high status branch of the field, academic psychology, abstract and isolated within its ivory tower, was never welcoming to women, and few were able to find a place there.

Problems similar to those described by Furomoto were perceived with extraordinary clarity by **Mary Wollstonecraft** in the late eighteenth century. Wollstonecraft may already be familiar to you as the mother of Mary Shelley, the author of *Frankenstein* (1818). However, our interest is in Wollstonecraft's *A Vindication of the Rights of Women* (1988 [1792]).

Universal Education

Wollstonecraft argued that women had the right to education, which they had previously been largely denied. She spoke out against those who believed that 'woman would be unsexed by acquiring strength of body and mind, and that beauty, soft bewitching beauty would no longer adorn the daughters of men. I am of a very different opinion, for I think that, on the contrary, we should then see dignified beauty, and true grace.' Wollstonecraft argued that 'Were boys and girls permitted to pursue the same studies together, those graceful decencies might early be inculcated which produce modesty without those sexual distinctions that taint the mind' (ibid., 165).

Although Wollstonecraft believed, as did empiricists such as Locke, that there were no innate ideas and that the mind is a blank slate or *tabula rasa* on which experience must write', she also believed that the properly educated mind could discover things for itself (Sapiro, 1992: 53–5). This ability to draw out the implications of what one had learned should be a principal goal of education. The capacity to think independently could only be fostered by an educational system that encouraged this form of behaviour and did not require children merely to imitate their teachers and blindly obey their instructions (ibid., 113).

To attain these goals, Wollstonecraft (1988: 167) proposed a system of education in which 'boys and girls might be educated together, absolutely free and open to all classes', at least for the younger children. Treating women equally in the educational system would undermine the tradition whereby women were 'shut out from all political and civil employments; for by thus narrowing their minds they are rendered unfit to fulfill the peculiar duties which nature has assigned them' (ibid., 169).

Although Wollstonecraft wanted women to break with some aspects of their traditional roles, she did not argue that they should abandon these roles altogether. 'The conclusion I wish to draw is obvious; make women rational creatures, and free citizens, and they will quickly become good wives, and mothers; that is—if men do not neglect the duties of husbands and fathers' (ibid., 178).

The Importance of Emotion

As Burns (1979) observed, Wollstonecraft had (for her time) a very sophisticated view of the relation between *emotion* and *reason*. Emotion has often been thought of as entirely a bodily process, less abstract and 'psychological' than reason. For example, the *Oxford English Dictionary* gives these two early meanings of the word *emotion*: 'a moving stirring perturbation (in physical sense)' and 'agitation or disturbance of mind, feeling, passion; any vehement or excited mental state'. A common stereotype is that women are more emotional and less rational than men. If emotional people are conceived of as susceptible to 'disturbances of mind', then this stereotype is very unflattering to women, not to mention dangerous to their well-being. Without accepting the stereotype, Wollstonecraft nonetheless accepted the notion that women were more influenced by their feelings than were men. However, she also introduced the idea that

emotions were not merely bodily 'agitations'. She suggested that feeling could also provide a point of view on a situation that supplemented the point of view given to us by reason alone. Wollstonecraft used the word **sensibility** to refer to this aspect of emotion. 'Sensibility is not a cold calculation of what is right; it is a spontaneous warmth of virtuous emotion. To use literary conventions, reason is the proper work of the head, sensibility is the proper work of the heart' (Sapiro, 1992: 65).

In the nineteenth and twentieth centuries, people became more comfortable with the notion that emotion can provide information about themselves and others that cannot be obtained in any other way. Phrases such as 'being in touch with our feelings' conveyed this sentiment. However, before the efforts of Wollstonecraft and others we will study later on, emotion did not have the same dignity as did other psychological process such as *reason* and *choice*. Throughout the nineteenth century, interest in emotion as a psychological process continued to grow, and in the twentieth century the psychology of emotion became a central part of the discipline.

The Utopian Tradition in Psychology

Wollstonecraft belongs to a somewhat neglected aspect of the history of psychology that historians such as Manuel (1966) and Morawski (1982) have identified as the **Utopian tradition** in psychology. Like Wollstonecraft, many psychologists actively sought to improve the well-being of themselves and others through changing the nature of the society in which they lived. Such social activism is characteristic of many twentieth-century psychologists, as we shall see in subsequent chapters.

Immanuel Kant (1724–1804)

Immanuel Kant conforms to one persistent stereotype of an intellectual, that of a person who is 'strongly influenced by ideas, though his ideas have their origin not in objective data but in his subjective foundation. He will follow his ideas . . . inwards and not outwards. . . . His judgment appears cold, inflexible, arbitrary and ruthless, because it relates far less to the object than to the subject . . . it always bypasses the object and leaves one with a feeling of the subject's superiority' (Jung, 1976 [1921]). As we will see, Kant tried to demonstrate that Hume's skepticism was wrong, and that one could reach definite conclusions through the use of reason. One of these conclusions was that we could arrive at certain necessary truths about our subjective experience, although nothing could be known about the world external to ourselves.

Kant was born and raised in Königsberg, in what was East Prussia. It is now called Kaliningrad and is in western Russia. Kant reportedly never left Königsberg, becoming a professor at the university in 1770:

> Kant led an uneventful life: no change, no travel, no reaching out for the unusual, not much interest outside his study room and university classroom. Kant's life was a life of thought. . . . Rain or shine, peace or war, revolution or counter-revolution had less affect on his life than a new book he read, and certainly counted less than a new idea that grew in his own mind. Kant's thoughts were to him the center of the universe, even more so than Descartes' *Cogito* was to Descartes. (Wolman, 1968: 229)

Kant's philosophy is often understood in contrast to Hume's skepticism, and, indeed, Kant credited Hume with making him think deeply about fundamental issues. Hume had shown that some concepts that we take for granted are actually quite empty. For example, Hume appeared to show that there really was no *self* and nothing corresponding to our concept of *causality* than mere correlation. In order to meet Hume's challenge, Kant had to show that such concepts were meaningful even though they were 'neither logically necessary, nor derived from experience' (Beck, 1950: x).

Kant's 'Second Copernican Revolution'

In order to discover the nature of our ideas, Kant recommended that we take an approach similar to that taken by **Copernicus** (1473–1543) in

his attempt to understand planetary motion. Copernicus's revolutionary way of understanding the solar system was to insist that the earth was not at its centre. 'Failing of satisfactory progress in explaining the movements of the heavenly bodies on the supposition that they all revolved around the spectator, he tried whether he might not have better success if he made the spectator to revolve and the stars remain at rest' (Kant, 1965 [1787]: 22). In other words, Copernicus completely changed the frame of reference within which planetary motion was explained. Similarly, Kant sought to change completely the frame of reference within which the origin of our concepts was understood. Kant changed the frame of reference used by empiricists such as Hume. They believed that our concepts were derived from events in the external world. Kant argued that it was a mistake to assume that a concept such as *causality* referred to something outside ourselves and insisted that our experience was actually shaped by our concepts rather than the other way around. To discover the nature of our concepts we need look no further than ourselves.

Kant's **second Copernican revolution** involves denying that our experience is completely determined by events outside ourselves. On the contrary, the person ultimately constructs his or her own experience. 'Instead of measuring the content meaning and truth . . . [of our concepts] by something extraneous which is supposed to be reproduced in them, we must find in . . . [our concepts] themselves the measure and criterion for truth and intrinsic meaning. . . . [Our concepts] are not imitations, but organs of reality, since it is solely by their agency that anything becomes an object . . . [and] is made visible to us' (Cassirer, 1946: 10). Without our concepts, we would not have experience. Our concepts make our experience possible.

This may sound mysterious, but the phenomena Kant has in mind are actually quite simple and obvious. Kant observed that everyone (not just scientists) tends to organize personal experiences in terms of causes and effects. We impose cause and effect relationships *on* the world, rather than observing them *in* the world. Perhaps you have had an experience of the sort that Kant had in mind.

For example, 'when a gust of wind blows a door shut, and at the same time an electric light happens to go on at the other end of a corridor, the impression of a causal relation is forced upon us' (Michotte, 1963: 16). Whenever we observe two events occurring close together in space and time there is a tendency for us to perceive one as causing the other. Our minds spontaneously and inevitably organize our experiences, using concepts such as causality. Another example that illustrates the tendency for us to impose our own organization on our experience is given in Box 2.3.

BOX 2.3

FINDING THE AREA OF A RECTANGLE

Look at A in the accompanying figure. Imagine that it is an inelastic string stretched tight around four small posts so that it takes the form of a square that is 2 inches by 2 inches. You know how to calculate the area of the square. You multiply 2 by 2 and get 4 square inches. Now look at B. In this figure the same string has been stretched tight around the same four posts, but the posts have been moved so that we now have a rectangle that is narrower and longer than in A. Now, quickly, answer the following question: Is the area of B equal to, larger than, or smaller than the area of A? If you are like most adults (including me when I was first shown this problem by A. Jonckheere), you will conclude that B has the *same* area as A. The reason you will give is that although the second figure is narrower than the first, it is also longer, and these changes compensate for each other. Therefore, the two areas must remain the same. Furthermore, you will persist in this conclusion as you are shown C and D, although you may begin to doubt yourself when you see E.

As it turns out, we are mistaken if we conclude that these figures all have the same area. We saw that A had an area of 4 square inches. Suppose that B is 0.5 inches longer, and therefore 0.5 inches less in height. That would make it 2.5 inches long and 1.5 inches wide. Multiply 1.5 by 2.5 and you will get 3.8 inches, which is less than the 4 square inches of the original figure. Similarly, suppose that C is another 0.5 inches longer and 0.5 inches less in height than B. That makes it 3 inches long and 1 inch wide, for an area of 3 square inches, or less than either of the previous figures. As a matter of fact, the figures get progressively smaller in area, as you can work out for yourself in the remaining cases.

Why do we make this mistake? A Kantian would give something like the following explanation. We do not rely on our perception of each individual rectangle to make a judgement about its area. Rather, we understand the area of *any* rectangular figure as being determined by multiplying the height and width of the figure. We apply this way of thinking to our perception of the figure. In general, it is *not* the things themselves, but the way that we think about them that determines the judgements we make.

The preceding problem is discussed by Kline (1985: 33), whose book contains a good introduction to Kant's view of mathematics. For another example of the way our perception and our reason can lead to opposite conclusions, see Benjafield (1969a).

Which figure has the largest area?

Kant was not suggesting that everyone organizes every aspect of experience in the same way. Individual experiences may be unique. 'When we say, "The room is warm, sugar sweet, and wormwood bitter," we have only subjectively valid judgements. I do not at all expect that I or any other person shall always find it as I now do' (Kant, 1950 [1783]: 47). However, in addition to having our own unique experiences, we can and do make judgements that are much more general. Kant gives the example of someone saying:

'When the sun shines on the stone, it grows warm.' This judgement, however often I and others may have perceived it, is a mere judgement of perception and contains no necessity; perceptions are only usually conjoined in this manner. But if I say, 'The sun warms the stone,' I add to the perception a concept of the understanding, namely, that of cause, which necessarily connects with the concept of sunshine that of heat. (Ibid., 49)

The conclusion that one thing (the sun) has caused another thing (the rock) to become warm is more than just a sequence of perceptions; it is a result of applying the concept of causality to one's perceptions. For Kant, this is not an isolated example but an illustration of the way that concepts shape our experience. As the example in Box 2.3 shows, our judgement is determined by the concepts we use to think about a situation, not simply by our 'impression' of the situation.

Can Psychology Be a Science Like Other Sciences?

Like other intellectuals of his day, Kant took Newtonian physics to be the model for any true science (Friedman, 1990). Kant was enormously impressed by Newton's ability to give his laws a mathematical expression, and claimed 'that in any particular theory of nature we can find only so much of real science as we can find mathematics . . . hence any theory of nature will contain only so much of real science as it permits the application of mathematics' (as cited by Cassirer, 1962 [1945]: 62). We have already seen how intimately the history of mathematics and science is interwoven. In Kant's case, the identification of science with mathematics means that psychology is necessarily excluded from the sciences (Mischel, 1967).

In order to see why Kant believed that psychology could never achieve the status of a true science, we must explore his distinction between the **external sense** and the **internal sense**. Our experience of what goes on outside of us is given to us through our external senses, such as vision. Our visual experience is organized spatially in relation to ourselves, such that things are near or far, high or low, left or right (Kant, 1968 [1768]; Bryant et al., 1992). Insofar as we can understand what goes on in this spatially extended world outside of us, this understanding is provided by disciplines like physics. The data of physics are given by our external senses, and Newton showed that mathematics can describe what is given by our external senses. However, our experience of what goes on *inside* us is not organized spatially, but temporally. Our subjective experience is organized in terms of *time*. We have a sense of things happening before and after this moment. Kant believed that psychology has as its subject matter the data of this internal sense, and he argued that these data cannot be organized mathematically. Therefore, the data of psychology cannot rest firmly on a mathematical foundation, and psychology can never be a true science. 'Since there can be no pure, mathematical science of mind for objects of inner sense, whose only form is time, we have no way of understanding why inner states must occur in the way they do' (Mischel, 1967: 603). Psychology can only provide a crudely empirical description of our subjective states and cannot provide us with any deep understanding of why our personal experiences are the way they are.

The notion that there can be no scientific study of our inner life is a recurrent theme in psychology. In what follows, we will see some psychologists attempt to show that a science of *subjective experience* really is possible. We will also see other psychologists attempt to show that psychology is actually *not* about inner experience at all, but about *behaviour*, which is something we experience through our external senses. Perhaps a science of behaviour is the answer, although Kant would not have thought so (ibid., 605). Still other psychologists are less concerned that psychology be a true science and more concerned that it faithfully represent the nature of our subjective experience. This last group most closely approximates the kind of psychology that Kant thought was possible. It is up to us to decide which of these alternatives, if any, adequately comes to grips with the problems Kant raised.

Charles Darwin (1809–82)

Like Kant, **Charles Darwin** thought deeply about the relation between people and the world in which they live. Unlike Kant, Darwin was much more interested in exploring the external world (Jung, 1921: 383). By thinking about what he found on his explorations, Darwin reached conclusions that helped bring about a revolutionary change in the way that many people think about themselves.

Anyone observing the behaviour of Charles Darwin when he was an undergraduate student would have been hard put to predict his future eminence as a great scientist. Although he came from a family with a rich intellectual tradition, he did not regard his own formal education as much of a preparation for the creative work he was to do later in his life (Gruber, 1981: 73). About his years attending Cambridge University (1828–31), Darwin later wrote:

> my time was sadly wasted there, and worse than wasted. From my passion for shooting and for hunting, and, when this failed, for riding across the country, I got into a sporting set, including some dissipated low-minded young men. We used often to dine together in the evening, though these dinners often included men of a higher stamp, and we sometimes drank too

much, with jolly singing and playing at cards afterwards. I know that I ought to feel ashamed of days and evenings thus spent but as some of my friends were very pleasant, and we were all in the highest spirits, I cannot help looking back to these times with much pleasure. (Darwin, 1958 [1892]: 19–20)

Thus described, Darwin's undergraduate experience sounds not very different from that of a great many undergraduates, both then and now. However, in common with many other former undergraduates, Darwin appeared to exaggerate 'the Bacchanalian nature of these parties' (F. Darwin, 1958 [1892]: 20), and his time at Cambridge may actually have given him a useful framework for his future work (Gruber, 1981: 82).

In some important ways Darwin's background resembles that of many highly innovative people. Simonton (1984, 1988) has demonstrated that people who make creative contributions to our culture often have the following characteristics:

- They suffer the loss of a parent when young.
- They receive neither too much nor too little formal education.

Darwin lost his mother in 1817, when he was eight years old (Darwin, 1958: 5), and his formal education stopped when he received his BA from Cambridge in 1831. Simonton (1984, 1988) speculates that the early loss of a parent forces children to think and do things for themselves, rather than simply take over their parents' ideas and habits. Of course, one needs a basic education to become acquainted with fundamental facts in a discipline, but too much education may lead to rigid habits of thought that stultify creativity. Darwin did not have this problem. Of course, by no means everyone who loses a parent or who attains a moderate level of education will become a successful innovator! Darwin also had other advantages, such as his family's intellectual tradition. Moreover, it was not so much Darwin's background as what he proceeded to do with it that brought about the theory of evolution.

The Voyage of the *Beagle*

In his autobiography, Darwin (1958: 6) observed that his 'taste for natural history, and more especially for collecting was well developed' even as a schoolboy. Thus, it is not entirely surprising to find Darwin serving as a naturalist aboard the **Beagle**, which was in the charge of a Captain Fitz-Roy. The *Beagle* left Plymouth, England, on 27 December 1831, bound for South America, and did not return to England until 2 October 1836. Darwin's job was to record the geological formations and collect specimens of the animals found in the various places the *Beagle* visited.

> During the first two years my old passion for shooting survived in nearly full force, and I shot myself all the birds and animals for my collection; but gradually I gave up my gun more and more, and finally altogether, to my servant, as shooting interfered with my work. . . . I discovered, though unconsciously and insensibly, that the pleasure of observing and reasoning was a much higher one than that of skill and sport. (Ibid., 29–30)

Darwin took a copy of the first volume of Charles Lyell's *Principles of Geology* (1969 [1830–3]) with him on his voyage. **Charles Lyell** had argued that the Earth was of a very great age, and that all the changes that had taken place since its beginning could be explained in terms of purely natural forces (Eiseley, 1987 [1956]: 67–8). This provided Darwin with a *historical* framework within which to think about how the population of organisms in an area changes:

> According to Lyell, change in fauna and flora could largely be explained in terms of organisms having moved from place to place, limited by barriers and ecological influences. The aim of biogeography, as Darwin was developing it, was to trace species to their places of origin in the light of their capacity for dispersal and the history of geological change. (Ghiselin, 1983: 65)

Darwin began to go beyond this simple historical framework as a result of observations he made as the voyage progressed. The most famous of these observations took place in 1835 in the Galapagos Islands, located about 650 miles off the west coast of Ecuador in South America. Darwin discovered some finches. 'The finches are of special interest, for although obviously closely related they have become separated off into at least 13 distinct species showing extraordinary modifications of the beak in accordance with different modes of life' (Hindle 1983: 67). This, together with other, similar observations, suggested that all species had not been created by God at the beginning of time, to remain invariant thereafter. Rather, it began to seem possible that new species could emerge as descendants of other species.

The Development of the Theory of Evolution

When Darwin returned to England, he began to ruminate about his findings. He first considered the emergence of different species in terms of the theory originally developed by **Jean Baptiste Lamarck** (1744–1829). Lamarck (1914 [1809]) developed the **law of the inheritance of acquired characteristics**, which held that animals can acquire characteristics in their lifetime that they can pass along to their immediate descendants. Useful habits acquired by an animal in one generation may not only be passed along to offspring, but the structure of the animal may change as a consequence. The most famous example used by Lamarck is the giraffe. The giraffe typically lives in regions devoid of grass, in which the only food source comes from trees. As a result of habitually reaching for leaves high up in trees, the giraffe has acquired both long legs and a very long neck. Lyell (1979 [1853]: 12–13) noted that Lamarck had also speculated on the possibility that humans had evolved from orangutans through a very slow process. As a result of 'the habit of climbing trees, and of hanging on by grasping the boughs with their feet as with hands', the forelimbs changed from being used as feet to being used as hands, and walking upright became necessary. Lamarckianism had a powerful influence during the nineteenth century, although, as we shall see, it was supplanted by Darwin's own theory.

More important than Lamarck in shaping Darwin's thinking was **Thomas Malthus** (1766–1834). Darwin read Malthus's *Essay on the Principle of Population As It Affects the Future Improvement of Society* in 1838 (Thomson, 1998). Malthus (1956 [1798]: 1193) had argued that 'the population has a constant tendency to increase beyond the means of subsistence.' According to Malthus's calculations, the food supply increases arithmetically, while the population increases geometrically. What this means is illustrated in Fig. 2.3, which is based on the same numbers used by Malthus. Suppose we start with a population that requires only as much food as is available. Over a period of 200 years, the population would increase to over 250 times what it was initially, while the food supply would only increase to a level nine times what it was initially. The necessary result is too many people competing for too little food. Some people will be losers, and will die as a result.

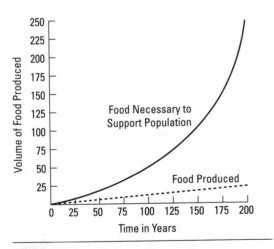

FIGURE 2.3
Mathus's calculation of the relationship between food produced and food necessary to support the population.

While Malthus's precise calculations may have been faulty, they still provided Darwin with the idea that it was necessary for individuals to compete for resources in order to survive (Ghiselin, 1983: 66). 'Malthus dichotomized nature into humankind on the one hand, and its food supply on the other. . . . Darwin was interested in describing all of nature, including humankind, in the same terms. Struggle is not only for food but against all the conditions of life' (Keegan and Gruber, 1983: 19). As a result of this struggle some species become extinct while others adapt and survive.

Darwin continued to refine his views, and eventually published the theory for which he became justly famous. The theory was based on **natural selection**, or the **survival of the fittest**.

> Let it also be borne in mind how infinitely complex and close-fitting are the mutual relations of all organic beings to each other and to their physical conditions of life; and consequently what infinitely varied diversities of structure might be of use to each being under changing conditions of life. Can it, then, be thought improbable, seeing that variations useful to man have undoubtedly occurred, that other variations useful in some way to each being in the great and complex battle of life, should occur in the course of many successive generations? If such do occur, can we doubt (remembering that many more individuals are born than can possibly survive) that individuals having any advantage, however slight, over others, would have the best chance of surviving and of procreating their kind? On the other hand, we may feel sure that any variation in the least degree injurious would be rigidly destroyed. This preservation of favourable individual differences and variations, and the destruction of those which are injurious, I have called Natural Selection, or the Survival of the Fittest. (Darwin, 1979 [1859]: 63–4)

The preceding quotation is from *The Origin of Species*, which Darwin did not publish until 1859, or 23 years after the return of the *Beagle* to

England. There has been a lot of speculation about why it took Darwin so long to announce his theory (Richards, 1983). Some have argued that Darwin was afraid of the social consequences of presenting a view that apparently contradicts traditional religious conceptions of the origin of human beings. Others have suggested that Darwin's theory emerged only slowly and required many years to become fully developed. Whatever the reasons, Darwin had the shock of his life when, on 18 June 1858, he received an essay from Alfred Russel Wallace (1823–1913). Wallace wanted Darwin's opinion of the essay, in which Wallace demonstrated that he understood the process of evolution in very much the same way that Darwin did. Darwin had previously confided some of his views on evolution to friends, such as the geologist Lyell, and they had warned him that if he did not publish his theory someone else would beat him to it. 'Darwin at once wrote to Charles Lyell: "Your words have come true with a vengeance—that I should be forestalled—I never saw a more striking coincidence. . . . So all my originality, whatever it may amount to, will be smashed, though my book, if it will ever have any value, will not be deteriorated, as all the labour consists in the application of the theory"' (Hindle, 1983: 67). Darwin was prepared to let Wallace get the credit, but it was arranged that the theory should be announced in a joint paper given to the Linnean Society on 1 July 1858 ('On the tendency of species to form varieties; and on the perpetuation of varieties and species by natural means of selection', by C. Darwin and A. Wallace). Darwin then wrote and published *The Origin of Species* in a little over a year.

It is important to be clear about the difference between *natural selection*, as Darwin described it, and the Lamarckian principle of *the inheritance of acquired characteristics*. Lamarck's view was that organisms attempt to adapt to their environments, and adaptations acquired during their lifetime can be passed along to their offspring. By contrast, Darwin proposed that the chief mechanism of evolution was what has come to be called *blind variation and selective retention* (Campbell, 1960).

Within each generation 'variation in nature is so inexhaustible that there are never two individuals that are completely identical and equally well adapted' to the environment in which they happen to find themselves (Mayr, 1991: 123). These variations are *blind*, in the sense that they occur by chance and without any foresight on the part of the organism as to their adaptive consequences. Those variations that happen to be adaptive tend to be *retained*, in that they 'have the greatest probability to survive, to reproduce, and to transmit their attributes to the next generation' (ibid.). Although Darwin allowed Lamarckianism a place in his theory, it became discredited as a theory of evolution (e.g., Dawkins, 1983, 1988) in favour of the principle of natural selection.

To see how the theory of evolution conflicted with established religious accounts of the origins of human beings, note the difference between the principle of natural selection and the world view of Aquinas we considered earlier. The conflict between 'Darwinism' and traditional theology has never been resolved, and a great many people continue to believe that human beings were created by God. In *The Origin of Species* Darwin left the door slightly open to creationism by admitting 'the possibility that the whole lawful system of material nature might have had a supernatural Creator, a First Cause, who then left all else to "secondary causes"' (Gruber, 1981: 210). However, Darwin never suggested that God directly intervened in the process of evolution once it had begun, and Darwin's views were persistently under attack by conventionally religious people throughout his lifetime. Nevertheless, Darwin was buried in Westminster Abbey, near Isaac Newton (Stone, 1982), a tribute to the immense impact of his work.

Darwin and Psychology

The influence of **evolutionary theory** on psychology has been very great indeed. As Heidbreder (1933: 106) observed, Darwinian theory implied that psychologists had to study people in terms of their 'development both genetic and phylogenetic, [their] position in the array of animal species, and the means by which [they] adapt themselves to [the] environment'. Each of these implications became an area of study in psychology. We will examine these areas in great detail in subsequent chapters and only briefly mention them here.

Comparative psychology. Darwinism led to the idea that there are important similarities between people and other animals. This suggests that a great deal can be learned about people by comparing them with other species. Thus, the study of animals should be part of psychology (e.g., Bitterman, 1967).

Individual differences. Another Darwinian idea to have a profound influence on psychology was *variation* between members of the same species (Herrnstein and Boring, 1966: 407). Individual members of a species differed from each other, and these individual differences determined how well or how poorly individuals adapted to the environment. The measurement of individual differences became the focus of a great deal of work in psychology (e.g., Anastasi, 1966).

Many other topics of study in psychology also received a Darwinian stamp. For example, Darwin's *The Expression of the Emotions in Man and Animals* (1955 [1872]) deeply influenced the psychology of *emotion*. Darwin (1964 [1959]) also discussed the role *instincts* play in human behaviour, and the instinct concept has been used in many areas of psychology, from ethology to social psychology (Beer, 1983). The study of *sexuality* was a central feature of Darwin's work (e.g., Ghiselin, 1966: ch. 9), as shown in his *The Descent of Man: Selection in Relation to Sex* (1955 [1871]). It is not surprising that sexuality subsequently became a preoccupation of many psychological theories, of which Freud's is the most obvious example. Finally, although *child psychology* began before Darwin, he still contributed a framework that has informed the work of many developmental psychologists (Vidal et al., 1983). However, Darwin's influence on developmental psychology was not as great as has sometimes been supposed (Charlesworth, 1992).

Studying the History of Psychology

Ixion's Wheel or Jacob's Ladder?

We have examined several famous thinkers who have left their mark on subsequent theories. Now we can look back over this history to see if there are any patterns in addition to those we have already considered in Box 1.2. In any overview of the history of thought, two contrasting patterns can be perceived. The distinguished historian Frank Manuel (1965: 4) called these the *progressive* and the *cyclical*: 'on the one hand the historical world seen as movement either to a fixed end, or to an indefinite end that defines itself in the course of the progression, history as novelty creating and always variant; on the other hand circularity, eternal recurrence, return to the beginning of things, sheer reiteration or similar recapitulation'. Manuel (1965) used Ixion and Jacob as personifications of this polarity. Ixion is a figure from ancient Greek mythology who was condemned to rotate forever on a wheel of fire. In the Bible (Genesis 28:12), Jacob 'dreamed that there was a ladder set up on the earth and the top of it reached to heaven.' Manuel (1965: 5–6) asked us to consider whether history is 'like Ixion in Hades tied to a perpetually revolving wheel' or like 'Jacob dreaming of the ladder that reaches up to the heavens?'

Progress in any discipline, including psychology, cannot be taken for granted. Psychology may not always get better and better. Sometimes psychology is cyclical. An idea may go out of fashion for a while, then get forgotten, and finally come back again as a 'new' idea. Berlyne (1975: 79) put it this way.

That many disputes now dividing psychologists are essentially rehashes of debates that have gone on for centuries, or for some cases for millennia, is hardly an original observation. In psychology, as in clothing, there is a limited number of possibilities. Nether garments must be based on the trousers principle, the skirt principle, or the loin cloth principle, and in each case, there is a finite number of discriminable gradations between floor length and zero. There is continuous oscillation among the possible alternatives, but there has to be some passage of time before what was once grotesquely frumpish can reappear as the refreshingly unconventional.

Knowledge of the history of psychology should put us in the position of being able to detect those parts of the current psychological scene that are genuinely novel and those parts that are recapitulations of previous ideas.

Of course, it is entirely possible that psychology both progresses *and* is cyclical. Ideas may keep being 'rediscovered', but at the same time those ideas may be understood in progressively more sophisticated ways. A *spiral* may be a useful symbol of such a process (e.g., Piaget, 1970: 124–5) in which ideas recur, but at higher and higher levels. The ideas of the people we have already considered will be reiterated again and again by the people we will now go on to consider. Modern thinkers 'have the advantage of time and can choose prototypes from a greater array of models. Moderns can learn from many more sources than could ancients, and though nature is no more prolific in genius . . . in one generation than in its predecessor, sheer accumulation of examples itself becomes an advantage' (Manuel, 1965: 66–7).

Person or *Zeitgeist*?

The ideas of psychologists do not come only from the past. Individual creativity also plays its part. In addition, it is impossible to neglect the role that 'prevailing ideologies and/or the socioeconomic situation of the period' play in shaping ideas (Mayr, 1991: 123). In addition to the contribution that an original thinker makes, it is necessary to understand each person's work in terms of the cultural context within which it takes place. This cultural context is called the **Zeitgeist**, or 'spirit of the times'. There is often a lot of controversy about whether an important idea is the result of one per-

son's originality or the inevitable outcome of forces acting within the culture at that time (e.g., Boring, 1950a). For example, is the theory of evolution the product of Darwin's genius, or would someone else (like Wallace) have produced it anyway, given the way ideas were developing in nineteenth-century European culture? We will need to be attentive to this kind of question and give due credit to the *person* where it is due, as well as acknowledging the role of the *Zeitgeist*.

Rediscovering the Past

When we study the history of psychology, we try to rediscover what each psychologist was attempting to accomplish. The history of psychology, like history generally, is not important simply because it lays the groundwork for what we have now. We should not regard all previous thinkers as obsolete, and we should guard against the danger of being too critical of the past. If we dwell on the weaknesses and failings of previous thinkers, then we may fail to understand them, and if we do not understand them, then we will lose an important part of our heritage. The great psychologists are like important works of art— by appreciating them we enrich ourselves. Earlier psychologists are still relevant, although it is up to us to connect what they had to say to our present concerns. To do this we must put aside our prejudices about what psychology should be and approach each theorist as sympathetically as we can. 'This means rethinking the thought' (Collingwood, 1946: 283) of the psychologists we are studying and trying to understand each theory on its own terms before we are critical of it.

There is much more to say about the relation between the history of ideas and psychology. However, now we will go on to review some of the major approaches to psychology in the nineteenth and twentieth centuries. As we go along, we will introduce some additional ideas about the nature of history as it applies to psychology. Then, in the last chapter, we will return to how the study of the history of psychology illuminates the nature of psychology itself.

IMPORTANT NAMES, WORKS, AND CONCEPTS

Names and Works

Beagle

Berkeley, George

Copernicus

Darwin, Charles

Descartes, René

Goethe, Johann Wolfgang von

Hobbes, Thomas

Hume, David

Kant, Immanuel

Lamarck, Jean Baptiste

Locke, John

Lyell, Charles

Malthus, Thomas

Mill, James

Mill, John Stuart

Newton, Isaac

The Origin of Species

The Subjection of Women

Wollstonecraft, Mary

Concepts

alchemy

association of ideas

British empiricists

Cartesian doubt

causality

Cogito, ergo sum

colour theory

dualism

empiricism

evolutionary theory

external sense

ghost in a machine

innate ideas

interactionism

internal sense

introspection

Ixion's wheel

Jacob's ladder

law of the inheritance of acquired characteristics

laws of motion

mental chemistry

natural selection

rationalism

reflection

Renaissance

rewards and punishments

second Copernican revolution

self

sensations

sensibility

survival of the fittest

'To be is to be perceived'

Utopian tradition

Zeitgeist

RECOMMENDED READINGS

Descartes

For a description of an approach to psychology that relies heavily on Descartes, see N.A. Stillings et al., *Cognitive Science: An Introduction* (Cambridge, Mass.: MIT Press, 1987).

Newton

The historian Frank Manuel has written about Newton with great psychological insight in *A Portrait of Isaac Newton* (Cambridge, Mass.: Harvard University Press, 1968) and *The Religion of Isaac Newton* (Oxford: Oxford University Press, 1974). C.U.M. Smith, 'David Hartley's Newtonian neuropsychology', *Journal of the History of the Behavioral Sciences* 23 (1987): 123–38, describes one of the ways in which Newton's ideas were imported into the psychology of Hartley (1705–57), who belonged to the school of British associationists.

The British Empiricists

J. Bennett, *Locke, Berkeley, Hume* (Oxford: Clarendon Press, 1971), provides an excellent review of the British empiricists. Much of contemporary neuropsychology has an associationist flavour, and this is well-captured by H. Buckingham, 'Early development of associationist theory in psychology as a forerunner to connection theory', *Brain and Cognition* 3 (1984): 19–34. J.S. Mill, in 1846, wrote what is perhaps the most famous guide to experimental method in 'A system of logic, ratiocinative and inductive', in J.M. Robson, ed., *Collected Works of John Stuart Mill*, vol. 7 (Toronto: University of Toronto Press, 1973). In that work he outlined methods of experimental inquiry that are still cited in logic and research methods texts. For example, see J. Benjafield, *Thinking Critically about Research Methods* (Boston: Allyn & Bacon, 1994).

Wollstonecraft

Over the years, Wollstonecraft has served as a beacon for many social scientists, including the American anthropologist Ruth Benedict, 'Mary Wollstonecraft', in M. Mead, ed., *Anthropologist at Work: Writings of Ruth Benedict* (Boston: Houghton Mifflin, 1959), 491–519. E.P. Thompson, in *Making History: Writings on History and Culture* (New York: Norton, 1994), provides a fine appreciation of Wollstonecraft and her social context.

Kant

For a taste of the kind of empirical psychology that followed Kant in the nineteenth century, see E.R. Hilgard, 'The trilogy of mind: Cognition, affection and conation', *Journal of the History of the Behavioral Sciences* 16 (1980): 107–17. Some of Kant's own writings are quite 'psychological', particularly his little book *Observations on the Beautiful and the Sublime*, trans. J.T. Goldthwait (Berkeley: University of California Press, 1960 [1763]). G. Hatfield, 'Kant and empirical psychology in the 18th century', *Psychological Science* 9 (1998): 423–8, provides several excellent examples of Kant's psychological observations. A thorough review of Kant's position on psychology as a science can be found in C.W. Tolman, 'Philosophical doubts about psychology as a natural science', in C. Green et al., eds, *The Transformation of Psychology: The Influences of 19th-century natural science, technology, and philosophy* (Washington: American Psychological Association, 2001), 175–93.

Darwin

A wonderful compilation of Darwiniana is available on a multi-media CD-ROM created by P. Goldie, *Darwin*, 2nd edn (San Francisco: Lightbinders, Inc.: 1997). This disk contains the text of several of Darwin's major works, as well as a Darwin bibliography and many intriguing images and sounds relevant to the study of evolutionary theory.

CHAPTER 3

THE NINETEENTH-CENTURY TRANSFORMATION OF PSYCHOLOGY

Introduction

At the beginning of the nineteenth century, many believed, with Kant, that psychology could never be a science. However, by the end of the nineteenth century, thanks in large part to the efforts of the people reviewed in this chapter, the possibility that psychology could be a truly scientific discipline seemed much more plausible. Green, Shore, and Teo (2001: xi–xvii) called this the 'transformation of psychology' and noted the importance of understanding the various processes whereby a more scientific approach to psychology came about. One important strand in this development was J.F. Herbart's attempt to cast a psychological theory in purely mathematical terms. Herbart was also one of the first to apply psychology to practical problems, by showing how his psychology implied a particular approach to education. Another scientific innovation was G.T. Fechner's **psychophysics**, which hypothesized a mathematically precise relation between stimulus values and sensation that could be tested using experimental data. Scientific work on the psychophysiology of perception led to important theories of colour vision by Hermann von Helmholtz, Ewald Hering, and Christine Ladd-Franklin. Finally, through the efforts of Francis Galton and Herbert Spencer, some of the more controversial implications of the theory of evolution were drawn out.

J.F. Herbart (1776–1841)

As we saw in the previous chapter, Kant did not believe that psychology could be a true science because it could not be mathematical. Although **J.F. Herbart** succeeded to Kant's position at the University of Königsberg, he differed from Kant by believing that mathematics was applicable to psychological events. Because of this belief, Herbart is often regarded as one of the earliest, if not the first, mathematical psychologist (Leary, 1980; Miller, 1964: 13).

In the last chapter we reviewed the many ways in which the *threshold* concept has been used in psychology. Herbart is usually credited with making this concept central to psychology by embedding it in a rich theory of mental life. Herbart was not only interested in what went on *above* the threshold of consciousness, but also in what went on *below* the **threshold of consciousness**. Events below the threshold of consciousness were *unconscious*, and, under the right circumstances, could become conscious. Herbart tried to show mathematically that these relationships were true.

Herbart's psychology rests on the assumption that all mental life is the 'result of the action and interaction of elementary ideas' (Ward, 1910). By elementary ideas, Herbart meant 'entirely simple concepts or sensations—e.g., red, blue, sour, sweet, etc.' (Herbart, 1966 [1891]: 395). In some respects, Herbart is similar to the associationists such as Hume (Hoffding, 1955 [1900]). However, Herbart went beyond the simple laws of association advocated by his predecessors. He suggested that ideas may be opposed to one another and act like forces upon each other. Such inconsistent ideas will tend to reduce the *intensity* with which each one is experienced. For example, as I am writing this, all my thoughts tend to be connected to Herbart's psychology. Any other thoughts, such as whether the Boston Red Sox will ever win a World Series again, tend to be suppressed by my preoccupation with Herbart. In general, ideas vary in intensity or clarity.

As the preceding example shows, some ideas *facilitate* each other while other ideas *inhibit* each other. The process of inhibition can be put into mathematical terms. (The following example is similar to that used by Ward [1910: 337] and by Boring [1950b: 259].) Consider two ideas A and B, of which A is the stronger. Suppose that the two ideas are inconsistent with one another and therefore inhibit each other. Obviously, A will inhibit B more than B will inhibit A because A is the stronger of the two. This means that A is experienced with a greater *intensity* than B, and another assumption of Herbart's psychology is that *intensity* can be quantified. This is very important, because, if it is true, then a mathematical treatment of mental life becomes possible.

Let us now see if we can work out exactly how much B is inhibited by its competition with A. The greater the difference in strength between A and B, the more A will inhibit B. If both ideas are roughly equal then B will be less inhibited than if A is much stronger than B. In any case, B will be inhibited by some amount. At this point, let us introduce a new variable called I. I is the amount by which each idea is weakened as a result of its competition with the other. To put it a different way, A will cause B to become less intense by a quantity equal to I. The more intense A is relative to B, then the greater will I be. Herbart cast this relationship in the form of the following equation:

$$\frac{A}{(A + B)} = \frac{I}{B}$$

The greater A is relative to the sum of A and B, then the greater I is relative to B. If we multiply both sides of the equation by B, then we then get this result:

$$\frac{(A \times B)}{(A + B)} = I$$

In order to see how much B will be inhibited by A, we must subtract I from B.

$$B - \frac{(A \times B)}{(A + B)} = B - I$$

This simplifies to:

$$\frac{B^2}{(A - B)} = B - I$$

This equation is significant because it shows that no matter how much B is inhibited by A, it will never be less than zero. A and B began as positive quantities, and the ratio of $B^2/(A+B)$ must be a positive quantity as well. This means that $B-I$ must also be positive, meaning that no matter how much B is inhibited by I, it must always be greater than zero. Herbart interpreted this to mean that one idea can never push another completely out of awareness, and ideas above the threshold of awareness never reach a state of complete balance, or *equilibrium* (Ward, 1910: 337). However, there are usually a great many ideas active at the same time, and Herbart's mathematical analysis suggested that two or more ideas acting together could drive another idea below the threshold of consciousness. Thus, consciousness would tend to consist of those ideas that mutually facilitate each other, while inconsistent ideas would tend to be below threshold. Any one idea may be kept outside of awareness if 'the field of consciousness is occupied by a long-formed and well-consolidated "mass" of presentations—as, e.g., one's business or garden, the theater, &c, which properly inhibit the isolated presentation if incongruent, and unite it to themselves if not' (ibid.). Herbart used the term **apperceptive mass** to refer to that set of ideas that *assimilates* ideas consistent with it and rejects ideas inconsistent with it.

Herbart (1966: 397) believed that 'all concepts strive against suppression, and certainly submit to no more of it than is absolutely necessary.' This striving for expression in consciousness is the source of the emotions. 'So far as it represents or conceives, the soul is called *mind*; so far as it feels and desires, it is called the heart. . . . *The disposition of the heart, however, has its source in the mind*' (ibid., 408). An unpleasant feeling will result if an idea is pressing to enter consciousness but is resisted. If, however, an idea pressing for expression finds several allied ideas, and consequently a welcome in consciousness, then this process is experienced as pleasant. 'Here is the source of the cheerful disposition, especially of joy in successful activity. Here belong various movements, instigated from without, which . . . favor one another as in the case of dancing and music. . . . [S]uch too is the insight based on understanding several reasons which confirm one another' (ibid., 411). Herbart's psychology, then, is very dynamic, with the contents of consciousness in constant flux, and ideas passing back and forth across the threshold of consciousness.

The process of **apperception** was central to Herbart's psychology, as well as to the thought of many of the other psychologists we will examine later on. The concept of apperception originated with Leibniz (1646–1716), who used it to refer to the process whereby the mind becomes fully aware of ideas. The *Oxford English Dictionary* gives the following as one definition of apperception: 'any act or process by which the mind unites and assimilates a particular idea (especially one newly presented) to a larger set or mass of ideas (already possessed), so as to comprehend it as part of the whole'. No idea is meaningful by itself; rather, it is understood in relation to the other ideas that make up the apperceptive mass.

Since the apperceptive mass is capable of considerable variation over time, it is always possible for an idea to be incomprehensible at first, but to become understandable later on. Thus it is that children come to understand better the precepts of their parents when they themselves become parents. Only when one assimilates experiences as a parent do parental ideas truly make sense. The same point can be made for anyone's point of view: understanding it requires the observer to have the equivalent apperceptive mass.

Herbart's Influence on Educational Psychology

Herbart believed that 'education's primary mission is to instill in the young the values held dear by the custodians of established social order, to believe, in short, in all things that law-abiding citizens of Christendom believe in, from truth and justice to service, duty, good works, and a healthy body and mind. Not knowledge, but character and social morality, should be the end of education' (Meyer, 1975: 236–7). These goals of education could be achieved through the application of Herbart's psychological theory to the pedagogical process. Herbart (as cited by Bantock, 1984: 153) put it like this: 'Pedagogics as a science is based on ethics and psychology. The former points out the goal of education; the latter the way, the means, and the obstacles.'

Herbart's **educational psychology** implied that instruction should proceed through four steps (Dunkel, 1970: 165). These were later extended to what are called 'the five ways' (Meyer, 1975: 238): preparation, presentation, association, generalization, and application.

1. *Preparation*. Given the centrality of apperception in Herbart's psychology, it is obviously necessary for the appropriate apperceptive mass to be engaged before any new material can be properly assimilated. One does not begin a class simply assuming that the students are already thinking about things they have learned previously that are relevant to the new information the teacher wishes to impart. You may have experienced teachers who keep this point in mind at the beginning of their classes. One contemporary mechanism for preparing students is the so-called 'advance organizer' (Ausubel, 1968; Mayer, 1983: 80), which is an outline summary of the topics to be covered in the lesson and primes the student for the new material. Herbart felt that it was important at the outset to make sure that the student was not distracted from what she or he was to learn, but focused clearly on the material at hand (Dunkel, 1970: 163).

The importance of the first stage of preparation has been recognized not only in education but in other areas as well. For example, its centrality was acknowledged in a famous description of the creative process introduced by Wallas (1926). There is no substitute for gathering as much relevant information as you can before embarking on any attempt to understand a topic or discover something new.

2. *Presentation*. Given that the stage is set, then the lesson can be sensibly introduced. Of course, Herbart and his generation did not have the educational tools available to them that we have today. Not only were there no computers, but there were no overhead projectors, either! Still, with Herbart's emphasis on maintaining *student interest*, he would have quickly seen the importance of employing whatever technology is available to engage the student when material is presented. 'Interest characterizes . . . the kind of mental activity which education ought to arouse, since it cannot be satisfied with mere knowledge. . . . He who holds his knowledge firmly seeks to extend it, has *interest* for it' (Bantock, 1984: 153).

3. *Association*. After the student has taken in the point of the lesson, the teacher should connect the new material with other relevant material. Recall that Herbart adopted much of the associationist psychology that we considered earlier. The educator could take advantage of these laws to embed new material in the context of what the student already knows. From Aristotle onward, *similarity* and *contrast* were regarded as fundamental principles of association. Thus, it was natural for Herbart to encourage teachers to point out similarities and differences between the current and earlier lessons (Meyer, 1975: 238).

4. *Generalization*. It is not enough for the student simply to have a set of associations—they must also be well organized. Much of what is taught in school is systematic, as in the 'grammar of a foreign language, the parts and sub-divisions of a science' (Dunkel, 1970: 166). Notice that systematization only comes after the student has acquired a set of ideas capable of being organized.

5. *Application*. Once something is understood, then the student should have some way to apply that knowledge. Knowledge should be to some purpose, and Herbart advocated putting ideas into practice. In fact, Herbart's educational psychology is itself an example of putting Herbart's own system into practice in the field of education. Herbart claimed that 'pedagogy has never been for me anything but the application of philosophy' (as cited by Dunkel, 1970: 195).

Herbart is important to the history of psychology in several ways. One obvious contribution is the emphasis he placed on the notion that ideas can move back and forth across a threshold of consciousness. This is an idea we will meet again in several different guises. A second contribution is his attempt to apply mathematics to psychology. While his particular application of mathematics to psychology did not attract many adherents, there are still those who believe that it is worth another look (Boudewijnse et al., 2001). Finally, Herbart's educational psychology was by no means the last attempt to apply psychological ideas to education. There has long been an intimate association between education and psychology, and we will see that many of the people we examine have profoundly influenced educational theory and practice.

G.T. Fechner (1801-87)

As much as anyone, **Gustav Theodor Fechner** is responsible for creating an approach to psychology that was seen as truly scientific. Of course, at this time, there were no psychology departments in universities, and to the extent that psychology was done at all, it was done by people trained in other fields. Fechner studied medicine in Leipzig, Germany, but found that he 'had lost my confidence in medicine. In part I did not feel that I had any practical talents in the field. I moved consequently into the literary field, which detracted me gradually from the medical profession' (Bringmann, DePace, and Balance, 1992: 2). His writing paid enough to allow him to study physics, and he eventually became a Professor of Physics at Leipzig University.

In his autobiography, Fechner describes a 'mysterious illness' that came upon him in 1839. 'I soon hurt my eyes, however, through experiments on subjective color phenomena, which required me to look for long periods of time directly into the sun through colored glasses. Eventually, I had to resign my position, because my condition developed into a complete aversion to light and resulted, together with my earlier mental exertions, in a disease of my head' (ibid., 3). Fechner's condition did not improve until 1843, at which time he began a 'new career' in which he lectured 'no longer in the field of physics, but [on] the greatest good, the relationships between body and soul, the field of psychophysics, esthetics, and the philosophy of nature' (ibid.).

Psychophysics

Fechner was a person of many talents and idiosyncrasies, and he had a mystical side to his character. His mysticism influenced his choice of topics to study and the way he interpreted what he found. One expression of this mysticism was his doctrine of **panpsychism**. This is the notion that mind permeates everything in the universe. Fechner's position was nicely summed up by Hoffding (1955 [1900]: 527).

I only have experience of my own soul; I can only infer the existence of other souls by way of analogy. What is to hinder me then from extending the analogy from men and animals to plants and heavenly bodies? . . . The transition from the animal to the plant world is so continuous that there is no justification for assuming so great an opposition between the two kingdoms as is connoted by animate and inanimate. The consciousness of plants may be as far below that of animals as the latter is below that of men. And why should not the heavenly bodies be animated? Men and animals are bound up with the earth, and the earth-soul may be related to the individual souls of men and animals as the earth-body is to their bodies. . . . Lastly, all souls are part of the highest, all-embracing soul, whose life and reality is manifested in the causal law; and the causal law is the principle of all particular natural laws, of all interconnection and all order in the universe.

Some readers may find this passage reminiscent of twentieth century ecological formulations that stress the mutual interdependence of all events (e.g., Lovelock, 1987). Indeed, Arnheim (1986: 40) described Fechner's view that 'everything organic and inorganic in the universe possesses a soul, including the earth itself and other planets', and referred to him as a 'deeply religious pantheist to whom we owe the most poetical ecology ever written'. This organic approach to the universe led Fechner to believe that 'the companionship of body and mind pervades the entire universe so that nothing mental is without its physical substratum while, conversely, a good deal of what happens physically is reflected in a corresponding mental experience' (ibid., 40–1).

Fechner's interest in the relation between physical and mental events should be seen against this religious background. Fechner assumed that there was an intimate relationship between consciousness (the mental) and events in the nervous system (the physical). He assumed that this relationship was one of **psychophysical parallelism**: 'A strict parallelism exists between soul and body in such a way that from one, properly understood, the other can be constructed' (Marshall, 1990: 46). The study of the relation between mind and brain was to be a part of what Fechner called *inner psychophysics* (Murray, 1993: 117–18). However, Fechner became most famous in psychology for his elaboration of what came to be called *outer psychophysics*. Outer psychophysics investigated the relationship between events in the external world and the experiences to which they give rise. Concretely, this involved the study of the connection between stimulus magnitudes and the intensity of the resulting sensations.

Fechner believed that the relationships between the brain and experience and between experience and events in the external world could be expressed mathematically. In this respect he stands in the long line of scientists, many of whom we have already considered, who believed that scientific knowledge is properly expressed by mathematical formulations. Fechner was particularly insistent on the notion that mathematics could be applied not only to inorganic systems, but equally well to living systems (Marshall, 1990: 47). He saw no contradiction between the application of mathematics to human experience and the possibility of individual freedom. Mathematical laws only set the limits within which the individual acts. A good example is 'a flag fluttering in the wind [which] shows a multitude of forms and movements and is thus capable of a certain incalculable freedom or uncertainty, . . . yet limits are set on the possibilities by the dimensions, the texture, and the fastening of the flag' (ibid., 48). Similarly, each one of us acts in particular ways that are unpredictable, but still constrained by very general laws.

What would such a general law look like? On 22 October 1850, in a moment of insight famous in the history of psychology, Fechner saw a way of expressing the relation between physical energy and mental activity. Suppose there is a change in some stimulus, such as a light in a room becoming brighter. To what degree will our experience mirror the change in the light stimulus? Fechner saw that the change in our experience would depend on the original magnitude of the stimulus, and not just on the magnitude of the change. Thus, if I have 10 candles in a room, and add one, that will make a bigger difference to my experience of the brightness of the room than if I have 1,000 candles in a room and add one candle. In the latter case, I may not notice the difference at all (Heidbreder, 1933: 81). Fechner intended this relationship to extend beyond simple physical stimuli, such as the intensity of light:

> Our physical possessions . . . have no value or meaning for us as inert material, but constitute only a means for arousing within us a sum of psychic values. In this respect they take the place of stimuli. A dollar has, in this connection, much less value to a rich man than to a poor man. It can make a beggar happy for a whole day, but it is not even noticed when added to the fortune of a millionaire. (Fechner, 1966 [1860]: 197)

Drawing on earlier work by **E.H. Weber** (1795–1878), Fechner formulated the relationship between stimulus magnitudes and the resultant experience as follows: 'A difference between two stimuli . . . is always perceived as equal . . . if its ratio to the . . . stimulus to which it is added remains the same, regardless of how the absolute size changes. For example an addition of 1 unit to a stimulus expressed as having a magnitude of 100 units is perceived the same as an addition of 2 to a stimulus of 200 units, of 3 to 300 units, and so on' (ibid., 112). Fechner called this relationship **Weber's Law** and characterized it as 'a main foundation for psychological measurement'. Weber's Law expresses the relation between a stimulus magnitude and the amount by which that magnitude must be changed in order for the subject to perceive a **just noticeable difference**, or JND. The law is usually written as follows:

$$\frac{\Delta I}{I} = K$$

This equation should be read as: *Delta I over I equals K for the JND*. ΔI, or *Delta I*, represents the amount by which a stimulus magnitude must be changed; *I* represents the original stimulus magnitude; and *K* is a constant. Thus, to return to our earlier example, if someone has $10, then giving that person $1 might very well make a difference to him. However, if the person already has $100, then adding $1 to his wealth may not constitute a just noticeable difference. It may take $10 before he feels that he has been noticeably enriched. To continue the series further, the lucky person who begins with $1,000 may not notice an increase in wealth until she has gained an additional $100. This example reduces to the following equalities:

$$\frac{1}{10} = \frac{10}{100} = \frac{100}{1000} = \frac{\Delta I}{I} = K$$

Of course, Weber's Law is merely a conjecture unless empirical methods can be used to verify it. Fechner developed three such methods that were to become staples of the emerging discipline of experimental psychology. These methods are described in Box 3.1.

Notice that Weber's Law makes sense if and only if we can regard our basic experiences, or sensations, as *quantifiable*. If sensations do not vary

---

BOX 3.1

FECHNER'S PSYCHOPHYSICAL METHODS

In his *Elements of Psychophysics*, Fechner (1966: ch. 8) outlined three methods for making psychophysical measurements.

1. *Method of just noticeable differences*. Also known as the *method of limits*, this procedure can be used to measure both the absolute threshold and the differential threshold. In its simplest form the method involves increasing or decreasing the magnitude of a stimulus until the subject reports a change. Thus, for example, one could have a device that emitted a tone the volume of which could be continuously varied (e.g., Woodworth and Schlosberg, 1954: 196). You could begin with the volume control completely off and then gradually increase the volume until a listener reported being able to hear the tone. You would then record the volume at which the listener began to report being able to hear the tone. Alternatively, you could begin with the volume control set quite high, and then gradually decrease the volume until the listener reports not being able to hear the tone. Once again, you would record the volume at which the listener stopped being able to hear the tone. After repeating these ascending and descending series several times, one can calculate the average volume at which the listener goes from being able to hear the tone to not being able to do so, or vice versa. This value is called the *absolute threshold*: the point above which the observer reports being able to perceive a stimulus, but below which the observer reports not being able to perceive it.

A more complex version of this method requires the observer to compare two stimuli. Thus, one could have two tones, one of which is clearly audible, while the other is noticeably lower in volume. You would then increase the volume of the second tone until the observer reports them as equal in volume, and then continue increasing the volume of the second tone until the observer reports it as louder than the first. The first tone does not vary in volume. This procedure

would be repeated, but with the second tone starting louder than the first. By averaging the results of ascending and descending series, you can determine the *difference threshold*, or the amount by which one stimulus must differ from another in order to be reported as greater or less in magnitude. The difference threshold corresponds to the just noticeable difference.

2. *Method of right and wrong cases*. This procedure is also called the *method of constant stimuli*, because it relies on a set of pre-selected stimuli that vary in magnitude. These stimuli are presented to the observer in a random order, and it is the observer's task to say whether or not each one is perceptible. The absolute threshold corresponds to that value of the stimulus which the observer reports being able to perceive 50 per cent of the time.

3. *Method of average error*. The method of average error is similar to the method of limits, in that it involves one stimulus that does not vary and another stimulus that does. However, in this case the variable stimulus is under the control of the observer and is not varied by the experimenter. For example, the observer could be shown a line of a given length and asked to adjust a variable line so that the two appear equal. This is called the **point of subjective equality**. There will almost inevitably be some error in the subjects' judgements, the average of which constitutes the difference threshold.

The psychophysical methods are not mere historical curiosities, but the foundation of measurement in experimental psychology. Many of the most important experiments we will review in subsequent chapters utilize methods that can be traced back to Fechner's psychophysical methods. We have already seen several times how fundamental the concept of a threshold is to psychology, and Fechner provided psychologists with methods with which to begin to measure thresholds.

in magnitude, then the entire enterprise of outer psychophysics is based on a misconception. In the nineteenth century many of Fechner's critics argued that 'mind was not possessed of magnitude and that mental measurement was an impossibility. . . . Introspection . . . does not show that a sensation of great magnitude ever contains other sensations of lesser magnitude in the way that a heavy weight may [supposedly] be made up of a number of smaller weights' (Boring , 1963d: 258). Such a refusal to go along with the fundamental assumption of psychophysics is called the **quantity objection** to psychophysics. The quantity objection has some points of similarity to Goethe's objection to Newton. Basically, the objection is that 'sensations do not stand in additive relations to one another and, so, the claim that one sensation is, say, ten times another in intensity, is meaningless' (Michell, 1997: 362). While stimuli may vary in magnitude, there is no introspective evidence that the resultant sensations vary in magnitude. Sensations may vary in quality, but not in magnitude. The great American psychologist William James (1983 [1890]: 515) put it this way: 'To introspection, our feeling of pink is surely not a portion of our feeling of scarlet; nor does the light of an electric arc seem to contain that of a tallow candle in itself.' As we have already seen, whether or not experience can be quantified has been a recurrent issue in psychology, although the quantity objection did not carry the day in the nineteenth century. Indeed, Fechner's methods were widely adopted and practised, and, as we will see, formed the basis of the development of an entire range of techniques for mental measurement.

Experimental Aesthetics

The experience of beauty is a fundamental feature of human life, although psychology has perhaps not attended to it as much as it warrants (Hilgard, 1987: 164). Be that as it may, the psychology of the arts is one of the oldest areas in psychology, in which many outstanding psychologists have done research (Kreitler and Kreitler, 1972). Fechner (1876) played a central role in founding a psychology of beauty, or what came to be called **experimental aesthetics**. To begin with, Fechner distinguished between an *aesthetics from above* and an *aesthetics from below*. 'Aesthetics from above' refers to the traditional approaches to aesthetics taken by philosophers and art critics. They approach art 'from above' by attempting to evaluate art according to standards derived from some theory of what art should be. By contrast, an 'aesthetics from below' is empirical: it depends on observation of spectators' responses to art in order to try to understand the effects that art has on people (Gilbert and Kuhn, 1972 [1953]: 525). 'Unlike philosophers who speculated about the nature of the beautiful, . . . Fechner hoped to furnish the missing factual base of aesthetics by determining what people in fact find beautiful' (Winner, 1982: 56). Fechner's most famous investigation in this area concerned the Golden Section, which we discussed in Chapter 1. His research persuaded him that objects displaying this proportion were more pleasing than objects displaying other proportions (Benjafield, 2001).

The distinction between 'aesthetics from above' and 'aesthetics from below' reflects a general trend in the development of experimental psychology in the latter part of the nineteenth century. The new breed of experimental psychologists thought of themselves as replacing speculation with observation. Experimental psychologists intended to replace windy philosophical treatises with factual investigations conducted under controlled experimental conditions. Their attempts to do so will be a central part of our story in future chapters.

Hermann von Helmholtz (1821-84)

Now we arrive at a figure who is one of the greatest scientists of the nineteenth century. The career of **Hermann von Helmholtz** was marked by 'enormous learning in physiology, physics and mathematics and his ability to bring all three fields to bear on any one subject' (Kline, 1962: vii). Helmholtz 'belong[s] to a dying age in which a full synthetic view of nature was still possible, in which one [person] could not only unify the practice and teaching of medicine, physiology, anatomy and physics, but also relate these sciences significantly and lastingly to the fine arts' (Margenau, 1954: i).

Helmholtz embodied the spirit of confidence in scientific progress that was so characteristic of the nineteenth-century scientist. This belief that scientific inquiry would lead to great benefits for humankind is well expressed in the following quotation, from an essay that Helmholtz wrote criticizing Goethe's attempts to understand colour.

> But we cannot triumph over the machinery of matter by ignoring it; we can triumph over it only by subordinating it to the aims of our moral intelligence. We must familiarize ourselves with its levers and pulleys, fatal though it be to poetic contemplation, in order to be able to govern them after our own will, and therein lies the complete justification of physical investigation, and its vast importance for the advance of human civilization. (Helmholtz, 1962 [1881]: 21)

Notice some important themes running through this quotation. Nature is described using mechanistic terms such as 'machinery', 'levers', and 'pulleys'. The scientific understanding of nature is 'fatal' to 'poetic contemplation'. Nature is something to be dominated, 'subordinated', and 'governed.' This view of the relation between science and nature has been widespread in many disciplines, including psychology. We will see many examples of psychologists who describe their goal in terms similar to those used by Helmholtz. However, this picture of the nature of scientific understanding has not gone unchallenged over the years, and we will also see more 'contemplative' psychologies.

Helmholtz and the Nature of Perception

Helmholtz's theorizing (ibid., 118) did not take place in a vacuum, and among those whose contributions he acknowledged was **Johannes Müller** (1801–58). Müller, who was not only one of Helmholtz's teachers but also an extremely influential figure in his own right, advanced a theory called the *specific energy of nerves*. Müller's doctrine was designed to explain the apparent fact that the same stimulus 'gives rise to different sensations in each sense.' Thus, for example, when I touch the back of my hand, I experience one kind of sensation that is quite different from the sensation I experience if I shut my eyes and press on my eyelid. In the latter case, I may experience 'a luminous circle; by more gentle pressure the appearance of colors may be produced, and one color may be made to change to another' (Müller, 1964 [1838]: 38). A tactile stimulus yields a visual experience when applied to the visual sense because each sense gives rise to its own characteristic kind of experience, regardless of how it is stimulated.

From Müller's doctrine it follows that we do not experience the external world directly, but that 'what, therefore, we directly apprehend is not the immediate action of the external exciting cause upon the ends of our nerves, but only the changed condition of the nervous fibers which we call the state of *excitation* or functional activity' (Helmholtz, 1962: 119). Helmholtz did not believe that these different experiences arose because the nerves of different senses had different properties. Rather, he argued that all nerves operate in the same way and transmit impulses at the same speed, which he estimated to be 100 feet/second. Different experiences arise when nerves connect different sense organs to different places in the brain. Helmholtz (ibid., 120) compared nerves to telegraph wires. All wires are the same, but each is capable of transmitting entirely different messages from sender to receiver.

In the case of vision, the optic nerve is connected to the retina. The retina contains receptors called rods and cones, so named because of their shape. Rods and cones are specialized to respond to light. Light varies in terms of wavelength, and these receptors in the retina are capable of picking up some of these wavelengths. The cones are the basis of colour vision, with the rods involved in the experience of light and dark. The 'cones allow us to distinguish colors by day and the rods enable us to see shapes by night' (Rossotti, 1983: 120). There are three types of cone, each one sensitive to a different range of the *visual spectrum*, or the range of wavelengths of light that are visible.

Figure 3.1 is similar to one used by Helmholtz (1961 [1909]: 13). Helmholtz's figure, like this one, was not based on real data but on hypothetical data of the sort that Helmholtz believed should be true. The horizontal axis represents the visual spectrum. Of course, as we saw in our earlier discussion of Newton, light is not itself coloured, but gives rise to the experience of colour. Thus, along the horizontal axis are the various colours of the spectrum. The three types of cone are represented by the lines *A*, *B*, and *C*. The vertical axis gives the relative degree to which the cones respond to different parts of the spectrum, with the maximal response arbitrarily set at 100. First of all, notice that each cone is capable of responding to some degree over a large part of the spectrum, and that cones differ in the extent to which they are generally sensitive to the entire spectrum. However, notice also that that cones labelled *A* have their most sensitive region at the 'blue' end of the spec-

trum; cones labelled *B* have their most sensitive region in the 'green' part of the spectrum, and cones labelled *C* have their most sensitive region at the 'red' end of the spectrum.

Helmholtz argued that the degree to which each cone was stimulated determined the colour we see. 'Pure red light stimulates the red-sensitive fibers strongly and the other two kinds of fibers feebly; giving the sensation red. . . . Pure yellow light stimulates the red-sensitive and green sensitive fibers moderately and the violet-sensitive fibers feebly; giving the sensation yellow' (ibid., 14). According to this theory, colours such as yellow have no specific receptor but derive from mixtures of the other receptors. As we will see below, this is a controversial aspect of Helmholtz's theory. Helmholtz credited Thomas Young (1773–1829) with being the originator of this theory, and so it is usually called the **Young-Helmholtz theory of colour perception**. The theory is also called the **trichromatic theory of colour perception** because it holds that three colours—red, green, and blue—are the most fundamental and that our perception of other colours is formed by blending these three in different proportions (Hurvich and Jameson, 1949).

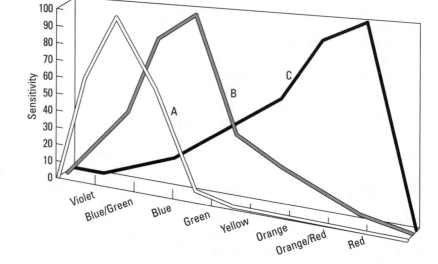

FIGURE 3.1
The relation between the visual spectrum and relative sensitivity in three types of cone, according to Helmholtz's theory.

Helmholtz (1954 [1885]) used similar principles to construct a theory of the perception of different tones. Sound waves vary in frequency. The higher the frequency the higher the pitch of the sound perceived. How are we able to perceive different pitches, such as different musical notes, for example? Helmholtz (1962: 135) suggested that the notes of a musical scale are analogous to colours, arguing that 'in the cochlea of the internal ear the ends of the nerve fibers lie regularly spread out side by side, and provided with minute elastic appendages (the rods of Corti) arranged like the keys and hammers of a piano. [E]ach separate nerve fiber is constructed to take cognizance of a definite note.' This is called a *place theory* because it assumes that nerves located at different places in the cochlea are responsible for the perception of different pitches. Although no longer believed to be entirely correct, aspects of Helmholtz's place theory were still incorporated in subsequent theories of pitch perception (e.g., Dowling and Harwood, 1986: 33).

Unconscious Inference

Helmholtz is also famous for his theory of how we perceive objects in the external world. At this point it would be useful to recall the *projective model of vision* and the discussion of the perception of pictures in Chapter 2. Helmholtz (1962: 158) noted, as had Leonardo da Vinci (1452–1519) before him, that each eye receives a slightly different picture of the external world. The two images painted on each retina represent slightly different points of view. Nevertheless, we perceive a single three-dimensional scene. Helmholtz demonstrated that we can integrate two different pictures of the world by pointing to the *stereoscope*, an invention of Charles Wheatstone (1801–75). The stereoscope is a device that presents two different views of a scene that can be fused when examined through special lenses, thus giving an impression of depth and solidity. It is an example of the many scientific instruments that began to be used in the nineteenth century and that greatly influenced psychological theorizing (Anderson, 2001).

Any theory of perception needs to explain how we are able to integrate the two different retinal images so as to yield our experience of a world in three dimensions. This problem is similar to the one posed by Berkeley, and Helmholtz's solution is also similar to that proposed by Berkeley (Pastore, 1971: 161). 'We always believe that we see such objects as would, under conditions of normal vision, produce the retinal image of which we are actually conscious' (Helmholtz, 1962: 177). We infer, on the basis of previous experience, that particular objects in the external world have given rise to the images on our retinas. The result of this inferential process is the three-dimensional world we experience. Notice that we are not aware of the inferences we make, a fact that leads to this process being called **unconscious inference**. The concept of unconscious inference has had a long life in perceptual theory, making its appearance in many theories over the years (e.g., Gregory, 1970: 30; Rock, 1983).

Helmholtz's (1962: 179) explanation of perception points to a useful distinction between two kinds of knowledge. On the one hand, knowledge enables us to do things, such as ride a bicycle or play a violin. It is very difficult to *say* precisely how one executes skills like this. We may not be able to put this kind of knowledge into words, and so it is, in a sense, 'unconscious'. This kind of knowledge is to be contrasted with knowledge that can be put into words, and of which we are fully aware, such as knowing that Helmholtz's first name is 'Hermann'. This particular distinction between conscious and unconscious knowledge will be considered at greater length further on in the text.

Ewald Hering (1834–1918)

Ewald Hering (1961 [1878]) is famous for formulating a competing theory to Helmholtz's theory of colour perception. Recall that, for Helmholtz, yellow was not a primary colour, but was derived through the blending of other colours. However, Hering, along with many others, noted that yellow was not experienced as a blend of other colours.

Rather, it seemed to be as much a primary colour as red, green, and blue. Hering also wanted a theory that would capture the distinction between achromatic and chromatic colours. Achromatic colours cover the range between black through grey to white. Chromatic colours have hue, such as red, green, yellow, and blue. Hering invented what came to be called an *opponent process theory of colour vision* (Hurvich and Jameson, 1957). Hering imagined that the visual system was based on three pairs of antagonistic processes. The pairs are yellow-blue, red-green, and white-black, the last being responsible for achromatic colours. In the absence of stimulation, all pairs give rise to the experience of grey, which represents a state of balance between opposing processes. Light acts on each pair to yield one of its component colours but inhibit the other. Thus, we cannot experience a 'reddish green' because red and green form an antagonistic pair. However, one can experience a 'greenish yellow' or a 'reddish blue,' because these colours can both be activated at the same time (ibid., 400). The Hering theory was quite successful in explaining a number of important colour phenomena, such as negative after-images. If you stare at a coloured patch (e.g., green) for about 30 seconds and then transfer your gaze to a white background, you are likely to see the opposite colour (e.g., red) projected onto the white surface. From the viewpoint of Hering's theory, the after-image occurs as balance is restored after excitation of the green component and inhibition of the red component. Of course, the process could work in the reverse manner, by staring at red and subsequently experiencing an after-image of green.

Christine Ladd-Franklin (1847–1930)

Christine Ladd-Franklin is a particularly interesting figure because she became an eminent scientist at a time when women were rigorously excluded from the academic and scientific communities. Furomoto (1992) has documented the many professional barriers and difficulties with which Ladd-Franklin had to deal. For example, she

did all the work for a Ph.D. in logic and mathematics at Johns Hopkins University but was not awarded the degree because she was a woman (ibid., 180). Regular university positions were closed to her because for most of her career she was a married woman, and the place of married women was supposed to be in the home. However, as Furomoto observed, Ladd-Franklin had the strength of purpose to become an influential scientist partly because she came from a family with a history of promoting the rights of women, and partly because her husband supported her efforts. Those who remembered her (e.g., Hilgard, 1987: 124) reported that she was a particularly strong-willed advocate of her own work.

Ladd-Franklin (1929) is remembered for her theory of colour perception, which was somewhat more sophisticated than Helmholtz's and Hering's theories. The theory was an evolutionary one, which is best understood in relation to Figure 3.2. Initially, vision would have been sensitive only to achromatic colours ranging from white to black. The rods are thus representative of the earliest stage of the evolutionary development of vision. The next stage consists of the emergence of cones sensitive to yellow and blue. Some of the cones sensitive to yellow undergo a further specialization to become cones sensitive to red and green.

Evidence in favour of the Ladd-Franklin theory comes from the study of **colour-blindness**, a common form of which is to be unable to see red and green but to be able to see yellow and blue. To

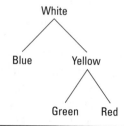

FIGURE 3.2
Ladd-Franklin's evolutionary theory of colour perception.

explain this fact, Ladd-Franklin invoked a widely used principle to the effect that the last system to evolve is the first to show the effects of degeneration. This is a sort of 'last in, first out' principle that R. Brown (1958: 297) has called the **law of progressions and pathologies**. According to this principle, since the red/green system is the last to evolve, it should be the first to show the effects of pathology, leaving behind only the more primitive yellow/blue system. Other theorists, as we shall see, make use of the law of progressions and pathologies to explain diverse sets of phenomena.

Francis Galton (1822–1911)

Francis Galton was born in England, a cousin of Charles Darwin's, and one of the most versatile and prolific scholars in the history of psychology. His contributions are many and varied, and some of his opinions are still controversial. In what follows we will sample some of his work in areas as diverse as memory and individual differences.

Hereditary Genius

Reading Darwin's *Origin of Species* was a very important event in Galton's life (McClearn, 1991). His travels in other countries were another important influence, for his experience among other cultures created a curiosity about 'the mental peculiarities of different races' (Galton, 1965 [1869]: 239). More important still may have been his childhood educational experiences, which included exposure at the age of eight to a 'brutally competitive boarding school' where he was '"demoted to a lower class in Latin"', and subsequent attendance at a series of schools in which he experienced 'much misery and mediocre performance' (Fancher, 1998: 102). It may be that Galton, who was from a 'wealthy and privileged background . . . could not easily blame his own relative failure on environmental deprivation', and was 'sensitized to the importance of innate intellectual differences much more through his experience of his own failures and limitations than of his

triumphs' (ibid., 103). Whatever the reasons, Galton developed the hypothesis that 'ability seemed to go by descent' and that 'genius was hereditary' (1965: 239). He stated his theory as follows:

> I propose to show . . . that a man's natural abilities are derived by inheritance, under exactly the same limitations as are the form and physical features of the whole organic world. . . . The arguments by which I endeavor to prove that genius is hereditary, consist in showing how large is the number of instances in which men who are more or less illustrious have eminent kinsfolk. (Ibid., 240)

Galton believed that appropriate evidence in support of his theory would be to show that there was a link between a person's *reputation* and the family to which that person belonged, with people of outstanding reputation tending to run in families. A person's reputation was supposed to be an index of 'natural ability', and by 'reputation' Galton meant 'the opinion of contemporaries, revised by posterity—the favorable result of a critical analysis of each man's character' (ibid., 242). In order to assemble a group of worthwhile candidates in such diverse categories as judges, military commanders, and poets, Galton took 'as an index of natural ability the appearance in such handbooks of eminence as *Dictionary of Men of the Time*. From these biographical encyclopedias Galton drew a sample . . . spanning two centuries' (Kevles, 1985: 3). For each category, Galton found to his satisfaction that eminent people tend to be related to other eminent people.

Galton remarked on the fact that an interesting feature of his data was that eminent fathers tend to have eminent sons to a greater extent than eminent grandfathers have eminent grandsons. This was presumably due to what came to be known as **Galton's law**, which 'states that the two parents contribute between them on average one-half of the total heritage of the offspring, the four grandparents one-quarter, and so on' (Bulmer, 1998: 579). Thus, eminent parents contribute less of their 'natural ability' to their grandchildren than to their children, and even less to their great-grandchildren.

Before exploring some of the social implications that Galton drew from his studies, it should be noted that his conclusions do not necessarily follow from his data. It is not obvious that 'reputation' and 'natural ability' must go together (Kevles, 1985: 4). After all, one's 'reputation' may be the result of a great many factors, including the possibility that being born into the upper classes provides one with a 'head start' that is not inherited so much as it is purely social. One's social class may be a very important determinant of how well one does in life. However, Galton did not see it that way. To him, all abilities clustered together and were innately determined. Thus, Galton believed that people of genius were also physically superior as well. 'A collection of living magnates in various branches of intellectual achievement is always a feast to my eyes; being as they are, such massive, vigorous, capable looking animals' (Galton, 1965: 248).

Eugenics

To Galton, the clear implication of his studies was that society should encourage selective breeding of humans. The process whereby the human race was to be improved through the production of superior offspring was called **eugenics**, a term Galton coined in 1883. By 'eugenics', Galton (1973 [1883]: 17) meant 'the study of the agencies under social control that may improve or impair the racial qualities of future generations, either physically or mentally'. The theory of evolution provided Galton with a context within which to justify a eugenic approach to social planning. As Fancher (2001) observed, eugenics became a 'secular religion' for Galton. Whereas formerly people had been misguided by conventional religious views, now society could rationally plan its future under the tutelage of scientific eugenics (Kevles, 1985: 12).

The eugenic movement that Galton founded became extraordinarily influential in the early twentieth century. 'In America, thousands of people filled out their "Record of Family Traits" and mailed it to Charles B. Davenport's Eugenics Record Office, at Cold Spring Harbor, Long Island' (ibid., 58). In Canada, 'few scientists or doctors . . . were not drawn to the notion that the breeding of humans followed the same . . . laws and was as predictive in nature as that of other sexually reproducing organisms' (McLaren, 1990: 23). In general, eugenicists were opposed to the emerging feminist movement. Galton himself was an ardent anti-feminist and an opponent of birth control, and those who adhered to his racialist views believed that 'the greatest anti-social act committed by the better type of woman was the avoidance of pregnancy. . . . the finer females, in restricting family size, were snuffing out the strains of hereditary intelligence . . . . the better sort of woman was shirking her maternal duty' (ibid., 21).

In his work on 'hereditary genius' Galton spawned a number of issues that continue to resonate in psychology. One of them is the recurrent question of the nature of **intelligence**, which Galton identified with 'natural ability' and believed to be innate. Precisely what 'intelligence' is and how it is transmitted from one generation to another are topics that have been hotly debated ever since Galton.

Statistics

The Normal Distribution

Galton helped to introduce statistical analysis as an important aspect of many forms of psychological inquiry. One idea that is central to many forms of statistical analysis is **normal distribution**. In Figure 3.3, a drawing of a device similar to one used by Galton (Stigler, 1986: 276), a metal pellet is dropped in the opening at the top. Below this opening are several rows of pins. The pellet will hit a pin in each row, being deflected to the left or right each time it hits a pin. Eventually, the pellet will end up in some position at the bottom of the apparatus. Suppose we drop several pellets in this manner. The pellets will tend to pile up at the bottom in the way shown in Figure 3.3. Most of the pellets end up more or less in the middle of the device, fewer fall

FIGURE 3.3
Galton's device for demonstrating the normal distribution.
Source: Stigler (1986). Copyright © 1986 by the President and Fellows of Harvard College. Reprinted by permission of the publishers.

a bit further away, and fewer still fall at the extreme ends of the instrument. There is an exact mathematical description of this kind of distribution, but for our purposes we need only observe that this normal distribution characterizes the way in which events are often distributed in the real world. Notice that this distribution is *symmetrical*, with equal numbers of events on the left as are on the right. Measurements, such as height and weight, may turn out to be distributed in this fashion.

Galton himself made a great many measurements of such things as keenness of eyesight, breath capacity, strength of hand squeeze, height, armspan, and weight (Johnson et al., 1985). He was keenly interested in discovering a way of calculating the degree to which such measurements were *correlated*.

Regression Towards the Mean

According to the *Oxford English Dictionary*, 'regression' means 'the action of returning to a place or point of departure'. The *OED* notes that the word has the following technical sense in genetics:

regression occurs when children 'slip back toward the average of the population from which the parents were chosen'. To understand what this means, consider Figure 3.4. The line labelled *M* represents the average or *mean* height of parents of a set of parents sampled from the British population in the nineteenth century. The left vertical axis represents the parents' height. You can read the graph by first noting the parents' height. Thus, at the point labelled *A* the parents' height is less than 65 inches. Observe that the children's height at the corresponding point *C* is closer to the mean value, *M*. Now look at the opposite end of the distribution, at point *B*, where the parent's height is close to 72 inches. Here, the children's height (point *D*) is closer to the mean. You should be able to verify for yourself that for all values of parents' height, the children's height is closer to the mean. In general, the children tend to regress towards the mean.

Regression towards the mean occurs as a mathematical necessity whenever two variables are not perfectly correlated (Cohen and Cohen, 1983: 45). Galton (1889, as cited in Senders, 1958: 106), described it as follows:

> The law of Regression tells heavily against the full hereditary transmission of any gift. Only a few out of many children would be likely to differ as widely as the more exceptional of the two parents. The more bountifully the Parent is gifted by nature, the more rare will be his good fortune if he begets a son who is endowed yet more largely. But the law is even-handed: it levies an equal succession-tax on the transmission of badness as of goodness. If it discourages the extravagant hopes of a gifted parent that his children will inherit all his powers; it no less discountenances extravagant fears that they will inherit all his weakness and disease.

Memory

Galton undertook to examine his own memory in great detail, employing techniques that have developed into widely used experimental

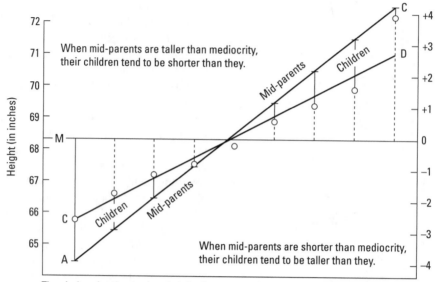

The circles give the average heights for groups of children whose mid-parental heights can be read from the line AB. The difference between the line CD (drawn by eye to approximate the circles) and AB represents regression towards mediocrity.

FIGURE 3.4
Rate of regression in hereditary stature. The deviates of the children are those of their mid-parent as 2 to 3. Source: Galton (1886: 253).

procedures. He was surprised at how many of his memories consisted of 'childish recollections, testifying to the permanent effect of many of the results of early education' (Galton, 1973 [1883]: 131). One of the techniques Galton used to generate memories was to take walks 'during which time I scrutinized with attention every successive object that caught my eyes, and allowed my attention to rest on it until one or two thoughts had arisen through direct association with that object; then I took very brief mental note of them, and passed on to the next object' (Galton, 1970 [1879]: 27). As a result of these observations, he found that:

> samples of my whole life had passed before me, and that bygone incidents, which I never suspected to have formed part of my stock of thoughts, had been glanced at as objects too

familiar to awaken the attention. I saw at once that the brain was vastly more active than I had previously believed it to be, and I was perfectly amazed at the unexpected width of the field of its everyday operations. (Ibid., 26)

Galton discovered that individual events could serve as the cues for **autobiographical memories**, or memories of events in one's life. A variant of Galton's technique for eliciting autobiographical memories is still widely used (e.g., Crovitz, 1970; Crovitz and Schiffman, 1974; Crovitz et al., 1991).

As a result of his experiments, Galton ended up being impressed by the 'multifariousness of the work done by the mind in a state of half-unconsciousness, and the valid reason they afford for believing in the existence of still deeper strata of mental operations sunk wholly below the level of consciousness, which may account for such mental phenomena as cannot otherwise be explained' (1970: 35). There is a similarity between some of Galton's views and those of such subsequent thinkers as Sigmund Freud (Roth, 1962), and we will explore this connection more thoroughly later on.

Herbert Spencer (1820–1903)

Herbert Spencer was one of the most influential thinkers in the world during the latter part of the nineteenth century. Although the phrase '**survival of the fittest**' was used by Darwin and is typically associated with him, Spencer coined the phrase in 1852. His most influential work was *First Principles*, in which he laid out a grand theoretical scheme intended to be true 'not of one class of phenomena but of *all* classes of phenomena' (Spencer, 1880 [1862]: v). Spencer made it clear that his ideas predated Darwin's, although they were often mistakenly attributed to Darwin:

> As the first edition of 'Origin of Species' did not make its appearance until October, 1859, it is manifest that the theory set forth in this work and its successors had an origin independent of, and prior to, that which is commonly assumed to have initiated it. (Ibid., vi)

Spencer's theory was an evolutionary theory in the broadest sense, intended to apply to the inorganic, organic, and 'super-organic'. By 'super-organic', Spencer meant societies (ibid., 273). Indeed, his application of evolutionary concepts to society played an important part in the emergence of sociology.

Much of *First Principles* was concerned with articulating what Spencer called 'the law of evolution'. He believed that evolution was a process whereby a system moved from 'an indefinite, incoherent homogeneity, to a definite coherent heterogeneity' (ibid., 329). While this may at first appear to be gobbledygook, in fact Spencer had specific phenomena in mind when he proposed this principle. Whether we are discussing the evolution of the solar system, of a person, or of a culture, there is an initial state in which the system is simple and undifferentiated. The system initially lacks definite parts and is a homogeneous whole. As evolution proceeds, the system develops parts, and these parts become increasingly interdependent.

Spencer gave a large number of examples of this process. Our solar system has passed from being initially an undifferentiated whole to consisting of a number of different bodies (planets, their satellites, and the sun) that are all in balance with one another. The child begins as a relatively simple creature, initially capable of only the most concrete forms of thought, and evolves into the more complex adult, increasingly capable of abstract thought that co-ordinates a wide range of actions. Primitive societies are much simpler in their organization than are modern industrial societies, which are regulated by 'governmental, administrative, military, ecclesiastical, legal' classes that would be inconceivable to a 'barbarous' society (ibid., 275).

Spencer's way of thinking about the evolution of the mind points to many themes that would be taken up by successive generations of psychologists:

> If the doctrine of evolution is true, the inevitable implication is that Mind can be understood only by observing how Mind is evolved. If creatures of the most elevated kinds have reached those highly integrated, very definite, and extremely heterogeneous organizations they possess, through modifications upon modifications accumulated during an immeasurable past—if the developed nervous systems of such creatures have gained their complex structures and functions little by little; then, necessarily, the involved forms of consciousness which are the correlatives of these complex structures and functions must have arisen by degrees. And it is impossible truly to comprehend the organization of the body in general, or of the nervous system in particular without tracing its successive stages of complication; so it

must be impossible to comprehend mental organization without similarly tracing its stages. (Spencer, 1968 [1855]: 181–2)

In particular, Spencer argues that no aspect of a creature can be understood without an evolutionary perspective. By an evolutionary perspective, Spencer means 'tracing its successive stages'. As we will see, the tracing of stages of development became an important aspect of both comparative and developmental psychology.

Social Darwinism

For Spencer, social evolution and progress amounted to the same thing. Since evolution was inevitable, so progress was inevitable. **Equilibration** was the process whereby societies regulated themselves by balancing opposing forces. The relation between supply and demand is an example of one such balancing process. Eventually, a society will evolve in which there is an 'equilibrium between man's nature and the conditions of his existence' (Spencer, 1880: 442). In such an equilibrated society, 'the individual has no desires but those which may be satisfied without exceeding his proper sphere of action, while society maintains no restraints but those which the individual voluntarily respects. The progressive extension of the liberty of citizens and the reciprocal removal of political restrictions are the steps by which we advance toward this state' (ibid., 444). So long as the evolutionary process is left to work itself out naturally, without interference, there will eventually be established a society 'of the greatest perfection and complete happiness' (ibid., 448).

As the preceding quotations demonstrate, Spencer argued that the state should not interfere with the evolutionary process. This position came to be known as **social Darwinism**, the meaning of which is essentially that individuals should be left to their own devices. Those who win the struggle for survival should do so because of their own strengths. Those losing the

struggle for survival should not be prevented from dying out. Systems for keeping the losers afloat, such as state welfare programs, would be an artificial imposition on a natural process. However, as Hofstadter (1979 [1955]: 393) observed, Spencer 'was not opposed to voluntary private charity to the unfit, since it had an elevating effect on the character of the donors and hastened the development of altruism.'

There has long been a debate about whether or not Darwin himself accepted the principles of social Darwinism. That he appears to have done so is revealed in a letter he wrote in 1872 in which he complained about 'our Trades-Unions, that [insist that] all workmen,—the good and the bad, the strong and the weak,—should all work for the same number of hours and receive the same wages' (Weikart, 1995: 611). He regarded such attempts to 'exclude competition' as a 'great evil for the future progress of mankind' (ibid.).

It should come as no surprise that successful American business people, such as John D. Rockefeller and **Andrew Carnegie**, took up social Darwinism with enthusiasm (Hofstadter, 1979: 397). Carnegie's espousal of 'the **gospel of wealth**' is a particularly important expression of this ideology:

> The Socialist or Anarchist who seeks to overturn present conditions is to be regarded as attacking the foundation upon which civilization itself rests, for civilization took its start from the day when the capable, industrious workman said to his incompetent and lazy fellow, 'If thou dost not sow, thou shalt not reap,' and thus ended primitive Communism by separating the drones from the bees. (Carnegie, 1979 [1900]: 399–400)

The 'rugged individualism' characteristic of Andrew Carnegie and late nineteenth-century America provided a social context within which a peculiarly American psychology emerged. That psychology was called *functionalism*, and we will see how it developed in Chapter 7.

IMPORTANT NAMES, WORKS, AND CONCEPTS

Names and Works

Carnegie, Andrew

Elements of Psychophysics

Fechner, G.T.

Galton, Francis

Helmholtz, Hermann von

Herbart, J.F

Hering, Ewald

Ladd-Franklin, Christine

Müller, Johannes

Spencer, Herbert

Weber, E.H.

Concepts

apperception

apperceptive mass

autobiographical memories

colour-blindness

educational psychology

equilibration

eugenics

experimental aesthetics

Galton's law

gospel of wealth

intelligence

just noticeable difference

law of progressions and pathologies

normal distribution

panpsychism

point of subjective equality

psychophysical parallelism

psychophysics

quantity objection

regression towards the mean

social Darwinism

survival of the fittest

threshold of consciousness

trichromatic theory of colour perception

unconscious inference

Weber's Law

Young-Helmholtz theory of colour
   perception

RECOMMENDED READINGS

Herbart

Herbart's educational ideas are explored more thoroughly in H.B. Dunkel, *Herbart and Education* (New York: Random House, 1969). G.-J. Boudewijnse, D.J. Murray, and C.A. Bandomir show how Herbart's mathematical psychology is still a useful theory of some important phenomena of memory in 'Herbart's mathematical psychology', *History of Psychology* 4 (1999): 163–93.

Fechner

A classic discussion of Fechner is by E.G. Boring, 'Fechner: Inadvertent founder of psychophysics', in R.I. Watson and D.T. Campbell, eds, *History, Psychology and Science: Selected Papers by E.G. Boring* (New York: Wiley, 1963), 126–31. A solid overview of the development of psychophysics is D.J. Murray, 'A perspective for viewing the history of psychophysics', *Behavioral and Brain Sciences* 16 (1993): 115–86. S. Link, 'Rediscovering the past: Gustav Fechner and signal detection theory', *Psychological Science* 5 (1994): 335–40, shows how relevant Fechner's mathematics is for contemporary psychology, and laments the fact that few psychologists have had enough mathematical training to be able to appreciate Fechner's work.

Helmholtz, Hering, Ladd-Franklin

A review that deals with many of the topics considered important by these three figures is given by M.S. Livingstone, 'Art, illusion and the visual system', *Scientific American* 258 (1988): 78–85.

Galton

A good account of the relation between Galton's life history and his orientation to psychology is R.E. Fancher, 'Biographical origins of Francis Galton's psychology', *Isis* 74 (1983): 227–33. Fancher has also written about a fascinating attempt by Galton to use civil service examinations as a measure of intelligence: 'Galton on examinations: An unpublished step in his invention of correlation', *Isis* 80 (1989): 446–55.

Spencer

Spencer's classic work in psychology is *Principles of Psychology* (New York: Appleton, 1897).

CHAPTER 4

WUNDT AND HIS CONTEMPORARIES

Introduction

Historians of psychology typically regard **Wilhelm Wundt** as a figure of the first importance. His eminence was such that he attracted scholars from around the world to his laboratory to learn his introspective techniques. In this chapter we will pay particular attention to the way in which introspection was practised by Wundt and others at that time. Wundt also invented a non-experimental approach called 'cultural psychology' that was a precursor of social psychology. Both his experimental and cultural psychologies were challenged and extended by other psychologists, notably by Ebbinghaus's pioneering studies of memory and the Würzburg school's elaboration of introspective psychology.

Wilhelm Wundt (1832–1920)

Wundt is a pivotal figure in the history of psychology. Born in Germany, Wundt studied with both Müller and Helmholtz before becoming a professor at Leipzig in 1875. For many years, Wundt's fame in psychology rested on two facts. The first is that he founded what is often called the *first laboratory in experimental psychology*, at Leipzig in 1879. The second is that his laboratory attracted a great many young scholars, often Americans, who then went on to develop psychology elsewhere (Benjamin et al., 1992). The influence Wundt had on other scholars guaranteed him a place of eminence in any history of psychology. In fact, a survey of historians of psychology (Korn et al., 1991) placed Wundt first in a ranking of the most eminent psychologists of all time. A comparison of Wundt's ranking with other well-known psychologists is given in Box 4.1.

Wundt's (1973 [1912]: 151ff.) approach to psychology extended well beyond the laboratory. As far as he was concerned, laboratory research was only appropriate for relatively simple psychological processes, an example of which will be considered below. More complex psychological processes, such as our ability to use language, could not be understood using experimental, laboratory methods. Rather, they required observations of the products of language and thought as they occurred naturally (Blumenthal, 1975). Thus, in the beginning, Wundt established the precedent that at least two kinds of method are necessary in psychology. One was laboratory-based experimentation, and was suited to the investigation of simple psychological phenomena. The other kind of method involved naturalistic observation, and was suited to the exploration of psychological processes as these were influenced by social and cultural factors (Danziger, 1983).

Investigations in the Laboratory

Wundt's laboratory procedures involved **introspection**. It may seem intuitively obvious that introspection should be a useful psychological method, but, beginning with Wundt, a large part of the history of psychology is concerned with attempting to develop a scientifically respectable introspective method. Wundt himself was acutely aware of the problems associated with any introspective method. To begin with, he made a distinction between two forms of introspection: self-observation and inner perception (Danziger, 1980: 244). Self-observation of the sort casually engaged in by everyone cannot be the basis of a scientific psychology because it is open to personal bias. **Inner perception** comes closer to the

BOX 4.1

CAN EMINENCE BE MEASURED?

Korn et al. (1991) surveyed prominent historians of psychology. A part of the survey asked these historians to list those psychologists they considered to be the 10 most important of all time, in rank order. After averaging the scores, the resulting ranking was as follows: Wilhelm Wundt; William James; Sigmund Freud; John B. Watson; Ivan Pavlov; Hermann Ebbinghaus; Jean Piaget; B.F. Skinner; Alfred Binet; and G.T. Fechner. We have already considered one of these 'top 10' figures in the last chapter (Fechner). In addition to Wundt, both Ebbinghaus and Binet have been considered in this chapter. The others will all be introduced in subsequent chapters. At the very least, this ranking indicates that we should take Wundt's work very seriously indeed.

Asking psychologists to rank order the eminence of other psychologists is a tradition in psychology, going back to the work of James McKeen Cattell (1903), who obtained rankings of leading American psychologists in 1903. Cattell's original 'top 10' were: William James; J. McK. Cattell; Hugo Münsterberg; G. Stanley Hall; J. Mark Baldwin; Edward B. Titchener; Josiah Royce; George T. Ladd; John Dewey; and Joseph Jastrow. We will deal with several of these psychologists in later chapters, but note that from this list only William James makes the current 'all-time' list. This shows how ephemeral such rankings can be.

Haggbloom et al. (2002) attempted to construct a list of the most eminent twentieth-century psychologists using a variety of measures, such as becoming president of the American Psychological Association. They acknowledge that their study was 'biased in favor of American psychologists'. Nevertheless there was substantial agreement between their list and the list compiled by Korn et al. (1991).

Some of the respondents to Korn et al. expressed misgivings about attempting to rank order psychologists at all. Such procedures may tend to reinforce existing biases and overlook important but not widely known psychologists. Thus, Korn et al. argue that the following should be included on any 'top 10' list: Francis C. Sumner was 'the first black man to receive the doctorate of philosophy degree in psychology, a feat accomplished in spite of innumerable social and physical factors mitigating against such achievements by black people in America' (Guthrie, 1976: 177; Sawyer, 2000). Margaret Floy Washburn was the author of *The Animal Mind* and the first woman to earn a Ph.D. in psychology. She also overcame innumerable social barriers. Kenneth B. Clark and Mamie Phipps Clark carried out an impressive series of studies of race, one of which influenced a major US Supreme Court decision on desegregation (Korn et al., 1991: 792).

required method because it involves deliberately observing one's own mental processes. However, such observations would still be too subjective to be trustworthy unless they were made under strictly controlled conditions. This is why the experimental method was so important to Wundt. By doing experiments, one can present a participant with a simple, objective stimulus condition and have the participant report on the experiences that result. It is obviously important that these experiments be kept as simple as possible, so that

the experiment can be easily repeated and the participant's observations can be checked by other observers (Mischel, 1969: 23).

A detailed description of Wundt's laboratory was given by a Belgian psychologist, J.J. Biervliet, writing in 1892. He observed that Wundt 'invariably . . . spends his afternoon at the laboratory. From time to time he visits the groups of workers: always simple and affable, he listens to the remarks, examines the installations, criticizes a detail and suggests improvement' (Nicolas and

Ferrand, 1999: 199). At the time that Biervliet gave his account, there would typically be about 20 persons of varying backgrounds and nationalities working in the laboratory. They were divided into groups, each of which worked on a different problem. Each group had one member who was the chief experimenter as well as one or more members who served as experimental participants:

> The head of a group is an important person; the success of the project depends largely upon him, his persistence, precision, initiative, sagacity. The participant or participants also have an important role in this success: the fundamental quality required from them is absolute sincerity. A participant must above all be conscientious; he must react naturally without bias, especially without preconceived ideas. (Ibid., 200)

Let us now become acquainted with Wundt's experimental method by replicating one of his experiments ourselves. Wundt's experiments often required the use of apparatus, and one piece of apparatus that Wundt (1973 [1912]: 2ff.) discussed at length was the *metronome*. As you know if you have ever taken music lessons, a metronome is a device that can be set to emit a sound, or *beat*, at a regular interval. The beat can be made faster or slower, and the musician can use these beats to guide his or her playing. Most metronomes today are electronic, but in Wundt's day metronomes looked like the one shown in Figure 4.1. A clockwork metronome consisted of 'an upright standing pendulum, on which a sliding weight is attached. . . . If the weight is fixed at the upper end of the pendulum, the beats follow each other at an interval of two seconds; if at the lower end, the interval is shortened to about a third of a second' (ibid., 2).

If you have access to a metronome—either a clockwork or an electronic metronome will do—try the following exercise with a partner, with each of you taking turns being the 'participant' and the 'experimenter'. Set the metronome so that the beats occur about once a second. If you are the

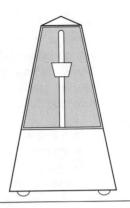

FIGURE 4.1
A metronome.
Source: Benjafield (1994: 7). Copyright © 1994 by Pearson Education. Reprinted by permission of the publisher.

'participant', you should begin by being aware of the fact that you are not to listen to the metronome in the way that you would if you were using it under normal circumstances (e.g., while playing the piano). Rather, as 'participant' your task is to attend carefully to the experiences that the metronome gives rise to in you. When the experimenter says 'Ready', then close your eyes and prepare yourself to attend to these experiences. What are your experiences as the metronome beats? Try to say what these experiences are.

At first this task yields a very wide range of reactions. One of the most common is that it is difficult to see what it is that the task is designed to elicit. That is one of the reasons why Wundt used *trained participants*. Participants need to be informed about what it is they are supposed to be experiencing before they can do this kind of task properly. So, here is a hint: try to experience the beats *without* emphasizing every second beat, in the way that we hear a clock go 'tick-tock' with the emphasis on the 'tock'.

Especially if you are using an electronic metronome, the successive beats have exactly the same *physical* characteristics. However, the successive beats do not have the same *psychological* characteristics. 'For we notice in this experiment that it is really extraordinarily difficult to hear the beats in absolutely the same intensity, or, to put it in other words, to hear unrhythmically. Again and again we recur to the ascending or descending beat. We can express this phenomenon in this sentence: Our consciousness is rhythmically disposed' (ibid., 5).

Why is rhythm such a central feature of our experience? Wundt observed that a great many aspects of our lives are rhythmically organized, from breathing to our heartbeat, from walking to running. These activities provide a background against which the metronome beat is experienced. This context shapes our experience of the beats. The rhythmic way we experience the beats illustrates the process of **apperception**, whereby we organize and make sense out of our experience. Our experience is not simply a sum of the individual impressions (such as individual beats) to which we attend, but is a **creative synthesis** of those impressions. Creative synthesis refers to the fact that, through apperception, our experience becomes a unified whole and not just a series of elementary sensations. As we noted in Chapter 3, in the discussion of Herbart, apperception is a concept that has been widely used in psychology to explain how our experience is integrated.

As a result of our metronome experiment, we can see that the flow of experience can be described as a sequence of stages or levels (e.g., Blumenthal, 1977: 16). We begin with individual beats, which we *apprehend*. By *apprehension*, Wundt (1973: 35) meant the process whereby individual impressions enter consciousness. The *span of apprehension* referred to how many impressions we could be aware of at one time, and Wundt (ibid., 31) thought that this number was about six. For example, we could be aware of about six beats at any one time. Investigations into the span of apprehension have been a central part of experimental psychological research ever since (e.g., Miller, 1956), and we will come across this topic again in Chapter 14. Apperception follows apprehension, as we attend to those events we have apprehended. These two processes are by no

means the whole story. From Wundt's perspective, *emotion* was also a central feature of mental life. In fact, we can demonstrate this by continuing on with our metronome experiment a little further.

The Tridimensional Theory of Feeling
Suppose we set the metronome at the slow speed that Wundt mentioned: about one beat every two seconds. What do you experience when the metronome is beating out that particular rhythm? Of course, you can hear the beats, one after the other, but is there anything else in your experience in addition to your perception of the beats? Wundt (1973: 53) observed that immediately after you hear one beat, you begin to anticipate the occurrence of the next one. You experience increased *tension* until the next beat occurs. However, this tension disappears once you hear next beat, at which point you experience *relief*. In addition, this slow rhythm tends to make you feel a bit sad, or *depressed*. By contrast, what do you experience if we speed the metronome up, to two or three beats a second? Now the rhythm is no longer depressed; rather, it gives rise to a feeling of *excitement*.

Wundt found that by manipulating the speed of the metronome, you can discover a set of basic feelings. So far we have found two dimensions along which feelings can vary: *tension-relief* and *excitement-depression*. Wundt also noted that some rhythms strike as *pleasant* while others strike us as *unpleasant*. This results in Wundt's famous **tridimensional theory of feeling**. It is illustrated in Figure 4.2. Any feeling can be thought of as located within the three-dimensional space. Wundt believed that this model was completely general. 'We find everywhere the same pairs of feelings that we produced by means of the metronome' (ibid., 59). In fact, variants of Wundt's three-dimensional model have been supported and extended by numerous other investigators (Blumenthal, 1977: 108).

Wundt did not believe feelings were incidental accompaniments to other psychological processes. Rather, he believed that emotion was a central aspect of all psychological processes:

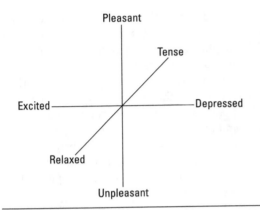

FIGURE 4.2
Wundt's tridimensional theory of feeling.
Source: Benjafield (1994: 9). Copyright © 1994
by Pearson Education. Reprinted by permission
of the publisher.

According to classical Wundtian theory, emotion is the primary source of all experience and is the primordial form of consciousness, both in the life of the individual and in the historical evolution of living organisms. This view finds some support in the observation that the parts of the nervous system that are associated primarily with emotional reactions are, in the evolutionary sense, the oldest parts, and among the earliest structures to develop in the fetus. (Ibid., 103).

In Wundtian psychology, there was a close relationship between emotion and **volition**, or acts of the will. Wundt (1973: 63) argued that the will was, in fact, an emotional process: 'There is no act of volition in which feelings of greater or less intensity . . . are not present.' Whether a process was best described as simply emotional or as also involving an act of the will depended on how the emotion was expressed. An example used by Wundt is of a person who displays an emotion such as anger in the way that he or she looks, but who does not act on the basis of the anger. Such a case is to be distinguished from that of a person who hits another person out of anger with that person. In such a case there is a simple motive

behind the action, and then 'we call the volitional process an impulsive act' (ibid., 65). However, when there are conflicting emotions, then acts of the will develop more slowly and are called **voluntary acts**. We all experience this sort of thing when we are uncertain about what to do and mull over different alternatives until we reach a decision. 'We look upon the will as our most private possession, the one that is most identical with our inner nature itself . . . at bottom our will coincides with our "ego"' (ibid., 68).

Psychophysical Parallelism

Wundt believed in a form of psychophysical parallelism that differed somewhat from the rigid doctrine proposed by Fechner, which we considered in the previous chapter. Wundt agreed that 'there is no psychical process, from the simplest sensation and affective elements to the most complex thought-processes, which does not run parallel with a physical process' (ibid., 186). However, there was not a point-for-point correspondence between every mental event and every event in the nervous system. Mental structures had to be understood in terms their own laws of combination, and so mental events could not be entirely explained by physical events. Psychological explanation was complementary to physiological explanation. Both psychology and physiology study the person, but from two sharply different points of view. Physiology treats the person as an object, to be understood in the way that other physical objects are understood. Psychology, by contrast, deals with the experiencing participant and has a 'universal importance, since all mental values and their development arise from immediately experienced processes of consciousness, and therefore can alone be understood by means of these processes' (ibid., 197–8).

Cultural Psychology

Wundt was quite clear about the fact that experimental investigations, of the sort we have considered above, 'cannot be sufficient to account for the special characteristics and phenomena of the development of thought. To do this we must turn our attention to this development itself, as it is shown in the documents of the spoken expression of thought at different stages of consciousness' (ibid., 151). Now we are dealing with Wundt's *Volkerpsychologie*, a word sometimes translated as 'folk psychology' perhaps translates better as 'cultural psychology'. Wundt (as cited by Farr, 1983: 294) characterized **cultural psychology** as the study of 'those mental products which are created by a community of human life, and are, therefore inexplicable in terms merely of individual consciousness, since they presuppose the reciprocal action of many.'

Wundt explicitly rejected the possibility of studying the development of thought by studying the development of children's thinking. Such a developmental approach is pointless, because a child develops within a particular culture, and cultures vary widely from the primitive to the advanced. Child development is not invariant across cultures, but is a product of the culture within which development takes place. Thus, in order to understand complex mental phenomena, we must study the artifacts of particular cultures. Language is one such cultural artifact that is a particularly important index of the mental life of a culture.

Wundt's aim in creating a cultural psychology was to 'trace the evolution of mind in man' (ibid., 295). To do so, one needed to adopt in psychology the same approach that Darwin had adopted in biology. 'The variety of species which were still extant was sufficiently rich to provide Darwin with the raw materials he needed to develop his theories. Wundt took as his raw material the varieties of human nature around the world as these were reflected in the anthropological accounts available to him' (ibid.). It was Wundt's hope that the conclusions of cultural psychology 'would converge with the findings that had been obtained through studying individuals in the laboratory' (Danziger, 1983: 309).

In addition to theorizing about the cultural development of language, Wundt also had a fairly sophisticated theory of the way individuals produce and understand their language that anticipated many later theories (Blumenthal, 1970: 17). This theory made use of the concept of apperception that we considered above. Remember that apperception involves understanding something as a whole. When we speak we begin with some such general idea. This idea is then divided into its component parts. This process is illustrated in Figure 4.3, in which a general impression is partitioned into a subject and a predicate. For example, imagine that you are listening to music with your roommate. You think the music is too loud, and you want to tell her so. You initially have an overall impression of what it is you wish to say, without having any particular words in mind. This overall impression, or 'simultaneous cognition' as Wundt (1970 [1912]: 22) would have called it, may be all that we are ever aware of at the time. Without our awareness, the process of creating a sentence takes this overall impression and transforms it into a more differentiated representation to which words can be attached to form a sentence. This process may generate a simple sentence containing just a subject ('The music') and predicate ('is too loud'), or something more complex. In order to understand a sentence we reverse the process and synthesize an idea out of the parts of the sentence. Thus, speaking and understanding language involves a

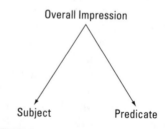

FIGURE 4.3
A tree diagram of a general idea divided into its component parts.

hierarchical process that moves back and forth between general ideas and particular words.

Wundt's Influence

To a large extent, Wundt was a figure against whom many subsequent psychologists reacted negatively (Danziger, 1990). As we shall see, even those who professed to be faithful to his ideas often actually distorted them (Blumenthal, 1975; Brock, 1993). However, due to recent reappraisals, Wundt's cultural psychology in particular is being appreciated again for its recognition that the human mind is inevitably a product of social and historical forces, and cannot be studied in isolation from the social context within which it develops (Farr, 1983: 296).

Wundt's cultural psychology involved the comparative study of different cultures, and this kind of work has occasionally been linked to racism. Certainly, there were forces in Germany during the Nazi period after 1933 that attempted to establish a racial psychology that characterized some cultures as inferior to other cultures. However, this does not appear to be at all true of Wundt's cultural psychology, and so it cannot be regarded as a precursor to Nazi doctrines. Wundt's cultural psychology 'had no room at all for studies of "national character" . . . Wundt was interested in psychological processes which he took to be universal . . . [and] was at pains to point out that he did not consider the intelligence of "primitive man" to be inferior to that of "civilized man". . . . [In Wundt's work one finds] a great deal of discussion about "humanity" and "human nature" but nothing at all about racial or biological differences' (Brock, 1992: 210).

Hermann Ebbinghaus (1850–1909)

Hermann Ebbinghaus was educated at the University of Bonn and subsequently travelled extensively in England and France. By chance, he came across a used copy of Fechner's *Elements of Psychophysics* at a bookseller's in Paris. As a result

of reading Fechner, Ebbinghaus was impressed by the potential for applying objective methods to the study of psychological processes. He went on to conduct an intensive series of investigations of learning and memory that became an important focus of research for many subsequent generations of psychologists (Gorfein and Hoffman, 1987).

The Experimental Study of Learning and Remembering

Ebbinghaus pioneered the use of **nonsense syllables**, which consist of a consonant followed by a vowel followed by a consonant, such as 'pib' or 'wol'. He argued that there were good reasons not to study the way in which meaningful material, such as poetry or prose, is learned. Such material has a wide of variety of characteristics that may influence the learning process in unpredictable ways: 'the content is now narrative in style, now descriptive, or now reflective; it contains now a phrase that is pathetic, now one that is humorous; its metaphors are sometimes beautiful, sometimes harsh; its rhythm is sometimes smooth and sometimes rough' (Ebbinghaus, 1964 [1885]: 23). Nonsense syllables are relatively meaningless, and so are relatively uninfluenced by previous learning. Any one nonsense syllable is no more or less difficult to learn than any other. Studying the ways in which people learn nonsense syllables appeared to Ebbinghaus to provide a window on the way that learning and memory occur in their simplest and most basic forms. By using nonsense syllables, Ebbinghaus hoped to discover fundamental laws of learning. Moreover, the use of nonsense syllables provided a quantifiable measure of learning and memory in terms of such variables as the number of syllables remembered and the number of trials required to learn a list of a given length.

In his experimental work, Ebbinghaus acted as his own participant. Nowadays we might regard this as inevitably leading to bias, but Ebbinghaus was so fastidious in his methods that his findings have proved to be remarkably resilient over the years. Many other investigators have obtained essentially the same results. Ebbinghaus's experiments involved constructing lists from a pool of 2,300 nonsense syllables, and all 2,300 were used before any were repeated. The experiments took place between 1879–80 and 1883–84. In learning a list of nonsense syllables, Ebbinghaus would go through the list from beginning to end, reading the syllables at a rate governed by a metronome at 150 beats per minute.

Ebbinghaus's work on *forgetting* has been enormously influential (Slamecka, 1985). In one of his experiments, he read and reread lists of 13 nonsense syllables until he could recite each list perfectly twice from memory. After various intervals, he then determined how long it took him to relearn a list. Naturally, the longer the time since the original learning, the longer it took to relearn a list. From these experiments he was able to estimate how much had been forgotten after different periods of time. In general, forgetting was greatest immediately after learning, followed by a more gradual decline. Ebbinghaus's results have often been replicated by other experimenters, and can be summarized in the famous **forgetting curve**, an example of which is shown in Figure 4.4.

Ebbinghaus believed that when he learned a list of items, associations appeared to be formed not only between adjacent items but also between all items in the list. This appeared to confirm a hypothesis of Herbart's that all the members of a series of items were associated with each other.

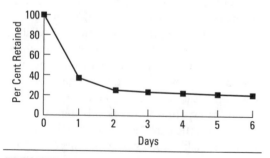

FIGURE 4.4
The Ebbinghaus forgetting curve.

'The strongest connections bound adjacent ideas and those that linked nonadjacent ideas were called remote associations' (Slamecka, 1985: 416). The concept of **remote associations** has been very influential over the years. It is consistent with a conception of the mind as a vast network of connections of varying strength. The ability to use remote associations has been linked to creativity (e.g., Mednick, 1962), the hypothesis being that the ability to recover remote associations will allow the person to experience ideas that do not occur very often to people but are potentially valuable.

Ebbinghaus's lasting reputation derives from the fact that he applied the experimental method to the study of the formation of associations. We have already seen that many theorists, from Aristotle to Hume, have written about the importance of associations. No one prior to Ebbinghaus had provided experimental evidence bearing on the associative process, and 'the significance of Ebbinghaus's work was recognized as soon as it appeared' (Hilgard, 1964).

Mary Whiton Calkins (1863–1930) and the Invention of 'Paired Associates'

Mary Whiton Calkins is another pioneer in the experimental study of the formation of associations. Although she has never received the same degree of recognition as Ebbinghaus, the technique she invented became a standard method in the study of human learning. She also 'reported many experimental effects that were rediscovered and recognized as fundamental much later' (Madigan and O'Hara, 1992: 170).

An example of Calkins's technique is given in Table 4.1. Instead of simply learning a list of individual items, Calkins had her participants learn *pairs* of items. This technique came to be called the **paired associates method**, although Calkins herself never used the phrase. By means of this method, it was possible for Calkins to attempt to determine experimentally which factors were the most important determinants of learning. In a typical paired associates experiment, the participant is first shown a list of pairs of items, after which the participant is given one of the members of the pair, and asked to give the first response that comes to mind. For example, in the paired associates list in Table 4.1, different colours are paired with different numbers. However, the colour violet is paired with the number 26 once, but with the number 61 three times. The test series requires the participant to say the first number that comes to mind upon seeing each colour and gives a measure of the importance of frequency in determining the participant's response. Frequency, or repetition, has long been considered an important determinant of the strength of associations, and Calkins's technique introduced a way of investigating variables such as frequency experimentally.

Calkins's interest in the role of frequency in learning was not merely academic. She believed that this kind of work could eventually lead to practical applications. 'The prominence of frequency is of course of grave importance, for it

TABLE 4.1
Example of Calkins's (1896) Experimental Materials: Paired Associate List to Test Frequency Effects

Serial Position	Study Series		Test Series
	Colour	Number	Colour
1	Green	47	Blue
2	Brown	73	Light Grey
3	Violet	26	Strawberry
4	Light Grey	58	Green
5	Violet	61	Violet
6	Orange	84	Orange
7	Blue	12	Brown
8	Violet	61	Medium Grey
9	Medium Grey	39	Light Grey
10	Violet	61	
11	Light Green	78	
12	Strawberry	52	

Source: Madigan and O'Hara (1992).
Copyright © 1992 by the American Psychological Association. Reprinted by permission.

means the possibility of exercising some control over the life of the imagination and of definitely combating harmful or troublesome associations' (Calkins, 1966 [1896]: 534). Here we see an anticipation of what became a major justification for experimental psychology: that it would ultimately enable us to control a person's learning history so that 'harmful or troublesome associations' could be eliminated and socially beneficial associations acquired instead. We will see how other experimental psychologists developed this theme later on in the text.

The experimental psychology of learning was far from being Calkins's focus for her entire career. Rather, she was also interested in the concept of the **self**. Calkins saw the self as 'first of all a "totality, a one of many characters," secondly, "a unique being in the sense that I am I and you are you", thirdly "an identical being (I the adult self and my ten year old self are in a real sense the same self)," and yet also "a changing being (I the adult self different from that ten year old)"' (Furomoto, 1991: 62–3). By regarding psychology as the study of the self, Calkins was attempting to create a more personal psychology that she conceived of as co-existing with the more impersonal aspects of experimental psychology (Wentworth, 1999: 121).

Like Ladd-Franklin, who we considered in the last chapter, Calkins's task was made more difficult because of prevailing attitudes towards women. While she did all the work for a Ph.D. at Harvard, she was denied it because she was a woman. Nevertheless, she went on to become the first woman president of the American Psychological Association in 1905. Her career did not have a lasting impact on psychology, and 'in slightly more than ten years after her death, psychology had essentially forgotten Mary Calkins. . . . She did not teach at a major university, but rather at a small women's college, she did not direct a single Ph.D. study, since Wellesley did not have a doctoral program. That is why Mary Calkins never founded a dynasty. This is why Mary Calkins was forgotten' (Stevens and Gardner, 1982: 88).

Franz Brentano (1838–1917)

Franz Brentano became a Catholic priest in 1864 and began working at the University of Würzburg. After struggling with religious questions for many years, Brentano left the priesthood in 1873. He was appointed as a professor at the University of Vienna in 1874, where he lectured for 20 years. In 1880 he chose to marry a prominent Viennese woman. The marriage was awkward because of a law stating that former priests could not marry. In order to facilitate the union, Brentano resigned his professorship. He subsequently never regained the status of professor in Vienna, although he continued to live and work there until 1895 (Kraus, 1976 [1926]). Then he moved to Florence, where he continued to write on psychology virtually until his death. One of Brentano's most productive students was **Carl Stumpf**, who went on to do important work in the psychology of music and himself influenced many important figures in psychology, as we shall see.

Brentano defined the subject matter of psychology by distinguishing mental phenomena from physical phenomena. Every mental phenomenon involves a **mental act**, of which 'hearing a sound, seeing a colored object, sensing warm or cold' are examples. By contrast, physical phenomena are 'a color, a shape, a landscape, which I see; a musical chord, which I hear; heat, cold, odor, which I sense; as well as comparable images, which appear to me in my imagination' (Brentano, 1968 [1874]: 480).

Brentano's distinction between mental and physical phenomena may not appear particularly obvious at first, and so, to clarify it, let us go back to the metronome experiment with which we began this chapter. When we were introspecting in a Wundtian manner, we were careful to attend to our own experiences. Thus, we focused on the experiences that the metronome gives rise to in us. Brentano, however, would ask us to do something different. We should try to understand the *act* of listening that takes place. When we *listen* to the metronome, the *act* of listening should be our

focus of interest, rather than that to which we are listening. This focus on mental acts meant that Brentano's approach was called (not surprisingly) **act psychology**.

Mental acts 'can properly be named only by an active verb. They fall into three fundamental classes; those, namely, of Ideating (I see, I hear, I imagine), of Judging (I acknowledge, I reject . . .), and of Loving-Hating (I feel, I wish . . . I desire) . . . . [W]e must always bear in mind that the psychical phenomenon is active, as a sensing or a doubting or a recalling or a willing' (Titchener, 1968 [1921]: 84–5). Every mental act involves 'reference to a content . . . [and] includes something as object . . . in judgment something is affirmed or denied, in love [something is] loved, in hate [something] hated, in desire [something] desired' (Brentano, 1968: 483). The technical term for this feature of mental acts—that they are always pointing towards some content—is that mental acts are *intentional*.

Brentano believed that psychology could adopt an empirical approach towards the study of mental acts, by researchers observing them as they occurred. By insisting that the most basic feature of mental life is that it is intentional, Brentano laid the groundwork for what came to be known as **phenomenological psychology**. As developed by Brentano's student Stumpf and later by **Edmund Husserl** (1965 [1910]), the phenomenological method is an attempt to describe consciousness as it presents itself to us, without any presuppositions as to its nature or purpose. Husserl developed Brentano's concept of **intentionality** and argued that, by comparing a number of similar experiences, we can intuitively grasp their essential nature (Klein and Westcott, 1994: 136). A phenomenological study of consciousness shows that we always have 'directedness—that is, our consciousness is always as if there were an object', even when that object does not exist, as when we imagine Count Dracula (Føllesdall, 1982: 36). To the extent that our experience is intentional, then it makes sense to characterize people as goal-oriented, purposive creatures who have expectations about what sorts of things they will experience. Such a characterization of people is in sharp contrast to many of the associationist psychologies we have already examined, and phenomenological psychology tends to regard persons as quite distinct from physical objects to which we do not ascribe consciousness. Phenomenological approaches tend not to be experimental but to rely on an intuitive description of experience. Such approaches have been quite common throughout the twentieth century, and we will examine some of them in later chapters.

The Würzburg School

During the first decade of this century, a group of psychologists at the University of Würzburg began studying complex mental processes by means of introspection. Remember that Wundt did not believe that anything but elementary mental processes could be studied by the experimental method, and so what the Würzburg group was attempting flew in the face of Wundt's conception of psychology (Humphrey, 1951: 31).

The mentor of the group was **Oswald Külpe**, but the ones who did the actual experiments included A. Meyer and J. Orth (1964 [1901]), N. Ach (1951 [1905]), and K. Bühler (1951 [1907]). The method they developed came to be called *systematic experimental introspection*. This method was described by Külpe (1964 [1912]: 214) as follows: 'Observation itself is a particular act, a committed activity of the ego. No other activity can be executed next to it at the same time. Our mental efficiency is limited, our personality is a unitary whole. But observation can take place after the completion of a function and can make it the object of self perception.' The method Külpe described came to be called **retrospection** because participants (who were usually the Würzburgers themselves) looked back on their experiences after they occurred and then described them.

To get some idea of the sort of thing that the Würzburg group was doing, here is a version of one of their experiments. In order to do this little experiment, you will need a partner, who should write a number between 1 and 9 down on a piece of paper but not let you see what it is. After your partner has done this, I would like you to think of a number between 1 and 9 yourself. Pick any number. Once you have chosen the number, think about adding the number your partner has written down to the number you have chosen. Once you have this task clearly in mind, ask your partner to show you the number she/he wrote down, add it to your number, and report the result. Repeat this exercise several times. Sometimes try to add the numbers, sometimes subtract them, and sometimes multiply them. After each trial, retrospectively examine your experience, and see if you can describe what you experienced as you added (or subtracted, or multiplied) the two numbers.

What the Würzburgers discovered was that the mental operations corresponding to activities such as addition or subtraction were not easy to put into words. Moreover, there did not seem to be any images that consistently corresponded to such activities. Thus, in the previous exercise, you can easily imagine a number (e.g., 5), the task (add 3), and the solution (8), but it is not easy to say what comes in between the task and the solution. The Würzburgers were surprised by this result, and called such experiences **imageless thoughts**.

The notion that thought could occur that was not accompanied by imagery called some previous theories of mind into question. Had not Aristotle himself believed that all thought was accompanied by images? In fact, many psychologists were (and still are) convinced of the primacy of imagery, and the fact that imagery seemed to be irrelevant to important mental activities was a controversial result. It is worth noting that **Alfred Binet**, who was later to become famous for his work developing intelligence tests, independently reached conclusions similar to those of the Würzburgers. After doing experiments on the experiences aroused by listening to a sentence, he remarked on 'the contrast between richness of thought and poverty of imagery . . . [and] the image is only a small part of the complex phenomenon to which we give the name thought' (Binet, 1969 [1903]: 213, 218).

However, there was more to the Würzburgers' psychology than imageless thought. These investigators were beginning to realize, as had Binet (ibid., 221), that, to a large extent, 'thought is an unconscious act of the mind.' This is clearly shown by the work of Ach on **determining tendencies**. To understand what a determining tendency is, let us briefly reconsider our arithmetic experiment. Suppose you are thinking about the number 7, and your task is to *add* the next number. If the next number is 6, then you get 13 as the result. Now suppose the first number is 7, but your task is to *subtract* the next number. If the next number is 6, then you get 1 as the result. The task (adding or subtracting) *determines* what you do with the two numbers. Determining tendencies give thinking a direction, and in this case correspond to the idea we have of the goal we are trying to achieve (e.g., 'add two numbers'). Notice that determining tendencies can operate independently of the content of thought. Operations such as adding and subtracting can be applied to any numbers.

Ach attempted to demonstrate that determining tendencies can operate unconsciously in an experiment on *post-hypnotic suggestion*:

The following suggestion was given to subject G. in deep hypnosis: 'Later on I will show you two cards with two numbers on each. To the first card you will react with the sum, to the second with the difference of the numbers. When the card appears you will immediately, and of your own will, say the correct number, without thinking of what I have now told you.' . . . Thereupon G. was awakened from hypnosis . . . after a few minutes of indifferent conversation I showed G. a card with the numbers 6/2. G. immediately said '8'. To the second card, 4/2, he immediately said '2'. I asked G.—showing him the first card—'Why did you say 8'? 'Just happened to say it' . . . 'How about this one?' (showing the second card). 'It was just accidental that I said 2' . . . 'Didn't you think that 4 − 2 = 2?' 'No.' (Ach, 1951: 17–18)

The work of the Würzburg group introduced several complications into psychology at the turn of the century. Introspection could no longer be regarded as a simple procedure investigating simple phenomena. At least some important mental processes appeared to be inaccessible to introspection because they were unconscious. These complications would have far-reaching consequences for psychology, as we shall see.

IMPORTANT NAMES, WORKS, AND CONCEPTS

Names and Works

Binet, Alfred

Brentano, Franz

Calkins, Mary Whiton

Ebbinghaus, Hermann

Husserl, Edmund

Külpe, Oswald

Stumpf, Carl

Wundt, Wilhelm

Concepts

act psychology

apperception

creative synthesis

cultural psychology

determining tendencies

forgetting curve

imageless thoughts

inner perception

intentionality

introspection

mental act

nonsense syllables

paired associates method

phenomenological psychology

remote associations

retrospection

self

tridimensional theory of feeling

volition

Würzburg school

RECOMMENDED READINGS

Wundt

A good overview of Wundtian approaches and of those approaches we will consider as we develop the topic of introspection further is provided by W. Lyons in 'The transformation of introspection', *British Journal of Social Psychology* 22 (1983): 327–42, and Lyons, *The Disappearance of Introspection* (Cambridge, Mass.: MIT Press, 1986). B. Nerlich and D.D. Clarke, 'The linguistic repudiation of Wundt', *History of Psychology* 1 (1998): 179–204, discuss the fate of Wundt's approach to language. Wundt's use of the metronome is but one example of the use of instruments to gather data. Many of the instruments from early experimental psychology are intrinsically interesting and are outlined by R.B. Evans, 'Psychological instruments at the turn of the century', *American Psychologist* 55 (2000): 322–5.

Ebbinghaus, Calkins

H.L. Roediger edited an issue of the *Journal of Experimental Psychology: Learning, Memory and Cognition* 11 (1985) that reviews and updates Ebbinghaus's contribution. K. Danziger provides a masterful discussion of the differences between Wundt's and Ebbinghaus's

approaches to the study of memory: 'Sealing off the discipline: Wilhelm Wundt and the psychology of memory', in C. Green et al., eds, *The Transformation of Psychology* (Washington: American Psychological Association, 2001), 45–62. Calkins wrote many books in philosophy, and her introduction to G. Berkeley, *Selections* (New York: Scribner's, 1929), ix–li, is particularly interesting because her attitude towards Berkeley is clearly that of a kindred spirit, who, like her, had a 'conception of the universe as personal'.

Brentano

For a thorough overview of Brentano's influence, see A.C. Rancurello, *A Study of Franz Brentano* (New York: Academic Press, 1968).

Würzburg School

An interesting development of the Würzburg approach concerned the exploration of religious experience using introspective techniques. See D.M. Wulff, 'Experimental introspection of religious experience', *Journal of the History of the Behavioral Sciences* 21 (1985): 131–50.

CHAPTER 5

WILLIAM JAMES

Introduction

William James (1842–1910) published **The Principles of Psychology** in 1890. It has been called 'a classic . . . probably the best general review of the subject that has yet been written' (Ayer, 1968), and it has continued to influence psychological thought since its first publication (Estes, 1990). A great many of the important figures we will review in this text received their introduction to psychology by reading James's book. You may recall from our discussion of 'eminence' in the previous chapter that James was rated the most eminent American psychologist in 1903, and was second on the 'all-time' list after Wundt. Thus, James has been traditionally regarded as a figure of considerable importance, particularly in American psychology.

William James was born in New York to a wealthy family of liberal, democratic values with intense and wide-ranging interests (Ross, 1992). His brother Henry (1843–1916) became a well-known and influential novelist. From early childhood, the family visited Europe often, and James received a very thorough education. As a young adult, he felt depressed and aimless, a condition that often recurred. In 1861 James began studying at Harvard, first in chemistry and finally in medicine, in which he earned his degree in 1869. He began to teach physiology at Harvard in 1872. He was 30 years old, and it was his first job. James proved to be 'a great success in the classroom. Having been included in intellectual discussions from an early age in his liberal household, James was at ease with students and they with him. His varied background and his attempts to relate class material to life situations were appealing to students. The breadth of his experiences and reading, his ability to communicate, and his engaging style added to his popularity' (Ross, 1992: 18).

James began writing *The Principles of Psychology* in 1878. It took him 12 years to finish it. When it was finally published, it proved to be a great success, and James's reputation as the most outstanding American psychologist of the time (or possibly any time) was secure. James 'wanted to uncomplicate the concept of mind and remove unwarranted assumptions and artificial restrictions' (Bjork, 1997: 155), and to a very large extent he was successful. Partly because *Principles* is such a central work in the history of psychology and partly because it is so beautifully written, it is well worth reading the entire work. Each of its two volumes is almost 700 pages long (cf. Lindsley, 1969)—all we can do here is indicate some of the reasons why this book has been so important to psychology.

The Principles of Psychology

Although each of the chapters of the *Principles* is worth reading, in what follows we will dwell on those chapters that have been, and continue to be, widely cited by others in subsequent work in psychology.

Habit

James observed that people are largely creatures of **habit** and that the formation of habits depends on **plasticity**. Plasticity is an extremely useful word in psychology and refers to the ability of an organism to alter its behaviour as circumstances change. James made the point that habits come about as organisms adapt to their surroundings and remain relatively constant as long as conditions do not change in any important way. In this formulation one can see James's Darwinian approach. Habits, like other psychological phenomena, can often be understood in terms of their role in the adaptive life of the organism. One function of a habit is to make our behaviour more efficient. Once an action has become habitual, then we no longer need to pay as much attention to it (James, 1950 [1890]: I, 114).

James regarded habit as a socially conservative force, and said that it was 'the great flywheel of society'. Here James is using 'flywheel'—a large wheel attached to a machine that serves to regulate the motion of the machine and to store up energy—metaphorically to indicate that habits perform a similar functions in the organism. Without ingrained habits, society would be anarchic. To a large extent, James believed, our habits are crystallized early on in life. 'Habit . . . dooms us all to fight out the battle of life upon the lines of our nurture or our early choice. . . . [Habit is something] from which a man can by-and-by no more escape than his coat sleeve can suddenly fall into a new set of folds . . . in most of us, by the age of thirty, the character has set like plaster, and will never soften again' (ibid., 121).

James's book was not just an academic exercise, but also contained practical suggestions throughout. In the case of habits, James observed that it was crucially important to 'make automatic and habitual, as early as possible, as many useful actions as we can' (ibid., 122). Not only does this enable us to focus on more serious matters, but it also liberates us from having to decide every minute detail of our lives. When we are first acquiring a habit, it is important to be consistent and not allow ourselves to sway from the path we have chosen. We should also form useful habits, and this is facilitated by doing 'a little gratuitous exercise every day' (ibid., 126). While this advice may sound gratuitous, James's point is that such an activity is like money in the bank. When you need to draw on reserves of self-discipline, they will be there.

The Methods and Snares of Psychology

James's approach to psychology was to consider every issue in as open-minded a fashion as he could. 'It was his opinion that nothing that pre-sented itself as a possibility should be dismissed without a hearing' (Heidbreder, 1933: 157). Thus, *Principles* not only considers topics that one would expect to find in any introductory psychology text-book, but also sympathetically reviews material concerned with such topics as freedom of the will that were often missing in subsequent treatments of psychology.

Introspection—'the looking into our own minds and reporting what we there discover'—seemed to James (1950: I, 185) to be the most natural and obvious psychological method. He did not doubt that introspection presented difficulties to the observer, and readily admitted that it was prone to error. However, he also argued that it was like any other form of observation in this respect. No method is perfect, but introspection was an indispensable source of data in psychology.

Many historians see James as a precursor to *phenomenology*. As you may recall, phenomenology is the method that follows from the work of Brentano and Husserl. James anticipated that method by not 'imposing a set of prior categories on experience' but 'by observing experience itself and letting experience dictate the categories' (MacLeod, 1969b: v). James may be said to differ from later phenomenologists by presenting his psychology 'in simple English instead of in an obscure jargon' (ibid., vi). James said that the **psychologist's fallacy** was to confuse 'his own standpoint with that of the mental fact about which he is making his report' (James, 1950: I, 196). No theory should stand between the psychologist and the observations she/he makes. Insofar as possible, we should let the facts speak for themselves. 'For James . . . the data of experience were intrinsically interesting. His great gift was [that] he could observe, describe, and render recognizable the nuances of experience that all of us have had' (MacLeod, 1969b: ix).

However, James is much more than a phenomenologist. He argued that psychology was a natural science, and that the minds the psychologist studies were objects in the natural world just like any other kind of object. Remember that James was trained as a physiologist, and his *Principles of Psychology* is full of physiological explanations of mental processes. James assumed a correspondence between 'the succession of states of consciousness and the succession of total brain processes', but precisely how mind and brain 'hang indubitably together . . . no mortal may ever know' (James, 1950: I, 182). In this, as in all other matters, James did not state unequivocal and final opinions, but always tentative, provisional formulations.

James was not much of an experimentalist. Although he acknowledged the importance of the **experimental method**, he never took much interest in it himself. James also acknowledged the **comparative method**, by which we gather data on different species and different cultures in the hope that the data from one will throw light on the others. Even in James's day a great deal of comparative data was gathered by means of surveys and questionnaires. James was obviously skeptical of such an atheoretical, data-driven approach. There is no guarantee that gathering a mountain of data will by itself yield greater understanding. 'Comparative observations, to be definite, must usually be made to test some pre-existing hypothesis; and the only thing then is to use as much sagacity as you possess, and to be as candid as you can' (ibid., 194).

One of the most characteristic features of James's method is the astute use of metaphor. As Gentner and Grudin observed, metaphor is not just a literary device. Metaphors have been widely used in psychology, notably at the time in which James was writing, the period during which psychology was emerging as a discipline. One function of such metaphors 'is to convey an overall sense of complexity or potential richness without necessarily specifying precise' relations between the phenomena under discussion (Gentner and Grudin, 1985: 189). In support of this notion, Gentner and Grudin cite James (1950: I, 6)) to the effect that 'at a certain stage of the development of every science a degree of vagueness is what best consists with fertility.' A good example of James's vague but fertile metaphors is the one with which we will now deal: the stream of thought.

The Stream of Thought

By the phrase '**stream of thought**', James did not mean to describe only intellectual events. The word 'thought' should be taken to refer very broadly to all of our experiences. James published a shorter version of *Principles* (1962 [1892]) in which the chapter on the stream of thought was renamed 'the stream of **consciousness**', and that is perhaps a better title. James (1950: I, 225) listed five characteristics of the stream of consciousness, and we will deal with each of them in turn.

1. 'Every thought tends to be part of a personal consciousness' (ibid., 225). 'No thought ever comes into direct *sight* of a thought in another personal consciousness than its own' (ibid., 226). James's point is that every thought is *my* thought, and I never have someone else's thought. This may at first seem unquestionably true, but after a moment's reflection one may wonder what James would say about multiple personalities? James considered these to be 'secondary personal selves' which 'still form conscious unities, have continuous memories, speak, write, invent distinct names for themselves' (ibid., 227). Thus, any thought is always someone's thought, and there is no thought apart from the personal self who has it, even if one person may have many selves.

2. 'Within each personal consciousness thought is always changing' (ibid., 225). The stream metaphor allows James to make a point that goes back to Heraclitus, whom we considered in the first chapter. Heraclitus said that 'You cannot step into the same river twice, for other waters and yet others go ever flowing on' (Wheelwright, 1966: 71). Similarly, James said that 'no state once gone can recur and be identical with what it was before' (ibid., 230). Just as a stream is never the same twice, so consciousness is never the same twice. We can be conscious of the same thing on more than one occasion, but our experience of that thing is never the same on two different occasions. 'For an identical sensation to recur it would have to occur the second time in an unmodified brain' (ibid., 232), and

that is an impossibility. Consequently, it is foolish to look for elementary, recurrent units of consciousness, such as the 'ideas' about which psychologists such as Herbart theorized. 'A permanently existing "idea" . . . which makes its appearance before the footlights of consciousness at periodic intervals, is as mythological an entity as the Jack of Spades' (ibid., 236).

3. 'Within each personal consciousness thought is sensibly continuous' (ibid., 225). From the stream metaphor, it also follows that consciousness occurs 'without breach, crack or division' (ibid., 237), because streams flow continuously. Of course, James then has to deal with the apparent fact that consciousness is interrupted by periods of unconsciousness, such as sleep. James argues that there is still a feeling of continuity that arches over such interruptions.

> When Peter and Paul wake up in the same bed, and recognize that they have been asleep, each one of them mentally reaches back and makes connection with but *one* of the two streams of thought which were broken by the sleeping hours. As the current of an electrode buried in the ground unerringly finds its way to its own similarly buried mate, across no matter how much intervening earth; so Peter's present instantly finds out Peter's past, and never by mistake knits itself onto that of Paul. (Ibid., 238)

James intentionally used the stream metaphor because of his belief in its superiority to other metaphors that had been used previously (ibid., 239). Consciousness is not adequately described as a *train of thought*, or a *chain of thought*, because these metaphors imply that consciousness can be broken up into separate 'links' connected together. Whether or not James was right in this, he recognized the importance of choosing the right metaphor for how it will subsequently influence one's thinking about a phenomenon (Gentner and Gentner, 1983).

Here is another metaphor. Consciousness is 'like a bird's life' because 'it seems to be made of an alternation of flights and perchings' (James, 1950: I, 243). What James means is that there are places where the stream of consciousness flows at different rates. If a river is wide it flows slowly; where it is narrow it speeds up. James called the places where the stream flows slowly *substantive parts*, and the places where it flows quickly *transitive parts of consciousness*. In order to see what James means, imagine being in Vancouver. Now imagine being in Halifax. The thoughts you have of Vancouver and Halifax are likely to be substantive states, in that you imagine particular states of affairs that you could easily describe. However, the transition from imagining Vancouver to imagining Halifax is less easy to describe, and corresponds to what James meant by a transitive state. It is 'very difficult, introspectively, to see the transitive parts for what they really are' (ibid.), and they tend not to have names. Our language is well-suited to describing substantive parts, but poor at providing us a way of describing transitive parts.

The stream of consciousness does not have a well-defined edge, and it is difficult to say where consciousness ends and unconsciousness begins. James (ibid., 258). spoke about events of which we are dimly aware lying beyond the **fringe of consciousness**. A good example of something beyond the fringe occurs when we attempt to remember someone's name, but just cannot quite come up with it. This has been called the **tip-of-the-tongue phenomenon** (Brown and McNeill, 1966), and James described it as follows:

> Suppose we try to remember a forgotten name. The state of our knowledge is peculiar. There is a gap therein; but no mere gap. It is a gap that is intensely active. A sort of wraith of the name is in it, beckoning us in a given direction, making us at moments tingle with the sense of our closeness, and then letting us sink back without the longed for term. If the wrong names are proposed to us, this singularly definite gap acts immediately so as to negate them. They do not fit into its mould. And the gap of one word does not feel like the gap of another, all empty of content as both might

seem necessarily to be when described as gaps. When I try vainly to recall the name of Spalding, my consciousness is far removed from what it is when I vainly try to recall the name of Bowles. (James, 1950: I, 251)

Over the years, there have been several different experimental techniques used to elicit the tip-of-the-tongue state. If you want to experience it yourself, try naming the Seven Dwarfs (Meyer and Hilterbrand, 1984).

    4. 'Consciousness always appears to deal with objects independent of itself' (James, 1950: I, 225). Consciousness 'is cognitive, or possesses the function of knowing' (ibid., 271). This point is closely related to the point made by Brentano—that consciousness is intentional. James insisted that the object of our thought was experienced as an 'undivided state of consciousness' and rejected the associationist claim that thought can be analyzed into components. To see what James means, examine Figure 5.1. It is a representation of the thought that occurs as you say 'I am the same I that I was yesterday.' Each of the numbers 1 through 9 stands for a particular instant in the process.

> If we make a solid wooden frame with the sentence written on its front, and the time-scale on one of its sides, if we spread flatly a sheet of India rubber over its top, on which rectangular co-ordinates are painted, and slide a smooth ball under the rubber in the direction from 0 to 'yesterday', the bulging of the membrane along this diagonal at successive moments will symbolize the changing of the thought's content. . . . Or, to express it in cerebral terms, it will show the relative intensities, at successive moments, of the several nerve processes to which the various parts of the thought object correspond. (Ibid., 283)

Although you only have one thought in mind from the beginning to end of the utterance, the various parts of the utterance pass smoothly from one to the other supported by a continuously flowing brain process. Such holistic neurological

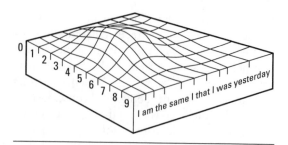

FIGURE 5.1
James's illustration of the unity of consciousness. Source: James (1950 [1890]: 283).

models have a strikingly contemporary flavour (e.g., Schull, 1992).

    5. 'It is interested in some parts of these objects to the exclusion of others, and welcomes or rejects—*chooses* from among them, in a word—all the while' (James, 1950: I, 225). James observed that many things go on around us of which we could be aware but that we appear not to notice. The world around us contains an enormous amount of information, and we attend to only a tiny fraction of it.

> Let four men make a tour of Europe. One will bring home only picturesque impressions—costumes and colors, parks and views and works of architecture, pictures and statues. To another all this will be non-existent; and distances and prices, populations and drainage arrangements, door and window fastenings, and other useful statistics will take their place. A third will give a rich account of the theaters, restaurants and public balls, and naught beside; whilst the fourth will perhaps have been so wrapped in his own subjective broodings as to tell little more than a few names of places through which he passed. (Ibid., 286)

The fact of selectivity raises several questions that have been extensively explored ever since James's time. For example, what determines the selections we make? James suggested that one crucial determinant was what we considered to be ours. We are interested in something to the extent that we feel it to be close to ourselves. 'The altogether unique kind of interest which each human mind feels in those parts of creation which it can call "me" or "mine" may be a moral riddle, but it is a fundamental psychological fact' (ibid., 289).

The Consciousness of Self

In *Psychology: Briefer Course*, James (1962: 189) observed that 'whatever I may be thinking of, I am always at the same time more or less aware of myself, of my personal existence. At the same time, it is *I* who am aware; so that the total self of me . . . [is] partly known and partly knower, partly object and partly subject.' The self has two parts. One part knows things, including oneself. James called that part the 'I'. The other part is what I know about myself, and James called that part the 'me'. The part called 'me' was characterized by James as the **empirical self**, while the part called 'I' was the **pure ego**. James divided the empirical self into three parts: the material self, the social self, and the spiritual self.

The Material Self
The **material self** consists of all those *things* you would call yours. Some parts of the material self feel closer to you than do others. Your body is the most intimate part of your material self, then come possessions such as your clothes. Also included in your material self are people you regard as yours, such as your mother, your father, your brother or sister. There will be wide variations among people in terms of what constitutes their material self and how important each part is to them. For example, at one time in a young person's life, a collection of baseball cards might become a central feature of the material self, and if it was lost or stolen the person might feel that a part of himself (or herself) had been lost.

The Social Self
Our **social self** is tied to those occasions when other people recognize us. Although each of us can imagine cases in which we would prefer to be incognito, we usually want to be recognized, and 'no more fiendish punishment could be devised, were such a thing physically possible, than that one should be turned loose in society and remain absolutely unnoticed by all the members thereof' (James, 1950: I, 293). James made a shrewd observation when he noted that ' we have as many social selves as there are people who know us' (ibid., 294), implying that each of us shows different sides of ourselves depending on the company we keep. The opinions of others shape our opinion of our self, and since the opinions of others are not always consistent, so our social self need not be terribly consistent but may contain many incongruent roles.

The Spiritual Self
The **spiritual self** refers to a person's 'inner or subjective being' (ibid., 296). It does not refer to the 'soul', but to all of the conscious experiences that we own as ours. Of all these experiences, our feelings seem to come closer to this private self than do our thoughts. We can 'literally feel' the spiritual self's 'presence in our nodding or shaking heads as we agreed or disagreed with what someone was telling us' (Coon, 2000: 91). James discussed one feeling in particular, self-esteem, or the degree to which we feel positively about ourselves. He noted that self-esteem can be calculated by the following formula.

$$Self\text{-}esteem = \frac{Success}{Pretentions}$$

'Such a fraction may be increased as well by diminishing the denominator as by increasing the numerator. To give up pretensions is as blessed a relief as to get them gratified', and we tend to give up our pretensions whenever 'disappointment is incessant and the struggle unending' (James, 1950: 310–11). Many a dieter, or smoker, will know exactly what James means!

The Pure Ego
Recall that Hume denied the existence of personal identity. Rather, all we have, by Hume's account, is

our experiences, or what James called the 'spiritual self'. James also struggled with the question of whether or not one can say anything about a self that exists over and above our experiences. He noted that our 'sense of personal identity' is based on the resemblance of experiences to one another in a 'fundamental respect' (ibid., 334). We feel that these experiences are similar and belong to each of us alone. But what 'pure ego' lies behind these experiences, and is responsible for the continuity we experience? James concludes that there is nothing of the pure ego that we can observe. The pure ego, if it exists, cannot turn around on itself and observe itself (ibid., 343). The empirical self is the only one about which we have any direct knowledge. Consequently, the pure ego cannot be a part of a scientific psychology based on empirical observation.

Attention

James's descriptions of **attention** were still cited by theorists 100 years after the publication of *Principles* (e.g., LaBerge, 1990). One of the passages most frequently cited is the following:

> Everyone knows what attention is. It is the taking possession by the mind, in clear and vivid form, of one out of what seem several simultaneously possible objects or trains of thought. . . . It implies withdrawal from some things in order to deal effectively with others, and is a condition which has a real opposite in the confused, dazed, scatter-brained state which . . . is called *distraction*. (James, 1950: I, 403)

James appreciated the complexity of attention. For example, he realized that *inattention*, or the process whereby we do not pay attention to what we are doing, was extremely common, and described how some

> very absent-minded persons in going to their bedroom to dress for dinner have been known to take off one garment after another and finally get

into bed, merely because that was the habitual issue of the first few movements when performed at a later hour. (Ibid., 115)

The execution of habitual, or *automatic*, acts when our behaviour is not under attentional control has been the subject of extensive research over the years. One aspect of this topic in which James was keenly interested was **automatic writing**. In its simplest form, automatic writing involves not paying attention to what you are writing. Box 5.1 outlines the reasons why this activity is interesting, and gives a brief review of some of the research devoted to it.

The Emotions

Perhaps no part of James's psychology has been more misunderstood that his theory of the **emotions** (Ellsworth, 1994). This theory is often called the **James-Lange theory** because a similar viewpoint was independently advanced by the Danish philosopher **C.G. Lange** (1834–1900). The theory appears to have been systematically misinterpreted for decades. Read carefully the following passage from *Principles* and try to formulate for yourself exactly what the theory is. In what follows, the phrase 'the coarser emotions' refers to 'big' emotions such as *grief, fear, rage*, and *love*.

> Our natural way of thinking about these coarser emotions is that the mental perception of some fact excites the mental affection called the emotion, and that this latter state of mind gives rise to the bodily expression. My theory, on the contrary, is that the bodily changes follow directly the perception of the exciting fact, and that our feeling of the same changes as they occur IS the emotion. Common-sense says, we lose our fortune, are sorry and weep; we met a bear, are frightened and run; we are insulted by a rival, are angry and strike. The hypothesis here to be defended says that this order of sequence is incorrect, that the one mental state is not immediately induced by the other, that the

BOX 5.1

AUTOMATIC WRITING

Automatic writing refers 'either to instances where writing occurs while the writer is preoccupied with something else . . . or to situations in which, although the individual is aware of the writing, he does not feel he is its author' (Koutstaal, 1992: 6). James studied automatic writing in the 1880s, but one of the most famous explorations of automatic writing was made by Gertrude Stein and L.M. Solomons at Harvard in the 1890s (Hirst et al., 1978). Stein is a particularly noteworthy investigator because of her subsequent impact on twentieth-century culture. She presided over a salon in Paris in which she knew many of the people who were to become the most important artistic figures of the time. Stein also wrote in a manner that was influenced by the study of automatic writing.

Stein's automatic writing experiments, like many others, involved the use of a planchette, similar to that used in a Ouija board. In one variant of these experiments, subjects would be given a task, such as reading a novel, while the writing hand rested on the planchette. 'Solomons and Stein found that . . . writing movements rapidly became automatic and did not interfere with the subject's giving his full attention to his reading' (Koutstaal, 1992: 14). They also explored situations in which subjects had to take dictation while reading a story. After much practice, subjects could take dictation automatically (i.e., without being aware of the fact that they were doing so) for brief periods.

Automatic writing is problematic because it goes against the intuition that we can only pay attention to one thing at a time, and that if we are required to do two complex tasks, then we must switch our attention back and forth between the two. James (1950: 299) believed that automatic writing implied 'that the processes in one system give rise to one consciousness, and those of another system to another simultaneously existing consciousness'. If something like this was true, then we would have a state of affairs called *divided attention*.

Decades after Gertrude Stein's work, divided attention was again explored by Spelke et al. (1976), who replicated one of the Solomon and Stein studies by training two subjects to read short stories and copy dictated words. This task was extremely demanding at first, but subjects who kept at it for several weeks were found to have a performance level when they did both tasks simultaneously that was as good as their performance when doing only one of the tasks. Further studies confirmed and elaborated these findings. (e.g., Hirst et al., 1980). The conclusion—that people appear to be able to learn to divide their attention between multiple complex tasks—should not be too surprising. One real-world example of such a feat is the simultaneous translator, who listens to one language while simultaneously translating it into another language (Hirst et al., 61). Can you think of any other examples?

bodily manifestations must first be interposed between. (James, 1950: II, 449–50)

James's theory has typically been interpreted to mean that 'emotions are *nothing but* our sensation of bodily changes' (Ellsworth, 1994: 222). James's point was actually more subtle, and he put it thus: '*if we fancy some strong emotion, and then try to abstract from our consciousness of it all the feelings of its bodily*

symptoms, we find we have nothing left behind' (James, 1950: II, 451). James recognized that many people would be unable to understand his point, which was that an emotion without bodily sensations is not an emotion worthy of the name.

What about the 'finer' emotions, such as aesthetic experiences, or what Martindale (1984) called the small emotions. These might include such experiences as 'the pleasure induced by a sunset, a painting, an elegant mathematical proof, or a piece of music' (Martindale and Moore, 1988: 661). While James did recognize that some people *might* have aesthetic experiences that would be dependent only on cortical events, he hesitated to call them emotions: 'cerebral processes are almost feelingless, so far as we can judge, until they summon help from parts below' (James, 1950: II, 472).

Another common misinterpretation of James's theory of emotion is that the bodily sensations occur directly as a response to a stimulus and are not mediated by the person's interpretation of the situation (Ellsworth, 1994: 223). However, if you read the quotation from James that begins this section, you will see that the bodily changes are contingent upon *perception* of the emotion-provoking stimulus. For James, perception involved apprehending the meaning of the situation. Perceiving a bear is different from perceiving a baby, and the different meanings entailed by these perceptions necessarily lead to different bodily responses and thus to different emotional experiences. James's position is not inconsistent with those theorists who have stressed the primary role of appraisal in determining emotional experience (.e.g., Lazarus, 1984).

Nevertheless, the reaction to James's theory focused on the role of the body in determining emotion. The most famous criticisms were proposed by **Walter B. Cannon** (1871–1945), who did several studies showing that changes in the state of the viscera (internal organs) were not necessary for emotion to occur. However, 'James is falsely credited with saying that feeling is defined by the perception of differing *visceral* patterns' (Mandler, 1979: 97). In fact, James included bodily reactions of all sorts, including voluntary movements, as determinants of feeling (Izard, 1977: 55). Nevertheless, Cannon's work was generally taken to be very damaging for James's theory.

Will

William James was prone to depression, and it was during one such period—in 1870—that he resolved to lift himself out of it, partly by choosing to believe in free will. James did not believe that we could freely choose to do anything whatsoever. Rather, our will can make a difference when we are in a conflict situation:

> We know what it is to get out of bed on a freezing morning in a room without a fire, and how the very vital principle within us protests against the ordeal. Probably most persons have lain on certain mornings for an hour at a time unable to brace themselves to the resolve. We think how late we shall be, how the duties of the day will suffer; we say 'I *must* get up, this is ignominious,' etc.; but still the warm couch feels too delicious, the cold outside too cruel, and the resolution faints away and postpones itself again and again just as it seemed on the verge of bursting the resistance and passing over into the decisive act. Now how do we *ever* get up under such circumstances? If I may generalize from my own experience, we more often than not get up without any struggle or decision at all. We suddenly find we *have* got up. (James, 1950: II, 524)

James believed that this example illustrated in miniature the nature of the will. The exercise of the will 'requires the absence of conflict. . . . [James] was taking his stand against Victorian will power, the exercise of a separate faculty called "will power" that must have failed him dismally in his own life and led him into the paralysis which expressed itself in his depressions' (May, 1969: 77).

James's post-Victorian preoccupation with **will power** is well-illustrated by his support of the self-help movements that flourished as the twentieth century began. The notion that one could help oneself by following simple principles was enormously attractive to many people, including James, who wanted to believe 'that everyone was capable of personal change and self-control' (Simon, 1992: 34). Consider the example of Horace Fletcher, an advocate of the practice of chewing each mouthful of food 32 times. This regimen enabled Fletcher to lose 60 pounds within five months, and he was an enthusiastic prosely-tizer, so much so that the ritual came to be known as *Fletcherizing*. Many people took up the habit, and James said of Fletcher's practices that 'it is impossible to overestimate their revolutionary import' (Simon, 1992: 38). 'The "revolutionary import" to which James referred was a new perception of the human body. . . . Portliness, in James's time, reflected wealth and power. Now Fletcher was [saying] that a slim, muscular body reflected true power—will-power, which was the quintessence of power' (ibid.). In the attitude of William James towards Horace Fletcher we see the beginnings of the modern American perspective on will power and self-control as learnable skills rather than inherited faculties. It is an interesting fact that James was an important influence on one of the founders of Alcoholics Anonymous (*Alcoholics Anonymous*, 1976: 569; Delbanco and Delbanco, 1995).

Other Topics

As we observed earlier, in both *The Principles of Psychology* and other works James showed a deep interest in topics that later were not considered part of mainstream American psychology. These topics included **parapsychology** and **religious experience** (e.g., James, 1958 [1902]). Spiritual-ism flourished in the late nineteenth century, and James was convinced that at least some of the spiritualistic phenomena were worth investigating. These included trances and communication with spirits of the dead (e.g., James, 1950: I, 396). James, who had been an early supporter of the American Society for Psychical Research, took the attitude that psychologists 'should simply study phenomena presented to them—which included telepathy and spiritualistic phenomena—and describe the functional relationships among them' (Coon, 1992: 147).

Most of James's colleagues in psychology, both then and now, would have preferred it if such topics were not considered a legitimate part of the discipline. However, issues such as parapsychol-ogy appear to be subjects that simply will not go away (e.g., Bem and Honorton, 1994; Schmeidler, 1992), and so perhaps it is better to face them squarely, as James did, than to insist that such areas of investigation are off limits to a scientific psychology.

James (1968 [1908]) believed that a funda-mental distinction between people was **tough-mindedness versus tender-mindedness**. The tough-minded person tends to place great store in facts and is materialistic, pessimistic, and skepti-cal. The tender-minded person tends to believe in principles and is idealistic, optimistic, and reli-gious. People who are clearly one or the other may have an easy time understanding their experience. However, these opposites can be blended in the same person, as they appear to have been in James: 'the interesting fact is that James himself cuts sharply across this classification. In some ways he is markedly tough-minded; an extreme empiricist . . . a materialist . . . a skeptic. On the other hand, he is temperamentally optimistic, reli-gious, a believer in free-will. . . . What he wanted therefore was to make the best of both worlds . . . [and] reconcile idealism and materialism' (Ayer, 1968: 191–2).

James was familiar with the work of Sigmund Freud (Taylor, 1999a: 466) and met Freud when the latter visited America in 1909. About this meet-ing, Freud said that it 'made a lasting impression on me. . . . I shall never forget one little scene that occurred as we were on a walk together. He stopped suddenly, handed me a bag he was carry-ing and asked me to walk on, saying that he would catch me up as soon as he had got through an attack of angina pectoris which was just coming on. He died of that disease a year later; and I have always wished that I might be as fearless as he was in the face of approaching death' (Jones, 1963: 260–1). One member of Freud's entourage recalls James as being 'very friendly to us and I shall never forget his parting words . . . "The future of psy-chology belongs to your work"' (ibid., 261). Whether or not James's judgement was correct in this instance is the subject of the next chapter.

IMPORTANT NAMES, WORKS, AND CONCEPTS

Names and Works

Cannon, Walter B.

James, William

Lange, C.G.

Stein, Gertrude

The Principles of Psychology

Concepts

attention

automatic writing

comparative method

consciousness

emotions

empirical self

experimental method

fringe of consciousness

habit

introspection

James-Lange theory

material self

parapsychology

plasticity

psychologist's fallacy

pure ego

religious experience

social self

spiritual self

stream of thought

substantive versus transitive parts

tip-of-the-tongue phenomenon

tough-mindedness versus tender-mindedness

will power

RECOMMENDED READINGS

The following papers update some of James's concepts with respect to late twentieth-century developments. On the self: H. Markus, 'On splitting the universe', *Psychological Science* 1 (1990): 181–4; on consciousness: E.R. Hilgard, 'Levels of awareness: Second thoughts on some of William James' Ideas', in R.B. MacLeod, ed., *William James: Unfinished Business* (Washington: American Psychological Association, 1969), 45–58, and J.F. Kihlstrom and K.M. McConkey, 'William James and hypnosis: A centennial reflection', *Psychological Science* 1 (1990): 174–8; and on emotion: G. Mandler, 'William James and the construction of the emotions', *Psychological Science* 1 (1990): 179–80. A good review of contemporary approaches to free will is A.A. Sappington, 'Recent psychological approaches to the free will versus determinism issue', *Psychological Bulletin* 108 (1990): 19–29. H.E. Adler, 'William James and Gustav Fechner: From rejection to elective affinity', in M. Donnelly, ed., *Reinterpreting the Legacy of William James* (Washington: American Psychological Association, 1992), 253–62, compares James's philosophy with that of Fechner and shows some surprising similarities.

CHAPTER 6

FREUD AND JUNG

Introduction

Freud and Jung became household names in the twentieth century, and in this chapter we will explore the reasons for their fame. One reason was their invocation of the 'unconscious' as an explanatory concept. As we have already seen, many psychologists, such as Herbart, had used the unconscious in their theories, but none had done so quite as effectively as Freud. Psychoanalysis emphasized the role of unconscious processes in such diverse phenomena as dreams, psychopathological symptoms, and religion, and the unconscious appeared to many to be an explanatory framework of great power. Even within the psychoanalytic movement, however, there were many critics of the theory, and one in particular, Carl Jung, became Freud's best-known challenger. Jung's theory also emphasized the role of the unconscious, but emphasized its more positive, spiritual aspects in a way that many found arcane but that others found inspiring.

The Unconscious

In this chapter we will be dealing with a group of psychologists who made the *unconscious* a household word. However, many others prior to the twentieth century also theorized about the unconscious, and many alternative meanings attach to this word today. Because it is such a central concept in psychology (Ellenberger, 1970), we would do well to be as clear as we can about the various possible meanings of the word 'unconscious' before we explore the intricacies of psychoanalytic and related theories.

There is no single definition of the word 'unconscious' because it has meant so many different things to different people at different times. In what follows, we will examine the recent history of the meaning of 'unconscious' in the way that Natsoulas (1978) used the *Oxford English Dictionary* (1989) as a guide to the various meanings of 'consciousness'. The *OED* is organized historically, with each entry tracing the historical development of the various senses of a word. In the entry for 'unconscious' the *OED* provides four basic senses of the word:

- 'Not conscious or knowing within oneself; unaware, regardless, heedless'.
- 'Not characterized by, or endowed with, the faculty or presence of consciousness'.
- 'Not realized or known as existing in oneself'.
- 'Not attended by, or present to, consciousness; performed . . . without conscious action'.

At first these various senses of the word may seem quite similar, and indeed they do shade into one another. However, the various ways in which 'unconscious' has been used involve rather different psychological assumptions that have far-reaching consequences for both theory and practice.

Meaning #1: Not conscious or knowing within oneself; unaware, regardless, heedless.

The simplest use of 'unconscious' is to refer to those beings that lack consciousness entirely. Thus, it might be supposed that inanimate matter is totally devoid of consciousness, although Fechner would not have agreed. Besides, drawing the line between those things that are conscious and those that are not conscious (i.e., 'unconscious') has never been easy. Are animals truly unconscious, as Descartes believed?

A more interesting way of using the word 'unconscious' is to refer to beings that are capable of consciousness, but who are not conscious of some particular event or class of events. The *OED* offers a good example of this sense of the word: 'unconscious model, i.e., one taken unawares with a detective camera'. Another illustration from the *OED* is the case of animals that, 'never having been disturbed, . . . were unconscious of danger.' This meaning of 'unconscious', while covering a great many cases, has not been of interest to psychologists because it refers to events that leave no psychological trace in the person.

Meaning #2: Not characterized by, or endowed with, the faculty or presence of consciousness.

This sense of 'unconscious' is more complex and closer to the way in which some psychologists have used the word. The *OED* quotes William James (1950: I, 199) from *The Principles of Psychology*, where he refers to 'sleep, fainting, coma, epilepsy, and other "unconscious" conditions'. 'Temporarily devoid of consciousness' is an important variant of this sense of the word. According to this reading of the word's meaning, we may be unconscious for awhile but return to consciousness later. However, this particular sense of the word has never excited the curiosity of psychologists as much as the following, which the *OED* lists as another variant of the second sense of the word. However, this meaning is so important to psychologists as to almost merit a category of its own.

Meaning #2a: Applied to mental or psychic processes of which a person is not aware but which have a powerful effect on his [or her] attitudes and behaviour . . . processes activated by desires, fears, or memories which are unacceptable to the conscious mind and so repressed; also designating that part of the mind or psyche in which such processes operate.

The *OED* labels this meaning as peculiarly psychological, and associates it specifically with 'Freud's psychoanalytic theory'. To illustrate this meaning of the word, the *OED* cites Freud (1959b [1912]:, 25): 'The term unconscious, which was used in the purely descriptive sense before, now comes to imply something more. It designates not only latent ideas in general, but especially ideas with a certain dynamic character, ideas keeping apart from consciousness in spite of their intensity and activity.' This quotation is from a paper Freud wrote in English for the Society for Psychical Research. In that paper Freud introduces this particular meaning of 'unconscious' partly because it seems to him to be required by the phenomena of hypnosis, in particular *post-hypnotic suggestion*. Freud described one case as follows:

> While he was in a hypnotic state, under the influence of a physician, he was ordered to execute a certain action at a certain fixed moment after his awakening, say half an hour later. He awakes, and seems fully conscious and in his ordinary condition; he has no recollection of his hypnotic state, and yet at the pre-arranged moment there rushes into his mind the impulse to do such and such a thing, and he does it consciously, though not knowing why. (Ibid., 23)

In fact, there is an intimate relationship between Freud's meaning of 'unconscious' and the concept of hypnosis, which itself developed out of the work of **Anton Mesmer** (1734–1815), after whom hypnotism was formerly called 'mesmerism'. Mesmer attributed hypnotic effects to a force called **animal magnetism**.

A widely held oversimplification of the history of hypnotism has been that the concept of 'animal magnetism,' a quasi-electrical fluid responsible for certain interesting phenomena, was displaced in the second half of the nineteenth century by the concept of 'hypnosis,' which was in turn closely linked to newly emerging notions about the unconscious mind.

But in fact ideas about the unconscious mind, or dissociated or relatively independent streams of consciousness, initially emerged in the context of animal magnetism . . . and were well advanced long before hypnotists took them over. (Gauld, 1992: 159)

Although this quotation treats the *unconscious mind* and *dissociated streams of consciousness* as equivalent, Freud (1959b: 25–6) was clear about the fact that this is not what he meant by the term. He argued that 'we have no right to extend the meaning of this word so as to make it include a consciousness of which its owner is himself not aware', and ridiculed the idea of an 'unconscious conscious', presumably because it was an oxymoron. Nevertheless, it has not always been easy to disentangle 'hidden streams of consciousness' (Gauld, 1992: 395) from what is meant by the 'unconscious'.

Freud was also at pains to distance himself from conceptions of the unconscious such as that of Herbart. Freud (1959b: 25) said that his conception of the unconscious differed from the notion that 'every latent idea was so because it was weak and that it grew conscious as soon as it became strong.' Latent ideas that present themselves to consciousness as they gain strength were to be called preconscious to distinguish them from truly unconscious ideas.

Meaning #3: Not realized or known as existing in oneself.

Here we have a different approach to the nature of 'unconsciousness' that blends together some of the former meanings of the word. Unlike the first sense of the term, this sense suggests that what is unconscious is psychologically real. However, unlike the second sense, this sense suggests that what is now unconscious may never have been conscious. Thus, the unconscious contains what has yet to become conscious. This includes unrealized potentialities of both a positive and a negative character. This sense of the

unconscious sounds most like what Jung (1933: 19) meant by the term:

The unconscious is not a demonic monster but a thing of nature that is perfectly neutral as far as moral sense, aesthetic taste, and intellectual judgment go. It is dangerous only when our conscious attitude towards it becomes hopelessly false. And this danger grows in the measure that we practice repressions.

Meaning # 4. Not attended by, or present to, consciousness; performed, employed, etc., without conscious action.

This meaning of 'unconscious' was perhaps best captured by J.R. Angell (1978 [1906]) in his famous presidential address to the American Psychological Association. In that address, he defined 'conscious' as 'accommodatory activity' (p. 87) and argued that 'consciousness [is] substantially synonymous with adaptive reactions to novel situations' (p. 89) and that 'no real organic accommodation to the novel ever occurs, save in the form that involves consciousness' (pp. 89–90). This makes of consciousness the 'primary accommodative process' (p. 101). This way of conceiving of consciousness leads directly to a conception of unconscious processes as responsible for regulating our behaviour in familiar situations: 'consciousness is constantly at work building up habits out of coordinations imperfectly under control; . . . as speedily as control is gained the mental direction tends to subside and give way to a condition approximating physiological automatism' (p. 89). Although not usually associated with Angell, his distinction between *controlled* (conscious) and *automatic* (unconscious) processes became a staple of late twentieth-century psychology (e.g., Shiffrin and Schneider, 1977). We will return to Angell in the next chapter when we explore American functional psychology.

The 'unconscious' clearly is a complex but rich concept. We must keep this complexity in mind as we now turn to explore the thought of those who have made such extensive use of this concept.

Sigmund Freud (1856–1939)

Sigmund Freud (1950 [1935]: 13) believed that his Jewish ancestors had lived for many years at Cologne, but 'as a result of a persecution of the Jews during the fourteenth or fifteenth century, they fled eastwards, and that, in the course of the nineteenth century, they migrated back from Lithuania . . . into German Austria. When I was a child of four I came to Vienna, and I went through the whole of my education there. At the "Gymnasium" I was at the top of my class for seven years; I enjoyed special privileges there, and was required to pass scarcely any examinations.' Freud noted that as a young person 'the theories of Darwin . . . strongly attracted me.' At university he experienced anti-Semitism: 'I found I was expected to feel myself inferior and an alien because I was a Jew' (ibid., 14), an experience that toughened him for the role of independent thinker that he was later to play. Freud graduated as a Doctor of Medicine in 1881, after entering university in 1873. In 1886, Freud felt well enough established that he could marry Martha Bernays, 'the girl who had been waiting for me . . . for more than four years' (ibid., 23).

Among Freud's most influential teachers was **Ernst Brücke**, who taught Freud neurology. Brücke was himself a student of Johannes Müller and an associate of Helmholtz. Brücke believed that 'no other forces than the common physical-chemical ones are active in the organism' and that these are 'reducible to the forces of attraction and repulsion' (Amacher, 1965: 10). This was a theme that often expressed itself in Freud's work, as we shall see.

In 1885 Freud went to Paris to study with **Jean-Martin Charcot** (1825–93), one of the great neuropsychological figures of the age. Charcot worked at the Salpêtriére, an institution first made famous in the history of psychiatry by Phillippe Pinel (1745–1826), who had freed the inmates from their chains. Charcot's clinical work had continued to expand the reputation of the Salpêtriére. Charcot specialized in studying **hysteria**, a condi-

tion that had also been investigated by **Joseph Breuer**, whom Freud had met while working in Brücke's laboratory. Hysteria was long believed to be exclusively a woman's disease. Primitive theories of hysteria attributed symptoms to a 'wandering womb' that moved about in a woman's body. Before Charcot, few medical professionals took it seriously.

Hysteria

Although hysteria has been described in many and various ways, the most interesting form of it, for our purposes, is called *conversion hysteria*. In such cases, the patient will have a physical symptom, such as paralysis or lack of feeling in a part of the body. One such symptom is called *glove anaesthesia*, in which the patient has no sensation in the hand below the wrist. Suppose that this symptom cannot be explained neurologically, because not only is there no observable neural damage, but, in any case, no possible pattern of injured nerves that could conceivably account for the symptom (Freud, 1959d [1893]: 54). Such cases were often thought to be malingerers, consciously inventing the symptom to avoid work. Notice two alternative explanations of the symptom: either it is due to a neural disorder or the patient is making it up. There is, however, a third possibility (McIntyre, 1958: 9). Perhaps the patient is not consciously playing the part of someone with a symptom, but rather the symptom is determined by forces of which the patient is unconscious. If we accept this line of reasoning, then we are forced to ask, 'What must the unconscious be like in order to produce symptoms like this?'

One famous case in the history of psychoanalysis was a woman given the pseudonym Anna O. who was treated by Breuer beginning in 1880, and whose real name was Bertha Pappenheim (Freeman, 1980; Kimball, 1998). The first symptom Breuer found Anna O. to be displaying was paralysis of both legs and the right arm. Breuer diagnosed hysteria, since there were no apparent physiological reasons for the symptoms. Many physicians, including Breuer and Charcot, used hypnosis to treat hysteria, and Breuer hypnotized Anna O. He discovered, and subsequently told Freud, that her symptoms disappeared if she was encouraged to talk about them while hypnotized. Freud himself began to adopt this procedure with hysterics and published an account of this *cathartic method* with Breuer (Breuer and Freud, 1959 [1893]). **Catharsis** is a concept that originated with Aristotle, who used it to refer to the experience of emotional purging that occurs in the spectator who witnesses a strong emotion being acted in a play. In psychotherapy, the term came to mean the process whereby the expression of an emotion removes its pathological effect. Notice that the implication of this formulation is that a 'pent-up affect' (ibid., 41) can have pathological consequences by being converted into symptoms (as in *conversion hysteria*). Few ideas were more influential in the twentieth century than this one!

Freud went on to develop his own therapeutic procedures. He gave up on hypnosis, partly because it occasionally led to awkward situations. One patient, for example, 'as she woke up on one occasion, threw her arms round my neck', and while Freud (1950: 48) 'was modest enough not to attribute the event to [his] own irresistible personal attraction', he realized that it was necessary for patients to be as aware as he was of what was happening in the therapeutic situation. 'So I abandoned hypnotism, only retaining my practice of requiring the patient to lie upon a sofa while I sat behind him, seeing him, but not seen myself' (ibid., 49).

The new method led Freud to develop a new way of understanding hysteria. He began to see hysterical symptoms as the result of sexual trauma that had occurred in early childhood. 'These *infantile* experiences are . . . *sexual* in content'; they are 'sexual experiences undergone by the patient personally, of sexual intercourse (in a wide sense)' (Freud, 1959f [1896]: 197). It is important to realize that at this point Freud believed in the 'reality of the infantile sexual scenes' and that patient's recovered memories referred to events they 'must

actually have experienced' (ibid., 200). At the time, Freud based this conclusion on a sample of 18 cases—6 men and 12 women. One of Freud's innovations was to regard hysteria as potentially a male as well as a female disorder.

Freud argued that the symptoms of the hysteric were the result of **repression**. Repression is a process whereby the person actively forgets something she or he has experienced, but that would be too painful to recall. However, a memory trace of the event still exists, although it has become unconscious. The unconscious memory is the source of the person's symptom. Under the right conditions, the person can re-experience the repressed experience and relieve the symptom. As we have seen, Freud originally believed that these repressed memories were of episodes of infantile sexual abuse that had actually taken place. However, Freud later decided that he had been too credulous, and that the descriptions of sexual abuse provided by his patients were actually fantasies. These fantasies represented infantile wishes on the part of the patients. For example, a male child might fantasize about having sexual relations with his mother, a condition Freud termed the **Oedipus complex**, after the mythological Greek king who killed his father and married his mother. Such fantasies, rather than actual seductions, were the true source of the person's neurotic symptomatology.

There has been a great deal of controversy over whether or not Freud's patients had actually experienced sexual abuse or were recalling imaginary incidents. Some (e.g., Masson, 1992 [1984]) have argued that Freud 'covered up' the true incidence of sexual abuse by depicting it as imaginary. Freud's motive for doing so might have been because his medical colleagues took a dim view of his original theory, and he believed his career to be threatened (Gleaves and Hernandez, 1999). However, others have argued that there is actually no evidence that Freud's colleagues attempted to ostracize him (Esterson, 2002), and consequently Freud's change of mind cannot be due to pressure from his colleagues. Gleaves and Hernandez

(2002: 97) suggest that 'the only reasonable conclusion that one can reach regarding Freud's initial discoveries of abuse is that nobody knows for sure what happened.' They further observe that 'as long as child sexual abuse elicits heated debate, so will Freud's seduction theory' (ibid., 92).

The Project for a Scientific Psychology

Freud was not only a clinician. During his university student days, he was torn between becoming a researcher or a practising physician. Later on, his clinical work provided him with material that he used to construct psychoanalytic theory. One of his first theoretical efforts was *Project for a Scientific Psychology*, written in 1895 and published posthumously in 1950. This work was written in neurological language, and one of its goals is to explain the nature of consciousness in neurological terms (Pribram and Gill, 1976: 19). Freud believed that the principle of inertia could be applied to the nervous system. In this context, you should recall our discussion of Newton's laws in the first chapter, one of which said that things tend to remain at rest unless some force makes them move. If you apply this law to the nervous system, then the nervous system tends to remain at rest unless something forces it to act. It is the *primary process* of the nervous system to discharge energy as it accumulates and return to a state of relative inertia.

As energy accumulates in the organism, the person wishes for objects that would reduce the level of tension in the system, and primary processes can result in the person hallucinating such an object. Of course, imagining an object is not as gratifying as actually having it, and the person must develop *secondary processes*, which are ways of getting what one wants in the real (as opposed to the imagined) world. Secondary processes involve inhibiting primary processes and using some energy to develop reliable means for gratifying wishes in accordance with the demands of reality. Thus, while primary processes only follow the **pleasure principle**, secondary processes follow the **reality principle**.

Things do not always go as they should, however. A traumatic experience, such as sexual assault, can precipitate the use of energy to maintain repressed memories. This means that energy cannot be discharged in the usual way. As energy accumulates in the system, without being appropriately discharged, then the person is at risk for displaying symptoms such as those found in hysteria. Hysterical symptoms are a way of defending oneself against the memory of a traumatic experience, and it is the goal of psychoanalytic psychotherapy to overcome the patient's **resistance** to remembering such an experience (Knight, 1984).

Cathexis is the name for the process whereby we become attached to activities that will gratify wishes. The process whereby we give up such attachments came to be called **countercathexis**. When our wish for something is repressed then it is countercathected. Countercathexis amounts to forgetting that we want a particular thing. We will discuss these processes further below.

Project for a Scientific Psychology served as a kind of draft of Freud's preliminary ideas. Although it was not published in Freud's lifetime, it nonetheless contained many concepts that continue to be influential (Bilder and LeFever, 1999).

The Interpretation of Dreams

In many ways, it is in *The Interpretation of Dreams* (1965 [1900]) that Freud set out his theory most clearly. The first part of the book presented a selective review of previous work on dreams and dreaming (Lavie and Hobson, 1986). In Chapter 7, Freud presented his own theory that 'certain memories actually cause dreams', a view that later came to be 'so widely accepted that it constitutes a major article of belief in American popular and literary culture, not to mention its pervasive influence within clinical psychiatry' (McCarley and Hobson, 1977).

Freud's theory of the dream process is best understood with reference to Figure 6.1, a representation of what is called Freud's dynamic model. The triangle represents different types of mental event. At the top is the **conscious system**, containing all those things of which we are aware. The **preconscious system** contains all those things of which we are not now aware, but of which we could become aware. Here might be located memory traces of such things such as your telephone number, for example. The **unconscious system** contains those things of which you are not aware and cannot directly become aware. Notice that the preconscious system intervenes between the unconscious system and the conscious system, and nothing can become conscious without first passing through the preconscious system. The unconscious does not have direct access to the conscious system (e.g., Kubie, 1961). Moreover, the unconscious system is inhibited, or *censored*, such that repressed material cannot normally gain access to consciousness through the preconsious.

Figure 6.1 represents the relationship between these systems for an adult. However, the state of affairs for a newborn is different. In that case, the censor has no influence, and unconscious material gains free access to consciousness. Freud argued that when an adult dreams, then **regression** occurs. Regression means 'returning' or 'going back to'. Dreams are the outcome of a regressed state, in which unconscious wishes are relatively more able to avoid censorship. However, they must still pass through the preconscious, and the dream as we experience it is an amalgam of unconscious wishes and preconscious material. Disguised by preconscious material, the dream does not transparently express an unconscious wish. That is why a dream must be interpreted if it is to divulge the unconscious wish it represents.

What we experience when we dream is called the **manifest content**. What we discover by analyzing a dream is called the **latent content**. In psychoanalysis, dreams may be interpreted through the technique of **free association**, a procedure whereby the patient begins by thinking about a dream and then saying whatever comes to mind, without censoring anything. With the help of the analyst, and honest hard work on the part of the patient, the meaning of the dream may gradually become clear. It is important to realize that Freud

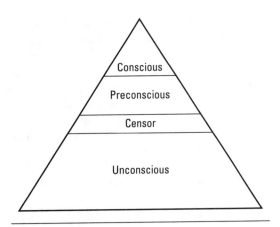

FIGURE 6.1
A representation of Freud's dynamic model.

did not advocate a mechanical approach to the analysis of dreams. He pointed out that a dream is not like a rebus—a puzzle consisting of a series of pictures. By translating each picture, you arrive at the meaning of the puzzle. For example, if there is a picture of a baseball, a team, and an oar, then you can put all three parts together and get ball-team-oar, or 'Baltimore'. By saying that dream analysis was *not* like this, Freud was insisting that a particular dream had to be interpreted in the context of the rest of the patient's life, and a symbol that meant one thing in one patient's dream might mean something quite different in another patient's dream.

While it is natural to emphasize the contribution that the unconscious makes to the dream, it is also important to appreciate the contribution of the preconscious. Freud compared the unconscious to a capitalist, who has lots of money but does not know what to do with it. The preconscious is like an entrepreneur, who has lots of good ideas but no money. They both need each other to accomplish their own ends, and so they join forces to produce a dream. In this analogy, money = energy. By coming together in a dream, the unconscious and preconscious dissipate some energy. Freud often used economic analogies like this.

Evidence for the role of preconscious material in dreams was provided by **Otto Pötzl** (1960 [1917]), who used a technique that subsequently proved to be very influential in the study of preconscious and unconscious processes. Pötzl's procedure involved showing participants pictures (e.g., temple ruins at Thebes) tachistoscopically. A tachistoscope is a device that allows a visual stimulus to be presented so briefly (e.g., one-hundredth of a second) that a participant may have difficulty saying what has been shown. Pötzl believed that such briefly exposed scenes subsequently influenced the content of his participant's dreams. This was in line with Freud's speculation that things that happened to us during the day but to which we pay little attention—the so-called *day residue*—end up in the preconscious available for further processing in a dream (Freud, 1965: 197).

The use of briefly exposed stimuli to study unconscious processes was extremely common throughout the twentieth century (e.g., Kihlstrom, 1987). Among the topics elaborated in this way was *subliminal perception*, the process whereby subthreshold stimuli are supposed to have subsequent effects on behaviour (e.g., Greenwald et al., 1991). Although such explorations have not always been conducted within the theoretical framework of psychoanalytic theory, they do follow historically from Freud's ideas (Westen, 1998)

The Development of the Personality

As his theory matured, Freud came to believe that *sexual instincts* dominated a person's development from the very beginning of life. **Libido**, or sexual energy, does not have sexual intercourse as its only object, but in the beginning is quite diffuse. The first object in which libido is invested is the person's own body. There are **erogenous zones**, such as the mouth, which provide the child's original sources of pleasure. Sucking on the mother's breast, for example, may be the first form of gratification. The child will focus on the mother's breast and other parts of her body during this **oral stage**. The **anal stage** begins when the child begins to be

able to control the anal sphincter and derive pleasure from this function also. Subsequently, the genitals become the child's focus in the **phallic stage**. The **genital stage** begins with puberty and the attempt to find a suitable sexual partner.

It is important to realize that the progression through these **psychosexual stages** is almost never without its problems. In a lecture called 'Some thoughts on development and regression-aetiology', Freud (1977 [1920]: 339–57) compares his theory with some general features of evolutionary theory. He agrees that there is a 'general tendency of biological processes to variation', so that over time living forms will alter their modes of adaptation. Each of the stages of development is an attempt at adaptation, but not all of them will work equally well. Some of the person's early attempts to adapt will not be entirely successful, and so the person will not completely pass through the developmental stages. Freud suggests that parts of these adaptations 'will be permanently held back' (ibid., 339) and as a result the person will become more or less *fixated* at that stage.

To clarify the developmental process, Freud makes use of the analogy to what happens 'when, as often happened in early periods of human history, a whole people left' one area and migrated to another (ibid.). He points out that it is overwhelmingly likely that not everyone who started out on the journey will arrive at the final destination of the group. Some individuals will choose to remain at various 'stopping places' along the route. Similarly, individual development is like a migration with various stopping places along the route. These stopping places are times when the person becomes attached to something or someone. When that attachment is given up (i.e., counter-cathected), then a part of the person is left behind, so to speak. As we are forced to move on, we leave a part of ourselves still connected to our earlier, childish attachments.

A central implication of Freud's analysis is that we do not give up an attachment unless we must do so (Toman, 1960). To revert to the analogy with migration, it is likely that people usually immigrate from one country to another because they have to, not because they freely choose to. So far as we know, everyone in North America, including Native people, is either an immigrant or descended from people who migrated from somewhere else in the world. Since recorded history, we have a continuous record of people coming here to escape the conditions they faced in their mother country. If they had remained where they were, they might have starved or faced political persecution or worse. Thus, it was necessary for them to give up their attachments in the mother country and form new attachments here. But notice that the old attachments seldom wither away completely. People tend to keep alive the customs of the mother country, at least for a generation or so, and perhaps even return to the homeland under certain conditions. Similarly, when a child develops and must give up its original attachments for new ones, it still retains some affection for the old ways. The old attachments must have been somewhat gratifying, even if they were in some deeper sense truly awful. If a child survives to adulthood then there must have been *some* wishes gratified in childhood, otherwise the child would have died (ibid., 16). Under the right conditions the adult may return to these childhood sources of gratification, just as an immigrant may return to his or her homeland for a visit, no matter how deprived they may have been there. Thus, **fixation** at early stages of development is almost a necessity of development. Later on in life the person may *regress* to these earlier stages. Regression is particularly likely when the person meets powerful 'external obstacles' (Freud, 1977: 341). For example, the death of a spouse might trigger regressive behaviour. Fixation and regression are complementary processes. If a person is strongly attached to a particular object, then he or she is likely to regress to that attachment if other gratifications are lost. As Freud put it, continuing the analogy with migration, 'if a people which is in movement has left strong detachments behind at the stopping places on its migration, it is likely to retreat to these stopping places if they have been defeated or have come up against a

superior enemy. But they will also be in the greater danger of being defeated the more of their number they have left behind on their migration' (ibid., 341) Thus, successful development depends on being able to form new attachments and not remain too attached to childish things.

The fact that we all remain somewhat attached to childish things illustrates a phenomenon Freud (1957 [1920]) called **repetition compulsion**. We are always trying to replicate the original conditions under which our wishes were gratified. The members of our families are usually, in this culture, our original sources of gratification, no matter how awful they may have been to us in other ways. If we survive to adulthood then we must have had at least some minimal gratifications from them. As a result, we inevitably strive to form relationships that duplicate our original family relationships (Toman, 1971). This is why people sometimes make the same mistakes over and over again, and seem not to be able to learn from experience.

The Structure of the Personality

Figure 6.2, which is similar to one presented by Freud (1964 [1933]: 78), contains the conscious, preconscious, and conscious systems represented in Figure 6.1. However, blended in with these systems are the structural aspects of the personality—id, ego, and superego. The **id** is 'the dark, inaccessible part of our personality . . . a chaos, a cauldron full of seething excitations. . . . It is filled with energy reaching it from the instincts, but it has no organization . . . only a striving to bring about the satisfaction of the instinctual needs' (ibid., 73). The **superego** represents the standards that other people have imposed on the person, and that the person has made his/her own. A convenient way of thinking about the superego is that it does not contain your own wishes but, rather, the wishes that other people have for you (Toman, 1960: 89). Freud sympathetically described the 'poor **ego**' that 'serves three severe masters and does what it can to bring their claims and demands into harmony with one another. No wonder that

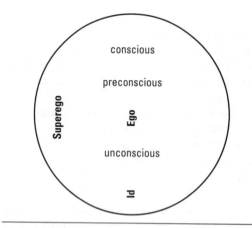

FIGURE 6.2
Freud's structural model.

the ego so often fails in its task. Its three tyranni-cal masters are the external world, the super-ego and the id' (Freud, 1964: 77). Corresponding to these three masters are three forms of anxiety: 'If the ego is obliged to admit its weakness, it breaks out in anxiety—*realistic anxiety* regarding the exter-nal world, *moral anxiety* regarding the super-ego and *neurotic anxiety* regarding the strength of the passions in the id' (ibid.).

Notice that in Figure 6.2 there are no sharp demarcations between the various parts of the per-sonality, and that id, ego, superego do not corre-spond to unconscious, preconscious, conscious. For example, parts of the ego are unconscious. Think of acts such as walking, which you carry out more or less automatically but are still regulated by the ego as you move about in the external world. Thus, the unconscious contains more than repressed wishes. Notice also that part of the super-ego is unconscious. We are usually unaware of the many ways in which we have taken our values from other people and the subtle ways in which these values unconsciously regulate our behaviour.

As Arnheim (1986: 141) has observed, Freud's way of representing the structure of the personal-ity, as shown in Figure 6.2, illustrates a common feature of theoretical thinking, not just in psychol-ogy but in any area of inquiry. Freud represented the structure of the personality in terms of a visual image that could be drawn. As the saying goes, 'A picture is worth a thousand words.' The 'mental model' (Gentner and Stevens, 1983) in Figure 6.2 served to guide Freud's thinking. Of course, the number of possible models of the mind is innu-merable—Freud's is by no means the only one pos-sible. Indeed, as we go along, you should watch out for other mental models that have served other theorists in the way that Freud's model served him.

Religion and Culture

In his theorizing about religious practices, Freud (1946 [1913]) often used examples drawn from the work of others, notably Wundt's cultural psy-chology and the cultural anthropology of **Sir James G. Frazer** (1854–1941). One of Frazer's most influential ideas is discussed in Box 6.1. Of course, Freud gave a distinctive twist to his expla-nations of widely observed cultural practices such as the **incest taboo**. The word 'taboo' originated in Polynesia, and entered the English language as a result of the voyage of Captain Cook in 1777. It was used to refer to sacred practices or prohibi-tions of which incest is an example. In explaining why there is a universal taboo against incest, Freud elaborated a suggestion of Darwin's to the effect that primordial humans lived in small groups, each dominated by the strongest male. In such a **primal horde**, the dominant male might drive out the other males, who would then have to seek mates elsewhere. Freud added the speculation that the weaker males might join together and kill the leader. This band of brothers would then be faced with the fact that none of them individually could replace the person they had killed. Partly out of a sense of guilt, and partly to survive as a group, they would all have to give up any interest in their female kin. Not only would the incest taboo be the result of the primal murder, but so, too, would be the beginnings of a religious attitude in which an imaginary father substitutes for the now dead one and becomes not only the source of hope and protection, but also of fear, awe, and dread. Given enough time, more universal religious maxims, such as 'Thou shalt not covet thy neighbour's wife', eventually develop out of the primitive conditions of the primal horde.

Because Freud emphasized the role that sexuality plays in determining our actions, many people have assumed that he took a laissez-faire attitude towards sexual behaviour and was in favour of loosening whatever restrictions there may be against the direct expression of such instincts. If anything, however, Freud (1953 [1927], 1961 [1930]) took the opposite position, stressing the importance of providing culturally sanctioned outlets for the instincts. Nowhere is this position clearer than in a letter written to Albert Einstein in 1932 in response to a letter from Einstein written as a part of series of exchanges sponsored by the League of Nations.

Freud began by outlining what he took to be the primordial way in which people settle disputes—by the use of violence. As we have evolved, we have confirmed that 'the superior strength of a single individual could be rivaled by the union of several weak ones' (Freud, 1959e [1932]: 275). The rule of law at this stage of evolution is made possible by the fact that the group can exact revenge on any individual who 'gets out

---

BOX 6.1

MAGICAL THINKING: THE INFLUENCE OF SIR JAMES FRAZER (1854–1941)

Sir James Frazer's (1959 [1911]) social anthropology had a profound influence on not only social science but also the arts in the twentieth century. Among those who have confessed their intellectual debt to him are Sigmund Freud and T.S. Eliot (Vickery, 1973). Frazer provided detailed examples of superstitious ways of behaving that exemplified what came to be called *magical thinking*.

Someone who thinks magically acts as if events in the world are regulated by two laws: the *law of similarity* and the *law of contagion*. The first of these laws leads the magical thinker to believe that causes are similar to the effects they produce. The law of similarity leads 'the magician to infer that he can produce any effect he desires merely by imitating it in advance' (Frazer, 1959: 5). The law of similarity is a source of magical power, as in the 'consumption of lion flesh by Hottentots to induce courage and strength', but it also leads to numerous fears, such as 'the ancient Greek belief that eating the flesh of the wakeful nightingale would prevent a man from sleeping; . . . avoidance of hedgehog by adult males in Madagascar, so that they will not become shy and retiring; . . . avoidance of deer by Dyak males so as not to become timid' (Rozin, 1990: 101).

The law of contagion leads the magical thinker to believe that things that have once been in contact continue ever afterwards to act on each other (Frazer, 1959: 5). 'Perhaps the last relic of such superstitions which lingered about our English kings was the notion that they could heal scrofula by their touch. The disease was accordingly known as the King's Evil; and . . . we may perhaps conjecture that the skin disease of scrofula was originally supposed to be caused as well as cured by the king's touch. . . . Dr. Johnson was touched in his childhood for scrofula by Queen Anne' (Frazer, 1909: 15).

Frazer (1909: 2) believed that magical thinking often had a beneficial effect, in that it promoted respect for the monarchy, private property, marriage, and human life generally. However one evaluates such superstitious behaviour, there is little doubt that it is not a relic of so-called 'primitive' cultures but is still a feature of everyday life. The work of Paul Rozin (Rozin et al., 1985; Rozin et al., 1986; Rozin and Fallon, 1987) demonstrates the continuing prevalence of such thinking.

of line'. However, to be effective the group must maintain itself over time by means of 'emotional ties . . . feelings of unity which are the true source of its strength' (ibid., 276). Nevertheless, there will inevitably be situations that lead to violence as a result of conflicts within the group or between rival groups.

In his letter to Freud, Einstein had wondered why it appeared to be so easy to arouse the wish to go to war, and Freud responded with his own belief that people's lives are ultimately ruled by two instincts, the **life instinct** (Eros) and the **death instinct** (Thanatos). The former is a constructive tendency to build things up, while the latter is a destructive tendency to tear things down. Freud regarded this formulation as 'no more than a theoretical clarification of the universally familiar opposition between Love and Hate which may perhaps have some fundamental relation to the polarity of attraction and repulsion that plays a part' in physics (ibid., 281). Here we should pause to recall that Freud began his career as a scientist who subscribed to the belief, held by Helmholtz, Brücke, and others, that all phenomena could ultimately be understood in terms of the fundamental forces of attraction and repulsion. Freud's postulation of a death instinct can be seen as the culmination of his attempt to remain true to this vision (Shakow, 1969: 94).

Few of Freud's own followers, and even fewer non-psychoanalysts, ever accepted the hypothesis of a death instinct. However, Freud himself saw it as a necessity in order to explain the awesome carnage witnessed in an event such as World War I, for example. He also believed that the goal of the life and death instincts were, at bottom, the same. Just as the erotic tendencies operate to reduce tension, so its opposite tends to return us to our 'original condition of inanimate matter' (Freud, 1959e: 282). Such a state would be, of course, completely tension free.

Regardless of how seriously one takes the notion of a death instinct, one might nonetheless agree with Freud that some mechanism is required to deal with aggressive tendencies, and that the best safeguard is the development of emotional attachments between people. In this connection Freud quoted the Bible: 'Thou shalt love thy neighbour as thyself', but observed that such a state of affairs can only be brought about through indirect means, if at all. Even though culture causes us problems by inhibiting the expression of instinctual urges, it is still our best guard against the irrationality of war. Culture provides 'a strengthening of the intellect, which is beginning to govern instinctual life', and so 'whatever fosters the growth of culture works at the same time against war' (ibid., 287).

Freud's Death

The analogy Freud made between development and migration applies in a particularly concrete way to the end of Freud's own life. When the Nazis came to power in Germany, psychoanalysis was not viewed with great favour, particularly since it had been invented by a Jew. The Nazis annexed Austria in 1938, and it became more and more dangerous for Freud to remain in Vienna. Many of Freud's followers were concerned that he leave for a safer place, but Freud stubbornly held fast. The necessity for leaving did not become obvious to Freud until his daughter, Anna, to whom he was very attached, was interrogated by the Gestapo. Soon after that episode the Freuds left Vienna for England. Freud's sojourn there was brief. He had suffered from cancer of the palate since at least 1923, and had previously arranged with his personal physician, Max Schur, to assist him in dying when the time came. Freud's suffering was intense, and he finally decided that there was no point in going on. He died after a dose of morphine on 23 September 1939.

Freud and America

In 1909, Freud lectured on psychoanalysis at Clark University in Worcester, Massachusetts. Freud's visit was well-publicized (Fancher, 2000: 1026) and by 1915 the psychoanalytic approach had become reasonably well-known in America

(Hornstein, 1992). Many psychologists were impressed, and historians of psychology in the first half of the twentieth century (e.g., Heidbreder, 1933; Boring, 1950b) counted Freud's theory among the most important of psychological theories (Shakow and Rapaport, 1964: 73). However, there was considerable resistance to Freud's approach, particularly from academic psychologists (Fancher, 2000: 1026). This resistance had two sources. One arose from the fact that academic psychologists were accustomed to laboratory evidence being used to support a theory, and there was a relative absence of experimental evidence in support of psychoanalytic theory. 'To the analyst, science had nothing to do with method, with controlling variables or counting things. What made something scientific was that it was true. . . . The efforts of [experimental] psychologists, with their bulky equipment and piles of charts and graphs, seemed superficial and largely irrelevant [to the psychoanalyst]' (Hornstein, 1992: 254–5). Added to this incommensurability of method was the attitude, so clearly stated by Freud, that in order to understand psychoanalysis, you had to be psychoanalyzed yourself.

> It is in general so hard to give anyone who is not himself a psychoanalyst an insight into psychoanalysis. You can believe me when I tell you that we do not enjoy giving an impression of being members of a secret society and of practising a mystical science. Yet we have been obliged to recognize and express as our conviction that no-one has a right to join in a discussion of psychoanalysis who has not had particular experiences which can only be obtained by being analyzed oneself. (Freud, 1964: 69).

This is a particularly pernicious argument, because it places the psychoanalyst in a win/win situation in relation to critics of the theory. If you approve of the theory then you are an insightful person. If you disapprove of the theory, then you are just resisting the truth and are in need of analysis yourself! Many academic psychologists found this attitude reprehensible and, as we will see in later chapters, demanded more objective standards for the validation of psychoanalysis or, for that matter, any other theory.

There were other forces that distanced academic psychologists from psychoanalysis. Especially in America, to a very large extent only physicians were eligible to be trained as psychoanalysts, and those trained in psychoanalysis tended to be active in private practice rather than in academic settings (Shakow and Rapaport, 1964: 195). However, although psychoanalytic theory was not easily assimilated by academic psychology departments, many prominent psychologists availed themselves of psychoanalytic therapy. Some of them published accounts of their analysis in a symposium in the *American Journal of Psychology* (American Psychological Association, 1953 [1940]):

> By its very nature the symposium could not provide systematic data. It did, however, offer a forum for the presentation by psychologists of a wide variety of material, ranging from views about the psychoanalytic process itself, through reports of actual experiments on psychoanalytic themes, to suggestions for revision of psychoanalytic theory. Even the most impersonal of the reports were sufficiently detailed to give some indication of the effects of the analytic process on the participants. The symposium leaves one with the distinct impression of important contributions to psychology from psychoanalysis. (Shakow and Rapaport, 1964: 77–8).

If discussions of psychoanalytic therapy helped embed psychoanalysis in psychology, so did the fact that psychoanalytic concepts began to appear in introductory textbooks, although they were often presented without much discussion of psychoanalytic theory itself (Hornstein, 1992: 259). However, what is taught in an introductory course in psychology is an important index of the extent to which particular ideas occupy a central place in a discipline (e.g., Morawski, 1992), and psychoanalytic concepts became a core part of the discipline in the sense that students were expected to know something about them. As Hornstein (1992: 261) observed:

> American psychology has always been distinguished by an uncanny ability to adapt itself to cultural trends as quickly as they emerge. Once it became clear that the public found psychoanalysis irresistible, psychologists found ways of accommodating to it. Instead of concentrating all their efforts on criticism, they identified those parts of the theory that were potentially useful to their own ends and incorporated them.

In future chapters, we will see examples of how psychologists incorporated psychoanalytic concepts into their own theories.

Freud's Critics within Psychoanalysis

Consider what the following quotation reveals about Freud's proprietary attitude towards psychoanalysis.

> For psychoanalysis is my creation; I was for ten years the only person who concerned himself with it. . . . no-one can know better than I what psychoanalysis is, how it differs from other ways of investigating the life of the mind, and precisely what should be called psychoanalysis and what should be described by some other name. (Freud, 1959c [1914]: 287)

It should come as no surprise that Freud did not tolerate dissent within the psychoanalytic movement. One of the chief dissenters, C.G. Jung, founded his own version of psychoanalysis that we will consider below. Others also created distinctive versions of the theory. Among the most prominent was **Alfred Adler** (1870–1937). Like many of the dissidents, Adler was uncomfortable with the notion that sexuality was the be-all and end-all of human existence, and instead chose to emphasize the role that **feelings of inferiority** play in human development.

Adler's emphasis on inferiority draws attention to the dimension of dominance-submission as a particularly important aspect of human affairs. Rather than regard erotic urges as the prime mover of human behaviour, Adler focused on the centrality of power. Adler spoke of 'the absolute primacy of the will to power . . . which asserts itself more forcibly . . . the stronger the inferiority feeling of the child' (Ansbacher and Ansbacher, 1964: 111).

Among the forces that influence feelings of inferiority, Adler believed that **birth order** was particularly important. He pointed out that 'it is a common fallacy to imagine that children of the same family are formed in the same environment', and that because of 'the order of their succession' each child was born into a different situation (ibid., 376). Based on his clinical experience, Adler gave thumbnail sketches of the typical personality to be found in each sibling position, and these make entertaining reading (ibid., 377–82). However one evaluates these characterizations there can be no doubt that birth order subsequently became an intensively investigated variable (e.g., Schachter, 1959; Toman, 1971).

Freud and Women

One of the persistent criticisms of Freud is that he was a misogynist. Certainly, many women have felt compelled to distance themselves from what Freud himself acknowledged was largely a male-centred psychology. In fact, Freud did not directly address differences between men and women until 1923, which is relatively late in his theoretical development (Appignanesi and Forrester, 1992: 399). Freud then advanced the infamous hypothesis concerning **penis envy**: women want to have a penis and feel incomplete without one. Many women have subsequently found this suggestion either preposterous or hilarious, or perhaps both (e.g., Steinem, 1994).

While women often disavowed psychoanalysis (including Breuer's patient Anna O., who eventually became a prominent feminist), there were also many women who managed to develop their own ideas within a modified form of psycho-analysis (Sayers, 1991). Among these was Freud's daughter, **Anna Freud**.

Anna Freud (1895–1982)

Much has been written about the closeness of the relationship between the founder of psychoanalysis and his daughter. She has been described as 'her father's secretary, nurse, and main exponent of his ideas. But she also went beyond them' (Sayers, 1991: 145). The ideas for which she became best known concerned the **defence mechanisms** (A. Freud, 1946 [1936]), those procedures that protect the ego from the disruptive influences of unconscious wishes. As we have already seen, repression is the basic mechanism for keeping id impulses under control. However, the ego must often resort to other devices in order to maintain control successfully. Among the best known of these are *displacement*, *projection*, *rationalization*, and *reaction formation*.

Displacement is a way of redirecting an impulse towards a safer target. The classic example of displacement is the person who wishes to murder his or her boss but is afraid to express this anger directly for fear of losing a job. Therefore, the individual may take out anger on the family pet or, worse yet, children and other vulnerable people who are less able to retaliate.

Projection involves attributing one's own unacknowledged wishes to someone else. If you cannot face the fact that you wish to have sex with someone, then you may find yourself thinking that the other person wants to have sex with you. If you unconsciously want to murder someone, then you may find yourself worried that the other person wants to murder you. Of course, in cases such as these, you may feel the need to take precautions against what you believe to be the evil impulses of the other person, and this may lead to some very strange behaviour.

Rationalization is a way of making excuses for oneself when one behaves in a way that is inconsistent with the ego's conception of itself. Imagine a teacher who thinks of himself as a brilliant pedagogue, but who always fails more students in his class than any other teacher. The truth may be that the teacher actually hates his students and expresses this by giving them undeservedly low marks. The students may perceive this fact themselves, and curse the day that fate landed them in this teacher's class. The teacher, however, may be reluctant to face the truth about himself, and instead complain about *his* bad luck in always being given such bad students to teach. Alternatively, the teacher may claim that he is the only teacher in the school with proper standards, and that he is just trying to keep the traditional academic integrity of the school from eroding. If you think about this example for a moment, you will see how difficult it may be to tell the difference between someone who is rationalizing and someone who is telling the truth. Both people sincerely believe what they say, but the rationalizer is deceiving both himself and his audience.

Reaction formation allows the ego to recruit additional energy in the service of repressing a wish. The ego does this by vigorously expressing the opposite behaviour to that which would occur if the unconscious wish was given free reign. Suppose you truly love (or hate) someone but cannot face this about yourself, let alone express it. One way of dealing with such a state of affairs is to express the opposite of what you really (i.e., unconsciously) feel. Typically, reaction formation is said to lead to exaggerated forms of behaviour. Perhaps you have experienced the attentions of someone who appears to think you are an absolutely wonderful person, so much so that you begin to wonder if their feelings can possibly be genuine.

The defence mechanisms are good examples of the sort of behaviour that interested not only Anna Freud, but psychoanalysts generally. The defence mechanisms beautifully illustrate the psychoanalytic premise that behaviour is not always what it seems to be. Like a dream, the meaning of behaviour is never transparent. That is why behaviour, like the dream, requires *interpretation*, because its true meaning may be the opposite of what it at first appears to be. Moreover, you are not in a good position to interpret your own behaviour because you are probably deceiving yourself. Only an objective outsider—a psychoanalyst, for example—will be able to interpret your behaviour properly (MacIntyre, 1958). The prevalence of interpreting other people's behaviour may be seen as largely due to the influence of psychoanalysis on twentieth-century culture (Trilling, 1972: 140–57). Men and women alike grew accustomed to interpreting each other's behaviour, often, without realizing it, along psychoanalytic lines. Finally, psychoanalytic interpretation became so commonplace that it no longer captured the popular imagination in the latter half of the twentieth century, as even Anna Freud (1969) was forced to conclude. However, as the twentieth century progressed, new popular psychotherapies emerged that provided ordinary people with alternative frameworks within which to interpret behaviour (Rosen, 1977), and we will examine some of them in Chapter 13.

Karen Horney (1885–1952) and the Psychology of Women

Karen Horney was born and educated in Germany, where she became a medical doctor in 1913. Although she started out as a more or less orthodox psychoanalyst, she gradually developed her own unique theory. In 1932 she moved to the United States. Horney has been described as one of 'the most important women in the history of psychology. A towering intellect, the courage of her convictions, creative imagination, and a genuinely rebellious spirit led to her dramatic secession from orthodox psychoanalysis. She became the first woman to found an independent psychoanalytic society, the American Institute for Psychoanalysis. She contributed brilliant, integrative, and original theories: a theory of neurosis, theories related to personality development, and a radical theory of the psychology of women' (Stevens and Gardner, 1982). There was renewed interest in Horney towards the end of the twentieth century with the publication of important books about her and her work (e.g., Quinn, 1987; Westcott, 1986).

Horney argued that the typical male analyst did not see women accurately, but in a distorted, juvenile way (Appignanesi and Forrester, 1992: 437). If a woman envied a man, it would not be so much because of his penis, but because of the superior status society accords the masculine role (Greenglass, 1982: 51). Moreover, men may also envy women, a condition Horney called **womb envy**. By this Horney meant concretely that men may envy women for their ability to have children, and, more abstractly, that men may envy women for their creativity. 'This "womb envy" is expressed by men in the form of disparagement of women's natural achievements and glorification of the practical achievements of men' (Greenglass, 1982: 248).

Horney (1950: 366) 'discarded Freud's theory of instincts' and regarded neurosis as the outcome of the child's response to **basic anxiety**, which was defined as a 'feeling of being isolated and helpless toward a world potentially hostile'. The child, and later the adult, tries to deal with this anxiety in three ways. The first is *moving towards people*, a pattern of behaviour in which the person behaves in a self-effacing, compliant manner towards others; *moving away from people*, in which the person attempts to live in isolation and maintain an attitude of indifference to what goes on; and *moving against people*, in which the person maintains an attitude of hostile vindictiveness against others. It is normal for all of us to engage in these forms of behaviour, which only become neurotic when the person is no longer able to be flexible, maintaining a rigid adherence to only one pattern of behaviour and engaging in it in an exaggerated fashion. Notice that each of these *neurotic types* involves a way of relating to people, and thus Horney's theory places great emphasis on the importance of interpersonal relationships.

Self-realization does not exclusively, or even primarily, aim at developing one's special gifts. The center of the process is the evolution of one's potentialities as a human being; hence it involves—in a central place—the development of one's capacities for good human relations. (Ibid., 308)

Horney (ibid., 370–1) believed that her psychology was different from Freud's in three ways. First, Freud underestimated the importance of social factors in determining personality. Second, Freud generally overestimated the role of sexuality. Third, Freud overemphasized the role of early childhood experiences. By suggesting that there are constructive forces in people that enable them to change neurotic patterns and live authentically as their real selves, Horney believed that she had created a more optimistic alternative to Freudianism.

C.G. Jung (1875–1961)

Jung's Relationship with Freud

Carl Jung was trained as a physician, and in the early phase of his career he practised psychiatry at the Burgholzli clinic in Zurich. The chief of staff at the Burgholzli was **Eugen Bleuler**, who coined the term **schizophrenia** to describe that terrifying condition in which the person seems totally cut off from normal reality. The Burgholzli was a prestigious facility, and it has been suggested that Freud was initially receptive to Jung because of Freud's wish to recruit members of prestigious institutions to the psychoanalytic cause (Zaretsky, 1994).

Jung discovered Freud's psychoanalytic theory by reading *The Interpretation of Dreams* and began writing to Freud (McGuire, 1974). One of his first letters concerned **Sabina Spielrein**, who, among other things, was a patient and co-worker of Jung's. Spielrein was also much more, and her fascinating story is briefly summarized in Box 6.2. Jung visited Freud in Vienna in 1907 and the two men became close friends. Freud began to see Jung as his successor as leader of the psychoanalytic movement. In 1909, Jung accompanied Freud to America, where both gave lectures at Clark University. Jung's lecture concerned the technique of *word association* he had

developed for diagnosis (e.g., Jung, 1974 [1904]). Jung's association experiments involved measuring the reaction time to a series of stimulus words. Words that required a long time to give an association were clues to the person's areas of difficulty.

During the period that Freud and Jung were getting along with each other, they wrote often. In those days, it was very common for people to exchange letters on a regular basis. The postal system was reliable and swift, and a letter from Jung in Zurich could be answered by Freud in Vienna in a few days. Let us examine two letters written towards the end of their friendship. On 11 November 1912, Jung wrote Freud upon returning from another visit to America. In the following extract from the letter, the symbol ΨA refers to 'psychoanalysis', a common abbreviation in both Freud's and Jung's correspondence.

I gave 9 lectures at the Jesuit (!) University of Fordham, New York—a critical account of the development of the theory of ΨA. . . . Naturally, I also made room for those of my views which deviate in places from the hitherto existing conceptions, particularly in regard to the libido theory. *I found that my version of ΨA won over many people who until now had been put off by the problem of sexuality in neurosis.* (McGuire, 1974: 515; emphasis added)

On 14 November 1912, Freud replied as follows:

Dear Dr. Jung,
I greet you on your return from America, no longer as affectionately as on the last occasion in Nuremburg—you have successfully broke me of that habit—but still with considerable sympathy, interest and satisfaction at your personal success . . . . *You have reduced a good deal of resistance with your modifications, but I shouldn't advise you to enter this in the credit column because, as you know, the farther you remove yourself from what is new in ΨA, the more certain you will be of applause and the less resistance you will meet.* (Ibid., 517; emphasis added)

BOX 6.2

SABINA SPIELREIN (1885–1941)

Sabina Spielrein is a good example of a woman who does collaborative work with men but who fails to receive appropriate credit. 'A passionate idealist, a woman of immense strength of character and resilience, Spielrein was the first woman psychoanalyst of significance, and she was until very recently almost entirely forgotten' (Appignanesi and Forrester, 1992: 205). Appignanesi and Forrester and Carotenuto (1982) have reminded us of some of the remarkable facts of her life.

Born in Russia, she began to study medicine in Zurich in 1904. As a result of some sort of problem, she was admitted to the Burgholzli, where she was treated by Jung. After being discharged, she began working with Jung on his word association experiments. Spielrein and Jung became erotically involved, and Jung wrote to Freud, apparently in an attempt to elicit Freud's help in extricating himself from the relationship. The resulting correspondence among the three makes fascinating reading and is contained in Carotenuto (1982).

Spielrein became a psychoanalyst and wrote papers that contained ideas later developed by Freud in his theorizing about a death instinct. Her work also influenced Jung's theorizing about the bipolar nature of the mind.

Spielrein's contributions went well beyond the psychoanalytic arena. Not only did she work on the development of language, but after moving to Geneva she became Jean Piaget's analyst. Piaget is, of course, one of the most famous twentieth-century developmental psychologists, and we will consider his work in detail later on.

After returning to Russia, Spielrein met A.R. Luria and L.S. Vygotsky, two of the giants of Russian psychology. It is entirely possible that she influenced these men as well.

Appignanesi and Forrester (1992: 226) write of her untimely end: 'In 1924 she moved back to her home town of Rostov and taught at the local university. . . . When Rostov was captured by the invading German army in November, 1941, all the Jews of the city, including Spielrein and her two daughters, were taken to the synagogue and shot.'

Jung is proposing a fundamental change in the libido concept (discussed below), and Freud, as usual, is not receptive to any alterations in what he regards as *his* theory. In addition, Freud believes that Jung is disowning the essential parts of psychoanalysis and is offering the public a sugar-coated version that is easier to swallow. As we now move on to discuss Jung's theory, keep Freud's attitude in mind, and see to what extent you think it fits Jung's revision.

The Difference between Freud and Jung

Recall that Freud had advanced the idea that the basic motivating force in human life is libido, which Freud regarded as sexual energy. Jung wanted to desexualize the concept of the libido. Freud felt that such a change would rob psychoanalysis of one of its most basic insights. The two

could not reach an accommodation, and communication between them eventually broke down completely. The change in the libido concept that Jung proposed was to equate it with **psychic energy**, which was the total 'life force' in the person. Although it might be expressed sexually, it was not solely, or even basically, sexual. Thus, Jung's concept of libido is much broader than Freud's. This 'life force' could be a source of inspiration and growth, not just a drive for pleasure.

Analytical Psychology

Jung left the psychoanalytic movement and founded his own theoretical school, called **analytical psychology**, or, as it is came to be called, **archetypal psychology** (e.g., Hillman, 1972).

Extraversion and Introversion

After his break with Freud, Jung spent many years working on his book *Psychological Types*, which was published in 1921. In it, Jung formulated the distinction between **introversion** and **extraversion** that has since become so well-known. These opposing tendencies are examples of what was, for Jung, a general feature of mental life: bipolar distinctions always underlie psychological processes, and every process is capable of moving in opposing directions (Dallett, 1973).

The introvert-extravert distinction refers to the way in which different people relate to the world. Jung (1971 [1921]: 427) described the typical extravert as someone who is obviously interested in what goes on in the environment. 'Extraversion is an outward-turning of the libido . . . a transfer of interest from subject to object.' By contrast, 'introversion means a turning inward of libido. . . . Interest does not move towards the object but withdraws from it into the subject' (ibid., 453). Jung's student, Jolande Jacobi, summarized the relation between introversion and extraversion:

> Extraversion is characterized by a positive relation to the object, introversion by a negative one. In his [or her] adjustment and reaction pattern, the extravert orients himself [or herself] predominantly by the outward, collective norms, the spirit of the times, etc. The attitudes of the introvert, on the other hand, are determined mainly by subjective factors. Often he [or she] is poorly adjusted to [the] environment. The extravert thinks, feels, and acts in relation to the object; . . . displaces . . . interest from subject to object and orients [herself or] himself primarily by the world outside. . . . For the introvert the subject is the basis of orientation, while the object plays at most a secondary, indirect role. (Jacobi, 1968: 18–19)

We could say that the introvert is more 'subjective' than the extravert, who is more 'objective'. Suppose an introvert and an extravert are in the same situation. The introvert regards the subjective experience of the situation as more important than the situation itself. By contrast, the extravert experiences a situation directly, as of value in its own right (Shapiro and Alexander, 1975). The introvert can be characterized as moving away from the world. This movement is not simply negative, because the introvert is simultaneously moving towards what Jung called the **collective unconscious**. In the collective unconscious are characteristics possessed by the species as a whole. It is indifferent to the individual ego, but rather expresses the most general tendencies there are; it corresponds to what we all have in common. 'We have to distinguish between a **personal unconscious** and an impersonal or transpersonal unconscious. We speak of the latter also as the *collective unconscious*, because it is detached from anything personal and is entirely universal, and because its contents can be found everywhere' (Jung, 1956 [1943]: 76).

The personal unconscious is analogous to what Freud meant by 'the unconscious', and 'contains lost memories, painful ideas that are repressed, . . . subliminal perceptions, . . . contents that are not yet ripe for consciousness', while the collective unconscious 'is the object which the libido chooses when it is freed. . . . It follows its own gradient down into the depths of the unconscious, and there activates what has lain slumbering from the beginning. It has discovered the hidden treasure upon which mankind ever and anon has drawn, and from which it has raised up its gods and demons' (ibid., 76–7).

We can begin to grasp the limitless nature of what Jung meant by the collective unconscious by examining Figure 6.3. About that diagram, Jung (1969: 21) said:

> If you suppose [the line between A and A¹] to be the threshold of consciousness, then you would have in D an area of consciousness referring to the ectopsychic [i.e., external] world B. . . . But on the other side, in C, is the *shadow-world*. There the ego is somewhat dark, we do not see into it, we are an enigma to ourselves. We only know the ego in D, we do not know it in C.

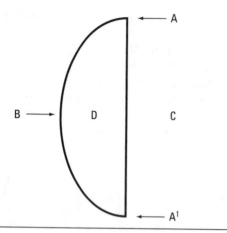

FIGURE 6.3
Jung's representation of the relation between consciousness, the external world, and the inner world.
Source: Jung, C.G.; *The Symbolic Life*–Volume 18.
© 1976 Princeton University Press, 2004 renewed PUP. Reprinted by permission of Princeton University Press.

Therefore we are always discovering something new about ourselves. Almost every year something new turns up which we did not know before. We always think we are now at the end of our discoveries. We never are. We go on discovering that we are this, that, and other things, and sometimes we have astounding experiences.

As Rycroft (1969) has pointed out, it is instructive to compare Jung's diagram with Freud's structural model (Figure 6.2). Both Freud and Jung conceive of the mind using spatial metaphors. As we observed earlier, the use of such metaphors can be a great aid to the theorist's thinking. They should not be taken literally, but rather as metaphorical models of the mind.

Archetypes
It is through exploration of the collective unconscious that one becomes aware of the existence of **archetypes**. According to the *Oxford English Dictionary*, the word 'archetype' originally meant 'the pattern or model from which copies are made;

a prototype'. There is a similarity between the concept of archetypes and Platonic ideas, although unlike Platonic ideas, archetypes have not only a cognitive function but also an emotional aspect (Jacobi, 1971: 49). From Jung's viewpoint, the mind is not a blank slate at birth, but meets life with archetypal predispositions to perceive, feel, and act in particular ways. The action of the archetypes is very general, in that they organize our experience without completely determining its content. They are innate organizational tendencies that are dynamic and emotional, carrying with them general feeling qualities. We never encounter archetypes directly, but rather particular images shaped by them.

Here is an example of how an archetype functions, adapted from Jacobi (1968: 44) and Campbell (1964: 73–4). We are all capable of imagining a hero. Close your eyes and imagine the person who, of all your personal acquaintances, best exemplifies a hero. The image you have is the sort of thing we are now interested in. These images will obviously be different for different people, and different for one individual at different times. But they will all be related to one another in that they will all express the archetype of 'the hero'. In addition to people of your own acquaintance, you could have images of heroes whom you may never have encountered. These might include famous warriors or politicians (Pierre Trudeau, John F. Kennedy), people who fought for civil and political rights (Mahatma Gandhi, Martin Luther King Jr), or someone who struggled for a cause despite great adversity (Terry Fox). You could also have images of heroes you may have discovered as a child through the media, such as Batman or Catwoman, as well as mythical heroes such as Hercules. The contribution the archetype makes to each image is greatest the more it is removed from actual people and situations. However, to a greater or less extent, the archetype will shape every image, even those we have of real people. No image is simply a copy of what is given by the external world. Images vary from those that are relatively 'extraverted' (i.e., that largely conform to an external reality) to those that are relatively 'introverted' (i.e., that largely conform to an inner reality). Neither is more 'accurate' than the other. Each reflects its own reality. The extraverted image is faithful to the outer reality, while the introverted image is faithful to the inner reality.

It is difficult to say how many archetypes there are, although Jungians typically argue that the number is finite and corresponds to our most 'fundamental experiences incurred . . . since primordial times. . . . They are the same in all cultures. We find them recurring in all mythologies, fairy tales, religious traditions, and mysteries' (Jacobi, 1968: 47). Among the archetypes most frequently discussed in the Jungian literature are the **anima** and the **animus**. The anima is the masculine image of femininity, while the animus is the feminine image of masculinity. Each of us has a mask, or **persona**, that constitutes our public self. To the extent that we identify with this mask, we will be cut off from those parts of ourselves that are inconsistent with it. Someone whose persona is excessively masculine may be totally unaware of his (her) feminine side, represented by the anima, while someone whose persona is excessively feminine may be totally unaware of her (his) masculine side, represented by the animus. These unacknowledged parts of the person exist in the 'shadow world' represented in Figure 6.3. It is a major part of a person's life work to integrate these opposing parts of the personality into a coherent whole.

Balancing Opposites

In many psychological theories, the goal of the organism is said to be tension reduction. As we saw earlier, in the standard psychoanalytic theory of motivation, our basic motive is to eliminate the 'unpleasure' that occurs as libido accumulates, and to do this we seek objects that will reduce tension. No doubt there is some truth to this notion, but Jung thought that the true situation was somewhat more complex. He believed that the overriding goal of the person was to balance the opposing tendencies contained within. The integration of these

opposites was the person's major task. By proposing the **union of opposites** as a basic process, Jung is echoing a theme that, as we saw in the first chapter, has been sounded for a long time. Indeed, Jung was a formidable scholar and not only drew on Western sources but also from Eastern traditions such as Taoism (e.g., Jung, 1950).

We can illustrate how this balancing process might work using the extraversion-introversion distinction. Jung argues that it is most common for the person to be extraverted at first, but somewhere around mid-life to begin to turn inward and become more introverted. The shift from extraversion to introversion is not only a shift in the orientation to the external world, but also a shift in orientation to the inner world. This means increased attention to the collective unconscious. If this process works well, it does not involve simply an oscillation from objective observation to the cultivation of an 'inner vision'. Rather, it involves an integration into a unified whole of both orientations, a union of opposites.

Jung's concept of a union of opposites was drawn in part from medieval alchemy. **Alchemy** was primitive chemistry, and involved the search for a way of turning lead into gold. One part of alchemy became modern chemistry. However, alchemy itself is still relevant because of its symbolic value. Jung believed that the alchemical search for gold symbolically represented the search for a union of the opposing parts of ourselves. The process whereby this union is achieved is symbolically represented not only in alchemy, but also in countless myths and legends, such as the search for the Holy Grail. The process of Jungian psychotherapy was intended to facilitate this quest for wholeness. To have the person produce art can be an important part of this process. Among the most interesting forms of art are *mandalas*, or balanced structures expressing the person's unified self.

The Four Functions

Jung's description of psychological processes was organized along bipolar dimensions. We have already noted one such distinction, extraversion-

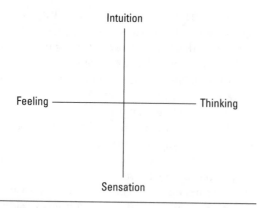

FIGURE 6.4
The four functions.

introversion. For Jungians, another important distinction is that between *perception* and *judgement*. There are two perceptual functions, *sensation* and *intuition*, as well as two judgemental functions, *thinking* and *feeling*. Figure 6.4 illustrates how these pairs stand in opposition to one another. Typically, the person specializes in one of these functions, in which case the opposite function remains relatively primitive. Thus, someone might favour thinking as a way of making judgements, which would mean that he or she evaluates something in terms of whether it is true or false. In that case, the person's feeling function, which evaluates things in terms of good versus bad, might be underdeveloped. Alternatively, someone might specialize in intuition, the process that grasps situations as whole. In that case, the sensation function, which deals with particular facts, might be underdeveloped.

Since a function can be either extraverted (looking outward) or introverted (looking inward), a great many possible combinations exist. Jung's typology (e.g., Briggs and Myers, 1976) became extremely popular in business and in education as a way of representing individual differences (e.g., Benfari, 1991), although academic psychologists had serious doubts about it (e.g., Stricker and Ross, 1964).

The Collective Unconscious and the External World

At first glance it appears that nothing could be more unlike the external world than the collective unconscious. The external world seems to be 'objective', while the collective unconscious is 'subjective'. However, Jung sometimes called the collective unconscious the *objective unconscious*, because, like the external world, it is relatively neutral with respect to the individual ego. At bottom, the external world and the collective unconscious are both aspects of the same underlying reality. Jung believed that the collective unconscious can be a rich source of inspiration.

Here is an example of the creative process of the sort that Jungians liked, although we must remember that a Jungian explanation of this example is by no means the only one.

> The German chemist Friedrich A. Kekulé said that many of his early insights into the nature of chemical bonds and of molecular structure arose out of idle reveries in which he spontaneously experienced kinetic visual images of the dancing atoms hooked up to form chainlike molecules. Kekulé's cultivation of this visionary practice culminated in his celebrated dream in which one of these snake-like, writhing chains suddenly twisted into a closed loop as if seizing its own tail; thus was the startled Kekulé provided with his long sought answer to the problem of the structure of benzene—a structure fundamental to all of modern organic chemistry. (Shepard, 1978: 126)

Jungians might approach this example as follows. Dreams and fantasy often reveal the effects of the collective unconscious. When we stop consciously attending to a problem, then ideas fall below the threshold of awareness and can make contact with archetypal material in the collective unconscious. One such archetypal image is the *uroboros*, the snake eating its tail, of which the art historian Ernst Gombrich (1965: 46) said: 'This image which stands for time can tell us in a flash what discursive argument can only enumerate, such as the proposition that time is swift, that time in its turning somehow joins the beginning to the end, that it teaches wisdom, and brings and removes things.' The uroboros is an ancient symbol found in diverse cultures. In Kekulé's dream it organizes his real-world problem, giving it the structure necessary for him to see the solution. In general, archetypal material that emerges in dreams or fantasy can restructure mundane thinking, which can then be mapped back onto the world in a productive way. Introverted images can help us understand the extraverted reality. From Jung's viewpoint, the fact that archetypal structuring of our thinking can help us in our dealings with the external world should not surprise us. Because the collective unconscious and the external world are part of nature, they share the same reality. Jung referred to this commonality as reflecting the ultimately *psychoid* nature of reality, meaning that nature is neither mental nor physical, neither inner nor outer, but everything at once.

Many people in the arts, sciences, and religion were drawn to Jung's ideas. One example is the physicist Wolfgang Pauli (1955). He pointed out that we cannot take so introverted an attitude that we are ignorant of the external world. However, if we want a unified world view, then we must recognize that introverted experience plays a significant role in the genesis of scientific ideas. Scientific creativity requires a relatively more introverted attitude than has customarily been advocated in modern science. The extraverted attitude, says Pauli, enables us to fit our ideas to reality, while the introverted attitude accesses the archetypal images that inform scientific ideas to begin with. Pauli argues that great scientists such as Kepler have understood the importance of balancing both sides of the equation.

As we saw when we reviewed Pythagorean ideas in Chapter 1, one of the most salient aspects of scientific thought in the West has been the application of mathematical ideas to the external world.

Jungians, such as Marie-Louise von Franz (1974: 18–19), argued, as had Pauli, that basic mathematical ideas 'should be included in Jung's concept of archetypal ideas. . . . If we accept Pauli's contention that certain mathematical structures rest on an archetypal basis, then their isomorphism with certain outerworld phenomena is not so surprising. For we know that archetypes engender images and ideas . . . which lie at the basis of [our] grasp of the outer world, and that they serve to release generally adequate adaptation reactions (comparable to the patterns of behavior in animals) that are probably not dependent on anything radically different from the basic structure of the physical world itself.' Thus, exploration of the collective unconscious may bring to light mathematical structures that regulate not only mental events but also physical and biological ones.

Synchronicity

Jung and Jungians generally are prepared to explore topics that other psychologists regard as far removed from their usual concerns. One of these areas of inquiry is synchronicity. Few of Jung's ideas are more obscure yet at the same time more influential than this one. Simply stated, **synchronicity** refers to meaningful coincidences. These are cases in which events seem to be connected to one another although they are not causally related. Almost everyone can report experiences of this sort, and most people resist explaining them as merely due to chance (Falk, 1989). Here is an example from Jung (1973 [1960]: 22):

A young woman I was treating has, at a critical moment, a dream in which she was given a golden scarab. While she was telling me this dream I sat with my back to the closed window. Suddenly I heard a noise behind me, like a gentle tapping. I turned round and saw a flying insect knocking against the window-pane from outside. I opened the window and caught the creature in the air as it flew in. It was the nearest analogy to a golden scarab that one finds in our latitudes, a scarabaeid beetle the common rose-chafer (*Cetonia aurata*) which contrary to its usual habits had evidently felt an urge to get into a dark room at this particular moment. I must admit that nothing like it ever happened to me before or since, and that the dream of the patient has remained unique in my experience.

One could treat such an incident as merely a coincidence and not read very much into it. However, Jung (who was interested in parapsychology throughout his life) insisted on the meaningfulness of such coincidences. He suggested that events may be meaningfully connected in a noncausal manner, through the collective unconscious. Mysterious as such a formulation sounds, it attracted many adherents (e.g., Koestler, 1974).

IMPORTANT NAMES, WORKS, AND CONCEPTS

Names and Works

Adler, Alfred
Anna O.
Bleuler, Eugen
Breuer, Joseph
Brücke, Ernst
Charcot, J.-M.
Freud, Anna

Freud, Sigmund
Horney, Karen
Jung, Carl G.
Mesmer, Anton
Psychological Types
Spielrein, Sabina
The Interpretation of Dreams

Concepts

alchemy
analytical (archetypal) psychology
anima and animus
animal magnetism
archetypes
basic anxiety
birth order
catharsis
cathexis and countercathexis
collective unconscious
conscious system
death instinct
defence mechanisms

erogenous zones
extraversion
feelings of inferiority
fixation
free association
hysteria
id, ego, superego
incest taboo
introversion
latent content
libido
life instinct
magical thinking

Concepts (continued)

manifest content

Oedipus complex

oral, anal, phallic, and genital stages

penis envy

persona

personal unconscious

pleasure principle

preconscious system

primal horde

psychic energy

psychosexual stages

reality principle

regression

repetition compulsion

repression

resistance

schizophrenia

synchronicity

unconscious system

union of opposites

womb envy

RECOMMENDED READINGS

Freud and His Precursors

For a fascinating review of mesmerism in nineteenth-century Britain, see A. Winter, *Mesmerized: Powers of Mind in Victorian Britain* (Chicago: University of Chicago Press, 1998). Overviews of Freud's life and influence are P. Gay, *Freud: A Life for Our Time* (New York: Norton, 1988), and F.J. Sulloway, *Freud: Biologist of the Mind* (New York: Basic Books, 1979). For Anna Freud, see E. Young-Bruehl, *Anna Freud: A Biography* (New York: Summit, 1988). A good example of the fascination that Freud had for ordinary Americans is a letter to Freud written in 1927 by 'a young woman working as a stenographer in a large Midwestern city'. Even though Freud had never met her, he took the time to respond to her request for his opinion about a disturbing dream of hers. See L.T. Benjamin and D.N. Dixon, 'Dream analysis by mail: An American woman seeks Freud's advice', *American Psychologist* 47 (1996): 123–31.

Although psychoanalysis has historically played a central role in the treatment of mental illness, it is also interesting to explore those attempts to deal with this problem before psychoanalysis came on the scene. For a sample of some nineteenth-century practices, see C.L. Krasnick, '"In charge of the loons": A portrait of the London, Ontario Asylum for the Insane in the nineteenth century', *Ontario History* 74 (1982): 138–84; S.E.D. Shortt, *Victorian Lunacy: Richard M. Bucke and the Practice of Late Nineteenth-Century Psychiatry* (Cambridge: Cambridge University Press, 1986).

Jung

A good introduction to Jung is his autobiography, *Memories, Dreams and Reflections* (New York: Vintage, 1965). R. Noll presents a controversial but highly readable characterization of the Jungian movement as a substitute for religion in *The Aryan Christ: The Secret Life of Carl Jung* (New York: Random House, 1997). S.L. Drob, 'Jung and the Kaballah', *History of Psychology* 2 (1999): 102–18, argues that Jung's ideas drew, directly and indirectly, from the Jewish mystical tradition.

CHAPTER 7

STRUCTURE OR FUNCTION?

Introduction

This chapter is mainly concerned with developments in the United States as the nineteenth century ended and the twentieth century began. This was a period during which psychology began to be established at universities, as illustrated by Titchener's extremely influential laboratory for the study of mental structure at Cornell. However, a more functional psychology was also making its appearance in areas as various as education and business. In addition, World War I provided the occasion for the first mass testing of recruits using intelligence tests, an activity that became central to psychology in later decades. Finally, an emphasis on the evolution of mental functions meant that the study of animals became increasingly important in the discipline.

Edward B. Titchener (1867–1927)

Born in England, **Edward B. Titchener** graduated from Oxford before going to Leipzig to study with Wundt from 1890 to 1892. He then went to Cornell, in Ithaca, New York, where he established a psychological laboratory. Titchener's work was similar to Wundt's experimental psychology in many ways. However, the complexity of Wundt's approach to psychology was lost in Titchener's much simpler approach. Moreover, like many academic psychologists, Titchener was unsympathetic to psychological explanations that invoked concepts such as 'the unconscious', which he believed to be an explanatory fiction. The result is a psychology that has few points of contact with the Freudian and Jungian concepts we considered in the previous chapter. Indeed, by considering

Titchener at this point we can see just how broad is the range of possible psychologies.

Like Wundt, Titchener distinguished psychology from other disciplines such as physics in terms of the different *point of view* taken by psychologists. What Titchener meant can best be grasped by using one of his own examples, the Muller-Lyer illusion shown in Figure 7.1. The horizontal line on the left is actually the same length as the horizontal line on the right. If you doubt this, get a ruler and measure each line. Measuring the line with a ruler is what a physical scientist would do in order to determine the true length of a line. However, from the point of view of an ordinary person simply reporting how long the two lines appear to be, then the line on the left is obviously longer than the line on the right. The physicist gives us a description of 'experience as altogether independent of any particular person; we will assume that it goes on whether or not anyone is there to have it', while the psychologist gives us a description of experience 'as altogether dependent upon the particular person' (Titchener, 1966a [1910]: 601). This means that the proper method for psychology will be **introspection**, the process whereby individuals describe their experience.

This way of defining the subject matter of psychology leads to the definition of mind as 'the sum-total of human experience considered as dependent upon a nervous system' (ibid., 602).

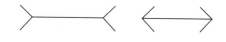

FIGURE 7.1
The Muller-Lyer Illusion.

Human experience is embodied in the sense that it cannot exist apart from someone's nervous system. However, Titchener did not reduce human experience to events in the nervous system. Rather, events in the nervous system run parallel to those in human experience, but should not be seen as causing them. The analogy Titchener used was that the nervous system bears the same relation to our mental processes as a map does to our experience of a journey. Consider what your experience is like when you take a trip by car from one city to another. Perhaps you will take a map along, particularly if you have not made the trip before. Without reference to the map, all you have are your particular experiences as you travel along. By looking at the map, you can get a deeper understanding of where you are, where you have been, and where you are going. The map improves your understanding of the journey you are taking, but is not a cause of your journey. Similarly, by referring to events in the nervous system we may be able to explain mental processes without regarding those events in the nervous system as causing mental processes. This is what Titchener meant by **psychophysical parallelism**.

The truly academic nature of Titchener's approach to psychology can be seen by considering what he believed to be the proper scope of the discipline. Titchener believed psychology to be, first and foremost, the study of the 'generalized human mind' by means of experimental introspection (Heidbreder, 1933: 125). Let us take the various parts of this statement and examine them in turn.

By 'generalized', Titchener meant that psychology was to develop principles that were true of *all* minds, not just some minds. Notice that this rules out the study of the peculiarities of individual minds, and, as we shall see, Titchener's attitude towards the study of *individual differences* was a source of considerable controversy, partly because the study of deviant minds is left out as well. While Titchener acknowledged that many interesting cases of unusual mental processes occur, these were not to be used to form the basis of psychology. Thus, Titchener begins in a very different place

than did Freud, for example, for whom the study of so-called *abnormal psychology* was a central part of psychological inquiry.

Psychology is essentially the study of adult, human minds, and this means that it is only peripherally concerned with the study of children or animals. Interestingly, Titchener did not believe that only humans have minds. Rather, he argued that 'the range of mind . . . appears to be as wide as the range of animal life' (Titchener, 1966a). One of his students, Margaret Floy Washburn, wrote an influential book on the psychology of animals. Titchener himself did do work on a number of topics in comparative psychology (Dewsbury, 1997a), even seeking 'information on bird song in an effort to differentiate rival theories of its evolution' (Dewsbury, 1992: 210). However, animal psychology was not, from Titchener's viewpoint, a central feature of the discipline.

By saying that psychology was the study of 'mind', Titchener was taking a position that may have seemed obvious at the time, but that became increasingly problematic. *Mind* began to seem to other psychologists to be a very slippery category, and, as we shall see, they began to redefine the discipline in ways that took the mind out of it.

Is psychology only an 'experimental' discipline? Remember that Wundt had argued that experimentation could only carry psychology so far, and that other forms of observation were equally important. However, by insisting on the necessity of *experimentation*, Titchener was taking a position that a great many academic psychologists subsequently espoused, but that was nonetheless the focus of continuous controversy.

What about 'introspection'? Is introspection the only legitimate method in psychology? Many psychologists began to question introspection as a method, even if it was practised under rigorously controlled conditions. If introspection is to be rejected as the primary psychological method, what is to take its place?

Thus, all parts of Titchener's approach to psychology look to be controversial. In many ways, this is Titchener's major contribution to American academic psychology. By defining his position and that of his opponents with extraordinary clarity, Titchener provided other psychologists with a benchmark against which they could measure their own orientation (e.g., Heidbreder, 1933: 150–1). Let us now briefly examine the content of Titchener's psychology and see why so many psychologists subsequently defined their psychology in opposition to it.

Structuralism

Titchener's psychology was often called **structuralism**, because it aimed to uncover the elementary structure of mind. However, since Titchener's day, there has been another intellectual movement called 'structuralism', which included such figures as the great Swiss developmental psychologist Jean Piaget. Titchener's structuralism and Piaget's structuralism have virtually nothing to do with one another.

Tweney (1987) has divided Titchener's career into four phases. In the first phase during the 1890s, Titchener established the basic characteristics of his introspectionist approach. Then, for most of the first decade of this century, Titchener was preoccupied with methodological issues. The subsequent period until 1915 was taken up with defending himself against various critics. Finally, he made some radical changes to his previous beliefs. Thus, Titchener, like most people, went through several changes throughout his professional career.

During his first phase, Titchener tried to differentiate between a *structural* and a *functional* psychology. He approached this topic by means of an analogy with biology, which is shown schematically in Figure 7.2. Among other things, biology has both structural and functional parts. The structural part of biology is anatomy, in which 'we may inquire into the structure of an organism, without regard to function' (Titchener, 1966c [1898]: 35). For example, we may attempt to understand the anatomical structure of the eye without worrying about what function the eye

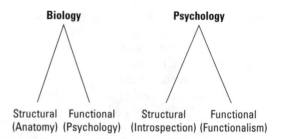

FIGURE 7.2
Titchener's distinction between structure and function.

serves. After understanding anatomy, we may then turn to physiology for an understanding of the function of organs such as the eye. Anatomy logically precedes physiology. Similarly, in psychology one can take a structural or functional approach. The subject matter of psychology is consciousness, and it may be understood in terms of what it is (its underlying structure) or what it does (its function). Naturally, we should know what consciousness *is* before we try to say what it is for. We can discover the structure of consciousness through introspective experimentation. A functional psychology should be postponed until we have a solid structural basis for psychology.

We ordinarily experience perceptions, ideas, and emotions. By means of introspection, these 'were reduced to their characteristic elements by means of analysis, just as the chemist breaks down complex substances into further unanalyzable substances' (Evans, 1973: 84). When it comes to saying what this underlying structure of consciousness is, Titchener (1966c: 41) argued that 'everyone admits that *sensations* are elementary mental processes' and underlie our perceptions. *Images* also figured large in Titchener's system. Ideas were believed always to be accompanied by images. In this context, recall that the British empiricists regarded mental life as being compounded out of elementary units like sensations, and Titchener had been trained in that tradition at Oxford. Titchener's psychology is a variant of the British associationist psychology.

In addition to sensations and images, Titchener believed that *affection* was the elementary process underlying emotion. Wundt had developed quite an elaborate tridimensional theory of feeling, but Titchener eventually simplified the number of affective dimensions into just one, *pleasant-unpleasant*.

Titchener's *Experimental Psychology*

During his second phase, Titchener (1971a [1902], 1971b [1905]) produced his **Experimental Psychology: A Manual of Laboratory Practice**. This is a remarkable set of volumes, and it offers interesting comparisons with texts currently being used in experimental psychology. Titchener lays out in great detail how a beginning student in experimental psychology is to acquire the fundamental skills of the discipline. 'A psychological experiment consists of *an introspection or a series of introspections made under standard conditions*' (Titchener, 1971a: I, xiii). Of course, in order to introspect properly, the student must learn the appropriate vocabulary.

> The importance of good terminology can, from the point of view of the teacher and student, hardly be overestimated. A rose by any other name would smell as sweet; but we do not teach botany by smell. The teacher of psychology is required, in a very limited time, to bring . . . pupils within the circle of science; to start them psychologizing, to train them in method, to give them facts and uniformities. How much of his success must depend upon his choice of words, and how completely is the beginner at the mercy of his phrasing! (Titchener, 1971b: II, cl)

Titchener is here attempting to confront a problem that was to bedevil introspectionism. The problem arises when students are to be taught the language to use when describing their experience (Mischel, 1969). What words should be used? Titchener (1971b: II, cli–clii) said that 'a good terminology should be absolutely transparent, letting the facts be seen through the words', and suggested 'the terms chosen must neither be familiar terms which bring with them misleading associations, nor terms so unfamiliar that their assimilation would itself be difficult.'

Students must be taught a new language if they are to introspect properly because ordinary language typically describes events in the external world, and not our experience of those events (Boring, 1963d: 256). When we pick up two objects, for example, we do not say 'this complex of cutaneous and organic sensations is more intensive than that one, but that this box or package is heavier than this other' (Titchener, 1971b: II, xxvi). Describing the object rather than one's experience of the object was called the **stimulus error**, and students had to be trained to avoid it. However, critics of introspectionism argued that it was never really clear precisely how the person learning to introspect was to choose one word as opposed to another, and that the language of experimental introspection was imprecise and potentially unreliable.

The content of Titchener's experimental psychology was divided into two parts: *qualitative* and *quantitative*. The former is the sort of experiment most frequently associated with introspectionism and includes the study of sensation, affection, attention, perception, and the association of ideas. As we have already seen, sensation and affection were regarded as elementary processes. Attention was 'a state of consciousness' in which 'events attended-to are the clearest and most distinct', while 'events attended-from are unclear and indistinct, relegated, as it were, to the background of consciousness' (ibid., 109). Perception ' is an aggregate, or group of sensations' (ibid., 127). The study of the association of ideas allowed students to examine experimentally the formation of associations according to traditional associationist laws such as frequency and recency. Finally, the quantitative part of Titchener's experimental psychology consisted largely of the psychophysical methods associated with Fechner, which we reviewed in Chapter 3.

Titchener and the Imageless Thought Controversy

During his third phase Titchener defended himself against such critics as the Würzburgers. This group of psychologists reported that introspection often yielded nothing more clear and distinct than *imageless thoughts*. The concept of an imageless thought was inconsistent with Titchener's way of analyzing mental processes, since he had maintained that ideas were always accompanied by images. The Würzburgers' analysis implied that some important mental processes may be 'unconscious' and therefore inaccessible to introspection. Workers in Titchener's laboratory, however, were able to find that so-called imageless thoughts were not really imageless at all. Titchener argued that sensitive introspection disclosed kinesthetic sensations, perhaps arising from the speech musculature as the person spoke silently to him/herself while introspecting (Humphrey, 1951: 121).

The controversy over imageless thought tended to bring experimental introspection into disrepute, since there were different introspectionist laboratories apparently coming up with entirely different results. However, the results of Titchener's work in this area were not entirely negative. As Tweney (1987: 47) has observed, Titchener's work on imageless thought 'had a direct influence on the later work by [Edmund] Jacobson on the progressive relaxation technique.' Jacobson's work is of considerable intrinsic as well as historical interest, and is reviewed in Box 7.1.

Titchener and the Dimensions of Consciousness

During his fourth phase, Titchener developed an abstract approach to the study of consciousness. Rather than conceive of the structure of consciousness in terms of elements such as sensations, Titchener began to stress the analysis of consciousness in terms of dimensions. Titchener was concerned with 'the number and nature of the dimensions of the psychological world, just pre-

cisely as the physicist is concerned with mass and time and space as the dimensions of his physical world' (Rand, 1973: 87).

Titchener never settled the question of precisely what and how many **dimensions of consciousness** there were, and he died before producing the great work on the subject that many of his students expected. Some hint of what that work might have been like is given in a posthumous publication (Titchener, 1972 [1929]). Fortunately, one of his most famous students, E.G. Boring (1963a [1933]: ch. 2), published an account of what he took to be some of Titchener's central views in which he singled out four dimensions for discussion: **quality**, **intensity**, **extensity**, and **protensity**. These dimensions all refer to sensory experience. Quality refers to variation in basic experiences, such as different colours or tastes. Intensity refers to the strength of an experience, such as how strong an odour is. Extensity is best seen in relation to senses such as touch (ibid., 28), in which an experience can vary across a wide area. Protensity refers to the duration of a sensory experience in time.

Boring noted the *phenomenological* nature of the dimensional approach to experience, and many other commentators have also suggested that before his death Titchener had been moving away from elementarism towards phenomenology.

> The transition . . . to the doctrine of dimensions is so easy that one is apt to lose sight of the fact that [it] combines the freedom of phenomenology with the systematic organization of abandoned elementarism. The description of consciousness now resembles the description of a picture. With a picture one simply describes the qualitative-intensive-extensive pattern. For consciousness one adds the protensive dimension and extends the qualitative account over the various sense-departments. (Ibid., 30)

Titchener's Influence

Boring's *Physical Dimensions of Consciousness* developed Titchener's doctrine of conscious dimensions

BOX 7.1

EDMUND JACOBSON AND PROGRESSIVE RELAXATION

Edmund Jacobson's book *You Must Relax* (1977) is a relatively recent popularization of his *Progressive Relaxation*, which was originally published in 1929. As mentioned in the text, Jacobson's investigations were strongly influenced by working in Titchener's laboratory at Cornell. Historically, Jacobson's work is interesting not only because of its association with the introspection espoused by Titchener but also because it was continued at the University of Chicago with the support of the functional psychologist Harvey Carr (Jacobson, 1925).

Like Titchener, Jacobson emphasized the importance of using participants who are 'accomplished in the method of observing . . . sensory and imaginal experiences', and claimed that properly trained individuals will find that 'thought-processes and other intellectual activities always involve experiences of sensation and images, including sensations from muscles' (Jacobson, 1938: 193). Jacobson argued that 'the activity of thinking . . . to the best of our present knowledge consists physiologically (chiefly or entirely) of a series of sensations, images and neuromuscular . . . tensions' (ibid., 195).

Jacobson observed that stress and tension were a central feature of modern life, and made use of introspective techniques to attempt to reduce tension. To uncover and eliminate muscular tension, he pointed out the importance of avoiding what Titchener had called the *stimulus error*. People who want to reduce tension must focus on muscular *sensations* and not imagine what the muscle itself is doing. The participant 'should report first the processes experienced and second what he is thinking about. If the latter alone is reported, he fails to distinguish the process of tenseness and therefore does not know what and where to relax' (ibid., 196).

In order for people to be able to relax, they must first stop paying attention to their thoughts and attend instead to the sensations that underlie them. Jacobson argued that by first discovering muscular tensions and then progressively relaxing them, the person will find that disturbing thoughts will diminish. Tension is not to be reduced by thinking about one's problems. Rather, relaxation will lead to less thinking about one's problems! While Jacobson recognized the similarity of some of his views to Eastern meditative techniques, he believed that his practices were not borrowed from them but were rooted in experimental science.

along more physicalistic lines. 'We are not yet ready to give up the conscious dimensions. We need them now, but I think we are already seeing how it can come about that we shall eventually be able to do without them' (ibid., xii). Thus, in the end there was little left of the content of Titchener's system to influence subsequent generations of psychologists. Moreover, as we shall see later on, Titchener's method of introspection received less and less support as other psychologists proposed other methods. However, his proposition that psychology was first and foremost an *experimental* discipline continued to receive widespread support in American academic psychology. Here again, his student Boring (1929, 1950b) was influential. His *History of Experimental Psychology* has been a widely used text for many years and presents psychology as a fundamentally experimental discipline.

Functionalism

It did not take long for opposition to Titchener's structuralism to make itself felt. **Functionalism** is the name of one of the forms this opposition took. Functionalism is usually characterized as one of the schools of psychology. A 'school' is a 'group of scholars or researchers whose approach to a field of study is . . . structured around a particular point of view' (Reber, 1985: 669). Titchener's structuralism is one example of a school, and Freud's psychoanalysis is another. Typically, the members of one school are more or less intolerant of the members of another school. As we shall see, functionalism is not as pure an example of a school as is structuralism or psychoanalysis, because it was much more open to alternative viewpoints and less well organized than other schools (Heidbreder, 1969). In spite of its ill-defined nature, there are still some characteristic attributes of a functional psychology.

Functionalism is a distinctively American psychology. To the extent that it has a birthplace, it is at the University of Chicago. If there is a grandparent of functionalism, it is William James, whose open-minded attitude towards psychology was widely shared by functionalists.

Functionalism deliberately sets out to violate the strictures that Titchener tried to place on psychology. It is open to methods alternative to introspection, and in fact is quite eclectic, that is, it attempts to select the method of solution to fit the particular problem. Eclectics are not bound by any one approach but borrow methods as the need arises.

As the name implies, functionalists are particularly interested in what function psychological processes serve. Heavily influenced by Darwin, functionalists focus on how organisms adapt to their environment (ibid., 39). Functionalism attempts to be practical as well as scholarly. This means that functionalists are often actively interested in topics such as education and in applied psychology generally.

With these broad, orienting attitudes in mind, let us now examine the work of some of the major functionalists.

John Dewey (1859–1952)

John Dewey did his undergraduate work at the University of Vermont, where physiology attracted his greatest interest. He then did a Ph.D. in philosophy at Johns Hopkins, graduating in 1884. In 1894, Dewey joined the University of Chicago, where he remained for 10 years. At Chicago he was chair of the Department of Philosophy, Psychology and Education. From 1904 until 1930 Dewey was at Teacher's College, Columbia University, New York.

Critique of the Reflex Arc Concept

Dewey's (1963 [1896]) paper 'The reflex arc concept in psychology' presents the basic ideas that were to inform his subsequent approach to psychology and education. Dewey's paper not only contains a criticism of the reflex concept—a concept that goes back at least to Descartes—as elementaristic and mechanistic, but also provides a positive statement of a more organic approach to psychological phenomena.

Dewey argued that the reflex was inappropriately understood as a stimulus followed by a central process followed by a response. The true fact of the matter was that 'sensory stimulus, central connections and motor responses [should] be viewed, not as separate and complete entities in themselves, but as divisions of labor, functioning factors, within the single concrete whole' (ibid., 253). In order to illustrate what he meant, Dewey made use of James's (1950: I, 25) example of a baby who 'sees a candle-flame for the first time, and . . . extends his hand to grasp it, so that his fingers get burned.' One might identify two stimuli and two responses in this situation. First, the candle flame is a stimulus that elicits the grasping as a response. Then the intense heat of the flame is another stimulus that reflexively causes the response of suddenly withdrawing the hand. Such an analysis seems intuitively obvious, and yet it is precisely this sort of analysis that Dewey believed to be wrong.

Dewey suggested that a stimulus does not elicit a response, but rather a stimulus is created by the organism through the act of paying attention to something. The candle does not exist as a stimulus until the organism sees it. 'Now if this act, the seeing, stimulates another act, the reaching, it is because both of these acts fall within a larger coordination; because seeing and grasping have often been so bound together to reinforce each other, to help each other out, that each may be considered practically a subordinate member of a larger coordination' (Dewey, 1963: 254). The reflex arc conception is false insofar as it regards stimulus and response as distinct elements in a chain of events, when in fact they mutually influence one another to the extent that 'the arc . . . is virtually a circuit' (ibid., 255). For Dewey, to interpret stimulus and response 'as separate existences in a causal sequence is a characterization that is not real but rather "read into" the process by the psychologist' (Backke, 2001).

Figure 7.3 illustrates these two contrasting conceptions of the relation between stimulus and response. The standard conception is given in A. Notice that the stimulus (S) elicits the response (R) directly through the central connection (symbolized by an arrow). What Dewey proposed is represented in B. Here the stimulus and response determine each other. What constitutes a stimulus depends on what you are doing at the time. 'The fact is that stimulus and response are . . . teleological distinctions, that is distinctions of *function*, or part played with reference to reaching, or maintaining an end' (Dewey, 1963: 260, emphasis added). The relation between stimulus and response cannot be seen in isolation from the other activities of the organism of which it is a part, but must be understood in terms of its function in enabling the organism to achieve its goals. How I respond to a candle will depend on what I am doing at that moment. If I am trying to shed addi-

tional light on the situation, then I will do one thing; if I am trying to warm my hands, then I will do something quite different.

Although Dewey's paper was written in 1896, it anticipates later twentieth-century developments that we consider in later chapters. As has often been pointed out (e.g., Dennis, 1948: 355), Dewey not only articulated a functional approach to the analysis of psychological phenomena, but also anticipated one of the criticisms of behaviourism, as we shall see in Chapter 8. Moreover, his emphasis on the necessity of seeing individual responses in relation to the goals of the organism as a whole is similar to one of the tenets of Gestalt psychology, which will be considered at length in Chapter 9.

Dewey's Influence on Educational Practice

Dewey's presidential address to the American Psychological Association laid down the foundations of what was to become his influential approach to psychology and education. Dewey pointed out that teachers are strongly influenced by whatever psychological assumptions they make about children and the educational process, and singled out two issues that he believed to be particularly important for teachers to understand.

In the first place, children and adults are different in that the adult is already in possession of cognitive abilities that the child is only in the process of developing. Children are not like adults, only smaller. Children should be 'busy in the formation of a flexible variety of habits whose sole immediate criterion is their relation to full growth, rather than in acquiring certain skills whose value is measured by their reference to specialized technical accomplishments' (Dewey, 1978 [1900]: 67). It is difficult to overemphasize the influence on twentieth-century educational practice of this contention of Dewey's. Dewey argued *against* teaching the '3 R's' as 'technical acquisitions which are to be needed in the specialized life of the adult' and argued *for* curriculum reform in which the goal is 'the facilitation of full normal growth, trusting to the result in growth to provide the instrumentalities

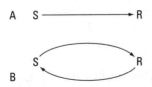

FIGURE 7.3
Two different conceptions of the reflex.

for later specialized adaptation' (ibid.). Thus, Dewey challenged 'the ideal of *formal discipline*', which advocated that children master a discipline such as mathematics in the form in which it would be useful to them as adults. Such a curriculum is marked by 'the excessive use of logical analytical methods' and assumes that children possess 'ready-made faculties of observation, memory, attention, etc.' (ibid.).

Although children are different from adults in terms of the abilities they bring to the educational situation, they are similar to adults in that they achieve 'power and control . . . through realization of personal ends and problems, through personal selection of means and materials which are relevant, and through personal adaptation and application of what is thus selected' (ibid., 68). The problems on which the child works in school should not be rigidly set by others; they should at least in part be selected by the child. Children differ from one another in terms of what is relevant to them at any particular time, and the curriculum must pay attention to the particular context within which individual children live.

Dewey became identified with the movement known as **progressive education**. Advocates of progressive education developed a reputation for schools that imposed no discipline on pupils and allowed children to study whatever they wanted. This is not what Dewey had actually advocated. Far from believing that teachers had no responsibilities, he thought that teachers had a greater responsibility for providing their pupils with 'experiences that are worthwhile':

> Traditional education did not have to face this problem; it could systematically dodge this responsibility. The school environment of desks, blackboards, a small school yard was supposed to suffice. There was no demand that the teacher should become intimately acquainted with the conditions of the local community, physical, historical, economic, occupational, etc., in order to use them as educational resources. A system of education based upon the necessary connec-

tion of education with experience must, on the contrary, if faithful to its principle, take these things constantly into account. This tax upon the educator is another reason why progressive education is more difficult to carry on than was ever the traditional system. (Dewey, 1970 [1938]: 234)

A good summary of Dewey's educational views is that the classroom 'is conceived and constructed to simulate the conditions under which the epistemological and political ideals of a democratic society are best learned and practiced' (Cahan, 1992: 208).

James R. Angell (1869–1949)

James R. Angell studied with both Dewey and James, and became Professor of Psychology at Chicago in 1894. Angell was known as one of the chief proselytizers for a functional psychology. Indeed, there are few clearer or more famous statements of the functionalist orientation than Angell's (1978 [1907]) presidential address to the American Psychological Association.

Angell observed that functionalism possessed the 'peculiar vigor which commonly attaches to Protestantism of any sort', meaning that functionalism was a protest movement. Of course, the orthodoxy against which it was protesting was Titchener's structuralism. However, Angell realized that functionalism was not merely a protest movement, but had historically important ancestors, including Aristotle, Spencer, and Darwin. Aristotle is mentioned because of his belief that human behaviour was purposeful and could only be understood in relation to the goals the person was trying to achieve. Spencer and Darwin provide an evolutionary/biological context within which to understand the purpose, or function, of psychological processes.

Angell argued that the 'mental contents' of which Titchener spoke were 'evanescent' and, therefore, an insecure foundation upon which to construct psychology. Psychological functions are far more obvious and durable. Consciousness is not to be searched for its contents but appreciated for its function. Consciousness is an *accommodative process*, a feature we considered briefly in our discussion of the unconscious in Chapter 6. Saying that consciousness is the primary accommodative process means that consciousness controls our adaptation to novel situations. Psychology studies the ways in which mental processes facilitate adjustment to the environment as it changes.

Methodologically, Angell did not believe in restricting psychology to laboratory investigation. Psychology has a lot to learn from comparative psychology, genetic (developmental) psychology, and the study of pathology. In all these areas, it is desirable to adopt a functional approach. This is particularly true in genetic psychology, where the adoption of longitudinal as opposed to cross-sectional studies means that one can begin to understand how psychological functions develop over time. (We will consider the rich history of developmental psychology in Chapter 12.)

Angell did not lay down any dogmatic classification of psychological functions, but suggested that the old division of the mind into cognition, emotion, and the will was an 'intrinsically biological' division with 'the first reporting to us the outer world, the second our general organic tone and the third supplying experiences of our motor activity by means of which voluntary control is developed.' In the end, however, Angell acknowledged that different psychologists might find it necessary to use different classificatory systems depending on their particular interests. By saying this Angell demonstrated the eclectic and pragmatic nature of functional psychology. Functionalism 'means today a broad and flexible and organic point of view in psychology' (ibid., 103).

Robert S. Woodworth (1869–1962)

Robert S. Woodworth had a strong background in both mathematics and physiology before beginning to teach psychology at Columbia in 1903. Even after his retirement in 1942 he continued to

be extremely productive. Woodworth's career exemplifies the maturation of functional psychology from a protest movement into an established form of psychological inquiry. Functional analysis ceased to be anything special, and 'the general orientation . . . became firmly established in American psychology, not as the special concerns of any one group or school, but as obviously having a place in the pursuits proper to psychology. Before long they were simply taken for granted' (Heidbreder, 1969: 48–9).

Woodworth wrote an introductory text, called *Psychology*, that 'sold over 400,000 copies between 1922 and 1939, thereby assuring Woodworth's financial well-being during this period' (Winston, 1990: 394). A more significant contribution from a historical viewpoint was Woodworth's *Experimental Psychology* (1938), which was a thorough review of the literature on topics ranging from psychophysics to the psychology of thinking. 'Between 1938 and 1954, nearly 44,000 copies of *Experimental Psychology* were sold in the United States and Canada. . . . The revised edition (Woodworth and Schlosberg, 1954) sold over 23,000 copies between 1954 and 1959. . . . Assuming conservatively that half of the books were reused by other students, nearly 100,000 North American psychology majors and graduate students used Woodworth as their guide for experimental research. . . . The *Experimental Psychology* textbook thus served as a major element of socialization for new recruits to the discipline' (Winston, 1990: 394).

The S-O-R Framework

Woodworth proposed that experiments were concerned with the relationship between stimulus (S), response (R), and the subject or organism (O). The experimenter manipulates a stimulus and observes O's response to it. In Titchener's *Experimental Psychology*, O did not stand for 'organism' but for 'observer'. However, as introspection declined as a method, the subject in an experiment was no longer treated as an observer who reported on his or her mental processes, but as an 'organism' that responded to stimuli, and this was the meaning of O that came to be adopted (e.g., Woodworth and Schlosberg, 1954: 2). The task of the experimenter is to discover what goes on between S and R.

The S-O-R formula seems to contradict Dewey's recommendation that R be seen as interacting with S, and not simply as determined by S. However, Woodworth took into account the interactive nature of the organism's relations with the environment by means of another formula: W-O-W. In this formula, O stands for organism as before and W stands for world or environment. 'The environment does things to the individual, and the individual does things to the environment. . . . This interaction goes on continually. . . . Since the interaction works both ways, we could just as well transpose the formula and write O-W-O' (Woodworth, 1940: 23).

Another important concept in Woodworth's system was **set**. 'Set' is similar in meaning to the 'determining tendency' of the Würzburgers. 'An individual often prepares to act before beginning the overt effective action', as when sprinters take their mark on the starting line (ibid., 29). There are many different kinds of set. For example, there are preparatory sets, as illustrated by the sprinters, executive sets that guide the organism through a sequence of responses as when you drive a car; and goal sets that represent what the organism aims to achieve. Woodworth regarded sets as temporary organizations in the brain that act 'by facilitating some responses, while preventing or inhibiting others . . . . While looking eagerly for a lost object you do not notice sounds that at other times would surely attract your attention. Readiness for one act is at the same time unreadiness for other acts' (ibid., 33).

Woodworth used the idea of 'sets' to combine the S-O-R formula and the W-O-W formula. This 'combined formula' was:

$$W\text{—}S\text{—}Ow\text{—}R\text{—}W$$

The 'small w attached to O symbolizes the individual's adjustment to the environment, [or] set'

(ibid., 36). By means of this formula, Woodworth was able to represent the notion that the S-O-R relationship is nested within the W-O-W relationship. The world is full of stimuli, but only those for which the organism is set will be important in determining responses. These responses in turn change the world, creating a new environment with new stimuli. This process goes on continuously.

Woodworth nicely illustrates both the strengths and weaknesses of a functional psychology. On the one hand, it was an extremely broad orientation, welcoming a variety of methods and topics. On the other hand, its theoretical formulations were criticized for being vague and imprecise (e.g., Henle, 1986). For example, E.J. Gibson (1941) explicitly targeted the concept of 'set' as being too vague to be of much explanatory value.

Intelligence Testing

Functionalism created a climate in America within which applied psychology could flourish. One of the best examples of the application of psychological methods to practical problems is the emergence of the *intelligence test* as a prominent feature of American life. Francis Galton, the eugenicist, had already begun the study of intelligence in the United Kingdom. The study of intelligence in Britain was carried forward by Charles Spearman (1863–1945) and Cyril Burt (1883–1971), and we will consider their efforts in Chapter 10. However, our concern now is to trace the development of intelligence testing in the United States.

James McKeen Cattell (1860–1944)

James McKeen Cattell trained with Wundt at Leipzig and subsequently became acquainted with Galton's methods for studying individual differences during a year spent at Cambridge in England. Galton's influence on Cattell was decisive, and he devoted much of his career at Columbia University to the further development of measures of individual differences. Cattell's tests were similar to those that Galton had originally

TABLE 7.1

Examples of Cattell's Mental Tests

Test	Description
Dynamometer pressure	Strength of hand squeeze
Rate of movement	How quickly the hand can be moved a distance of 50 cm
Sensation of areas	Two-point threshold: How far apart on the skin must two stimuli be in order to be detected as two, and not just one
Pressure causing pain	Amount of pressure applied to the forehead at which the subject reports pain
Least noticeable difference in weight	Psychophysical procedure using two weights, one in each hand
Reaction time for sound	Time required to respond to a sound
Time for naming colours	Time required to name different coloured papers (red, green, yellow, blue)
Bisection of a line	The accuracy with which a 50-cm line can be divided into two equal parts
Judgement of time	The accuracy with which a 10-second interval can be estimated
Letter span	The number of letters that can be repeated after hearing a series

pioneered, and in 1890 Cattell was the first to introduce the term *mental test*.

A partial list of Cattell's (1948 [1890]) tests is given in Table 7.1. These are by and large measures associated with psychophysics and quantitative experimental psychology. Few of these items will strike you as familiar from intelligence tests that you may have taken yourself. In fact, Cattell's measures did not relate very closely to academic performance, which is something that a valid measure of intelligence might be expected to do (Mayrhauser, 1992: 248). A *valid* measure is one that measures what it purports to measure, and Cattell's measures seemed to be of questionable validity. Consequently, Cattell's measures did not end up forming the backbone of intelligence tests as these were subsequently developed.

In any case, Cattell's mental tests were not his most significant achievements. In addition to being able to lay claim to being the first person appointed as a professor of psychology (as opposed to philosophy or physiology), he was responsible for awarding the Ph.D. to many students who subse-

quently became important figures, including two of the persons we are considering in this chapter, Woodworth and Thorndike. Moreover, 'he became a psychological statesman. He was the first psychologist elected to the National Academy of Science, he became the editor and owner of *Science*, the leading general scientific publication, and he organized and published *American Men of Science*, still the leading directory in the field' (Watson, 1979: 215). Cattell was also one of the movers and shakers who helped organize the American Psychological Association in 1892, and he became its president in 1895 (Clifford, 1973 [1968]: 236). Finally, Cattell specialized in the 'order of merit' procedure, whereby items are ranked in terms of their worth. We have already encountered one of his rankings in Box 4.1.

Alfred Binet (1857–1911)

Not only did **Alfred Binet** contribute to the experimental psychology of thinking, as we saw in Chapter 4, but he also invented the most influential form of intelligence test. This test was developed in Paris, in collaboration with **Theophile Simon**.

> In October, 1904, the Minister of Public Instruction named a Commission which was charged with the study of measures to be taken for insuring the benefits of instruction to defective children. . . . They decided that no child suspected of retardation should be eliminated from the ordinary school and admitted to a special class without first being subjected to a pedagogical and medical examination from which it could be verified that because of the state of his intelligence, he was unable to profit . . . from the instruction given in the ordinary schools. (Binet and Simon, 1965a [1905]: 30)

Binet was a member of the Commission, and to comply with its directive he and Simon created a test designed to discriminate between normal and subnormally intelligent children. They defined intelligence as:

> a fundamental faculty the alteration or lack of which is of the utmost importance for practical life. This faculty is judgment, otherwise called good sense, practical sense, initiative, the faculty of adapting oneself to circumstances. To judge well, to comprehend well, to reason well, these are the essential activities of intelligence. (Binet and Simon, 1965b [1905]: 38)

Notice the *functional* nature of the definition—intelligence is 'practical sense', 'the faculty of adapting oneself to circumstances', and consists of 'activities' such as reasoning and comprehension. Some items from the Binet and Simon (1915 [1911]) test are shown in Table 7.2. These are a far cry from the more 'structural' items used by Cattell. Binet and Simon were careful to base their scale on a substantial body of empirical research. Their items are 'arranged in a real order of increasing difficulty' (Binet and Simon, 1965c [1908]), in the sense that children tend not to fail items at a lower level and then pass items at a higher level.

TABLE 7.2

Example of Binet and Simon's items

Age	Item
3	Give family name
4	Repeat three numbers
5	Compare two weights
6	Distinguish morning and afternoon
7	Describe a picture
8	Give a day and date
9	Name months of the year in order
10	Criticize absurd statements
12	Describe abstract words
15	Give three rhymes for a word in one minute
Adult	Give three differences between a president and a king

Moreover, of '203 children studied individually . . . 103 pupils . . . have exactly the mental level that we attribute to their age; 44 are advanced; 56 are' below their age level (ibid., 44). The Binet-Simon scale allows children to be compared in terms of their **mental age**, which is determined by the age level of the items a child can pass.

The Binet-Simon scale seemed to many people in the United States to be just the sort of thing they were looking for. **Lewis M. Terman** (1877–1956) developed the most successful adaptation of the scale for the American context. Terman did this work at Stanford University, and so this version of the Binet test was called the **Stanford-Binet**. One of Terman's (1948 [1916]) most durable innovations was the **intelligence quotient** or IQ. The IQ was itself an adaptation of a suggestion by the German psychologist William Stern (1871–1938) that a useful measure of intelligence could be obtained by dividing the person's mental age (MA) by his/her chronological age (CA). Terman made use of Stern's (1967 [1912]: 453) idea in his equation for IQ.

$$IQ = \frac{MA}{CA} \times 100$$

The formula means that 'normal' children will have IQs of 100. Terman (1948: 489) obtained Stanford-Binet IQ scores for 905 children between the ages of 9 and 14 and reported that they were approximately normally distributed. Moreover, there was a significant relationship between IQ and such variables as teachers' estimates of children's intelligence, suggesting that the test had some validity. Partly because of these properties, the Stanford-Binet became a widely accepted test of intelligence.

Intelligence Testing in the United States Army

As the saying goes, 'It is an ill wind that blows nobody good', and while World War I was a disaster for the world as a whole, it was a boon for the emerging profession of psychology in the United States. The United States declared war on Germany in April 1917. That same month **Robert M. Yerkes** (1876–1954) was appointed chair of a committee to investigate how psychology could contribute to the war effort.

> As mobilization for World War I approached, Yerkes got one of those 'big ideas' that propel the history of science: could psychologists possibly persuade the army to test all its recruits? If so, the philosopher's stone of psychology might be constructed: the copious, useful, and uniform body of numbers that would fuel a transition from dubious art to respected science. Yerkes proselytized within his own profession and within government circles, and he won his point. As Colonel Yerkes, he presided over the administration of mental tests to 1.75 million recruits during World War I. Afterward he proclaimed that 'mental testing helped win the war.' (Gould, 1996: 223–4)

The tests that Yerkes and his group developed were derived from many sources, including the Binet tests. If a soldier could read and write, then he would be given the *Army Alpha*. Among the items on this form of the test were analogies like 'Washington is to Adams as first is to ____.' 'Nearly one third of the men examined were unable to read or write, or else did so poorly to be classed as illiterate, and to these was given a special examination prepared for illiterates' (Garrett, 1948: 31). This second test was called *Beta*, and contained such items as pictures with something left out that the examinee would have to complete (e.g., a profile with a nose missing). Alpha and Beta could be administered in groups, but if a soldier managed to fail Beta, then he would be given an individually administered Binet-like test. Gould observes that at least some items on all these tests can be seen as culturally biased. For example, the analogy given above requires some knowledge of United States history. Another item singled out by Gould (1982: 349) is the following multiple choice question: 'Christy Mathewson is famous as a: writer, artist, baseball player, comedian', which also requires some familiarity with the culture of the United States.

The question of cultural bias is important because of the interpretations sometimes made when the data were analyzed and reported after World War I (Yerkes, 1921 [1948]; Brigham, 1923). One controversial finding concerned *national differences in intelligence*. For example, men who were originally from such countries as England, Scotland, Holland, and Germany scored higher than men originally from such countries as Greece, Russia, Italy, and Poland. One interpretation of these results follows from the fact that immigrants from the former group tended to have been in the United States for a longer time. Perhaps 'foreign-born men, long exposed to American customs, language, and ways of life are enabled thereby to make higher scores' (Garrett, 1948: 51–2). Others, however, preferred an alternative interpretation—that these results reflected innate differences in intelligence between racial groups. Gould (1982) has argued that this hereditarian interpretation was widely influential and was one of the reasons for the passage of the Immigration Act of 1924, which discriminated against some groups in favour of others by 'imposing quotas on immigration based on the percentage of immigrants from each country as of the census of 1890. Using the 1890 census effectively excluded many immigrants from southern and eastern Europe, which had sent most of its refugees to America after 1890, in favor of those from northern and western Europe' (Snyderman and Herrnstein,1983: 991). However, Snyderman and Herrnstein were unable to find very much documentary evidence that intelligence test results were an important part of the decision-making process that led Congress to pass this Act, and they concluded that racism in the testing movement and the Immigration Act 'do not appear to be causally related to each other' (ibid., 994), but that both reflect attitudes that may have been prevalent in the United States at that time.

Another widely interpreted result from the Army data was that, generally speaking, black soldiers had lower intelligence test scores than whites. One interpretation of this difference is that the black recruits were educationally disadvantaged. However, many observers chose to give this finding a hereditarian interpretation, arguing that blacks were innately less intelligent than whites. The hereditarian interpretation was challenged by the black scholar Horace Mann Bond (Urban, 1989: 325), who showed, among other things, that blacks 'from some northern states, namely Illinois, New York, Ohio, and Pennsylvania, scored higher than did whites from the southern states of Mississippi, Kentucky, Arkansas, and Georgia.' This finding is not easily interpreted along strictly hereditarian lines.

What Is 'Intelligence', Anyway?

Controversy over the degree to which intelligence is innate or acquired has been and continues to be a fixture of debate in psychology. Gould (1982: 151) observed that Binet never regarded 'intelligence' as a single, scalable entity, but rather as a collection of different skills. However, it is easy to believe that because we have one word, 'intelligence', then there must be one thing to which it refers. The question of whether or not intelligence is one thing or many things is not easy to answer, and we will examine some of the difficulties inherent in this question in a later chapter. For now we will only deal with answers to this question that emerged in the aftermath of World War I.

During this time one of the most influential answers was proposed by the ubiquitous Edwin G. Boring, who had been one of the members of Yerkes's team. Boring's paper was originally published in *The New Republic*, and was intended to educate the general public concerning the meaning of 'intelligence'. He argued 'that intelligence as a measurable capacity must at the start be defined as the capacity to do well in an intelligence test. Intelligence is what the tests test' (Boring, 1969 [1923]: 26). Even though the correlation between the tests and performance in real-world situations is not perfect, that only means that each real-world situation requires special skills other than intelligence. Intelligence is one thing: what **intelligence tests** measure. Notice that this formulation places great emphasis on the importance of the tests themselves. The tests *define* intelligence.

After World War I, the intelligence test became progressively embedded in American culture. In its various forms, such as the Scholastic Aptitude Test, it exercised enormous influence over the lives of countless people. One of the best known of late twentieth-century researchers on intelligence, Robert J. Sternberg (1992: 134), suggested that 'the intelligence test of today is quite similar to that of Alfred Binet.' That is, in spite of variations in form and content, intelligence tests tended to be similar to the one originally invented by Binet. Intelligence may not be only one thing, but intelligence tests did tend to be only one thing!

Sternberg pointed out that 'testing is today, and has been for many years, a market driven industry. Testing companies are no different than any other business in their desire to maximize' both sales and profits (ibid.). This means that a central issue for companies that produced tests was 'What do

BOX 7.2

MARKET FORCES THAT DETERMINE INTELLIGENCE TESTS

Sternberg (1992: 135) has identified 10 characteristics of intelligence tests that those who create and market these tests must meet to satisfy the educational institutions that are the principal consumers.

1. *Predicting achievement.* The main use of intelligence tests is to predict school achievement.
2. *Reliability.* Tests scores should be relatively stable over time. No one can afford the time or money to give the same test again and again.
3. *Standardization.* Administrators are concerned about how . . . their schools their students compare with other schools. Thus, they need accurate norms.
4. *High correlation with other, similar tests.* When a decision is made to switch tests one year, the administration wants to know that the tests used in the past will provide scores that are at least roughly comparable to the tests of the present.
5. *Ease of administration.* Group tests need to be administered by teachers with little or no training in psychological testing.

6. *Ease of interpretation.* The interpreters of the test scores may have little or no knowledge about psychological testing, so the results must be easily and readily understood.
7. *Objectivity of scoring.* Administrators do not want to get into arguments with parents over 'right answers'. Thus, the test questions must be clear and leave no room for debate about which answers are correct.
8. *Perceived fairness.* The tests should be perceived to be fair and hence not biased in favour of one group (e.g., ethnic, gender) over another.
9. *Cost effectiveness.* The tests should be as cheap as possible and yield information worth at least what they cost.
10. *Legal defensibility.* The tests should be legally defensible should their use be brought to court.

Adapted from R.J. Sternberg, 'Ability tests, measurements, and markets', *Journal of Educational Psychology* 84 (1992): 134–40. Copyright © 1992 by the American Psychological Association. Reprinted with permission.

consumers of intelligence tests want?' Sternberg accounted for the remarkable durability and popularity of intelligence tests by the way in which they had been sensitive to what the market for such tests required. Sternberg identified 10 market forces that shaped the nature of intelligence tests. These are given in Box 7.2. It is important to realize that the intelligence test not only was shaped but also was maintained by the kind of market forces Sternberg identified. The intelligence test was not a purely intellectual exercise designed entirely to provide scientific data. Perhaps we can generalize on the basis of this example. As Sternberg (ibid., 135) pointed out, it is possible to regard psychology generally as being at least partly responsive to market

forces. Although market forces will determine some aspects of psychology more than others, we should ask ourselves what the market forces were for each aspect of psychology.

Psychology in Business

At the same time as the mental testing industry was beginning to develop, the application of psychology to problems of interest to business was also emerging as a discipline in its own right. Two names often associated with this aspect of applied psychology in the United States are Hugo Münsterberg (1863–1916) and Walter Dill Scott (1869–1955). Münsterberg was trained by Wundt and came to Harvard in 1892. Although originally expected to be primarily a laboratory worker, Münsterberg later demonstrated that he had wide-ranging interests. He published popular books on topics as diverse as psychology and the law and psychology in industry. Scott was also a student of Wundt's and had the same sort of protean career as did Münsterberg. He was particularly interested in developing mental tests that were suited to the business environment (Von Mayrhauser, 1989) and founded the Scott Corporation, which was devoted to providing psychological services to business.

While Münsterberg and Scott are undoubtedly important figures in this area, it is instructive to compare the work of Frederick W. Taylor with that of Elton Mayo. Together they define the range of services that psychology was able to offer the business community.

Frederick W. Taylor (1856–1915)

Frederick W. Taylor displayed an interest in the efficiency of human movement early in life. The story goes that as a college student he changed the game of baseball by introducing overhand as opposed to underhand pitching (Brown, 1954: 12). Overhand pitching was a much more efficient and effective way of doing the job, and showing people how to do things more efficiently and effectively became Taylor's life work. While working as an engineer, he became distressed with the amount of inefficiency he observed in the way that manual labourers performed their tasks and set about to eliminate 'awkward, inefficient, or ill-directed movements' (Taylor, 1967 [1911]: 5). Taylor argued that the interests of worker and employer were identical, not antagonistic. If workers were trained to produce goods in the most efficient manner possible and given raises as their output increased, then workers would get more money and employers would reap higher profits.

One of the most famous examples of Taylor's method took place at the Bethlehem Steel Company. There were 80,000 tons of pig iron that had been sold and needed to be loaded onto rail-way cars. Workers typically loaded 12.5 tons a day, a number Taylor believed could be increased to 47.5 by using efficient methods. Taylor began by selecting a workman, whom he called Schmidt, 'who had been observed to trot home for a mile or so after his work in the evening about as fresh as he was in the morning. . . . He also had the reputation of . . . placing a very high value on a dollar' (ibid., 44). Thus, Schmidt was a well-conditioned, highly motivated individual, and selecting the best workers is an essential part of Taylor's system. Schmidt had been earning $1.15 a day and was asked if he would like to earn $1.85 a day for loading pig iron. After answering in the affirmative, he was told to 'do exactly as this man tells you to-morrow, from morning till night. When he tells you to pick up a pig and walk, you pick it up and you walk, and when he tells you to sit down and rest, you sit down. You do that straight through the day' (ibid., 46). Taylor had already figured out what the most efficient blend of work and rest would be, and Schmidt 'was told by the man who stood over him with a watch, "Now pick up a pig and walk. Now sit down and rest. Now walk—now rest, etc."' (ibid., 47). This regime produced 47.5 tons loaded at day's end. Taylor proceeded to induct additional workers and eventually 'was able to decrease the number of workers needed to load wagons at the steel company from 500 to 140, increase daily earnings by 60 per cent, and save the firm about $75,000 a year' (Brown, 1954: 15).

Taylor called his system **scientific management**, and characterized its most important feature as follows. 'The work of every workman is fully planned out at least one day in advance, and each man receives in most cases complete written instructions, describing in detail the task which he is to accomplish, as well as the means to do the work' (Taylor, 1967: 39). Workers did not always take kindly to having someone stand over them with a watch, particularly since the goal of Taylor's method was not only to increase the output of individual workers but also to reduce the total number of workers required, as occurred in one project involving girls inspecting ball bearings for bicycles in which 'thirty five girls did the work formerly done by one hundred and twenty.' Thus, one assumption of Taylor's technique is that 'personal ambition always has been and will remain a more powerful incentive to exertion than a desire for the general welfare' (ibid., 95).

Taylor's methods were developed further by the husband and wife team of Frank and Lillian Gilbreth. Frank Gilbreth first made his mark in 1909 by analyzing the motions of bricklayers and reducing these motions from a languid 18 to a crisp 5. This type of analysis, whereby 'needless motions can be entirely eliminated and quicker types of movements substituted for slow movements', has been called **time and motion study** (ibid., 80). The life of the Gilbreths was made the subject of a 1950 movie called *Cheaper by the Dozen* starring Clifton Webb as Frank and Myrna Loy as Lillian Gilbreth.

Elton Mayo (1880–1949)

Elton Mayo became famous because of some work he did not himself begin. In 1926, the National Research Council had made a curious discovery in its investigation of the effect on worker output of changing levels of illumination in the Western Electric Plant in Hawthorne, Illinois. The particular workers studied made telephone relays, and so the measure of output is simply the number of relays produced per week. One part of the study, described later by Mayo (1960 [1933]: 53–4), involved two rooms of workers, in one of which the level of illumination was systematically varied, while in the other illumination remained constant. One would expect no change in output for the group for which the lighting stayed the same and might expect the group being subjected to variation in illumination to show changes in performance as a result of this manipulation of an important environmental variable. However, both groups showed roughly the same level of output regardless of illumination. In a certain sense, the experiment was a failure because it did not show any effect of changing illumination

upon performance. 'Somehow or other that complex of mutually dependent factors, the human organism, shifted its equilibrium and unintentionally defeated the purpose of the experiment' (Mayo, 1960: 54).

Mayo, who was at Harvard in the Department of Industrial Research from 1926 until 1947, became part of a group called in to investigate further. This time 'no attempt was made to test for the effect of single variables. Where human beings are concerned one cannot change one condition without inadvertently changing others—so much the illumination experiment had shown' (ibid.). Briefly stated, Mayo's research seemed to show that no matter what one did to change working conditions, output went up. For example, more rest pauses, reduced rest pauses, going home early, even returning to the original work conditions all resulted in increased output when introduced (Brown, 1954: 71–2). This phenomenon came to be known as the **Hawthorne effect**: any change in work conditions increases output.

While there has been considerable debate about the generality and limitations of the Hawthorne effect, Mayo's explanation of it was quite influential. The investigators were paying attention to the workers in the Hawthorne plant, and this act of paying attention was important to the workers themselves. For example, workers were interviewed using a technique Mayo (1960: 93–4) compared to that used by Jean Piaget, the great Swiss developmental psychologist whose own work we will examine in Chapter 12. One aspect of Piaget's technique was to be open and attentive to the interviewee's concerns and not simply work through a list of prepared questions. 'Attentive listening' (Hsueh, 2002) to workers' concerns in this unstructured way seemed to have a beneficial effect. As his studies progressed, Mayo began to realize that work was an inherently *social* activity, regulated by the group to which the worker belongs. The workers in the Hawthorne study appeared to have developed a feeling of pride in the accomplishments of their group as a whole. This suggested that business needs to work with such groups to ensure worker co-operation in attaining corporate goals.

The contrast between Taylor and Mayo represents in part a difference in philosophical assumptions concerning human nature. Taylor assumed that the individual was motivated by self-interest, while Mayo saw the individual as motivated by the concerns of the group to which the person belonged. Taylor's focus was on individual behaviour seen as a collection of bodily movements, while Mayo's focus was on behaviour as determined by the quality of one's interpersonal relationships. These differences are not peculiar to industrial psychology, but represent fundamental differences in orientation that reveal themselves again and again in the work of the various psychologists we will examine in subsequent chapters.

Comparative Psychology

Comparative psychology is that branch of the discipline that attempts to understand the evolution of behaviour through the comparison of different species. We noted at the end of Chapter 2 that comparative psychology was a logical outgrowth of Darwinism, and so it is not surprising to discover that functional psychology was open to the comparative point of view (Dewsbury, 2000: 751).

George John Romanes (1848–1894) is often considered to be the founder of a comparative approach to psychology. Although born in Canada, Romanes became famous for work done in Britain. Romanes (1977 [1883]: 2) wrote about his procedure for studying animals as follows:

What is the kind of activities that may be regarded as indicative of mind? I certainly do not so regard the flowing of a river or the blowing of the wind. Why? First, because the objects are too remote in kind from my own organism to admit of drawing any reasonable analogy between them and it; . . . they afford no evidence of feeling or purpose. In other words, two conditions require to be satisfied before we even begin to imagine that observable activities are indicative of mind:

first, the activities must be displayed by a living organism; and secondly they must be of a kind to suggest the presence of two elements which we recognize as the distinctive characteristics of mind as such—consciousness and choice.

Thus, Romanes regarded 'mind' as the subject matter of comparative psychology, and he considered drawing analogies between human and animal mental processes to be the proper method. Romanes himself described his psychology as *anthropomorphic*, meaning that it involved projecting human characteristics onto animals. 'The mental states of an insect may be widely different than those of a man, and yet most probably the nearest conception that we can form of their true nature is that which we form by assimilating them to the only mental states with which we are acquainted' (ibid., 10).

Romanes believed that it was reasonable to apply this method because there 'must be a psychological, no less than a physiological, continuity extending throughout the length and breadth of the animal kingdom' (ibid.). The hypothesis of **continuity** is very important, because it implies that there are no qualitative differences between humans and other species. We can find in other species characteristics similar to ourselves, although other creatures may very well display a more primitive form of these characteristics.

Romanes's psychology was criticized for being *anecdotal* in that it consisted largely of stories about animals, 'often provided in the form of letters and even rumors regarding the feats of members of this or that species . . . there is no instance of experimentation' (Robinson, 1977: xxii). Romanes's great competitor in late nineteenth-century comparative psychology was **C. Lloyd Morgan** (1852–1936), another British naturalist, who adopted a more experimental approach to the study of animal behaviour. While Morgan acknowledged that one could interpret animal behaviour in terms of the observer's own subjective experience, he also stressed the importance of the objective observation of behaviour. He saw each as complementing the other.

One oft-cited example of Morgan's approach is his analysis of the behaviour of his dog, Tony, who, 'when he wanted to go out into the road, used to put his head under the latch of the gate, lift it, and wait for the gate to swing open' (Morgan, 1979 [1894]: 184). The observer of such behaviour should not interpret it as meaning that the dog 'perceived how the end in view was to be gained, and the most effective means for effecting his purpose' (ibid.). By carefully observing the way in which the dog learned how to get out of the yard, Morgan found that Tony had hit upon the correct response more or less by chance, after sticking his head between the bars of the fence until the latch was accidentally lifted. On subsequent occasions, the dog did not go immediately and open the latch, but only gradually perfected this habit and eliminated incorrect responses. 'It was nearly three weeks . . . before he went at once and without hesitation to the right place and put his head without any ineffectual fumbling beneath the latch' (ibid.). Thus, it makes no sense to interpret the dog's action as the outcome of 'reasoning'. A much simpler explanation is possible, namely that the dog gradually acquired the correct response through a process we could call trial and error.

Morgan's greatest claim to fame is his *canon*. A 'canon' is a rule that regulates the way one is supposed to investigate something. Lloyd Morgan's canon is intended to guide the way in which one interprets observations of behaviour:

In no case may we interpret an action as the outcome of the exercise of a higher psychical faculty if it can be fairly interpreted as the outcome of the exercise of one which stands lower on the psychological scale. (Morgan, 1968 [1894]: 468)

Morgan's canon has usually been interpreted as a **principle of parsimony**. Such principles, which go back at least to William of Ockham (1300–50), assert that our explanations of any phenomenon should be kept as simple (parsimonious) as possible. In the case of the explanation of

animal behaviour, we should not invoke complex human mental processes such as 'reasoning' when simpler explanations such as 'trial and error' will do. However, as Costall (1993: 117) pointed out, Morgan's canon did not rule out 'the interpretation of a particular activity in terms of the higher processes, if we already have independent evidence of the occurrence of these higher processes in the animal under consideration.' Morgan's canon was not intended to prohibit anthropomorphic explanations, but only to limit them to cases in which they appeared to be necessary.

Edward L. Thorndike (1874–1949)

Edward L. Thorndike was the son of a clergyman in Lowell, Massachusetts. This fact is relevant because Thorndike was not only an American pioneer in comparative psychology, he was also a typical late nineteenth-century American scientist in that 'among Americans born around 1870 . . . the striking fact is that a clergyman's household, combined with a New England setting, was the best predictor of a future career in science' (Clifford, 1973 [1968]: 233). This is partly because at the time 'organized religion was losing stature in the nation's social and intellectual life . . . [and] science was usurping its place in academic disputations and attracting college graduates away from ministerial careers' (ibid., 234). Thorndike's career exemplified that of the zealous scientist for whom science was an all-consuming passion. 'In 1934 Thorndike was chosen President of the AAAS [American Association for the Advancement of Science]; except for economist W.C. Mitchell in 1928, no other social scientist headed this professional organization of the whole body of scientists since Thorndike's tenure until . . . 1966' (ibid., 237).

In an autobiographical sketch, Thorndike described the beginning of his research as a graduate student at Harvard when he

suggested experiments with the instinctive and intelligent behavior of chickens as a topic, and this was accepted. I kept these animals and conducted the experiments in my room until the landlady's protests became imperative. [William] James tried to get a few square feet required for me in the Laboratory, and then the Agassiz Museum. He was refused, and with his habitual kindness and devotion to underdogs and eccentric aspects of science, he harbored my chickens in the cellar of his own home for the rest of the year. The nuisance to Mrs. James was, I hope, somewhat mitigated by the entertainment of the two youngest children. (Thorndike, 1949b [1936]: 2–3)

Thorndike subsequently completed his doctoral work on **animal intelligence** at Columbia under Cattell. 'The motive for my first investigations of animal intelligence was chiefly to satisfy requirements for courses and degrees. Any other topic would probably have served me as well. I certainly had no special interest in animals' (ibid., 3–4). The fact that Thorndike had no passionate interest in working with animals, and yet did work that became central to psychology, is a lesson that many students would do well to heed! You do not need to work on a topic that you regard as crucial to your being in order to make a significant contribution.

Learning as the Formation of Connections

Thorndike's work on animal intelligence (1948 [1898], 1998 [1898]) used equipment that became both famous and controversial. These pieces of apparatus were the **puzzle boxes**, contraptions Thorndike assembled out of wooden crates and assorted odds and ends (Burnham, 1972). Remember that this was before the time when researchers might expect to have grants to support their efforts, and many, like Thorndike, built all their apparatus themselves. One of the boxes is illustrated in Figure 7.4. A cat would be placed in the box, with food outside. If the cat pulled on a loop or other device, then the door would open

and the animal would be freed. Thorndike described the cat's behaviour as follows:

When put into the box the cat would show evident signs of discomfort and of an impulse to escape from confinement. It tries to squeeze through any opening; it claws and bites at the bars or wire; it thrusts its paws out through any opening and claws at everything it reaches; it continues its efforts when it strikes anything loose and shaky; it may claw at things within the box. It does not pay very much attention to the food outside, but seems simply to strive instinctively to escape from confinement. . . . The cat does not look over the situation, much less *think* it over, and then decide what to do. It bursts out at once into the activities which instinct and experience have settled on as suitable reactions to the situation 'confinement when hungry with food outside.' The one impulse, out of many accidental ones, which leads to pleasure, becomes strengthened and stamped in thereby, and more and more firmly associated with the sense-impression of that box's interior. (Thorndike, 1979 [1898]: 255–6)

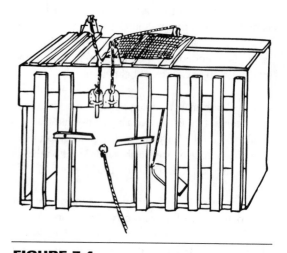

FIGURE 7.4
One of Thorndike's puzzle boxes.
Source: Thorndike (1948 [1898]).

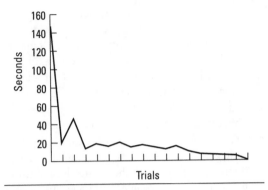

FIGURE 7.5

A learning curve similar to those reported by Thorndike in his study of cats solving a puzzle box. The vertical axis represents the number of seconds the cat spends in the box before escaping.

Notice that Thorndike acknowledges that the animal has an instinct to escape from confinement. By 'instinct', Thorndike meant anything the animal does in a situation that is experienced for the first time. In the puzzle box, instinct is not enough to provide the cat with the means to escape. However, the animal does not reason its way out of its predicament, but accidentally does the right thing. Thorndike studied several cats, and plotted the time it took for them to escape from the puzzle box on successive trials. Such learning curves tended to look like Figure 7.5. Thorndike observed that these learning curves did not suddenly improve, but rather the amount of time the animal spent in the box gradually and irregularly got to be less and less. This suggested that the animal did not suddenly realize what it had to do in order to free itself, but that the connection between the animal's situation and the response that freed it was gradually stamped in. What Thorndike's data demonstrated to him was 'the wearing smooth of a path in the brain, not the decision of a rational consciousness' (ibid., 256).

For Thorndike, learning involved the formation of connections in the brain between situations and actions, and he invented the **law of effect** to explain the formation of these connections. Over the course of Thorndike's career, the law of effect took different forms, with a late form being 'that the immediate consequence of a mental connection (in particular, a satisfying state of affairs following a connection and belonging to it) can work back upon it to strengthen it' (Thorndike, 1949d [1933]: 13). By a 'satisfying state of affairs', Thorndike (ibid., 14) meant 'one which the animal does nothing to avoid, often doing things to maintain or renew it'. The influence of a satisfier on a connection was presumed to be direct, and did not require the subject to realize that a particular connection had been rewarded. 'It is, on the contrary, as natural in its action as a falling stone, a ray of light, a line of force, a discharge of buckshot, a stream of water, or a hormone in the blood' (ibid., 15).

Thorndike took the cat's behaviour in a puzzle box to be paradigmatic of what happens when any animal (including human animals) learns anything. All learning involved the formation of connections, and connections were strengthened according to the law of effect. With Thorndike's work, learning began to come to the forefront in American psychology as the most important psychological process.

> Man's power to change himself, that is, to learn, is perhaps the most impressive thing about him. . . . Civilization is, indeed, the chief product of human learning. Homes and tools, language and art, customs and laws, science and religion are all created by changes in the minds of men. Their maintenance and use also depend on human modifiability—the ability of man to learn. If that were reduced by half . . . most of human civilization would be unusable by the next generation and would soon vanish off the face of the earth. (Thorndike, 1966 [1931]: 3)

For Thorndike, a person's capacity to learn was limited by his or her general level of intelligence, as measured by an intelligence test. Intelligence is the ability to form connections, and humans are the most evolved animal because they are, in general, able to form more connections than any other animal. However, there are great individual differences in 'general intelligence', which Thorndike believed to be innately determined. This view made Thorndike (ibid., 199–200) sympathetic to eugenics, since we should 'provide the intellect of man with higher and purer sources than the muddy streams of the past. If it is our duty to improve the quality of what is learned and the means of learning it, it is doubly our duty to improve the original inborn ability of man to learn.'

Thorndike stands in the tradition of associationist psychology, one of his innovations being the study of the formation of associations in animals under experimental conditions. Thorndike's theory is often called *connectionism*, a model of the nervous system as a telephone switchboard with a vast network of connections between inputs and outputs (Pribram, 1981). One might have expected Morgan to have approved of the simplicity of Thorndike's system, but in fact he was critical of the evidence upon which Thorndike built his theory, in particular the original experiments with cats in puzzle boxes. Morgan (as cited by Costall, 1993: 120) wrote that 'the conditions of his experiments were perhaps not the most conducive to the discovery of rationality in animals if it exists. The sturdy and inconvincible advocate of reasoning (properly so-called) in animals may say that to place a starving kitten in a cramped confinement of one of Mr. Thorndike's box-cages, would be more likely to make a cat swear than to lead it to act rationally.' Similar criticisms were voiced by other animal psychologists (Maier and Schneirla, 1964 [1935]: 358–63; Stamm and Kalmanovitch, 1998). Thorndike's reputation, however, did not depend solely on his animal work. Over the span of his career he published extensively on topics in human learning that generally supported his original conclusions.

The implications of Thorndike's work for education were considerable, as was his influence on educational practice (Beatty, 1998). A famous study done with Woodworth investigated the degree to which learning would transfer from one situation to another. For example, if participants were trained to pick out 'words containing certain combinations of letters (e.g., s and e)' (Thorndike and Woodworth, 1948 [1901]: 391), would such training generalize to words containing other letter combinations? In general, the results did not show very much *transfer of training* from one situation to another. The educational implications of such a result were that students should not be taught the principles that applied to one situation in the hope that they will be generalized to novel situations. Rather, the specific components of each skill need to be taught separately. For example, when a child is taught arithmetic, then the teacher should 'analyze arithmetical learning into the unitary abilities which compose it, showing just what, in detail, the mind has to do in order to be able to pass a thorough test on the whole of arithmetic' (Thorndike, 1949c [1922]: 165). Although Thorndike's psychology was quite different from Dewey's, they both helped undermine the traditional curriculum that emphasized learning subjects such as Latin in the hope that the acquisition of general principles would provide the student with rules that could be applied to situations encountered in everyday life as an adult (Ellis, 1979 [1965]: 72–3).

In many ways, Thorndike exemplified the functional psychologist by having an evolutionary viewpoint, being interested in individual differences, and attempting to apply his findings. In other ways, however, Thorndike's work anticipated the movement we will examine in the next chapter. By demonstrating the important role of animals in experimental research and emphasizing the importance of learning while de-emphasizing the importance of 'higher mental processes', Thorndike helped lay the groundwork for behaviourism.

IMPORTANT NAMES, WORKS, AND CONCEPTS

Names and Works

Angell, James R.

Binet, Alfred

Cattell, James McKeen

Dewey, John

Experimental Psychology: A Manual for Laboratory Practice

Mayo, Elton

Morgan, C. Lloyd

Romanes, George John

Simon, Theophile

Taylor, Frederick W.

Terman, Lewis M.

Thorndike, Edward L.

Titchener, Edward B.

Woodworth, Robert S.

Yerkes, Robert M.

Concepts

animal intelligence

comparative psychology

continuity

dimensions of consciousness

functionalism

Hawthorne effect

intelligence quotient (IQ)

intelligence tests

introspection

law of effect

mental age

mental test

principle of parsimony

progressive education

psychophysical parallelism

puzzle boxes

quality, intensity, extensity, protensity

scientific management

set

Stanford-Binet

stimulus error

structuralism

time and motion study

RECOMMENDED READINGS

Titchener

Titchener often became embroiled in colourful disputes with those who did not share his views. See D.L. Krantz, 'The Baldwin-Titchener controversy: A case study in the functioning and malfunctioning of schools', in Krantz, ed., *Schools of Psychology* (New York: Appleton-Century-Crofts, 1969), 1–19.

Dewey

Dewey was an extremely prolific writer. One book that captures the flavour of his ideas in a popular format is *Individualism Old and New* (New York: Minton, Balch, 1930), which is an extension of articles he originally wrote for *The New Republic*.

Angell and Functionalism

The essence of the functional approach exemplified by Angell and to a large extent by the other theorists in this chapter is also found in many more recent approaches to the teaching of psychology. A good example is P. Gray, *Psychology*, 4th edn (New York: Worth, 2002), a popular introductory textbook that attempts to understand all psychological phenomena (e.g., fear of the dark) in terms of the functions they serve.

Woodworth

Woodworth's S-O-R framework owed much to the work of Ernst Mach (1838–1916), whose emphasis on the importance of understanding 'functional relations' was very influential. See A.S. Winston, 'Cause into function: Ernst Mach and the reconstruction of explanation in psychology', in C.D. Green et al., eds, *The Transformation of Psychology* (Washington: American Psychological Association, 1991), 107–31. Woodworth also wrote a text in the history of psychology that went through many editions: *Schools of Psychology* (New York: Ronald, 1931). In it he demonstrated his tolerant, middle-of-the-road approach to controversial issues. However tolerant he may have been towards alternative points of view in psychology, Woodworth regarded many of his Jewish graduate students as the possessors of 'cultural and personal differences' that made them potentially unsuitable to be professors. Woodworth's anti-Semitism, however, was less virulent that that of many other psychologists of the day. See A.S. Winston, 'R.S. Woodworth's letters of reference and employment for Jewish psychologists in the 1930s', *Journal of the History of the Behavioral Sciences* 32 (1996): 30–43.

Binet and Intelligence Testing

Despite Binet's path-breaking work in both experimental psychology and intelligence testing, he never received an academic appointment. The story of Binet's attempts to secure such an appointment is well told by S. Nicolas and L. Ferrand, 'Alfred Binet and higher education', *History of Psychology* 5 (2002): 264–83. Apparently this failure occurred partly because Binet was not well enough connected in academia and partly because of the tendency of French academics not to recognize psychology as an independent discipline. R.E. Fancher, *The Intelligence Men: Makers of the IQ Controversy* (New York: Norton, 1985), provides a thorough review of the issues and persons involved in the measurement of IQ.

Taylor and Industrial Psychology

R.M. Barnes, *Motion and Time Study: Design and Measurement of Work*, 6th edn (New York: Wiley, 1968), provides a compendium of the techniques that have evolved from Taylor's work. A review of the influence of the Hawthorne study is given by H.A. Landsberger, *Hawthorne Revisited: Management and Worker, Its Critics and Developments in Human Relations in Industry* (Ithaca, NY: Cornell University Press, 1958). R. Kanigel, *The One Best Way: Frederick Winslow Taylor and the Enigma of Efficiency* (New York: Viking, 1997), is a thorough overview of Taylor's life and work. The link between Mayo and Piaget is analyzed by Y. Hsueh, 'The Hawthorne experiments and the introduction of Jean Piaget in American industrial psychology, 1929–1932', *History of Psychology* 5 (2002): 163–89.

Comparative Psychology

A classic introduction to the history of the psychology of animals is C.J. Warden et al., *Introduction to Comparative Psychology* (New York: Ronald, 1934).

Thorndike

Thorndike (1949b: 11) was particularly interested in 'the science and teaching of language', and began 'with the humble task of counting the frequency of occurrence of English words, publishing the facts for a ten-million count in 1921 and an extension of it in 1931. Dr. Irving Lorge and I brought out a greatly extended and improved count in 1944.' This word count has been cited countless times by psychologists interested in language, and is worth perusing if only to see how much labour went into the project, illustrating Thorndike's remarkable capacity for hard work. See E.L. Thorndike and I. Lorge, *The Teacher's Word Book of 30,000 Words* (New York: Columbia University Press, 1944).

BEHAVIOURISM

Introduction

Behaviourism was, and in some ways still is, one of the most dominant approaches to psychology, particularly in the United States. Several different orientations were accommodated under the broad umbrella of 'behaviourism'. Some who thought of themselves as behaviourists, such as the Americans John B. Watson and B.F. Skinner, argued that behaviour could be explained without recourse to either introspection or physiology. However, others, such as the American Karl Lashley and the Russian Ivan P. Pavlov, believed that physiology and psychology were complementary. Another Russian, Vladimir Bekhterev, created an ambitious system in an attempt to explain all forms of behaviour from the individual to the social. Although behaviourists differed from each other in many ways, what they all had in common is just what their name suggests: they regarded behaviour as the only proper subject matter and rejected subjective experience as a legitimate topic in psychology.

Thorndike had done much to create a climate in which comparative psychology could flourish. It is an obvious but nonetheless important point to realize that animals cannot be asked introspect, and so comparative psychology implicitly called into question introspection as a psychological method. You cannot ask animals to explain their own behaviour, as you can with people. Animal behaviour is something that the psychologist can only observe, and comparative psychology implicitly promoted the objective observation of behaviour (e.g., Krech, 1962: 41). Thorndike himself, however, never entirely moved away from describing behaviour as having a subjective aspect. That is why he should be seen as a transitional figure, occupying a middle ground between those functionalists who were untroubled by including introspection as a proper psychological method and those investigators we will explore in this chapter who called for the total abandonment of subjectivity in favour of an entirely objective description of behaviour. This movement, usually called *behaviourism*, 'originated independently in America and in pre-Revolutionary Russia. In both countries one of the sources was animal research. In Russia this source was Pavlov's work on conditioned reflexes' (Bauer, 1952: 53).

Ivan P. Pavlov (1849–1936)

Like Thorndike, **Ivan P. Pavlov** was the son of clergyman. He originally set out to become a priest like his father but abandoned this pursuit after reading a Russian translation of Darwin and becoming interested in natural science (Windholz, 1997: 941). He developed a keen interest in physiology, and in 1883 became a medical doctor. However, his great passion was scientific research, which he carried out with such skill and ingenuity that he was awarded the Nobel Prize in 1904 for his work on the physiology of the digestive system (Pavlov, 1997 [1897]). He subsequently became famous for his work on so-called conditioned reflexes, which we will discuss in detail below.

When Pavlov was a student, he lived with his brother, who apparently took care of all of Pavlov's daily requirements, including buying Pavlov's clothes. Pavlov married Serafima Karchevskaya in 1880 and thereafter was as dependent on her as he had formerly been on his brother (Gantt, 1928: 14–15). In this respect, Pavlov was extremely fortunate to have other people around him whose efforts on his behalf freed him to devote himself to research.

Like Thorndike, when Pavlov began his work with animals he would often take them home with him because of a lack of facilities at the university. However, as his career progressed he was able to command more resources, and eventually had an Institute of Experimental Medicine constructed for him in 1891 (ibid., 16). Pavlov's devotion to his research made a strong impression on those who worked for him. Gantt quotes the following story from one of Pavlov's assistants, which describes an incident that occurred during the Russian Revolution in 1917.

> During the revolution it was very difficult to get to the laboratory at all, because besides other things there was often shooting and fighting in the streets. However, Pavlov was generally present, even though nobody else was. One of those days when I was about ten minutes late for an experiment, I found Pavlov already there punctually, though no one else had come. Seeing that I was not on time, he immediately lit into me with his customary vivaciousness. 'Why are you late, Sir?' I asked him if he did not know that there was a revolution going on outside. 'What difference does a revolution make when you have work in the laboratory to do!' (Ibid., 25)

Pavlov's international fame as a scientist meant that he was relatively immune to persecution after the Communist takeover in Russia. Moreover, Pavlov's work on the physiology of the central nervous system using the procedure he called conditioned reflexes seemed to fit the temper of the times. 'Pavlov's work captured the fancy of many prominent persons and . . . *Pravda*, the central organ of the [Communist] Party, said that the doctrine of conditioned reflexes was one of the foundations of **materialism** in biology, and *Izvestia*, the government organ, devoted a special laudatory article to Pavlov's work' (Bauer, 1952: 54–5). Materialism is the doctrine that physical events constitute the only reality. Pavlov himself never subscribed to a simple-minded materialism, saying instead that 'We are now coming to think of

the mind, the soul and matter as all one, and with this view there will be no necessity for a choice between them' (cited by Gantt, 1928: 25).

Conditioned Reflexes

It is important to realize at the outset that for most of his career Pavlov thought of himself as a physiologist, and not a psychologist. He regarded his chief inspiration to have come from the work of the Russian physiologist I.M. Sechenov (1829–1905), who published a book on *Cerebral Reflexes* in 1863. Sechenov had proposed that mental life should be understood entirely in physiological terms and that the reflex was the appropriate unit of explanation. Pavlov (1960 [1927]: 3) dissociated himself from the psychology of the time, observing that psychologists as prominent as William James and Wundt did not claim that psychology was even close to being a science. Physiology clearly *was* a science and the physiologist had no need for psychology.

Interestingly, Pavlov (1928: 39–40) did acknowledge that ' some years after the beginning of the work with our new method I learned that somewhat similar experiments on animals had been performed in America, and indeed not by physiologists but by psychologists . . . and now I must acknowledge that the honor of having made the first steps along the path belongs to E.L. Thorndike. By two or three years his experiments preceded ours'. However, Pavlov believed that his work was completely different in orientation than Thorndike's, which he characterized as focusing on behaviour to the exclusion of exploring the causes of behaviour in the central nervous system. By contrast, Pavlov regarded his approach as a more balanced blend of both the study of behaviour and physiology. He believed that it was best to approach psychological questions through physiology, rather than to do psychology first and then try to find physiological explanations.

The experiments that made Pavlov a household word developed as a result of something he noticed while observing the action of salivary glands. Saliva would be secreted not only in the presence of food, but also by 'the dish in which it is presented, the furniture upon which it is placed, the room, the person accustomed to bring it, and the noises produced by him' (ibid., 52). The connection between food and salivation seems natural and inevitable, but how should one account for the power of stimuli such as furniture to elicit a response such as salivation with which furniture has no necessary connection?

To understand such phenomena, Pavlov made a distinction between **unconditioned reflexes** and **conditioned reflexes**. A reflex is unconditioned if the same response always occurs in the presence of the same stimulus. Food is an **unconditioned stimulus** and salivation is an **unconditioned response** to the food. Thus, 'unconditioned' means that the connection is unconditional:

> Our starting point has been Descartes' idea of the nervous reflex. This is a genuine scientific conception, since it implies necessity. It may be summed up as follows: An external or internal stimulus falls on some one or other nervous receptor and gives rise to a nervous impulse; this nervous impulse is transmitted along nerve fibres to the central nervous system, and here, on account of existing nervous connections, it gives rise to a fresh impulse which passes along outgoing nerve fibres to the active organ. . . . Thus a stimulus appears to be connected of necessity with a definite response, as cause with effect. (Pavlov, 1960: 7)

The unconditioned reflexes corresponded to the instincts of the animal. Pavlov preferred the term 'unconditioned reflex' because it was less vague and more directly descriptive of the nervous system. There were a large number of unconditioned connections. In addition to the obvious ones we will consider below, Pavlov listed such reflexes as defence, freedom, and purpose. Each of these is intended to refer to specific behaviours. For example, the reflex of defence is the animal's spontaneous reaction to anything that threatens it;

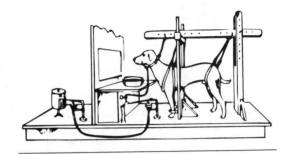

FIGURE 8.1
Pavlov's experimental apparatus.
Source: Yerkes and Morgulis (1909: 264).

the reflex of freedom occurs when the animal is confined and attempts to escape; the reflex of purpose is observed when the animal attempts to attain something of value to it.

Conditioned reflexes are *conditional* in the sense that they only occur under certain conditions. The best way to see the relationship between conditioned and unconditioned reflexes is with reference to Figure 8.1. This figure represents the famous experimental situation in which a dog is fitted with a harness and a surgically implanted device used to collect salivary output. A typical experimental procedure consisted of sounding a tone, followed by the presentation of food to a hungry animal. After repeated pairing of the tone with the food, the tone by itself will come to elicit salivation. The tone has become a **conditioned stimulus**, and the saliva it elicits is a **conditioned response**. The experimental procedure allows for the formation of a conditioned reflex. The relation between conditioned and unconditioned connections is represented in Figure 8.2.

Here are three important facts about conditioning.

1. A conditioned response is typically smaller in magnitude than an unconditioned one. In the experimental situation described above, the amount of saliva elicited by the tone is usually less than the amount of saliva elicited by food (Kimble, 1961: 53).

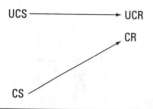

FIGURE 8.2
The relation between conditioned and unconditioned reflexes. UCS, unconditioned stimulus; UCR,
unconditioned response; CS conditioned stimulus;
CR, conditioned response.

2. If a conditioned reflex has been formed, and
    then the conditioned stimulus is repeatedly
    presented by itself, in the absence of the
    unconditioned stimulus, then the conditioned
    response will eventually cease. This phenom-
    enon is called the *extinction* of a conditioned
    response (Pavlov, 1960: 297).
3. Suppose that a conditioned response has
    been extinguished and the animal has been
    returned to its home cage. If the animal is
    then brought back to the experimental situa-
    tion after a rest, the previously extinguished
    conditioned response may return. The phe-
    nomenon whereby a previously extinguished
    conditioned response returns after an interval
    during which it has not been tested is called
    spontaneous recovery (Kimble, 1961: 82–3).

These facts about conditioning were not mere
curiosities, relevant only to the laboratory situation. The power of Pavlov's experiments rested in
the way that his findings could apparently be
generalized from the laboratory to situations outside the laboratory. The experiments formed the
basis for Pavlov's speculations about the adaptive
nature of the conditioning process in the real
world. Unconditioned reflexes are not by themselves sufficient to ensure the survival of the
organism. For example, the animal must not only
eat food when it is given to it, but also must be

able to find food for itself. Consider an animal
hunting for prey. It must follow signs that lead it
to its quarry. This is exactly the function of
conditioned stimuli: they are *signals* that guide
the animal to an unconditioned stimulus. As long
as these signals are reliable, then the animal
continues to respond to them. However, the environment is always changing. The essence of
adaptability is the ability to be flexible and change
one's responses as the environment changes.
Thus, when conditioned stimuli fail to lead to
unconditioned stimuli, then extinction occurs.
The key thing about conditioned stimuli is that
they form *temporary* connections that are *inhibited*
when they become unreliable signals (Pavlov,
1928: 123). However, just as a reliable signal may
become unreliable, so an unreliable signal may
once again become reliable as the environment
fluctuates. Spontaneous recovery provides the
organism with an opportunity to 'check out' a
signal that may have become reliable again.
Although conditioning is often portrayed as a
rigid, mechanical process, it is important to see
that Pavlov's view was that conditioning enables
the organism to form an adaptive, flexible
relationship with its environment.

Pavlov (1928: 24–5; 1960: 123) used the
analogy of a central telephone switchboard to
explain how cortical connections functioned in the
conditioning process. It is obviously inefficient to
have connections between each phone and every
other phone. Far better to have phones connected
through a central switchboard. Similarly, while
there are some inborn connections in the nervous
system (the unconditioned reflexes), new connections are continuously being formed through the
cerebral hemispheres.

Speech

Higher-order conditioning occurs when a second
conditioned stimulus is paired with a conditioned stimulus that has already been established
(Pavlov, 1960: 33). This process is represented
diagrammatically in Figure 8.3. This procedure

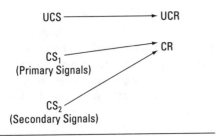

FIGURE 8.3
Higher-order conditioning.

leads to two levels of signals. The **primary signalling system** consists largely of sensory stimuli, such as the tone we described above. In humans, the **secondary signalling system** plays a crucial role, because it consists largely of *words*. Words name primary signals. A single word can stand for an entire class of signals and thus greatly extend the range of stimuli to which a person can respond. For example, the word 'pencil' is not just a label for a particular pencil, but a label for all pencils, and having learned to write with one pencil, you can generalize to any other pencil you come across. It is speech that most differentiates humans from other animals, and gives them their greater flexibility and power over the environment.

Obviously for man speech provides conditioned stimuli which are just as real as any other stimuli. At the same time speech provides stimuli which exceed in richness and many-sidedness any of the others, allowing comparison neither qualitatively nor quantitatively with any conditioned stimuli which are possible in animals. Speech, on account of the whole preceding life of the adult, is connected up with all the internal and external stimuli which can reach the cortex, signaling all of them and replacing all of them, and therefore it can call forth all those reactions of the organism which are normally determined by the actual stimuli themselves. (Ibid., 407)

Temperaments and Psychopathology

Pavlov believed that the fundamental cortical processes were **excitation** and **inhibition**. In order to be properly adjusted to the environment, it is necessary to inhibit all but those responses that are appropriate to the current situation. '[T]his is of the greatest importance in our life as well as in the life of animals; . . . that under any given circumstance and at any moment a certain activity must be manifested, but in another situation, inhibited. Upon this principle is founded the highest orientations of life. In such a way, a continual and proper balancing of these two processes lays the basis of a normal life for both man and animal. These two opposite processes . . . [are] coexistent and are equally important in nervous activity' (Pavlov, 1928: 373).

Pavlov observed great individual differences between animals in terms of the ease with which they formed conditioned reflexes. At one extreme was an *excitatory* group, which is easily conditioned, while at the other extreme is an *inhibitory* group, which is difficult to condition. Pavlov (ibid., 376) believed that this dimension characterized differences between people also. In attempting to characterize such individual differences in human terms, Pavlov drew on the work of Hippocrates (c. 460 BC–377 BC), who had classified people into four temperaments: choleric, sanguine, phlegmatic, and melancholic. Pavlov regarded the four temperaments as arranged on a scale from extremely excitatory (choleric) to extremely inhibitory (melancholic), with the sanguine and phlegmatic in between. The excitatory/inhibitory imbalance of the extreme temperaments is associated with pathology, by contrast with the relative equilibrium of the middle temperaments. Pavlov described the choleric temperament as 'pugnacious, passionate and easily and quickly irritated,' while the melancholic 'believes in nothing, hopes for nothing, in everything he sees only the dark side, and from everything he expects only grievances.' The sanguine and phlegmatic types stand 'in the golden middle . . . well-equilibrated and therefore healthy [and] stable' (ibid., 377).

Vivisection and Anti-vivisectionism

Pavlov often performed surgery on his animals to prepare them for his experiments, and he was acutely aware of the fact that many people found such experimental work on live animals to be objectionable. The dissection of live animals is called *vivisection* and the movement against the use of live animals in research was called *anti-vivisectionism*. Pavlov (ibid., 21) justified such procedures, which occasionally did result in 'painful and violent deaths of animals', by saying that there was no other way to understand how the nervous system worked. It was necessary to sacrifice some animals in order to benefit mankind. Pavlov also noted that animal experimentation was a small source of pain compared to the consequences of recreational hunting and the slaughter of animals for food. Further discussion of this issue is in Box 8.1.

Vladimir M. Bekhterev (1857–1927)

The objective approach in Russia was also carried forward by Bekhterev's **reflexology**, an extremely

---

BOX 8.1

ANIMAL RIGHTS

A persistent issue in psychological research is the proper treatment of animals. Experimentation on animals goes back a long way. We noted in Chapter 2 that in the seventeenth century Descartes treated animals merely as machines with no feelings. This is an attitude that many people would find offensive today (e.g., Plous, 1996).

Experimental work on live animals has often been seen by members of the general public as giving researchers an opportunity to use techniques that would be unacceptable if performed on humans. For decades, some people have feared that what is done to research animals today will be done to people tomorrow, particularly to people who are not in a position to object to maltreatment. Thus, over the years there has been a concern in some quarters that researchers who use animal subjects may be abusive to animals, and ultimately to people. An excellent review of the early period of this controversy is by Lederer (1985).

Subsequently, the controversy over animal experimentation entered a new phase. The nature of the debate is well illustrated by the reaction to an article by Johnson (1990). Johnson argued that there are two contrasting views of what constitutes ethical treatment of research animals. The first he called *animal welfare*, and the second *animal rights*.

- **Animal welfare** is consistent with the Judeo-Christian tradition, which has always maintained that, while people are of greater value than animals, people have a responsibility to promote the welfare of animals. However, from this viewpoint, it is ethical to use animals in research that will benefit people. Without animal subjects, we will be forced to abandon research 'that would have saved lives or eased the pain' of people who may be suffering from one disorder or another (Johnson, 1990: 214). Of course, the use of animals in research should be as humane as possible, with no unnecessary suffering. This would be the position that researchers like Pavlov adopted.
- The **animal rights** activists adopt a different value system. People are not necessarily superior to other life forms. For example, both people and animals are capable of experiencing pain. Pain is a great leveller. It is immoral to inflict pain on any animal, human or otherwise. Application of this principle eliminates research with animals that would not be ethical if done with humans.

What do you think?

ambitious attempt to explain all behaviour, from the individual to the social, in terms of the reflex concept. **Vladimir Bekhterev** regarded the individual as a system of energy transformation and exchange, in much the same way as did Freud. However, Bekhterev regarded his method as more objective than Freud's. He rejected the study of subjective aspects of the mind in favour of studying its observable products, such as speech and social behaviour.

Bekhterev believed that the basic laws of physical science could be applied to explain behaviour at all levels, from the individual to the social. For example, gravitational attraction not only applies to inanimate objects but also to 'individuals who have similar internal and external characteristics [and] are mutually attracted' (Bekhterev, 2001 [1921]: 311). Another example is the law of 'equal and opposite reaction', which explains, for example, why 'every new social movement meets with some form of opposition' (ibid., 317). Similarly 'inertia . . . causes any movement, once it has developed, to tend to be popularized across the whole collective, attracting more and more individuals in the manner of a snowball that grows unlimitedly as it rolls through snow' (ibid., 365), leading eventually to 'old tattered ideas hold[ing] on to their influence for a long time, taking the form of a prejudice' (ibid., 377).

While Bekhterev proudly regarded his psychology as 'objective', most American psychologists of the time judged it to be vague. Pavlov's approach was seen as more truly objective. As a result, Pavlov became the iconic Russian psychologist in America, while Bekhterev's more ambitious psychology faded into the background. However, due to the work of Lloyd Strickland, who was responsible for producing recent editions of Bekhterev's *Collective Reflexology*, there have been signs of renewed interest (Bakhurst, 2001; Benjafield, 2002a; Rumbaugh, 1996).

In spite of the fact that Bekhterev's more ambitious research program did not find universal favour, it should be remembered that Bekhterev, even more than Pavlov, was initially responsible for the interest in conditioning shown by early twentieth-century psychologists. This was because Bekhterev developed a technique for studying *associated motor reflexes* in both dogs and humans. The technique involved applying electrical shock to, for example, a person's finger resting on a metal surface. The response was withdrawal of the finger upon being shocked. This response could come to be elicited by a signal that had preceded the shock, and Bekhterev called this the **association reflex**. (Le Ny, 1964: 23). Bekhterev's procedure was extensively used by J.B. Watson, whose American form of behaviourism we will examine next. Indeed, during 1914–15, Watson himself devoted a seminar 'to the translation and discussion of the French edition of Bekhterev's work' (Hilgard and Marquis, 1940: 9).

John B. Watson (1878–1958)

John B. Watson is one of the most colourful figures in the history of twentieth-century psychology in the United States. He was born in South Carolina, the son of a boisterous father who was more often away from home than not, and a mother who, as a devout Baptist, hoped that young John B. Watson would become a preacher. As we shall see, Watson did indeed become a preacher of sorts, although his message went against received wisdom.

Watson attended Furman University, graduating in 1899. He was ambitious, and in spite of a mediocre record managed to get accepted as a graduate student at the University of Chicago. As we saw in the last chapter, Chicago was the home of functional psychology, and Watson worked with J.R. Angell, among others. However, the ideas of Jacques Loeb (1859–1924) also made quite an impression on him (Buckley, 1989: 40–1; Weizmann, 2001: 230). Loeb had himself been influenced by the great scientist-philosopher Ernst Mach (1838–1916), who regarded science as the search for functional relations (Winston, 2001). For Loeb, functional relations in psychology describe the dependence of behaviour on particular stimulus conditions. A good example is

Loeb's interest in **tropisms**—movements under the direct control of a stimulus. An example would be a tendency for an animal to turn towards light. A tropism in an animal is conceived of as 'a forced response, in the sense that the organism is governed by the . . . stimulus in a mechanical way, just as pressing a switch in an electrical circuit turns on an appropriate light bulb' (Tavolga, 1969: 77). Loeb was a materialist and believed that mechanisms similar to tropisms governed all behaviour.

Watson's doctoral dissertation was in animal psychology. He used white rats as subjects, a relatively novel practice at the time, but one that became widespread later on (Wertz, 1994). Among other things, Watson investigated the behaviour of rats in mazes, a method not invented by Watson but that also became extremely common in psychology. Watson received his Ph.D. in 1903.

> He was the youngest to have earned that degree from the University of Chicago. Yet he felt what he called his 'first deep-seated inferiority,' which grew into years of jealousy, when he was told by Dewey and Angell that his doctoral exam was inferior to that of Helen Thompson Wooley, who had graduated two years before. Watson was often a willing mentor to his female students, but he was extremely uncomfortable with women as professional peers. (Buckley, 1989: 45–6)

After receiving his degree, Watson stayed on at Chicago. He married a student there named Mary Ickes in 1903, and they had a daughter in 1905. Watson was never happy with the level of support for his research that he received from the university administration, and he moved to Johns Hopkins University in 1908, where he was appointed as a full professor at age 29.

The head of Watson's department at Hopkins was James Mark Baldwin, whose work on developmental psychology we will consider in Chapter 12. For now, however, Baldwin is relevant only insofar as he played a part in Watson's career.

Watson's animal work had been attracting much favourable attention, and Baldwin was enthusiastic about adding Watson to his department. Baldwin also had other enthusiasms. 'In the summer of 1908, Baldwin had been caught in a police raid on a "coloured house" of prostitution. He gave a false name to the police and the charge was eventually dropped' (Pauly, 1979: 38). Baldwin would have been out of the woods, except that the mayor of Baltimore nominated him for the school board, apparently not aware of Baldwin's escapade. At that point, somebody blew the whistle and Baldwin's indiscretion became widely known. The upshot was that the trustees of Johns Hopkins asked Baldwin to resign, and he left the country.

As we have observed before, 'It is an ill wind that blows nobody any good', and Baldwin's misfortune was Watson's great chance. He became head of the department, which provided him with the platform he needed to achieve his ambitious goals. He began to do the work that would transform psychology in the United States.

Psychology as the Behaviourist Views It

In 1913, Watson published a paper that challenged psychologists to change virtually every aspect of their discipline as it was then being practised. Watson (1966 [1913]: 70) began the paper by saying that 'psychology as the behaviorist views it is a purely objective experimental branch of natural science.' The rest of the paper laid out the consequences of taking this proposition with utter seriousness.

The first consequence is that psychology is not in any way the study of consciousness. The comparative psychologist studies behaviour without any reference to consciousness and in so doing is leading the way for psychologists who study humans. Human behaviour can and should be studied in the same way as animal behaviour. A part of Watson's message was that it is time finally to replace the unreliable method of introspection with the reliable, objective observation of behaviour: 'The time seems to have come when psychology must discard all reference to consciousness; when it need no longer delude itself into thinking that it is making mental states the object of observation' (ibid., 74).

Functional psychology was also to go by the boards. It was a vague grab bag of topics and methods, ill-suited to a scientific psychology. By including discussion of 'mind', it simply muddies the waters. Questions about the relation between mind and body are relics of 'philosophical speculation' and 'need trouble the student of behavior as little as they trouble the student of physics. . . . I can state my position here no better than by saying that I should like to bring my students up in the same ignorance of such hypotheses as one finds among the students of branches of science' (ibid., 76). Evidently there would be no courses in the history of psychology for Watson's students!

Watson's psychology would begin with 'the observable fact that organisms, man and animal alike, do adjust themselves to their environment by means of hereditary and habit equipments' (ibid.). These adjustments are responses to particular stimuli, and the prediction of behaviour is a realistic possibility given an understanding of *stimulus-response relationships*. Psychology, according to Watson, concerns itself with the *prediction and control of behaviour*. This makes of psychology not just an experimental discipline, but also a truly applied discipline. Psychology is able to provide 'the educator, the physician, the jurist and businessman' with information that will be useful in their professions (ibid., 78).

At the end of his paper, Watson made a statement that is undoubtedly true. 'If you grant the behaviorist the right to use consciousness in the same way that other natural scientists employ it— that is, without making consciousness a special object of observation—you have granted all that my thesis requires' (ibid., 83). Watsonian behaviourism comes down to this: a real science uses consciousness to make observations, it does not observe consciousness itself. Watson never denied the existence of consciousness or that observers were conscious. He only denied that observers in

psychology should act differently from observers in any other science. A scientific psychology would have as its subject matter the behaviour of organisms, no more and no less.

Watson's message had a profound impact on other psychologists, many of whom felt that it was a breath of fresh air. In place of the interminable quarrels about what psychology was and how it should go about its business, Watson promised a clear and simple solution. Just study behaviour; forget about the rest, and all will be well.

Watson's 1913 paper is the first in a series of what might be called his **promissory notes** (Soyland, 1994: 230–1). In the context of the history of science, a promissory note is a claim that if a certain research direction is followed, then the results will be worthwhile. Promissory notes are quite common in the history of science, and certainly in the history of psychology. Throughout his career Watson issued several promissory notes, and here is an example of the rhetoric he used to try to persuade people to accept the promise of behaviourism:

> I should like to go one step further now and say, 'Give me a dozen healthy infants, well-formed, and my own specified world to bring them up in and I'll guarantee to take any one at random and train him to become any type of specialist I might select—doctor, lawyer, artist, merchant-chief and, yes, even beggar-man and thief, regardless of his talents, penchants, tendencies, abilities, vocations, and race of his ancestors.' I am going beyond my facts and I admit it, but so have advocates of the contrary and they have been doing it for many thousands of years. Please note that when this experiment is made I am to be allowed to specify the way the children are to be brought up and the type of world they have to live in. (Watson, 1962 [1930]: 104)

Although some people had reservations about his radical **environmentalism**, many were quite happy to accept Watson's promissory note. Of course, such a promissory note must pay off at some point with real research findings. What was the content of the psychology Watson actually proposed, and did it live up to its promise?

Watson's Psychology

Conditioning

In 1916, Watson wrote a paper in which he reflected on his earlier criticisms of introspection and said that it was now necessary to 'suggest some method which we might *begin* to use in place of introspection. I have found, as you easily might have predicted, that it is one thing to condemn a long-established method, but quite another thing to suggest something in its place' (Watson, 1970 [1916]: 35). However, he had not only been reading about the work of Pavlov and Bekhterev, but also was beginning to use their methods in his own laboratory. At that point, Watson had gathered data on 'eleven human subjects, one dog and seven chickens'. Although he was concerned about the validity of using conditioning methods with humans who might 'get the drift of what is expected of them as the experiment proceeds' (ibid., 44, 46), he felt confident that conditioning would be useful with a variety of types of subjects and topics in psychology. Gradually, Watson became more and more closely identified with conditioning.

> Not only was Pavlovian conditioning a practical, objective, and deterministic framework in which to cast as much of psychology as one's imagination encompassed, but it was built upon the reflex itself, Watson's first love in psychological analysis. The marriage was a natural, and there were no impediments to it.
>
> Watson's conversion to the conditioned reflex went hand in hand with a change in the scope of his behaviorism. Instead of a mere faction within an academic discipline, it became a program for social control and improvement. During the 1920's, Watson's books became more and more concerned with practical questions . . . [and] were usually compilations . . . of articles

that had appeared in various popular magazines . . . [such as] 'The behaviorist looks at instincts' (*Harper's*, 1927); 'Feed me with facts' (*Saturday Review of Literature*, 1928); 'The weakness of women' (*The Nation*, 1928); 'Can we make our children behave?' (*Forum*, 1929); 'It's your own fault' (*Collier's*, 1928); 'The heart or the intellect?' (*Harper's*, 1928); 'Are parents necessary?' (*New York Times*, 1930). (Herrnstein, 1973 [1967]: 111)

Emotional, Manual, and Verbal Habits

In his book *Behaviorism*, Watson (1962: 197) argued that humans are unique in the animal kingdom because of the variety of useful habits they can form through conditioning. These habits are of three kinds: (1) *visceral* or *emotional* habits; (2) *manual* habits; and (3) *laryngeal* or *verbal* habits. Let us consider each of these in turn.

Emotional Habits

Watson (ibid., 141) was contemptuous of James's theory of emotion because it relied on introspective evidence gathered from adults. The only way to study emotion is to examine very young children and see what emotional responses are elicited by what stimuli. Watson (ibid., 152–4) came to the conclusion that humans come equipped with three emotional responses tied to particular stimuli—**fear**, **rage**, and **love**. Obviously, by these three words Watson did not mean any kind of subjective experience. They referred to unlearned responses. Fear was a baby's reaction in the presence of a sudden, loud sound or when it suddenly loses support: 'there is a catching of breath, clutching with the hands and crying' (ibid., 153). Watson's example of rage is the behaviour elicited when the body is restrained, and involves 'stiffening of the whole body . . . and holding of breath' (ibid., 154). Love responses occur in the baby through the stimulation of 'erogenous zones, such as the nipples, the lips and the sex organs' that results in behaviours such as 'gurgling and cooing' (ibid., 155).

Little Albert

These primitive emotional responses constitute the platform upon which a much more complicated variety of emotional responses is built. Watson and Rosalie Rayner described a procedure for producing conditioned emotional reactions. The subject on their experiment is one of the most famous in the history of American psychology, Albert B., or Little Albert, as he came to be called, an eleven-month-old infant who was 'the son of one of the wet nurses in the Harriet Lane Hospital. He had lived his whole life in the hospital' (Watson, 1962: 159). At first, the child was quite happy to touch any object brought near to him. However, 'a fear reaction could be called out . . . by striking a hammer upon a suspended steel bar' behind the child (Watson and Rayner, 2000 [1920]: 280). By pairing this sound with the sight of a white rat, Albert could be made to show a fear reaction to the rat as well. Watson and Rayner reported that this fear reaction subsequently transferred to other white, furry things, such as a rabbit and a Santa Claus mask. Watson (1962: 163–4) called these generalizations 'undifferentiated emotional reactions', and believed that they were particularly characteristic of 'most of us in infancy . . . many adults, especially women . . . [and] all primitive peoples'. However, he also believed that with proper training people could be taught to differentiate between the original fear-producing stimulus and those that had become fear-producing accidentally. It is, of course, one of the goals of psychotherapy to attempt to rid a client of unnecessary fears. As we will see in a subsequent chapter, Watson and Rayner's study has often been cited as a classic precursor of psychotherapeutic procedures deriving from theories of conditioning (Rilling, 2000).

Manual Habits

By 'manual habits', Watson (1962: 197) meant the entire range of muscular responses including those in the 'trunk, legs, arms and feet'. Stimuli are forever eliciting manual responses of one sort or another. The act of responding to one stimulus places the person in a new stimulus situation that elicits another response, and so on. Through repetition, manual habits form that allow for a smooth transition from one situation to another. Watson (ibid., 212) advocated the 'formation of early work habits in youth', believing this to be the 'most reasonable explanation we have today not only for success in any line, but even for genius.' When it came to the acquisition of a skill, Watson advocated *distributed practice*, as opposed to continuous or *massed practice*. Practice is distributed if the number of trials is spread out, with inter-trial intervals in which no work is done on the task. For many skills, it appears that distributed practice leads to better results.

Verbal Habits

Watson loved to make exaggerated claims and then retract them just a little bit. One such claim is 'thought is nothing but talking to ourselves' (ibid., 238). This claim was often taken to mean that thinking is nothing but movements in the larynx, but Watson denied that this is what he actually meant, although he admitted to having said it 'for pedagogical purposes'. What he actually meant was that thought and internal speech are one and the same. Internal speech can be generated by any number of muscular activities, including movements in the larynx. For example, people who know sign language may speak to themselves using minute movements of their fingers. The point was not that thought took place in the larynx, but that verbal habits, however realized, constituted thinking. In support of this contention, Watson pointed out that young children talk out loud, even when alone. Under the pressure of socialization, this speech becomes silent, and although still present it is hard to notice. Thinking is this subvocal speech, and involves running off verbal habits that enable us to accomplish things that range from recalling the words of a song to planning our day.

Speech is an example of a chain of responses, sentences consisting of one word after another. As such, speech is but one example of a very large class of **serially ordered behaviours**. We are constantly performing complex tasks that require us

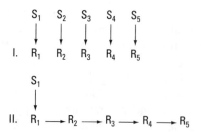

FIGURE 8.4
Watson's model of serially ordered behaviour.

to generate responses in the proper sequence. Driving a car and playing the piano are only two examples. Watson believed that the process whereby such habits are formed worked in the way that is illustrated in Figure 8.4. First there is a sequence of stimuli, each of which elicits a response in the manner depicted in Part I of the figure. With repetition, the first stimulus by itself is capable of setting off the entire chain. Each response in the chain serves as the stimulus for the next response, as shown in Part II of Figure 8.4. Watson's example of this process was playing the piano. At first, every note on the page elicits a key press, but with practice you can look at the first note and then play the entire piece without looking at the music (ibid., 257).

Watson believed that it was an important function of internal speech to guide these serially ordered acts. For example, as you drive a car you might be able to catch yourself as you covertly say things that serve as stimuli for your actions. However, there are some things we do that are not under verbal control. Watson had a special role for behaviours for which we have no verbal label, which he called the *unverbalized*. There are any number of infantile responses to which a verbal label never becomes attached. For example, 'what child has ever verbalized its incestuous attachments?' (ibid., 263). If that last remark sounds like Freud, that is because Watson appropriated Freudian ideas and recast them in a behaviourist mode (Rilling, 2000). For Watson, the unverbal-

ized was what Freud had called the 'unconscious' (Watson, 1962: 262). The 'unconscious' occurred of necessity because early childhood experience took place before the child could verbally label any of its experiences.

Watson and Rosalie Rayner

Rosalie Rayner, the graduate student with whom Watson had done the Little Albert study, was not only his co-worker. Rayner was 'the daughter of a prominent Baltimorean who some years earlier had donated $10,000 to the University, and niece of a former US senator. Watson left his wife in April 1920; he and Rosalie were seen together so much that many thought they were married. . . . When Mrs. Watson sued for divorce she submitted as evidence a number of letters Watson wrote "breathing affection" to Rosalie; excerpts were printed in the Baltimore *Sun*' (Pauly, 1979: 39). The Johns Hopkins administration reacted to Watson's case similarly to the way it reacted to the Baldwin case. Watson was asked to resign, and he did so. Many of his former colleagues disowned him, although a few thought that the punishment did not fit the crime.

Watson's Second Career in Advertising

Watson and Rayner were married on New Year's Eve in 1920 (Buckley, 1989: 132) and moved to New York. There he worked first for the J. Walter Thompson advertising agency and then for William Esty & Co. until he retired in 1946 (Herrnstein, 1973). The step from academia to advertising was not so great for Watson as it might have been for other professors. As we have already seen, Watson was keenly interested in developing a psychology that could be of use in the real world, and what could be more of an applied psychology than advertising? Advertisers wanted to be able to provide 'a controlled and predictable body of consumers', and who better to provide this than Watson, 'who claimed to have the techniques that could be used to predict and control human behavior' (Buckley, 1982: 211).

Watson recommended to his colleagues that they take advantage of conditioned responses. 'To insure the appropriate reaction from the consumer, tell him something that will tie up with fear, something that will stir up a mild rage, that will call out an affectionate or love response, or strike at a deep psychological or habit need' (ibid., 212). To accomplish this goal, Watson relied on several now well-known techniques. In general, these techniques did not sell a product on the basis of its intrinsic virtues, but rather attempted to associate positive features with the product. For example, Watson employed experts and celebrities who would recommend the product in advertisements, and himself played this role in advertisements for coffee and toothpaste (ibid., 215–16). One might wonder whether merely repeating a commercial that paired a positive figure with a commodity would be sufficient to establish an association, but a great deal of subsequent research suggests that 'mere exposure' to a stimulus may very well be enough to cause it to become positively evaluated (Bornstein, 1989). At any rate, Watson was a great success in his second career, widely respected by his colleagues in the business world.

As time went on, the attitudes of Watson's former associates in academia softened. Finally, in 1957, Watson was given a citation by the American Psychological Association, which read as follows.

> To Dr. John B. Watson, whose work has been one of the vital determinants of the form and substance of modern psychology. He initiated a revolution in psychological thought, and his writings have been the point of departure for continuing lines of fruitful research. (Watson, 1962: iii)

Karl S. Lashley (1890–1958)

Karl S. Lashley had a background in biological science, receiving his undergraduate training at the University of West Virginia and then doing his Ph.D. with the geneticist Herbert S. Jennings

at Johns Hopkins. Lashley then did postdoctoral studies with John B. Watson. The two became great friends, and a part of their subsequent correspondence is discussed in Box 8.2. Throughout his entire career, Lashley considered himself to be a behaviourist (Hebb, 1980), even though, as we shall see, his interests diverged considerably from Watson's.

Cortical Localization of Function

Watson and Lashley 'developed different interests in conditioning research. . . . Lashley's interest was in finding out how conditioned reflexes are represented in the nervous system' while Watson was never very interested in the physiology of the nervous system (Bruce, 1991: 311). Lashley initially thought that it might be possible to 'understand the physiological processes underlying the establishment of conditioned reflexes and to trace such reflexes through the brain' (Bruce, 1986: 34). Lashley's endeavour should be seen in the context of a long-standing controversy in psychology, called the **localization of function controversy**.

Lashley was by no means the first person to wonder where particular psychological functions were located in the nervous system. As Krech observed, the attempt to discover which parts of the brain are specialized for which tasks goes back at least to Franz Joseph Gall (1758–1828) and his student, J.G. Spurzheim (1776–1832). Gall and Spurzheim promoted **phrenology**. A phrenological chart, which purports to represent the locations of various psychological functions, is shown in Figure 8.5. Although Gall and Spurzheim's charts are not taken seriously any longer, their underlying premises still deserve consideration.

Their argument reduced to three basic principles: (1) The brain is the sole organ of the mind. (2) The basic character and intellectual traits of man are innately determined. (3) Since there are differences in character and intellectual traits among individuals as well as differences in various intellectual capacities within a single

---

BOX 8.2

WATSON AND LASHLEY:
THE BOYS OF SUMMER, OR SOMETHING ELSE?

John B. Watson destroyed most of his correspondence, but some letters written in the 1950s to and from Karl Lashley survived (Dewsbury, 1993). In these letters Watson and Lashley freely express their personal views on a variety of issues, including women and race. They probably never thought about the possibility that their letters would be made available to a wider audience. Today their views would be called 'politically incorrect'. For example, Lashley 'made several racist remarks concerning blacks' (ibid., 267) and concluded some of his letters with the phrase 'Heil Hitler and apartheid' (Weidman, 1999: 164).

Weidman (1999) has raised the question with respect to these letters about the relevance of the personal views of Lashley and Watson to their work in psychology, and by extension has called into question all the personal views held by psychologists. Dewsbury (1993: 264) suggested that 'we must be very careful when judging the acts and views of scientists of another era from the perspectives and values of our own', and noted that Lashley and Watson were 'products of their time, as we all are'. Can we explain the theoretical orientation of a psychologist as an extension of his or her personal and political life, or is scientific activity a purely objective matter? The standard answer is that the political beliefs of scientists have nothing to do with their scientific work. Weidman (1999: 162) countered, however, that 'science and politics are on an equal footing . . . they develop together and are always complexly intertwined.'

Dewsbury (2002a, 2002b) and Weidman (2002) have continued their debate. What do you think?

---

individual, there must exist differentially developed areas in the brain, responsible for these differences! Where there is variation in *function* there must be variation in the controlling *structures*. (Krech, 1962: 33)

Gall and Spurzheim's method for locating functions in the brain was highly speculative. They believed that the more highly developed a function, the larger it would be. Furthermore, the larger a function, the more it would manifest itself as a protrusion on the skull. Thus, one could divine a person's strengths and weaknesses by examining the shape of skull. Phrenology had a powerful impact on nineteenth-century cultural practices, and many paying customers relied on the advice of phrenologists (Sokal, 2001). In spite of the obvious weakness of their method, the underlying hypothesis that specific functions are localized in specific parts of the brain has guided much subsequent research (e.g., Gardner, 1983; Sarter et al., 1996).

Lashley began his studies of localization in 1916 with **Shepherd Ivory Franz** (1874–1933). Franz was an expert in the technique of **ablation**, whereby parts of the cortex are destroyed and the results observed. If functions were localized in the cortex, then the effect of ablation of cortical tissue should depend on the area destroyed. However, on the basis of his observations, Franz (1912: 328) believed that 'mental processes are not due to the independent activities of individual parts of the brain, but to the activities of brain as a whole' and that 'it would appear best and most scientific that we should not adhere to any of the phrenological systems.'

Lashley and Franz studied the effects of ablation of the frontal lobes in rats. Their technique was to make 'small holes in the animal's skull rather than opening up the skull, and determine by later histology precisely where the lesions had occurred' (Bruce, 1986: 38), thus determining the effect of such lesions on the retention of a simple learned

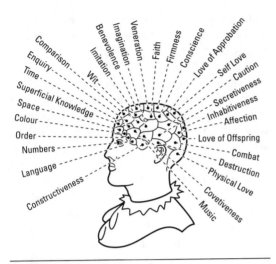

FIGURE 8.5
A phrenological chart.
Source: Krech and Crutchfield (1958: 481).
Copyright © 1958 by David Krech and Richard
S. Curtchfield. Copyright © 1969 by Alfred A.
Knopf, Inc. Reprinted by permission of Hilda Krech.

maze habit. Their results persuaded them that as long as sufficient tissue remained after the operation, then the location of the tissue was irrelevant.

In 1917, Lashley moved to the University of Minnesota. Largely as a result of work at Minnesota and elsewhere, he published a classic in the area of localization of function, **Brain Mechanisms and Intelligence** (1929). This research developed further the procedures he had learned from Franz. Lashley lesioned the cortex of rats in different places and to different degrees. He reasoned that 'if there were reflex paths transversing the cortex . . . then surgery would destroy them' (Weidman, 1994: 166). Lashley (1929: 74) observed the ability of rats to learn or remember such tasks as finding their way through mazes of different levels of difficulty, and found that performance in simple mazes was not greatly affected by brain damage. Rather, performance declined as the difficulty of the task increased and/or the amount of brain damage increased. Lashley summarized the implications of his results:

What is the evidence that the cortex itself contains the definite specialized synapses which are demanded by the reflex theory? Small lesions either produce no symptoms or very transient ones, so that it is clear that the mechanisms for habits are not closely grouped within small areas. When larger areas are involved, there are usually amnesias for many activities. . . . After injuries to the brain, the rate of formation of some habits is directly proportional to the extent of the injury and independent of the position within any part of the cortex. (Lashley, 1978 [1930]: 271)

There was no evidence for specialized connections developed as a result of learning in the brain. Rather, neither learning nor memory is 'dependent upon the properties of individual cells'; instead, these are functions of 'the total mass of tissue' (ibid.). These results came to be formulated as the *law of mass action* (learning and memory depend on the total mass of brain tissue remaining) and the *law of equipotentiality* (even though some areas of the cortex may become specialized for certain tasks, within limits any part of an area can do the job of any other part of that area). Lashley used the metaphor of an electric sign as a model to explain his findings. The 'functional organization plays over' cortical cells 'just as the pattern of letters plays over the bank of lamps in an electric sign' (ibid.). A single bank of bulbs in an electronic sign can be used to display any number of messages, and similarly the cortex can be organized in any number of ways depending on circumstances.

While Pavlov had attempted to approach psychological problems through physiology, Lashley attempted to do the reverse. He argued that:

psychology is today a more fundamental science than neurophysiology. By this I mean that the latter offers few principles from which we may predict or define the normal organization of behavior, whereas the study of psychological processes furnishes a mass of factual material to which the laws of nervous action in behavior must conform. . . . For immediate progress it is not very important that we should have a correct theory of brain activity, but it is essential that we shall not be handicapped by a false one. (Ibid., 282)

Needless to say, Pavlov was not pleased with the direction in which Lashley's work had taken him. In his talk to the International Congress of Psychology in 1929, Lashley had advanced a 'vigorous attack on Pavlovian reflex theory. . . . Afterwards, Pavlov denounced Lashley's lecture so vehemently that his interpreter, trying to keep up with the 20-minute tirade, finally gave up and said simply at the end of it, 'Professor Pavlov said: No!' . . . [For Pavlov] to have had one of the foremost behaviorists of the time reject his ideas so thoroughly must have been a bitter disappointment' (Bruce, 1991: 314).

The Problem of Serial Order in Behaviour

The importance of Lashley's work on the localization of function problem would have ensured his place in the history of psychology. However, Lashley went on to do other work that may in the long run turn out to be his most important (e.g., Bruce, 1994). The best expression of this work was in a paper Lashley presented in 1948 and published in 1951.

Recall that Watson had proposed that a chain of responses, such as a sentence, consisted of a sequence of responses cued by an initial stimulus. Watson's theory was that in such a chain each response was cued by the preceding response. It was just such an *associative chain theory* that Lashley criticized.

Animals are almost always engaging in serially ordered acts such as speaking, writing, playing the piano, or running through a maze, and any adequate explanation of behaviour must explain the way sequences of behaviour become organized. Lashley pointed out that any associative chain theory has difficulty explaining phenomena such as *priming* of responses. A response

sometimes occurs earlier in a sequence than it would if it was elicited by the immediately preceding stimulus. One of Lashley's examples was typing 'wrapid writing' rather than 'rapid writing'. The 'w' in 'writing' had been *primed*, or activated, before the word 'rapid' had been typed. 'Not infrequently words are introduced which should occur much later in the sentence, often five or six words in advance' (Lashley, 1951: 119). Lashley also discussed Spoonerisms, which are errors named after an Oxford professor (William Archibald Spooner, 1844–1930) about whom many stories were told. He was supposed to have said such things as 'You have tasted your worm' to a student who had wasted his term, and to have discussed 'the weight of rages' when he meant to speak about the rate of wages (Augarde, 1991: 206). In the first example, the 't' in 'term' was primed before the sentence was uttered and intruded earlier in the sequence. 'In these contaminations, it is as if the aggregate of words were in a state of partial excitation, held in check by the requirements of grammatical structure, but ready to activate the final common path' (Lashley, 1951: 119). Some central organization of such sequences is required that is different from the peripheral stimulus-response process postulated by Watson's theory.

Lashley's ideas were ahead of his time. Citations of his serial order paper continued to increase long after it was published in 1951 (Bruce, 1994: 94). His ideas about the necessity of central control of behaviour anticipated later developments, when cognitive psychology challenged behaviourism for hegemony in the field of psychology. These developments will form an important part of our story in Chapter 14.

B.F. Skinner (1904–90)

The Nature of Behaviourism

The three theorists we have considered in detail thus far demonstrate that the orientation to psychology called 'behaviourism' was able to accommodate a variety of approaches. Both Lashley and Pavlov considered physiological explanations of behaviour to be a necessity, but Watson thought that the study of behaviour was sufficient in its own right. Lashley and Pavlov differed from each other with respect to the primacy of physiology, with Pavlov regarding psychology as dependent on physiology and Lashley seeing it the other way around. Although behaviourists differ in some ways, what they all have in common is just what their name suggests: they all regard behaviour as the only subject matter and reject subjective experience as a legitimate topic in psychology. We now come to **B.F. Skinner**, regarded by many as the foremost behaviourist of all time. As we shall see, Skinner shared more with Watson than with either Pavlov or Lashley.

Skinner's Radical Behaviourism

Skinner was not only a behaviourist, but also one of the most famous American psychologists of any persuasion in the twentieth century (Rutherford, 2000). Terms associated with Skinner have become a part of the English language. Herrnstein (1977) pointed out that 'Skinner box' was an entry in *Webster's Third New International Dictionary*. More recently, the *Oxford English Dictionary* (1992) has entries for 'Skinner' ('The name of the American psychologist . . . used to indicate the theories or methods concerned with conditioning human or animal behaviour associated with him; esp[ecially] as *Skinner box*, a box in which an animal is isolated, equipped essentially with a bar or other device that it learns to use either to obtain a reward or to escape punishment'), 'Skinnerian', and 'Skinnerism'. Herrnstein (1977: 593) also remarked on a survey conducted by a popular magazine 'to determine the 100 most important people who ever lived: Jesus Christ was first, and Skinner was about 40th, not far from Luther and Calvin.'

In a paper marking the fiftieth anniversary of Watson's (1913) paper 'Psychology as the Behaviorist Views It,' Skinner (1964: 81) paid homage to 'John B. Watson who made the first clear, if rather noisy, proposal that psychology should be regarded simply as a science of behavior'. It is proper to see Skinner as the true inheritor of Watsonian behaviourism. For both of them, the most important thing a psychologist needs to understand is that mental events do not explain behaviour. For Skinner, the 'central argument' was 'that behavior which seemed to be the product of mental activity could be explained in other ways' (ibid.).

Skinner believed that consciousness was a form *of* behaviour, and not a mysterious process responsible *for* behaviour. It is unscientific to conceive of people as having minds that control their behaviour. The notion that people have minds is rooted in the animism of primitive people. **Animism** is the belief that all objects, including plants and animals, have souls. Animism arose in primitive societies as a way of explaining such phenomena as dreams. Dreams seemed to simple-minded folk to be the result of the soul leaving the body and wandering through other worlds. Eventually, people began to believe in a soul, and even brilliant philosophers like Descartes defended the notion. People took it for granted that there was 'a little person in the head', or **homunculus**, that controlled our behaviour. From Skinner's viewpoint, this is only a primitive explanation of behaviour. To believe that a soul controls our behaviour simply postpones an explanation of behaviour. After all, once you say that the soul controls behaviour, then you are left with the problem of answering the question, 'What controls the soul?' All mentalistic explanations have the same problem: They never reach a full understanding of the causes of behaviour. If we believe that behaviour is a product of mental activity, then we are the victim of old-fashioned beliefs.

We need to realize that all events are in principle public events. Even events 'within the skin' (ibid., 84) would be open to public observation if we had sophisticated enough measuring devices. Behaviours inside the skin are still behaviours. There need be no 'private' events known to the person alone. We may falsely believe that behaviours are 'private' if we are not aware of the stimuli that are controlling them, but our feelings of privacy and self-control are illusory.

The Behavior of Organisms

Skinner first came to widespread attention when he published *The Behavior of Organisms* in 1938. In that book he made a distinction between *respondent* and *operant* behaviour. Respondent behaviour is the kind of behavior Pavlov studied. It is behaviour elicited by a known stimulus. By contrast, operant behaviour has no known eliciting stimulus. Operant behaviour may be studied by means of the apparatus known as a **Skinner box**, which is a sophisticated version of one of Thorndike's puzzle boxes. A white rat is placed in the box, which has a lever protruding from one side. At some point the rat will press the lever. The stimulus that elicits lever pressing is unknown. However, the experimenter has arranged things such that when the rat presses the lever, then a food pellet will be dispensed into the food tray. The food pellet is a *reinforcing stimulus* for pressing the lever. Reinforcing a response will increase the probability of its future occurrence. 'A reinforcing stimulus is defined as such by its power to produce the resulting change. There is no circularity about this; some stimuli are found to produce the change, others not, and they are classified as reinforcing and non-reinforcing accordingly' (Skinner, 1938: 62). Skinner's studies of the *reinforcement* of lever pressing were extensions of Thorndike's studies of cats in a puzzle box. In general, Skinner's investigations of the role of reinforcement in regulating human behaviour have been extremely influential.

According to Skinner, behaviour is regulated by *three-term contingencies* (Mazur, 1990: 121): the environment provides a *stimulus* situation, which elicits a *response*, which is followed by a *reinforcing stimulus*. Reinforcing stimuli may be either rewards or punishments. In general, rewards are environmental consequences that make the behaviour more probable, and punishments make behaviour

less probable. While the presence of a reward is 'positively reinforcing', its removal constitutes a form of 'negative punishment'. While the presence of a punishment depresses behaviour, its absence constitutes what Skinner called **negative reinforcement**: whatever behaviour caused the removal of the punishment is reinforced. Kimble (1993) has pointed out that this terminology can be quite confusing, and it is important to realize that *negative reinforcement* and *punishment* are not the same thing. 'Punishment' occurs when an aversive stimulus occurs as a consequence of a response. 'Negative reinforcement' occurs when a response gets the organism out of a noxious situation. Kimble's example is being told that 'if you do well enough on the earlier exam, then you don't have to take the final' (ibid., 254).

Skinner (1984: 477) considered learning to involve the natural selection of behaviours in a manner analogous to the evolutionary process. 'What we call behavior evolved as a set of functions furthering the interchange between the organism and environment. In a fairly stable world [behaviour] could be as much a part of the genetic endowment of a species as digestion, respiration, or any other biological function.' However, two processes evolved to deal with novel environments. 'Through respondent (Pavlovian) conditioning, responses prepared in advance by natural selection could come under the control of new stimuli. Through operant conditioning, new responses could be strengthened ("reinforced") by events which immediately followed them.'

Notice that the events *immediately* following behaviour have the greatest impact, while events that occur later on will have far less effect. In education, for example, children will be shaped by the immediate consequences of their actions in the classroom more than by the grades they get at the end of the year. 'Immediate reinforcement singles out some particular recent behavior, while long-run reinforcement is ambiguous, not indicating which of thousands of previous behaviors is responsible for it' (Platt, 1973: 643).

A Case History in Scientific Method

When Skinner, in *A Case History in Scientific Method* (1956), discussed the ways in which he made his discoveries, he applied the principles of his own psychology to his own creativity. He offered the following list of 'unformalized principles of scientific practice'. While at first these principles may sound frivolous, they are actually serious points about how psychologists actually do research, as opposed to how psychologists are taught that they should do research.

- 'When you run into something interesting, drop everything else and study it' (ibid., 223). In the course of doing research on one topic, Skinner accidentally discovered something intriguing. He put aside his original research question to take up this new one. Notice how Skinner's behaviour as a scientist was being regulated by its immediate consequences. Scientists learn in the same way that everyone else learns.
- 'Some ways of doing research are easier than others' (ibid., 224). Skinner recounts how he invented a precursor to the Skinner box because he did not want the trouble of constantly handling the animals in his experiments. So he built a piece of apparatus that fed the animal and kept track of its responses without his intervention. By keeping things simple, Skinner had also managed to create an apparatus that gathered very useful data.
- 'Some people are lucky' (ibid., 225). An accidental feature of the apparatus Skinner built was that it allowed him to keep track of the cumulative frequency with which the animal responded. These cumulative frequency curves showed how the animals' rate of responding was a function of different *schedules of reinforcement*. A schedule of reinforcement is 'a specification of the way in which reinforcers occur in time. Some simple schedules include *fixed ratio* (the last of a certain

number of responses is reinforced), *variable ratio* (the required number varies from one reinforcer to the next), fixed interval (the first response after a certain period of time has elapsed is reinforced), and variable interval (the interval varies from one reinforcer to the next)' (Skinner, 1980: 361; emphasis added). One of Skinner's most important contributions has been the extensive exploration of schedules of reinforcement as they influence behaviour, not only in the Skinner box but also in everyday life. For example, 'hunting and fishing are on a variable-ratio schedule. Incentive wages contain ratio elements. The craftsman or private contractor is essentially on piecework' (ibid., 195).
- 'Apparatuses sometimes break down' (Skinner, 1956: 225). As Epstein (1991) noted, Skinner's approach to creativity emphasized *generativity*: behaviour is inevitably and spontaneously novel, and thus we are continuously being presented with new opportunities to explore. When something goes wrong, it is an opportunity to learn something new.

All of Skinner's principles of research can be summarized by one word: *serendipity*, or 'the art of finding one thing while looking for something else' (Skinner, 1956: 227). Serendipity is defined by the *Oxford English Dictionary* as 'the faculty of making happy discoveries by accident'. The dictionary notes, as does Skinner, that the word was coined by Horace Walpole, an eighteenth-century British politician. Walpole used it to refer to people who 'were always making discoveries, by accident and sagacity, of things they were not in quest of'. In this statement Walpole is drawing attention to a feature of serendipity that is not always brought out, namely that it not only involves luck, but also requires sagacity. **Sagacity** is defined by the *OED* as the 'aptitude for investigation or discovery; keenness and soundness of judgment in the estimation of persons and conditions, and in the adaptation of means to ends'. Thus, Skinner's discoveries are not due to chance alone. Someone less sagacious than Skinner would never have realized what he or she had discovered.

The 'Baby Tender'

Like Watson, Skinner always explored the practical implications of his psychology. Many of his innovations and recommendations have been controversial, although the controversy surrounding some of his projects was not always of his own making. For example, consider his use of an *air crib* or 'baby tender' that he built for his second daughter, Debbie. 'Air entered through filters at the bottom and, after being warmed and moistened, moved upward through and around the edges of a tightly stretched canvas, which served as a mattress. A strip of sheeting ten yards long passed over the canvas, a clean section of which could be yanked into place in a few seconds' (Skinner, 1979: 275). Skinner built the baby tender in response to his wife Yvonne's concern that caring for a child during its first year was very onerous. Anyone who has parented a child during its first year will share Yvonne's concerns! 'When Debbie came home, she went directly into this comfortable space and began to enjoy its advantages. She wore only a diaper. Completely free to move about, she was soon pushing up, rolling over, and crawling. She breathed warm, moist filtered air, and her skin was never waterlogged with sweat or urine. Loud noises were muffled (though we could hear her from any part of the house), and a curtain pulled over the window shielded her from bright light when she was sleeping' (ibid., 276).

Like Watson before him, Skinner wrote about his innovative approach to child-rearing in the popular press, in particular the *Ladies Home Journal* (Skinner, 1945b). Upon doing so, Skinner discovered a fact that many popular writers also discover when their work is published, namely that it is often highly edited (and therefore potentially misleading), and its impact may not be what you intend. For example, the title of the article was 'Baby in a box', a title chosen by the editor, not by

Skinner. There were newspaper, radio, and film reports of the Skinners' home life, some of which led to 'the impression that we used a baby-tender to keep Debbie out of the way as a trouble-maker. . . . As people began to hear of the baby-tender by word of mouth, misunderstanding spread. Details of Debbie's actual life and the care we gave her were lost in the retelling. . . . It was natural to suppose that we were experimenting on our daughter as if she were a rat or a pigeon' (Skinner, 1979: 304–5). The rumours about Deborah Skinner's fate persisted for many years, and may even exist today. However, Deborah Skinner herself never attributed any negative consequences to her experience with the air crib, and there is no evidence that it harmed her in any way (Bjork, 1993: 133; Rutherford, 2000: 390).

Teaching Machines

Skinner's belief in the power of **positive reinforcement** was nowhere more evident than in his advocacy of what came to be called **teaching machines**. He argued that 'the most serious criticism of the current classroom is the relative infrequency of reinforcement' (Skinner, 1962 [1954]: 25), pointing out that a single teacher cannot possibly reward a classroom of students often enough so that a complex subject such as mathematics is properly learned. The usual classroom situation is reinforcing only when the child does the work required in order to avoid punishment of one kind or another, and this situation is far from ideal. 'In this welter of aversive consequences, getting the right answer is in itself an insignificant event, any effect of which is lost amid the anxieties, the boredom, and the aggressions which are the inevitable by products of aversive control' (ibid.). He suggested that a curriculum should be designed so that the correct responses constituting a discipline like mathematics could be developed systematically. Students should be reinforced for each response in a sequence that gradually builds up a discipline.

To provide such *programmed learning*, Skinner and his students built on ideas that had been advanced much earlier by Sidney Pressey (1926), who had described 'devices . . . which at once inform a student about the correctness of his answer to a question, and then lead him to the right answer' (Pressey, 1962 [1950]: 113). J.G. Holland, one of Skinner's associates, described how such a program was implemented at one university:

> At Harvard there is a self-instruction room with ten booths, each containing a machine. The student gets one set of material from the attendant and places it in the machines. He closes the machine and begins his studies.
>
> This machine presents one item of material at a time. The subject reads the statement which has one or more words missing and he completes the statement by writing in the answer space. He then raises the lever and a small shutter opens revealing the correct answer, and simultaneously his answer is moved under glass where it can be read and compared with the new-exposed correct answer. After comparing his answer with the correct answer the student indicates to the machine, with an appropriate movement of the lever, whether his answer was correct or incorrect and the next item appears in the window. All items answered wrong are repeated after he completes the set of items. Correctly answered items are not repeated.
>
> A critical feature of this machine is that it provides immediate reinforcement for correct answers. Being correct is known to be a reinforcer for humans. . . . In machine teaching reinforcement is immediate. (Holland, 1962 [1959]: 35–6)

This approach was criticized, as Skinner foresaw, by those who regarded it as treating children mechanically and not leading to 'understanding' but only to rote learning. Skinner saw these criticisms as misguided, since the machines were designed precisely to influence behaviour directly, and not deal with ephemeral matters such as 'understanding'. After all, from a behaviourist standpoint, 'understanding' was nothing but the appropriate behaviours. However, many parents resisted the use of 'machines' for teaching their children, believing they would necessarily be a cold and inadequate substitute for a human teacher (Rutherford, 2003: 11). In any case, much of what teaching machines were designed to do was later taken over by computer-aided instruction, which involved techniques adopted from cognitive psychology, an approach quite different from Skinner's that we will consider in detail in Chapter 14.

Skinner's Utopian and Dystopian Views

In his Utopian novel, **Walden Two**, Skinner (1948) envisioned a community regulated entirely by positive reinforcement. The original 'Walden' had, of course, been described by Henry David Thoreau, in 1854. Thoreau's 'Walden' evoked 'the theme of the sage who makes a voluntary break with society in order to discover his genuine self in a context of solitude and nature' (Frye, 1966: 46). Skinner's version of Utopia also involves a break with conventional society, but there is nothing solitary about it. Skinner's Utopia 'is an environment in which people just naturally do the things they need to do to maintain themselves (with something to spare for the future) and treat each other well, and then just naturally do a hundred other things they enjoy doing because they do not *have* to do them. And when I say natural, . . . I simply mean positively reinforced. The labor we save in Walden Two is the unnecessary labor forced upon people by a badly designed environment' (Skinner, 1987: 41). To the charge that behaviour controlled by positive reinforcement is not voluntary, Skinner replied that concepts like 'freedom' and 'dignity' are no more than feelings. One of his characters says that 'in Walden Two we behave under relatively undemanding contingencies of reinforcement, and we feel free' (ibid., 39).

Walden Two received mixed reviews, but it has continued to be widely read. Skinner wrote it in one summer, and some critics have suggested that it is not entirely serious (Frye, 1966: 32). However, the subsequent course of Skinner's career demonstrated his very serious concern about the drift of modern society. Platt (1973: 652) pointed out that Skinnerian theory is very good at describing some well-known situations in which people get 'started in some direction . . . that later proves to be unpleasant or lethal, and that they see no easy way to back out of or avoid.' One example is the so-called 'tragedy of the commons' (Hardin, 1968). Suppose that people are allowed freely to graze their cattle on public land. The more cows you graze, the more rewarding it is monetarily. However, the number of cows soon exceeds the number that can be supported. The consequence is that everyone loses because the free public pasturage has been exhausted. As Platt points out, the fact that one's actions are controlled by their immediate positive consequences can lead to a future that no one wants. You will undoubtedly be familiar with many examples of this scenario. Platt defined a behavioural trap as occurring when 'there is an opposition between the highly motivating short-run reward or punishment . . . and the long-run consequences' (Platt, 1973: 643). Smoking and overeating are possible examples of such traps.

A description of a society that is the opposite of a Utopia is called a **dystopia**, (e.g., Mumford, 1966), and towards the end of his life Skinner began increasingly to characterize the dystopian features of modern life in the West.

> Many of those who live in the Western democracies enjoy a reasonable degree of affluence, freedom, and security. . . . In spite of their privileges, many of them are bored, listless or depressed. They are not enjoying their lives. They do not like what they are doing; they are not doing what they like to do. In a word, they are unhappy. (Skinner, 1986: 568)

Skinner never swerved from his commitment to positive reinforcement as the best agent for social control, but he regarded contemporary Western societies as having created problems for themselves by moving away from important behavioural principles. Skinner argued that primitive people lived like other primates, hunting, gathering, and building shelters. However, 'a unique evolutionary step' occurred with the emergence of language because 'people could then tell as well as show each other what to do (Skinner, 1957). Extraordinarily complex social environments or cultures evolved [and these cultures] eroded the close relationships between organisms and the environment' (Skinner, 1986: 568). Culture comes to intervene between the organism and its environment, and the consequences, from Skinner's viewpoint, are not all good.

To understand why the development of our culture has had maladaptive consequences, Skinner (ibid., 569) believed that we needed to distinguish between the *pleasing* effects of reinforcement and the *strengthening* effects of reinforcement. Something can be pleasing but not strengthen any particular behaviour. Skinner argued that our culture provides us with things that please us, but that do not strengthen adaptive behaviour. What Skinner had in mind is quite straightforward, and an example is the salary system. It is pleasant to get a paycheque, or an allowance if you are a child, at the end of some time period, such as once a month or once a week. However pleasing such a monetary reward is, it does not strengthen any particular behaviour because it is not linked to any particular behaviour (ibid., 570). The key word is 'particular'. For example, a teacher gets paid for 'teaching', which is not a particular behaviour, but rather a class of behaviours (e.g., preparing reading lists, answering students' questions, preparing lectures, marking exams, and so on). Some behaviours may be more effective in producing learning than others, and only rigorously tying effective behaviours to 'reward' will strengthen them. As Skinner argued, 'If students do not learn is it their fault? No, their teachers have not arranged effective instructional contingencies. Is it then the teachers' fault? No, the culture has not arranged effective contingencies for them' (Skinner, 1980: 27).

Skinner was particularly concerned about the ease of access to rewarding activities such as television, movies, and a veritable cornucopia of food. All these things could be enjoyed without having to do anything to achieve them, and that is just the problem. Late twentieth-century North Americans seemed to have reached a state in which they could be rewarded for doing nothing at all. 'How much richer would the whole world be if the reinforcers in daily life were more effectively contingent on productive work' (Skinner, 1986: 573). Precisely how one would have effected the changes Skinner saw as necessary was not clear, but a worthwhile exercise would be to think through the ways in which social policy would have changed if Skinner's views had been taken seriously. What would have happened to child-rearing practices? Education? Communications? The family?

IMPORTANT NAMES, WORKS, AND CONCEPTS

Names and Works

Bekhterev, Vladimir
Brain Mechanisms and Intelligence
Franz, S.I.
Lashley, Karl S.
Loeb, Jacques

Pavlov, Ivan P.
Skinner, B.F.
Walden Two
Watson, John B.

Concepts

ablation
animal rights
animal welfare
animism
association reflex
conditioned reflexes
conditioned response
conditioned stimuli
dystopia
environmentalism
excitation
fear, rage, and love
homunculus
inhibition
localization of function controversy

negative reinforcement
phrenology
positive reinforcement
primary signalling system
promissory notes
reflexology
sagacity
secondary signalling system
serially ordered behaviours
Skinner box
teaching machines
tropisms
unconditioned reflexes
unconditioned response
unconditioned stimulus

RECOMMENDED READINGS

Pavlov

D.P. Todes presents an intriguing account of Pavlov's development in 'From the machine to the ghost within: Pavlov's transition from digestive physiology to conditional reflexes', *American Psychologist* 52 (1997): 947–55. G. Windholz, a leading Pavlov scholar, describes both the context within which Pavlov worked as well as some of the more subtle aspects of the theory in 'Pavlov and the Pavlovians in the laboratory', *Journal of the History of the Behavioral Sciences* 26 (1990): 64–74, and 'Pavlov's conceptualization of the dynamic stereotype in the theory of nervous activity', *American Journal of Psychology* 109 (1996): 287–95.

Watson

The experiences of Watson and Rayner's son are recounted in M.J. Hannush, 'John B. Watson remembered: An interview with James B. Watson', *Journal of the History of the Behavioral Sciences* 23 (1987): 137–52. Two volumes edited by R.H. Wozniak provide a useful introduction to early behaviourist writings: *Theoretical Roots of Early Behaviorism* and *Experimental and Comparative Roots of Early Behaviorism* (London: Routledge/Thomes Press, 1993).

Lashley

D.O. Hebb of McGill University was one of Lashley's most influential students. His *The Organization of Behavior* (New York: Wiley, 1949) has influenced generations of neuropsychologists, particularly in Canada. Hebb originally wanted Lashley to collaborate with him on this book, but Lashley refused (Hebb, 1980: 296). We will consider Hebb's work further in Chapter 11.

Skinner

For teaching machines, see L.T. Benjamin, 'A history of teaching machines', *American Psychologist* 43 (1988): 703–12. F.S. Keller presents a summation of Skinner's contributions in 'Burrhus Frederic Skinner (1904–1990)', *Journal of the History of the Behavioral Sciences* 27 (1991): 3–6. Skinner's *Beyond Freedom and Dignity* (1971) elicited widespread public reaction that is well described by A. Rutherford, 'B.F. Skinner's technology of behavior in American life: from consumer culture to counterculture', *Journal of the History of the Behavioral Sciences* 39 (2003): 1–23.

CHAPTER 9

GESTALT PSYCHOLOGY

Introduction

Gestalt psychology draws on ideas that have their roots in German culture. The 'Gestalt' concept itself was introduced by Goethe and had various meanings throughout the nineteenth century (Ash, 1995: 85ff.). The Gestalt psychologists took **Gestalt** to mean that there are many important phenomena, in disciplines as diverse as physics and psychology, 'whose characteristic properties cannot be reduced to the sum of their so-called parts' (Arnheim, 1998: 22). Our perception of everyday objects, such as tables and chairs, cannot be reduced to a set of sensations, and our behaviour, such as walking towards a destination, cannot be understood merely as a series of muscle movements. The approach of the Gestalt psychologists put them in opposition to associationists and behaviourists of all kinds. Strikingly different from the psychology practised in the United States, the holistic approach of Gestalt psychology was nonetheless very influential in all aspects of psychology, from the individual to the social.

When we turn to Gestalt psychology we encounter something radically different from either the introspectionism of Titchener or the behaviourism of Watson. In fact, Gestalt psychologists regarded both of these approaches as varieties of the same mistaken orientation to psychology. The differences between introspectionism and behaviourism, while important to their practitioners, were trivial compared with the fact that both exemplified a 'science intent upon a systematic collection of data, yet often excluding through that very activity precisely *that* which is most vivid and real in the living phenomena it studies. Somehow the thing that matters has eluded us' (Wertheimer, 1967a [1925]: 1). The 'thing that matters', which was missing from other approaches to psychology, was an appreciation of the fact that a psychological phenomenon is a *Gestalt*: an integrated whole that could not be understood solely in terms of the parts that made it up. Our experience of a melody, for example, is more than the sum of the individual notes. The melody is a whole, a unity, a Gestalt. Approaches such as introspectionism and behaviourism take things apart and analyze them to try to understand them from the bottom up, in terms of elements such as sensations or stimuli. Gestalt psychologists believed that such an approach is doomed to failure. 'There are wholes, the behavior of which is not determined by that of their individual elements, but where the part[s] are themselves determined by the intrinsic nature of the whole' (ibid., 2). There was no adequate translation of the German word 'Gestalt', and consequently it entered the English language as a term referring to unified wholes.

Another important way in which Gestalt psychology differed from American approaches such as functionalism and behaviourism was that it was less obviously concerned with practical applications and more attuned to topics, such as aesthetics, that had been relatively unappreciated by American psychology. American psychologists such as Watson and Skinner tended to view their scientific mission in terms of 'technological manipulation and control' of behaviour, while the Gestalt psychologists viewed science first and foremost 'as an attempt to understand and appreciate order in nature' (Ash, 1995: 411).

Gestalt psychology has many precursors, and we will consider some of them later in this chapter. However, it would be just as well to begin by considering a specific phenomenon—apparent motion—that marks the beginning of Gestalt psychology as a distinctive movement. The theoretical importance of this phenomenon was first appreciated by Max Wertheimer, who is usually considered to be the founder of Gestalt psychology.

Max Wertheimer (1880–1943)

The career of **Max Wertheimer** did not begin with the invention of Gestalt psychology. Born in Prague, he did his doctoral dissertation in 1904 at the University of Würzburg. His dissertation topic concerned the use of the *word association method* for the detection of complexes, a topic that was central to the development of Jung's career. Wertheimer and Jung squabbled about just who was the inventor of the method. Some recent opinion favours Wertheimer (Michael Wertheimer et al., 1992). However, Wertheimer's research interests subsequently moved in the direction that was to lead to the founding of Gestalt psychology. In particular, Wertheimer's studies at the University of Frankfurt of a form of apparent motion called 'phi phenomenon' attracted great attention.

Phi Phenomenon

Wertheimer was very skilful at using demonstrations to illustrate the Gestalt psychologists' contention that when we perceive things we tend to do so holistically. A **demonstration** is a simple, easily observed phenomenon, usually requiring only minimal apparatus, and that has the same effect for almost everyone. Figure 9.1 illustrates the famous Gestalt demonstration, called **phi phenomenon**. The two lights can be alternately turned on by means of the switch. Each light casts a different shadow on the screen. However, at the right rate of alternation, a participant does not see *two* shadows, but *one* shadow moving back and forth. 'So what?' you might think, and psychologists before Wertheimer did not think that apparent motion was a very interesting topic. They tended to give it an explanation like this: 'I regard this second object as identical with the first and conclude that the first has simply moved from the one place to the other' (Köhler, 1969

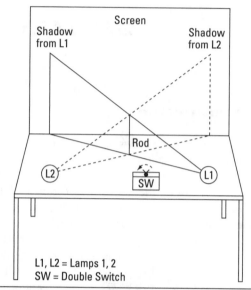

FIGURE 9.1
Apparatus to demonstrate apparent motion.
Source: Kohler, Wolfgang; *The Task of Gestalt Psychology*, © 1969 by Princeton University Press, 1997 renewed PUP. Reprinted by permission of Princeton University Press.

[1967]: 70). This explanation holds that apparent motion occurs as a result of an inference. However, Wertheimer insisted that the experience of apparent motion did not include any inferences. Rather, if one took the experience seriously, as it presented itself and without any theoretical bias, then you discovered a *perception* of motion, even though no stimulus moved. Wertheimer argued that there was a lot to be learned from phenomena like these.

For one thing, demonstrations such as phi phenomenon constituted evidence that our perception is not just a copy of the stimulus. Rather, our experience tends to be as simple as possible. Thus, when conditions allow, we perceive one thing moving, rather than two things flashing on and off.

The Minimum Principle

The phi phenomenon demonstrated to the Gestalt psychologists that experience could be simpler and

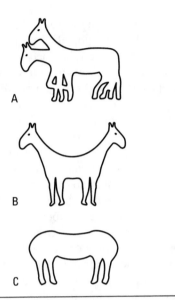

FIGURE 9.2
Simplicity versus likelihood.
Source:. Leeuwenberg and Boselie (1988).
Copyright © 1988 by the American Psychological
Association. Reprinted with permission of the
author and the APA.

more unified than the stimulus conditions giving rise to the experience. Instead of seeing two separate events, you see only one moving event. This illustrated a very general law—called the **minimum principle** (Köhler, 1967 [1920])—that not only applied to perception but to the organization of other systems as well.

The Gestalt psychologists pointed out that the minimum principle means that we do not perceive what is actually in the external world so much as we tend to organize our experience so that it is as simple as possible. This tendency towards simplicity is illustrated in Figure 9.2. Leeuwenberg and Boselie (1988) observed that one could see the shape shown in Figure 9.2A as either one rather strange animal, or as two horses, and we tend to see two horses. Since we have seen horses before, then we should be ready to see horses now, and so the fact that we see horses is not surprising. Notice further, however, that our perception is following the minimum principle because seeing two animals

that overlap is a less complex alternative than seeing one animal with two heads and extra legs. Thus, sometimes the simplest perception is also the most realistic one. However, in B and C we tend to see the simplest alternative rather than the most realistic one. We see one animal with two heads, or one animal with no heads, even though we are not likely ever to have encountered such creatures in the world. This illustrates the Gestalt contention that simplicity is a principle that guides our perception and may even override the effects of previous experience (e.g., Gottschaldt, 1967 [1926]).

The minimum principle has been investigated for a long time (Beck, 1982) and is one of the Gestalt ideas that has received support. Experience may tend towards the simplest possible state for the same reason that any system tends towards simplicity (Hatfield and Epstein, 1987). The laws that govern processes in the nervous system are, after all, the same laws that govern what happens in any other realm. From a Gestalt viewpoint, simplicity and coherence in experience emerge for the same sort of reason that they emerge in other structures. In an organism, simplicity in experience is the necessary outcome of basic processes in the brain. We will consider additional implications of this idea later in this chapter.

Precursors of Gestalt Psychology

Although Goethe introduced the term 'Gestalt', a more direct forerunner of Wertheimer's ideas was **Christian von Ehrenfels** (1859–1932), who suggested that experiences, such as that of a melody, should be understood as composed of individual sensations, such as those corresponding to the individual notes, plus a *Gestalt quality* that provided the form of the experience, i.e., the melody as a whole. Wertheimer rejected the existence of Gestalt qualities superimposed on sensations. In fact, Wertheimer rejected the existence of sensations as such. One could not understand experience by beginning with elementary units, such as sensations, because 'in psychology . . . the possibility of advance requires a procedure "from above", *not* "from below upward." Thus the comprehension of whole properties and whole-conditions *must* precede consideration of the real significance of "parts" (Wertheimer, 1967a: 15). One had to begin with a Gestalt and understand how parts are determined by the whole of which they are a part. This was not only true in psychology, but in other areas as well, such as physiology. 'The cells of an organism are *parts* of the whole and excitations occurring in them are thus to be viewed as part-processes functionally related to whole-processes of the entire organism' (ibid.). What was true of the individual organism was also true of the relations between people. 'When a group of people work together it rarely occurs . . . that they constitute a mere sum of independent Egos. Instead the common enterprise often becomes their mutual concern and each works *as* a meaningfully functioning part of the whole' (ibid., 6).

One of the true ancestors of Gestalt psychology is Kant, whom we considered in Chapter 2. Recall that Kant argued against the associationist notion that our experience was derived from events in the external world. Kant argued that our experience was a construction, not a mirror of external events. Kant believed that we impose cause and effect relationships *on* the world, rather than observing them *in* the world. Whenever we observe two events occurring close together in space and time there is a tendency for us to experience one as causing the other. Notice how similar Kant's view of causality is to the way in which we experience apparent motion. We spontaneously and inevitably see one thing moving when there are in fact two stationary objects. The phi phenomenon is an example of the tendency for us to impose an organization on our experience. Just as Kant opposed the associationist psychologies of the British empiricists, so the Gestalt psychologists opposed neo-associationist psychologies such as those espoused by structuralists and behaviourists.

Another movement with which Gestalt psychology had much in common is **phenome-**nology. As we saw in Chapter 4, Edmund Husserl (1965 [1910]) developed phenomenology as a philosophical method designed to describe consciousness as it presents itself to us, without any presuppositions as to its nature or purpose. It was this type of description of direct experience that Gestalt psychologists practised, rather than the type of description carried out by trained introspectionists. 'We call this kind of observation "phenomenology," a word that has several other meanings that must not be confused with ours. For us phenomenology means as naive and full a description of direct experience as possible' (Koffka, 1935: 73). The Gestalt psychologists made a sharp distinction between their phenomenological methods and introspection, which 'became unpopular in America because American psychologists saw its barrenness. But in their justified criticism they threw out the baby with the bath . . . tending to leave out phenomenology altogether' (ibid.). Thus, the Gestalt psychologists refused to go along with behaviourists like Watson and ban the study of experience altogether. Rather, they saw phenomenology as different from trained introspection because it was less biased and very useful as a starting point in psychological investigation. We will see as we go along precisely how the Gestalt psychologists used the phenomenological method.

The Laws of Perceptual Organization

The configurations in Figure 9.3 illustrate the **Gestalt laws of organization**. These laws, presented by Wertheimer (1958 [1923]), were intended to describe the basic ways in which we organize our experience as simply and coherently as possible. 'When we are presented with a number of stimuli, we do not as a rule experience a number of individual things. . . . Instead larger wholes . . . are given in experience; their arrangement and division are concrete and definite' (Wertheimer, 1967b [1923]: 72). For example, compare rows A and B in Figure 9.3. In line B there is a tendency to group the dots in pairs, but there is no such ten-

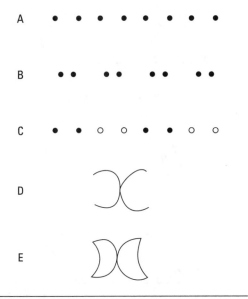

FIGURE 9.3
Examples of the Gestalt laws of organization.
Source: Palmer (1992: 437). Copyright © 1992, with
permission from Elsevier.

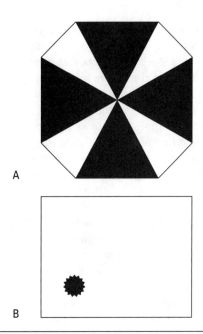

FIGURE 9.4
Which area is figural?

dency in A. This example illustrates the Gestalt law of *proximity*: we tend to group things together that are close together in space. In C, however, even though the dots are equidistant, we see them in pairs because of the law of *similarity*. In D, we see two lines crossing. We do not see 'two angles meeting at a point' (Palmer, 1992: 438). The principle operating here is called *good continuation*. However, in E, we *do* see two forms meeting at a point. This is because of the principle of *closure*, a very important gestalt principle stating that we tend to make our experience as complete as possible. To summarize: the Gestalt psychologists believed that *proximity*, *similarity*, *good continuation*, and *closure* are examples of principles that govern how our experience is organized (e.g., Coren and Girgus, 1980).

Figure and Ground
Another basic principle of perceptual organization is the distinction between figure and ground. In order for perception to occur it must be organized into something that stands out and to which we

pay attention (the figure) displayed against a background to which we tend not to pay attention. The importance of the distinction between figure and ground was discovered by Edgar Rubin (1958 [1915]). What is figural at any one time depends on many factors. Consider the configuration shown in Figure 9.4A. It is probably easiest to see a black cross as figure against a white background, but it is also possible to see a white cross against a black background. Whichever area is background appears to pass beneath the figure. This feature of figure/ground organization can be seen in Figure 9.4B. At first one might see a black seal displayed against a white background. However, it is also possible to see the black area as a cut-out of the white foreground revealing the black surface underneath.

Productive Thinking

Among Wertheimer's most influential works was ***Productive Thinking*** (1959). We considered one of the examples from that book in Figure 1.6. You may want to go back and review that problem now. Wertheimer liked to point out that improper teaching methods lead to a rote memorization of solutions that do not transfer well to new situations, while good teaching methods lead to a deep understanding of the structure of a problem. Such understanding involves grasping the Gestalt of a problem—how the parts of a problem are related to each other. Another Gestalt psychologist, George Katona, described this distinction:

> There are two kinds of learning. Connections established by the conditioned-reflex technique or by repeating the same contents or responses over and over again, as in all forms of drill, are characteristic of one kind of learning. Then we draw a thick dividing line. On the other side of the barrier we find processes of learning that are described by such expressions as 'apprehension of relations,' 'understanding of a procedure,' 'insight into a situation.' . . . 'Senseless' may be written on one side of the line where there is the depository of connections, and 'meaningful' on the other side, where the achievement brought about by learning may be called understanding. (Katona, 1967 [1940]: 5–6).

The difference between 'structurally blind' teaching methods and those that teach students principles that can be generalized to new situations is illustrated by the problem shown in Figure 9.5.

Students can be shown the parallelogram in Figure 9.5A and taught how to find its area by dropping a line from the upper left corner and a line from the upper right corner, and then connecting the base line to meet the second perpendicular. The area of the parallelogram is found by multiplying the height by the width of the new figure. Wertheimer (1959: 14–16) shows that students can learn this procedure by rote without understanding. In such a case, students will have a hard time generalizing the solution to a parallelogram such as that in Figure 9.5B. They can drop a line from the left-hand corner, but since it falls out-

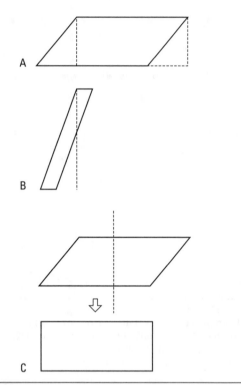

FIGURE 9.5
Finding the area of a parallelogram.

side the figure they do not know what to do. These 'structurally blind' students do not understand the nature of the solution. In order to teach the solution in a holistic manner, Wertheimer had students cut out the figure of a parallelogram from a piece of paper, and then tape together the two diagonal ends of the parallelogram to form a tube. When the tube is cut, the result is a rectangle, as shown in Figure 9.5C. Students can then understand that the parallelogram and the rectangle are equivalent, and thus the reason for multiplying the height by the width to get the area. Such structural understanding will generalize to any parallelogram. 'If we ask whether these features are learned, are acquired in accordance with the traditional associationist conception of past experience, this seems improbable indeed in the light of experiments concerning Gestalt laws, etc. They center in laws of organization and reasonable structure; they are an outcome of the structural way of working of our mind and brain rather than of blind associations' (ibid., 63).

Gestalt Psychology as a Philosophy

The Gestalt approach was not limited to psychology, but was also a theory of knowledge as well as a theory of ethics (e.g., Wertheimer, 1961a [1934], 1961b [1935]). 'Science is the will to truth. With the will to truth it stands or falls. Lower the standard even slightly and science becomes diseased at the core. Not only science, but [people]. The will to truth, pure and unadulterated, is among the essential conditions of [our] existence; if the standard is compromised [we] easily become a kind of tragic caricature of [ourselves]' (Wertheimer, 1961a: 19).

Wertheimer contrasted the Gestalt theory of truth with the correspondence theory of truth, according to which a statement is true if it corresponds to the facts and false if it does not. For example, consider a statement such as 'Linda assaulted Lisa.' The statement is true if Linda did indeed assault Lisa and false if she did not. However, such a simple theory of truth cannot be the whole story. Suppose Linda did not commit the act of assault herself, but hired someone else to do the dirty work. Is Linda guilty of assault or not? Usually we would regard Linda as guilty even though she did not physically perform the act. If Linda said, 'I did not assault Lisa', she would be telling the truth according to the correspondence theory. However, she would be lying according to the Gestalt theory.

The difference between the two theories can be illustrated by means of Figure 9.6. There is a fundamental difference between *pieces* and *parts* (Krecz, 1986). In general, parts are related to a whole, while pieces are arbitrary fragments. The heart is a part of your body, but a splinter is just a piece of wood. Something can be understood piecemeal, or as a part of a larger whole. 'Let us indicate piecemeal truth and falsity by t and f; and by T and F what we have called the real truth, in which the statement and its object are considered as parts in their related wholes' (Wertheimer,

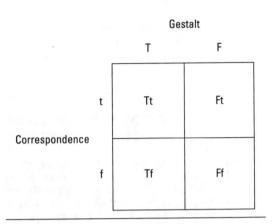

FIGURE 9.6
The Gestalt part-whole theory of truth compared to the correspondence theory of truth.

1961a: 21). In the preceding example to say Linda did not assault Lisa is to speak the truth in a piecemeal way (t). To say that Linda did not assault Lisa is to speak falsely in a deeper sense (F). Thus, in Figure 9.6, something can be true when considered merely as a piece (t), but false as a part (F). Something can also be false as a piece (f), but true as a part (T), 'for example an excellent caricature. It may be wrong in practically every detail and yet be a truer representation of its object than a photograph which is accurate in every detail' (ibid., 23). Similarly, to say that Linda assaulted Lisa is false as a piece (f), but true as a part (T).

An interesting consequence of the Gestalt theory of truth is that a fact can change its meaning depending on the context within which it is seen. To return to the Lisa/Linda example, we might at first believe that Linda did not assault Lisa if we were with Linda at the time and know that she was nowhere near the site of the assault. However, as our horizon expands we may become aware of new facts that change our original belief about Linda. As we see her behaviour as part of a larger whole, then our perception of her may change. At first we may understand things piecemeal, but then have our understanding radically changed as we see the part/whole relationships that actually determine a situation.

While Wertheimer was technically the founder of Gestalt psychology, the movement was essentially a group effort. Some facts about the members of the group, and their migration from Germany, are given in Box 9.1.

BOX 9.1

GESTALT PSYCHOLOGISTS MIGRATE TO THE UNITED STATES OF AMERICA

Other scholars joined Max Wertheimer, most notably Wolfgang Köhler, who had been trained in physics, Kurt Koffka, who wrote a classic text in Gestalt psychology, and Kurt Lewin, whose work was to have a profound influence on social psychology. We will consider their individual contributions in later sections of this chapter.

> Köhler, in 1920, became acting director, and soon afterward director, of the Psychological Institute of the University of Berlin. Wertheimer was already there, as was Kurt Lewin, whose work bears a significant relationship to Gestalt psychology. From that time until the coming of the Nazis to power, Gestalt psychology flourished. Graduate students were coming to the institute from a number of countries; the *Psychologische Forschung*, the journal of the Gestalt psychologists, was founded, and work was progressing in many directions. (Henle, 1986 [1977]: 119)

Robert M. Ogden (1877–1959), Dean of Arts and Sciences at Cornell, 'was the first and principal proponent of Gestalt psychology in America. He . . . brought Gestalt psychologists to his faculty as visiting professors. Koffka was a visiting professor . . . during 1924–1925; Köhler . . . in 1926 and again . . . in 1928; and Lewin . . . for two years, 1933–1935' (Dallenbach, 1959).

Many people associated with the Gestalt movement left Germany because they found life under the Nazis intolerable. A good example is Köhler. Because he was not a Jew, he was not dismissed from his university position. However:

> On November 3, 1933, the government decreed that professors must open their lectures with the Nazi salute. Köhler flipped his hand in a caricature of the salute and said:
> 'Ladies and gentlemen, I have just saluted you in a manner that the government

has decreed. I could not see how to avoid it.

> 'Still, I must say something about it. I am a professor of philosophy in this university, and this circumstance obligates me to be candid with you, my students. A professor who wished to disguise his views by word or by action would have no place here. You could no longer respect him; he could no longer have anything to say to you about philosophy or important human affairs.
> 'Therefore I say; the form of my salute was until recently the sign of very particular ideas in politics and elsewhere. If I want to be honest, and if I am to be respected by you, I must explain that, although I am prepared to give that salute, I do not share the ideology which it usually signifies.' (Henle, 1986 [1978]: 229)

Eventually, Köhler resigned from the Psychological Institute (Ash, 1995: 338). A Nazi director was appointed, and the Gestalt-trained students and assistants went elsewhere. Many of them ended up in settings very different from a university laboratory. Far from functioning as a unified whole, the Gestalt psychologists ended up being scattered throughout America and other parts of the world. You can imagine what an enormous adjustment they had to make. Although deeply appreciative of their welcome in the United States, they were also faced with learning the ways of a new culture at a time when their research should have been at its peak. Moreover, at that time in the United States, behaviourism was rampant, and behaviourism was not congenial to Gestalt ideas (Sokal, 1984). It was difficult under these circumstances to begin to train the next generation of Gestalt psychologists, and to a large extent there never was a next generation. However, Gestalt ideas percolated through American psychology, as we shall see, and not only had an effect but continue to influence psychological thinking.

Wolfgang Köhler
(1887–1967)

We have already considered some of the facts of Köhler's life in Box 9.1, but one additional fact is extremely important: During World War I **Wolfgang Köhler** was marooned on Tenerife, in the Canary Islands. He had been appointed Director of the Anthropoid Station there in 1913, and 'with the outbreak of World War I, he was effectively confined there, a circumstance that left him isolated but did not interfere with his scientific activities. Indeed this was an extraordinary productive period' (Asch, 1968a: 110–11). While on Tenerife Köhler did the work that was to result in one of his most influential publications, *The Mentality of Apes* (Köhler, 1956 [1925]).

The Mentality of Apes

Köhler described his work as concerned with testing 'the intelligence of the higher apes . . . whether they do not behave with intelligence and insight under conditions which require such behavior' (ibid., 3). Chimpanzees were useful subjects because they could be placed in an experimental situation and required to solve a problem that they may never have faced before. Köhler described the behaviour of one of his chimpanzees, Sultan, who was in a cage with fruit outside beyond his reach. There was a small stick in the cage, and a longer stick just outside the bars. The longer stick:

cannot be grasped with the hand. But it can be pulled within reach by means of the small stick. Sultan tries to reach the fruit with the smaller of the two sticks. Not succeeding, he tears at a piece of wire that projects from the netting of his cage, but that, too, is in vain. Then he gazes about him; (there are always in the course of these tests some long pauses, during which the animals scrutinize the whole visible area). He suddenly picks up the little stick once more, goes up to the bars directly opposite to the long stick, scratches it towards

him with the [small stick], seizes it, and goes with it to the point opposite to the objective, which he secures. From the moment his eyes fall upon the long stick, his procedure forms one consecutive whole . . . [and] follows, quite suddenly on an interval of hesitation and doubt. (Ibid., 155–6).

To Köhler, the behaviour Sultan displayed was insightful. Köhler provided examples of insight in different problem situations using different animals. By **insight**, Köhler meant the ability to understand how the parts of a situation are related to one another. Insight occurred spontaneously and suddenly, and involved a perceptual restructuring of the situation. The animal suddenly saw how to solve the problem. Insightful problem-solving was an all-or-none phenomenon: the animal saw the solution or it did not.

Köhler's chimpanzee experiments should be compared to Thorndike's puzzle box experiments, which we considered in Chapter 7. Thorndike's cats appeared to him to show no signs of anything that could be called insight, and they learned to escape by trial and error. Why is there such a difference between the results of Köhler and Thorndike? The Gestalt psychologists argued that Thorndike's cats had been placed in a situation in which there was nothing to be understood. How can a cat possibly understand the relation between pulling on a string and escaping from a box, since it is an entirely arbitrary relationship created by the experimenter. All the cat can do is respond by trial and error, and that is what it falls back on.

Some observers believed that Köhler's studies were persuasive. 'Taken as a whole, the behavior of the chimpanzee in solving these problems excludes interpretation in terms of accident or previous learning. . . . When all of the evidence is considered, one becomes convinced that the ape behaved intelligently or had what Köhler called *insight* into the situation' (Maier and Schneirla, 1964 [1935]: 469). However, other critics, particularly in America, felt that Köhler's experiments lacked the quantitative rigour of Thorndike's, and that his definition of 'insight' was too vague to make of it a scientific concept. In spite of these reservations, the concept of insight continued to be a focus of research (e.g., Metcalfe and Wiebe, 1987), albeit a controversial one (e.g., Weisberg and Alba, 1981).

The Nature of Learning

In a paper charmingly entitled 'Simple structural functions in the chimpanzee and the chicken', Köhler (1927 [1918]) considered a form of learning that was to prove problematic for associationist psychologists. The logic of Köhler's experiments is illustrated in Figure 9.7. Suppose chickens are presented with two shades of grey, labelled A and B 'Training' as shown in the top of Figure 9.7. Suppose further that the chickens are trained to peck at A (by placing corn on A, for example, but not on B). What has the chicken learned? From an associationist viewpoint, there has been a learned connection formed between the response of pecking and the stimulus A. Now look at the pair labelled A and C 'Test' in the top half of the figure. If, after training, the chicken is presented with these two stimuli, neither of which has corn on them, which will it choose to peck at? (Of course, in such an experiment the position of the two stimuli relative to each other must be systematically varied.) Since it learned to peck at A in the training phase of the experiment, should it not peck at A in the test phase? Actually, the chicken tends to peck at C. This is surprising from an associationist viewpoint, because the animal has not been reinforced for pecking at C, and so it should be a neutral stimulus (symbolized by '0').

Now consider the situation in the lower part of Figure 9.7. Once again the animal is trained to peck at the stimulus labelled A, but in the test phase the stimulus to which the animal learned *not* to respond is paired with a previously neutral stimulus. In this case the animal does not respond to the neutral stimulus, but to the stimulus to which it had learned not to respond.

From a Gestalt viewpoint, these results are not at all surprising. This is because the animals are responding to the *relationships* between stimuli, not

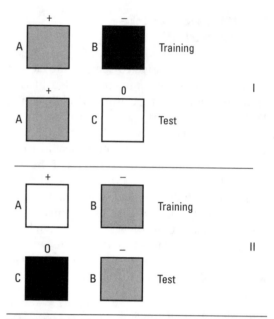

FIGURE 9.7
Köhler's transposition experiment.

to the stimuli themselves. Thus, in the situation in the top of Figure 9.7, the animal learns to respond to the *lighter* of two stimuli. Consequently, when faced with a choice between A and C, it chooses C because it is the lighter of the two. Similarly in the bottom portion of Figure 9.7, the animal learns to respond to the lighter of two stimuli, and so chooses B in the 'test' phase. Of course, the experiment could be done by training animals to choose the darker of two stimuli, in which case they would have chosen the darker stimulus on the test. It is only when one considers the relations between the parts of the situation—the Gestalt—that the animals' behaviour becomes comprehensible.

The ability to take a relationship acquired in one situation and apply it in another situation is called **transposition**. Transposition is a very important phenomenon as far as the Gestalt psychologists are concerned. Transposition of relationships is what enables someone to transfer what they have learned in one situation to another situation, as in the 'area of a parallelogram' problem we considered earlier. Köhler thought that his experiments showed that Gestalt principles do not apply only to humans but also in comparative psychology.

The Concept of Isomorphism

Before becoming a psychologist, Köhler had been trained as a physicist, and he developed definite ideas concerning how theoretical physics and psychology should inform each other (Arnheim, 1998). Köhler believed that there were parallels between the phenomena of psychology and those of physics. He liked to quote eminent physicists such as Clerk Maxwell and Max Planck to the effect that modern physics begins with whole systems and then proceeds to understand parts of those systems (e.g., Köhler, 1969: 60–2). For example, 'an electric circuit is a system precisely because the conditions prevailing at any given point are determined by those obtaining in all the other parts' (Köhler, 1967 [1920]: 19). Köhler (1969 [1967]: 77) argued that the Gestalt approach 'agreed with perfectly clear procedures and facts in natural science. In a sense, Gestalt psychology has . . . become a kind of application of field physics to essential parts of psychology and brain physiology.'

Köhler used the phrase 'field physics' to refer to the study of those regions, such as magnetic fields, that exert their influence over an entire area and that cannot be understood simply as a sum of local effects. From a Gestalt viewpoint, the brain was such a region, in which fields of electric current determined our experience.

> By this we mean that the neural functions and processes with which the perceptual facts are associated in each case are located in a continuous medium; and that the events in one part of this medium influence the events in other regions in a way that depends directly on the properties of both in their relation to each other. This is the conception with which all physicists work. The field theory of perception applies this simple scheme to the brain correlates of perceptual facts. (Köhler, 1960 [1940]: 55)

Field theory required a novel approach to the relation between experience and the brain, which Köhler named **isomorphism**. Isomorphism is a variant of psychophysical parallelism, the doctrine of the mind-brain relation held by many previous psychologists, including Titchener. Isomorphism goes beyond simple parallelism by claiming that there is not a simple point-for-point correspondence between events in the brain and events in experience. Rather the correspondence between brain and mind was *structural*: brain processes and experience shared the same Gestalt.

If isomorphism is correct, then changes in the structure of brain processes should yield corresponding changes in the structure of experience. Köhler (1971 [1965]; Köhler and Wallach, 1944) did some controversial experiments in an attempt to demonstrate this relationship. The general spirit of these investigations can be gathered by examining the configuration in Figure 9.8. This is a famous figure called a **Necker cube**, named after a geologist, Louis Albert Necker (1964 [1832]), who was the first to remark on its psychologically interesting properties. When you focus on the cube face labelled ABCD, then that face seems to be in the foreground. Eventually, however, the figure will reverse itself, and the face labelled EFGH will come to the foreground. Köhler's idea was that such alterations were produced as a result of prolonged inspection of a figure. The cortical representation of the figure becomes *satiated* (fatigued), or only weakly capable of supporting electrical fields, and so another part of the cortex then begins to represent the figure. As the cortical representation changes, so too does one's perception of it.

Köhler's satiation theory was roundly attacked by prominent psychologists, including Karl Lashley (Lashley et al., 1951) and Roger Sperry (Sperry and Milner, 1955). Using different procedures, Lashley and Sperry attempted 'to disturb the flow of visual currents in monkeys and cats, and then gave these animals tests with visual patterns, between which

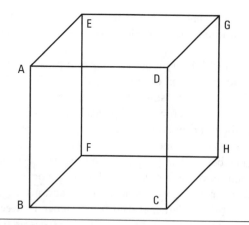

FIGURE 9.8
A Necker cube.

they had learned to choose before those measures were taken' (Köhler, 1965: 280). The fact that the animals could still make the discriminations between patterns in spite of the supposed disruption of brain currents was taken as evidence against Köhler's theory. 'Although Köhler subsequently argued that serious objections could be raised against these experiments, they were generally accepted as decisive by the psychological community, thus sounding the death knell for his theory of brain interaction through electrical fields' (Palmer, 1990: 291).

Although the specifics of Köhler's brain theory faded away, the general orientation remained viable. 'Even though Gestalt ideas about electrical fields were erroneous, the more general proposal that the brain is a dynamic system . . . —physical *Gestalten* in Köhler's terminology—may turn out to be correct' (Rock and Palmer, 1990: 90). In the last two decades of the twentieth century, there was a great deal of interest in *neural networks*, systems of neurons that function in a way analogous to the way Köhler described physical Gestalten. The dynamics of such systems appeared to be able to explain such Gestalt phenomena as unstable figures, of which the Necker cube is an illustration (Palmer, 1990). Thus, some of Köhler's ideas

remained alive, after having been totally written off. This is a good example of how ideas get recycled in psychology. A few years prior, no one would have predicted the resurrection of these particular ideas, and so this case also demonstrates the difficulty of predicting which ideas are good candidates for recycling.

Kurt Koffka (1886–1941)

Kurt Koffka attended the University of Berlin, but before going there 'he spent a year at the University of Edinburgh, where he came under the influence of several outstanding British scientists and scholars. This student year abroad, in addition to perfecting his use of the language, brought him in close touch with English-speaking people and laid the foundation for the international scientific recognition that was to be his' (Harrower, 1983: 253). This international recognition largely stemmed from a book he wrote in 1935, *Principles of Gestalt Psychology*, that became known as the 'Bible' of Gestalt psychology and a classic in the history of psychology (Henle, 1987).

Principles of Gestalt Psychology

Koffka's book introduced several important concepts. One was the distinction between the *geographic* and the *behavioural environment*. Koffka (1935: 27–8) presented an anecdote to clarify this distinction. Apparently a man had crossed a snow-covered plain and, upon reaching the other side, met another man. The second man expressed amazement that the first man had been foolhardy enough to cross a newly frozen lake. At which point the first man, realizing that he had crossed a lake rather than a plain, had a heart attack and died. The man's behaviour had been determined by his understanding of what his environment was. His behaviour was not determined by what the environment actually was.

The **geographic environment** is the environment as it 'actually is'. It is the environment that geographers tell us about, and it is the environment in which physical stimuli exist. The **behavioural environment** is the environment that actually determines our behaviour, and it can be quite different from the geographic environment. In the example of the man crossing the lake, the behavioural environment was different from the geographic one. It was only when the geographic environment entered the man's behavioural environment that it affected him (i.e., he had a heart attack). The behavioural environment contained the person's **phenomenal world** of lived experience. While the word 'phenomenal' has as one of its meanings 'extraordinary', in this context it refers to things as they are experienced—phenomena.

My behaviour can be an item in my behavioural environment, or it can be an item in someone else's behavioural environment. That is, I may understand my behaviour one way, and someone else may understand my behaviour in another way (ibid., 40). As psychologists we must be careful to understand someone else's behaviour in terms of that person's behavioural environment, not in terms of our own.

Why Do Things Look as They Do?

This was the fundamental psychological question as far as Koffka was concerned. Things do not appear to us as they 'really are', as items in the geographic environment. In fact, it is necessary to distinguish *distal stimuli*, which are things as they exist in the geographic environment, from *proximal stimuli*, which are the effects that distal stimuli have on the surface of a receptor organ. For example, we must distinguish between the actual, rectangular shape of a table top (a distal stimulus) from the shape it projects onto the surface of our retina (a proximal stimulus). The proximal stimulus may not be at all rectangular in form and will change as we move about in the geographic environment. (We considered this problem briefly in Box 1.4.)

Proximal stimuli are our only source of information about events in the 'real world', since we are not in direct contact with distal stimuli. Since proximal stimuli are almost always changing, how do we manage to experience a stable, coherent world? This question is particularly interesting in relation to the **perceptual constancies**, which refer to the fact that our *perception* of the properties of objects remains the same even though the proximal stimulus may change. For example, *shape constancy* refers to the fact that the perceived shape of an object (e.g., a table top) remains the same regardless of our viewing angle. *Size constancy* refers to the fact that the size of an object appears the same regardless of its distance from us (a problem addressed by Berkeley, and that we considered in Chapter 2). We do not perceive a car as getting smaller as it retreats down the road, but only as getting further away. How are such phenomena possible? The Gestalt answer, as presented by Koffka, is that the parts of the perceptual field remain in the same relationships to one another as the proximal stimulus changes. Thus, a car that is close to us can be compared in size with trees close to us. As we move away from that car, its size relative to the trees around it remains the same. Invariant relationships of this sort make the constancies possible.

The Growth of the Mind

The Gestalt psychologists are often said to be 'nativists'. However, this is actually not true: 'The Gestalt psychologists are not nativists. They do not accept the nativism-empiricism dichotomy; there is a third class of factors, invariant dynamics, that applies to all of nature' (Henle, 1986 [1977]: 123). In Köhler's words, 'An enormous part of the business of living can never, as such, have been affected by the changes introduced during evolution' (Köhler, 1969: 87). He continues: 'Why so much talk about inheritance, and so much about learning—but hardly ever a word about invariant dynamics? It is this invariant dynamics . . . which keeps organisms and their nervous systems going' (ibid., 90).

The charge of nativism has been levelled at the Gestalt psychologists because such principles as the Gestalt laws of organization seem to be 'innately determined' and not the result of learning.

However, the Gestalt psychologists did not conceive of such principles as the Gestalt laws of organization as being 'innately determined' in the sense of being the result of genetic programming. Rather, the Gestalt laws of organization were the necessary consequence of the operation of physical laws. Just as soap bubbles tend towards a spherical shape because of the operation of the minimum principle, so too does our perception tend towards *pragnanz* (good form) because of the operation of the minimum principle. The minimum principle is a physical law, and it would be a mistake to use either 'innate' or 'learned' to refer to such laws.

In *The Growth of the Mind*, Koffka presented a Gestalt approach to child psychology. Here he reviewed the competing approaches to the study of children, such as behaviourism, and presented the Gestalt alternative. He argued that the earliest experiences of children are figure/ground relationships, such as a 'luminous point set off from a uniform background; something cold at a place upon the skin set off from the usual temperature of the rest of the skin; the too cold or too warm milk in contrast with the temperature level of the mouth-cavity' (Koffka, 1959 [1928]: 146). Thus, Koffka rejected the associationist view that the earliest experiences were simple sensations. Moreover, Koffka claimed that infants did not have to learn the emotional meaning of their perceptions. Percepts have expressive qualities, or *physiognomic properties*, that are understood even by very young children.

In the middle of the first year the reaction to a 'friendly' face is quite different from the reaction to an 'angry' face. Furthermore, this difference is of a kind which obliges us to conclude that 'friendly' and 'angry' faces are phenomenal facts to the infant, and not mere distributions of light and shade. It seems quite impossible to explain this behavior by experience, upon the assumption that these phenomena arise from an original chaos of sensations in which single visual sensations combine with one another, together with pleasant or unpleasant consequences. (Ibid., 148–9).

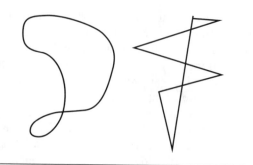

FIGURE 9.9
Which is the maluma and which is the takete?

A demonstration of Köhler's (1959 [1947]: 133–4) is often used to make the point that percepts have intrinsic emotional meanings. Köhler showed participants shapes like those in Figure 9.9 and asked them which one was the 'maluma' and which one was the 'takete' (pronounced takaytay). Generally speaking, participants have no difficulty assigning the 'maluma' label to figures like that on the left and the 'takete' label to figures like that on the right. Both the figure and the label seem to go together naturally, even though one may never have experienced them together before. The naturalness of the pairing of label and figure follows from the fact that both have the same expressive quality: soft and round for the 'maluma' sound and shape, and sharp and jagged for the 'takete' sound and shape. From a Gestalt viewpoint, physiognomic properties are intrinsic features of percepts and do not need to be learned.

Subsequent investigations of infant perception (e.g., Kellman and Spelke, 1983) suggested that infants may very well be capable of perceiving configurations at a very young age. However, there did not appear to be much evidence that infants' perception tended to follow the Gestalt laws of organization. Even though infant perception does appear to be well-organized, principles other than those proposed by the Gestalt psychologists may be necessary to explain it.

Kurt Lewin (1890–1947) and the Emergence of Social Psychology

Kurt Lewin began to study at the University of Berlin in 1910. He did his Ph.D. dissertation at the Psychological Institute under the relaxed supervision of Carl Stumpf:

> Stumpf gave his students an unusual degree of freedom, though to some it might seem more accurate to say 'lack of attention.' The thesis topic Lewin had selected was presented to Stumpf by an assistant, while Lewin himself waited in another room to learn if it would be acceptable. Lewin could not remember having ever discussed the matter with Stumpf between the time the assistant relayed word that his subject was approved and the day of his final examination four years later. (Marrow, 1969: 8)

However, at the Psychological Institute, Lewin was influenced by the emerging group of Gestalt psychologists. Decades later he openly disagreed with some aspects of Gestalt theory, such as its emphasis on physiological explanations of psychological events. Nevertheless, although he developed his own unique approach, his theory always bore the mark of the Gestalt influence. Lewin was also profoundly influenced by the neo-Kantian philosopher, Ernst Cassirer, who believed that people represent their experience by means of diverse **symbolic forms**, such as art, language, and mathematics (Gardner, 1982a). Each symbolic form is a different way of representing reality. Symbolic forms create the world we live in, in the sense that we do not experience the world except through them. Symbolic forms are not immutable, but develop throughout history and in the life of the individual. Cassirer's ideas were fundamental to Lewin's subsequent theory construction.

Before Lewin eventually migrated to the United States he had already developed an international reputation. In the United States, Lewin worked first at Cornell from 1933 to 1935, and then at the University of Iowa, 1935–44. In 1944 he became the Director of the Research Center for Group Dynamics at MIT. The German pronunciation of 'Lewin' sounds like 'Laveen'. After being in the United States for some time, Lewin began using an Americanized pronunciation of his name, which sounds like 'Loo-in' (Marrow, 1969: 177).

Lewin's aim was to create a practical psychology that took into account social influences on individual behaviour. One of his earliest interests was in humanizing Taylorism, the approach to work efficiency we considered in Chapter 7. Lewin argued that job satisfaction was an indispensable component of job performance. If a job was psychologically satisfying, then work was likely to be done efficiently. Here we can see an enduring theme in Lewin's work—an emphasis on understanding a person's behaviour as a function of personal goals. Lewin's theory of motivation is one of his major achievements.

As befits a theory with a Gestalt orientation, Lewin (e.g., 1951) called his approach a **field theory**. By a 'field' Lewin meant all the forces acting on an individual at a particular time. In psychology, the field in which we are interested is the person's **life space**. A 'life space' consists of the 'totality of facts which determine the behavior (B) of an individual at a certain moment. The life space (L) represents the totality of possible events. The life space includes the person (P) and the environment (E)' (Lewin, 1936: 216). This leads to the following formula:

$$B = f (P, E)$$

This formula may be read: 'Behaviour is a function of the person and the environment.' Remember that the person and the environment are both understood as part of the life space. If an event is not a part of the life space, then it cannot influence behaviour. Thus, Lewin's concept of a life space is similar to Koffka's concept of a behavioural environment. There are differences between the two conceptions, however. In Lewin's formulation, the person did not have to be aware of an event for it to be a part of the life space:

> Although Lewin held that phenomenal properties must be included in the psychological environment and although he favored use of participants' accounts of the world as they experience it, he did not *equate* the psychological environment with the phenomenal world. His basic criterion was whether any given fact had an effect on behavior, not whether it appeared in conscious awareness. He explicitly asserted that the life space should include within it 'unconscious' determinants of behavior. (Cartwright, 1959: 68)

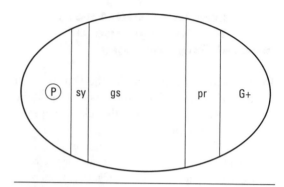

FIGURE 9.10
A life space. P, person; sy, senior year; gs, graduate school; pr, practice; G+, goal with positive valence.

Lewin's psychology is concerned with describing the parts of the life space and how these parts interact to produce behaviour. To describe the life space, Lewin made use of a version of *topology*, that branch of geometry concerned with the relations between parts of a space. This approach allowed Lewin to go beyond a verbal description of a life space and to represent life spaces by means of figures such as that in Figure 9.10, which is similar to one of Lewin's (1936: 48) examples. This figure represents some of the parts, or *regions*, of the life space of a person who wants to become a clinical psychologist. The person is a part of the life space, located in a particular region. The person, whom we will suppose is a junior, can imagine the tasks that lie ahead. These tasks represent *barriers* to the achievement of the final goal of becoming a clinical psychologist. Thus, the person must satisfy the requirements of entering senior year, at which time the person will be in a new region (sy). Getting into graduate school (gs) is the next barrier, and setting up a practice (pr) after graduating is the final barrier. The goal (G) provides a positive *valence* throughout the entire process. Valences may be positive or negative, and act as forces on the person in the life space.

Notice that in this example some of the regions of the life space are imaginary situations in the future. Events in the life space may be, but

need not be, representations of events in the real world. Events in the real world belong to what Lewin called the *foreign hull* that surrounds the life space. The life space itself has a membrane that is more or less *permeable* to events in the foreign hull. Some life spaces are highly permeable, while others are relatively impermeable. In the latter case, the person may seem to others to live in a world of his/her own. Remember, only events in the life space at the current time can influence behaviour.

In Figure 9.10, the person is represented inside a simple oval. However, one could represent the person in more detail. It was one of Lewin's principles of development that people tend to become more *differentiated* over time. Thus, children have a relatively simple, undifferentiated structure, while adults have a more differentiated structure. There may be regions of the person that are relatively inaccessible, corresponding to what other theorists term the 'unconscious'. Although there is a tendency towards *equilibrium* between regions, at any one time energy may not be distributed evenly throughout the person. Needs create *tension*, and consequently disequilibrium. The person acts to reduce this tension, but a particularly interesting situation for Lewin was the so-called 'barrier problem', in which a person must initially move away from an object with positive valence. For example, imagine a child who sees a desirable toy in another room through a plate-glass window. The child cannot move directly towards the object because the window is an impermeable barrier. Rather, the child must turn away from the toy, exit the current room, and then enter the room with the toy. Turning away from an object with positive valence creates tension in the person. However, by doing so the child is able in the end to reduce tension by achieving the desirable object. Being able to tolerate increased tension in the short run in order to relieve tension in the long run is an important developmental achievement.

The Zeigarnik Effect

The way tension influences psychological processes was masterfully delineated by one Lewin's students, **Bluma Zeigarnik** (1967 [1927]: 300), who asked the question, 'What is the relation between the status in memory of an activity which has been interrupted before it could be completed and of one which has not been interrupted?' Zeigarnik gave participants a series of tasks, half of which were interrupted before the person could complete them. After the experiment, participants were asked to recall the tasks they had been given. Generally speaking, participants remembered the interrupted tasks best.

> When the [participant] sets out to perform the operations required by one of these tasks there develops within [the participant] a quasi-need for completion of that task. This is like the occurrence of a tension system which tends towards resolution. Completing the task means resolving the tension system, or discharging the quasi-need. If a task is not completed, a state of tension remains and the quasi-need is unstilled. The memorial advantage enjoyed by interrupted tasks must be due to this continuation of the quasi-need. (Ibid., 305–6)

The **Zeigarnik effect** is interesting in part because it shows that it is not necessarily the most rewarding experiences that we tend to remember best. The Zeigarnik effect suggests instead that tension created within a region of the person will tend to persist, and cause us to remember unfinished business. You might want to see if this is true of your own experience. After an examination, which questions do you tend to recall first— the ones you know you answered correctly, or the ones you may have not answered correctly or did not have time to finish?

Group Dynamics

As Lewin's career progressed, he became increasingly interested in exploring applied, social issues. This led to the advocacy of **action research**, which refers to a program of research designed not only to gather data but also to lead directly to social change. Lewin (e.g., 1946; Lewin and Grabbe, 1945) recognized that new methods were required to overcome barriers to social change. It was not enough to attempt to change individuals, but rather the group within which the individual functioned had to undergo a transformation. The person is to the group as a part is to the whole, and a change in the dynamics of the group will also change the way the individual perceives and acts. The study of **group dynamics** became a central focus for Lewin and his group of researchers.

The interest in group dynamics spawned a very consequential experiment in what came to be called **sensitivity training**, or T-groups, where the 'T' stands for training. The spark for these groups came from the Connecticut State Inter-Racial Commission, which asked Lewin to assist in 'training leaders and conducting research on the most effective means for combating racial and religious prejudice in communities' (Marrow, 1969: 210). A group was assembled consisting of people who would be responsible for attempting to effect the desired changes. The most dramatic discovery of the resulting workshops was the effect on group members of feedback on their behaviour. As successive group experiments were conducted at what became the National Training Laboratories in Bethel, Maine, it began to appear as if the T-groups might be powerful agents of change (Benne, 1964). Being given the opportunity of 'seeing yourself as others see you' provided group participants with a valuable source of information about the effects of their behaviour on others. This in turn appeared to make participants more tolerant and accepting of both themselves and others. The T-group was subsequently taken up with enthusiasm by humanistic psychologists, whom we will consider in Chapter 13.

Fritz Heider (1896–1988)

Gestalt psychology shaped the thinking of some of the most influential social psychologists of the twentieth century, including **Fritz Heider** and Solomon Asch (Fiske and Taylor, 1991). We will discuss Asch in the next section. Heider had worked at the University of Berlin when the Gestalt movement was in its prime. Heider (1958: 4) acknowledged Lewin as a major influence on his thinking. He subsequently migrated to the United States and, after a period working at Smith College with Koffka, spent many years at the University of Kansas.

Heider's psychology of interpersonal relations begins with an analysis of **common-sense psychology**: 'In everyday life we form ideas about other people and about social situations. We interpret other people's actions and we predict what they will do under certain circumstances. Though these ideas are usually not formulated, they often function adequately' (ibid., 5). An inspection of common-sense psychology shows that several concepts are at the heart of the way people usually understand interpersonal relations. These include *giving versus taking; benefits versus harms;* and *liking versus disliking.* While this list is far from exhaustive, such concepts constitute dimensions along which our interpersonal experience can vary. One pole of this dimension tends to be psychologically positive, while the other is psychologically negative (Osgood and Richards, 1973).

Heider was particularly interested in the process whereby people tend to achieve **balanced states** in their relations with others. 'By a balanced state (or situation) is meant a harmonious state, one in which the entities comprising the situation and the feelings about them fit together without stress' (Heider, 1958: 180). A balanced state is a good Gestalt, while an unbalanced state may 'leave us with a feeling of disturbance that becomes relieved only when change within the situation takes place in such a way that a state of balance is achieved' (ibid.). Balanced and unbalanced states are easily represented by means of triads, which represent the relations between a person (*p*), another person (*o*), and a thing (*x*). A series of such *p-o-x* triads is shown in Figure 9.11. The triad at the top left represents a situation in which there are positive relations between all three components of the triad. For example, suppose you (*p*) like your roommate (*o*), and you both like to eat a vegetarian diet (*x*). This is a balanced state, and there is no need to change it. The triad at the top right is more problematic. Suppose that in this case you (*p*) like your roommate (*o*) as before, and your roommate is still a vegetarian, and so likes a meatless diet (*x*). You, however, have become tired of not eating any meat, and so your relation to the meatless diet (*x*) is negative. This is an unbalanced situation, and will set in motion processes designed to change the situation. In general, an unbalanced situation is one in which the product of the three relations is negative. Thus, in this triad a negative times a positive times a negative is negative. Notice that there are several things you could do to restore balance. For example, you could decide that you were mistaken about your roommate, and that you do not really like her after all. This would change the sign of the *p-o* relation to negative, and now a negative times a negative times a negative is positive. The situation is now balanced.

The triad at the lower left in Figure 9.11 is also balanced. In such a situation you (*p*) have a negative relation with another person (*o*), but a positive relation with something (*x*). This is balanced by the negative relation the other person has with *x*.

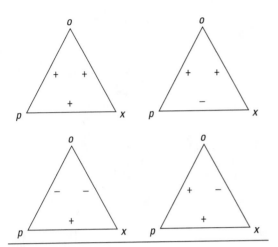

FIGURE 9.11
Examples of Heider's p-o-x triad.

For example, suppose you dislike your roommate, and your roommate dislikes vegetables, while you are a vegetarian. The final triad is unbalanced, however, because you (*p*) bear a positive relation to both *o* and *x*, while *o* and *x* bear a negative relation to each other. Suppose that you like your roommate and you are a vegetarian, but she hates vegetables. In this situation, there will be pressure to change one or more of these relationships. Perhaps you could persuade her to become a vegetarian.

Notice that the stress that produces change is generated by the structural relations between the parts of a triad. It is the Gestalt tendency towards *pragnanz*, or 'good form', that regulates interpersonal processes, just as it regulates most processes from a Gestalt viewpoint (Asch, 1968b: 166).

Solomon Asch (1907–96)

Solomon Asch was born in Warsaw but moved to New York City in 1920 (Gleitman et al., 1997). He did his graduate work at Columbia, where he studied under Woodworth. As a graduate student he learned a bit about Gestalt psychology and was drawn to it. He subsequently met and was influenced by Wertheimer, and then went to Swarthmore

College, which had become an unofficial 'headquarters' of Gestalt psychology, mostly because Köhler had settled there. After leaving Swarthmore, Asch was the founding director of the Institute for Cognitive Studies at Rutgers (Ceraso et al., 1990).

In addition to being the author of a standard text (Asch, 1952), Asch became known for two lines of research in social psychology: **forming impressions of personality** and **conformity**. We will consider both of these in turn.

Forming Impressions of Personality
Asch's (1946; Asch and Zukier,1984) studies of social cognition are consistent with a basic premise of Gestalt psychology, which is that we tend to experience events as coherent and related to one another. In the social sphere, the corresponding premise is that we experience people as psychological units. Concretely, this means that the individual attributes of people are treated as parts of an overall Gestalt. We do not perceive others as being merely the sum of their pieces. To illustrate this point, consider one of Asch's (1946) experiments. Participants were presented with one of two lists of traits. One group of participants heard a person described as 'intelligent, skillful, industrious, *warm*, determined, practical and cautious', while another group of participants heard a person described as described as 'intelligent, skillful, industrious, *cold*, determined, practical and cautious'. Notice that the difference between the two lists lies in only one word, *warm* in the first list and *cold* in the second list. Although the two lists differed by only one feature, the impressions formed by the two groups of participants were strikingly different. The group given the *warm* list formed an impression of the target person as someone who was 'wise, humorous, popular and imaginative', while the participants given the *cold* list formed an impression of the target person as not possessing these qualities. Thus, 'a change in one quality produces a fundamental change in the entire impression' (Asch, 1952: 210). People do not form an impression by simply adding up pieces of information about

others. If that were the way we form impressions, then changing only one attribute would have only a small effect and not alter the entire impression. Rather, we appear to relate personal qualities to each other as parts to a whole.

Conformity

Asch (ibid., 257) characterized the relation between a person and a group as a 'part-whole relation that depends on the recapitulation of the structure of the whole in the part'. This means that a group exerts its influence on an individual to the extent that the individual takes on the viewpoint of the group as a whole. Asch was particularly interested in situations in which a group member adopts the opinion of a group, even when this group opinion is clearly erroneous.

In a famous series of experiments, Asch (1955, 1956) presented groups of participants with a series of line judgement tasks. The groups consisted of seven to nine men each, and all but one of the group members were confederates of the experimenter. The confederates made incorrect judgements on some of their line judgements. For example, Figure 9.12 shows the standard and comparison lines for the trials on which the confederates deliberately chose the wrong line. Thus, the confederates would say that a 3¾-inch standard line was equal to a 3-inch comparison line, when it is obviously equal to the 3-inch comparison line. What about the one group member—the critical participant—who was not in on the deception? This person is 'in the position of a *minority of one* against a *wrong and unanimous* majority. Perhaps for the first time this person found a massed majority contradicting the clear evidence of his senses' (Asch, 1956: 3).

The results showed that the critical participants conformed to the majority's erroneous judgement on approximately 37 per cent of the trials. About 25 per cent of the participants never agreed with the majority on any trials, while some individuals conformed at every opportunity. Asch reported that individual differences were quite consistent across trials. The compliant participants appeared to be less self-confident, while the inde-

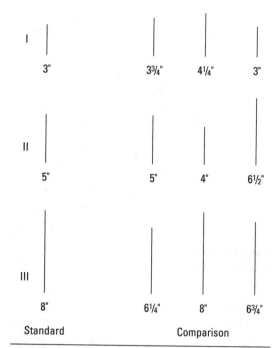

FIGURE 9.12
Standard and comparison lines.
Source: Asch (1956: 7).

pendent participants trusted their own experience. Asch (1955: 34) concluded that while 'life in society requires consensus', that 'consensus, in order to be productive, requires that each individual contribute independently out of his experience and insight.' The high rate of conformity 'raises questions about our ways of education and about the values that guide our conduct.' Would Asch's results be the same today?

Asch also did ground-breaking research in areas that did not utilize techniques peculiar to social psychology. One of these studies is reviewed in Box 9.2.

Kurt Goldstein (1878–1965)

Kurt Goldstein was one of the founding editors of *Psychologische Forschung*, the Gestalt psychologists' journal, and shared many of the Gestalt

BOX 9.2

FRAME OF REFERENCE

In 1992, the *Journal of Experimental Psychology: General* reprinted a series of 'classic articles' 'as part of the centennial celebration of the American Psychological Association' (Hunt, 1992: 403). One article so honoured was by Asch and Witkin (1992 [1948]), which refined some observations that had originally been made by Wertheimer (1912). The problem that Asch and Witkin explored involved the Gestalt notion of **frame of reference**. We perceive the orientation of objects in relation to a particular context. What counts as a vertical or as a horizontal direction is not determined absolutely, but depends on the frame of reference within which directions are understood. This frame of reference is not determined solely by the orientation of our bodies in relation to gravity. For example, as Asch and Witkin (1948: 325) observe, 'In [a] plane, disorientation may be so severe that the person can be upside down and perceive himself and the plane as upright, or suddenly see the sky where he believes the earth should be, and so on.' To demonstrate the power of frame of reference, Asch and Witkin asked participants to set a line to the vertical or horizontal orientation. Ordinarily this is a task that can be accomplished with great precision. However, in their experiment, the line is set with a rectangular frame, and the frame is tilted by 22°. In one condition,

the line is moved off the horizontal and gradually moved by the experimenter. The subject's task is to say when the line is oriented horizontally, that is, in line with the floor of the room in which the subject is standing. It turns out that the frame of reference tends to influence participants' judgements, so that they deviate from the 'true' horizontal and are more consistent with the frame provided. Thus, even vertical and horizontal directions, quite fundamental features of experience, are influenced by the context of which they are a part.

The concept of a frame of reference has been applied to many more situations in addition to space perception (Rock, 1992). One significant direction of research was to study individual differences in susceptibility to frame effects (e.g., Witkin et al., 1954). Those who were strongly affected by the frame of reference were termed *field dependent*, while those who were less influenced by the frame were termed *field independent*. This difference was extensively explored in relation to other personality characteristics, such as the tendency to be independent, have control of one's impulses, and have high self-esteem. The guiding idea of such research is that all aspects of the person, from perception to personality, are interrelated and influence each other.

psychologists' orienting attitudes. A physician, Goldstein had wide-ranging interests and collaborated with and influenced both psychologists and philosophers. 'Upon Hitler's assumption of power in 1933, Goldstein was briefly jailed, then released on condition he leave the country' (Simmel, 1968: 7) He lived in Amsterdam for a while and then moved to New York City where he was in private practice and affiliated with Columbia University. Subsequently he moved to the Boston area, where he became a close friend of Karl Lashley (ibid., 9).

Organismic Theory

Goldstein developed his distinctive approach partly through his attempts to rehabilitate thousands of brain-damaged soldiers who were casualties of World War I. He believed that associationist psychology was a barrier to understanding the brain-damaged person (Goldstein, 1967: 151). For example, the organism should not be conceived of as consisting of a set of separate mechanisms such as the reflex. In fact, reflexes did not operate independently of other organismic activity, but needed to be understood in relation to the activity of the whole organism. 'Practically nowhere can a simple stimulus response relationship, corresponding to the strict reflex concept, be directly observed' (Goldstein, 1963 [1939]: 79).

Rather than take an associationist approach, 'it is of the utmost importance that one evaluate any aspect of the human organism in relation to the condition of the organism in its totality. On this understanding is based what I have called *self realization*. The trend toward self-realization is not merely a stimulus but a driving force that puts the organism into action' (Goldstein, 1967: 151). Goldstein believed that self-realization, which he also called **self-actualization**, was the only drive that regulated behaviour. As we shall see in a later chapter, the concept of self-actualization was taken up and developed by humanistic psychologists such as Abraham Maslow.

> Under various conditions, various actions come into the foreground; and while they thereby seem to be directed toward different goals, they give the impression of independently existing drives. In reality, however, these various actions occur in accordance with the various capacities which belong to the nature of the organism, and occur in accordance with those instrumental processes which are then necessary prerequisites of the self-actualization of the organism. (Goldstein, 1963 [1939]: 197–8)

The **organismic approach** meant that the investigator should not evaluate behaviour mechanically, according to a set formula. For example, it made no sense to give a standardized test to a brain-damaged patient and simply count the right and wrong answers. One needed to observe all the behaviours that the person presented, 'giving no preference in the description to any special one' (Goldstein, 1967: 151). Description should be as full and painstakingly complete as possible. Although Goldstein invented tests to be used with brain-damaged patients (e.g., Goldstein and

Scheerer, 1941), these were intended to provide the investigator with a sample of the range of a patient's behaviour, which was then to be interpreted holistically.

The Abstract Attitude

Goldstein made a distinction between abstract and concrete performance.

> In 'concrete' performances a reaction is determined directly by a stimulus, is awakened by all that the individual perceives. The individual's procedure is somewhat passive, as if it were not he who had the initiative. In 'abstract' performances an action is not determined directly and immediately by a stimulus configuration but by the account of the situation which the individual gives to himself. The performance is thus more a primary action than a mere reaction, and it is a totally different way of *coming to terms with the outside world*. The individual has to consider the situation from various aspects, pick out the aspect which is essential, and act in a way appropriate to the whole situation. (Goldstein, 1963 [1940]: 59–60; emphasis added)

Pathology, in forms as disparate as brain damage and schizophrenia, undermines the **abstract attitude**. Such patients can respond only to the concrete properties of their current situation, they cannot imagine alternative possibilities. Goldstein (ibid., 54–5) described a patient who was asked to repeat the sentence 'The snow is black.' The patient was unable to do this without hesitating before the word 'black' or changing it to 'white'. Snow, after all, is not actually black. It requires an abstract attitude to imagine the possibility that snow *could* be black. The absence of an abstract attitude undermines the person's ability to come to terms with the world. The person lacking such an attitude is particularly susceptible to **anxiety**, which is an experience of dread. Anxiety differs from fear in that anxiety has no object, while fear is always fear of something. People may experience anxiety if they cannot adequately deal with the environment in which they find themselves. By only behaving concretely, damaged individuals can protect themselves from the catastrophic reaction that would result if they confronted the myriad possibilities that the world affords, and with which the abstract attitude enables healthy individuals to deal.

IMPORTANT NAMES, WORKS, AND CONCEPTS

Names and Works

Asch, Solomon

Goldstein, Kurt

Heider, Fritz

Koffka, Kurt

Köhler, Wolfgang

Lewin, Kurt

Principles of Gestalt Psychology

Productive Thinking

The Mentality of Apes

von Ehrenfels, Christian

Wertheimer, Max

Zeigarnik, Bluma

Concepts

abstract attitude

action research

anxiety

balanced states

behavioural environment

common sense psychology

conformity

demonstration

field theory

forming impressions of personality

frame of reference

geographic environment

Gestalt

Gestalt laws of organization

group dynamics

insight

isomorphism

life space

minimum principle

Necker cube

organismic approach

perceptual constancies

phenomenal world

phenomenology

phi phenomenon

self-actualization

sensitivity training

symbolic forms

transposition

Zeigarnik effect

RECOMMENDED READINGS

J.D. Seaman, 'On phi-phenomena', *Journal of the History of the Behavioral Sciences* 20 (1984): 3–8, provides historical background to research on apparent motion. Gestalt psychology is often confused with Gestalt therapy, which borrowed some of the concepts of Gestalt psychology, but applied them, along with other ideas from psychoanalysis, in a much looser way than was intended by the Gestalt psychologists themselves. See M. Henle, 'Gestalt psychology and Gestalt therapy', *Journal of the History of the Behavioral Sciences* 14 (1978): 23–32. Gestalt psychology has also had a profound influence on the psychology of art. A classic work is R. Arnheim, *Art and Visual Perception* (Berkeley: University of California Press, 1974). The possibility that Köhler was a German spy while he was marooned on Tenerife is explored in R. Ley, *A Whisper of Espionage: Wolfgang Köhler and the Apes of Tenerife* (Garden City Park, NY: Avery, 1990). M. van Elteren, 'Kurt Lewin as filmmaker and methodologist', *Canadian Psychologist* 33 (1992): 599–608, provides a fascinating account of the films that Lewin made in Berlin to illustrate various psychological issues, particularly the world of childhood. On Heider, see especially his *The Life of a Psychologist: An Autobiography* (Lawrence: University of Kansas Press, 1983). A detailed case history that beautifully illustrates the organismic method is E. Hanfmann et al., 'Case Ianuti: Extreme concretization of behavior due to damage of the brain cortex', *Psychological Monographs* 57, 4 (1944). For how the Gestalt psychologists were precursors of those who developed cognitive psychology, a topic we cover in Chapter 14, see C.D. Green, 'Where did the word "cognitive" come from anyway?', *Canadian Psychology* 37 (1996): 31–9, and D.J. Murray, *Gestalt Psychology and the Cognitive Revolution* (London: Harvest Wheatsheaf, 1995).

RESEARCH METHODS

Introduction

The search for the proper scientific method for psychology has been a part of its history at least since the nineteenth century. As we have already seen, numerous methods were developed, ranging from introspection to behavioural observation. In the early part of the twentieth century a new philosophy of science emerged. Called logical positivism, this approach appeared to justify a behaviourist methodology and cast doubt on Gestalt and psychoanalytic methods. Equally important was the development of statistical methods, which came to be widely accepted as providing the rules for designing experiments and understanding their results. The problem of ethics in research was made very salient due to possible cases of scientific fraud in psychology. Finally, the relation between methods for experimental and non-experimental data was also a topic of serious concern.

Virtually every student who majors in psychology must take a course in research methods. These methods have not existed since the beginning of time, but they do have a definite history. Psychology depends on particular *investigative practices* that generate 'products that count as scientific knowledge' (Danziger, 1987: 14). We have already met several of these investigative practices as we considered specific psychological practitioners. For example, Titchener was known for the investigative practice called introspection, while Watson was known for the investigative practice called methodological behaviourism. Each particular investigative practice must be justified in terms of prevailing standards at the time it is introduced. The research methods employed by one generation of psychologists may strike later generations as either obsolete or flawed. In this chapter we will consider some of the ways in which investigative practices developed in the first half of this century.

Philosophy of Science

Logical Positivism

In the 1920s a philosophy appeared that had a profound influence on psychology. This philosophy goes under various names, one of which is **logical positivism**, a philosophy that began with a group of physicists, logicians, and mathematicians working in Vienna. They were called the Vienna Circle, and they tried to formulate general principles for gathering knowledge, taking these rules from successful knowledge-gathering disciplines, such as physics and chemistry.

A good example of the application of logical positivism to psychology is a paper by **Rudolf Carnap** (1959 [1935]). Carnap, like other logical positivists, emphasized that knowledge is embodied in language. Thus, any science is at bottom a set of statements referring to observations. The truth of these statements must lie in their correspondence with these factual observations. How can we check to see if the statements we make are in correspondence with the facts? There must be a procedure for verifying statements. The truth or falsehood of statements must be objectively (i.e., publicly) determinable. This kind of thinking led to the **verification principle**, which stated that the meaning of a statement is its method of verification. 'Thus, whenever we ask about a sentence, "What does it mean?", what we expect is instruction as to the circumstances in which the sentence is to be used; we want a description of the conditions under which the sentence will form a true proposition, and of those which will make it false' (Schlick, 1962

[1938]: 30). From this viewpoint, unless we can describe a procedure for verifying our statements, then they are of no value; they are meaningless.

According to Carnap, when we do experiments, then our observations should be described by **protocol sentences**, which refer to publicly observable events. A meaningful statement is a statement that can be translated into these protocol sentences. If you are unable to translate a statement into protocol sentences then it is not a meaningful statement. Moreover, once you have translated a statement into protocol sentences, then the protocol sentences *are* the meaning of the statement. There is no *surplus meaning*, in that statements never mean more than the protocol sentences to which they refer.

To illustrate the procedure that Carnap is recommending, let us reconsider Wundt's experiment with metronomes that we considered in Chapter 4. Suppose that, as the experimenter, I play the metronome at a very slow speed (one beat every two seconds). Suppose further that I say, 'This metronome speed makes the participant feel sad.' How can a statement like that be meaningful, since I cannot observe the participant's emotional experience? However, if you think about it for a minute, you can see what appears to be a way out of this problem. How do you usually find out that someone is sad? Is it not by observing what they say and do? If someone says he or she feels sad, and if the person's facial expression is downcast and posture is slumped, then you might feel justified in saying 'That person feels sad.' Notice that all of your observations would have been objective: what the person says and his/her facial expression and posture. In Carnap's terms, your descriptions (of what the person said and of facial expression and posture) would be *protocol sentences*. These descriptions give meaning to your statement 'That person is sad.' Similarly, in Wundt's experiment, the experimenter can say, 'The participant feels sad' and mean by it that the participant says 'That beat makes me feel sad.' What the participant *says* is publicly observable. From Carnap's viewpoint, Wundt was mistaken in believing that the data of

psychology consisted of private experiences. In fact, the data of psychology consist of publicly observable occurrences in the form of behaviour, which includes verbal behaviour such as saying 'I feel sad.' Carnap's argument was consistent with the views of behaviourists such as Watson, who had argued that while introspection was inadmissible as an investigative practice, verbal reports could be studied simply as behaviour and not as referring to 'mental' phenomena.

Carnap went further and argued that psychology involved what he called **dispositional concepts**. Dispositional concepts are descriptions of lawful relationships between independent and dependent variables. Such statements have the following form: If X then Y, where X is a stimulus and Y is some behaviour. Thus, the following is a dispositional concept: If the metronome is played at one beat every two seconds, then the participant will say 'That beat makes me feel sad.'

Dispositional concepts are capable of being falsified. As a result of the influence of philosophers such as Karl Popper (1965), **falsifiability** came to be regarded as an important characteristic of scientific concepts. As long as your observations are consistent with a dispositional concept, then they can be retained as laws. However, should observations be inconsistent with a dispositional concept, then they must be replaced with a more likely alternative. This alternative can then be tested against publicly observable data until it is falsified. For Popper it was falsifiability that distinguished genuinely scientific approaches from non-scientific ones (McGinn, 2002).

Operationism

Psychologists were also influenced by another viewpoint quite similar to Carnap's recommendation that all psychological concepts ultimately refer to publicly observable occurrences. That viewpoint is usually associated with the physicist Percy Bridgman (1927) and is called **operationism** (Boring, 1945). Operationism requires the investigator to specify how a concept is to be measured.

Such specifications are called **operational definitions**. For any psychological concept whatsoever, a researcher should be able to give an operational definition of it. Thus, an operational definition of a concept such as *intelligence* might be the score a person obtains on an intelligence test (e.g., Boring, 1969 [1923]). Operational definitions were regarded as a way of making sure that psychological concepts refer to publicly observable events.

Where Did Psychologists Stand?

Logical positivism and operationism were welcomed most warmly by behaviourist psychologists. Indeed, we will see in the next chapter how a group of psychologists called *neo-behaviourists* explicitly developed theories in accordance with the tenets of logical positivism and operationism. Of the psychologists we have already considered, B.F. Skinner embraced operationism the most warmly (Green, 1992; Rogers, 1989). Skinner (1945: 271) argued that behaviourism was 'nothing more than a thoroughgoing operational analysis of traditional mentalistic concepts'. Skinner's point was that by defining concepts such as 'reward' in a completely objective, publicly observable way, behaviourists had rendered psychological concepts in a scientific manner.

Gestalt psychologists appeared to be damaged by the new philosophy of science. This was because of their preoccupation with the world as it is experienced, a subjectivity that cannot be expressed directly within a logical positivist framework. Gestalt concepts such as 'life space' evidently had surplus meaning, since no operational analysis of them could rid them of their reference to lived experience. By and large, the Gestalt psychologists resisted logical positivism and operationism as being *complete* philosophies of science, and argued for the continued inclusion of subjective experience as a legitimate part of psychology. The fact that operationism became widely accepted, particularly in America, was another reason why Gestalt psychology was relatively unacceptable for many psychologists.

Psychoanalysis was another movement that was roundly criticized by adherents of logical positivism and/or operationism. For example, Skinner (1961 [1953]: 121) said that 'Freud appears never to have considered the possibility of bringing the concepts and theories of a psychological science into contact with the rest of physical and biological science by the simple expedient of an operational analysis of terms.' Thus, psychoanalysis was out there on its own, speaking a language that had little or no scientific meaning because its concepts were not given scientific definitions. Many philosophers of science were just as critical. 'The theory is stated in language so vague and metaphorical that almost anything appears to be compatible with it' (Nagel, 1960: 41). This is to say that psychoanalytic theory is untestable. No matter what happens, the theory can be made to explain it. The process of deriving hypotheses that can be falsified is not possible in principle because the theory is too imprecise. Apologists for psychoanalysis agreed that the theory was in need of 'data obtained in controlled experiments', but argued that the theory was extremely complex and could not easily be given an operational analysis without oversimplifying it (e.g., Rapaport, 1959: 159–63). However, academic psychologists were largely unsympathetic to the psychoanalysts' call for patience, believing instead that the theory was simply unfalsifiable (Crews, 1996, 1998).

In general, the rise of logical positivism and operationism coincided with the dominance of behaviourism in America. Methodological behaviourism met the requirements of scientific method as prescribed by operationists, and until the end of the 1950s methodological behaviourism seemed to most academic psychologists to be common sense.

Criticisms of Operationism

Critics of operationism, such as **Sigmund Koch** (1917–96) (Leary et al., 1998), have claimed that some psychologists, including the ones we will examine in the next chapter, went overboard in their enthusiasm for operational definitions. Koch

(1992: 265) observed that Bridgman himself was less of a doctrinaire operationist than were many psychologists. 'From an early point on, Bridgman repeatedly indicated that operations are necessary conditions for meanings, not *sufficient* ones. More he *stressed*—constantly and emphatically—that he was not advocating a theory or method of *definition* . . . but only a method for analyzing, perhaps sharpening, the meanings of concepts *already in place*. He did not advocate "operational *definition*" but rather "operational *analysis*", or "operational *method*".' On this account, operationism was not a way of creating psychological concepts, but one way among many of analyzing their meaning. The meaning of a psychological concept would not be reduced to its operational definition, but could mean more than the operations used to investigate it. Koch cited the following paragraph from Bridgman (1940: 36) to convey this point:

> The process that I want to call scientific is a process that involves the continual apprehension of meaning, the constant appraisal of significance, accompanied by a running act of checking to be sure that I am doing what I want to do, and of judging correctness or incorrectness. This checking and judging and accepting, that together constitute understanding, are done by me and can be done by no one else. They are as private as my toothache, and without them science is dead.

This contrast between the personal, subjective and the impersonal, objective sides of scientific inquiry was echoed in the distinction between the *context of discovery* versus the *context of justification* (Gigerenzer, 1991; Reichenbach, 1938). The thinking that leads to the *discovery* of a method for investigating a problem may be quite different from the thinking that goes into presenting a completed study for consumption by the rest of the scientific community. The latter involves *justifying* the investigative procedure that was used, rather than explaining how the investigator came up with it in the first place. Operationism in psychology placed great emphasis on the context of justification, and

as we shall see in later chapters, many psychologists began to feel that too much of the subjective side of psychological inquiry had been sacrificed in the process.

Experimental Methods

Statistical Inference

As Gigerenzer and Murray (1987: 18) pointed out, experiments done in Wundt's day consisted largely of exhaustive descriptions of individual cases, with no explicit rules for making generalizations. Such experiments proved to be not very convincing to most twentieth-century academic psychologists, partly because, as we saw earlier, Wundt's experiments appeared to rely on subjective interpretation that seemed, to many scholars, to be unscientific. Some psychologists, such as Ebbinghaus and Thorndike, pioneered the use of graphs to represent their data, a technique that stood the test of time (Smith et al., 2000). However, the most influential development in the analysis of experimental data was the work of Sir R.A. Fisher, who is generally acknowledged to be one of the most important methodologists of all time (Rao, 1992).

R.A. Fisher (1890-1962)

Fisher's Approach to Designing Experiments

R.A. Fisher was an English gentleman who made his major contributions in the 1920s, and so the research that amused him might not appeal to everyone today. For example, one experiment he considered involved evaluating the claim made by 'a lady [who] declares that by tasting a cup of tea she can discriminate whether the milk or the tea . . . was first added to the cup' (Fisher, 1991 [1925]: 11). This must have been a person of some refinement and gentility, since few people would claim to be able to tell whether the milk or the tea had been added first! It is useful to consider how one would put such claims to an experimental test.

In designing an experiment to test tea-tasting ability, Fisher proposed to give the participant eight cups of tea, four with milk added to tea, and four with tea added to milk. In Fisher's experiment, the participant knows that there will be four cups of each kind, but the order in which the cups are given to the participant is *random*. A random order is not 'determined arbitrarily by human choice' (ibid.) but by a purely chance procedure such as rolling dice. Why did Fisher insist on a random order? One reason is that a random order of presentation makes it possible to determine how likely the participant is to make the correct choices by chance alone. It turns out that there are 70 different orders in which the cups can be presented, and so the participant has one chance in 70 of making the correct choices. The odds are heavily against the participant accomplishing this task by chance alone. Thus, should the participant make the correct choices, we would feel fairly secure in believing that the participant did not make the correct choices by chance.

Fisher notes that we could make the task even more difficult to accomplish by chance alone by increasing the number of cups. Alternatively, we could make the task easier to accomplish by chance alone by decreasing the number of cups. What degree of chance are we willing to accept? Fisher proposed that researchers adopt a criterion of one chance in 20, or 5 per cent. To illustrate what this means, consider a tea-tasting experiment in which there are six cups. As Fisher points out, there are 20 different ways in which the six cups can be presented. Therefore, if a participant gets the order right, there is only a one in 20, or 5 per cent, likelihood that the participant did it just by luck.

The Null Hypothesis

According to Fisher, when we do an experiment we typically assume that any differences between the experimental conditions are due only to chance; that is, we establish a **null hypothesis**. In this case, 'null' means 'no difference'. In the

tea-tasting experiment, the null hypothesis is that the order in which milk and tea are mixed makes no difference. Should the participant guess the sequence of cups correctly, then we may reject the null hypothesis, which 'is never proved or established, but is possibly disproved, in the course of experimentation. Every experiment may be said to exist only in order to give the facts a chance of disproving the null hypothesis' (ibid., 16).

There has been much controversy surrounding the concept of the null hypothesis (Cohen, 1994; Gigerenzer and Murray, 1987; Tryon, 2001; Wilkinson and the Task Force on Statistical Inference, 1999). One key aspect of the null hypothesis is that it can only be rejected, and never accepted. One can only falsify the null hypothesis. By so doing, one does not confirm an alternative research hypothesis. This point is worth re-emphasizing. If the data allow the psychologists to reject the null hypothesis, then that does not mean that any particular alternative hypothesis is correct. It only means that the null hypothesis is apparently false. Thus, Fisher's concept of a null hypothesis is consistent with an emphasis on falsifiability. Psychological hypotheses can only be falsified, they cannot be proved. A hypothesis that is not falsified is provisionally retained and subject to future test.

From a statistical viewpoint, Fisher realized that the decision to reject the null hypothesis is not a completely straightforward matter. As we saw above, Fisher recommended that we tolerate a 5 per cent chance of making the wrong decision. In the tea-tasting example, a participant who guessed all six cups correctly would enable the investigator to reject the null hypothesis, because there would only be a 5 per cent chance that the investigator was making a mistake. However, Fisher believed that doing the experiment only once is not as persuasive as *replicating the results*. If the participant could guess all six cups correctly over and over again, then that would be more persuasive than simply getting the order right once. However, the experimenter would still need to be mindful of the kind of bias reviewed in Box 10.1.

BOX 10.1

THE 'CLEVER HANS' PHENOMENON

The story of Clever Hans is one of the most famous in the history of psychology, and has played an important role in challenging psychologists' methodological practices (Suls and Rosnow, 1988). Hans was a horse who could answer questions by tapping his hoof. For example, if asked the sum of 3 plus 2, the horse would tap 5 times. Hans could also answer questions of much greater complexity, and was a truly mysterious phenomenon in his day. By the use of careful observation and experimental procedure, a psychologist named **Oscar Pfungst** (1911) showed how Hans did it. For one thing, Pfungst discovered that the kind of spectators made a difference. If the spectators knew the right answer to the question Hans was asked, then Hans would also get the right answer. However, if the spectators did not know the right answer, then Hans did not know either. It turned out that Hans was picking up information from the spectators' behaviour. They would make subtle head movements when Hans reached the right answer. Hans was apparently being influenced by this behaviour, not arriving at answers on his own.

The importance of the 'Clever Hans phenomenon' to psychological research was emphasized in a series of articles by Robert Rosenthal (1966, 1967), who pointed out that experimental participants may play the role of 'Clever Hans', picking up subtle cues from the experimenter that tell the participant what the experimenter expects the participant to do. In other words, the experimenter may unwittingly bias the outcome of the experiment. There may be subtle interactions between experimenter and participant such that each one influences the other's behaviour in ways that may escape notice. By the 1960s experimental psychologists began to realize that elaborate precautions may be necessary to eliminate the Clever Hans phenomenon, such as double-blind procedures to ensure that neither the experimenter nor the participant knows into what experimental condition the participant has been placed.

Suppose, for example, that we are interested in testing the efficacy of aspirin in preventing heart attacks. One way to do so would be to divide participants randomly into two groups. One group would take aspirin regularly, while the other would take a placebo (i.e., something that looks just like aspirin but has no known effect) regularly. If aspirin has a real effect, then those who take it regularly will have fewer heart attacks than those who take the placebo. It is essential that neither the experimenters nor the participants know who is in which group (i.e., they are both 'blind'). If the participants know into which group they have been placed, then their expectations may bias the results. Similarly, the experimenters may (consciously or unconsciously) influence the results to make them come out in accordance with their expectations. The study just described has actually been done, with aspirin having a small but positive effect (Rosnow and Rosenthal, 1989: 1279).

Although Fisher realized that the 5 per cent level of significance was completely arbitrary, many psychologists adopted it as an article of faith. By the end of the 1950s, the achievement of 'statistically significant' results was an established goal of psychological research, and to a large extent 'the quality of research [was] measured by the level of significance' because of a belief that 'the level of significance reflects the degree of confidence that the result is *repeatable* and that it specifies the *magnitude* of the effect. However, both assertions are incorrect' (Gigerenzer and Murray, 1987: 23–4). Statistical significance, as Fisher understood, is no substitute for repeatability. Gradually, criticisms of the reliance on significance testing began to appear (e.g., Bakan, 1966), but many psychologists continued to rely on the practice nonetheless (e.g., Rosnow and Rosenthal, 1989: 1277).

Correlational Methods

By no means all academic psychologists adopted experimental methods. Many psychologists made use of **correlational methods**. Although, strictly speaking, correlational methods have the same underlying principles as experimental designs (Cohen, 1968), they are a sufficiently different tradition to merit separate treatment (e.g., Cronbach, 1978 [1957]; Hilgard, 1987: ch. 20). In a typical correlational study, the investigator obtains a number of different measures on a set of participants. Correlational methods are usually traced back to Francis Galton. For example, in a study we referred to in Chapter 3, Galton obtained measures for several hundred English participants in the nineteenth century (Johnson et al., 1985: 887). These included social class and physical measures such as height. For Galton's data, social class can be measured by different occupations, ranging from professional (e.g., physicians) to unskilled workers. There was a very close relationship between social class and the physical measures, with upper-class participants being larger, leading to hypotheses about the possible causes of such differences (e.g., better diet for upper-class participants).

Charles Spearman (1863–1945)

One of the central figures in the development of correlational methods was **Charles Spearman**, who did most of his work at the University of London. Together with Cyril Burt, he laid the groundwork for what became **factor analysis** (Lovie and Lovie, 1993). Factor analysis begins with a set of correlations between a number of measures, such as different mental tests. Factor analysis consists of statistical procedures for deriving a number of underlying factors to describe the structure of the set of correlation coefficients. As a result of his analysis of the pattern of correlations between different tests of mental abilities, Spearman (1904) proposed what came to be called a **two-factor theory of intelligence**. This theory held that:

every individual measurement of every ability . . . can be divided into two independent parts. . . . The one part has been called the 'general factor' and denoted by the letter g; it is so named because, although varying freely from individual to individual, it remains the same for any one individual. . . . The second part has been called the 'specific factor' and denoted by the letter s. It not only varies from individual to individual, but even for any one individual from each ability to another. (Spearman, 1970 [1932]: 75)

The two-factor theory is illustrated in Figure 10.1. It is a hierarchical model, in which **general intelligence**, or **g**, underlies a set of specific abilities. The specific factors are represented by the abilities to do well in different school subjects, such as French, English, Mathematics, and Music. Spearman found that these specific abilities were all correlated with each another, such that people who tend to do well in one specific ability tend to do well in the others, and vice versa. However, the inter-correlations between specific abilities are not perfect. Each specific ability was seen as determined in part by g and in part by circumstances specific to that ability. Thus, someone could have a high level of g but varying specific abilities. Spearman was able to formulate a statistical criterion that enabled him to estimate the amount of g that contributed to each specific ability.

Spearman believed that g represented the amount of **mental energy** available to an individual. This was a general, unspecific energy that

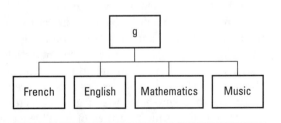

FIGURE 10.1
Spearman's two-factor theory of intelligence.

could be directed towards the specific abilities. The specific abilities were regarded as engines that were driven by g. Spearman argued that the overall level of g was innately determined. After reviewing a wide range of sources, including the Army Alpha data we considered in Chapter 7, he concluded:

> On the whole, there has been found a large body of evidence that races do differ from one another, at any rate in respect of g. And there have been some indications—as yet hardly decisive—that such differences persist even when the members of the respective races are living in the same environment, educational and otherwise; to this extent, then, the cause would appear fairly traceable to inheritance. Nevertheless such racial differences, even if truly existing, are indubitably very small as compared with those that exist between individuals belonging to one and the same race. (Ibid., 380)

Spearman exercised considerable influence on the way succeeding generations of psychologists have regarded intelligence. Many subsequent commentators argued that 'when the term intelligence is used it should refer to g, the factor common to all tests of complex problem solving' (Jensen, 1972: 77). When it came to estimating the effects of education on intelligence, Spearman concluded that heredity was more important than education in determining g, but that the specific factors could be shaped by schooling.

Cyril Burt (1883–1971)

Cyril Burt was Spearman's co-worker. Burt apparently invented some of the basic statistical techniques underlying factor analysis (Loehlin, 1992: 21), although his precise role is controversial (Lovie and Lovie, 1993), as are so many things about him. The use of factor analysis allowed Spearman to claim that g was a general factor underlying all specific measures of intelligence. Although Burt believed in a somewhat more complex theory of intelligence than did Spearman, he

nonetheless endorsed the hypothesis that g was the most important factor in intelligence.

Throughout its history, g has been a controversial concept. Burt believed that tests of g could be used to identify the educational setting for which the child was best suited. If g was believed to be inherited, such a practice would mean that schools would be stratified on the basis of inherited ability. An additional consequence of believing that g is inherited is that it would appear to be foolish to try to improve g by means of educational interventions, such as providing remedial programs for those whose test scores are low. Thus, there are serious social policy consequences of the belief that intelligence is inherited. Burt was clearly on the side of those who believed in streaming education so as to put those who tested high on intelligence tests in different streams than those who tested low on such tests.

Burt retired from his position at the University of London in 1950. However, after his retirement he continued to publish papers containing data purporting to demonstrate that g was largely inherited. His most provocative data came from studies of identical (monozygotic) twins reared apart. Such twins are genetically the same, and are traditionally a much sought after source of information concerning the degree to which genes determine behaviour (Loehlin, 1989). Burt reported that for monozygotic twins reared together, there is a very high correlation between intelligence test scores, and that this correlation is only slightly lower for monozygotic twins reared apart. 'The correlations of identical twins with their elder or younger sibs usually averaged about .40–.50; the correlations between identical twins themselves often rose to .70 or over, even when they had been reared apart' (Burt, 1972: 179). Data like these reinforced the notion that changing the environment will produce relatively little change in intelligence and that genetic determinants are the most important.

In a paper written on the occasion of receiving an award from the American Psychological Association, but published one year after his death, Burt (1972) reviewed his accomplishments over a career that had spanned the first six decades of this century. He repeated his argument that differences in g reflected differences in the potential of the individual's brain, and, as such, were similar to other inherited biological capacities. Burt concluded that 'each individual's innate capacity sets a fixed upper limit to what in actual practice he is likely to achieve', but he qualified this conclusion by saying that 'a given genetic endowment is compatible with a whole range of developmental reactions and consequently of acquired attainments. All a knowledge of a child's genetic endowment permits us to infer are the limits of the range' (ibid., 188).

The Burt Scandal

One of the key assumptions underlying research methods is that they will be practised honestly. The user of the research literature should be able to assume that the data were not only gathered in a competent way, but that they are being honestly reported. Intentional falsification of the data strikes at the heart of the scientific enterprise. In one of the most consuming scandals of twentieth century psychology, it is precisely such fraud that Burt was accused of perpetrating. The following account of the history of the Burt scandal draws heavily on the scholarship of Franz Samelson (1992, 1993, 1996, 1997).

Precisely when Burt's reputation began to unravel is a matter of debate, but an important event was Leon Kamin's (1974) claim that Burt's published data were not credible. Kamin began reviewing Burt's work in 1972 (Kamin, 1977) and discovered, as did others, that 'a correlation would have the same value in different articles, but the number of cases would differ' (Green, 1992: 328). Incidents like this suggested that the data might have been invented. The possibility that Burt may have been less than honest was made more credible when a British journalist, Oliver Gillie, was unable to verify that several people whom Burt had listed as having gathered data for him ever existed or ever gathered such data. Gillie (1977: 257) called for the establishment of a committee of the

British Psychological Society 'to consider the problem of how better to facilitate the exposure of fraud in science and how to maintain the highest standards of scientific work and teaching'. Shortly thereafter the final nail in Burt's coffin appeared to have been driven by Leslie Hearnshaw (1979), whose biography of Burt charged that he had published fraudulent results favourable to his case under a pseudonym and had published work with a co-author who apparently did not exist. Moreover, Hearnshaw alleged that Burt had painted a false picture of his role in the invention of factor analysis by aggrandizing his contribution and denigrating Spearman's. At that point, the evidence against Burt seemed, to many, to be conclusive. The prevailing attitude was exemplified by a statement published in the British Psychological Society's Bulletin (1980: 71–2), flatly stating that 'Burt was guilty of deception', including 'falsification of the early history of factor analysis' and 'production of spurious data on monozygotic twins'.

The Burt case, however, was not yet closed. Other investigators, such as Robert B. Joynson (1989) and Ronald Fletcher (1991), argued that the charges against Burt were exaggerated in some cases and not proven in others. For example, many other psychologists have portrayed themselves in a more favourable light than the facts may have warranted (Green, 1992: 329), and psychologists are not alone in this failing. Publishing under a pseudonym is also something that many other psychologists and non-psychologists have done. However, there were still more arguments against Burt's veracity. Tucker (1997), as a result of a thorough examination of the possible sources of Burt's data, concluded that there was 'little doubt that he committed fraud'. Finally, Butler and Petrulis (1999: 159) presented evidence that Burt revised his papers in ways that 'misrepresented his work'.

In the end, the question of whether or not Burt's data were falsified has had little bearing on the question of whether or not g is inherited. To a large extent those who believed before the scandal that g was inherited, continued to believe it afterwards (e.g., Herrnstein and Murray, 1994: 12), arguing that even if Burt's data were to be discarded there would still be ample other findings that made the same case. Others were far less sure that the remaining data require the interpretation that g exists at all, let alone that it is inherited (e.g., Neisser et al. 1996: 81, 97).

From the perspective of the history of psychology, the Burt affair is important because of the lessons it has to teach us about what happens when someone's reputation is called into question. One such lesson is that such controversies are often conducted in an emotional atmosphere, and are not always resolved by discovering the 'true facts'. Rather, the disputants take definite points of view and point to facts that they believe are consistent with their point of view (Wisdom, 1957: 155). Once a point of view on a controversial issue has been publicly taken, it is difficult for the combatants to back down. Moreover, as Audley (1980) and Samelson (1992, 1993) have observed, arriving at a judgement about a person's reputation is a quasi-judicial process that invokes a host of legalistic concepts, including the right of the accused to be judged innocent until proven guilty beyond a reasonable doubt. Each participant's judgement is inevitably driven by social factors, such as whether or not one was acquainted with the accused. Presumably those who actually knew or worked with Burt would be more likely to defend him than those who never knew him or who held different beliefs. Such social factors can be important not only in cases such as Burt's, but also in determining whether or not any viewpoint in psychology will be accepted or rejected (Joynson, 2003). We will return to issues of this kind in the last chapter.

Louis Leon Thurstone (1887-1955)

Factor analytic techniques were developed in the United States by **L.L. Thurstone** (1938) of the University of Chicago. Thurstone's approach differed markedly from that of Spearman and Burt in that he wanted to uncover a set of mental abilities that were relatively independent of each other rather than to measure g. He searched for tests that would measure a particular mental ability, but that would be unrelated to other mental abilities. The result of his efforts was a set of six **primary mental abilities**: verbal (e.g., vocabulary), number (e.g., arithmetic), spatial (e.g., identifying a design), word fluency (e.g., thinking of words of a particular type), memory (e.g., remembering a series of digits) and reasoning (e.g., following a rule) (Cronbach, 1960: 256–7).

Thurstone's approach de-emphasized the importance of g. Rather than treating g as the most important form of intelligence, Thurstone regarded his list of six abilities as more useful than g. In understanding an individual's mental abilities it was more important to examine that person's *profile* of abilities than to try to summarize his/her intelligence in a single number.

Mental profiles have been determined for over half a million high school children in Chicago and it has been found that all possible combinations occur in the profiles. The records show many hundreds of interesting case histories. A boy who was a poor reader was considered a dunce by his teachers. His mental profile showed that he had the highest score on Space and Reasoning, and high scores in all other factors except the verbal factor V. His teachers changed their attitudes when they saw that his handicap was quite specific. . . . It requires often considerable insight of the examiner to relate the mental profile to the circumstances of each case, but there is no question but that the profile is more helpful than the IQ in the interpretation of educational and behavior problems. (Thurstone, 1965 [1948]: 64)

Thurstone (1978 [1934], 1944), along with other factor analysts, did not employ the technique only on tests of mental abilities. In principle, factor analytic procedures can be applied to any set of correlations between different measures.

TABLE 10.1
List of Adjectives Used in Thurstone's Study

persevering	impetuous	suspicious	tactful
crafty	fickle	courageous	careless
awkward	domineering	stern	tidy
self-important	frank	headstrong	precise
determined	pessimistic	jealous	systematic
friendly	spiteful	generous	cheerful
patient	quiet	dependable	conscientious
sarcastic	disagreeable	faithful	grasping
congenial	reserved	reserved	satisfied
hard-working	refined	solemn	cynical
stubborn	unnatural	earnest	courteous
capable	bashful	talented	unconventional
tolerant	self-reliant	frivolous	quick-tempered
calm	broad-minded	eccentric	
peevish	haughty	ingenious	
religious	submissive	accommodating	

Source: Thurstone (1934: 13).

Thus, factor analysis was seen as able to address 'the old problem of classifying the temperaments and personality types' (Thurstone, 1978: 285). One approach to this problem was to make lists of 'the many hundreds of adjectives that are in current use for describing personalities and temperaments' (ibid., 289). An example of such a list is shown Table 10.1. Participants were asked to think of 'a person they knew well, and underline every adjective that s/he might use in a conversational description of that person' (ibid., 293). Averaged over many participants, such data give some idea of the degree to which different words are used together. Factor analysis showed that five factors apparently explained the structure of these correlations. Thus, for example, *friendly* and *congenial* go together, as do *patient* and *calm*, *persevering* and *hard-working*, *self-reliant* and *courageous*, and *self-important* and *sarcastic*. The five factors may be taken as representing the underlying structure of the way our understanding of other people is organized. Factor analytic studies such as Thurstone's generated a remarkable amount of research (e.g., McCrae et al., 1993).

Lee J. Cronbach (1916–2001) and 'The Two Disciplines of Scientific Psychology'

Lee J. Cronbach (1978 [1957]), in his presidential address to the American Psychological Association, reviewed the development of research methods in psychology through the middle of the twentieth century. He saw psychology not as a unified discipline, but as consisting of two distinct methodological approaches. He called them *experimental psychology* and *correlational psychology*. Cronbach traced this division back to Wundt's distinction between experimental psychology and cultural psychology, with the former adopting laboratory methods and the latter examining correlations as they exist in the 'real world'. As this distinction evolved, it came to be represented by one science that attempted to 'discover the general laws of mind or behavior' and another science 'concerned with individual minds' (ibid., 440). As we have already seen, experimental psychology came to rely on the analysis of experimental data using statistical approaches advocated by Fisher.

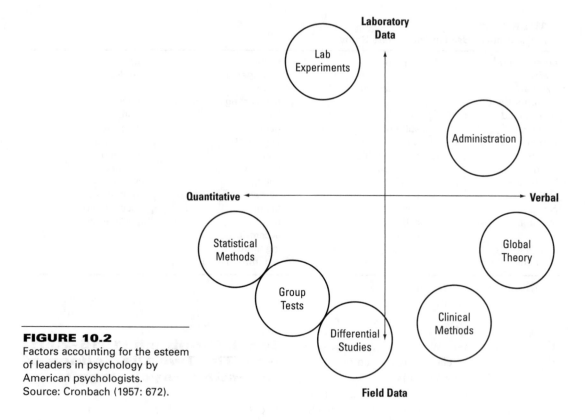

FIGURE 10.2
Factors accounting for the esteem
of leaders in psychology by
American psychologists.
Source: Cronbach (1957: 672).

Correlational psychology devised measures of individual differences, such as tests of intelligence, that could be administered in applied settings, such as schools, and then analyzed using techniques such as factor analysis.

In order to represent the methodological distinctions present in psychology around mid-century, Cronbach presented a model of the distinctions that separate psychologists. The model is shown in Figure 10.2, based on data originally gathered by Thorndike (1954) of psychologists' assessments of those psychologists who had made the greatest contributions. Cronbach's factor analysis of Thorndike's data revealed two factors. The most important factor in the present context is the vertical one, *laboratory data* versus *field data*. As the diagram indicates, laboratory experiments are most characteristic of the former, while the study of individual differences (differential studies) are most characteristic of the latter. The wide separation of these two in terms of this factor demonstrates how differently psychologists regarded workers in these two areas. The second factor in Cronbach's model is *quantitative* versus *verbal*, which distinguishes most clearly between those psychologists who rely on numbers (e.g., statistical methods) as opposed to those whose medium is language, such as psychologists who write about theories. Other groups of psychologists, such as those who employ group tests of individual differences, exemplify blends of both rather than one factor or another. Ideally, one could locate the preferences of any psychologist within this two-dimensional space.

Cronbach pointed out that these methodological preferences of psychologists had resulted in stable groups consisting of 'personality, social, and child psychologists' on the one hand and 'perception and learning psychologists' on the other (ibid., 439). Moreover, each group tended to take a dim view of the activities of the members of the other group. 'Individual differences have been an annoyance rather than a challenge to the experimenter. His goal is to control behavior . . . [and] individual variation is cast into that outer darkness known as 'error variance'. . . . The correlational psychologist is in love with just those variables the experimenter left home to forget' (ibid., 441).

The experimenter is concerned with the effects of particular experimental treatments on behaviour. To the extent that all participants do not respond in the same way to the treatments, the experimenter may feel that he has not got proper control over all the relevant variables. However, the correlational psychologist is interested precisely in understanding the fact that all participants do not respond in the same way to the same treatment. This is particularly clear in applied psychology. 'The job of applied psychology is to improve decisions about people. The greatest social benefit will come from applied psychology if we can find for each individual the treatment to which he can most easily adapt. This calls for the joint application of experimental and correlational methods' (ibid., 449).

The idea that individuals with different aptitudes may respond differently to different treatments came to be called **aptitude treatment interaction**. To investigate such interactions, Cronbach proposed the model shown in Figure 10.3. In this model, the treatments used by experimenters can be of two types: control of the past situations that the organism has experienced, and control of the present situation in which the organism is placed. Psychometric information refers to measures of individual differences that enable the investigator to make much more refined predic-

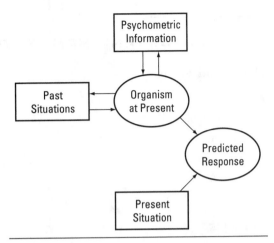

FIGURE 10.3
Theoretical network to be developed by a unified discipline.
Source: Cronbach (1957: 685).

tions about the responses an organism will make to past and present treatments. Notice the arrows leading both to and from 'Past Situations' and 'Psychometric Information'. These represent the fact that the effect of past situations and/or variables being measured by psychometric information depends on the current state of the organism, and vice versa.

Cronbach's call for a unified discipline was only partially successful, and in succeeding chapters we will see some psychologists championing one side of the discipline or the other. When Cronbach wrote his paper, psychology consisted of 'two solitudes' (a phrase used in another context by MacLennan, 1945), a condition that to some extent persisted throughout the twentieth century. In the next chapter we will examine the history of learning theorists whose exemplification of the experimental approach was extraordinarily influential, and who, Cronbach argued, had been too narrow. Then we will turn to the history of developmental and humanistic psychology, each of which tended to involve the study of the individual case.

IMPORTANT NAMES, WORKS, AND CONCEPTS

Names and Works

Burt, Cyril

Carnap, Rudolf

Clever Hans

Cronbach, Lee J.

Fisher, R.A.

Koch, Sigmund

Pfungst, Oscar

Spearman, Charles

'The two disciplines of scientific psychology'

Thurstone, L.L.

Concepts

aptitude treatment interaction

correlational methods

dispositional concepts

factor analysis

falsifiability

general intelligence/mental energy (*g*)

logical positivism

null hypothesis

operational definitions

operationism

primary mental abilities

protocol sentences

two-factor theory of intelligence

verification principle

RECOMMENDED READINGS

More information about the history of research methods may be found in J. Benjafield, *Thinking Critically about Research Methods* (Boston: Allyn & Bacon, 1994) and Benjafield, 'Research methods: A history of some impor-tant strands', *Archives of Suicide Research* 6 (2002): 5–14. A good history of the role of statistical reasoning in mod-ern life is G. Gigerenzer et al., *The Empire of Chance* (Cambridge: Cambridge University Press, 1989).

CHAPTER 11

THEORIES OF LEARNING

Introduction

As a result of the influence of psychologists such as Thorndike and Watson, the psychology of learning became a major interest of American psychologists in particular. Research on learning began to accumulate, and, beginning in the 1940s, a brilliant series of textbooks on the subject by Ernest Hilgard marked the arrival of what is often called 'The Age of Learning Theories'. The learning theories of Guthrie, Hull, and Tolman were at the core of American academic psychology. Although different from one another in some ways, they all shared the assumption that learning was the basic psychological process. This period also saw the emergence of D.O. Hebb's neuropsychological approach to learning, which revived physiological psychology after a period of neglect. Roger Sperry's Nobel Prize-winning work on learning in organisms with 'split brains' also helped usher in the beginnings of contemporary neuroscience. The breadth of learning theories was well illustrated by Albert Bandura's 'social learning' approach to such phenomena as imitation.

Ernest R. Hilgard (1904–2001)

Hilgard was an important researcher in a number of areas in psychology, as well as a prolific textbook writer (Leary, 2002). Textbook writers can be extremely important to a pluralistic discipline such as psychology because they articulate for both students and teachers the different strands that make up an emerging discipline and point the way towards future developments. Of all the psychology textbook writers in the twentieth century, **Ernest R. Hilgard** was arguably the most important. Not only did Hilgard write an introductory

text (Hilgard, 1953) that was rated in the 1970s as 'the most successful academic textbook in sales' (Laberge, 1994: 184), as well as a history of American psychology (Hilgard, 1987) that 'served as both a chronicle of our discipline and a graduate-level introductory textbook' (Kihlstrom, 1994: 179), but he also wrote a series of textbooks on learning that 'substantially organize[d] and structured an entire research discipline for generations to come' (Bower, 1994: 181). Hilgard and Marquis's *Conditioning and Learning* (1940; Kimble, 1961), as well as the successive editions of his review of *Theories of Learning* (Hilgard, 1948, 1956; Hilgard and Bower, 1966, 1975; Bower and Hilgard, 1981), defined the era that we will consider in this chapter (Fuchs, 1997). The last three editions of *Theories of Learning* were written with **Gordon H. Bower**, who became a renowned theorist in his own right.

Hilgard's *Theories of Learning* 'became the defining survey textbook for hundreds of teachers who organized their lectures around it. It also served as a prototype for later survey textbooks and courses in social, personality, and developmental psychology' (Bower, 1994: 181). When Hilgard wrote the first edition of *Theories of Learning* in 1948, he included those theorists listed in the first column of Table 11.1. Represented in that list are several theorists and approaches we have already considered, such as Thorndike, Skinner, Gestalt psychology, and functionalism. While we will not consider Thorndike, Skinner, and Gestalt further, we will elaborate on functional as well as other approaches to learning because there are important details about them that we need to understand. However, we will spend much of our time in this chapter dealing with those approaches that recur in all of the editions of *Theories of Learning*, and that may thus be

TABLE 11.1

Topics of the Various Editions of Theories of Learning

First (1948)	Second (1956)	Third (1966)	Fourth (1975)	Fifth (1981)
Thorndike	Thorndike	Thorndike	Thorndike	Thorndike
Guthrie	Guthrie	Guthrie	Guthrie	Guthrie
Hull	Hull	Hull	Hull	Hull
Tolman	Tolman	Tolman	Tolman	Tolman
Skinner	Skinner	Skinner	Skinner	Skinner
Gestalt	Gestalt	Gestalt	Gestalt	Gestalt
Functionalism	Functionalism	Functionalism	Functionalism	Functionalism
Lewin	Lewin			
Wheeler's organismic theory/Field theories				
	Freud	Freud	Freud	
	Mathematical models	Mathematical learning theory	Mathematical learning theory	Mathematical learning theory (Estes)
		Pavlov	Pavlov	Pavlov
		Information processing models	Information processing models	Information processing models
		Neurophysiology of learning	Neurophysiology of learning	Neurophysiology of learning
		Learning and instructional technology	Learning and instructional technology	Learning and instructional technology
			Piaget	

thought of as being of particular historical significance. These core theories include the work of Guthrie, Hull, and Tolman.

Before beginning our discussion of Guthrie, Hull, and Tolman, we should explore a bit further the structure of the topics in Table 11.1. The following points are particularly notable.

Kurt Lewin and organismic/field theories are the only topics in the first edition to subsequently be dropped. To some extent, this material was incorporated into other chapters in subsequent editions, but much of it simply disappeared because it was seen as no longer relevant to the learning theories of the day (Hilgard, 1956: v; Hilgard and Bower, 1966: v).

Freud made his appearance in the second edition because he 'so influenced psychological thinking that a summary of theoretical viewpoints, even in a specialized field such as the psychology of learning, is incomplete without reference to him' (Hilgard, 1956: 290). Hilgard was known as a 'generous skeptic' in relation to psychoanalysis, 'one who holds the discipline of psychoanalysis to the canons of scientific methods, but who preserves a respectful interest in the mysterious and the unknown' (Holzman, 1994: 191).

Pavlov does not have a chapter devoted to him until the third edition. His inclusion there is due to 'a resurgence of interest in his views, particularly as represented in current developments from the

USSR, with recognition given to the significance in human learning of the "second signaling system" (language)' (Hilgard and Bower, 1966: v). The 1960s saw a resurgence of interest in Soviet psychology as well as in topics such as language, and we will explore the emergence of the psychology of language in Chapter 14.

In the second edition, mathematical approaches to the construction of learning theories are introduced, and coverage of them continues in subsequent editions. By the fifth edition the major practitioner of mathematical learning theory, William K. Estes, had a chapter of his own.

Topics such as information-processing and neurophysiological theories, as well as applications to education, were introduced in the third edition and continued to grow thereafter. We will review one major contributor to the neurophysiological approach, D.O. Hebb, below. Information-processing theories will be considered in Chapter 14 on cognitive psychology.

Jean Piaget figures in the fourth edition because his theory 'provides, as does Freud, a larger context in which to view the acquisition of knowledge and competence as a consequence of growth and interaction with the physical and social environment' (Hilgard and Bower, 1975: 318). Although Piaget's theory had been around for decades it was not really until the 1960s that it began to take hold in the United States. We will consider Piaget's developmental theory in detail in Chapter 12. Both Freud and Piaget were dropped from the fifth edition, 'regrettably . . . because a survey of teachers using the text indicated that those chapters were not being used in the typical course in learning theory' (Bower and Hilgard, 1981: vi).

E.R. Guthrie (1886–1959)

E.R. Guthrie (1959: 161) was trained in logic and the philosophy of science, an experience that led him to conclude that 'the laws of logic are conventions and not laws of thought.' This conclusion made him 'impatient with the notion that

there can be any completely rigorous deduction, or ultimate validity in an argument. This skepticism colors my notions of the nature of scientific facts and scientific theory.' As a result, Guthrie's theory of learning is presented in a relatively informal way. Moreover, early in his career Guthrie's 'chief interest lay in undergraduate teaching, a fact that probably accounts for a strong bent toward simplification which, with some justification, has been described as oversimplification' (ibid.). The result is a straightforward theory of learning that has one principle at its core, that of **contiguity**.

Contiguity

Guthrie (1961 [1930]: 19–20) wondered if there was 'a single formula which can be made to include all or most of the established generalizations concerning the nature of learning? If there is such a formula it will in all probability be some form of the ancient principle of association by contiguity in time, which has been a part of all theories of memory and learning since before Aristotle, and has retained its essential character in spite of a variety of names, such as "conditioning," [and] "associative memory".' Guthrie stated this principle as follows: 'A combination of stimuli which has accompanied a movement will on its recurrence tend to be followed by that movement' (Guthrie, 1960 [1952]: 23). Notice that Guthrie's basic principle proposes that 'combinations of stimuli', rather than stimuli singly, act on the organism to produce movements. Many stimulus patterns may have the potential to produce movement, but only some of them are actually effective. The latter are termed *cues* or *signals*.

Guthrie observes that movements are different from acts, a point that goes back to Aristotle, and that we considered in the first chapter.

> Playing a tune on the piano is an act. The act is accomplished by movements but it can be accomplished by a wide variety of movements. The naming of the act does not specify the move-

ments. An armless man can learn to play skillfully with his feet. On different occasions a tune can be given a radically different fingering by a player using his hands. . . . The difference between act and movement is of vital importance in learning theory because our accepted notion of the mechanism of response is that nerve impulses actuate muscular contraction, and if association or conditioning is to be related to changes in the nervous system it is specific movement patterns which must be dealt with. (Ibid., 27–8)

Repetition

By saying that conditioning involves the formation of associations between stimulus patterns and movements, Guthrie places his account of learning well within the traditional associationist principles stretching from Aristotle to Pavlov. However, Guthrie did not agree with the traditional associationist view of the effect of repetition on learning. The typical view was that repetition acts to strengthen the connection between stimulus and response. Guthrie argued instead that repetition provides the opportunity for additional stimuli to become associated with a response. 'The habit of smoking is in reality made up of thousands of habits. The sight of tobacco, the smell of it, the mention of it, finishing a meal, finishing an office task, looking at the clock, and innumerable other situations have all become signals for smoking' (ibid.). Once a habit has been associated with a large number of different stimuli, it is, of course, that much harder to change it.

Reward

Guthrie proposed a unique way of explaining the effect that reward or reinforcement has on behaviour. He does not question the fact that rewards influence behaviour, but does not agree with the notion that reinforcement acts to strengthen the connection between stimulus and response. Rather, reward acts to prevent the animal from unlearning the association formed just prior to the

reward. For example, in the sequence signal → response → reward, the reward terminates the signal, and allows it to be the only signal connected to the response. Consider Thorndike's puzzle box here. The behaviour that allows the cat to escape is the last response to be performed before reward. The response does not have the opportunity to become connected to some other signal.

> When a signal has been followed by a response that prevents the signal from recurring, there is no opportunity . . . for the attachment of that signal to other responses. If an association is established, it is secure . . . until the [signal] is again present and a different [response] is introduced. The association is protected from unlearning . . . . This makes specific the nature of a reward or reinforcement. They are defined in terms of straight association by contiguity. They protect learning that has occurred by making unlearning impossible. (Guthrie, 1959: 171)

One-Trial Learning

Bower and Hilgard (1981: 87) observed that 'it was part of the charm of Guthrie's writing that it was closely in touch with everyday life and provided amusing but cogent suggestions for meeting the problems of animal training, child rearing, and pedagogy.' In particular, Guthrie proposed ingenious methods for breaking undesirable habits. Guthrie's basic approach was characteristically simple: 'The simplest rule for breaking a habit is to find the cues that initiate the action and to practice another response to these cues' (Guthrie, 1960: 115). Crafts et al. (1950: 320) provided examples consistent with Guthrie's principles, such as the old advertising slogan, 'Reach for a Lucky instead of a sweet.' This slogan appeared at a time when eating candy was a less desirable habit than smoking, and now the advice might be 'Reach for a carrot stick instead of a smoke.' In either case, the principle remains the same: a different response must be connected to the same cues. Another practical example is given in Box 11.1.

BOX 11.1

CHANGING UNDESIRABLE HABITS

Here is another example of the practical nature of Guthrie's style of thinking. It is adapted from Guthrie (1960 [1952]: 18), and was also discussed by Bower and Hilgard (1981: 87–8). Imagine a school-age child who has developed the following sequence of habits. Whenever the child comes through the door and enters the house, she throws her coat on the floor and then goes downstairs and watches television. The parent of this child tries everything to get the child to hang her coat up before she does anything else. Thus, the parent makes the child come back upstairs and hang the coat up before she can continue watching television. However, this fails to change the coat-throwing habit. The parent threatens additional punishment, and even rewards such as a favourite food if only the child will hang her coat up before she watches television. Nothing works. From a Guthrian viewpoint, trying to solve this or other problems through rewards and punishments is wrong-headed. What is needed is a careful analysis of the cues leading to the undesirable behaviour. In fact, we can represent the undesirable sequence of cues and responses as follows.

Enter the house → Throw coat on floor → Go downstairs

The problem is to make another response— 'Hang coat up'—the first response after 'Enter the house'. This can be achieved, Guthrie says, by having the child come back upstairs, put her coat back on, go outside the house, come back in the house, and hang up her coat. This means that hanging up her coat is now the first response made upon entering. Notice how Guthrie's proposal, like his other advice, is based on a meticulous attention to the details of the cues and responses in the problem situation.

Clark L. Hull (1884–1952)

Like so many other psychologists, **Clark L. Hull** entered the discipline as a consequence of reading William James. He received his Ph.D. from the University of Wisconsin in 1918, and, after working in a variety of areas in psychology, his characteristic approach began to crystallize in 1929 when he began working at the Institute of Human Relations at Yale University. By then, Hull had become a proponent of the principles of conditioning and opposed to the Gestalt approach (Mills, 1988). However, he realized that conditioning could only be the mechanism responsible for the process of learning. In addition, a learning theory needed to provide an understanding of the organism's motives if it was to be credible. The process of conditioning provided an explanation of how learning occurred, while the process of motivation allowed one to understand why learning occurred when it did.

Hull's motivational theory was based on the concept of **drive**. He defined 'any persistent and intense stimulus, external or internal, as a drive, that is, a motivation' (Shakow and Rapaport, 1964: 136). The way the drive concept worked in Hull's system will be explored in detail below, but many observers have remarked on the similarity between Hull's drive concept and basic psychoanalytic hypotheses about motivation (e.g., Toman, 1960). It is of historical interest to note that while he was developing his theory between 1936 and 1942, Hull held a series of seminars concerned with integrating his behaviourist approach to learning with Freudian psychoanalytic theory. Hull was critical of psychoanalytic theory for not being sufficiently rigorous, but encouraged the attempt to 'formulate for ourselves various sharply defined alternative hypotheses which are consistent with current psychoanalytic views' (Shakow and Rapaport, 1964: 139). Among the members of these seminars were John Dollard and Neal Miller, who later wrote

Personality and Psychotherapy (1950), a book that attempted to provide an integration of learning theory and psychoanalysis.

The Formal Structure of Hullian Theory

It is difficult to imagine a more stark contrast than that between Guthrie's and Hull's theories of learning. Whereas Guthrie's approach was almost folksy with its use of simple, practical ideas, Hull's (1943, 1952) theory of learning was abstract and technical. Whereas the relation between theory and data in Guthrie's approach was largely informal, the relation between theory and data in Hull's approach was intended to be quite precise. Hull tried to mimic what he took to be the form of theory construction and testing that had been successful in other sciences. Thus, Hullian theory illustrates the kind of procedures recommended by logical positivists (Bergman and Spence, 1941; Spence, 1944).

The Hypothetico-Deductive Method

Hull attempted to create a mathematical theory from which could be deduced the facts of learning. The theory consisted of *postulates* that are intended to describe the basic laws of behaviour. The postulates contain descriptions of *intervening variables*, a concept originally introduced by Tolman (1951 [1935]). These intervening variables represent hypothetical processes that occur inside the organism and are supposed to govern behaviour. From the postulates, one can deduce *theorems*, which are experimentally testable hypotheses about behaviour. This may all sound obscure, but the way it worked in practice was quite straightforward. If experimental data are consistent with the theorem, then the postulates are retained unchanged. However, if a theorem is falsified, then the postulates must be changed. New theorems can be derived and tested from the new set of postulates. This process goes on and on, with the postulates being improved as a result of experimentation. Of course, the postulates must also be consistent with

one another. The procedure we have just described is called the *hypothetico-deductive method*, because the theorems that are *deduced* from the postulates are *hypotheses* that can be tested experimentally.

Postulates

Hull believed that organisms were born with unlearned stimulus response connections, much like Pavlov's unconditioned connections. The unlearned connections are able to satisfy some of the organism's needs but need to be supplemented by learned connections. New connections are formed as a result of reinforcement. Hull's theory of reinforcement was an elaboration of Thorndike's law of effect. A **primary reinforcer** is any stimulus that results in a reduction in drive. For example, food reduces hunger and is thus a primary reinforcer. A **secondary reinforcer** is a stimulus that initially has no reinforcing properties but acquires them through association with a reinforcing stimulus. Money is an example of a secondary reinforcer. By itself it is only a piece of paper or metal that causes no reduction in drive. However, because money allows one to acquire primary reinforcers, such as food, it becomes a reinforcing stimulus itself.

To see how the concepts in Hull's theory were related to each other, we first need to list the major intervening variables in the theory.

Drive (D). This is the major motivational concept in Hull's theory. Drive tends to increase as a function of the amount of time that has elapsed since the last reinforcement. Hunger is the paradigmatic example. After being fed, the level of drive drops. The level of drive then increases until the animal is fed again. Of course, drive does not continue to increase forever. After a certain period, if the animal has not been fed then drive tends to drop off. For example, if an animal is starved for a long period, it will begin to wither away.

Habit strength ($_SH_R$). The definition of **habit strength** illustrates very nicely the attempt at precision in Hull's system. Habits are learned connections between stimuli and responses. In line with the law of effect, habits are formed as a result of reinforcement. However, Hull did not leave it at that, but formulated a precise mathematical definition of habit strength as a function of the number of reinforcements. This definition may be stated in the form of an equation (Hull, 1952: 8).

$$_SH_R = 1 - 11^{-aN}$$

This equation should be read as follows: 'habit strength ($_SH_R$) is equal to 1 minus 11 to the minus aN, where N is the number of times a response to a stimulus has been reinforced, and a has a constant value of about .03.' So defined, habit strength varies between zero and 1. Other intervening variables in Hull's system were given precise definitions like this, but they will not be presented here. The mathematical definition of habit strength is enough to give you the general idea of the ambitious nature of Hull's theory.

Stimulus-intensity dynamism (V). This intervening variable refers to the amount of energy possessed by a stimulus that impinges on the organism.

Incentive motivation (K). Incentive motivation is defined in terms of the amount of reward (such as food or money) that follows a response.

The foregoing intervening variables combine to yield *reaction potential* ($_SE_R$), which is the amount of energy available for a response. The way in which these variables combine is defined precisely. They are assumed to multiply together to give reaction potential, as follows:

$$_SE_R = {_SH_R} \times D \times V \times K$$

While variables such as D, V, K, and $_SH_R$ act so as to energize the organism, there are other variables that inhibit responding. These variables are listed below.

Reactive inhibition (I_R). Everyone is familiar with the fact that as we behave we become fatigued. The more the organism responds, the more fatigued it will get, and the greater will reactive inhibition be. Reactive inhibition acts as a negative drive that is reduced by not responding.

Conditioned inhibition ($_SI_R$). By resting, or doing nothing, the organism reduces reactive inhibition. The reduction in reactive inhibition, or fatigue, is reinforcing. Doing nothing is rewarding. The organism develops a negative habit, or conditioned inhibition, that tends to make it less likely to respond.

These last two intervening variables combine with the first set to yield a more complete equation for reaction potential. This equation may be stated as follows (Logan, 1959: 323).

$$_SE_R = {_SH_R} \times D \times V \times K - {_SI_R} - I_R$$

Other intervening variables make the equation even more complicated, but this version of it is sufficient for our purposes. The first four intervening variables on the right-hand side of the equation ($_SH_R \times D \times V \times K$) contribute to the vigour with which the organism responds, while the last two intervening variables ($_SI_R - I_R$) detract from the vigour with which the animal responds. The first four intervening variables may be thought of as excitatory, while the last two are inhibitory.

One may wonder whether or not equations like Hull's could actually be used to make very precise predictions about behaviour. In fact, only relatively crude predictions were made in practice. Some of these predictions were actually quite interesting. For example, imagine a situation in which the organism has a well-developed habit and is in a heightened drive state. Surely this means that the organism will respond no matter what the values of the other variables? Not so. Notice that the value of reaction potential ($_SE_R$) cannot be positive if any one of the first four variables is zero. Thus if incentive is zero, the animal will not respond, regardless of the value of the other variables. Intuitively, this makes sense. Thinking of it in anthropomorphic terms, no matter how hungry you were, you would be unlikely to work for someone else if you were not going to get paid for it. We will explore this example further when we contrast Hull's theory with that of Tolman.

Kenneth W. Spence (1907–67)

Kenneth W. Spence (1956, 1960) worked so closely with Hull on the development of the theory that it was sometimes called the Hull-Spence approach. One of his earliest and most significant contributions to the Hullian way of thinking was his attempt to explain Köhler's transposition experiments (Spence, 1937). Köhler (1927) did experiments that appeared to show that animals learned *relationships between* stimuli and did not learn responses *to* particular stimuli. These experiments involved training animals to respond to one of two stimuli in a series. Thus, an animal might be rewarded for responding to the larger of two stimuli. Subsequently, the animal was presented with another choice between two stimuli, one of which was the stimulus for which it had been rewarded and the other a stimulus that was still larger than the first. The animal responded to the new stimulus even though it had never been rewarded for doing so, and ignored the stimulus for which it had previously been rewarded.

Spence realized that Köhler's Gestalt explanation of transposition was a threat to an associationist form of explanation such as Hull's. Figure 11.1 indicates Spence's simple yet powerful alternative to Köhler's explanation. As we noted earlier, in Hullian theory an animal's tendency to respond to a stimulus is the outcome of two opposing tendencies, one excitatory and one inhibitory. Figure 11.1 represents an experiment in which an animal

is initially rewarded for choosing the larger (256 cm^2) as opposed to the smaller (160 cm^2) of two stimuli. From an associationist viewpoint, the animal will learn an association between the response and the 256 cm^2 stimulus. In Hullian terms, the animal will form a habit of some strength between the 256 cm^2 stimulus and the response. This habit will generalize to other stimuli similar to the one that is rewarded. Thus, the excitatory tendency will be strongest to the stimulus for which the animal is rewarded and gradually diminish as the difference between the original stimulus and other stimuli increases. This *generalization gradient* is the topmost curve in Figure 11.1. The animal will also learn to inhibit its response to the stimulus for which it is not rewarded. This inhibitory tendency will be strongest at the 160 cm^2 stimulus and gradually diminish as stimuli become less similar to that stimulus. This gradient of inhibition is the lower curve in Figure 11.1.

While the generalization curves are theoretically derived, they permit some precise predictions. The difference between the excitatory and inhibitory gradients for any particular stimulus represents the net reaction potential for that stimulus. Compare this difference for the 409 cm^2 stimulus and the 256 cm^2 stimulus. Notice that it is greater for the 409 cm^2 stimulus than for the 256 cm^2 stimulus. Thus, given a choice between these two stimuli the animal should choose the 409 cm^2 stimulus. This result is what Köhler found, and upon which he based his anti-associationist

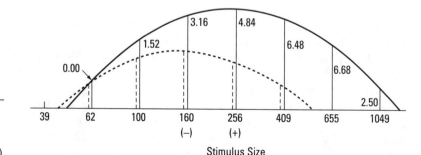

FIGURE 11.1
Curves of excitation and inhibition.
Source: Spence (1937: 433).

theory of transposition. However, Spence provided a neo-associationist framework within which to explain Köhler's finding that animals will sometimes respond to stimuli for which they have not been rewarded and ignore stimuli for which they have been rewarded. Such an analysis provided support for those who believed that theories of learning based on conditioning principles were best able to explain the data.

Spence's analysis of transposition was by no means his only contribution. The study does illustrate, however, the way in which a Hullian form of theory appeared in the beginning to be able quite elegantly to explain interesting experimental data. One can easily see why so many young psychologists were attracted to it at the time.

Charles E. Osgood (1916–91)

Charles E. Osgood (1980: 342) did his graduate work at Yale, beginning in 1940 when he 'got swept up, just like everyone else, into the monumental edifice of learning theory that Clark L. Hull was building.' However, Osgood extended the Hullian approach in a highly original direction. Hull had postulated the existence of what

Osgood (1952) called *mediational processes* that intervened between stimulus and response. Mediational processes guided the organism's reactions. Osgood saw in these mediating processes a way of explaining how stimuli acquired meaning for an organism. The formation of mediational processes was hypothesized to occur in the manner illustrated in Figure 11.2.

The notation used by Osgood in Figure 11.2 is as follows. The letter S with a dot on top represents some stimulus object to which the organism responds (R_T). Osgood's example is a spider, which elicits a complex, and perhaps highly emotional, reaction. The letter S surrounded by a box represents a *sign*, which can come to evoke the same kind of reactions as the stimulus with which it is paired. Thus, in Figure 11.2 the sign might be the word 'spider'. When paired with an actual spider, as when a child attaches the word 'spider' to an actual spider, the word will come to evoke a fraction of the reaction evoked by the original stimulus itself. In this way words come to be meaningful, not only by denoting stimulus objects, but also by evoking the internal responses elicited by those objects. These internal responses constitute the first part of a mediating process, labelled $r_m \rightarrow s_m$

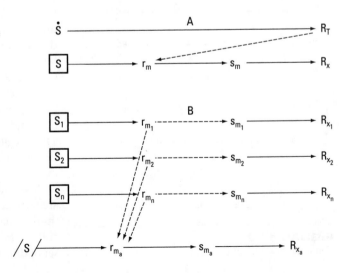

FIGURE 11.2
The development of a mediational process.
Source: Osgood (1952: 205).

in the figure. The internal response (r_m) is itself a stimulus (s_m) that guides the organism's future behaviour. In this case, mention of the word 'spider' can lead to a mediating process of disgust and/or fear that in turn leads to withdrawal (R_X).

The Semantic Differential

As the preceding example shows, mediating processes in humans are often associated with words. From Osgood's perspective, these mediators carry the meanings of words, particularly their emotional or affective meanings. Osgood's great contribution was to provide a way of measuring this aspect of meaning. This was the **semantic differential** technique (Osgood et al., 1957). In its usual form, the semantic differential asks you to rate a person, thing, or event on a set of seven-point bipolar scales such as those given in Figure 11.3.

The task requires you to make a series of judgements about something (in this case, 'spider'). If your reaction to 'spider' is best charac-

terized as 'extremely unpleasant', then you would mark the interval closest to the unpleasant end of the scale. If you thought it was only 'quite unpleasant', 'slightly unpleasant', or 'neither pleasant nor unpleasant', then you would mark intervals increasingly close to the centre of the scale. After you fill out a number of such scales, the result is a profile of how these dimensions go together for you for this concept ('spider'). It may initially strike people as odd to be asked to rate a concept like 'spider' on scales such as 'happy vs sad'. However, almost everyone who has accepted the task finds that this can be done without too much difficulty. The scales are intended to capture aspects of a person's emotional, or affective, reaction to a concept. For one person, this reaction might be 'unpleasant', and relatively neutral on the other scales. For another, it might make them feel 'timid' and 'weak'. The point is that a particular concept will be rated differently by different people, and so we can get a measure of individual differences in the affective meaning of particular concepts. However, suppose we obtain, as did Osgood, a large number of ratings of different concepts by different people on different scales in different cultures. It turns out that ratings tend to be correlated across scales.

Factor analysis, discussed in Chapter 10, begins with a set of correlations between a number of measures, in this case ratings of concepts. Using factor analysis one can derive a number of underlying factors that describe the structure of this set of correlation coefficients. In fact, Osgood found three important clusters of dimensions (e.g., Osgood et al., 1975). Within each cluster, the dimensions go with one another more than they do with dimensions from the other sets. The first, and largest, set consists of dimensions such as *pleasant-unpleasant*, *good-bad*, and *happy-sad*. Osgood called these the *evaluative* (E) set of dimensions. The second set contains dimensions such as *strong-weak*, *bold-timid*, and *hard-soft*, and are termed the *potency* (P) set of dimensions. The third set has dimensions in it such as *active-passive* and *excitable-calm*, and represent an *activity* (A) set of dimensions.

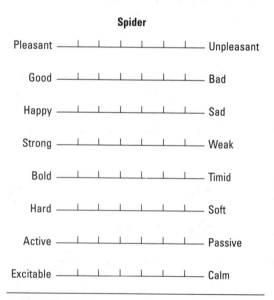

FIGURE 11.3
Semantic differential scales.

Osgood et al. (1957: 72–3) speculated about why evaluation, potency, and activity, and not some other factors, emerge as the important aspects of affective meaning. They pointed out the importance of these three factors in our experience. Evaluation is 'based on the bedrock of rewards and punishments both achieved and anticipated'; potency 'is concerned with power and the things associated with size, weight, toughness, and the like'; while activity is 'concerned with quickness, excitement, . . . agitation and the like'. These three dimensions represent answers to questions such as 'How much pleasure or pain is it likely to give us' (evaluation); 'How strong is it relative to us?' (potency); and 'What do we have to do to deal with it?' (activity). 'Survival, then and now, depends upon the answers' (Osgood et al., 1975: 395).

As Osgood et al. (1975: 394) observe, there is a close similarity between their three factors and Wundt's tri-dimensional theory of feeling, which we considered in Chapter 4. Evaluation corresponds to Wundt's pleasantness-unpleasantness dimension, potency corresponds to tension-relaxation, and activity to excitement-depression. Wundt and Osgood used strikingly different methods, and Osgood did not set out to replicate Wundt's findings. The correspondence between the two is, thus, all the more striking.

Osgood's semantic differential technique generated an enormous amount of research. By 1969, there were at least 1,500 studies related to it (Osgood, 1980: 354). Semantic differential studies uncovered intriguing similarities in affective meaning across cultures, as reported by Osgood et al. (1975). For example, *courage* and *success* are consistently rated as positive on all three of evaluation, potency, and activity, while *tree* and *knowledge* are positive on evaluation and potency but negative on activity. For a majority of cultures, concepts such as *freedom*, *girl*, and *love* are evaluatively positive but *hunger*, *snake*, and *thief* are evaluatively negative. In terms of potency, *progress* and *sun* are positive while *bird* and *egg* are negative. *Fire* and *game* are positive on activity while *sleep* and *stone* are negative. It is interesting to note that words

that one might expect to be emotionally neutral, such as 'egg', nonetheless elicit affectively toned responses. This shows that virtually everything has an affective meaning for us.

Osgood believed that his cross-cultural research was relevant to issues of 'meaning and survival of the human species in the nuclear age', and saw himself as 'trying to bring a strategy for reducing international tensions, based on psychological principles, into the awareness of the public at large and people in government in particular' (Osgood, 1980: 360). The fact that many concepts elicited the same subjective reaction cross-culturally was evidence for a widely shared set of meanings. In spite of important individual and cultural differences, it appeared that people had a great deal in common in terms of the way they feel about many basic events. It was Osgood's hope that research such as his would facilitate successful communication between people and cultures and thus reduce international tensions.

E.C. Tolman (1886–1959)

E.C. Tolman became converted to behaviourism in 1914 while a graduate student at Harvard. However, the behaviourism he developed was quite different from that of Watson. His theory was a 'common-sense mentalistic psychology—or what the gestalt psychologists have called phenomenology—in operational behavioristic terms. Köhler has called me a cryptophenomenologist. He is probably right. What I wanted was a behavioristic psychology which would be able to deal with real organisms in terms of their inner psychological dynamics' (Tolman, 1959: 94). Tolman's psychology is primarily a blend of methodological behaviourism and Gestalt psychology, with other influences, such as psychoanalysis, also a part of the mix.

In general, Tolman adopted a much looser and more speculative formulation than did Hull. Tolman's attitude towards the relation between research and theory in psychology can be gleaned from a paper he wrote towards the end of his career:

The system may not stand up to any final rules of scientific procedure. But I do not much care. I have liked to think about psychology in ways that have proved congenial to me. Since all the sciences, and especially psychology, are still immersed in such tremendous realms of the uncertain and the unknown, the best that any individual scientist, especially any psychologist, can do seems to be to follow his own gleam and his own bent, however inadequate they may be. In fact, I suppose that actually this is what we all do. In the end, the only sure criterion is to have fun. And I have had fun. (Tolman, 1959: 152)

In spite of the apparently whimsical nature of this remark, Tolman was a very serious investigator whose influence lasted well beyond his lifetime (Garcia, 1997). However, it is important to note that his description of how he *actually did* research contrasts sharply with the way in which philosophers of science such as the logical positivists said that we *should* do research. As we observed in Chapter 10, there is a difference between the *context of discovery* and the *context of justification* (Reichenbach, 1938; Gigerenzer, 1991). The thinking that leads to the *discovery* of a method for investigating a research problem may be quite different from the thinking that goes into presenting a completed study for consumption by the rest of the scientific community. Tolman's statement nicely illustrates this difference. With that in mind, let us explore some of Tolman's major concepts.

Purposive Behaviour

The subject matter of Tolman's (1967 [1932], 1951) behaviourism is behaviour described with reference to the goal that the animal is seeking. Tolman made an important distinction between **molar** and **molecular** descriptions of behaviour. A molecular description of behaviour is in terms of specific muscular and glandular reactions, while a molar description is in terms of what the behaviour is intended to accomplish. This distinction is quite similar to Aristotle's distinction, considered in the

Chapter 1 and discussed earlier in relation to Guthrie, between *movements* and *actions*. Descriptions of movements are at the molecular level, while descriptions of actions are at the molar level. Examples of behaviour described at the molar level are 'a rat running a maze; a cat getting out of a puzzle box; a man driving home to dinner; a child hiding from a stranger; . . . my friend and I telling one another our thoughts and feelings—*these are behaviors* (qua *molar*). And it must be noted that in mentioning no one of them have we referred to, or, we blush to confess it, for the most part even known, what were the exact muscles and glands, sensory nerves, and motor nerves involved. For these responses had other sufficiently identifying properties of their own' (Tolman, 1967: 8). Because Tolman attempted to explain molar behaviour, his approach is called **purposive behaviourism**.

Cognitive Maps

As far as Tolman was concerned, the explanation of purposive behaviour required an understanding of how an animal represented its environment.

We believe that in the course of learning, something like a field map of the environment gets established in the rat's brain. . . . Secondly, we assert that the central office itself is far more like a map control room than it is like an old-fashioned telephone exchange. . . . [S]timuli . . . are not connected by just simple one-to-one switches to the outgoing responses. Rather, the incoming impulses are usually worked over and elaborated in the central control room into a tentative, cognitive-like map of the environment. And it is this tentative map, indicating routes and paths and environmental relationships, which finally determines what responses, if any, the animal will finally release. (Tolman, 1951: 245)

Cognitive maps contain *expectancies*, which are representations of what the animal is likely to find by following the different routes represented in the map. Expectancies are integrated into *sign*

Gestalts, which are representations of the way one event leads to other events in the cognitive map. One of Tolman's examples of sign Gestalts concerns the way in which the perception of an object leads to the representation of different possibilities: "'this chair if sat on will lead to rest' . . . ; or "that chair, if placed against the wall, can be stood upon like a stepladder to reach this picture"; or "yonder chair, if placed over there, if placed near such and such other furniture, will form an aesthetically pleasing whole"; or "this chair, if kicked out of the way, will conduce to the catching of yonder escaped white rat"; and the like' (ibid., 80). Thus, one important class of sign Gestalt relationships concerns the representation of the uses to which objects can be put, or *means-end expectations*.

The Place versus Response Controversy

A good illustration of how cognitive maps function is given in an experiment by Tolman, Ritchie, and Kalish. This experiment was selected by the editors of the *Journal of Experimental Psychology* as a classic article and reprinted as part of the centennial celebration of the American Psychological Association. The experiment bears on a controversial issue that was called the **place versus response controversy** (Amundson, 1985). From Tolman's viewpoint, the issue concerned what an animal learns. Does learning consist of the formation of stimulus-response connections, or does it consist of the formation of expectations, as Tolman believed? If learning means the acquisition of stimulus-response connections, then animals would learn specific responses to specific stimuli. If learning means the acquisition of expectations, then animals would learn a cognitive map that contained representations of the *place*, or location, of themselves in relation to different objects in the environment. In order to try to settle this question, Tolman, Ritchie, and Kalish did a study of maze learning in rats that began with the simple maze shown in Figure 11.4.

Approximately 50 rats were trained to follow the path from A through C, D, E, and F to the

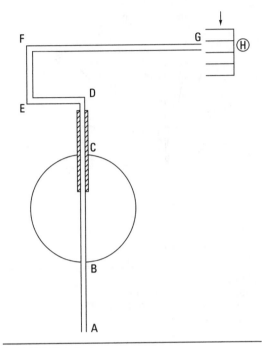

FIGURE 11.4
Apparatus used to train rats.
Source: Tolman et al. (1992: 430).

goal—box G—where they were fed. H is a small light. This maze was then replaced with the one shown in Figure 11.5. Notice that the path the animals had learned to run before was now blocked. Where did the rats go instead? It turned out that '36 percent chose path No. 6 which ended at a point four in. to the left of the place where the food box entrance had been during the [training] trials. This path No. 6 was, of all the paths offered, the most direct path to the former goal location' (Tolman et al., 1992 [1946]: 431). No other path was chosen by anything like this number of rats. 'One should note the frequencies on paths No. 9 and 11. These two paths are the ones that are most similar, or spatially closest to, the original path on which the rats were practiced during the . . . training. The *combined* frequencies of these two paths is only nine percent' (ibid.,

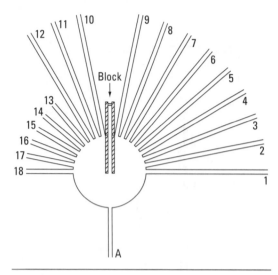

FIGURE 11.5
Apparatus used to test rats.
Source: Tolman et al. (1992: 431).

431–2). Thus, the rats did not try to execute the *response* they had learned so much as they tried to find the *location* where they expected to find food. One could say that the animals had formed a cognitive map that enabled them to navigate through the new terrain in which they found themselves.

The place versus response controversy was one of a number of contentious issues in the age of learning theories. Another instructive example—the latent learning controversy—is reviewed in Box 11.2.

Like so many controversies in psychology, the place-response and latent learning controversies were never really decided. In this respect, these controversies illustrate a more general feature of theoretical dispute in the age of learning theories. Many controversial issues, including the transposition controversy we considered earlier, were collected and analyzed by Goldstein,

---

BOX 11.2

LATENT LEARNING: A CASE HISTORY IN PSYCHOLOGICAL EXPLANATION

Tolman and Hull were great competitors in the psychology of learning. They offered different explanations for well-known phenomena. Their battles are highly representative of the age of learning theories. One of the best known concerns the nature and explanation of **latent learning**.

As we considered earlier, *habit strength* was an intervening variable in Hull's system. Habit strength referred to the connection between a stimulus and a response, and was postulated to increase gradually whenever an animal was rewarded for responding to a stimulus. For example, suppose that a food-deprived animal, such as a hungry white rat, is placed in the start box of a maze similar to the one in the figure below. Eventually the animal will reach the end of the maze and be fed. From Hull's perspective, this means that there will be an increase in the strength of the habits that connect the stimuli from the maze to the correct

responses that enable the animal to reach the food. Thus, turning left, right, right, left, left, right are the responses that the animal needs to learn. Hull would predict that the time it takes the animal to go from start box to goal box would decline gradually as a function of trials. This hypothesis was deduced from Hull's theory and can be tested experimentally. In fact, experiments in which animals were rewarded on each trial showed the kind of continuous improvement that Hull's theory predicted. The data seem to support the notion that habit strength increases continuously as a function of trials on which the animal is rewarded. However, these data are not the whole story.

As we have already seen, Tolman's view of the nature of learning was radically different from Hull's. Tolman argued that learning involved the formation of *expectations* rather than the formation of habits, and that these expectations could be learned in the absence of

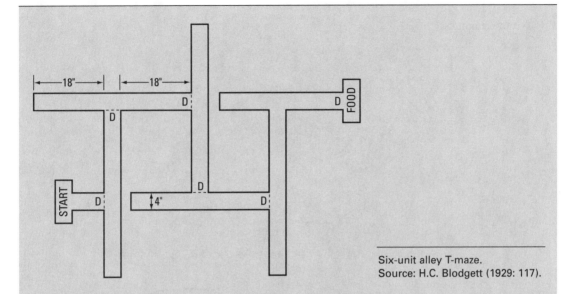

Six-unit alley T-maze.
Source: H.C. Blodgett (1929: 117).

reward. Thus, simply by exploring the maze, an animal could learn what to expect at each point in the maze. The animal might not demonstrate that it had learned anything until it became important for it to do so. What are the consequences of the difference between the hypotheses of Tolman and Hull? Consider the following figure, which contains data from an experiment by Tolman and Honzik (1930). This graph shows data from three groups of rats, each of which was allowed to run once a day through a maze similar to the one shown in the first figure. One group, called HR for 'hungry-reward', was fed every time it reached the food box. Notice that this group behaves just as Hull would have predicted. They go through the maze faster and faster on successive days until they have apparently learned the maze thoroughly and there is no further improvement. Another group, called HNR for 'hungry no reward', also behaves just as Hull would have predicted. This group receives no reward when they reach the end of the maze, and they show no improvement as the days pass, indicating that they may not have learned anything. But wait a minute. Look at the curve for the group labelled HNR-R, for 'hungry no reward-reward'. This group is not rewarded for the first 10 days. These rats behave just like the no-reward group during this period.

According to Hull's theory, they should not have learned anything, because they have not been rewarded. However, when the rats are rewarded on the eleventh and subsequent days, then they very rapidly begin to perform as well as the rats who have been rewarded all along. It is as if these rats learned the maze without reward, but did not display their learning until they were rewarded for doing so. This phenomenon was called *latent learning*. Results such as these led Tolman to make a distinction between *learning*, which could occur without reward, and *performance*, which was influenced by reward. Perhaps you can discover instances of latent learning in your own experience. Can you not learn something without anyone else knowing that you have learned it, like the rats in the HNR-R group. And, again like the rats in that group, do you usually show what you have learned only when it is important for you to do so?

The controversy over latent learning demonstrates how an experiment can provide data that allow a researcher to argue in favour of one theoretical interpretation rather than another. The controversy between Hull and Tolman also illustrates how non-human participants can be used to provide data bearing on a theoretical dispute that is quite general and not restricted to only one species. Hull's and Tolman's

continued

BOX 11.2 (continued)

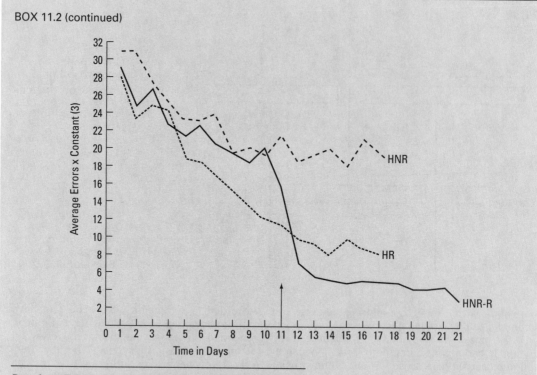

Data from Tolman and Honzik's 'latent learning' experiment.
Source: Tolman (1948: 195).

theories were intended to apply to any species whatsoever, not just to rats or just to people. Although Tolman's theory was challenged on many occasions and eventually was replaced by other theories, the underlying assumption that behaviour is guided by expectancies has proved to be remarkably popular (e.g., Olton, 1992). We will see in a later chapter how Tolman's cognitive approach was developed by others and emerged in the form of cognitive psychology.

Krantz, and Rains. By 1965, most of these issues were 'considered "dead," but it becomes clear in re-examining them that many of them are by no means settled. Research in these fields seems to have petered out without actually clearly resolving the issues' (Goldstein et al., 1965: vi). Goldstein et al. point out that these controversies illustrate the fact that psychology does not progress simply as a result of the steady accumulation of knowledge. There is a certain amount of trial and error involved in psychology, and some blind alleys are simply abandoned after they have been explored. This seems to have happened with much of the research conducted during the age of learning theories. In Chapter 15 we will explore in more detail the extent to which this may be a more general feature of the history of psychology.

The Verbal Learning Tradition

Functionalism and Verbal Learning

The first four editions of *Theories of Learning* (Hilgard, 1948, 1956; Hilgard and Bower, 1966, 1975) included a chapter on functionalism. This chapter typically provided a brief history of the functional school at Chicago and a discussion of Woodworth's contributions. Functionalism was characterized as experimental and associationist in orientation. In the fifth edition (Bower and Hilgard, 1981), the chapter on functionalism was replaced with a chapter called 'Human Associative Memory', and the authors observe that 'the verbal learning tradition [is] the strongest modern issue from Functionalism' (ibid., vi).

Of course, the verbal learning tradition goes back to Ebbinghaus and his studies using nonsense syllables. Variants of these studies continued more or less continuously after Ebbinghaus, as we observed in Chapter 4. Many used the method of paired associates invented by Mary Calkins. Studies of **verbal learning** were concerned with uncovering the basic laws of the formation of associations in humans. E.S. Robinson wrote an influential account of basic associationist principles and suggested that:

> the general law [of association] should be written as follows:
> A = f (x, y, z ...)
> where A is associative strength [and] x, y, z, etc. are such factors as time-interval, frequency of repetition, the state of other existing connections, sensory intensity, affective intensity, and other factors demonstrably related to associative strength. Thus, associative strength is a function of some combination of these factors. (Robinson, 1964 [1932]: 129)

Robinson's formulation illustrates the meaning of the word 'function' in the context of verbal learning. It refers to the study of the formation of associations 'as a function' of different variables such as the ones on Robinson's list. There have been innumerable studies in the verbal learning tradition since Ebbinghaus, and in this section we can only indicate with one or two examples some of the directions taken by this line of research.

Acquisition

Recall our earlier discussion of Guthrie, in which we considered his view that repetition provides the opportunity for a learner to acquire a connection, but does not strengthen a connection already formed. A series of experiments conducted by **Irvin Rock** (1922–95) explored the hypothesis of *one-trial learning* in a particularly provocative way. Rock's experiments (Rock, 1957; Rock and Heimer, 1959; Steinfeld and Rock, 1968) were regarded as classics in many quarters (e.g., Hilgard, 1987: 213).

These experiments called into question an intuition that many of us have about the nature of learning. This intuition can be summarized in terms of the following proverb: 'Practice makes perfect.' We often believe that repeating something we wish to learn over and over will gradually lead to our being able to remember it. This intuition seems to imply that if we were given a list of unfamiliar items to learn, then we might learn a little bit the first time we read through the list, a little bit more the next time we read through the list, and so on, until finally we would have learned the entire list after a suitable number of repetitions. This view of learning implies that it is a *gradual* process and that connections are gradually strengthened.

In light of the foregoing, imagine the following experiment (Rock, 1957). First, make up a set of 50 items, consisting of letter-number pairs, such as L-12, or double-letter-number pairs, such as JJ-48. Then, suppose we have two groups of participants, a control group and an experimental group. The control group is given a list of 12 letter-number pairs to learn. The list is a random sample from the 50 original letter-number pairs. Each of the letter-number pairs is presented on a separate card.

After the participant has seen the entire list, he or she is shown each letter, and asked to recall the appropriate number. This procedure is repeated until the participant either recalls all the numbers correctly or does so badly that the experiment must be terminated before the participant can get them all correct.

Now let us consider how the experimental group is treated. On the first trial, they receive the same set of letter-number pairs as did the control group. After trial 1, however, the pairs that the participant did not get correct are removed, and new pairs substituted for them. Thus, suppose the participant got 5 correct after trial 1. Then the remaining pairs are deleted, and the participant is given a new list of 12 items containing the 5 pairs he or she got right, plus 7 new pairs. This procedure is repeated, with incorrect items being substituted for errors on each trial, until the participant gets all the numbers correct or until the experimenter runs out of new items.

In Rock's original experiment, it turned out that, on average, participants in both groups took virtually the same number of trials to learn the list (about 4.5). This result is surprising because the experimental group is not given the chance to practise on incorrect items until they are correct. Rather, they are always having to learn some new items until they get all the items right. The results were taken by Rock (1957: 193) to suggest that 'repetition plays no role in the formation . . . of associations, other than that of providing the occasion for new ones to be formed, each on a single trial.'

There were several arguments directed against Rock's experimental procedure (e.g., Postman, 1962; Underwood et al., 1962). As was the case in other areas of the psychology of learning, it was difficult to tell whether or not a particular position carried the day. However, Rock's work focused attention on a methodological problem and helped to explore the limits of a particular type of experimental procedure. The question of whether learning is all-or-none or continuous began to be seen as a much more complex issue as a result of Rock's work. In a general way, this was the lesson learned

from much of the work in human associative memory from this period.

Serial Learning

> How does a person manage to learn a succession of responses in a fixed order? The pianist who must play the proper series of notes, or the experimental participant who must master the appropriate sequence of verbal items, is faced with much the same task. What are the processes which underlie the accomplishment of such tasks? This is the problem of serial learning, and it has been studied with human participants mainly through the presentation of lists of nonsense syllables or unconnected words. (Slamecka, 1967: 61)

When participants are asked to learn lists of nonsense syllables, 'it is found that the syllables in the middle of the list are learned more slowly than are those at the two ends, and in general the initial syllables are learned more rapidly than are the final ones' (McCrary and Hunter, 1953: 151). This is a stable, reliable result, found for just about any kind of material learned under a wide variety of conditions. The reason for the existence of such *serial position curves* was intensively investigated for many years.

While the serial position curve might seem to be a rather esoteric topic, it does turn up in some 'real-world' contexts. For example, Roediger and Crowder (1982 [1976]) showed that when participants are asked to recall as many of the presidents of the United States as they can, then the result is a serial position curve, with participants tending to recall both early and recent presidents more frequently than those in the middle of US history. The exception to this rule is the heightened tendency to recall Lincoln, presumably because of his historical prominence. However, Roediger and Crowder note that even this apparent exception can be explained by a principle from verbal learning called the *von Restorff effect* (von Restorff, 1933; Hunt, 1995), which holds that an item that has distinguishing properties will be more likely to be recalled. People are likely to know more about Lincoln than, for example, Van Buren, Grant, or Garfield. Lincoln's distinction will make him stand out as a relatively unique figure in the list of presidents.

The Fate of Verbal Learning

In spite of attempts to apply principles discovered through the study of verbal learning, many observers began to grow impatient with the area. One of the most active and influential students of verbal learning, **Benton J. Underwood** (1915–94), observed that by the 1960s the area of verbal learning had acquired the reputation of being 'dull, narrow, sterile and, in a manner of speaking, deals with a form of learning that is almost intellectually demeaning' (Underwood, 1964: 51–2). While Underwood believed that such an opinion was unjustified, it was clear by that time that the area of verbal learning was not enjoying the prestige that once attached to it. A symposium on *Verbal Behavior and General Behavior Theory* (Dixon and Horton, 1968) brought together several well-known students of verbal learning as well as several critics of the area. The upshot of the conference was that the adequacy of an associationist approach to the study of learning—verbal or otherwise—was called into question. The conveners of the conference, in reviewing the contributions made by the participants, concluded that 'a revolution is certainly in the making' (Horton and Dixon, 1968). That revolution was the so-called *cognitive revolution*, which we will review in Chapter 14.

D.O. Hebb (1904–85)

The Emergence of Neuroscience

D.O. Hebb was a Canadian whose career was largely spent at McGill University in Montreal, and who was the first foreign president of the American Psychological Association (Hebb, 1960). As a young man Hebb wanted to be a novelist and sup-

ported himself through teaching. It was not until the age of 30 that he went to Chicago to study psychology with Karl Lashley. In 1935, Lashley moved to Harvard, and Hebb went along as his student, graduating with the Ph.D. in 1936. About Lashley's influence, Hebb (1980b: 287) said, 'Lashley was my model—Lashley the biological scientist interested in the mind.' Years later, when Hebb wanted to write a general neuropsychological theory, he asked Lashley to collaborate on it (Bruce, 1996), 'but Lashley was entirely uninterested and remained skeptical of the whole thing' (ibid., 296). Hebb (1949) went on to write *The Organization of Behavior* by himself. Although a separate chapter was never devoted to Hebb in any of the editions of *Theories of Learning*, Hilgard (1993: 72) selected Hebb as one of those psychologists who made lasting contributions to psychological theory in the second half of the twentieth century, and singled out *The Organization of Behavior* as having 'revitalized physiological psychology, which had been in the doldrums for years'.

The Organization of Behavior

Hebb's theory was one of **neuropsychology** in that it combined aspects of psychology, such as learning theory and Gestalt psychology, with neurophysiology (Hochberg, 1988: 64). Hebb (1959: 628) described the essence of his theory as follows:

> The key conception is that of a *cell assembly*, a brain process which corresponds to a particular sensory event, or a common aspect of a number of sensory events. This assembly is a closed system in which activity can 'reverberate' and thus continue after the sensory event which started it has ceased. Also, one assembly will form connections with others, and it may therefore be made active by one of them in the total absence of the adequate stimulus. In short, the assembly activity is the simplest case of an *image* or an *idea*: a representative process. The formation of connections between assemblies is the mechanism of association.

Cell assemblies constitute physiological mediating processes and are responsible for representing stimulation. They consist of neurons that have become associated as a result of being active simultaneously. Hebb postulated that the mechanism of association occurred through growth at the synapse, or junction between two neurons. 'The fundamental physiological assumption of learning is that whenever an impulse crosses a synapse it becomes easier for later impulses to do so. More precisely: when a neuron A fires, or takes part in firing, another neuron B, some change occurs in A or B or both which increases A's capacity to fire B in the future. The change might be an enlargement of a synaptic knob; or it might be some chemical change' (Hebb, 1958: 103). This hypothesis has become known as the **Hebb rule** (e.g., McClelland et al., 1986: 36), even though 'this postulate is one of the few aspects of the theory he did not consider completely original. Something like it had been proposed by many psychologists, including Freud in his early years as a neurobiologist' (Milner, 1993: 127).

Cell assemblies represent the basic units of experience that themselves become connected into **phase sequences**. A phase sequence 'amounts to one current in the stream of thought' (Hebb, 1959: 629). Different phase sequences will occur depending on the circumstances. Thus, cell assemblies represent particular events, while phase sequences constitute how these events are organized in a particular situation:

> The sight of a stimulus object may arouse many different trains of thought; which one it does arouse is determined by the already existing central processes which (so to speak) select among these possibilities. . . . [T]he course of thought can have some continuity and directedness, since at each moment the processes now going on tend to pick out, from among the many perceptions of the environment that are possible, only those that are relevant to the activities that have gone before. (Hebb, 1958: 106)

Hebb (1960, 1968) believed that the way cell assemblies represent our experience is well illustrated by the phenomenon of **phantom limbs**. A phantom limb occurs in an adult whenever an active body part, such as an arm or leg, is amputated. The person will still experience the missing body part as 'being there', even though he/she knows perfectly well that it is missing. Marianne L. Simmel (1956) had shown that the probability of the occurrence of a phantom limb following amputation increases steadily with age, until it reaches nearly 100 per cent in adults. In Hebb's (1960) terms, phantom limbs occur as a result of a process whereby each of us develops over time a *body image* that constitutes our representation of our bodies. This body image is the result of cell assemblies that are responsible for representing the typical state of various parts of our body. These cell assemblies will become associated with each other over time and eventually form a stable system, or *body schema*. Any part of the system can cause other parts to fire. Thus, even in the absence of direct stimulation from a missing limb, the person can still experience that limb because the cell assemblies responsible for representing it can still become active. 'No excitation can originate in the missing hand, but the same excitation in principle can arise higher in the pathway by spontaneous firing of the neurons at level X in [Figure 11.6]. If [the participant] S now reports pain in his imaginary hand we are not dealing with any different mechanism, in brain function, than when a normal S reports pain. Report of "sensation" from a phantom limb is not introspective report' any more than 'a dog's yelp when his tail is trod on' is introspective report (Hebb, 1968: 467). Such *vocal responses* are objective, behavioural occurrences under the control of physiological processes.

Motivation

Hebb was particularly interested in understanding how the cognitive neuropsychological processes we have already considered are related to motivational processes. He emphasized the

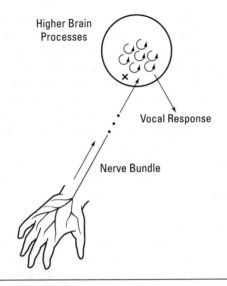

FIGURE 11.6
The relation between normal sensation and the phantom limb.
Source: Hebb (1968: 467). Copyright © 1968 by the American Psychological Association. Reprinted with permission of the publisher.

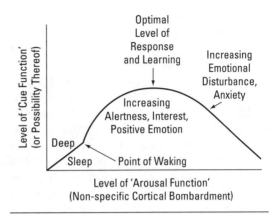

FIGURE 11.7
The relation between arousal and cue functions.
Source: Hebb (1955).

importance of the **arousal system**, 'the nonspecific or diffuse projection system of the brain stem, which was shown by Moruzzi and Magoun (1949) to be an *arousal* system whose activity in effect makes organized cortical activity possible' (Hebb, 1955: 248). Arousal functions in a manner analogous to drive; it 'is an energizer, but not a guide; an engine, but not a steering gear' (ibid., 250). While stimuli have a *cue function* that serves to guide behaviour, their effectiveness is determined by the organism's arousal level at the time of their occurrence. This relationship is illustrated in Figure 11.7.

Hebb's diagram proposes that performance will be optimal when arousal is moderate. Low levels of arousal mean the organism takes too little interest in its environment; too much arousal and the organism is paralyzed by competing response tendencies. Hebb, in common with many other psychologists (e.g., Berlyne, 1960),

argued that the organism will try to maintain an optimal level of arousal, that is, neither too high nor too low. This may require seeking out arousal-producing situations when arousal is too low, as well as satisfying needs that may produce states of high arousal. Hebb's (1958: 176) hypothesis that it is important to the organism to avoid 'a too-easy or monotonous environment' led to one of his most famous lines of research, involving **sensory deprivation**.

Experiments in Sensory Deprivation

The Korean War occurred during the early 1950s, a period when there was an intense interest in the phenomenon of **brainwashing**. The *Oxford English Dictionary* defines 'brainwashing' as 'the systematic and often forcible elimination from a person's mind of all established ideas, especially political ones, so that another set of ideas may take their place; this process regarded as the kind of coercive conversion practiced by certain totalitarian states on political dissidents.' Some former prisoners of war returned to the United States and Canada apparently having been the victims of brainwashing, and its causes were of obvious interest.

One of the conditions of brainwashing appeared to be keeping the person in extreme isolation, without normal stimulation. Hebb and his research group at McGill, funded in part by the Canadian Department of National Defence (Payne, 1986), attempted to mimic such conditions. Paid undergraduate student volunteers served as participants, and were placed in bed in isolation chambers, 'wore translucent but not transparent goggles; heard a constant slight buzzing sound from a small speaker in the foam-rubber pillow except when the experimenter was on line with a question; and wore long cardboard cuffs from the middle of the forearm to beyond the fingers. Thus they received much sensory stimulation, but all of it unpatterned, except in the tests or occasional requests for information' (Hebb, 1980a: 96). For this reason Hebb preferred the term **perceptual isolation** rather than *sensory deprivation*.

Four results from experiments like these were widely reported and believed (Suedfeld and Coren, 1989: 18). The first result is that after two or three days the participants who experienced perceptual isolation began to have hallucinations. The second result is that the same participants were more likely to believe propaganda than was a group of control participants who were also paid undergraduate student volunteers. The control participants listened to propaganda 'advocating belief in ghosts and poltergeists as well as clairvoyance and telepathy' (Hebb, 1980a: 97), but they were less likely to be influenced by it. The third result is that the perceptual isolation participants were less able to think about problems, and the fourth is that the perceptual isolation participants bailed out of the experiment quickly, terminating the session well before the experimenter had scheduled it to end.

One of the most frequently cited reports of the McGill studies of perceptual isolation was Woodburn Heron's *The Pathology of Boredom* (1957). As Suedfeld and Coren (1989: 18) point out, this title has 'come to characterize the field in the minds of many non-specialists'. The topic of sensory deprivation became a staple of under-

graduate education in psychology, and the McGill studies, done in the 1950s, were the standard references in introductory psychology textbooks even in the 1980s. Suedfeld and Coren observe that the McGill studies continued to be cited even though subsequent research tended to show that their results could not be replicated, and they conclude that 'introductory textbook authors have been captured by the dramatic reports of hallucinations, emotional distress and perceptual and cognitive deficits that emanated from the McGill reports. . . . Perhaps textbook authors have ignored the past 25 years of research in order to retain a "good story"' (ibid., 24–5).

The fate of the McGill sensory deprivation studies is instructive in several ways. Not the least of these is the fact that once a particular view of a phenomenon becomes embedded in introductory courses, it is hard to dislodge it, no matter what subsequent research demonstrates. Certain ways of thinking may attain the status of 'what everybody knows' and may be very difficult to modify.

Another neuroscientist, who came on the scene somewhat later than Hebb and who also had a profound influence on neuropsychological theorizing, was Roger Sperry. His work is discussed in Box 11.3.

Albert Bandura (1925–)

Albert Bandura was born in Alberta, Canada, and did his undergraduate degree at the University of British Columbia. He then did his Ph.D. at the University of Iowa, where he was influenced by Kenneth Spence. Bandura developed 'a strong interest in conceptualizing clinical phenomena in ways that would make them amenable to experimental test, with the view that as practitioners, we have a responsibility for assessing the efficacy of our procedures' (Evans, 1976: 243). Bandura is generally regarded as having constructed a persuasive synthesis of different approaches to learning as well as providing a framework within which applied psychologists can operate (e.g., Bower and Hilgard, 1981: 461–72).

BOX 11.3

ROGER SPERRY AND THE SPLIT BRAIN

Roger Sperry (1913–94) did an MA in psychology at Oberlin, completed a Ph.D. in Zoology at Chicago in 1941, and did post-doctoral work with Karl Lashley. He received the Nobel Prize in 1981. Although he had a most distinguished career, he never forgot the influence of those who had been his teachers. In particular he was mindful of the influence of his Oberlin psychology professor, Ronald H. Stetson, himself a student of William James. Indeed, it was after Sperry read William James 'at a very tender grade school age' that he became 'imprinted on the mind-brain problem' (Sperry, 1995: 505).

Beginning with the third edition of *Theories of Learning*, Hilgard and Bower (1966, 1975; Bower and Hilgard, 1981) included a discussion of Sperry's work on *interhemispheric transfer*. As shown in the figure below, this work initially involved severing the optical chiasm in cats with the result that information coming from the right eye was projected only onto the visual areas of the right hemisphere, and information from the left eye projected only onto the visual areas of the left hemisphere. When the corpus callosum is also severed, then no information is transferred between the hemispheres, and each hemisphere appeared to be 'a separate mental domain operating with complete disregard—indeed with a complete lack of awareness—of what went on in the other. The *split brain* animal behaved . . . as if it had two entirely separate brains' (Sperry, 1964: 43).

continued

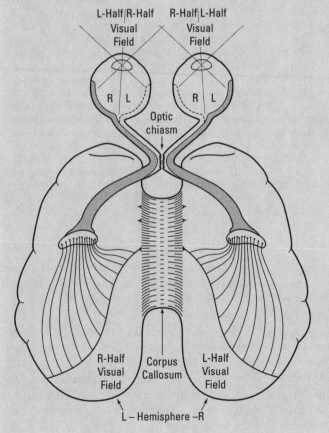

Effect of sectioning crossed fibres in optic chiasm.
Source: Sperry (1961). Copyright © 1961 AAAS. Reprinted by permission of the author.

BOX 11.3 (continued)

Sperry's work broadened considerably when he was able to study humans whose corpus callosum had been severed by neurosurgeons in the hope of alleviating epilepsy. In a series of clever experiments, Sperry and his associates showed not only that 'the two hemispheres of the brain had unique capabilities' but also that 'the combination of both hemispheres working together produced a unified state of consciousness that amounted to more than the simple additive effects of the two hemispheres alone' (Puente, 1995: 941). Sperry's work led to an avalanche of research attempting to discover the 'unique capabilities' of each hemisphere. It had been known at least since the time of Paul Broca (1824–80) and Carl Wernicke (1848–1905) that the left hemisphere was typically associated with linguistic functions. Split-brain research seemed to many to lead to the more general conclusion that the left hemisphere managed 'analytic' (e.g., verbal, rational) tasks and the right hemisphere 'holistic' (e.g., nonverbal, intuitive) tasks (Jaynes, 1976: 100–25; Martindale, 1981: 286–7). However, it subsequently became clear that there was no simple division of labour between the two hemispheres (Gardner, 1982b: 278–85).

In the final phase of his career, Sperry's attention turned to issues of the greatest generality, such as the nature of consciousness and human values (Erdmann and Stover, 2000 [1991]; Stover and Erdmann, 2000). Sperry argued that consciousness was an emergent property of the brain, not reducible to or predictable from other features of the brain. (We came across emergent properties before in our discussion of J.S. Mill's mental chemistry in Chapter 2.) Once consciousness emerges, then it can have an influence on lower-level functions, a process that may be termed emergent causation (Erdmann and Stover, 2000: 50). Sperry (1987: 165) recognized a 'mutual interaction between neural and mental events' such that 'the brain physiology determines the mental events' but is in turn 'governed by the higher subjective properties of the enveloping mental events.' The mind was seen as supervenient, meaning that mental states may 'exert downward control over their constituent neuronal events—at the same time that they are being determined by them' (Sperry, 1988: 609).

Sperry's view of consciousness led him to a new way of understanding human values. 'If conscious mental values not only arise from but also influence physical brain action, it then becomes possible to integrate subjective values with objective brain function and its physical consequences' (ibid., 610). Science and values need not belong to separate realms of discourse, but their study can be mutually complementary (Stover and Erdmann, 2000: 97–127). Sperry's later work on consciousness and values influenced and was influenced by many of the ideas we will consider in Chapter 13 (Humanistic Psychology) and Chapter 14 (Cognitive Psychology).

Social Learning Theory

Bandura has been a leading exponent of **social learning theory**, also known as 'social cognitive theory'. A landmark in the development of this approach was *Social Learning and Personality Development*, written by Bandura with his student Richard Walters. In that book, they 'outlined a set of social-learning principles that emphasize the role of social variables to a greater extent than existing learning theories and consequently appear more capable of accounting for the development and modification of human behavior' (Bandura and Walters, 1963: vii). They called their approach *socio-behaviouristic*.

Social learning theory stressed the importance of **modelling** in shaping a person's learned behaviour. Bandura (e.g., 1986: 46–9) was careful to differentiate between imitation, identification, and modelling. Imitation refers to occasions when one person mimics another person's specific behaviours, while identification refers to a much vaguer process whereby one person may attempt to take on the entire personality of another person. As a concept, modelling is broader than imitation and more precise than identification.

Modelling takes place through a process called **observational learning**. Observational learning refers to the fact that a person can acquire novel responses through the observation of another person's actions. The acquisition of new words by children is a small-scale example of such a process. Children hear someone else use a word in a particular context and are then able to use the word appropriately themselves. Bandura and Walters reported on several experiments attempting to demonstrate that observational learning occurs in a wide range of situations. For example, children who observed a model who behaved aggressively towards a dummy later showed more aggressive behaviour themselves than did other children who observed a more inhibited model (Bandura et al., 1961). Bandura has drawn out the social implications of such modelling, pointing out the potential for both positive and negative influences stemming from the availability of a wide range of models through media such as television. The increase in airplane hijacking after the first occurrence in the US in 1961 is an example of the negative effects of observational learning (Bandura, 1986: 172). However, there are innumerable positive effects. 'On the basis of modeled information, people acquire, among other things, judgmental standards, linguistic rules, styles of inquiry, information processing skills, and standards of evaluation' (ibid., 102).

Behaviour Modification

Bandura has made his name partly as a result of his use of modelling techniques to modify behaviour in clinical and other applied settings. Of course, **behaviour modification** did not originate with Bandura. Everyone acknowledges the pioneering work of **Mary Cover Jones** (1896–1987), who developed the techniques described by Watson and Rayner that we considered in Chapter

8 (Jones, 1924a, 1924b). In one study, Jones worked with a boy, named Peter, who was afraid of furry objects. She arranged to have a caged rabbit present, but at some distance, while the boy was fed. The distance between the boy and the rabbit was decreased on subsequent occasions. Eventually, the boy was able to tolerate being in close proximity to the rabbit, even when it was uncaged. This technique was subsequently refined and named **systematic desensitization** (e.g., Wolpe, 1958). Bandura and Walters (1963: 243) noted that Jones (1924a) also 'explicitly used the method of social imitation in overcoming children's fears. Fear-reduction was produced by having other children behave in a non-anxious manner in the presence of the avoided object. Jones also demonstrated that a fear could be acquired through social imitation, a finding which suggests that exposure to models who suffer, are punished, or exhibit fear in the course of performing a deviant act may be an effective means of producing conditioned fear reactions, which may be lacking in underinhibited children.'

Bandura compared the relative efficacy of using operant conditioning or modelling to change behaviour. He suggested that operant conditioning procedures, which had been advocated by B.F. Skinner, were inefficient because they require the person to emit the desired behaviour so that it can be reinforced. 'In cases in which a behavioral pattern contains a highly unique combination of elements selected from an almost infinite number of alternatives, the probability of occurrence of the desired response, or even one that has some remote resemblance to it, will be zero' (Bandura, 1965: 312). By contrast, Bandura referred to the use of models to provide clients with the opportunity to learn through observation as an example of 'no-trial learning', a process of response acquisition that is highly prevalent. . . . [O]ne does not employ trial-and-error or operant conditioning methods in training children to swim, adolescents to drive an automobile, or in getting adults to acquire vocational skills. Indeed, if training proceeded in this manner, very few persons would ever survive the process of socialization.'

In an influential review, Mischel (1968: 225) stated the argument from the perspective of social learning theory: 'An effective behavior change program . . . must assure that the person learns the necessary response patterns, and that the environment provides the cues necessary to evoke those responses. Exposure to the behavior of appropriate models is one of the most effective ways to enhance the acquisition of new behavior patterns and skills.' Mischel cited a study by Bandura, Grusec, and Menlove (1967) as a particularly powerful demonstration of the efficacy of observational learning:

> In one study, groups of preschool children who were intensely afraid of dogs observed a fearless peer model who displayed progressively stronger and more positive approach behavior to a dog. In the course of eight brief sessions the model exhibited increasingly longer and closer interactions with the dog in accord with a prearranged program of graduated steps. The model progressed from briefly petting the dog while the latter was safely confined in a play pen to ultimately joining the dog in the playpen. The results revealed significantly greater approach behavior on the part of children who had watched the non-anxious model when compared to their peers in control groups. (Mischel, 1968: 225)

It is hard to imagine a more faithful replication and extension of Mary Cover Jones's original findings.

Reciprocal Determinism

A recurrent issue in psychology is whether the person or the situation is more important in determining behaviour (Bowers, 1973). Bandura (1978: 345) maintained that the social learning perspective provides a resolution to this controversy because it 'analyzes behavior in terms of reciprocal determinism', an approach that is different from other forms of explanation in psychology. Reciprocal determinism assumes neither that the environment controls behaviour, as did B.F. Skinner, nor that people are free to do as they wish. Rather, the person, the environment, and behaviour interact so as to determine each other. 'In the social learning view of interaction . . . behavior, interpersonal factors and environmental influences all operate as interlocking determinants of each other' (ibid., 346). Bandura used television viewing as an example of reciprocal determinism.

> Personal preferences influence when and which programs, from among the available alternatives, individuals choose to watch on television. Although the potential televised environment is identical for all viewers, the actual televised environment depends on what they select to watch. Through their viewing behavior, they partly shape the nature of the future televised environment. Because production costs and commercial requirements also determine what people are shown, the options provided in the televised environment partly shape the viewers' preferences. Here, all three factors—viewer preferences, viewing behavior, and televised offerings—reciprocally affect each other. (Ibid.)

IMPORTANT NAMES, WORKS, AND CONCEPTS

Names and Works

Bandura, Albert

Bower, Gordon H.

Conditioning and Learning

Guthrie, E.R.

Hebb, D.O.

Hilgard, Ernest R.

Hull, Clark L.

Jones, Mary Cover

Osgood, Charles E.

Spence, Kenneth W.

Sperry, Roger

The Organization of Behavior

Theories of Learning

Tolman, E.C.

Rock, Irvin

Underwood, Benton J.

Concepts

arousal system

behaviour modification

brainwashing

cell assemblies

cognitive maps

contiguity

drive

habit strength

Hebb rule

latent learning

modelling

molar and molecular descriptions of behaviour

neuropsychology

observational learning

perceptual isolation

phantom limbs

phase sequences

place versus response controversy

primary reinforcer

purposive behaviourism

secondary reinforcer

semantic differential

sensory deprivation

social learning theory

systematic desensitization

verbal learning

RECOMMENDED READINGS

Guthrie

A good summary of Guthrie's approach may be found in his *The Psychology of Human Conflict* (New York: Harper & Row, 1938).

Hull

Another important psychologist in the Hullian tradition was Daniel E. Berlyne of the University of Toronto. His *Structure and Direction in Thinking* (New York: Wiley, 1965) is a scholarly tour de force that combines the Hullian approach with European approaches.

Tolman

For an intriguing account of how Tolman has been interpreted over the years, see F. Ciancia, 'Tolman and Honzik (1930) revisited or the mazes of psychology (1930–1980)', *Psychological Record* 41 (1980): 461–72. One of Tolman's most productive and influential associates was Isidore Krechevsky, who subsequently changed his name to David Krech. Appreciations of Krech's contributions are given by N.K. Innis, 'David Krech: Social activist', in G.A. Kimble and M. Wertheimer, eds, *Portraits of Pioneers in Psychology*, vol. 3 (Hillsdale, NJ: Erlbaum, 1998), 295–306, and L. Petrinovich and J.L. McGaugh, eds, *Knowing, Thinking, and Believing: Festschrift for Professor David Krech* (New York: Plenum, 1976).

Verbal Learning

Another well-known study of one-trial learning is by W.K. Estes, 'Learning theory and the new mental chemistry', *Psychological Review* 67 (1960): 207–23. Good reviews of verbal learning research are L. Postman and G. Keppel, eds, *Verbal Learning and Memory* (Baltimore: Penguin, 1969) and N.J. Slamecka, ed., *Human Learning and Memory* (Oxford: Oxford University Press, 1967).

Hebb

Another important experimental technique used by Hebb's group to investigate cell assemblies involved *stabilized retinal images*. See R.M. Pritchard, W. Heron, and D.O. Hebb, 'Visual perception approached by the method of stabilized images', *Canadian Journal of Psychology* 14 (1960): 67–77. Hebb's classic book is now available again after being out of print since 1966. See D.O. Hebb, *The Organization of Behavior* (Mahwah, NJ: Erlbaum, 2002).

Bandura and Social Learning Theory

Another person identified with the social learning theory movement is Julian Rotter. See his *Social Learning and Clinical Psychology* (Englewood Cliffs, NJ: Prentice-Hall, 1954). Rotter helped introduce the distinction between *external versus internal locus of control*. This distinction refers to the degree to which people see themselves in control of the conditions influencing their behaviour. See Rotter, 'Generalized expectancies for internal versus external control of reinforcement', *Psychological Monographs* 80, 1 (no. 609). This construct generated an immense amount of research, as reviewed by H.M. Lefcourt: 'Internal versus external control of reinforcement: A review', *Psychological Bulletin* 65 (1966): 206–20, and 'Durability and impact of the locus of control construct', *Psychological Bulletin* 112 (1992): 411–14. Reciprocal determinism was criticized by D.C. Philips and R. Orton, 'The new causal principle of cognitive learning theory: Perspectives on Bandura's "reciprocal determinism"', *Psychological Review* 90 (1983): 158–65, with a reply by Bandura: 'Temporal dynamics and decomposition of reciprocal determinism: A reply to Philips and Orton', *Psychological Review* 90 (1983): 166–70.

CHAPTER 12

THE DEVELOPMENTAL POINT OF VIEW

Introduction

Most people associate developmental psychology with the study of children. However, in addition to the study of children, developmental psychology is also a way of looking at psychology as a whole. In this chapter we examine several theorists for whom the developmental approach was a point of view that encompassed everything that people can do, whether alone or in groups. Perhaps the early developmentalists such as G. Stanley Hall and James Mark Baldwin had the most general theories, but Heinz Werner's approach was also a very ambitious developmental theory. Each of the others, while attempting a general theory, is still best known for concentrating on a particular aspect of development: Jean Piaget for the development of logical thinking; L.S. Vygotsky for the development of language; Erik H. Erikson for stages in the life cycle; and Eleanor J. Gibson for the study of learning as a developmental process.

Developmental psychology represents not only a specific area of inquiry in psychology, but also a particular approach to the understanding of psychological phenomena. Developmental psychology and child psychology are not the same thing, although, to be sure, the study of children is and always has been a central part of the developmental approach. However, the **concept of development** is quite complex, and we need to be continuously mindful of the different ways in which this concept has been applied. We can begin to do this by acquainting ourselves with some of the meanings of 'development' listed by the *Oxford English Dictionary*. One important meaning is 'a gradual unfolding; . . . a fuller disclosure or working out of the details of anything, as a plan, a scheme, the plot of a novel'. We shall see that many developmental theorists

adopt such a definition of development as a process that unfolds according to a preset plan. However, other theorists regard 'development' as synonymous with 'evolution', and certainly do not see it as a process that is predetermined, but rather one that is fraught with chance occurrences. Still another variant is the meaning of 'development' as a process of 'bringing out the latent capabilities' of a person. Many developmentalists were (and are) social reformers who wished to ensure that the developmental process maximized the potential abilities of individuals. Some developmental theorists have regarded development as a process of 'advancement through progressive stages', and the question of whether or not there are discernible stages of development has always been a lively issue in this area. As we go along, we will see that there are still more variations on the meaning of 'development'. With that in mind, let us examine some of the major figures in the history of developmental psychology. In what follows you should bear in mind that in this context the word 'genetic', as in 'genetic psychology', has the same meaning as 'developmental'.

G. Stanley Hall (1844–1924)

The Theory of Recapitulation

One of the recurring themes in developmental theory is the idea of *recapitulation*. This idea is most closely identified with the German biologist and philosopher E.H. Haeckel (1834–1919). The famous slogan **ontogeny recapitulates phylogeny** captures Haeckel's central idea. 'Recapitulation' means 'to restate, review, or summarize', while 'ontogeny' refers to individual development and 'phylogeny' to the evolutionary development of a species. Haeckel's position can be stated as follows:

Ontogeny is the short and rapid recapitulation of phylogeny. . . . During its own rapid development . . . an individual repeats the most important changes in form evolved by its ancestors during their long and slow paleological development. (Gould, 1979: 76–7)

This principle has a long and complex history in biology, and has been the source of a great deal of controversy over the years. One concrete application of the principle was in embryology, where it was sometimes claimed that a human fetus undergoes a condensed form of our evolutionary development. Thus, one nineteenth-century thinker 'saw that, at a first stage [of ontogeny], the human brain resembled that of a fish; that at a second stage, it resembled that of reptiles; at a third, that of birds; and at a fourth, that of mammals, in order finally to elevate itself to that sublime organization that dominates all nature' (ibid., 47). The recapitulation principle was extended far beyond the confines of embryology and was also extensively used in other areas, including psychology. The foremost practitioner of recapitulation theory in developmental psychology was **G. Stanley Hall**.

Hall's Life and Career

Hall was born in a rural setting in Massachusetts, did his undergraduate work at Williams College, and subsequently went to Union Theological Seminary. He became a minister, but soon went on to pursue further studies. In 1878 he was awarded the first American Ph.D. in psychology after studying under William James at Harvard. Hall had voracious intellectual interests and explored a variety of disciplines during visits in Europe between 1870 and 1882 (White, 1992: 28). Hall then became professor of psychology at Johns Hopkins University in 1884, but is best known for being the founding president of Clark University in Worcester, Massachusetts (Sokal, 1990). Hall was president of Clark for 35 years, from 1888 until 1923. Among his many achievements were his founding of the *American Journal of Psychology* in

1887 and the American Psychological Association in 1892. Among Hall's most famous students was Lewis Terman, the inventor of the Stanford-Binet, whose work we considered in Chapter 7. Hall was also responsible for Freud's visit to Clark in 1909, which we noted in Chapter 6.

As a teacher, Hall believed that the study of the history of philosophy and psychology was particularly important because it 'deepens mental perspective . . . and rouses a love of many sides and points of view' (Bringmann, Bringmann, and Early, 1992: 287). As a historian of ideas, Hall adopted the personalistic approach, attempting to understand history in terms of the individuals who made it. This approach to the history of psychology was taken up by Edwin G. Boring, whom we have considered earlier as one of the most eminent historians of the discipline. Boring was a colleague of Hall's at Clark in 1919 (ibid.).

Hall's Recapitulationism

Hall's version of the recapitulation principle was informed by a deeply religious sensibility (Vande Kemp, 1992). Not only did he believe that an individual's course of development was a summary of racial history, but he also believed that the historical order in which religions emerged was indicative of their developmental status. Thus, the religious sentiments of a small child are particularly attuned to pagan nature worship, miracles, and myths. However, the developed mind will find itself to be more open to the kind of religious sensibility described by Hall:

This whole field of psychology is connected in the most vital way with the future of religious belief in our land. . . . The new psychology, which brings simply a new method and a new standpoint to philosophy, is, I believe Christian to its root and center; and its final mission in the world is . . . to flood and transfuse the new and vaster conceptions of the universe and of man's place in it . . . with the Scriptural sense of unity, rationality, and love. . . . The Bible is slowly being re-revealed as man's great text book in psychology—dealing with him as a whole, his body, mind, and will, in all the larger relations to nature, society—which has been misappreciated simply because it is so deeply divine. That something may be done here to aid this development is my strongest hope and belief. (White, 1992: 25)

Recapitulation and religion were linked in Hall's mind because he believed that it was only when people understand themselves as at the pinnacle of a long evolutionary process, which each person undergoes in a condensed form, that they can appreciate their destiny, which is to facilitate further evolutionary progression. Hall believed that the people most fit to lead in this endeavour were research psychologists, because they could provide the means for 'self-knowledge and self-control. . . . Psychology was instrumental to the attainment of the perfect social order, and the psychologist occupied a social role consistent with the special obligations of the field' (Morawski, 1982: 1084).

As Gould (1987: 139–40) observes, when it came to evidence for recapitulation, Hall pointed to childhood pleasures and fears. A child's love of the beach, for example, could be traced to that time when our evolutionary ancestors had lived in the sea. Similarly, a child's fear of snakes was a relic of ancient times when it was much more realistic to fear snakes and other reptiles. Great emphasis was laid on play as illustrating recapitulationist principles. Children's games were regarded as relics of what once in our history were adaptive activities. 'The child revels in savagery', in its 'tribal, predatory, hunting, fishing, fighting, roving, playing proclivities' (Hall, 1968 [1904]: 197).

Questionnaires

Hall and his co-workers gathered data on childhood activities through the use of **questionnaires**. Beginning in 1882, Hall (1948 [1883]: 256–7) 'undertook, soon after the opening of the Boston

schools in September . . . , to make out a list of questions suitable for obtaining an inventory of the contents of the mind of children of average intelligence on entering the primary schools of that city. . . . The problem first in mind was strictly practical; viz., what many children be assumed to know and have seen by their teachers when they enter school. . . . [K]indergarten teachers were employed by the hour to question three children at a time.' This procedure initially produced data on 200 children, which showed that 'there is next to nothing of pedagogic value the knowledge of which it is safe to assume at the outset of school life' (ibid., 275). Because of the highly variable and impoverished nature of many urban children's knowledge, Hall (1968) stressed the importance of acquainting them all with nature and myth, a task that parents should accept.

The deep and strong cravings in the individual to revive the ancestral experiences and occupations of the race can and must be met . . . by tales of the heroic virtues the child can appreciate. . . . So, too, in our urbanized hothouse life, that tends to ripen everything before its time, we must teach nature, . . . perpetually incite to visit field, forest, hill, shore, the water, flowers, animals, the true homes of childhood in this wild, undomesticated stage from which modern conditions have kidnapped and transported him. Books and reading are distasteful, for the very soul and body cry out for a more active, objective life, and to know nature and man at first hand. These two staples, stories and nature, by these informal methods of the home and environment constitute fundamental education. (Hall, 1968: 197)

Hall's questionnaire approach was extraordinarily influential. The method was taken up by many other students of child development, and a vast amount of data was collected. The **child study movement** was 'the most popular educational movement of the 1890s, with followers in two thirds of the states' (Zederland, 1988: 155). One of the consequences of this movement was the formation of a bond between psychologists and teachers who worked together in this context. This bond was one of the reasons why psychology became so strongly embedded in the American educational system.

Adolescence

Data collected through questionnaires were one of the foundations of Hall's work on adolescence, which was his most ambitious undertaking. Hall is known for drawing attention to **adolescence** as a period of *storm and stress* in human development (Vande Kemp, 1992: 295). The storm and stress of adolescence is caused by the transition from a relatively comfortable relationship with nature to a new, more civilized level of development.

> This long pilgrimage of the soul from its old level to a higher maturity which adolescence recapitulates must have taken place in the race in certain of its important lines long before the historic period, because its very nature seems to involve the destruction of all its products and extinction of all records. Just as the well-matured adult . . . has utterly lost all traces and recollection of the perturbations of the storm and stress period, because they are so contradictory and mutually destructive and because feelings themselves cannot be well-remembered, so the race must have gone through a long heat and ferment, of which consciousness, which best develops in stationary periods, was lost. (Hall, 1967 [1904]: 219)

Adolescence was a period of 'transformation and reconstruction'. Religious education had a particular importance during adolescence, and religious 'conversion was regarded as a normal outcome of the "storm and stress" of adolescence in individual and species, hastening the transformation from egocentrism to altruism. This theory inspired extensive research on conversion by several generations of psychologists of religion' (Vande Kemp, 1992: 295).

Recent evaluations of Hall's contributions to developmental psychology point out that he was much more than just a successful administrator and institutional innovator. As White (1992: 32–3) notes, Hall's questionnaires established the first '"normal science" of human development'. Hall also 'elaborated a social-biological conception of childhood' in which the underlying theme is that development involves increasingly elaborate 'forms of social participation'. Finally, as White (1992: 33) observes, Hall's conception of development as a process that unfolds according to its own schedule is a useful corrective to many subsequent attempts to speed up development in the mistaken belief that 'the faster the better'.

James Mark Baldwin (1861–1934)

We have already dealt with a part of Baldwin's life in our discussion of Watson in Chapter 8. **James Mark Baldwin** ran the Johns Hopkins psychology department until he was caught in a police raid on a 'colored house' of prostitution and was forced to resign. Following this incident he left the country, and Watson took over at Hopkins. There is, however, much more to Baldwin's career than this unfortunate occurrence might suggest (Horley, 2001).

Baldwin graduated from Princeton in 1884 and then went to Europe, where, among other things, he studied with Wundt and became a devotee of experimental psychology (Wozniak, 1982: 20). He then taught at Princeton and Lake Forest University, and received his Ph.D. from Princeton in 1888. In 1889 Baldwin became a chair at the University of Toronto, an event that 'represents the beginning of modern academic psychology in Canada' (Hoff, 1992: 692). Several figures at the University of Toronto subsequently became important for the history of psychology. Their work is outlined in Box 12.1.

Baldwin became unhappy with the level of support he received at Toronto and returned to Princeton in 1893 as professor of psychology. From

BOX 12.1

THE PSYCHOLOGY OF HUMAN DEVELOPMENT AT THE UNIVERSITY OF TORONTO

One of the most important figures in Canadian psychology in the first half of the twentieth century was **Edward A. Bott** (1887–1974), who became the first head of the Psychology Department at the University of Toronto in 1926. He remained in this position for a remarkable 30 years, until his retirement in 1956 (Myers, 1982: 81). Under Bott, psychology at Toronto had a community orientation similar to that of John Dewey, whose work we reviewed in Chapter 7 (Pols, 2001; 2002: 138). Rather than do research in university laboratories, Bott and his co-workers worked in schools and other community organizations. 'They believed that human beings attained fulfillment in their lives through continuously encountering opportunities for development and growth in their communities: at home, school and work. Psychologists advised parents, teachers, educational administrators, and managers how to foster mental health among the individuals for whom they were responsible' (Pols, 2001: 13).

Among the best-known members of the Toronto research group was **William E. Blatz** (1895–1964). Blatz initiated studies of the 'kinds of child-rearing practices that would foster mental health' (Wright, 1996: 202), by which he meant the attainment of a sense of security. Blatz was also the lead investigator of a developmental study of the Dionne quintuplets (Prochner and Doyon, 1997), who had been taken from their parents by the provincial government and placed in a nursery, where from the ages of approximately 1–4 years Blatz was able 'to plan and direct their daily routines' subject to some supervision from medical authorities (Wright, 1996: 204). Although such an arrangement would not meet the ethical standards of the early twenty-first century, it was consistent with the ethical norms of the 1930s. These norms held that 'the potential to further the good of humankind' outweighed other considerations in the field of child study (Prochner and Doyon, 1997: 105). Balancing the potential benefit derived from research against the possible harm that research may do to individuals is a perennial concern.

Blatz has been called 'perhaps the most colorful figure in the early history of Canadian psychology' (Wright, 1996: 199), a statement that not only reflects Blatz's engaging personality, but also the fact that he was one of the first psychologists to appear routinely on television in Canada. His child-rearing advice was widely heeded by a generation of Canadians.

1903 until 1912 Baldwin was at Johns Hopkins, until the scandal forced him to leave. 'After that incident, he spent little time in the United States, and his name seems to have been virtually blacklisted by the next generation of psychologists' (Cairns, 1992: 22). Baldwin then settled in France, and his ideas were taken up in Europe much more so than in America. In fact, he was a major influence on Piaget and Vygotsky (ibid., 21–2).

Psychology of Mental Development

As Wozniak (1982: 32) observed, Baldwin moved away from experimental, introspective psychology towards developmental psychology partly because he came to believe that mind developed in the individual and was not always present in the same form.

The older idea of the soul was of a fixed substance, with fixed attributes. . . . Under such a conception, the man was father to the child. What the adult consciousness discovers in itself is true, and wherein the child lacks it falls short of the true stature of soul life. . . . The old argument was this, . . . consciousness reveals certain great ideas as simple and original: consequently they must be so. If you do not find them in the child-mind, then you must read them into it.

The genetic idea reverses all this. Instead of a fixed substance, we have the conception of a growing, developing activity. . . . Are there principles in the adult consciousness which do not appear in the child consciousness, then the adult consciousness must, if possible, be interpreted by principles present in the child consciousness; and when this is not possible, the conditions under which later principles take their rise and get their development must still be adequately explored. (Baldwin, 1897: 2–3)

Developmental psychology allowed the psychologist to move beyond mere description of mental events, and to provide an explanation of them, in terms of their genesis. Complicated mental phenomena that appear in the adult may be traced to simpler activities in the child. In this respect, the study of children furnishes us with information that we could never get from animal psychology (ibid., 6). Baldwin did not, however, believe in a rigid set of developmental laws. Particular 'mental functions' did not emerge like clockwork at specific ages, and only very general norms could be formulated. However, child development normally progressed through invariant *stages*, such that one function emerges before another. For example, 'thought develops to a degree independently of spoken language' (ibid., 12).

Without committing himself to a strong view of recapitulationism, Baldwin (ibid., 15–16) nonetheless believed that there were analogies between phylogenesis and ontogenesis. It was possible to discern four 'epochs', or stages, through which both the species and the individual progress. Initially, organisms are concerned with basic sensations and are governed by pleasure and pain. The next stage provides the ability to represent objects and to have memories, but the organism is still quite passive. It is at the third stage that mental life becomes more active, 'self-controlled and volitional', while the final stage provides the opportunity for a fully 'social and ethical' being (ibid., 17). Baldwin presents a complex picture of

development as moving along both cognitive and social dimensions (Kohlberg, 1982).

According to Baldwin's theory, development occurs through a series of interactions between the child and the environment (Freeman-Moir, 1982: 128). He used many concepts that became familiar staples of developmental psychology, such as assimilation, accommodation, and imitation (Cairns, 1992: 19). **Assimilation** refers to the tendency to respond to the environment in familiar ways. Habits, which involve the tendency to repeat adaptive actions, are the chief process of assimilation. **Accommodation**, by contrast, is the tendency to respond to the environment in the novel ways that changing circumstances may require (Baldwin, 1897: 478–9). **Imitation** is the major way in which accommodation takes place. By imitating events in the environment the organism develops new responses. The relation between habit and accommodation is particularly important, because development involves maintaining existing adaptive responses on the one hand (assimilation), while producing novel adaptive responses on the other (accommodation). Over time, the child becomes able to respond to the environment in increasingly complex ways.

Heinz Werner (1890–1964)

Heinz Werner received his Ph.D. in 1914 from the University of Vienna. His original interests were in the psychology of art, and his investigations in that area were approached from a genetic point of view (Kaplan and Wapner, 1960). He joined the University of Hamburg in 1917, where he influenced and was influenced by a number of scholars we have considered in previous chapters, including William Stern, Fritz Heider, and particularly the neo-Kantian philosopher Ernst Cassirer. When the Nazis came to power, Werner left the University of Hamburg in 1933 and held a variety of positions in the United States until he was appointed as G. Stanley Hall Professor of Genetic Psychology at Clark University in 1949 (Franklin, 1990: 181). From his position at Clark, he attracted a number of colleagues and students who went on to become prominent developmentalists themselves, including Seymour Wapner, Bernard Kaplan, and Edith Kaplan. 'Werner created an atmosphere in which students were treated with unusual respect, and atypically for the times, women were regarded as the intellectual equals of men' (ibid., 184). Perhaps this atmosphere was responsible for the extraordinary devotion to Werner's ideas possessed by many of his former students (e.g., Glick, 1992).

The Comparative Psychology of Mental Development

Werner's best-known work, *The Comparative Psychology of Mental Development* (1961 [1926]), which was originally published in German, indicates that his approach to development was *comparative*, in the sense of examining the relation between developmental processes in different cultures as well as different species. Moreover, for Werner development is not restricted to the study of the development of individuals. 'Each field of psychology—the psychology of the individual and of the human race, animal and child psychology, psychopathology and the psychology of special states of consciousness—all these can be approached from the genetic standpoint' (Werner, 1961: 5). In addition to being comparative, Werner's approach was also *organismic*, meaning that 'behavior must be considered in relation to the context of total organismic activity' (Wapner, 1964: 198).

Precisely what it means to take a developmental point of view was most clearly articulated by Werner in his paper, 'The concept of development from a comparative and organismic point of view'. Development is defined in terms of the **orthogenetic principle**:

> wherever development occurs it proceeds from a state of relative globality and lack of differentiation to a state of increasing differentiation, articulation, and hierarchic integration. This principle has the status of a heuristic definition.

Though not itself subject to empirical test, it is valuable to developmental psychologists in leading to a determination of the actual range of applicability of developmental concepts to the behavior of organisms. (Werner, 1957: 126)

This last point is particularly important for understanding Werner's approach. The orthogenetic principle does not purport to be a statement of fact about development. Rather, it provides a framework within which development may be studied, and we will expand upon it as we go along.

> For Werner, development was not a substantive topic area. Rather, it was a way of studying things. Developmental theory was, from his perspective, not an explanation of changes that might be observed with age; it did not really have particularly much to do with age changes at all. It was rather a standpoint for interrogating phenomena. It was a set of questions that investigators posed to themselves about the nature of the phenomena they were studying. (Glick, 1992: 560)

The questions that Werner posed when analyzing phenomena developmentally included the following. Is development uniform or multiform? Is development continuous or discontinuous? Is development unilinear or multilinear? Is development fixed or mobile? Let us examine each of these issues in turn.

Uniformity versus Multiformity

Here the issue is whether 'behavior tends to converge from isolated units toward integrated wholes—i.e., toward uniformity', or whether it becomes increasing differentiated or 'multiform' (Wolff, 1960: 33). Examination of behaviour reveals that it develops in both ways, a fact that is well illustrated by a famous study by Werner and E. Kaplan (1952). Participants in this experiment were 8–13-year-old children who were given several tasks, of which the following is an example.

A corplum may be used for support.

Corplums may be used to close off an open place.

A corplum may be long or short, thick or thin, strong or weak.

A wet corplum does not burn.

You can make a corplum smooth with sandpaper.

The painter used a corplum to mix his paints.

After being presented with each sentence, the child was asked the meaning of 'corplum'. The percentage of children at each age who were able to identify 'corplum' as 'stick' steadily increased. Thus, the ability of children to identify word meanings as a function of the context in which they are used develops *uniformly* with age. However, the methods children use to arrive at a solution are quite varied, and demonstrate that the processes underlying development are *multiform*. Some children generate a unique solution for each sentence and only try to find a general solution at the end, while other children are always looking for a general solution.

The fact that multiple solutions can be generated for the same problem illustrates the importance of the distinction between *process* and *achievement* (Werner, 1937; E. Kaplan, 1983). Werner and his students were less interested in measurements that focused exclusively on achievements than they were in understanding the processes that enabled such achievements to take place. Thus, an intelligence test score considered by itself is a measure of achievement but achievement test scores by themselves do not tell the investigator very much about underlying psychological processes. A **process analysis** examines in detail and over time the way in which a person arrives at a particular achievement (E. Kaplan, 1983: 155). An example of such an analysis would be to carefully observe a child as he or she attempts to answer each item on an intelligence test, so as to be able to specify the means the person is using to attain particular ends. Such analyses are tailored to specific cases and rely less on standardized scores than on the analysis of the behaviour of individuals.

Continuity versus Discontinuity

The continuity-discontinuity issue has traditionally been a central one in developmental psychology (Lerner, 1986: 183–215). Werner (1957: 133) believed that developmental processes had both a continuous and a discontinuous aspect. That is, the child's ability to interact with the world in an increasingly differentiated (precise) and integrated (well-organized) way develops smoothly, but also shows *emergence*. By 'emergence' is meant that later forms of behaviour have properties not found in earlier forms. Such properties are called **emergent properties**, a notion we came across before in our discussion of J.S. Mill in Chapter 2 and Sperry in Chapter 11. Wolff (1960: 33) gives the development of intentional behaviour as an example of an emergent property. Children appear to suddenly develop the ability to set some of their own goals and attempt to achieve them. Thus, intentional behaviour is an emergent property, not reducible to previous behaviours, and shows development to be discontinuous as well as continuous.

Unilinearity versus Multilinearity

Although the orthogenetic principle implies that all developmental processes progress in the same way (unilinearity), it nevertheless permits individuals to develop in idiosyncratic ways (multilinearity). Werner (1957: 137) recognized the existence of individual differences in development, viewing them as 'specializations' or 'aberrations'. Werner uses the example of physiognomic perception, which we considered in the chapter on Gestalt psychology. Physiognomic perception involves experiencing the expressive quality of things, such as the friendliness of a face. While Gestalt psychologists believed that physiognomic properties are intrinsic features of percepts and do not need to be learned, Werner believed that physiognomic perception was a relatively 'primitive' form of representation. Children would be expected to 'physiognomize' perception, while adults would tend towards a relatively 'objective' form of representation (Werner and B. Kaplan, 1963: 106). While this is the general rule, there are nevertheless people, such as artists, who specialize in physiognomic perception, and who develop the ability to represent events physiognomically alongside the ability to represent events objectively. Thus, for Werner a 'primitive' process was an 'early' or 'primary' process, and need not be 'simple' or 'crude' (Franklin, 1997: 482).

An example of the unilinear aspect of development is the way in which organism-environment interactions progress (Werner and B. Kaplan, 1963: 9; Wapner, 1964: 196). The most primitive form of interaction involves *tropistic* and/or *reflexive* responses to physical stimuli. These are relatively rigid, biological processes that are early to emerge both phylogenetically and ontogenetically. From a Wernerian standpoint, the studies of behaviourists were preoccupied with this type of process. At the next level of development one finds *sensori-motor* forms of interaction, in which there is 'direct, motoric, concrete manipulation of objects' (Wapner, 1964: 196). Tool usage by apes would be an example of such a process. This type of interaction differs from the reflexive because the organism can now represent itself as different from the objects with which it deals and begin to use objects to attain goals. The development of a distinction between subject (self) and object (world) is a central developmental achievement. The third level of organism-environment interaction is *conceptual* or *contemplative*. This level is most characteristic of adult, human thought, and it permits the person to construct tools and symbols 'in the service of knowing about and manipulating the environment' (Werner and B. Kaplan, 1963: 9).

Fixity versus Mobility

Later developmental levels do not displace earlier ones. Rather, as development proceeds, earlier levels become subordinated to later ones. This is what the orthogenetic principle means by 'differentiation and hierarchic integration'. The organism attains a greater range of operations, but these are organized hierarchically so that later forms control earlier ones. This implies that earlier ways of behaving tend not to be fixed, but to be mobile enough to change when they become part of a new organization (Wolff, 1960: 34). This tendency is well expressed in the Bible (I Corinthians 13:2), 'When I was a child I spake as a child, I understood as a child, I thought as a child. But when I became a man, I put away childish things.' The adult still speaks and thinks, but usually does so in a way that is different from how he or she would have as a child.

Even if adults have attained a relatively advanced developmental level, adult behaviour may still not be fixed at that level. They may still sometimes behave in childish ways. Earlier modes of functioning 'may come to the fore when the organism is confronted with especially difficult and novel tasks: in such cases, one often finds a partial return to more primitive modes of functioning before progressing towards full-fledged higher operations; we may refer to this tendency as a manifestation of the *genetic principle of spirality*' (Werner and B. Kaplan, 1963: 8).

To be sure, there is a complexity to Werner's type of developmental analysis. He does not provide convenient age norms for the attainment of particular achievements, such as logical thinking. Such norms run counter to the kind of detailed, process analysis that Werner and his students believed was the best way to gain an understanding of development (Glick, 1992: 61–2).

Microgenesis

Werner believed that developmental analysis could be extended to phenomena that develop over relatively brief periods of time, even as short as a few milliseconds (e.g., Werner, 1935). Every psychological process, such as perceiving or speaking, takes time to unfold, and such **microgenetic processes** (Flavell and Draguns, 1957) have the same formal properties as do processes that develop over longer intervals, such as months or even years. This means that the orthogenetic principle can be applied equally to microgenetic and genetic processes. When it is initiated, a psychological process is global and undifferentiated and progresses towards increasing differentiation and articulation.

Werner (1935) pioneered the use of an experimental technique to investigate microgenetic processes in perception. Werner's procedure is best understood by examining Figure 12.1. If you had been a participant in this experiment, you would have been shown a disk, like that labelled 'first stimulus', for a brief period. Then you would have been shown a ring, like that labelled 'second stimulus'. The outer contour of the disk was the same as the inner contour of the ring, so that the ring fit exactly over the disk. Werner varied the time between showing the disk and showing the ring. When this interval was relatively long (over 200 milliseconds), the subject saw two stimuli, the first being the disk, followed by the ring. The most interesting cases occurred when the time between the two stimuli was relatively short (between 100

and 200 milliseconds). Under those circumstances subjects reported only seeing the ring, and did not report seeing the disk at all.

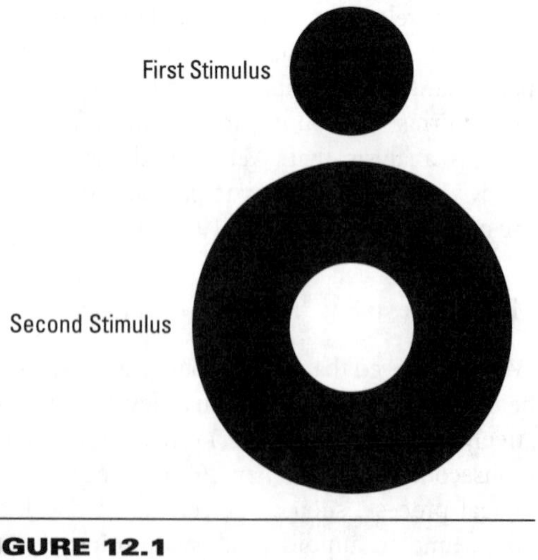

Werner explained this result in terms of the time it takes for a perception to be constructed. When the disk is presented the subject begins to perceive it from the centre outward. The last stage in the perception of the disk is the construction of its edge, or contour. Suppose that the ring is presented just as the disk contour is being constructed. Remember that the inner contour of the ring matches the contour of the disk. Consequently the process of construction of the inner contour of the ring will prevent the completion of the disk. Since the disk is not allowed to be fully constructed, there is no 'finished' object to be perceived, and consequently the disk is not seen. Notice how this experiment relies on a detailed 'process analysis' of the microgenesis of perception.

Jean Piaget (1896–1980) and Bärbel Inhelder (1913–97)

In the latter half of the twentieth century, many commentators shared the view that Piaget's theory was 'the most nearly complete systematization we have of how individuals develop, especially in the cognitive domain' (Sternberg, 1984: viii). The stature of **Jean Piaget** in the history of developmental psychology was probably unrivalled by any other theorist, and while he was alive he was perceived even by those outside of psychology as 'our leading scholar of child development, one of the most respected intellectuals in the world' (Gould, 1979: 144).

Born in Switzerland, Piaget began publishing on biological topics in 1907 when he was 11 years old. His career as a psychologist may be said to have begun in Paris in 1919, where he went to do postdoctoral studies after receiving a Ph.D. in natural science from the University of Neuchâtel. Piaget:

FIGURE 12.1
Werner's backward masking technique (1935).

was offered the opportunity to work in Binet's laboratory at a Paris grade school. Dr. Simon, who was in charge of the laboratory, suggested that Piaget might try to standardize [Sir Cyril] Burt's reasoning tests on Parisian children. Although Piaget undertook this project without enthusiasm, his interest grew when he began the actual testing. He found himself becoming increasingly fascinated, not with the psycho-metric and normative aspects of the test data, but with the processes by which the child achieved his [or her] answers—especially his [or her] *incorrect* answers. By adapting psychiatric examining procedures . . . he was soon using the *clinical method* which was later to become a kind of Piagetian trademark. (Flavell, 1963: 3)

Piaget returned to Switzerland in 1921 and eventually became Director of the Centre for Genetic Epistemology at the University of Geneva.

Although the theory that bears his name is pri-marily Piaget's creation, his associate, **Bärbel Inhelder**, helped develop it in the period following World War II (e.g., Piaget and Inhelder, 1969). In addition to making substantive contributions, 'she frequently attended international conferences where American psychologists met her and could converse easily with her, for her English was excel-lent' (Hilgard, 1993: 73). Thus, Inhelder played a crucial role in making Piagetian theory as wide-spread as it became (Gruber, 1998).

Genetic Epistemology

Piaget called his approach **genetic epistemology**, or the study of the development of knowledge. 'Genetic epistemology attempts to explain knowl-edge, and in particular scientific knowledge, on the basis of its history, its sociogenesis, and especially the psychological origins of the notions and opera-tions upon which it is based' (Piaget, 1968a: 1). For Piaget, knowledge is not simply the result of the application of innate categories to experience, in the way that Kant proposed. Nor does knowledge simply accumulate as a result of experience in the way that empiricists such as Locke, Berkeley, and Hume suggested. There are 'hereditary factors' such

as 'the constitution of our nervous system and of our sensory organs' that limit the kinds of experi-ences of which we are capable (Piaget, 1963: 2). However, our most important inheritance is the function of intelligence, which enables us to adapt to our environment. Intelligence is not fixed, but develops. The study of the way that intelligence develops is the subject matter of Piaget's psychology.

The Development of Intelligence

We discuss the development of intelligence in terms presented by Piaget in the introduction to his classic work, *The Origins of Intelligence in Children* (1963). Another useful translation of the same material, containing extensive explanatory footnotes by David Rapaport, is Piaget (1951).

The study of the development of the ability to think logically owes more to Jean Piaget than to anyone else. Logical thinking is the hallmark of intelligence. Intelligence is rooted in biological processes, which are themselves concerned with furthering the organism's adaptation. Adaptation is an *invariant function* of the organism. Organisms adapt by changing themselves in response to the environment in ways that are not random, but in doing so they reveal processes that exist at all levels of development. Piaget (1950: 6) uses the example of digestion to illus-trate how the organism changes with changing circumstances. A hungry organism takes in food, and the food is transformed to be used by the body. The organism *assimilates* the food by chang-ing it to suit its needs. Eventually the body returns to its original state, and the process begins all over again. Suppose, however, that the organ-ism's diet must change because the food it habit-ually ingests is no longer available. Now the organism, to adapt, will have to adjust to new foods. Such an adjustment is an *accommodation* of the organism to environmental change.

Assimilation and accommodation exist at all levels of adaptation, including intelligence. Intelligence involves assimilation because we must put things in terms we can understand in order to be able to deal with them. However, we cannot adapt merely by changing everything to fit our own way of doing things. We must also accommodate by changing our way of doing things so as to come to terms with reality.

Piaget singled out *play* as a relatively pure example of assimilation, and *imitation* as a relatively pure example of accommodation. 'Play . . . proceeds by relaxation of the effort at adaptation and by maintenance or exercise of activities for the mere pleasure of mastering them and acquiring a feeling of virtuosity or power' (Piaget, 1962: 89). When a child pretends, for example, that a broomstick is a horse and proceeds to 'ride' it all over the house, then the child is disregarding what the broomstick actually is and using it instead for his or her own purposes. By contrast with play, 'imitation is a kind of hyperadaptation, through accommodation to models' (ibid.). Imitation plays a central role in the acquisition of language, for example, which begins through the child's attempts to imitate sounds made by others. Neither play by itself nor imitation by itself is enough to guarantee our well-being. Assimilation and accommodation are opposing tendencies, each one as important as the other. Piaget emphasized the necessity of attempting to achieve a balance between assimilation and accommodation, a process he termed *equilibration*.

Piaget's Clinical Method

As indicated previously, Piaget's studies of the development of intelligence employed a **clinical method**. The method essentially consists of an open-ended series of questions designed to elicit the child's viewpoint on the subject of the investigation. The nature of the method is well illustrated in Piaget's (1976 [1965]) exploration of the way children understand the rules of the game of marbles.

> The experimenter speaks more or less as follows. 'Here are some marbles. . . . You must show me how to play. When I was little I used to play a lot,

but now I've quite forgotten how to. I'd like to play again. Let's play together. You'll teach me the rules and I'll play with you.' . . . It is important to bear in mind all possible contingencies of the game and to ask the child about each. This means that you must avoid making any sort of suggestions. All you need to do is to appear completely ignorant, and even to make intentional mistakes so that the child may each time point out clearly what the rule is. Naturally, you must take the whole thing very seriously, all through the game. . . . It is of paramount importance to play your part in a simple spirit and to let the child feel a certain superiority at the game (while not omitting to show by an occasional good shot that you are not a complete duffer). In this way the child is put at ease, and the information he gives as to how he plays is all the more conclusive. (Piaget, 1976 [1965]: 418–19)

The features of the method Piaget stresses with respect to investigating children's games—such as gaining the child's confidence, not appearing to be superior, asking questions about all aspects of the matter, and avoiding suggestions—are important features of the method when one is investigating any aspect of children's activity. The clinical method was criticized by many other developmentalists, especially those trained in America, who preferred more 'objective' methods, such as standardized tests. However, Piaget believed that the deficiencies of the clinical method were more than offset by the richness of the information it could provide when used by a skilled and perceptive observer. Piaget was also criticized for studying his own children, which he did from 1936 to 1945 (Wolff, 1960: 15), but it is far from true that Piagetian theory was based solely on such observations. Piagetian theory also drew on observations of a great many children made by psychologists not only in Geneva but from around the world. One such centre of Piagetian research was at the University of Montreal, under the direction of Adrien Pinard (1916–98).

Piaget's application of the clinical method to the study of the child's understanding of the rules of the game of marbles showed that these rules went through a sequence of stages. Initially, the child is concerned only with what it is possible to do with the marbles, a stage Piaget (1976: 430) calls 'simple individual regularity'. After the age of two, a new stage begins to emerge when the child imitates the rules he or she sees others follow. However, the child uses the rules in a personal way, without engaging in any co-operative activity, and Piaget calls this stage 'egocentric'. Around age 7, children begin a 'co-operative' stage by deciding together what the rules will be. However, the rules are formulated neither precisely nor consistently from time to time. The fourth and final stage emerges around age 11 when a consistent and enduring set of rules is subscribed to by all participants. Piaget calls this the stage of 'codification'. These particular stages are interesting in their own right as illustrating the development of an understanding of the social rules governing an area of interpersonal interaction. However, it was Piaget's contention that the development of rules of the game of marbles was also interesting because it illustrated general stages of intellectual development. For Piaget, there was an invariant sequence of stages that regulated all aspects of intellectual development.

Stages in the Development of Intelligence

Piaget believed that a crucial aspect of intellectual development was a discontinuous series of levels or **stages**. Stages are qualitatively different modes of psychological organization. Initially, the child responds concretely to particular situations, but by progressing through the developmental stages she or he becomes able to use general principles to deal abstractly with the world. Although the sequence of stages through which the child progresses is invariant, there are no firm age norms at which these must occur.

Sensorimotor period. During the first two years of life the child is initially able to interact with objects only in rudimentary ways but gradually shows a more intelligent approach to these interactions. For example, consider a child who is able to

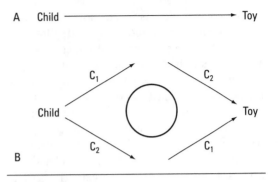

FIGURE 12.2
The attainment of associativity in sensorimotor intelligence.

crawl around on the floor and thus move from one location to another to attain a desirable object, such as a favourite toy. Obviously, the child will crawl directly from the first place to the second, provided there are no barriers. This situation is diagrammed in Figure 12.2A. The situation in Figure 12.2B is more interesting. In this case there is a barrier—a round table—between the child and the goal. Through active exploration of situations such as this, the child can begin to appreciate that the goal can be attained in different ways (e.g., Berlyne, 1965: 205). Two of these alternatives are diagrammed in Figure 12.2B. The child can crawl to its left (C_1) and then to the right after passing the barrier (C_2), or the child can crawl to its right (C_2) and then back to the left after passing the barrier (C_1).

Piaget's (1966: 41) point in analyzing situations such as this one is that the development of the ability to take detours reveals the beginnings of the development of logic. In this case we can see the roots of the concept of *associativity*. The child begins to realize that actions taken in different orders may lead to the same result. Thus, in our example, $C_1+C_2 = C_2+C_1$ in the sense that both orders bring the child to the same goal. Moreover, the child may return to its original position after having attained its goal, a sign of the beginnings of *reversibility*, which, as we shall see, is a central concept in Piagetian psychology.

Of course, there is much more going on in the **sensorimotor period** than the development of the ability to make detours! Another important achievement is the development of an awareness of *permanent objects*. Initially, the child makes no distinction between itself and objects in the external world. 'At about five to seven months, when the child is about to seize an object and you cover it with a cloth or move it behind a screen, the child simply withdraws his already extended hand' and acts as if the object ceased to exist (Piaget and Inhelder, 1968: 14). Subsequently, however, the child will look for the hidden object, demonstrating understanding of the fact that the object continues to exist even when it can no longer be seen. This marks the beginnings of the realization that the nature of the external world is not dependent on the child's activities. The emergence and continued refinement of objectivity is one of the hallmarks of the developmental process.

Preoperational period. Piaget described this stage as lasting roughly from two to seven years and having as its major feature the emergence of symbolic activity, including language. As a consequence of the 'symbolic function . . . the internalization of actions into thoughts becomes possible' (Piaget, 1957: 10). The child is no longer limited to merely doing things, but can now also begin to think about things. Piaget and Inhelder (1968: 53) point to *deferred imitation* and *symbolic play* as characteristic of this stage. Deferred imitation refers to the ability to imitate a model in its absence. Such imitation requires that the child be able to represent internally the model so as to be able to mimic it. **Symbolic play** refers to the ability to pretend that something is the case, as in the broomstick/horse example.

The **preoperational period** is also interesting and important for what it shows the child still to be unable to do (Piaget, 1957: 11). One of Piaget's (1968b; Piaget and Inhelder, 1973) most dramatic illustrations concerns the preoperational child's memory for ordered events. Piaget described one experiment as follows:

children are shown an ordered configuration, that is, 10 sticks, varying in size from about 9 to 15 centimetres, ordered from the biggest to the smallest. . . . The children are asked to have a good look, so that they will be able to draw it later. A week later, without showing them the configuration again, they are asked to draw or to describe verbally . . . what we had shown them before. Six months later, without seeing the configuration they were asked to do the same thing. (Piaget, 1968b: 3)

The interesting result of this experiment, and others like it, is that the quality of memory depends on the age of the child. After one week, the youngest children in the experiment (3–4 years) only remember that they were shown a set of sticks, but do not recall their relative lengths. Only the oldest children (6–7 years) remember that the sticks were ordered, or seriated, from small to large. The truly remarkable finding reported by Piaget and Inhelder is that six months later the younger subjects' memory has *improved*! Now children are able to report that the sticks had been in some kind of order, although their recall may not be perfect. Piaget and Inhelder interpreted such findings as meaning that memory changes as the child develops. 'Old' memories will be recalled in terms of the child's 'new' developmental level. The younger children initially could not represent seriation and so could not recall it. Later on they have developed the ability to represent an ordered series, and only then are they able to reconstruct what they had been shown. Piaget and Inhelder (1973: 409) took such findings as showing that individual psychological functions (such as memory) are not determined by the characteristics of particular experiences, but operate in accordance with the general intellectual level of the child.

Concrete operations. Children in the preoperational period easily confuse the classes to which events belong. Piaget (1957: 4) described an experiment in which children who were between 5 and 8 years of age were shown a set of 20 wooden beads. The beads were either *brown* or *white*, with the majority being brown. The children were asked if there are more brown beads or more wooden beads. Of course, this strikes adults as a silly question because all the beads are wooden. We know that the total number of wooden beads is greater than the number of brown ones, but the child is not at all sure of this. Rather, the child is likely to say that there are more brown beads than wooden ones because, after all, there are only a few white ones. This 'logic' may strike us as puzzling until we realize that the child lacks the concept of a superordinate class that contains the other two classes. Thus, suppose we consider A the class of wooden beads, $B1$ the class of brown beads, and $B2$ the class of white beads. As adults we immediately see that $A = B1 + B2$, and that $B2 < A$. However, the child does not yet appreciate that something can be the member of one class ($B1$) and of another (A) simultaneously. To the child $B1$ is larger than A, because if you take $B1$ from A, then only $B2$ is left, and $B1 > B2$. The child lacks a stable concept of a superordinate class.

It is during the period of **concrete operations** (roughly between 7–11 years) that children come to understand that something can be placed in one class (e.g., brown beads) and also in another class (e.g., wooden beads) at the same time. To put it more formally, children realize that something can belong to both a subordinate class (e.g., brown beads, white beads) and a superordinate class (e.g., wooden beads). An important next step is the **multiplication of classes**. Multiplication of classes becomes a possibility when the child realizes that something can belong to more than one superordinate class. For example, we can classify people in more than one way simultaneously. People can be classified by such dimensions as *gender* and *income* as well as any number of additional dimensions. An example is shown in Figure 12.3. Suppose we let A be one superordinate class (such as gender) and B be another superordinate class (such as income). We can further classify people as *men* (A1) or *women* (A2) and as *rich* (B1) or *poor* (B2),

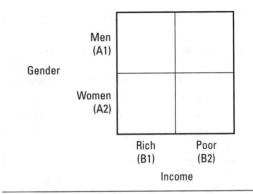

FIGURE 12.3
The multiplication of classes.

resulting in the four classes in Figure 12.3: rich men, rich women, poor men, and poor women.

Multiplication of classes is an example of an *operation*, or internalized action. Instead of actually manipulating object, such as placing them in boxes, the child can imagine what the results would be of carrying out the action. The stage of concrete operations gives the child much to think about, but all the child is able to think about are specific states of affairs. Operations at this stage are termed 'concrete' because they are 'not yet completely dissociated from the concrete data to which they apply' (ibid., 15).

Formal operations. Sometime around age 12 the child begins to be able to carry out **formal operations** on possible as well as actual events. For example, a multiplication of classes may be undertaken in a purely experimental manner. The child can imagine different possible independent variables, such as *income* and *gender*, and formulate hypotheses concerning their possible effects on behaviours of various sorts. These hypotheses can then be tested against observed data.

The two-by-two classification in Figure 12.3 is, of course, only one possibility. One could think of any number of alternative classes that could be multiplied, such as age (old vs young) or height (tall vs short). Depending on the situation, different classifications would be relevant. Moreover, there is no reason to be limited to multiplying only two dimensions. It is possible to imagine experiments that classify events using three or more variables (e.g., *gender* by *age* by *intelligence*).

Could one imagine multiplying all possible classes? That would result in a 'logical space' that contained all possible events. Wittgenstein put it like this: 'Logic deals with every possibility, and all possibilities are its facts. . . . If I know an object, I also know all its possible occurrences in states of affairs. . . . Each thing is, as it were, in a space of possible states of affairs. This space I can imagine empty, but I cannot imagine the thing without the space' (Wittgenstein, 1974 [1922]: 71). It is necessary to have a logical space within which to imagine some of the possibilities, and the development of formal operations makes this logical space possible. However, in any actual experiment, only a part of the logical space can be included.

Piaget as a Structuralist

Piaget was a part of a broad European intellectual movement called **structuralism** (Gardner, 1974; Lane, 1970). Other prominent structuralists include the anthropologist Claude Lévi-Strauss (1967), the linguist Roman Jacobson (1967), and the novelist/philosopher Umberto Eco (1989). The *Oxford English Dictionary* defines a *structure* as 'an organized body or combination of mutually connected and dependent parts'. While there are very great differences between individual structuralists, they all share the assumption that organized systems underlie and control all aspects of human experience, from art to politics and from child development to scientific reasoning (Lane, 1970: 13). Contemporary structuralism should not be confused with Titchener's psychology, which is sometimes given the same name.

Piaget (1970, 1973) emphasized that structures must be understood in terms of the way they develop over time. Developing structures are characterized by three properties: *wholeness*, *systems of transformations*, and *self-regulation*.

Wholeness

Structures are not merely compounds of elements. As in Gestalt psychology, structures are wholes and, as such, are not reducible to their parts. Unlike the Gestalt psychologists, however, Piaget did not believe that structures emerged spontaneously in experience. The structure of human experience must be understood in terms of the way it has developed, both historically and in the life of the particular person. Structures develop over historical time as well as within the life of individuals. The structure of the medieval mind was more limited than that of the modern mind in terms of what it was able to conceive. Nevertheless, mentalities at any level of development will be characterized by wholeness.

Systems of Transformations

The wholeness of structures is not static but dynamic. That is, the parts of structures are capable of being transformed into other parts of the same structure according to definite rules. For example, linguistic structures possess grammatical transformations that allow active sentences (e.g., 'The cat chased the dog') to be transformed into passive sentences (e.g., 'The dog was chased by the cat'). In arithmetic, numbers may be transformed into each other in a variety of ways. For example, 6 may be divided by 2 to get 3, or 1 may be added to 2 to get 3, and so on. These transformations are not arbitrary, but are parts of a self-regulating structure.

Self-regulation

Self-regulation is the key property of structures. A structure is self-regulating if 'transformations inherent in a structure never lead beyond the system but always engender elements that belong to it and preserve its laws' (Piaget, 1970: 14). Logical and mathematical structures are good illustrations

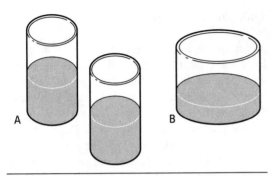

FIGURE 12.4
The conservation of quantity.

of self-regulation. In arithmetic, for example, you can transform numbers into each other through unambiguous transformations (addition, subtraction, multiplication, and division). If the transformations are applied properly, then the system always provides the correct answer. Moreover, every transformation has an inverse that enables the transformation to be undone. Thus, by dividing 6 by 2, you get 3, but you can get back to 6 again by multiplying 3 by 2. A perfect structure is reversible if it always allows you to get back to where you started, and such **reversibility** is an extremely important property of high-level structures.

By no means all structures are perfectly self-regulating, although there is a tendency for structures to become self-regulating. It is a large part of Piaget's genius to have described in considerable detail the processes whereby psychological structures develop self-regulation. One of his most famous examples is the achievement of **conservation**. There are many forms of conservation, but perhaps the best known is conservation of quantity, which is illustrated in Figure 11.4.

In a typical conservation task, a child is shown two glasses, each containing the same amount of fluid, as in Figure 12.4A. The fluid from one of the glasses is then poured into another glass of different dimensions, like the one in Figure 12.4B. Although the level of the fluid in the last glass is

different from the previous level, adults have no difficulty concluding that the amount of fluid in the glasses is the same. However, as parents know, five-year-old children may prefer the tall glass because it appears to them to contain more than the short, stubby glass. Such children are termed *preconservative*, because they do not understand that the quantity of liquid is conserved even though its appearance has changed.

The difference between the adult and the child demonstrates the difference between a self-regulating and a non-self-regulating structure. The adult realizes that even though the fluid is transformed when it is poured from one glass to another, these transformations could be reversed, returning everything to its original state. It is precisely this lack of awareness of reversibility that makes the child focus on one dimension, such as the height of the fluid, and not take other changes into account, such as the greater width of the fluid. The preconservative child cannot transform one situation into the other and back again. Rather, the child is *centred* on one aspect of the situation. To understand it properly, the child must become *decentred*, which involves allowing each dimension to correct the other one. A decentred view reveals the underlying reality behind changing appearances (Flavell, 1985: 96).

Can Development Ever End?

Although structures tend to develop in the direction of self-regulation, it is illusory to imagine that development can reach a point where it is complete. No matter what level of structure is attained, it is impossible for that level of structure to understand itself without progressing to a still higher level that includes the first. '[T]here is no "terminal" or "absolute" form because any content is form relative to some inferior content, and any form the content for some higher form' (Piaget, 1970: 140). This means that 'the ideal of a structure of all structures is unrealizable. The *subject* cannot be . . . a finished . . . structure; rather it is a center of activity. And whether we substitute "society" or "mankind" or "life" or even "cosmos" for "subject," the argument remains the same' (ibid., 142). Thus, living structures are in a continuous, never-ending process of construction.

L.S. Vygotsky (1896-1934)

Although **L.S. Vygotsky** died in the first half of the twentieth century, his ideas became more influential as the century progressed. One reason was that Vygotsky 'provides the still needed provocation to find a way of understanding man as a product of culture as well as a product of nature' (Bruner, 1986: 78). A noted Vygotsky scholar (Wertsch, 1985: 231) remarked that 'It may strike many as ironic that Vygotsky's ideas should appear so fruitful to people removed from him by time and space. . . . Instead of viewing this as paradoxical, however, it should perhaps be seen as a straightforward example of how human genius can transcend historical, social and cultural barriers.'

Vygotsky graduated from Moscow University in 1917, and was initially very interested in the relation between art and psychology (Vygotsky, 1971). He gradually began to focus on the psychology of teaching, particularly with respect to physically and mentally challenged children. It was during this period that he wrote what was to become his most influential work, *Thought and Language*. This work was not fully translated into English until many years after its appearance in Russian (Vygotsky, 1962 [1934]). He died of tuberculosis, bringing to a tragic close a brief but extraordinarily productive life (Luria, 1978).

Because of the time and place in which he worked, we should not be surprised to discover that Marxist ideas shaped Vygotsky's thinking (Teo, 2001: 197). However, it would be a mistake to criticize Vygotsky's theory merely because it has Marxist roots. Many of Vygotsky's ideas have been warmly welcomed in non-Marxist countries, such as the United States, because they can be applied to general developmental issues without raising questions of political ideology.

Thought and Language

An important assumption that Vygotsky borrowed from Marx was that 'historical changes in society and material life produce changes in "human nature" (consciousness and behavior)' (Cole and Scribner, 1978: 7). This means that the developmental process is inherently social (Wertsch and Tulviste, 1992: 548). Development is not entirely constrained by the nature of the nervous system and it cannot be understood on the level of individual development. Moreover, people cannot be studied in the same way one would study animals, because this would overlook the essentially social nature of human development.

> [H]uman behavior differs qualitatively from animal behavior to the same extent that the adaptability and historical development of humans differ from the adaptability and development of animals. The psychological development of humans is part of the general historical development of our species and must be so understood. (Vygotsky, 1978: 60)

A crucial difference between humans and other animals is the way that tools are used. A tool is anything that can be used to attain a goal. The distinctively human form of tool use involves language. Initially, language and action proceed independently of each other. 'The most significant moment in the course of intellectual development, which gives birth to the purely human forms of practical and abstract intelligence, occurs when speech and practical activity, two previously completely independent lines of development, converge' (ibid., 24). To illustrate this development, Vygotsky uses as an example a 4½-year-old child who is getting candy from a cupboard using a stool and a stick as tools. The child continually describes her action out loud as she carries it out, as if the speech was controlling her action. The development of such linguistic self-regulation was of particular interest to Vygotsky.

Vygotsky began his analysis of the development of language and thought by elaborating on Piaget's concept of **egocentric speech**, which is speech in which the young child 'talks to himself as though he were thinking aloud. He does not address anyone' (Piaget, 1959 [1923]: 9). From Piaget's viewpoint, egocentric speech is replaced around age 7 by socialized speech, in which the child 'really exchanges his thoughts with others' (ibid., 9–10). Vygotsky (1962: 136) studied egocentric speech in various contexts and concluded that it occurred when other children were around and that the young child did not yet distinguish between private speech and social speech.

Vygotsky believed that what Piaget called egocentric speech does not actually disappear, but becomes internalized as *inner speech*. Thus, Vygotsky distinguished between inner speech, or 'speech for oneself', and external speech, or 'speech for others' (ibid., 131). Inner speech comes to control mental life. It is as if we use inner speech to give orders silently, not to other people but to ourselves. Inner speech is condensed and vivid. Because the speaker and the listener are the same person, a lot can be taken for granted and everything does not need to be spelled out.

The less well you know someone, the more will your speech to them have all the properties of formal, grammatically correct external speech. However, people who know each other very well may speak in a way that has some of the characteristics of inner speech. Vygotsky made this point using an example from a story by Dostoevski, in which:

> a conversation of drunks . . . entirely consisted of one unprintable word (*The Diary of a Writer*, for 1873): 'One Sunday night I happened to walk for some fifteen paces next to a group of six drunken young workmen, and I suddenly realized that all thoughts, feelings and even a whole chain of reasoning could be expressed by that one noun, which is moreover extremely short.' (Ibid., 143)

Vygotsky (ibid., 140) gives a beautiful example, taken from Tolstoy's *Anna Karenina*, of the way that two people who share the same intimate context can communicate deeply without saying anything explicitly.

> 'I have long wished to ask you something.'
> 'Please do.'
> 'This,' he said, and wrote the initial letters: *W y a: i c n b, d y m t o n.* These letters meant: 'When you answered: it can not be, did you mean then or never' It seemed impossible that she would understand the complicated sentence.
> 'I understand,' she said blushing.
> 'What word is that?' he asked, pointing to the n which stood for never.
> 'The word is "never,"' she said, 'but that is not true.' He quickly erased what he had written and handed her the chalk, and rose. She wrote: *I c n a o t.*
> His face brightened suddenly: he had understood. It meant: 'I could not answer otherwise then.'
> She wrote the initial letters: *s t y m f a f w h.* This meant: 'So that you might forget and forgive what happened.'
> He seized the chalk with tense, trembling fingers, broke it, and wrote the initial letters of the following: 'I have nothing to forget and forgive. I never ceased loving you.'

The Zone of Proximal Development

One of Vygotsky's most enduring concepts is the **zone of proximal development**, which he defined as follows: 'It is the distance between the actual developmental level as determined by independent problem solving and the level of potential development as determined through problem solving under adult guidance or in collaboration with more capable peers' (Vygotsky, 1978 [1935]: 86). The actual developmental level may be determined by standardized testing. The potential developmental level requires more sensitive exploration on the part of a teacher to discover what the child is capable of discovering with assistance from an adult. Such a teacher might 'offer leading questions or show how the problem is to be solved and the child then solves it, or if the teacher initiates the solution and [then] the child completes it or solves it in collaboration with other children' (ibid., 85).

Vygotsky pointed out that two children can be at the same actual developmental level, but at different potential developmental levels. It is the potential developmental level that should guide the efforts of educators. Rather than simply teach to the actual developmental level, one should be enabling the child to reach his or her potential developmental level (El'konin, 1969: 168). 'What is in the zone of proximal development today will be the actual developmental level tomorrow— that is, what a child can do with assistance today she will be able to do herself tomorrow' (Vygotsky, 1978: 87).

Erik H. Erikson (1902-94)

Erik H. Erikson was born in Germany of Danish parents, who had separated before he was born. When Erikson was three his mother married a Dr Homburger, from whom Erikson gets his middle initial. As a young man Erikson travelled extensively in Europe, living as an artist. A friend from his school days became a teacher in a new school in Vienna that Anna Freud had helped to establish. In 1927, Erikson became associated with the school and began to develop his understanding of child development, although at this point he had no formal training in psychology. However, he undertook a psychoanalysis with Anna Freud and graduated from the Vienna Psychoanalytic Institute in 1933. In 1929, Erikson met and later married a Canadian, Joan Serson, who subsequently played an important role in the development of his theories (Coles, 1970: 13–31).

Partly because of the rise of Nazism in Europe, Erikson moved to Boston in 1933, where he became its first child psychoanalyst. He enrolled in, but never completed, a Ph.D. program at Harvard. Nevertheless, he both taught and did research at Harvard. He also spent time at Yale, where he came into contact with Clark Hull's research group. A fateful period involved a visit to a Sioux Indian reservation in South Dakota. '[H]is work with the Sioux Indians marked the beginning of a life-long effort to demonstrate how the events of childhood are affected by the inevitable encounter with a given society, whose customs affect the way mothers hold and feed infants, and later on bring them up to behave' (ibid., 37).

Erikson was at the University of California at Berkeley from 1939 until 1950, when he resigned over the requirement that all professors take a loyalty oath. (Like Erikson, Edward C. Tolman also refused to sign the oath.) While Erikson declared himself to be a non-Communist, he believed that as a matter of principle he should make a stand against what he perceived to be an infringement of the right of individuals to think and be judged independently of their political convictions. He eventually ended up back at Harvard, where he became a professor in 1960 and from which he retired in 1970.

Lifespan Developmental Psychology

Erikson created one of the most influential descriptions of the issues and crises that people generally face as their lives unfold. As one might expect, Erikson himself was heavily influenced by Freudian theories. As did Freud, Erikson emphasized the importance of early childhood experience in shaping the adult personality. However, in his major and best-known work, *Childhood and Society* (1950, 1963), Erikson went well beyond Freud to posit the existence of specific stages of development that occur throughout the entire life cycle, not just in childhood. Erikson's theory is one of the major reasons why developmental psychology is no longer concerned only with childhood but with those changes that occur throughout a person's life.

Epigenesis

Erikson called his theory **epigenesis**, meaning that developmental stages unfold in a necessary sequence.

> [A]nything that grows has a *ground plan*, and out of this ground plan the *parts* arise, each part having its *time* of special ascendancy, until all parts have arisen to form a *functioning whole*. . . . [I]n the sequence of his most personal experiences the healthy child, given a reasonable amount of guidance, can be trusted to obey inner laws of development. . . . Personality can be said to develop according to steps predetermined in the human organism's readiness to be driven toward, to be aware of, and to interact with a widening social radius, beginning with a dim image of his mother, and ending with mankind. (Erikson, 1959: 52)

Thus, the sequence of **developmental stages** is a 'progression through time of a differentiation of parts' (ibid., 53). However, Erikson was at pains to emphasize that this progression is modulated by the particular society in which the person develops. Moreover, 'the theory postulates a *cogwheeling of the life cycles*: the representatives of society, the caretaking persons, are coordinated to the developing individual by their specific inborn responsiveness to his [or her] needs and by phase-specific needs of their own' (Rapaport, 1959: 15). People are inherently social beings, and one of ways in which this is expressed is in the way that older people feel the need to care for younger ones.

> *Care* is a quality essential for psychosocial evolution, for we are the teaching species. Animals, too, instinctively encourage in their young what is ready for release, and, of course, some animals can be taught some tricks and services by man. Only man, however, can and must extend his solicitude over the long, parallel and overlapping childhoods of numerous offspring united in households and communities. . . . Once we have grasped this interlocking of the human life stages, we understand that adult man is so constituted as to *need to be needed* lest he suffer the mental deformation of self-absorption, in which he becomes his own infant and pet. (Erikson, 1964: 130)

While Erikson's developmental stages unfold over time and have an invariant order, it is difficult to be too specific about the times at which the stages emerge, because these will be at least somewhat different for each individual as a consequence of his or her own unique situation. At best we can make only general estimates for an ideal life cycle, which may only be imperfectly realized in the individual case. Moreover, as Erikson (1959) makes clear, the stages do not proceed like the links in a chain; rather, they may overlap. The person may begin working on a new stage before the current one is resolved.

The Eight Stages

Each stage in the life cycle presents the person with a definite task that must be solved at that time. At each stage the person is presented with alternative choices and, through important encounters with the physical and social environment, some resolution of the crisis occurs. The stages in an individual's life number eight (Erikson, 1963: ch. 7):

1. basic trust vs mistrust
2. autonomy vs shame and doubt
3. initiative vs guilt
4. industry vs inferiority
5. identity vs identity diffusion
6. intimacy vs isolation
7. generativity vs stagnation
8. integrity vs despair

In Erikson's scheme, each developmental stage involves pairs of opposing tendencies, one with a positive connotation (e.g., 'trust') and one with a negative connotation (e.g., 'mistrust'). From Erikson's point of view, the successful resolution of each developmental crisis is not seen as meaning that one of the opposites has 'won out' over the other. Rather, when a person successfully negotiates a critical period in development, the opposing tendencies are mixed in the right proportion, with an imbalance in favour of the positive (Erikson, 1963: 274). Although it is essential, for example, that the child develop a sense of basic trust in the world, 'to learn to mistrust is just as important' (Evans, 1976: 293). The content of each stage may be described as follows.

Basic trust vs mistrust. In the beginning the child is dependent on significant others for his/her well-being and comfort. The child's identity may be captured by the statement 'I am what I am given' (Erikson, 1959: 82). If the child receives a high enough quality of care during the first year of life, then the child will acquire a sense of confidence, a feeling that he can trust the world to be consistent and provident. As with the succeeding stages, too much of the positive quality (trust) can be unhealthy. There are certainly situations in which a skeptical attitude is appropriate, and so the best outcome is a balance between the two, but in favour of basic trust. A positive outcome at this stage gives the child *hope* (Erikson, 1963: 274).

Autonomy vs shame and doubt. The second and third years of life are associated with the achievement of self-control (e.g., becoming toilet-trained) and the beginnings of mastery of the external world. The child's identity at this stage depends on the emergence of *will power* (Erikson, 1962: 255) and may be characterized as 'I am what I will' (Erikson, 1959: 82).

Initiative vs guilt. Now the child is moving around in the environment more freely, begins to use language effectively, and can also start to imagine the sort of person she or he would like to become. Since play and imagination are so salient for the child at this stage (Erikson, 1972), the child's identity is closely tied to what it is possible to imagine becoming, as in 'I am what I can imagine I will be' (Erikson, 1959: 82). A successful

resolution of this stage gives the child a sense of *purpose* (Erikson, 1963: 274).

Industry vs inferiority. Once the child begins school, she or he becomes increasingly reliant on education to master the world. The child's self-definition now becomes 'I am what I learn' (Erikson, 1959: 82). The desirable outcome of this stage is a feeling of *competence* (Erikson, 1963: 274).

Identity vs identity diffusion. The problem of establishing a stable personal **identity** now comes to the fore. The young person has as a central concern the development of a sense of who he or she is, the maintenance of a stable conception of oneself and the way one is seen by others. Of course, this should not be a rigid, inflexible identity determined by peer pressure, but one that expresses and is tolerant of individuality (Erikson, 1959: 91). The ideal outcome at this stage is *faithfulness* to oneself and to others (Erikson, 1963: 274).

Intimacy vs isolation. After this sense of identity is established, it is possible to become genuinely intimate with others, as in marriage; and to maintain one's identity without becoming isolated from others. Erikson (1950: 266) suggested that at this stage one should ideally be capable of 'mutuality of orgasm . . . with a loved partner . . .with whom one is able and willing to share a mutual trust . . . and with whom one is able and willing to regulate the cycles of . . . work . . . procreation . . . [and] recreation so as to secure to the offspring, too, all the stages of a satisfactory development.' Erikson regarded this kind of *love* was an ideal to aim for rather than a universally achievable goal.

Generativity vs stagnation. Building on a solid sense of self and viable interpersonal relationships, the focus turns towards the contribution the person can make to society through creativity in a variety of spheres (e.g., as a parent, in a career). *Caring* is the dominant theme of a successful resolution of this period (Erikson, 1963: 274).

Integrity vs despair. As a person's work and family become established, the question of what one's life all adds up to begins to pose itself. 'Only he who in some way has taken care of things and people and has adapted himself to the triumphs

BOX 12.2

LIFE REVIEW AND REMINISCENCE IN PSYCHOLOGISTS

Some support for Erikson's eight-stage theory of lifespan development came from a study of autobiographical memories by Mackavey, Malley, and Stewart (1991). They analyzed the autobiographies of 49 well-known psychologists (31 men and 18 women), written when they were an average of 72 years of age, with a range of 54 to 86 years. From Erikson's viewpoint, this group of people should be at the eighth stage (integrity versus despair) and concerned with evaluating their lives, a process called *life review*. The evaluative process should lead them to *reminisce*, which means spending an increased amount of time remembering events from the earlier parts of life. Rubin, Wetzler, and Nebes (1986) reviewed evidence that supports the hypothesis that reminiscence increases after 50 years of age.

When a person reflects on one's life, it is likely that he or she will tend to remember episodes from periods in which decisions were made that had consequence for the rest of one's life (Mackavey et al., 1991: 52). By counting and dating 250 of these autobiographically consequential experiences (ACEs) in the 49 autobi-

ographies, Mackavey et al. derived a distribution of ACEs across the typical lifespan. About 80 per cent of these consequential experiences occurred between the ages of 18 and 35; relatively few were from early childhood or after age 50. Mackavey et al. suggested that these results can best be understood in the context of Erikson's theory of the role of identity in the life cycle (Erikson, 1959; Erikson and Kivnick, 1986). The most important choices in our lives (e.g., marriage, career) are typically made in late adolescence and young adulthood. These choices have crucial consequences for what happens to us later on. Consequently, it is natural for the process of life review to tend to focus on this period, as the person summarizes and evaluates what has been important and meaningful in his/her life.

Of course, one cannot be sure that how reminiscence seems to work for psychologists will mirror the trends found in other people. However, this research demonstrates that Erikson's theory could generate interesting research in contexts beyond that in which the theory was originally created.

and disappointments of being, by necessity, the originator of others and the generator of things and ideas—only he may know the fruit of the seven stages. I know of no better word for it than *integrity*' (Erikson, 1959: 98). After successfully negotiating the previous crises more or less well, the reward is the achievement of a measure of *wisdom* (Erikson, 1963: 274).

Erikson's theory is grounded in clinical observation, particularly of children at play. The theory has been quite fruitful in terms of generating research. An example of such research that is particularly relevant to the history of psychology is given in Box 12.2.

Eleanor J. Gibson (1910–2002)

Eleanor Jack Gibson (1980, 2002) did her undergraduate degree at Smith College, graduating in 1931. She met James J. Gibson, then teaching psychology at Smith:

at a garden party at the end of my junior year. It rained and we were happily stranded in a corner of a quadrangle where he was supposed to be shaking hands with parents of seniors as I offered them punch. He took me back to my dormitory in his ancient Model-T Ford, and the next day I hurried to the class dean's office and changed the following year's schedule to include his class in Advanced Experimental Psychology. It was a wonderful course and I fell in love with Experimental Psychology and with the instructor. (Gibson, 1980: 243)

Eleanor and James subsequently married, and both had a significant influence on American psychology. We will consider James J. Gibson's influence in a later chapter.

Eleanor Gibson also studied with Koffka at Smith, but she 'was not attracted by Gestalt psychology and yearned for what I thought of as "hard" psychology. I didn't like introspective methods. I wanted to be objective, as I thought of it then, and I wanted to work with animals and children' (Gibson, 1980: 245). Her interest in 'hard' psychology was well served by going on to study at Yale with Clark Hull, who was her Ph.D. dissertation supervisor.

After receiving her Ph.D., E.J. and J.J. Gibson worked together at Smith, where both were on the faculty. After World War II, they moved to Cornell, where J.J. Gibson was on the faculty, but Eleanor was listed only as a research associate. In those days many universities had nepotism rules that forbade husbands and wives both to be on the faculty. Over the years, many women were denied professional opportunities as a result of such rules. In Eleanor Gibson's case, she did not become a professor of psychology until 1966, when nepotism rules finally began to change (Pick, 1992: 789).

Perceptual Learning

One of E.J. Gibson's most enduring contributions has been her research concerning the way children learn to perceive their environment. In a classic paper, the Gibsons (1955) argued that learning to perceive has traditionally been conceived of as a process of **enrichment**. For example, associationist theorists such as Locke, Berkeley, and Hume believed that information that we receive through our senses is not intrinsically meaningful. Rather, it

was necessary to supplement immediate experience with previous experiences drawn from memory. A similar position was taken by Wundt and Titchener, when they argued that sensations were united by previous experience to form perceptions. Thus, according to these theorists, perceptual learning reflects the extent to which immediate experience is enriched by previous experience. We learn what the stimulus is that we are currently experiencing by associating it with other stimuli we have experienced in the past. For example, we are able to recognize the letter 'A' because it is similar to, and thus associated with, other stimulus configurations that have the same properties. Perceptual learning, from this viewpoint, is a matter of *generalization*.

By contrast with the enrichment theory, the Gibsons argued that **perceptual learning** was a matter of **differentiation**. Perceptual learning is not characterized by learning to place stimuli in equivalent classes. Rather, it involves becoming increasingly attuned to the specific events that make up the world. Before perceptual learning takes place, we overgeneralize and see things as similar to each other. Perceptual learning allows us to make distinctions between events that we were not initially able to make. The example of a wine connoisseur is used by the Gibsons to make this point. Someone who is skilled at wine tasting can discriminate between many more different wines than can someone who is just starting out, for whom all wines may taste the same.

To illustrate this process of differentiation Eleanor Gibson did an experiment that was reported in the Gibson and Gibson (1955) paper. The experiment made use of a set of 'scribbles', as illustrated in Figure 12.5. Casual inspection of the items shows them all to consist of a number of coils. However, these coils differ from each other in three ways. First, the number of coils varies from three to five. Second, the coils are more or less close together. Third, starting from the outermost coil, they spiral in a clockwise or counter-clockwise direction.

There were three groups of participants in this experiment. One group consisted of younger

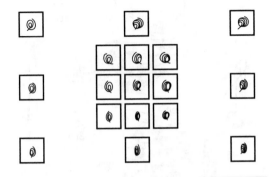

FIGURE 12.5
Nonsense items differing in three dimensions
of variation.
Source: Gibson and Gibson (1955: 36).

children between 6 and 8 years old; another group consisted of older children between 8.5 to 11 years; and a third group consisted of adults. A deck of cards was made up in which each card had one of the scribbles printed on it. In addition, there were also several other nonsense figures printed on cards and interspersed in the deck. One of the scribbles was selected as the target item, and shown to the participants. Their task was to select those items in the deck that were exactly like the target. After the first trial, the younger children named many more items as the same as the target (13.4) than did the older children (7.9), who in turn named more than the adults (3.0). Moreover, the adults took only an average of 3.1 trials to reach a perfect identification of the one coil that corresponded to the target. The older children took 4.7 trials, and many of the younger children failed to identify the target correctly during the course of the experiment.

This experiment demonstrates what the Gibsons meant by 'perceptual learning'. Initially, a number of stimuli are easily confused with one another. With repetition, stimuli can be differentiated from one another, although this occurs more quickly with adults than children.

Achievement of specificity involves the detection of properties and patterns not previously responded to. Detection of properties was illustrated in the scribble experiment, as the [participants] discovered the dimensions of difference. It would be hard to overemphasize the importance for perceptual learning of the discovery of invariant properties which are in correspondence with physical variables. The term 'extraction' will be applied to this process, for the property may be buried, as it were, in a welter of impinging stimulation. (Gibson, 1969: 81)

Gibson argued that differentiation has characterized both the evolutionary and developmental processes. Phylogenetically, different senses have emerged, each attuned to a different kind of stimulus dimension. These senses themselves have become increasingly able to pick up highly specific forms of information. Ontogenetically, perceptual learning enables the person to respond to increasingly differentiated aspects of the environment.

Reading
One of the most important developmental achievements is learning to read. Gibson (1991 [1965]; Gibson and Levin, 1975) explored this process in considerable detail. One question she has explored is 'How are words perceived?' This is a complicated question because words have several features that could be perceived by readers. What features allow a successful reader to differentiate rapidly one word from another? While words differ in length and shape, such cues are insufficient to be the entire basis of reading. Gibson et al. (1962) suggested that certain strings of letters were more pronounceable than others, and that **pronounceability** was a very important property of words that would-be readers learned to perceive. They observed that particular letters tend to go together in particular positions in words and that these spelling patterns are always pronounced in the same way. Thus, for example, 'glurck' is not an English word, but is pronounceable, while 'ckurgl' is not as pronounceable. This is because a spelling pattern such as 'gl' tends to begin

English words, while 'ck' tends to come at the end of English words.

Gibson et al. showed subjects non-words (like 'glurck') that are pronounceable and non-words that are less pronounceable (like 'ckurgl'). These stimuli were only exposed for very brief durations. Subjects were much more likely to perceive the pronounceable non-words than the less pronounceable ones. 'We conclude from these experiments that skilled readers more easily perceive as a unit pseudo words that follow the rules of English spelling-to-sound correspondence; that spelling patterns which have invariant relations to sound patterns function as a unit' (Gibson, 1991: 408). Subsequent research showed that the ability to perceive spelling patterns may already exist in a limited way in first-graders. There is clearly more to reading than simply the ability to pick up spelling patterns, and Gibson also investigated many additional aspects of the reading process. Nevertheless, her work on spelling patterns is a good illustration of her careful experimental approach to the discovery of developmentally important processes.

The Visual Cliff

Science often progresses through the invention of a new piece of apparatus that enables the investigation of an important process. Such an invention was the **visual cliff** introduced by Walk and Eleanor Gibson (1961). One version of the visual cliff is shown in Figure 12.6. The visual cliff enabled Gibson and her co-workers to investigate depth perception. As noted in Chapters 2 and 3, this classic problem has been addressed by a number of the most prominent figures in the history of psychology, from Berkeley to Helmholtz. The usual explanation of our ability to locate objects in space was that we infer, on the basis of previous experience, that particular objects in the external world have given rise to the images on our retinas. The result of this inferential process is the three-dimensional world we experience.

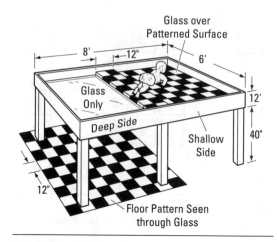

FIGURE 12.6
The visual cliff.
Source: Walk and Gibson (1961: 8).

Gibson's work with the visual cliff suggested a very different answer to this question. Gibson pointed out that the ability to see objects in depth is a highly adaptive skill:

> [O]ne universal requirement holds for all terrestrial animals, the necessity to avoid falling from high places. A long fall means death. Whether the avoidance is learned or innate the animal must be able to respond as soon as he attains free locomotion unguided by a parent. He must be able to see a drop-off, a falling-off place. (Gibson, 1969: 267)

The visual cliff is constructed as follows. A centre board is flanked by a shallow and a deep side. Both the shallow side and the deep side are covered by the same sheet of glass, which is strong enough to carry the weight of an experimental subject. The glass on the shallow side has a patterned surface directly underneath it, while the glass on the deep side has a patterned surface at some distance beneath it. A participant (animal or human) is placed on the centre board. The experimenter observes whether the animal has a tendency to move to the shallow side, the deep side, or both sides equally. If the animal is able to perceive depth, one would expect a preference for the shallow over the deep side.

Over the years, a number of infant animals, including rats, chickens, pigs, kittens, puppies, monkeys, turtles, rabbits, ducklings, lions, tigers, leopards, and humans, were tested on the visual cliff by a number of different investigators (ibid., 268). Animals whose natural mountain habitat requires them to avoid sharp drop-offs, such as snow leopards, sheep, and goats, show an avoidance of the deep side of the visual cliff at a very early age. Aquatic animals such as turtles and ducks do not show such a pronounced preference, presumably because their natural habitat enables them to swim over deep places, and so it is less important to avoid them.

Experiments with human infants between 6.5 and 14 months involved placing the infant on the centre board and having the baby's mother call to the baby from either side. Almost all those infants able to crawl would do so when the mother called from the shallow side, but they were very unlikely to do so to the deep side. It appeared that infants were able to perceive depth by the time they were able to crawl. This calls strongly associationist accounts of the development of space perception into question, since the infants did not appear to have to crawl around in the world in order to develop the ability to perceive depth. Walk and Gibson (1961) took their results to be consistent with the notion that depth perception does not have to be learned, although it is capable of becoming increasingly differentiated with experience.

Eleanor Gibson on the Future of Psychology

One outstanding feature of Eleanor Gibson's reputation was that of 'a consummate experimenter . . . . Throughout her career she has continued to be a model experimenter who has been widely recognized, for example, by her election to the National Academy of Science and the awarding to her of the National Medal of Science (1992)' (Pick, 1992: 792). Since its inception in 1962, the National Medal of Science had been awarded to a total of 304 recipients by 1992. Including Gibson, only 10 psychologists had received it (Kent, 1992: 15). 'She was cited for the National Medal of Science for her "conceptual insights in developing a theory of perceptual learning and for achieving a deeper understanding of perceptual development in children and basic processes in reading"' (ibid., 14).

In 1994, Gibson published an overview of the history of psychology over her last few decades as an active researcher. She observed that there was a great deal of general 'excitement in the air about the future of psychology in the 1930's', but that 'something went wrong with this youthful dream, about halfway into the century' (Gibson, 1994: 69). She presented a picture of psychology as lacking in coherence, and lamented the lack of 'a search for encompassing principles, ones that make sense of all the underlying relationships. I think many psychologists have given up on this, a hope we still shared 60 years ago' (ibid., 70). Gibson urged a new agenda, based on a developmental approach, that would restore a unity of purpose to psychology. This question of the perceived fragmentation of psychology, and possible remedies for it, will be taken up in Chapter 15.

IMPORTANT NAMES, WORKS, AND CONCEPTS

Names and Works

Baldwin, James Mark

Blatz, William E.

Bott, Edward A.

Childhood and Society

Erikson, Erik H.

Gibson, Eleanor Jack

Hall, G. Stanley

Inhelder, Bärbel

Piaget, Jean

The Comparative Psychology of Mental Development

Thought and Language

Vygotsky, L.S.

Werner, Heinz

Concepts

accommodation

adolescence

assimilation

child study movement

clinical method

concept of development

concrete operations

conservation

developmental stages

differentiation

egocentric speech

emergent properties

enrichment

epigenesis

formal operations

genetic epistemology

identity

imitation

microgenetic processes

multiplication of classes

ontogeny recapitulates phylogeny

orthogenetic principle

perceptual learning

preoperational period

process analysis

pronounceability

questionnaires

reversibility

sensorimotor period

stages

structuralism

symbolic play

uniformity versus multiformity

unilinearity versus multilinearity

visual cliff

zone of proximal development

RECOMMENDED READINGS

Hall

The standard biography of Hall is D.G. Ross, *Stanley Hall: The Psychologist as Prophet* (Chicago: University of Chicago Press, 1972). The relation between ontogeny and phylogeny continues to be explored by developmentalists. A good contemporary review of the topic is S. Strauss, ed., *Ontogeny, Phylogeny and Historical Development* (Norwood, NJ: Ablex, 1988).

Baldwin

At an early stage of his career, Baldwin became involved in a nasty dispute with Titchener over the nature of individual differences in reaction time. See J.M. Baldwin, 'Types of reaction' [1895] and 'The "type theory" of reaction' [1896], in J.M. Vanderplas, ed., *Controversial Issues in Psychology* (Boston: Houghton Mifflin, 1966), 144–55, 164–73, and E.B. Titchener, 'The type theory of the simple reaction' [1895] and 'The "type theory" of the simple reaction' [1896], in Vanderplas, ed., *Controversial Issues*, 155–64, 173–9. These lively papers still make good reading. Baldwin also became well known for a sophisticated argument that acquired characteristics, under certain circumstances, may be passed on to the next generation. This phenomenon became known as the 'Baldwin effect'. See J.J. Vonèche, 'Evolution, development, and knowledge', in J.M. Broughton and D.J. Freeman-Moir, eds, *The Cognitive-Developmental Psychology of James Mark Baldwin: Current Theory and Research in Genetic Epistemology* (Norwood, NJ: Ablex, 1982), 51–79.

Werner

Bernard Kaplan, who was Werner's student and colleague, wrote a provocative analysis of the relation between organismic, developmental, and historical forms of analysis: 'Strife of systems: tension between organismic and developmental points of view', *Theory and Psychology* 2 (1992): 431–43. Werner's experimental procedure became known as *backward masking* because one stimulus 'masks' a previous stimulus, preventing it from being fully perceived. See H. Werner, 'Studies on contour: I. Qualitative analyses', *American Journal of Psychology* 47 (1935): 40–64. Werner's technique was refined and used by numerous experimenters after his initial study, with the result that psychologists uncovered an impressive array of findings about microgenetic processes. See, e.g., A.J. Marcel, 'Conscious and unconscious perception: Experiments on visual masking and word recognition' and 'Conscious and unconscious perception: An approach to the relations between phenomenal experience and perceptual processes', *Cognitive Psychology* 15 (1983): 197–237, 238–300; Marcel et al., 'Laterality and reading proficiency', *Neuropsychologia* 12 (1974): 131–9.

The comparative approach of T.C. Schneirla (1902–68) is often compared to that of Werner, and there are important similarities between the two. See L.R. Aronson et al., *Development and Evolution of Behavior: Essays in Memory of T.C. Schneirla* (San Francisco: Freeman, 1970).

Piaget

A good overview of the area of cognitive development is R.S. Siegler, *Children's Thinking* (Englewood Cliffs, NJ: Prentice-Hall, 1986). An overview of Piaget's life and work from the perspective of the late twentieth century is given in a special section of *Psychological Science* edited by Brainerd. See C.J. Brainerd, 'Piaget: a centennial celebration', *Psychological Science* 7 (1996): 191–5.

Vygotsky

In addition to the original translation of Vygotsky's *Thought and Language* (1934) by Hanfmann and Vakar (Cambridge, Mass.: MIT Press, 1962), there is a newer translation by A. Kozulin: L.S. Vygotsky, *Thought and Language* (Cambridge, Mass.: MIT Press, 1986). Applications of Vygotsky's ideas to education and other areas are given in B. Rogoff and J. Wertsch, *Children's Learning in the Zone of Proximal Development* (San Francisco: Jossey-Bass, 1984). Erving Goffman, 'Response cries', *Language* 54 (1978): 787–815, provided interesting and amusing examples of cases in which inner speech, which is normally silent, will become public.

Erikson

Erikson wrote a number of studies of historically important figures, including Jesus, Luther, Hitler, and Gandhi. These studies are sympathetically reviewed by D.C. Andersen and L.J. Friedman, 'Erik Erikson on revolutionary leadership: Thematic trajectories', *Contemporary Psychology* 42 (1997): 1063–7. Erikson's own life came under critical scrutiny when it was revealed that he had a son born with Down's syndrome who was institutionalized and whose existence was apparently kept from other family members. See L.J. Friedman, *Identity's Architect: A Biography of Erik H. Erikson* (New York: Scribner's,1999), and H. Gardner, 'The enigma of Erik Erikson', *New York Review of Books*, 24 June 1999, 51–6. Gardner (p. 54) writes: 'Such revelations are one more painful reminder that excellent child clinicians (and psychologists) are not necessarily model parents.' R.M. Lerner, ed., *Developmental Psychology: Historical and Philosophical Perspectives* (Hillsdale, NJ: Erlbaum, 1982), contains a useful history of contributors to the lifespan approach other than Erikson.

Eleanor Gibson

A number of tributes to Gibson's work and influence are in A. Pick, *Perception and Its Development: A Tribute to Eleanor J. Gibson* (Hillsdale, NJ: Erlbaum, 1979). Other important figures in the history of developmental psychology are chronicled in *Developmental Psychology* 28 (1992). These include Nancy Bayley (J.F. Rosenblith, 'A singular career: Nancy Bayley', 747–58); John Bowlby and Mary Ainsworth (I. Bretherton, 'The origins of attachment theory: John Bowlby and Mary Ainsworth', 759–75); Arnold Gesell (E. Thelen and K.E. Adolph, 'Arnold L. Gesell: The paradox of Nature and nurture', 368–80); and Robert Sears (J.E. Grusec, 'Social learning theory and developmental psychology: The legacies of Robert Sears and Albert Bandura', 776–86). A particularly good introduction to and overview of developmental psychology is T. Keenan, *An Introduction to Child Development* (London: Sage, 2002).

CHAPTER 13

HUMANISTIC PSYCHOLOGY

Introduction

Humanistic psychology was not only a movement within academic psychology, but was also an essential part of cultural trends that characterized the 1960s. The founders of humanistic psychology, people like Abraham Maslow and Carl Rogers, became well known by the general public. The humanistic movement combined influences from European existentialism with the optimism characteristic of American psychology. By calling themselves the '**Third Force**', humanistic psychologists were attempting to distinguish clearly their approach from the other two 'forces', psychoanalysis and behaviourism. Humanistic psychologists believed that psychoanalysis was too pessimistic about human nature, and wanted to stress the importance of enabling people to attain their human potential. Humanistic psychologists also believed that behaviourists were too concerned with being objective and, as a result, ignored the richness of human experience.

In 1958, a book called *Existence* was published, edited by Rollo May, Ernest Angel, and Henri F. Ellenberger. This book introduced European existentialism to many American psychologists (e.g., Mahrer, 1996). Existentialism is difficult to define precisely. The *Oxford English Dictionary* characterizes **existentialism** as 'A doctrine that concentrates on the existence of the individual, who, being free and responsible, is held to be what he makes himself'. A particularly clear summary of existentialism was given by Mary Warnock:

Broadly speaking, we can say that the common interest which unites Existentialist philosophers is the interest in human freedom. They are all of them interested in the world considered as the environment of [people], who [are] treated as . . . unique object[s] of attention, because of [their] power to choose [their] own course of action. . . . [F]or existentialists, uniquely, the problem of freedom is in a sense a practical problem. They aim, above all, to show people *that they are free*, to open their eyes to something which has always been true, but which, for one reason or another may not always have been recognized, namely that [people] are free to choose, not only what to do on a specific occasion, but what to value and how to live. The readers of Existentialist philosophy are being asked, not merely to consider the nature of human freedom, but to *experience* freedom, and to practice it. (Warnock, 1970: 1–2)

Existentialism

Søren Kierkegaard (1813–55)

Søren Kierkegaard was a Danish philosopher who was preoccupied with the nature of human choice. In a work called **Either/Or**, Kierkegaard (1959 [1843]) presented the reader with two alternative ways of living one's life: the aesthetic and the ethical. The aesthetic way of life involves the search for sophisticated forms of pleasure. The arbitrariness of the aesthetic approach to living is well captured by the following quotation.

If you marry, you will regret it; if you do not marry, you will also regret it. . . . Laugh at the world's follies, you will regret it; weep over them, you will also regret that. . . . Hang yourself, you will regret it; do not hang yourself, and you will also regret that. . . . This . . . is the sum and substance of all philosophy. (Kierkegaard, 1959 [1843]: 37)

In spite of the melancholy nature of such sentiments, Kierkegaard did not believe that the ethical alternative of living by a rigorous set of idealistic principles was superior to the aesthetic way of life. Both the aesthetic and the ethical are equally justifiable. All choices are arbitrary because no objective rationale exists for one alternative over the other. In the end, one's choices are one's own.

To illustrate the *subjective nature of human choice*, Kierkegaard (1954 [1843]) considered the case of Abraham. In the Old Testament, Abraham was commanded by God to make a sacrifice of his son, Isaac. Abraham does not have to kill his son simply because God tells him to. God does not *make* him sacrifice his son; it is up to Abraham to choose to do so. Of course, it is *absurd* for Abraham to be presented with such a choice, and Kierkegaard argued that all people are confronted in one way or another with the absurd nature of human existence. Abraham could choose to sacrifice his son because of his *faith* in God. For Kierkegaard, such faith is itself absurd, but possible nonetheless. The **leap of faith** that makes one into a religious person is not grounded in any objective fact; it is a purely subjective act.

Friedrich Nietzsche (1844–1900)

The influence of **Friedrich Nietzsche** on European thought was considerable during his lifetime, and this influence continues to provoke and disturb people until this day. Nietzsche (1967 [1901]: 3) observed the emergence of **nihilism** in Europe, the notion that there are no absolute truths or values. Nietzsche believed that nihilism marked the end of Christianity. 'The time has come when we have to pay for having been Christians for two thousand years: we are losing the center of gravity by virtue of which we lived; we are lost for a while' (ibid., 20). In the place of Christianity, Nietzsche saw the emergence of **perspectivism**, the notion that there are any number of interpretations of reality, all of them equally valid (Greer, 1997). Perspectivism rejects the superiority of a scientific understanding of the world:

> Against positivism, which halts at phenomena—'There are only *facts*'—I would say: No, facts is precisely what there is not, only interpretations. We cannot establish any fact 'in itself': perhaps it is folly to want to do such a thing.
>
> 'Everything is subjective,' you say; but even this is interpretation. The 'subject' is not something given, it is something added and invented and projected behind what there is. Finally, is it necessary to posit an interpreter behind the interpretation? Even this is invention, hypothesis.
>
> In so far as the word 'knowledge' has any meaning, the world is knowable; but it is *interpretable* otherwise, it has no meaning behind it, but countless meanings.—'Perspectivism.'
>
> It is our needs that interpret the world; our drives and their For and Against. Every drive is a kind of lust to rule; each one has its perspective that it would like to compel all the other drives to accept as a norm. (Nietzsche, 1967: 267)

Nietzsche's argument that 'our needs . . . interpret the world' leads directly to his concept of the **will to power**. There is no objective description of reality, but all descriptions are intended to accomplish particular ends. 'Knowledge works as a tool of power. Hence it is plain that it increases with every exercise of power' (ibid., 266). Something that society as a whole takes to be true is only what powerful people want to be true. However, every individual is free to choose some other interpretation of reality in accordance with his or her own will to power.

If all experience is an interpretation and all interpretations reflect the will to power, then all experience is 'permeated with value judgments' (ibid., 275). No value judgement can be taken to be 'better' than any other. They are all 'beyond good and evil . . . . This world is the will to power—and nothing besides! And you yourselves are also this will to power—and nothing besides!' (ibid., 550).

Jean-Paul Sartre (1905–80)

Jean-Paul Sartre (1962 [1939]) was one of the greatest twentieth-century French intellectuals. His companion of many years, Simone de Beauvoir, will be discussed in a later chapter. After teaching in France for a number of years, Sartre lived in Berlin in the early 1930s, where he was influenced by Edmund Husserl. As we noted in Chapter 4, Husserl was a student of Franz Brentano's and had pioneered the phenomenological method. The phenomenological method is an attempt to describe consciousness as it presents itself to us, without any presuppositions as to its nature or purpose.

Sartre served in the French army and was captured by the Germans in World War II. After his release he was active in the French resistance movement. He published his major philosophical work, **Being and Nothingness**, in 1943. Sartre refused to accept the Nobel Prize for literature that he was awarded in 1964. This refusal was consistent with his general attitude of disdain for established cultural institutions. He was acquainted with, and contemptuous of, the work of academic psychologists who regarded their discipline as an objective, experimental science.

[T]he psychologist strictly forbids himself to consider the men around him as men *like himself*. . . . [H]is human nature will not be revealed in any special manner under the pretext that he *is* himself that which he is studying. Introspection here, like 'objective' experimentation there, will furnish nothing but facts. . . . [P]sychology, insofar as it claims to be a science, can furnish no more than a sum of . . . facts, the majority of which have no link between them. What could be more different, for instance, than the study of the stroboscopic illusion and the study of the inferiority complex? This disorder does not arise by chance, but from the very principles of the science of psychology. To wait upon the *fact* is, by definition, to wait upon the isolated; it is to prefer, positively, the accident to the essential, the contingent to the necessary, disorder to order. It is to discard, in principle, the essential as something in the future—'that is for later on, when we have collected enough facts.' The psychologists do not notice, indeed, that it is . . . impossible to attain the essence by heaping up the accidents. . . . If their only aim is to accumulate observations of detail there is nothing to be said, except that one can see little interest in the collectors' labours. (Sartre, 1962: 16–18)

Sartre (1966 [1943], 1957) adopted Brentano and Husserl's concept of *intentionality*, meaning that consciousness is always directed at something other than itself. We are always conscious of something, such as the sentence I am now writing and that you are now reading. Our intentions are revealed by our choices. We are always choosing to do one thing as opposed to another. Not only do we choose to do some things and not others, but we also choose to know some things and not others. We are what we have chosen to be, a fact Sartre sums up in the slogan 'existence precedes essence'. By this is meant that people are not predetermined and cannot claim that they had no choice but to become what they are.

Dostoievsky said, 'If God didn't exist, everything would be possible.' That is the very starting point of existentialism. Indeed, everything is permissible if God does not exist, and as a result man is forlorn, because neither within him nor without does he find anything to cling to. He can't start making excuses for himself.

If existence really does precede essence, there is no explaining things away by reference to a fixed and given human nature. In other words, there is no determinism . . . man is condemned to be free. Condemned, because he did not create himself, yet, in other respects is free; because, once thrown into the world, he is responsible for everything he does. (Sartre, 1957: 22–3)

Sartre placed great importance on honesty, both with oneself and with others. Self-deception arises when we do not take responsibility for our choices. Sartre regarded lying to oneself as a form of *bad faith*. Facing the truth about oneself may be painful, and Sartre acknowledged the fact that existentialism appeared to many to lead to a form of bleak despair, a life without illusions. However, Sartre (ibid., 51) regarded his approach as a form of **humanism** because it placed the person at the centre of the action, the only one responsible for his or her life.

Ludwig Binswanger (1881–1966)

Existentialism provided an alternative to psychoanalytic psychotherapy (May, 1958). This form of psychotherapy not only drew on such people as Kierkegaard and Nietzsche, but also on **Martin Heidegger** (1899–1976). Heidegger was a student of Husserl's and had also been an influence on Sartre. Heidegger was chancellor of the University of Freiburg in the early days of the Nazi regime, and for a few years following World War II he was forbidden to teach because of pro-Nazi sentiments he had expressed.

Heidegger's (1962 [1927]) fame rests on his analysis of Being, or *Dasein*. A person is fundamentally concerned with the fact that he or she is a **being-in-the-world**. People want to know what it means to be in the world and ask fundamental questions about the nature of existence. To be human is to *care* about the nature of existence, and such care is intrinsic to human beings. Heidegger believed that the phenomenological method is the only proper way to investigate the nature of being-in-the-world. A phenomenological description of consciousness reveals that people vary in the way that they are related to the world in which they live. Terms such as 'melancholy, boredom, fear, anxiety, and despair' refer to different ways of being-in-the-world (Schrag, 1967). The attempt to understand these moods as different ways of being-in-the-world constitutes the starting place for existential psychotherapy.

Ludwig Binswanger developed an existential approach to psychotherapy by building on Heidegger's basic ideas. Binswanger was originally trained as a psychoanalyst and then shifted to an existential approach. He recorded a conversation he had with Freud in 1927 in which they discussed a patient who had failed 'to take the last decisive step of psychoanalytic insight and to thus continue in his misery in spite of all previous efforts and technical progress. . . . I suggested that such a failure might only be understood as the result of something which could be called a deficiency of spirit, that is, an inability on the part of the patient to raise himself to the level of spiritual communication with the physician' (Binswanger, 1975: 1). Binswanger then went on to tell Freud that he was 'forced to recognize in man something like a religious category' that was fundamental in human beings (ibid., 2). People must make some spiritual commitment in order to make fundamental changes in themselves.

In his discussion with Binswanger, Freud, of course, did not agree with the notion that people are spiritual as well as biological creatures. However, Binswanger believed that a psychotherapist needs to attend to the spiritual side of the patient, 'who is his partner in the community of man and is another "human soul"' (ibid., 210). Such an understanding goes beyond mere scientific understanding of the person as a biological object. It 'inquires into the being of man as a whole' (ibid.), and requires 'a relation rooted equally in "care" and love. It is of the *essence* of being a psychiatrist, *therefore*, that he reaches beyond . . . *scientific* knowledge found in the fields of psychology, psychopathology, and psychotherapy. . . .The being of a psychiatrist . . . involves, therefore, the insight that . . . no "whole man" can be "grasped" with the methods of science' (ibid., 219–20).

Binswanger claimed that psychotherapy is not something that one can do with only a part of oneself, like 'a hobby or . . . some other scientific activity'. Rather, psychotherapy requires a total commitment to 'encounter and mutual understanding with his fellow man and . . . understanding human beings in their totality' (ibid., 220).

The Emergence of Humanistic Psychology

The American psychologists and psychotherapists who imported existentialism from Europe and modified it to suit their own purposes included Rollo May, Abraham Maslow, and Carl Rogers. We will consider each of them in detail below. Now, however, we will outline some features of their common reaction to existentialism. These reactions were expressed at a symposium on existential psychology held at a convention of the American Psychological Association in 1959 (May, 1961).

1. The American psychologists believed that existentialism added important dimensions to psychology. For May (ibid., 40), this meant a renewed 'emphasis on will and decision' as central psychological processes. For Maslow (1961: 53), it meant 'a radical stress on the concept of identity and the experience of identity'. For Rogers (1961a: 92), it signalled a concern with an 'existing, becoming, emerging, experiencing being'.
2. The American psychologists disagreed with the anti-scientific attitude expressed by many European existentialists. May (1961: 37) argued that existentialism was consistent with a broader conception of the nature of science than American academic psychologists usually adopt, and quoted one of the symposium participants as saying that 'Science offers more leeway than graduate students are permitted to realize.' Maslow (1961: 58) believed that existentialism would lead to the inclusion of 'raw experience' in a psychological science that would have to be radically revised. However, he hoped that existentialism would not 'turn into an antipsychology or into an antiscience' (ibid., 59). Rogers (1961a: 92) believed that existentialism could be approached scientifically and suggested that

an 'empirical research method' properly applied could investigate 'subjective qualities'.
3. In general, the Americans believed that the Europeans had been too pessimistic. This was especially true of Maslow (1961: 60), who called the attitudes of the most pessimistic existentialists 'high I.Q. whimpering on a cosmic scale'. In place of European pessimism, the American psychologists began to see on the horizon an optimistic new science of the experiencing person. 'It is possible that existentialism will not only enrich psychology. It may also be an additional push toward the establishment of another *branch* of psychology, the psychology of the fully evolved and authentic self and its ways of being' (ibid., 59).

Precisely what this new branch of psychology was to be like became clearer when many of the contributors to the 1959 symposium on existential psychology met in November 1964 at Old Saybrook, Connecticut, for the First Invitational Conference on Humanistic Psychology. 'Can the scientific functions of a humanistic psychological science be set forth?' was the central question before the conference (Bugental, 1965: 181). Papers presented by May (1965a), Maslow (1965), and Rogers (1965) were subsequently published in the *Journal of Humanistic Psychology*, which Maslow had helped found in 1961. Another contributor to the conference was George A. Kelly (1965), whose work we will review later in this chapter.

The papers from the Old Saybrook conference sounded several themes that were to become characteristic of humanistic psychology. One theme was to be critical of both behaviourist and psychoanalytic approaches to psychology. B.F. Skinner always figured prominently in any critique of behaviourism mounted by humanistic psychologists, who were adamant that human beings could not be regarded as governed entirely by stimulus-response connections (e.g., Rogers, 1964). Psychoanalysis was criticized for presenting a stunted view of the person as consumed by the necessity of reducing biological drives.

Humanistic psychologists were united in believing that there was more to being a person than either of these perspectives admitted. Because they saw themselves as going beyond behaviourism and psychoanalysis, humanistic psychologists often styled themselves as the Third Force (e.g., Bugental, 1964). One of the clearest spokespersons for humanistic psychology at this time was Charlotte Buhler, who described how humanistic psychology was different from either behaviourism or psychoanalysis:

> It conceives of man as living with intentionality, which means living with purpose. The purpose is to give meaning to life through interpreting it within a bigger context. Within this bigger context, to which the individual relates, he wants to create values. . . . [I]n humanistic psychology, the human being is conceived of as having a primary, or native orientation, in the direction of creating and of values. (Buhler, 1965: 55)

Rollo May (1909–94)

Rollo May was born in Ohio, graduating from Oberlin College in 1930. He studied with Alfred Adler in Vienna before attending Union Theological Seminary in New York, where he received a divinity degree in 1938 (Taylor, 1994). While studying for a doctorate in clinical psychology at Columbia he came down with tuberculosis and was required to spend a year and a half convalescing in a tuberculosis sanatorium, during which time he discovered in Kierkegaard's writings a description of 'anxiety as the struggle of the living being against non-being—which I could immediately experience there in my struggle with death or the prospect of being a life-long invalid' (May, 1961: 19).

In *The Meaning of Anxiety* (1950) and in his other widely read works (e.g., May 1953, 1969b), he elaborated on the nature and importance of **anxiety** as a modern phenomenon. 'In anxiety . . . we are threatened without knowing what steps to take to meet the danger. . . . [Anxiety is] the human

being's basic reaction to a danger to his existence or to some value he identifies with his existence' (May, 1953: 39–40). May distinguished between pathological, *neurotic anxiety* and *normal anxiety*. The former was the kind of anxiety Freud had discussed. The latter was seen as an inevitable response to the conditions of life in the middle of the twentieth century.

Normal anxiety results in 'bewilderment—this confusion as to who we are and what we should do' (ibid., 44). Modern people are confused and bewildered because the traditional values do not work any longer. Rugged individualism was fine for the nineteenth century, but it leads to isolation and loneliness in the modern urban context. The glorification of reason, which made sense in the early days of science, has led to a ruinous split between the intellect and other parts of the person, such as the emotions and the will. 'The upshot is that the values and goals which provided a unifying center for previous centuries in the modern period no longer are cogent' (ibid., 55). The task of the modern person is to rediscover a sense of self based on an exploration of one's existence.

The title of May's **Love and Will** conveys his approach to finding meaning in the modern world. Love and will represent those aspects of ourselves that have been pushed aside as a result of our preoccupation with the intellect. 'Apathy is the withdrawal of will and love, a statement that they "don't matter," a suspension of commitment' (May, 1969b: 33), and apathy is a central part of the modern condition. By apathy, May meant 'a state of feelinglessness, the despairing possibility that nothing matters' (ibid., 27).

Love is a necessary beginning in the movement away from apathy. May described the appearance of 'a new morality . . . of authenticity in relationship' that he witnessed in the 1960s and that claimed to be based on love. '[P]eople are not interested in money and success. . . . They seek an honesty, openness, a feeling, a touch, a look in the eyes, a sharing of fantasy.' Other people tend to be judged by their 'authenticity, doing one's own thing, and giving in the sense of making one's self available for the other' (ibid., 306). May was not entirely supportive of the morality he saw emerging in the 1960s. He believed that love by itself was not enough and suggested that the young people of the 1960s were emphasizing love at the expense of will precisely because their parents had done the opposite (ibid., 278). Although we often think of power and emotion as opposites, they do not need to be. While it is true that the exercise of willpower without love can be very destructive to oneself and to others, this is also true of love that does not discriminate between one person and another.

May argued that love and will both can and should support each other, and suggested that this could come about through *care*. Heidegger had observed that people *care* about the nature of their existence, and May (ibid., 289) proposed not only that the loss of such care is what creates apathy but also that the existence of care is what enables love and will to become conjoined. Care begins with love, but goes beyond it. It includes not only the ability to let one's actions be affected by one's immediate feelings, but also to 'mold and form one's self' over a long period of time (ibid., 279). Will is the process whereby the person makes judgements about the value of different alternatives and actively chooses between them. Without the discrimination that comes from will power, we treat every experience as equally valuable. We become passive consumers of experience. If all experiences are equally valuable, then they are all equally meaningless. It is only by actively choosing to have some experiences over others that our life becomes meaningful. This is reminiscent of William James's treatment of the will, and May regarded James as well as the existentialists as providing him with the basis of his approach to psychology.

> We love and will the world as an immediate, spontaneous totality. We *will* the world, create it by our decision, our fiat, our choice; and we *love* it, give it affect, energy, power to love and change

us as we mold and change it. This is what it means to be fully related to one's world. I do not imply that the world does not exist *before* we love or will it. . . . But it has no reality, no relation to me, as I have no effect upon it; I move as in a dream. . . . One can choose to shut it out . . . or one can choose to see it, create it. (Ibid., 324)

Abraham H. Maslow (1908–70)

Born in the Jewish slums in Brooklyn, **Abraham Maslow** overcame numerous obstacles to become one of the most broadly influential American psychologists of the century. After doing an undergraduate degree at City College of New York, he studied with Harry Harlow (1905–81) at the University of Wisconsin. Harlow's (1958) laboratory subsequently became famous for using monkeys to study the nature of attachment in primates. Maslow's doctoral dissertation concerned the relation between dominance and sexual behaviour in monkeys. He went on to Columbia Teacher's College, where he was employed by E.L. Thorndike. Thorndike gave Maslow an intelligence test, on which Maslow got the equivalent of an IQ of 195. Suitably impressed, Thorndike gave Maslow free rein to work on whatever topics interested him (Hoffman, 1988: 74). Maslow continued his research on dominance and sexuality, only this time by interviewing human participants.

The period between 1935 and 1940 was extremely important for Maslow. Living in New York City, he 'came to know and study with Adler . . . and Karen Horney in the field of psychoanalysis, and Kurt Goldstein, Max Wertheimer, and Kurt Koffka in Gestalt psychology' (ibid., 87). In some ways, the psychology Maslow went on to create is a blend of neo-Freudianism and Gestalt/organismic psychology. Maslow was also influenced by the anthropologist **Ruth Benedict** (1887–1948). Benedict's *Patterns of Culture* (1989 [1935]) has become a classic in cultural anthropology. As a result of Benedict's influence, Maslow spent a summer doing fieldwork on a Northern Blackfoot reservation in Alberta (Hoffman, 1988: 116).

Maslow (1964a) later acknowledged Benedict's influence in bringing home to him the importance of **synergy**, or the degree to which the needs of the individual are consistent with the demands of the culture. In a high synergy culture, being selfish also promotes the welfare of others, while in a low synergy culture the needs of the individual conflict with how the culture wants the individual to behave. It became a key assumption of Maslow's psychology that one should attempt to create synergic 'social institutions, whether in business, in an army, or in a university, in such a fashion that the people within the organization are co-ordinated with each other and are perforce made into colleagues and teammates rather than into rivals' (ibid., 161).

In 1951, Maslow became the founding chair of the Psychology Department at Brandeis, a non-sectarian university that had recently been founded by the American Jewish community. He retained his affiliation with Brandeis until 1969, when he became a resident fellow at the W.P. Laughlin Charitable Foundation in California. During his time at Brandeis he was responsible for hiring, among others, George Kelly and Ulric Neisser, both of whom made important contributions to psychology quite independent of Maslow's influence.

In many ways, Maslow's career illustrates the fate of humanistic psychology. Although his theory was never regarded as very respectable by academic psychologists, he was nevertheless elected to the presidency of the American Psychological Association in 1967. An index of his widespread popular influence is the fact that Maslow was the only psychologist to be named in a review of the most influential Americans of the previous 50 years conducted by a leading American mass-market magazine (Leonard, 1983). His influence on psychology as it is taught in psychology departments in universities was less than his influence on business, education, and the culture as a whole. We will return to the general question of the influence of humanistic psychology below.

The Hierarchy of Needs

Maslow's *Motivation and Personality* (1954) presented the theory of motivation that would eventually penetrate American culture so thoroughly that it would be taught as a part of the curriculum in many high schools. Consequently, most readers will already be familiar with Maslow's **hierarchy of needs**. Maslow defined **basic needs** in terms of their importance to the health of the person. Something is a basic need if it is required to preserve health, if its absence causes illness, if its restoration cures illness, and if it is freely chosen by a deprived person. Needs may be organized hierarchically in terms of the order in which they must be satisfied. Thus, the child is first preoccupied with satisfying his/her *physiological needs*. If a child lacks some bodily requirement it will do what it can to remedy that deficiency. For example, the child will strive to maintain the appropriate state of the blood with respect to its water content, salt content, sugar content, protein content, and so on (Maslow, 1954: 80). The child need not intentionally seek what is needed. Obviously, a child does not say, 'Oh, I need more salt', and then add salt to its diet. Rather, the child regulates itself without thinking, naturally and automatically.

Of course, in an environment where these needs are not met it is entirely possible for physiological needs to become a preoccupation. But what happens when these needs *are* met, when there is plenty of bread and the child's belly is usually full? At that point, Maslow said, a 'higher' need emerges. 'The higher need is a later . . . evolutionary development. We share the need for food with all living things, the need for love with (perhaps) the higher apes, the need for self-actualization (at least through creativeness) with nobody. The higher the need the more specifically human it is' (ibid., 147). Next to the physiological needs are the **safety needs**, which are the requirements we have for shelter, for relative peace and quiet, and for a modicum of comfort and stability. If these needs are met then we go on to the belongingness or **love needs**. A person requires

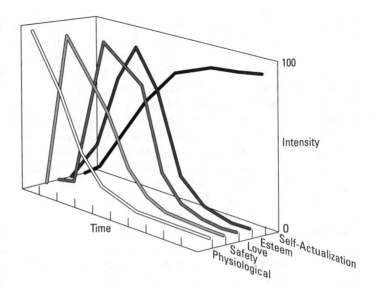

FIGURE 13.1
Maslow's hierarchy of needs.

affectionate relations with other people. Should these needs be satisfied, then the **esteem needs** emerge. These are requirements everyone has 'for adequacy, mastery and competence', and they lead to self-esteem. We also need the esteem of others, as manifested by 'status, dominance, recognition' (ibid., 90). If we manage to achieve all this, then the tendency towards **self-actualization** becomes increasingly salient. Maslow (ibid., 91–2) attributed the concept of self-actualization to Kurt Goldstein, and meant by it a person's 'desire for self-fulfillment' or the tendency 'to become everything that one is capable of becoming'. The tendency towards self-actualization manifests itself most clearly in what Maslow called the *cognitive-aesthetic needs*. These are 'needs to know and understand' things for their own sake and to be in the presence of and to create beautiful things (ibid., 93–8). These needs do not emerge only after the other needs are gratified—after all, preschool children spend a lot of time making art, as any parent should know. However, cognitive-aesthetic needs become increasingly important as the other, more basic needs are gratified.

Maslow argued that his theory of motivation was different from other motivational theories, such as Freud's. In other theories of motivation, needs are regarded as periodic, in the sense that gratifying a need reduces its intensity, which then builds back up, after which the need is gratified again, and so on. You cannot just gratify a need once and then be done with it. (It is nice to imagine the meal to end all meals, but such a meal does not exist. No matter how much you eat on one occasion, you will still have to eat again!) Maslow's system emphasizes the degree to which needs are not only periodic. Needs also emerge sequentially, as illustrated in Figure 13.1. The intensity with which different basic needs are experienced follows a particular order.

During the initial stage, when physiological needs are the most important, then that need system is at the centre of your life and is experienced the most intensely. Other needs are in the background. All the needs are there all the time, but you are most concerned with one type of need at any one time. When you are attending to your safety needs, for example, then you pay less attention to your esteem needs. When one need is more or less taken care of and you do not have to worry about it, then one of the others emerges to become your central concern. The tendency towards self-actualization is always there in the background, underlying all the other needs, but only comes to the fore after the other needs are gratified. Thus, after a need such as safety is more or less gratified, it is still present but is no longer a preoccupation. It could become a preoccupation if conditions change. A particular homeowner may not worry about housing needs as long as mortgage rates remain low. However, the same person could become preoccupied with shelter if mortgage rates go up dramatically and decent housing is no longer affordable. Thus, Maslow's theory regards human development as consisting of a hierarchy of stages, but, depending on the circumstances, one can go backward as well as forward.

The Self-actualizing Person

One of Maslow's (e.g., 1971: 23) most famous concepts is that of the **self-actualizing person**. Self-actualizing people have managed to satisfy their basic needs to a very great extent. To study self-actualizing people, Maslow recorded his observations of individuals such as Max Wertheimer and Ruth Benedict, who seemed to him to have gone beyond satisfying the lower needs. From these records he formulated a theory of the motivations of self-actualizing people. Maslow argued that at this higher level a different set of motives were important, which he called *metamotivations*. 'Meta' means beyond, and so metamotivations are motives beyond or above ordinary motives.

Maslow argued that self-actualizing people have different values from those held by ordinary people. The rest of us value that of which we are deprived. For example, people deprived of food value food, while people deprived of shelter value shelter. Maslow (1962) called such motivations **deficiency motives**. The self-actualizing person isn't deprived of such things as food, shelter, love,

or self-esteem. The self-actualizing person does not work to gratify deprivation motives. The work of such people is not something they feel they are being forced to do out of the necessity to satisfy their basic needs. They do not regard their work as drudgery, something from which they escape on the weekends. Self-actualizing persons feel that there is a harmony between themselves and their work, a good match between who they are and what they do for a job. Rather than having values based on real or imagined deprivation, the self-actualizing person has what Maslow (1962) called **Being values**, or B-values. B-values follow from the intrinsic worth of an activity.

In his studies of self-actualizing people, Maslow found that they do not rest on their achievements. Maslow (1971: 301) used words and phrases such as 'devoted', 'dedicated', 'people who have a calling, or a vocation, or a mission', and 'a passionate attachment to their work' to describe self-actualizing people. For Maslow, these are examples of B-values. For metamotivated individuals, their work is something that they feel they *must* do, in the sense that they feel it is their duty, a responsibility that they shoulder voluntarily. For example, a baby requires that someone take care of it, and a self-actualizing caregiver responds without begrudging the attention lavished on the child. To give another example, injustice requires opposition, and a self-actualizing lawyer responds to the challenge willingly, perceiving it as a personal necessity to do so. The self-actualizing person lives synergistically, with a correspondence between what he or she wants to do and what the situation demands.

> At this level the dichotomizing of work and play is transcended. . . . There is certainly no distinction between work and play. . . . If a person loves his work and enjoys it more than any other activity in the whole world and is eager to get to it, to get back to it after any interruption, then how can we speak about 'labor' in the sense of something one is forced to do against one's wishes? (Ibid., 304)

For the self-actualizing person, the distinction between work and play is irrelevant because, for this individual, work *is* play. Imagine that you owned a company. Would you not like to have employees who felt like this about their work? Perhaps this accounts for the popularity of Maslow among many people in business. Maslow occasionally pointed out that some self-actualizing people will be willing to work for no money at all, preferring not to be bothered with it, just like the members of some religious orders.

Metamotives and their corresponding B-values are the most advanced from an evolutionary or developmental point of view. However, this means that they are also the weakest, in the sense of being the last to emerge and the most easily destroyed. Nevertheless, if they are not gratified, then there will develop a state Maslow called *metapathology*. The metamotives are instinctual in the sense that if they are thwarted it will make you sick. The sicknesses that result are the sort of spiritual illnesses that have been described for millennia by religious people and philosophers (ibid., 316): alienation, boredom, apathy, despair.

Maslow (1964b: 38) argued that 'a large proportion of all affluent nations' have spiritual ailments. In spite of having their most basic needs satisfied, many people are not very happy. This is because a life based solely on the gratification of lower needs will strike people as not really worth living (ibid., 42). However, many people have become cynical about higher values, believing them to be 'a fake and a swindle' (ibid., 9). Maslow regarded such attitudes as partly responsible for spiritual illnesses. We should accept higher values as intrinsic parts of our being. B-values are not culturally determined, but are universal values, found in all the great religions.

Peak Experiences

Maslow (1962: ch. 6) is well known for promoting the concept of **peak experiences**, which have much in common with mystical experiences of a oneness with the world. 'The emotional reaction in the peak experience has a special flavor of wonder, of awe, of reverence, of humility and surrender before the experience as before something great' (ibid., 82). It is from peak experiences that many people become aware of the centrality of B-values in their lives. Peak experiences are intrinsically valuable, and many people regard such experiences as the most important they have ever had. While anyone can have a peak experience, they are more common in self-actualizing persons.

Peak experiences are similar to a childlike way of being-in-the-world. Children do not distinguish clearly between themselves and their environment. Similarly, a peak experience reduces feelings of alienation from the world and enhances the feeling that you are a part of a larger whole. However, peak experiences are more than just a regression to a childish way of experiencing. They represent 'a fusion of ego, id, super-ego, . . . of conscious and unconscious, . . . a synthesizing of pleasure principle and reality principle, a regression without fear in the service of the greatest maturity, a true integration of the person at all levels' (ibid., 91).

The Psychology of Science

Maslow's investigations of such topics as peak experiences and self-actualization were unorthodox, as he acknowledged himself (e.g., Maslow, 1954: 199). He described one of his studies as an:

> impressionistic, ideal, 'composite photograph' or organization of personal interviews . . . I have added together all the partial responses to make a 'perfect' composite syndrome. In addition, about fifty people wrote me unsolicited letters after reading my previously published papers, giving me personal reports of peak experiences. Finally, I have tapped the immense literatures of mysticism, religion, art, creativeness, love, etc. (Maslow, 1962: 67)

Not surprisingly, more orthodox academic psychologists took a dim view of what they regarded as a methodology that was too subjective and unreliable to produce any scientifically meaningful results. Maslow's response was to write *The Psychology of Science*, which was 'a critique of orthodox science . . . [that] rejects the traditional but unexamined conviction that orthodox science is *the* path to knowledge or even that it is the only reliable path' (Maslow, 1966: 1). In place of orthodox science, Maslow advocated a science with a number of features not always associated with scientific psychology. For example, he spoke of a *Taoistic science* that would be open and receptive to people, rather than attempting to predict and control them. He also advocated a *problem-centred* rather than a *method-centred* approach to psychology. Rather than apply the same methodology to all problems, the methods should be tailored to fit the problem. A logical positivist methodology was only suited to the exploration of very limited aspects of behaviour. The study of such topics as peak experiences could not be accommodated within traditional methods, but that does not mean that such experiences should be ignored. Rather, more *experiential methods* were required that involved the active participation of the researcher in the phenomenon being investigated. Scientists could not understand all phenomena from the outside, by being spectators rather than participants. To truly understand such phenomena as peak experiences you had first of all to experience them yourself.

Carl R. Rogers (1902–87)

Perhaps more than anyone else, **Carl Rogers** became synonymous with the practice of clinical psychology. As we shall see, there are good reasons for this, but the fact of the matter is that clinical psychology did not begin with Carl Rogers. Clinical psychology may be defined as 'a scientific and professional field that seeks to increase our understanding of human behavior and to promote the effective functioning of individuals' (Reisman, 1991: 3). As such, clinical psychology is not defined by any single approach, such as psychoanalysis.

Most people agree that the first person in the United States to define an area called 'clinical psychology' was **Lightner Witmer** (1867–1956) of the University of Pennsylvania (McReynolds, 1996, 1997). Witmer developed his conception of clinical psychology while working in schools. Clinical psychology was to be used to diagnose and treat deficiencies, practices he carried on at 'the first psychological clinic, actually the first child guidance clinic in the world', founded at the University of Pennsylvania in 1896 (Reisman, 1991: 38). Witmer developed courses in clinical psychology designed to demonstrate methods useful to would-be practitioners. These courses were the forerunners of the clinical training programs that subsequently became fixtures in many American graduate programs in psychology.

While mental testing has long been an activity central to the practice of clinical psychology, psychotherapy is perhaps even more closely associated with clinical psychology in the public's mind. Few people are more closely identified with the practice of psychotherapy than Carl Rogers (Lakin, 1998). Rogers entered the University of Wisconsin in 1919 intending to major in agriculture. An ardent Christian, he was chosen:

> to go to a World Student Christian Federation Conference in Peking, China. . . . Due to this six months' trip I had been able freely, and with no sense of defiance or guilt, to think my own thoughts, come to my own conclusions, and to take the stands I believed in. . . . From the date of this trip, my goals, values, aims, and philosophy have been my own and very divergent from the views which my parents held and which I had held up to this point. (Rogers, 1967: 351)

Rogers subsequently changed his major to history, graduating in 1924. He then went to Union Theological Seminary in New York, but eventually left the 'field of religious work [because], although questions as to the meaning of life and the possibility of the constructive improvement of life for individuals were of deep interest to me,

I could not work in a field where I would be required to believe in some specified religious doctrine' (ibid., 354).

While at Union Theological Seminary, Rogers had been taking some courses at Columbia University, one of which was in clinical psychology and taught by **Leta Hollingworth** (1886–1939), a figure of considerable historical importance in her own right. Hollingworth had been instrumental in the establishment of the American Association of Clinical Psychologists in 1917 (Street, 1994). In addition to being an authority in child clinical psychology, Hollingworth (1914a, 1914b) did foundational work on gender differences that 'undermined the hypothesis of male superiority . . . and arguments that women were dysfunctional during their menstrual cycle. . . . Work in this tradition died out around 1920 and did not become a focus within academic psychology again until the early 1970s' (Kimball, 1994). Thus, Hollingworth was a pioneer in the psychology of women, a topic we will consider more fully in Chapter 15. Rogers (1967: 355) described Hollingworth's influence on him: 'She was a warm human being, concerned about individuals, as well as a competent research worker. It was under her supervision that I first came in actual *clinical* contact with children— testing them, talking with them, dealing with them as fascinating objects of study, and helping to make plans for their welfare.'

After receiving his Ed.D. from Columbia, Rogers went to work at the Rochester Society for the Prevention of Cruelty to Children. Rogers (ibid., 358–61) described the 12 years he spent in Rochester as particularly formative ones during which he began to develop the style of psychotherapy that would eventually be called 'Rogerian'. In 1940 he moved to Ohio State University, where he established a 'practicum in counseling and psychotherapy' that may have been 'the first instance in which supervised therapy was carried on in a university setting' (ibid., 362). Subsequently, Rogers went on to the University of Chicago, where he established a counselling centre. In 1947, while at Chicago, Rogers was elected

president of the American Psychological Association. After a period at the University of Wisconsin, Rogers moved to California in 1964, first to the Western Behavioral Sciences Institute and then to the Center for Studies of the Person.

Client-Centred Therapy

In his presidential address to the American Psychological Association, Rogers (1978 [1947]) foreshadowed several aspects of what was to become *client-centred* or **non-directive psychotherapy** (Rogers, 1951, 1952). Quoting from a number of taped interviews between therapists and clients, Rogers outlined the ways in which his approach to therapy brought about change. He characterized the non-directive therapist's behaviour as expressing an attitude of 'warmth and understanding . . . [that] helps maximize the freedom of expression by the individual' (Rogers, 1978: 418). The therapist does not attempt to bias what the client has to say, and attempts to see the client's behaviour 'through his eyes, and also the psychological meaning it has for him. . . . Only a novelist or a poet could do justice to the deep struggles which we are permitted to observe from within the client's own world of reality' (ibid., 419).

Such openness and receptiveness on the part of the therapist came to be called *unconditional positive regard*, which Rogers (1961b: 62) defined as:

> the therapist's genuine willingness for the client to be whatever feeling is going on in him at that moment—fear, confusion, pain, pride, anger, hatred, love, courage, or awe. It means that he prizes the client in a total rather than a conditional way. By this I mean that he does not simply accept the client when he is behaving in certain ways, and disapprove of him when he behaves in other ways. It means an outgoing positive feeling without reservations.

In a nutshell, client-centred therapy provides the therapist with the opportunity to see 'the client as the client sees himself, to look at problems through his eyes' in an 'atmosphere of complete psychological security' (Rogers, 1952: 67). As a result of this empathic understanding the client spontaneously begins to 'reorganize the structure of self in accordance with reality and his own needs' (ibid.). A central notion in Rogers's theory of therapy was the **self-concept**, or the view the person had of himself or herself. A discrepancy between the person's self-concept and the way the person wished to be (the **ideal self**) was one source of discomfort. Rogers believed that non-directive therapy caused the self to become 'more positively valued, i.e., . . . more congruent with the ideal, or valued, self' (Rogers, 1961b: 235).

When humanistic psychology was just beginning, Rogers (e.g., 1965a: 5) often spoke of the importance of developing 'tough, dedicated, persistent, humanistic scientists', and it was characteristic of his work that he not only attempted to state his theory in as precise terms as possible (e.g., Rogers, 1959), but also tried to evaluate empirically his therapeutic approach. In his studies, Rogers sought to test the null hypothesis that clients do not change as a result of non-directive therapy. In the context of Rogerian psychotherapy, the null hypothesis is that the difference between the self-concept and the ideal self-concept is not different at the end of therapy than it was at the beginning of therapy.

In order to measure the self-concept and ideal self-concept, Rogers and his co-workers used a card-sorting technique. This technique uses 100 self-descriptive statements such as 'I am a submissive person'. 'I don't trust my emotions', 'I have an attractive personality' (Rogers, 1961b: 232). Before therapy (the pre-test) clients sorted the cards to represent themselves and then sorted the cards to represent the person they would like to be (ideal self). They repeated this procedure immediately after therapy (first post-test) and again some time later at a follow-up session (second post-test).

Rogers presented data that allowed him to reject the null hypothesis. The self and ideal self card sorts were typically more similar on both the post-tests than they were before therapy. One

difficulty in interpreting data such as these is that we do not know whether or not the outcome is merely due to repeated testing. Perhaps simply retaking the card-sorting test results in the observed results, and the findings may not be due to therapy at all. Rogers himself was acutely aware of this problem and spent a lot of time seeking proper evaluation of his psychotherapeutic approach. In the end, he was skeptical of the value of such research programs:

> Person-centered therapists were under pressure . . . to prove that our approach to therapy was effective. We gradually carried on more and more sophisticated studies to assess the outcomes. But when this was the sole purpose of the research, the results, even though the evidence of effectiveness was positive, were always disappointing. We found, as could have been predicted, that some clients were more successful than others, some therapists more effective than others. But assessment studies are not heuristic, do not lead forward. They offer almost no clues to the elements we need to know to improve therapy or to understand its process. (Rogers, 1980: 311)

In spite of his skeptical attitude towards evaluative research, his theory was the focus of many other psychologists' research efforts in a variety of areas. A typical example is given in Box 13.1.

Rogers remained an active participant in humanistic psychology well after the normal retirement date for most people. For example, in 1986 he visited the then Soviet Union together with his colleague, Ruth Sanford, where they came in contact with over 2,000 people. 'In Moscow and Tbilisi, Rogers and Sanford led day-long discussions with large groups and four-day encounter groups with 30–45 members. . . . After the Rogers and Sanford visit, a national Soviet television program carried a one-hour special on them' (Hassard, 1990: 27–8). Rogers's visit was a part of an exchange program begun in 1983 between the Association of Humanistic Psychologists and Soviet psychologists and educators.

BOX 13.1

CARL ROGERS'S THEORY OF CREATIVE ENVIRONMENTS

A persistent criticism of humanistic psychology has been that there is little empirical support for it. An exception is an article by Harrington et al. (1987) that provided some support for Carl Rogers's (1970 [1954]) theory of creative environments. According to this theory, a person is able to express him/herself most creatively under conditions of openness to experience, internal locus of evaluation, and an ability to toy with elements and concepts.

1. *Openness to experience.* This means a 'lack of rigidity . . . a tolerance for ambiguity . . . the ability to receive much conflicting information without forcing closure on the situation' (Rogers, 1970 [1954]: 143).
2. *Internal locus of evaluation.* This means that 'the value of his [or her] product is, for the creative person, established not by the praise or criticism of others, but by himself [or herself]' (ibid., 144).
3. *The ability to toy with elements and concepts.* This means the 'ability to play spontaneously with ideas, colors, shapes, relationships', and so on (ibid.).

In order for the person to develop these characteristics, he or she must be raised in an environment that has the following features:

- *Psychological safety*, whereby the individual is 'understood empathically'

and accepted as having 'unconditional worth', and where 'external evaluation is absent' (ibid., 147–8).
- *Psychological freedom*, which means that the individual is given 'complete freedom of symbolic expression' (ibid., 148).

Harrington et al. tried to determine if child-rearing practices such as these consistently lead to more open, creative adults. In their study, 106 families were studied over an 11-year period. At the start of the study, when the children in the families were about 3 years of age, the parents filled out a scale describing their child-rearing practices. A little later, parent-child interactions occurring while the parent taught the child a task were videotaped. There was also a set of ratings by trained observers and teachers of how creatively the children behaved at different ages.

Based on these data, it appeared to be the case that the more the child was raised in accordance with Rogerian principles, the more creative she or he tended to be rated. These relationships were partly due to the mother's child-rearing practices and partly due to the father's child-rearing practices. This study is consistent with Rogers's theory that 'Children raised by parents who provide conditions of psychological safety and freedom will develop their creative potential more fully than will children whose parents do not provide such conditions' (Harrington et al., 1987: 855).

Eugene T. Gendlin

Eugene Gendlin was a student of Carl Rogers at the University of Chicago who articulated the Rogerian viewpoint and its relation to other forms of psychology in a particularly clear way. Gendlin was also the first editor of the journal, *Psychotherapy: Theory, Research and Practice*, which was founded in 1963.

The key concept in Gendlin's exposition is **experiencing**, which is the 'flow of feeling, concretely, to which you can every moment attend inwardly, if you wish' (Gendlin, 1962: 3). Experiencing is a very complex 'felt apperceptive mass to which we can inwardly point' (ibid., 27). When we attend to our experiencing directly, then we have *felt meanings*.

Gendlin observed that the goal of many personality theories is to be able tell people who and what they are, as in 'You are an introvert' or 'You have an Oedipus complex.' Gendlin argued that this is the wrong approach. A person *is* 'the flow of experiencing. . . . For that is what you are inside, to yourself.' Thus, a humanistic approach facilitates the person's discovery of himself or herself through experiencing. Gendlin (ibid., 30–2) gave an extended example of what he meant by 'experiencing'. Imagine a situation in which you are trying to impress someone in that person's home. However, you drop something—a glass of red wine, say—on the brand new white rug. An observer might interpret your behaviour as revealing your unconscious hostility towards the other person. Gendlin believed that such interpretations from the outside were meaningless. Rather than accept the 'hostile' interpretation, you should attend to the felt meanings you had when you dropped the wine glass.

> If you refer directly to it . . . you will find much more in this . . . concretely felt experiencing. Perhaps you will now say that you felt apprehensive, lest that other person become impatient with you. His high position made you afraid. His secure ease also made you afraid, for he could afford to lose you, but you had to be glad to receive his time and attention. You would never blame him for your lowly position, of course, but you never do like being put into such a position. Of course, now that we discuss it, who likes to associate with someone on the basis of needing something from him which he may or may not want to give, and that—as you, of course, knew all along—was how it stood. What is more, we have all been in situations of this kind as children, and so you might feel some loss of adulthood when you must plead, appeal, or please. So it may well be as you attend directly to this aspect of experiencing, you find—as you use symbols along with your reference—that all these many meanings can truly be said of how you felt, and were aware of feeling. (Ibid., 32–3)

Experiencing is not limited to simple mental contents, such as sensations or ideas. Felt meanings occur prior to any words or concepts that we may use to interpret them. That is, felt meanings are preverbal and preconceptual. We can try to put these felt meanings into words, but words are often a poor translation of the felt meaning we experience. Consequently, there is a continuous interaction between experiencing and the words and other symbols we use to try to represent our experiencing. Our experiencing need not be represented only by words. Music, painting, dancing, and other forms of self-expression can also be appropriate ways of representing our experiencing.

In psychotherapy, the client is encouraged, with the support of the therapist, to try to represent felt meanings symbolically. This may involve a change in the way that the client has previously represented his or her experience. The meaning of our experience is something each of us creates through the symbols we use. These symbols should be true to our own experience. We should not try to make our experience fit the symbols we may have been taught by others to use when we describe ourselves. There are many different ways of representing our experience, and there are no fixed patterns to which everyone's experience must conform (Gendlin, 1981). The process of symbolically representing experience need never be completed, and so the process of creating oneself can be a life's work.

Encounter Groups

Recall our discussion of Kurt Lewin in the chapter on Gestalt psychology. Lewin had been instrumental in developing *sensitivity training*, or the so-called T-groups, and group members often dramatically changed their view of themselves as a result of feedback from other members of the group. T-groups, subsequently renamed **encounter groups** (Rogers, 1970), were taken up with enthusiasm by many humanistic psychologists as vehicles for enabling people to realize their full human potential.

Partly as a result of the use of encounter groups and other forms of therapy designed to enhance personal growth, humanistic psychology became virtually synonymous with what came to be called the **human potential movement**.

The encounter group was a setting in which people discussed themselves as freely and openly as possible. The original purpose of such groups had been to increase the accuracy of the participants' perceptions of themselves and others. However, it soon became clear that participants did not necessarily change in this manner. For example, Smith reviewed several studies showing that encounter group experience did not increase *empirical understanding*, which is 'the degree to which one person can predict another person's feelings, thoughts and behavior'. However, these studies also showed that encounter groups increased 'the degree to which a person feels close to, sympathetic with, and understanding of another person' (Smith, 1973: 32). While there was little evidence that encounter group experience increased the extent to which participants saw each other as unique individuals, it did tend to increase the extent to which participants saw themselves as similar to each other (e.g., Benjafield et al., 1976). Feelings initially thought to be too private to be expressed may, upon being expressed in the group, turn out to be met with accounts of similar experiences from others. Consequently, encounter group experience seemed to reduce feelings of alienation and to promote the sense that people are all fundamentally alike. Smith (1973: 32) argued that this kind of experience is 'more real to us, . . . more deeply desired, and probably more important to our personal survival than is empirical understanding.'

What Happened to Humanistic Psychology?

Humanistic psychology fit well with the *Zeitgeist* in American popular culture in the 1960s and 1970s. However, as the 1970s wore on, humanistic psychology began to attract more and more criticism (e.g., Rosen, 1977; Wertheimer, 1978). Much of this criticism came from outside humanistic psychology itself and focused on the large number of different 'therapies' that had emerged, as well as on what appeared to be a general lack of standards as to what constituted legitimate forms of therapy. Humanistic psychology seemed to be unable or unwilling to regulate these myriad approaches, and at least some consumers may have been damaged as a result (Wallach and Wallach, 1983). To many people—both psychologists and the lay public—it seemed as if 'anything goes'.

Some of the most trenchant criticisms of the human potential movement came from within humanistic psychology itself. A good example is Richard Farson's analysis of the state of humanistic psychology as the 1970s drew to a close. Farson had been a colleague of Carl Rogers at Chicago and helped to persuade him to join the Western Behavioral Sciences Institute in La Jolla, California. In retrospect, Farson lamented the fact that humanistic psychology had done little to build a truly humanistic science. Instead of 'systematic research or theory construction', humanistic psychology had witnessed 'a massive proliferation of therapies, and other experiential programs generally referred to as the human potential movement' (Farson, 1978: 7).

Humanistic psychology declined as a major force in academic psychology, partly because, as Farson observed, the leaders of humanistic psychology, such as Rollo May, Abraham Maslow, and Carl Rogers, moved away from university settings. This had the consequence that 'their theories have not been researched, expanded or revised, and their thinking has not been tested by the critical questioning that would come from students and university colleagues. . . . Moreover, they have not developed students who can extend their work into second and third generations of scholars and scientists' (ibid., 29).

To a large extent, the enthusiasm that fired humanistic psychology when it was founded had faded away by the end of the century. One prominent humanistic psychologist observed that 'the movement has failed to sufficiently infuse the traditional establishment of psychology; the universities, the journals, and major professional organization[s]' (Wertz, 1998: 65). However, humanistic psychology still continued to have an impact on popular culture. One had only to examine the offerings in the psychology or self-help sections of mass-market bookstores to realize that such topics as interpersonal relationships, marriage, work, and child-rearing were still of great concern to many people. Humanistic psychology shaped the way ordinary people thought about these issues. Can one say the same about many academic psychologies?

George A. Kelly (1905–67)

George Kelly attended the Old Saybrook conference that launched humanistic psychology in 1964, and the paper he gave there was later published in the *Journal of Humanistic Psychology* (Kelly, 1965). While Kelly's approach shared some of the characteristics of humanistic psychology, in other ways it was quite distinctive. The following captures one of the essential differences between Kelly and many humanistic psychologists.

> Because of the present uncertainty of its stand on experimental research, I fear there is a real danger of the recent humanistic psychology movement fizzling out. In their outright opposition to so much that is considered synonymous with 'scientific research' and 'experimental psychology,' humanists may convince themselves and others that they oppose research in general and experimentation in particular. Nothing could be more incongruous than for humanistic psychology to become frozen in this posture. What could be more vital to psychology than to recognize that experimentation is even more characteristically human than it is scientific? (Kelly, 1969a: 144)

Notice that Kelly associated being human with being a scientist. Kelly did not see scientific behaviour as something unnatural. Rather, Kelly (1955: 5) believed that people naturally wish to 'predict and control the course of events with which they are involved', just as scientists do. Kelly's psychology is largely the result of exploring the implications of the notion that **people are scientists**.

The Psychology of Personal Constructs

Kelly first came to widespread attention with the publication in 1955 of his two-volume work, *The Psychology of Personal Constructs*. The fundamental postulate of this theory is that 'A person's processes are psychologically channelized by the ways in which [that person] anticipates events' (Kelly, 1955: 46). By this, Kelly meant that the person 'ultimately seeks to anticipate real events. This is where we see psychological processes as tied down to reality. Anticipation is not merely carried on for its own sake; it is carried on so that future reality may be better represented. It is the future which tantalizes [the person], not the past. Always [the person] reaches out to the future through the window of the present' (ibid., 49).

Kelly believed that the process of anticipation was analogous to the way scientists behave when they are performing experiments to test hypotheses. People attempt to predict, or anticipate, the events they will encounter, just as scientists formulate hypotheses that are then tested against reality. In order to predict events, it is necessary for the person to be able to represent them. From Kelly's viewpoint, we do this by means of **constructs**. In its simplest form, a construct is a way in which two events are alike but different from a third event. 'If we choose an aspect in which A and B are similar, but in contrast to C, it is important to note that it is the same aspect of the three A, B and C that forms the basis of the construct' (ibid., 59). For example, if we have three acquaintances— Curly, Moe, and Larry—and we see Curly and Moe as similar in that they are *warm*, but different from Larry, who is *cold*, then the aspect underlying the comparison may be said to be *warmth* (cf. Benjafield, 1983).

It is essential to Kelly's psychology that 'people differ from each other in their construction of events' (Kelly, 1955: 55). Each person creates **personal constructs**, which are dimensions that may be unique to that individual. Personal constructs are idiosyncratic ways of noting similarities and differences. They are most obvious when people make distinctions using terms that are not opposites in any conventional sense, as in the following illustration. Suppose we ask someone to differentiate among three acquaintances—the ubiquitous Curly, Moe, and Larry. The person replies that Curly and Moe are *intelligent* and Larry is *lazy*. At first this may puzzle us. To understand it we inquire further and discover that, according to this person, Curly and Moe are also *rich*, and Larry is *poor*. Now we may be starting to get a better picture of what the construct *intelligent* versus *lazy* means to this person. We need not agree with his construction of Curly, Moe, and Larry to be able to understand how he sees them. It is through the pattern of relationships between the person's constructs that the meaning of particular constructs emerges (ibid., 56).

Once we have a feeling for how some of a person's constructs are related, then we can begin to make hypotheses about how the person might employ other constructs. In the example, since being *intelligent* and *rich* go together, as do being *lazy* and *poor*, then we might infer that this person believes that being intelligent goes with being hard-working. We might turn out to be wrong. Suppose the person says that only Curly *works hard*, and that Moe and Larry *take it easy*. In this case, the person's construct system has turned out to be more complicated than we anticipated. We could continue to probe the other person's constructs by asking for further construals. Kelly's point is that we try to understand someone else's construct system in the same way as we try to understand any other set of events. We try to antic-

ipate the other person's constructions, and modify our understanding of the person in the light of the results of these anticipations (ibid., 95–100).

In our running example, we have been considering a hypothetical person for whom the construct *intelligent versus lazy* is related to the construct *rich versus poor*. As a consequence of this linkage between the two constructs, if this person meets someone *rich*, then he or she will anticipate that the new acquaintance will demonstrate *intelligence* as well. Even if the other person's behaviour provides no evidence of intelligence, it may still be construed as intelligent in order to validate this prediction. Kelly (ibid., 510) used the term *hostility* to refer to the process of distorting evidence so as to preserve one's construct system, and likened hostility to the 'method of Procrustes, who was always stretching his guests, or cutting them down to a size to fit his bed' (ibid., 511). A hostile person does not behave as would a good scientist. In fact, poor scientists behave like Procrustes, forcing the facts to fit their theory rather than the other way around. People are better scientists when they are able to revise the linkages between their constructs in the light of new evidence. Thus, in our hypothetical example, finding a *rich* person who was *lazy* should lead to a looser relation between the two constructs.

According to Kelly (ibid., 117–19), the pattern of linkages between constructs takes a specific form that may be unique to the individual. On the basis of these linkages between our constructs we are able to explore reality and make predictions about what we will find there. These predictions may be falsified by the events we actually encounter, leading to a revision of the linkages between constructs, and thus a restructured construct system.

The Repertory Test

Personal constructs came to Kelly's attention as a result of his work as a psychotherapist in Kansas in the 1930s. He observed that his clients seldom described themselves in conventional terms. 'Each person seeks to communicate his distress in the terms that make sense to [that person], but not necessarily in terms that make sense to others' (Kelly, 1969b: 58). Kelly (1955: 4) observed that John Locke had begun to write *An Essay Concerning Human Understanding* (which we considered in Chapter 2) upon being 'struck by the unique imperceptiveness of his friends', just as Kelly was spurred to write *The Psychology of Personal Constructs* because of the uniqueness of the viewpoints his clients had demonstrated. Each person lives in a world that is somewhat unique, as revealed by the uniqueness of their personal constructs. It is vitally important that the psychotherapist somehow be able to construe the idiosyncratic constructions of the client.

One of Kelly's (ibid., ch. 5) most influential contributions was to invent a method of eliciting an individual's personal constructs. An example of this instrument is given in Figure 13.2. It is called a repertory grid test, and allows one to get some idea of how a person thinks about her/his acquaintances. The columns of the grid give 13 role titles, such as 'most successful person'. Kelly (ibid., 274) used a list of 22 role titles, while Figure 13.2 has only 13 role titles, taken from Benjafield and Green (1978). A participant taking this test starts by giving the name of one acquaintance who best fits the description of 'most successful person'. The participant then assigns names of other acquaintances to all the remaining role titles.

If you wish to have the experience of taking a repertory grid test, then you should begin by filling in names of your acquaintances that best correspond to the role titles, remembering that a name can be used only once. The column labelled 'self' refers to you. Now turn your attention to the rows. Each row of the grid gives you an opportunity to generate your own constructs. The first row has circles in the first three squares. 'This means that you are first to consider the people whose names' correspond to the first three role titles. 'How are two of them alike in some important way that distinguishes them from the third person? Keep thinking about them until you remember the important way in which two of them are alike and which sets them off from the third person. When you have decided which two it is, and the important way in which two of them are alike, put a checkmark ["✓"] in the two circles corresponding to the two who are alike. Do not put any mark in the third circle. Now write in the blank under "Construct" the word or short phrase that tells how these two are alike. Next write in the blank under "Contrast" what you consider to be the opposite of this characteristic. Now consider each of the other . . . persons whose names appear at the heads of [the columns]. . . . [W]hich ones also have this important characteristic? Put a checkmark "✓" under the name of each other person who has this important characteristic' (Kelly, 1955: 273).

This procedure is repeated for each row. The result is a pattern of checks and blanks, together with the names of constructs and contrasts. Kelly provided a rationale for each of the triplets he used, but in Figure 13.2 the triplets have been assigned arbitrarily. Thus, while Figure 13.2 can give you some idea of what filling out a repertory grid is like, it does not yield any interpretable data.

Research in Personal Construct Theory

It is an interesting quirk of history that Kelly's approach was not taken up by psychologists in the United States to anything like the degree it was adopted in Britain. 'By the late 1950s, [personal construct theory] had begun to attract adherents in Great Britain, and by the mid-1960s it was being vigorously debated, and applied by a small but devoted network of psychologists and psychiatrists. Despite its more recent origin, the British theory has grown rapidly, so that by 1980 as many British as American psychologists had published . . . twice in the theory' (Neimeyer, 1985: 40). It is generally agreed that the popularity of personal construct theory in Great Britain was largely due to the efforts of Don Bannister (e.g., Bannister and Bott, 1973; Bannister and Mair, 1968; Fransella and Bannister, 1977), who brought the theory to the attention of many clinical practitioners (e.g., Ryle, 1975).

Most Successful Person	Most Ethical Person	Happiest Person	Warmest Person	Strongest Person	Most Active Person	Most Unsuccessful Person	Unhappiest Person	Most Unethical Person	Coldest Person	Weakest Person	Most Passive Person	Yourself	Construct	Contrast
○	○	○												
			○	○	○									
						○	○	○						
									○	○	○			
○	○											○		
		○	○									○		
				○	○							○		
						○	○					○		
								○	○			○		
										○	○	○		
		○		○	○									

FIGURE 13.2
A repertory test.

Bannister's work drew attention to the many different ways in which a repertory grid can yield information about a person's construct system. For example, repertory grids can be used to measure a person's *cognitive complexity* (Bieri, 1955; Bannister and Mair, 1968: 70). 'The cognitively complex person is assumed to have a greater number of personal constructs to construe the behaviour of others, while the cognitively simple person has available relatively few personal constructs' (Bieri, 1961: 359). There are several possible measures of complexity (Adams-Webber, 1970; Fransella and Bannister, 1977: 61–2), but we will focus here only on one simple measure, just to get a rough idea of what kinds of measures are possi-

ble using the grid. Bieri (1961: 361) suggested that a person's construct system, as measured by a grid, may be said to be relatively *simple* if there are a large number of matches between the constructs (rows). It is possible to imagine a grid in which the same pattern of checks and blanks occurred for each construct. For example, suppose the two rows below were the first two rows from Figure 13.2 that had been filled in by a participant. The names of the acquaintances (columns) have been left out. The two rows represent checks and blanks for two constructs—pleasant versus unpleasant, and intelligent versus stupid. In this example, the constructs are perfectly correlated, since every time a role title is judged as *pleasant* it is also judged as *intelligent*, and every time a role title is seen as *unpleasant* it is also seen as *stupid*.

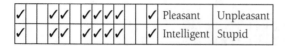

✓		✓	✓		✓	✓	✓	✓			✓	Pleasant	Unpleasant
✓		✓	✓		✓	✓	✓	✓			✓	Intelligent	Stupid

A great many such matches in a grid may indicate that the person is using only one construct, under different names (ibid.). Such a grid may reflect a construct system that is 'simple' because there is really only one distinction being made, regardless of what it is called (Ryle, 1975: 32). Contrast the situation just described with the one illustrated below. Here the match between constructs is far from perfect.

✓		✓	✓		✓		✓	✓			✓	Pleasant	Unpleasant
	✓	✓		✓			✓	✓	✓		✓	Intelligent	Stupid

This sort of relationship between constructs suggests that each construct is being applied in a relatively unique way. Each construct is being used to make a somewhat different distinction, and this is reflected by the different profile of checks and blanks in each row. People who are cognitively complex may be better able to see others as relatively unique individuals with idiosyncratic combinations of features (Bieri, 1961: 360). Particularly during the 1960s and 1970s, an extensive line of research both within personal construct theory and in social psychology generally was concerned with various ways to measure cognitive complexity and with determining whether or not it was related to the ability to make more precise, differentiated predictions (e.g., Mancuso, 1970; Warr, 1970).

Writing 20 years after Kelly's death, Jankowicz (1987: 484) observed that the flexibility of repertory grid methodology made it broadly useful in applied settings. 'The practice developed of taking as elements any well-defined set of mutually exclusive terms that are exemplars of the particular topic under investigation (Bannister and Fransella, 1971). The technique could then be used in any field of application in which a precise and explicit articulation of a person's construct system is required.' Among these fields of application, Jankowicz mentioned market research, an area in which it is particularly important to have an understanding of 'the idiosyncratic ways in which consumers construe products' (Jankowicz, 1987: 484). In general, the field of industrial-organizational psychology was particularly receptive to personal construct theory, although, here again, this influence was most pronounced in Britain. The repertory grid proved valuable to people who wish to respond to their clients 'in the individual's own language . . . rather than in the language of psychological expertise' (ibid., 486).

Qualitative Research Methods

The use of the repertory grid to tap the unique perspectives of individuals has been cited as an example of the kind of *qualitative research methods* that began to find favour in some parts of the discipline (e.g., Banister et al., 1994; Hein and Austin, 2001). Qualitative research methods are to be distinguished from quantitative research methods, such as those we considered in Chapter 10. Quantitative research methods 'aggregate the objects, events or persons under study' in the hope of being able to make general statements about people as a whole (Pyke and Agnew, 1991: 134). By contrast, qualitative research methods are not designed to test a particular hypothesis, but rather to develop a description of the way individuals represent the world they inhabit. 'Qualitative research methods are based on the assumption that humans do not so much respond to direct stimuli as they do to their interpretations of the information impinging on them. Thus we are constantly involved in an interaction process with environmental elements that we symbolically transform. These symbolic translations or meanings that humans attach to events must be studied if we are to understand the subsequent behavior' (ibid., 136). Since the repertory grid lends itself to the analysis of 'symbolic translations or meanings', it can fit quite nicely into the qualitative researcher's tool kit (Banister et al., 1994: ch. 5).

Qualitative research methods are obviously aimed at the same kind of understanding of the person that humanistic psychologists originally sought. They also belong to the same tradition as the case study approach adopted by some clinical psychologists and the kind of action research promulgated by Lewin, which we considered in Chapter 9. Qualitative research was also advocated by some feminist scholars, a topic to which we will return in the last chapter.

IMPORTANT NAMES, WORKS, AND CONCEPTS

Names and Works

Allport, Gordon
Being and Nothingness
Benedict, Ruth
Binswanger, Ludwig
Either/Or
Gendlin, Eugene T.
Heidegger, Martin
Hollingworth, Leta
Kelly, George A.
Kierkegaard, Søren

Love and Will
Maslow, Abraham
May, Rollo
The Meaning of Anxiety
Nietzsche, Friedrich
The Psychology of Personal Constructs
The Psychology of Science
Rogers, Carl
Sartre, Jean-Paul
Witmer, Lightner

Concepts

anxiety
basic needs
being-in-the-world
Being values
constructs
deficiency motives
encounter groups
esteem needs
existentialism
experiencing
hierarchy of needs
humanism
human potential movement
ideal self
leap of faith
love needs

nihilism
non-directive psychotherapy
peak experiences
people are scientists
personal constructs
perspectivism
repertory grid
role titles
safety needs
self-actualization
self-actualizing person
self-concept
synergy
'Third Force'
will to power

RECOMMENDED READINGS

Emergence of Humanistic Psychology

Gordon Allport (1897–1967) was a central figure in the development of a psychology of personality. Although not a member of the humanistic psychology movement, he was very much on the minds of many of those who developed what became humanistic psychology. Allport had earlier considered many of the themes that were to become central to humanistic psychology. In particular, Allport had stressed the importance of the distinction between *idiographic* and *nomothetic* approaches to the study of the person. On the one hand, psychology was a nomothetic science, meaning that it searched for general laws. On the other hand, psychology had to use idiographic methods, meaning that it was interested in the uniqueness of the individual. Allport's classic book, *Pattern and Growth in Personality* (New York: Holt, Rinehart and Winston, 1964), took the view that we should 'not deny the proposition that psychology seeks general laws', but drew 'attention to those laws and principles that tell how uniqueness comes about' (p. 572). Allport also did pioneering research on human values, another area of central concern to humanistic psychologists. The *scale of values* developed by Allport and colleagues has proved to be a very useful research tool in a wide variety of areas. See G. Allport, P.E. Vernon, and G. Lindzey, *Manual: A Study of Values* (Boston: Houghton Mifflin, 1960). For more on Allport, see I.A.M. Nicholson, 'Gordon Allport, character, and the "Culture of Personality"', *History of Psychology* 1 (1998): 52–68.

May

May's 'William James, humanism and the problem of will', in R.B. MacLeod, ed., *William James: Unfinished Business* (Washington: American Psychological Association, 1969), 73–92, is an analysis of James's psychology from the viewpoint of existential and humanistic psychology.

Maslow

Maslow's *Eupsychian Management* (Homewood, Ill.: Dorsey, 1965) gives an interesting perspective on the way his ideas could be applied in business settings. I.A.M. Nicholson, '"Giving up maleness": Abraham Maslow, masculinity, and the boundaries of psychology', *History of Psychology* 4 (2001): 79–91, argues that Maslow retained a 'masculine' orientation to psychology that conflicted with his attempts to create a broader and more inclusive science.

What Happened to Humanistic Psychology?

Some humanistic psychologists believed that it did not go far enough. By only attending to individual experience, it paid short shrift to those aspects of human experience that were universal and transcendent. This led to the founding of the *Journal of Transpersonal Psychology* in 1969. Transpersonal psychology tended to be quite respectful of religious and esoteric traditions, regardless of their origin. E. Taylor, *Shadow Culture: Psychology and Spirituality in America* (Washington: Counterpoint, 1999), places transpersonal psychology in its American historical context, while a collection of basic readings in this area is C.T. Tart, *Transpersonal Psychologies* (New York: Harper & Row, 1975).

Kelly

A thorough review of early research in personal construct theory is J.R. Adams-Webber, *Personal Construct Theory: Concepts and Research* (New York: Wiley, 1979). For an excellent overview of Kelly's life and work, see F. Fransella, *George Kelly* (London: Sage, 1995).

CHAPTER 14

COGNITIVE PSYCHOLOGY

Introduction

Like humanistic psychology, cognitive psychology emerged in part as a reaction to behaviourism. However, the 'tender-minded' constituency that had been attracted to humanistic psychology was quite different from that which initiated and developed cognitive psychology. The study of cognition appealed to academic psychologists who regarded themselves as 'tough-minded' scientists first and foremost. They regarded behaviourism as too narrow and wanted to replace it with an approach that not only integrated aspects of psychology that behaviourism appeared to leave out, but also was genuinely scientific. The emergence of information theory and computer science after Word War II provided a framework for cognitive psychology, as did Chomsky's revolutionary theory of language.

Cognition is a complex area of psychological inquiry that contains a large number of topics. The *Oxford English Dictionary* defines 'cognition' as the 'action or faculty of knowing'. Thus, cognitive psychology investigates those processes whereby we understand ourselves and our environment. These processes include attention, memory, concepts, imagery, problem-solving, reasoning, judgement, and language (e.g., Benjafield, 1997). These topics have all had a distinguished history in psychology, some of which we have reviewed in previous chapters. By and large, they were neglected during the behaviourist era in psychology because they appeared to be too 'subjective' to admit of scientific investigation. However, this situation began to change after World War II. In this chapter we will review the work of some of the individuals who made psychology cognitive again.

The Concept of 'Information'

One of the most momentous developments in the twentieth century was computer science and allied disciplines. Many psychologists attempted to determine whether concepts derived from computer science can be successfully applied in psychology. A computing machine can be seen as an *information-processing system*. The interesting question is: To what extent can people also be seen as information-processing systems? That is one of the central issues we will explore in this chapter.

Information is obviously a key concept in any discussion of computers, and a revolutionary change in the way this concept is used was brought about by information theorists such as Shannon and Weaver (1949). Intuitively, 'information is something that occurs when some person or machine tells us something we didn't know before' (Garner, 1962: 2). Information theorists went beyond this rough definition and proposed to measure the amount of information transmitted when an event occurs. An event can be any one of a number of possible occurrences, such as a coin coming up heads or tails. The basic idea was that 'any communicative act provides information only insofar as it reduces a condition of ignorance or uncertainty about the state of things under consideration' (ibid., 3). Thus, information is the opposite of uncertainty. Consider tossing a coin, for example. Before tossing the coin, we are uncertain about which alternative (heads or tails) will occur. After tossing the coin, our uncertainty is eliminated. Any event that reduces or eliminates uncertainty provides us with information.

Some situations contain more uncertainty than others. In the case of coin tossing, there are only two possible outcomes—heads or tails. In other situations, such as rolling a single die, there are six possible outcomes—the numbers 1 to 6. There is more prior uncertainty in the latter case than in the former, and consequently rolling a die provides more information than does tossing a coin. It is possible to quantify the amount of information provided by the occurrence of an event in terms of *bits*. 'Bit' is short for 'binary digit'. Imagine a situation, such as flipping an unbiased coin, in which we are uncertain about which of two equally likely events will occur. When one of the two events occurs, then we get one bit of information. Every time the number of equally likely alternatives doubles, then the number of bits goes up by one.

The relationship between the number of equally likely alternatives and the amount of information transmitted when one of the events occurs is illustrated in Table 14.1. (The situation becomes more complicated when the alternatives are not equally likely.) A popular illustration of this relationship is a guessing game in which one person thinks of a number and another person tries to guess it (ibid., 5). The number of bits corresponds to the number of questions you would need to ask in order to guess the right answer. For example, if I am thinking of a number between 1 and 8, you need 3 questions to find it. The correct strategy is to reduce the number of possibilities by half with each question. First, ask if it is above 4. If the answer is 'yes', then ask if it is above 6. If the answer is 'yes' again, then ask if it is above 7. If the answer is 'yes', then the number is 8, if it is 'no', then the number is 7. You can work out the scenario for other cases in Table 14.1 at your leisure.

Information theory provided a new model for the process of communication (Sperber and Wilson, 1986). This model described the process whereby information was *transmitted* through a *channel of communication*. The first stage in this process is *encoding*, or the transformation of the *input* into a form that can be transmitted. Thus, a telephone encodes the human voice into a set of

TABLE 14.1

Examples of the Relationship Between the Number of Equally Likely Alternatives and the Number of Bits

Alternatives	Bits
2	1
4	2
8	3
16	4
32	5
64	6
128	7
256	8
512	9
1024	10

signals that can be transmitted along telephone wires or some other medium. At the other end of the channel, the message is *decoded* into a form that can be used as *output* by the consumer of the information. This way of representing the flow of information in a system has been enormously influential, as we shall see.

Noam Chomsky (1928–)

Any theory of communication must provide an understanding of how languages function. Understanding the human ability to use language is one of the great challenges that faces psychology. This challenge was taken up by behaviourists, in particular by B.F. Skinner, who argued that language was governed by the same principles that regulated all other forms of behaviour. Words are responses elicited by stimuli, and as such are under the control of environmental reinforcement contingencies. Language is learned behaviour. When a child emits a sound and is reinforced for doing so, then the probability that the child will reproduce this utterance is increased. By reinforcing children for producing the appropriate utterances, parents can shape their children's speech so that it increasingly approximates their native language.

This behaviourist account of language was attacked by a young linguist from MIT named **Noam Chomsky** (1959, 1972b). In a review of Skinner's *Verbal Behavior* (1957), Chomsky argued that behaviourist principles could not explain any significant aspects of language. For example, people are continuously generating sentences that they have never spoken before, and Skinner's approach does not and cannot explain this fact. When people speak a sentence they cannot be doing so in response to a stimulus, since it would be impossible to learn all the stimulus-response connections required to enable people to speak a natural language. A natural language is a 'native' language, such as English, French, or Chinese. Any theory of language worth its salt must explain the fact that natural language is inherently creative, and no behaviourist theory can do so.

Syntactic Structures

Chomsky's critique of behaviourism attracted a great deal of attention from psychologists who, by the mid-1950s, had already begun to doubt the value of the behaviourist approach. However, those who were sympathetic to Chomsky's critical analysis were quite different from those who had been attracted to humanistic psychology. Chomsky's ideas appealed to academic psychologists who regarded themselves as scientists and empiricists. Chomsky not only dismissed behaviourism as lacking scientific content, but proposed to replace it with a genuinely scientific theory that could explain the basic facts of language.

The theory Chomsky proposed had been developed as a part of his doctoral dissertation at MIT. Even within linguistics, Chomsky's approach had been regarded as a radical departure from the prevailing wisdom, and consequently he had difficulty publishing his work. Gradually, however, scholars began to appreciate the originality and power of his approach. Chomsky (1957: 15) provided an account of aspects of language that were difficult for other theories to explain. For example, he pointed out that native speakers of English have

no trouble telling which of the following sentences is grammatical, even though both are meaningless.

Colourless green ideas sleep furiously.
Furiously sleep ideas green colourless.

Chomsky's point was that everyone has the 'ability to produce and recognize grammatical utterances' and that 'grammar is autonomous and independent of meaning' (ibid., 16–17). People have an understanding of grammar that allows them to discern whether or not an utterance is grammatical, even when they may never have heard anything like it before.

Ambiguity is another linguistic fact that Chomsky (1957: ch. 8) believed was particularly revealing. For example, consider the following sentences (Bigelow, 1986: 379):

Time flies like an arrow.
Fruit flies like a banana.

Most people interpret the first sentence such that 'time' is a noun and 'flies' is a verb. However, the second sentence is usually interpreted such that 'flies' is a noun. Ambiguity is very common in natural languages. Consider this sentence (Greene, 1972: 47):

The shooting of the hunters was awful.

We can interpret this sentence as meaning that the hunters were lousy shots or that the hunters were shot. How do we arrive at one interpretation or the other? To answer questions such as this, Chomsky proposed that language be understood in terms of levels. The particular words that make up a sentence constitute one level, called the **surface structure**. Although surface structures are spoken one word at a time, each successive word does not act as a stimulus for the next word in the sentence. Rather, the surface structure is derived from an underlying **deep structure** by means of grammatical transformations. Grammatical transformations are rules that replace one symbol with another. The following are examples of such transformations (Chomsky, 1957: 26; Greene, 1972: 35).

1. Sentence (S) → Noun Phrase (NP) + Verb Phrase (VP)
2. NP → Article (T) + Noun (N)
3. VP → Verb (V) + NP
4. T → the
5. N → boy, girl, fence, car, etc.
6. V → paints, jumps, etc.

Of course, these are by no means the only rules necessary, and they are only intended to illustrate the general idea. These rules permit the derivation of different surface structures, one of which is given in Figure 14.1.

The important thing to see about Chomsky's approach is that speech is produced by a hierarchical, top-down process that moves from deep to surface structure. When you hear a sentence, then you understand it by simply reversing the process and going from surface to deep structure (Chomsky, 1957: 48). Sentences that have similar surface structures (e.g., 'Time flies like an arrow' and 'Fruit flies like a banana') can have different deep structures and thus be understood in different ways.

Compare Figure 14.1 with Figure 8.4, which represents Watson's stimulus-response model of serially ordered behaviour. In Chomsky's model, language is not controlled by external stimuli but by an internally generated system of rules. There is nothing haphazard about the rules that govern language. Grammatical transformations have the same necessity as mathematical laws (e.g., Chomsky, 1967). However, although there are only a finite number of grammatical rules, they provide the means for generating an infinite number of possible sentences.

Cartesian Linguistics

Chomsky saw his theory as descended from that of Descartes, whose views we considered in Chapter 2. While Descartes believed that animals were like machines, he did not believe that *human*

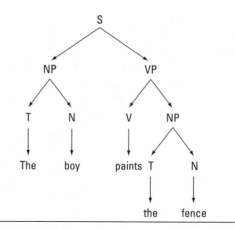

FIGURE 14.1
Derivation of a surface structure from a deep structure.

behaviour could be understood in a completely mechanical manner. People differ from both animals and machines in that they are much more flexible in response to changing circumstances. For example, we are able to speak in ways that are spontaneous and novel, something Descartes believed no animal or machine could be trained or made to do. It is precisely this aspect of Cartesian doctrine with which Chomsky (1965: 3) agreed. '[H]uman language is free from stimulus control and does not serve a merely communicative function, but is rather an instrument for the free expression of thought and for appropriate response to new situations' (ibid., 13).

Descartes also was a nativist, believing that our most human capacities are innate. This is also the position Chomsky took with respect to language.

The central doctrine of Cartesian linguistics is that the general features of grammatical structures are common to all languages and reflect certain fundamental properties of the mind. . . . There are, then, certain *language universals* that set limits to the variety of human language. . . . Such universal conditions are not learned; rather they provide the organizing principles that make language learning possible. (Ibid., 60; emphasis added)

All languages share common principles, and these principles are 'known unconsciously' by everyone (ibid., 63). When a child is exposed to a natural language, its task is not to learn the language from scratch but to 'discover which of the possible languages he [or she] is being exposed to' (Chomsky, 1972: 259). The child possesses a *language acquisition device* (ibid., 135) that comes equipped with a rich set of hypotheses about the grammatical structure of any possible natural language. Language acquisition occurs quite quickly because each child already has an elaborate theory of language that can be used to make sense of the linguistic data he or she hears. If the child did not innately possess such a language acquisition device, then the rapidity with which a child acquires the ability to generate novel utterances 'would be an impenetrable mystery' (ibid., 136).

Chomsky never regarded his research on language as complete, but continued to tune his theory and develop its implications (e.g., Chomsky, 1995). His approach received much support, although many of his critics charged that Chomsky overestimated the role of innate factors in determining the process of language acquisition. However, even those who disagreed with Chomsky's theory still had to pay attention to it. 'The story of psycholinguistics in the second half of the 20th century is to a large extent the story of the evolution of Chomsky's theory of grammar (Chomsky, 1957, 1965, 1980, 1986)' (Rosenberg, 1993: 15). Moreover, as we shall see, Chomsky's influence was not restricted to linguistics and the psychology of language. His emphasis on the importance of internal processes that operate more or less independently of external stimulus control was one of the factors that facilitated the re-emergence of an interest in the scientific study of mental processes. This renewed interest was one of the hallmarks of cognitive psychology.

George A. Miller (1920-)

George A. Miller was in the right place at the right time. Working at Harvard in the 1950s, Miller

(2003) came in contact with many of the central figures in what was to become cognitive psychology. He regarded 1956 as particularly important in the history of cognitive psychology, and singled out a symposium on information theory held at MIT that year as the occasion when the several strands that were to become cognitive psychology came together. In addition to Chomsky, the participants included Allen Newell and Herbert Simon, whose work in computer simulation we will discuss below. The year 1956 also marked the publication of *A Study of Thinking* by Jerome Bruner and his colleagues J. Goodnow and G. Austin. This book reintroduced the study of 'higher mental processes' to psychology after decades of neglect. We will review Bruner's contributions later on, but for now we will only note that in 1960 Bruner joined with Miller to open the Center for Cognitive Studies at Harvard. Over the next several years many such institutes and centres for cognitive studies were created at universities in the United States and throughout the rest of the world.

The Magical Number Seven

Miller (1953) was one of the first psychologists to become aware of and to use information theory in his research. A famous example of his work in this area was his paper, 'The magical number seven: plus or minus two' (Miller, 1967 [1956]), in which he considered experiments where an experimental participant was regarded as a 'communication channel', and the experimenter was interested in how much information can be accurately transmitted through this channel. This amount is called **channel capacity**. For example, a participant might be asked to estimate the magnitude of a stimulus dimension. The dimension might be anything from sounds of different pitch or loudness to tastes of different saltiness. In experiments like these, participants could discriminate between about seven different magnitudes, giving a channel capacity of about 2.5 bits of information. A similar result occurred in investigations of the *span of apprehension*. In Chapter 4, we noted that

Wundt (1973 [1912]: 35) had done research on this topic, which refers to how many items we can be aware of at one time. There have been many investigations into the span of apprehension since Wundt's day, and Miller's review of the literature suggests that we can hold about seven items in mind at one time. He called this the **span of immediate memory** (Miller, 1967: 34), and observed that the amount of information we can retain in this way is quite limited.

Of course, there is nothing magical about the number seven, although, with tongue in cheek, Miller (ibid., 42) drew attention to 'the seven wonders of the world, the seven seas, the seven deadly sins, the seven daughters of Atlas in the Pleiades, the seven ages of man, the seven levels of hell, the seven primary colors, the seven notes of the musical scale, and the seven days of the week'. In spite of (or perhaps because of) this refreshing willingness not to take oneself or one's research too seriously, Miller's analysis of psychological processes such as judgement and memory tempted many other psychologists to use information theoretic concepts in their own work. In addition, quite independently of Miller's work, psychologists in other countries, particularly in Britain, were also inventing new experimental paradigms to the process of communication. One of these paradigms is discussed in Box 14.1.

Plans and the Structure of Behavior

One of the first attempts to give cognitive psychology a coherent theoretical framework occurred with the publication of **Plans and the Structure of Behavior** by George Miller and his colleagues Eugene Galanter and Karl Pribram (Miller et al., 1960). In addition to information theory and Chomskyian psycholinguistics, Miller et al. drew on **cybernetics** for their core theoretical ideas. 'Cybernetics was defined by [the mathematician] Norbert Wiener as "the science of control and communication, in the animal and the machine"—in a word as the art of *steermanship*'

(Ashby, 1962: 1). Cybernetics was concerned with formulating general principles that control any system, whether organic or inorganic. One of the central concepts of cybernetics was *feedback*, a process in which the output of one part of a system effects another part of the system, which in turn effects the first part. The classic example of a **feedback loop** is a thermostat. Such a device is set to maintain a pre-set temperature. If the temperature falls below a certain level, then the thermostat sends a signal to the furnace that turns it on. The furnace then generates heat, which raises the temperature. When the temperature reaches its pre-set level, the thermostat turns the furnace off. This cycle can go on indefinitely, allowing the maintenance of a more or less steady state with respect to temperature.

Miller and his colleagues proposed that the feedback loop be regarded as the basic unit of behavioural control. They called these units TOTE **mechanisms**, short for test-operate-test-exit. A TOTE mechanism is illustrated in Figure 14.2. The mechanism works in the same way as a thermostat. First, the input is tested against a standard. If the input does not match the standard, then the system operates so as to reduce the discrepancy between the two. Once this difference is eliminated, then you exit from this routine.

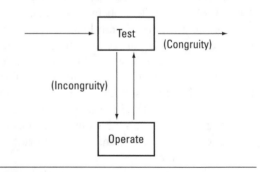

FIGURE 14.2
A TOTE mechanism.
Source: Miller et al. (1960: 26). Copyright © 1960 by G.A. Miller. Reprinted by permission.

BOX 14.1

DONALD E. BROADBENT AND DICHOTIC LISTENING

Donald E. Broadbent (1926–93) was born in Britain and served in the Royal Air Force in World War II. The RAF trained pilots in the United States, and while there he began to think of becoming a psychologist. Partly this was because, at that time, psychology was a much more common career in the United States than it was in Britain. As a pilot, he also became acutely aware of the way in which 'technology . . . was badly matched to human beings.' Airplanes and other machines were designed by engineers, and often did not take the psychology of the operator into account. The result was that machines were often difficult and/or dangerous to operate. This early interest in person–machine interactions signalled Broadbent's subsequent involvement in applied psychology, a practical approach he maintained throughout his career (Craik and Baddeley, 1995). An important component of applied psychology, particularly since World War II, has been the study of ways to improve the ease with which people can interact with machines. This area of inquiry is called *ergonomics* in Europe and *human factors* in the United States.

When Broadbent returned to Britain, he took up psychology at Cambridge, studying with, among others, Sir Frederic Bartlett, that giant of British psychology whose work we will review later on in this chapter. Broadbent's early research was driven by practical problems experienced by armed forces personnel. One such problem concerned 'those arising in communication centers, where many different streams of speech reached the person at the same time' (Broadbent, 1980: 54). This line of research led to one of the most influential papers in the history of experimental psychology. Broadbent (1992 [1952]: 125) created a task in which the participant was required to 'answer one of two messages which start at the same point in time, but one of which is irrelevant.'

The experimental technique Broadbent used is called **dichotic listening**. Participants were exposed to two verbal messages presented simultaneously by a tape recorder. The participant was required to answer questions posed in only one of the messages. When participants knew in advance which of two different voices contained the required message, then performance on this task was very good. Participants were clearly able to select relevant information and ignore irrelevant information. Broadbent suggested that this demonstrated the role of *attention* in the selection of information. As Broadbent (1980: 55) later noted, the concept of attention 'had hardly appeared in respectable circles for forty years', or since the demise of introspectionism.

Partly as a result of Broadbent's experiments and subsequent theoretical work (e.g., Broadbent, 1958), attention is now 'a vital component of work in cognitive psychology, cognitive science, and neuroscience. At a more general level, the dichotic listening studies helped fuel the cognitive revolution against behaviorism by pointing to the importance of implicit, unobservable mental representations and processes in understanding behavior. These studies are surely among the most important of the last 100 years' (Egeth, 1992: 124).

Broadbent also worked closely with Colin Cherry (1914–79), a Professor of Telecommunications at the University of London. Broadbent (1980: 59) described him as 'a leading activist in the early days of information theory, and his students were often doing work that might just as well have been done in a psychological laboratory.' Cherry, although not a psychologist, (1953) became well known in psychology for drawing attention to the **cocktail party phenomenon**, a topic that is still mentioned in virtually every introductory text. This phenomenon occurs when you are able to attend to one conversation in a crowded room in which many other conversations are going on. The ability to attend to one message while ignoring another has often been studied using a *shadowing task*, in which an experimental participant wears headphones and is given two messages, one in each ear. The participant 'shadows' one of the two messages by repeating it as it is heard.

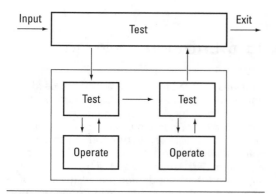

FIGURE 14.3
Hierarchical TOTE mechanisms.

The beauty of TOTE units is that they can be nested within one another to form hierarchies. Figure 14.3 illustrates this kind of structure. Such *hierarchical models* can be used to represent a variety of different activities. Miller et al. (1960: 36) give the example of hammering a nail, in which the superordinate test is whether or not the nail is flush with board. If not, then proceed to test the hammer. If the hammer is down, then raise it. When the hammer is up, then strike the nail. Then return to the superordinate test and determine if the nail is flush. If it is not, then go through the subordinate routines again. When the nail is flush, then exit. Another example might have as a superordinate test whether or not you have satisfied your BA requirements. The subordinate tests are whether or not you have satisfied your major and minor requirements. If not, then you take courses to pass these tests. When all tests are passed, then you exit university. Yet another example comes from using a recipe to make salad dressing (e.g., Green, 1982). The superordinate test could be whether or not the dressing passes a taste test. The subordinate tests refer to particular ingredients, such as oil and vinegar, which you add until you reach the appropriate amounts.

You can see that TOTE mechanisms lend themselves to modelling an enormous range of behaviours. Moreover, they can be much more complex than the simple cases we have considered. For example, when you are making salad dressing, you are likely doing so as a part of making a meal, which would constitute a still more superordinate TOTE mechanism. Making a meal is presumably nested within still more general goals, such as acquiring proper nutrition. Our more general TOTEs are called *strategies*, while our more concrete activities are called *tactics*. Our strategies tend to be relatively invariant. For example, we always need nutrition. However, our tactics tend to be quite variable, depending on the particular context. Thus, we do not always eat the same meal.

Hierarchically organized TOTE mechanisms make up our *plans*, which contain a hierarchically organized set of instructions for conducting all of our actions. Plans are like computer programs, which provide the instructions that tell a computer precisely what operations to perform. For Miller et al. (1960) cognitive psychology is the study of plans, which are the programs that regulate all of our behaviour. The similarity between people's plans and computer programs is a topic we will return to below. However, by now you should be able to see that plans, like computer programs, need not be rigid, inflexible procedures. Rather, plans, like computer programs, are able to adjust their operations as different conditions arise.

Subjective Behaviourism

How do you investigate people's plans? One way is to ask them what their plans are. Of course, this will not work in every case, because we simply are not aware of all of our plans. For example, our plans for speaking, in which Chomsky was so interested, are largely unconscious. However, Miller et al. (1960) advocated asking people to tell us about their plans as often as was feasible. The procedure they recommended was not introspection as it had been practised by Wundt and other introspectionists. Rather, they proposed the limited use of **thinking aloud**, a technique that had already been used by many psychologists interested in studying thinking (e.g., Claparède, 1933; Duncker, 1945). What people say when they are asked to think aloud is quite different from what they say when they are asked to introspect (e.g., Benjafield, 1969b), and so the two methods are not the same. Thinking aloud simply involves speaking while you are thinking and reporting directly on what you are thinking as it occurs.

Miller et al. (1960: 194) were willing to use methods such as thinking aloud since it 'has one great advantage in its favor, because language, with all its notorious shortcomings, is still the least ambiguous of all the channels open from one human being to another.' In spite of their willingness to try such apparently 'subjective' methods to investigate internal processes, Miller and his colleagues were not even remotely interested in abandoning the objective methods that had characterized behaviourism. Rather, they hoped to have the best of both worlds, and thus called their position (only half jokingly) **subjective behaviourism** (ibid., 211). This phrase—subjective behaviorism—describes quite nicely the attitudes of most of the founders of cognitive psychology.

Giving Psychology Away

In his presidential address to the American Psychological Association, Miller sounded a theme that is still resonating through psychology. He cautioned psychologists against using their expertise to act as agents of social control. Rather, he argued that 'understanding and prediction are better goals for psychology than is control—both for psychology and for the promotion of human welfare—because they lead us to think, not in terms of coercion by a powerful elite, but in terms of the diagnosis of problems and the development of programs that can enrich the lives of every citizen' (Miller, 1970 [1969]: 13–14). To accomplish these goals, Miller suggested that psychology be *given away*.

Our responsibility is less to assume the role of experts and try to apply psychology ourselves than to give it away to the people who really

need it—and that includes everyone. The practice of valid psychology by non-psychologists will inevitably change people's conception of themselves and what they can do. And when we have accomplished that, we will really have caused a psychological revolution. (Ibid., 16)

The social role of psychology in the United States was debated throughout the twentieth century. Miller argued that, while psychological science was something of which all citizens can and should become aware, professional organizations such as the American Psychological Association should not become involved in the promotion of social change. In 1991, George Miller was awarded the National Medal of Science.

Jerome S. Bruner (1915-)

Reading Jerome Bruner's (1980) autobiography is astonishing, because he appeared to have known virtually every prominent social scientist of his time in America and Europe. The list includes William McDougall, Margaret Mead, Clark Hull, Kurt Goldstein, Gordon Allport, Edwin Boring, Bärbel Inhelder, and Jean Piaget. The range of his acquaintances is matched by the range of his research interests. As we shall see, **Jerome Bruner** did seminal research on everything from perception and thinking to child development. Bruner himself believed that there is a consistent functionalist orientation across all these investigations that marked him 'as following the tradition of James, Dewey, McDougall, Vygotsky, and Tolman. . . . I am also a mentalist and have always felt that the banning of "mental" concepts from psychology was a fake seeking after the gods of nineteenth century physical sciences' (ibid., 146).

The New Look in Perception

In the 1940s and 1950s Bruner and his colleagues began a research program in perception that became known as the 'New Look'. More traditional approaches to perception had focused primarily on the stimulus and paid little attention to the role of the perceiver in determining the process of perception. Bruner's group investigated 'the effects of need, of interest, of past experience, on the manner of organization of the perceptual field' (Bruner and Klein, 1960: 63). The 'New Look' approached perception as a joint function of both the stimulus and the state of the organism.

A good example of the 'New Look' experiments is Bruner and Postman's (1973 [1949]) investigation of the perception of incongruous events. One of the central axioms of the 'New Look' was called the **minimax axiom**: people 'organize the perceptual field in such a way as to maximize percepts relevant to current needs and expectations and to minimize percepts inimical to such needs and expectations' (ibid., 69). Although people change their expectancies when the evidence requires them to, 'for as long as possible and by whatever means available, the organism will ward off the perception of the unexpected, those things which do not fit his [or her] prevailing set' (ibid., 70).

Events that do not fit our expectancies strike us as incongruous. Bruner and Postman examined people's reaction to incongruous events by altering a familiar stimulus. They constructed two sets of playing cards, one normal and the other containing trick cards that were printed with the colours reversed. For example, the three of hearts was printed in black, the two of spades in red, and so on. These are the incongruous stimuli. Participants saw both normal and trick cards presented tachistoscopically. As discussed in Chapter 6, a tachistoscope is a device that allows a visual stimulus to be presented for varying intervals, some so brief (e.g., 1/100 second) that participants may have difficulty saying what it is that they have been shown. In Bruner and Postman's experiment, each card was initially exposed for 1/100 second and then exposed at increasingly longer intervals until the participant recognized it.

One result was that participants required a longer exposure interval to recognize trick as

opposed to normal cards. This was supportive of the hypothesis that stimuli that conform to people's expectations are more easily seen than those that do not. The responses of individual participants to particular incongruous stimuli were also informative. Sometimes participants initially claimed to have seen a normal six of spades. As the exposure duration increased, they came to realize that the card was actually a red six of spades. Sometimes this realization was accomplished all at once, and sometimes it emerged gradually. However, the evidence was consistent with the notion that 'perceptual organization is powerfully determined by expectations built upon past commerce with the environment. When such expectations are violated by the environment, the perceiver's behavior can be described as resistance to the recognition of the unexpected or incongruous' (ibid., 82).

Bruner believed this experiment and others like it demonstrated the importance of **perceptual readiness**, or the degree to which one is prepared to perceive what is in the environment. Expectancies consist of categories into which the perceiver attempts to fit the input. One can fail to be ready to perceive what is there, in which case one's experience may not be a very good match for what is actually in the environment. This may be particularly true when we are perceiving other people.

> If, on the basis of a few cues of personal appearance, for example, one categorizes another person as dishonest, it is extremely difficult in most cases to check for the other cues that one would predict might be associated with instances of this category. . . . Moreover, there is also the likelihood . . . that available equivocal signs will be distorted so as to confirm the first impression. . . . The reticence of the man [or woman] we categorize as dishonest is seen as caginess; the honest man's [or woman's] reticence is seen as integrity and good judgment. (Bruner, 1973 [1957]: 32)

Bruner was drawing attention to what later came to be called 'putting a spin on events'. From this perspective, 'putting a spin on events' is a natural process in which everyone engages, not just politicians and their press secretaries. It is not necessary for us to intentionally 'put a spin' on events, but it can take place more or less automatically. This general idea has proved to be remarkably durable. As we shall see in the next chapter, many philosophers of science see 'perceptual readiness' or something like it as an important factor in the way scientists are prepared to relate scientific evidence to scientific theories (Anglin, 1973: xi).

The 'New Look' was criticized on methodological grounds because the experiments often lacked appropriate controls. By the end of the 1950s many psychologists believed that the 'New Look' had gone too far in emphasizing the internal, personal determinants of perception. However, while agreeing with many of the criticisms, Bruner and Klein (1960) responded that the 'New Look' had done much to correct an imbalance in the way perception had been studied and to open up new areas of investigation.

A Study of Thinking

Expectancies, as noted above, involve placing events into categories. One of Bruner's contributions was to initiate an experimental study of the formation of categories (Bruner et al., 1956). The process whereby categories develop is called **concept attainment**. The study of concepts had been relatively neglected during the behaviourist period, and the work of Bruner, Goodnow, and Austin in *A Study of Thinking* did much to make this study legitimate.

Any time we do not regard an event as unique but as belonging to a particular category, we are making use of concepts. For example, whenever something is seen as 'red', or as a 'musical instrument', or as a 'chair,' then it is being subsumed by a particular concept. You can see that the range and number of concepts is extremely great. Bruner et al. defined concepts as collections of attributes. Attributes of concepts were properties such as size, shape, or colour. Attributes could take on different values. Thus, 'size' could be 'big' or 'small'. An

event that contained all the attributes necessary for membership in the concept was called a 'positive instance', while an event lacking one or more of the required attributes was called a 'negative instance'. For example, a liquid containing the proper amounts of olive oil, vinegar, and spices could be a positive instance of the concept 'salad dressing', but a liquid consisting of just oil would be a negative instance.

Bruner and his colleagues investigated the process of concept attainment using a set of cards similar to those shown in Figure 14.4. Although the stimuli in Figure 14.4 are simpler than the ones they used, these are suitable for our purposes. The cards can be characterized in terms of three attributes: colour (grey or white); form (triangle or circle); and size (large or small). In a concept attainment experiment, the experimenter thinks of a concept like 'grey triangle' and the participant tries to guess it. This is not an experiment in parapsychology, since, as we shall see, the participant can ask questions and get feedback that leads to the solution. (What follows may remind you of the game of Mastermind, which this kind of

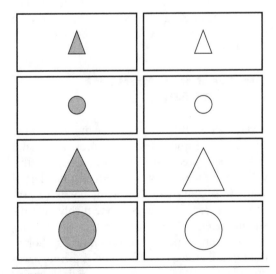

FIGURE 14.4
A set of cards for an experiment in concept attainment.

experiment actually resembles rather closely, as Laughlin et al. [1982] noted.) Bruner, Goodnow, and Austin observed that participants adopt particular strategies when they try to solve concept attainment problems like these. For example, suppose a participant is told that the card with the large, grey triangle is a positive instance. Then the participant can select another card that differs in one attribute, such as a large, grey circle. Upon being told that the large, grey circle is a negative instance, the participant can correctly infer that a card must have a triangle on it in order for the card to be a positive instance. By using strategies such as this, the participant can figure out what attributes are in the concept. By examining the choices participants make as they attempt to discover the concept, the experimenter can learn about the strategies people use as they form concepts.

Bruner, Goodnow, and Austin's (1956) work was subsequently criticized because the concepts they studied, like our example, were somewhat artificial. Subsequent work on concepts tended to focus on concepts that people actually use in everyday life (e.g., Rosch, 1978). Nevertheless, Bruner's work on concepts made it evident that 'higher mental processes' could be studied experimentally. Consequently, these experiments were important in setting the stage for subsequent work in cognition.

Sir Frederic Bartlett (1886–1969)

Psychology in Britain was for many years more attuned to the study of cognitive processes than it was in the United States. To no small extent, this was due to the work of **Sir Frederick Bartlett** of Cambridge University. Like many cognitive psychologists, Bartlett's interests were highly interdisciplinary, and he brought neurology, philosophy, and social anthropology to bear on his psychological work. Bartlett's classic study of memory was published in 1932, although the original experiments had been carried out much earlier, between 1914 and 1916 (Zangwill, 1972: 124).

One of Bartlett's best-known memory experiments used the **method of serial reproduction**. This method involves giving an experimental participant something to learn and remember. What the first participant remembers is then given to a second participant to learn and remember. What the second participant remembers is then given to a third participant, and so on. This method allows the experimenter to track the way in which memory changes over time with successive attempts at recall. Bartlett had participants, who were British, try to recall stories in his experiments. The following is a part of one of the stories, called 'The War of the Ghosts', which was adapted from an Amerindian tale.

One night two young men from Egulac went down to the river to hunt seals, and while they were there it became foggy and calm. Then they heard war-cries, and they thought: 'Maybe this is a war party.' They escaped to the shore, and hid behind a log. Now canoes came up, and they heard the noise of paddles, and saw one canoe coming up to them. There were five men in the canoe, and they said:

'What do you think? We wish to take you along. We are going up the river to make war on the people.'

One of the young men said: 'I have no arrows.'

'Arrows are in the canoe,' they said.

'I will not go along. I might get killed. My relatives do not know where I have gone. But you,' he said, turning to the other, 'may go with them.'

So one of the men went, but the other returned home.

And the warriors went on up the river to a town on the other side of Kalama. The people came down to the water, and they began to fight, and many were killed. But presently the young man heard one of the warriors say: 'Quick, let us go home: that Indian has been hit.' Now he thought: 'Oh, they are ghosts.' He did not feel sick, but he said he had been shot. (Bartlett, 1932: 65)

You should try to remember this story fragment, now that you have read it. You can imagine that by the time the story has been passed from one participant to another 10 times it would have undergone considerable modification. These changes in the story were not random, however, but showed systematic transformations. Over time, the story became increasingly conventional and rational from the point of view of the person trying to remember it. Information that does not fit in with this simplification tended to be omitted. At the same time, the story became more of an 'imaginative reconstruction' than a literal rendition (ibid., 213).

Bartlett's memory experiments are often contrasted with those of Ebbinghaus, which we reviewed in Chapter 4. Where Ebbinghaus used nonsense syllables, Bartlett used meaningful materials, such as stories. While Ebbinghaus's studies were masterpieces of experimental design and control, Bartlett's work is often thought to be more reflective of real-life memory processes. Although Ebbinghaus studied memory for individual items, Bartlett studied memory for meaningful discourse. Ebbinghaus's experiments lend themselves to a theory in which each item is stored separately in memory. Bartlett's experiments lend themselves to a theory in which individual items are not remembered in isolation, but as part of larger whole. To explain his results, Bartlett used the **schema** concept, which he borrowed from the neurologist Henry Head (1861–1940). By 'schema' Bartlett (ibid., 201) meant an 'active organization of past reactions' that provided a setting within which individual events were understood and remembered.

The schema is always actively adjusting to the current situation. Memory of the past is useful only to the extent that it can be adapted to suit the present needs of the organism. Bartlett (ibid., 201–2; 1958: 11) likened memory and other cognitive processes to *motor skills*, such as those involved in playing a sport. Suppose, for example, that you are at the plate in a baseball game and have two strikes against you. When you try to hit the next pitch, you do not try simply to repeat exactly the same swing that you made on the last pitch. Rather, your next swing attempts to adjust to the characteristics of the next pitch. A skilled hitter is able to make these kinds of adjustments and not simply do the same thing over and over again. Similarly, when we remember the past we do not simply re-experience it, but we reinvent it so that it fits the requirements of our current situation. Memory is a compromise between what we have actually experienced and what we imagine happened in the past. Ideas like this have been quite important in such areas of psychology as eyewitness testimony (e.g., Loftus and Palmer, 1974) because they suggest that we should not be too trusting of our own or other people's memories.

Although read and cited by American psychologists, Bartlett's work did not reach its greatest influence in American psychology until cognitive psychology began to establish itself there. From the new viewpoint that cognitive psychology provided, Bartlett's work not only made sense, but appeared to be foundational. This importance of Bartlett's influence on what was to become cognitive psychology was explicitly recognized by Ulric Neisser, to whose work we next turn.

Ulric Neisser (1928–)

Ulric Neisser received his undergraduate degree from Harvard, where he worked with George Miller. He then did a Master's degree at Swarthmore, which was still home to Gestalt psychologists such as Köhler. After completing a Ph.D. at Harvard, he took a position at Brandeis in 1957, where he was influenced by Abraham Maslow. While Maslow's humanistic orientation was not an explicit part of Neisser's cognitive psychology, it did express itself in Neisser's attitude that cognitive psychology was a more humanistic alternative to behaviourism (Baars, 1986: 273).

Although I never knew Neisser very well, I was a first-year graduate student in psychology at Brandeis in 1964 and have a recollection of a meeting where we all heard the faculty introduce themselves and describe their research interests.

I recall Neisser saying that he had been doing research in a variety of areas, and up until then had not been able to think of precisely in which area his research interests lay. However, he went on, he now believed that all his research interests could be seen as involving cognition and that he was beginning to think of himself as a cognitive psychologist.

Cognitive Psychology

It was not only Neisser who was beginning to think of himself as a cognitive psychologist. By the mid-1960s a great many academic psychologists were thinking of themselves in just that way. What was needed was a text that brought the several strands of research together that were to become cognitive psychology. This is what Neisser (1967) provided in **Cognitive Psychology**, which became the bible of the new psychology.

Near the beginning of his book, Neisser spelled out the relationship between cognitive processes and computer programs. His view of this relationship was to become standard for most cognitive psychologists.

> The task of a psychologist trying to understand human cognition is analogous to that of a [person] trying to discover how a computer has been programmed . . . if the program seems to store and reuse information, [we] would like to know by what 'routines' or 'procedures' this is done. . . . [We] will not care much [how] his particular computer stores information . . . [we] want to understand the program, not the 'hardware'. . . . We must be careful not to confuse the program with the computer that it controls. . . . A program is not a machine; it is a series of instructions for dealing with symbols: 'If the input has certain characteristics . . . then carry out certain procedures . . . otherwise other procedures . . . combine the results in various ways . . . store and retrieve various items . . . etc.' The cognitive psychologist would like to give a similar account of the way information is processed by people. (Neisser, 1967: 6–8)

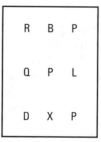

FIGURE 14.5
Stimulus letters similar to those used in Sperling's experiment (1960).

Neisser then traced the flow of information through the organism, beginning with the *icon*. The icon is a representation of a stimulus that persists even after the stimulus has ceased. Classic work on the icon had been done by Sperling (1960), who showed participants three rows of letters like those in Figure 14.5. The letters were exposed tachistoscopically, for 50 milliseconds. After a further 50 milliseconds, during which there is no stimulus, participants were asked to report either the top, middle, or bottom row of letters. Participants were able to do so, reporting that it was as if the letters were still there to be read. The phrase **iconic storage** was used to refer to a brief period during which information from a stimulus was preserved and available for further processing.

The next stage of information-processing Neisser discussed was **pattern recognition**, or the process whereby a stimulus is recognized as an instance of a particular category. Pattern recognition was difficult to understand from an information-processing point of view, because stimuli with very different physical characteristics will often end up being seen as instances of the same category. For example, letters can be presented in different fonts, such as 'b' and 'b', yet still be properly recognized, as in 'problem' and 'problem'. What kind of program is required to enable these stimuli to be recognized as equivalent? Neisser (1967: 84) reviewed research suggesting that pattern recognition relied on the *distinctive features* of stimuli. Distinctive features were those properties—such as the orientation of lines—that served to define a stimulus.

Attention was the next information-processing stage to be considered. Neisser distinguished between *preattentive processing* and *focal attention*. Preattentive processing was concerned with constructing 'the objects which later mechanisms are to flesh out and interpret' (ibid., 89). Before you can focally attend to something, it must first be constructed. Preattentive processes are similar to the Gestalt laws of organization (ibid., 90) and operate automatically to segregate objects in the visual field that can then be attended. A good demonstration of the automatic nature of preattentive processes is the fact that people can drive a car home along a familiar route without ever paying very much attention to what they are doing (ibid., 92). The investigation of automatic processing became a focus for many cognitive psychologists, and one of the standard experimental procedures for such investigations is described in Box 14.2.

BOX 14.2

JOHN R. STROOP AND THE STROOP TASK

Using the right test or experimental apparatus can allow us to explore psychological processes that might otherwise remain unknown to us. A good example is the **Stroop task** (Stroop, 1992 [1935]), which is one of the most useful research tools ever invented (MacLeod, 1992). The Stroop task is named after John R. Stroop (1897–1973), the psychologist who first introduced it. It consists of a list of colour names, such as yellow, red, blue, and green. Of course, it is easy to read colour names such as these. However, this task can become quite difficult if the colour names are printed in different colours. For example, suppose the word 'red' is printed in *blue*; the word 'green' is printed in *red*; the word 'blue' is printed in *green*; and so on. It turns out to be very difficult to name the colours in which the words are printed.

It would be instructive for you to create your own Stroop task by writing a list of 100 words in different colours. (You can make up your own list, or see Benjafield, 1994: 194–5). First try reading the colour names. Then try naming the colours of the words. You will find that the latter task is by far the more difficult of the two. One measure of the relative difficulty of the two tasks is how long it takes you to finish each one. Naming the colours of the words takes longer than reading the colour words themselves. As an experience, naming the colours seems to require you to inhibit the tendency to read the names.

Psychologists interested in information-processing have typically interpreted the Stroop phenomenon as reflecting the difference between *automatic* and voluntary or *controlled* processes (MacLeod, 1992). A skill that has been overlearned may tend to 'run itself off', in the sense that it will be exercised whether we want it to be or not. For example, once reading has become overlearned, then you read without thinking about it, as it were. In the Stroop situation, it is difficult not to read the words. Reading is an example of an *automatic process*. Such a process 'takes care of itself'. We do not need to pay attention to it in order for it to be done properly. By contrast, *controlled processes* require our attention if they are to be done properly (Shiffrin and Schneider, 1977). Naming the colours in which the words are printed is an example of a controlled process. The Stroop task has proven to be an invaluable device for investigating the distinction between automatic and controlled processes. As MacLeod (1992) observes, the impact of the Stroop task can be measured by the fact that over 700 studies have employed it since it was introduced in 1935.

Stroop invented his test as a part of his doctoral dissertation at George Peabody College in Nashville. He was by no means the first psychologist to have explored this topic. 'In fact, it was imported from philosophy into psychology by James McKeen Cattell (1886) for his own dissertation, which was supervised by Wilhelm Wundt' (ibid., 14). Stroop himself took little interest in research after completing his dissertation, but 'devoted his attention to religion for the rest of his life', writing seven books on biblical topics (ibid., 13).

Subsequent chapters in Neisser's *Cognitive Psychology* dealt with what were to become the staples of this approach: visual and auditory imagery; speech perception; echoic memory (an analogue to the visual icon); verbal memory; and psycholinguistics. Finally, Neisser (ibid., ch. 11) proposed a 'cognitive approach to memory and thought'. Here he considered and rejected the **reappearance hypothesis**, which is the notion that information is retrieved from memory in the form in which it is stored. This is a view that Neisser traced back to the British empiricists. He attributed to them the belief that ideas are copies of previous experiences and are retained in memory through being associated with other ideas. On the associationist account, when we remember the past, then we are re-experiencing it. Against the reappearance hypothesis, Neisser cited William James (1890: I, 236): 'A permanently existing "idea" . . . which makes its appearance before the footlights of consciousness at periodical intervals, is as mythological an entity as the Jack of Spades.' Neisser (1967: 279) himself agreed with Bartlett's view that 'reorganization and change are the rule rather than the exception in memory.'

Elaborating on Bartlett's theory, Neisser (ibid., 284) proposed what he called the **utilization hypothesis**. 'There are no stored copies of finished mental events, like images or sentences, but only traces of earlier constructive activity. . . . [W]e store traces of earlier cognitive acts, not of the products of those acts. The traces are not simply "revived" or "reactivated" in recall; instead the stored fragments are used as information to support a new construction' (ibid., 285–6). Neisser drew an analogy between the process of reconstruction and what a paleontologist does when reconstructing an animal. The paleontologist may have only a few bones from which to imaginatively reconstruct the animal. Obviously, the fewer the fragments upon which to base the reconstruction, the more possible 'memories' we can reconstruct. That is why there is so little difference between memory and imagination.

At the end of *Cognitive Psychology*, Neisser (ibid., 304) considered the fact that the study of the so-called 'higher mental processes', such as thinking and creativity, had thus far in the history of psychology proven to be very difficult to investigate. He suggested that 'a really satisfactory theory of the higher mental processes can only come into being when we also have theories of motivation, personality, and social interaction. The study of cognition is only one fraction of psychology, and it cannot stand alone' (ibid., 305).

The effect of Neisser's book was somewhat ironic. Rather than approach the study of cognition as 'only one fraction of psychology', many psychologists enthusiastically seized on the experimental study of cognitive processes, but treated them as if they existed in isolation from other psychological processes. Neisser himself became skeptical of the changes he had been partly responsible for consolidating. By the 1970s, cognitive psychologists began to seem to him to be focusing on details of interest mainly to academics, not on the importance of cognitive processes as they occurred in the real world (Baars, 1986: 282). Moreover, Neisser began to be influenced by the ideas of Cornell's James J. Gibson. Gibson's ideas not only influenced Neisser, but are both distinctive and important enough in their own right to merit a consideration of them here.

James J. Gibson (1904–79)

We considered some of the more important aspects of Gibson's life when we reviewed Eleanor Jack Gibson's work. **James J. Gibson** spent several years at Smith College, where Kurt Koffka was an important influence, and he 'came to share Koffka's conviction that the problems of perception were the central problems of psychology' (Neisser, 1981: 214).

Gibson's approach to perception was highly distinctive. He did not agree with traditional approaches that treated the stimulus as if it had no intrinsic meaning (Gibson, 1960). Other theorists treated a visual stimulus, for example, as if it consisted only of wavelengths of light. If that is all there is to a visual stimulus, then the process of perception must enrich that stimulus somehow in order for us to end up perceiving a world of meaningful objects. Gibson (1966: 245) did not believe that stimuli were impoverished sources of information, a point he made by distinguishing between two meanings of the word 'information'. In the information-processing model of communication that we considered above, we receive information about the external world in the form of 'signals' that we must 'encode' in order to 'process' the information contained in them. Thus, in the standard information-processing model, there is a lot of 'internal processing' required to make information meaningful. Information-processing psychology, like Gestalt psychology and introspective psychology before it, makes the assumption that what we perceive is the result of adding meaning to a stimulus. By contrast, Gibson believed that information about the world could be directly picked up. The perceiver does not need to add anything to the information available in the world. Rather, enough information is available to enable the person to perceive the world directly.

Gibson (1950, 1966) argued for the creation of an *ecological* approach to perception that would describe environmental stimulation at the appropriate level. Describing stimuli only in the language of physics left out levels of description that were relevant to perception. 'The environment consists of *opportunities* for perception, of *available* information, of potential stimuli. Not all opportunities are grasped, not all information is registered, not all stimuli excite receptors. But what the environment *affords* an individual in the way of discrimination is enormous, and this should be our first consideration' (Gibson, 1966: 23). Gibson described a number of *stimulus gradients* that provided information about the environment. A gradient is an 'increase or decrease of something along a given dimension' (Gibson, 1950: 73). Simple examples of stimulus gradients are given in Figure 14.6. It is easy to see

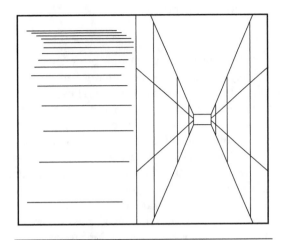

FIGURE 14.6
Stimulus gradients that give rise to the perception of depth.

the gradient on the left as a receding pathway and the converging lines on the right as a hallway. By looking around you, you can probably observe similar gradients, such as the changing distances between floorboards or the changing texture of a rug as it recedes from you (cf. Gibson, 1966: 254–5) Gibson (1950: 88–9) argued that these kinds of information are readily available in the environment, especially as we move around in it.

Gibson also believed that the meaning of objects and events can be perceived directly through what he called **affordances**. 'I have coined this word as a substitute for *values*, a term which carries an old burden of philosophical meaning. I mean simply what things furnish, for good or ill' (Gibson, 1966: 285). Thus, stairs afford climbing, food affords eating, ice affords skating, and so on. Of course, one has to learn the affordances of objects, but affordances are still tied to the properties of objects. Gibson's is a theory of *information pickup*, in which learning means becoming progressively more attuned to what the environment affords us.

Cognition and Reality

As was mentioned previously, Neisser (1976) turned away from information-processing psychology because he believed that it had become too narrowly academic in its orientation. He turned towards Gibson's ecological approach and argued that cognitive psychology needed to have more **ecological validity**. The concept of ecological validity had originally been introduced by Egon Brunswik (1903–55) (1956) to refer to the extent to which the information available to a perceiver is truly representative of the environment. Neisser used 'ecological validity' in a broader sense to mean that a theory should have 'something to say about what people do in real, culturally significant situations. What it says must not be trivial, and it must make some kind of sense to the participants themselves' (Neisser, 1976: 2). An oft-cited example of an ecologically valid study is Bahrick's (1984) study of long-term retention of Spanish learned as a second language. Instead of studying what participants learn in a laboratory, Bahrick studied what ordinary people had learned in school. This is the kind of study Neisser called for when he noted that higher education:

> depends heavily on the assumption that students remember something valuable from their educational experience. One might expect psychologists to leap at the opportunity to study a critical memory problem so close to hand, but they never do. It is difficult to find even a single study, ancient or modern, of what is retained from academic instruction. Given our expertise and the way we earn our livings, this omission can only be described as scandalous. (Neisser, 1978: 5)

By no means did all cognitive psychologists appreciate being scolded in this manner, and the issue of ecological validity continued to be hotly debated (e.g., Loftus, 1991). However, to guide those who wished to do ecologically valid research, Neisser (1976: 21) proposed a cyclical model of cognition. Rather than completely accept Gibson's view that the perceiver simply picks up information available in the environment, Neisser insisted that the perceiver possesses a schema that represents what the person was likely to find in the environment. This schema directs the person's exploration of the environment. As the environment is explored, the person encounters information that is expected as well as information that is unexpected. The latter kind of information is capable of modifying the schema so as to increase the accuracy with which it represents the environment. Thus, the cycle begins with the schema directing exploration of the environment, which brings the person into contact with information, which in turn corrects the schema, and so on.

Herbert A. Simon (1916–2001)

Herbert A. Simon (1980, 1991) was one of the most protean intellectuals of the century. He received the Nobel Prize for economics in 1978, yet his Ph.D. is in political science (from the University of Chicago), and he has also made important contributions to cognitive psychology. Simon has been a force for change in social science generally. Throughout his career, his work has been characterized by an ability to apply logical and mathematical techniques to complex problems. A good example of the interdisciplinary nature of his approach is a paper he wrote on spurious correlation and the nature of causality (Simon, 1954). This paper not only provides a good introduction to Simon's thought, but also illustrates one of the reasons why computers have become so central to psychology and to social science generally.

Spurious Correlation and the Nature of Causality

The relation between correlation and causality is traditionally one of the most difficult problems in the history of thought. Recall our consideration of this problem in Chapter 2, when we reviewed Hume's argument that there is nothing more to causality than an observed correlation between two events. Simon noted that every undergraduate course in statistics teaches students that a correlation between two variables does not mean that the two variables are causally related. Students are taught that correlations can often be spurious. A **spurious correlation** occurs whenever the correlation between two variables is due to a common cause. Consider the correlation between academic achievement and height in schoolchildren. Such a correlation is spurious because both academic achievement and height increase with age (Pedhazur and Schmelkin, 1991: 215).

Simon pointed out that the concept of a spurious correlation implies the existence of a true correlation, in the sense of a correlation that represents a causal relationship. How can one distinguish between a spurious and a true correlation? He addresses this question by considering some of the possible relationships between three variables. Suppose we calculate the correlation between two variables, X and Y, and find it to be significantly different from zero. We can then speculate that the observed correlation may be due to spurious causes. That is, perhaps there is a third variable, Z, that accounts for the observed correlation between X and Y. To investigate this possibility, we can make use of a statistical technique, called partial correlation, that allows us to calculate the correlation between X and Y with the possible effect of Z removed. Suppose that the correlation between X and Y is zero when the effect of Z is removed. There are then two possibilities.

One possibility is that the correlation between X and Y resulted from the effect of Z on X and on Y, and hence is spurious. This would be the case for our earlier example of the relation between academic achievement (X) and height (Y) being due to the effect of age (Z) on both variables. This case is illustrated in Figure 14.7A, in which the arrows represent causal relationships.

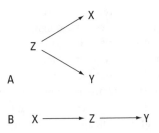

FIGURE 14.7
Possible causal relations between three variables.

However, another possibility is that Z intervenes between X and Y, such that the effect of X on Y is mediated by Z. To illustrate this possibility, we will use a variant of an example Simon (1954) considered. Imagine a hypothetical study of a number of corporations in which three variables were measured. X represents the percentage of employees in each corporation who are married; Y is the average number of absences per week per employee; and Z is the average number of children per employee. Suppose that, when we do the study, we discover a high correlation between X and Y. However, the correlation between X and Y is virtually zero when the effect of Z is taken into account. In this case, we would not want to conclude that the correlation between X and Y is spurious. Rather, we would conclude that there is a causal chain connecting X to Z and then to Y. Z intervenes between X and Y because marriage (X) often results in children (Z) (who make demands of one sort or another on parents' time), which in turn increases absenteeism (Y). This case is represented in Figure 14.7B.

As Simon pointed out, the same pattern of correlations leads to opposite conclusions in the two cases. It is not the statistical evidence by itself, but the assumptions we make about the situation we are investigating that determines the conclusions we draw from the statistical evidence. There are many possible relations between three variables other than the ones we have considered. Moreover, social scientists often want to investigate systems that contain many more than three variables. Untangling the possible causal relationships in such complex systems is a very difficult matter. The analysis of complex systems would be impossible without the availability of computer programs that perform the appropriate analyses. The advent of the computer after World War II made possible an entire range of statistical analyses that would have earlier been inconceivable.

> The ubiquity of computers and the diverse functions they perform belie the prediction made about 40 years ago by the RAND corporation 'that because computers were so large and expensive, no more than 12 corporations in the United States would ever need or be able to afford one' (Brzezinski, 1984: 7). . . . Within sociobehavioral sciences, the use of computers for data management and analysis come most readily to mind. As is well known, however, the diverse uses to which computers can be put in research, academic, and clinical endeavors are virtually limitless, including such activities as information retrieval and exchange, presentation of stimuli in research settings, simulations, artificial intelligence, authoring systems, computer-aided instruction, computerized testing, and counseling applications. (Pedhazur and Schmelkin, 1991: 342)

Computer Simulation

Of all the applications of computers in social science, perhaps none has been more controversial that the computer simulation of psychological processes. Herbert Simon, along with his colleague **Allen Newell** (1927–92), was at the forefront of computer simulation for many years. However, the technique of computer simulation had originally been proposed by the British mathematician **Alan Turing** (1912–54).

Turing's Test

People often discuss the question 'Can computers really think?' This is a deep question, and possibly indeterminable. Turing (1950) proposed that we not try to settle this question through endless discussion, but pay more attention to a concrete situation that illustrates the problem underlying the question. The concrete situation he considered is called the 'imitation game' (Gunderson, 1964).

Turing described a game involving three people: A man and a woman, who are in one room, and an interrogator who is in another room. The interrogator is linked to the others by means of a computer terminal. Thus, the interrogator is able to ask questions of the man (let us call him Frank) and/or the woman (let us call her Annette), and they are able to reply using the computer interface. The object of the game is for the interrogator to be able to distinguish between the replies of the man and the replies of the woman.

You might think that this would be a trivial task for the interrogator, because the only question that needs to be asked of either respondent is 'Are you Frank or Annette?' However, just like ordinary people, the players of this game can lie. Thus, this game is not as easy as it appears to be at first. Now suppose that we make a change. In place of one of the people, we install a computer. Suppose, for example, we remove the man and replace him with a computer we also name 'Frank'. The computer has been programmed to answer questions in the same way that Frank would. The interrogator's job is still to distinguish between Frank and Annette, but now one of the respondents is a computer while the other is a person. Suppose that the interrogator could not reliably tell which was which. Then, according to Turing, we would have programmed the computer so that it could successfully play the imitation game. The computer would have passed **Turing's test**, and the computer program would be an adequate model of the psychological processes that are involved when one person answers another person's questions.

By no means everyone has been persuaded that Turing's test is the right way to construct a psychological model. Over the years, a lot of ink has been spilled over the question of whether or not a computer program can ever be a realistic model of psychological processes. However, regardless of how we feel about this question, there has still been an enormous amount of work undertaken by psychologists, such as Herbert Simon, who use some version of Turing's test as a methodological tool for evaluating a psychological theory. Notice that it is not the computer itself that constitutes the psychological model, but the computer *program* that actually is the model. Beginning in the 1950s Simon and his colleagues began to put Turing's ideas into practice.

> Computers, then, could be general symbol systems, capable of processing symbols of any kind—numerical or not.
>
> This insight, which dawned on me only gradually, led Al [Newell] and me even more gradually to the idea that the computer could provide the formalism we were seeking—that we could use the computer to simulate all sorts of information processes and use computer languages as formal descriptions of those processes.
>
> In the summer of 1954, I taught myself to program the 701, IBM's first stored program computer, and computers were much on my mind. . . . Al and I had a long discussion of the possibility of simulating human thinking by computer. (Simon, 1991: 201)

The fruit of Simon and Newell's discussions was a series of computer simulations of human thinking. The programs they wrote were among the first examples of **artificial intelligence**. A summary of their efforts was published in Newell and Simon (1972). Among the first simulations they produced was a program to play chess (Newell et al., 1958). Although such programs are commonplace now, they were considered to be extremely innovative in the 1950s. The simulation

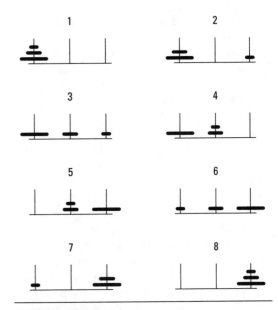

FIGURE 14.8
Solution for the three-disk version of the Tower of Hanoi problem.

of more mundane forms of human thought was accomplished through the use of toy problems, such as the Tower of Hanoi problem (e.g., Simon, 1975; Anzai and Simon, 1979). In one form of this problem there are three pegs on a board, with three disks on the leftmost peg. The person's task is to transfer all three disks to the rightmost peg by moving one disk at a time to one of the other pegs. The person is not allowed to put a larger disk on a smaller disk. Moreover, you cannot move a disk that is covered by another disk.

A version of the problem is illustrated in Figure 14.8, which gives the moves required for the solution. Although it might seem like a trivial exercise to simulate the solution of such problems on a computer, you should remember that the goal is to program the computer so that its behaviour is indistinguishable from that of a person. Thus, the program should not necessarily solve the problem in the best way possible, but in the same way as would a person.

Research using toy problems proceeds by having the person think aloud (Newell and Simon, 1972; Simon, 1979), the technique we described earlier in this chapter. Ericsson and Simon (1980; 1984) pointed out that thinking aloud involves *concurrent verbalization* and not *retrospective verbalization*. Concurrent verbalization involves saying what you are thinking while you are thinking it. This is not as difficult as it seems; you simply 'think out loud.' By contrast, retrospective verbalization in-volves trying to recall what you were thinking after it has occurred. This technique is obviously more open to error and is more like introspection than is con-current verbalization. Concurrent verbalization can provide a useful description of the process of thinking. A fragment of a thinking-aloud protocol is given below, from Anzai and Simon (1979: 138). The participant is trying to solve a five-disk version of the Tower of Hanoi puzzle. You might find it instructive to try this yourself.

1. I'm not sure, but first I'll take 1 from A and place it on B.
2. And I'll take 2 from A and place it on C.
3. And then, I take 1 from B and place it on C. (The interrogator asks, 'If you can tell me why you placed it there.')
4. Because there was no place else to go, I had to place 1 from B to C.
5. Then, next, I placed 3 from A to B.
6. Well . . . first I had to place 1 to B, because I had to move all disks to C. I wasn't too sure though.
7. I thought that it would be a problem if I placed 1 on C rather than B.
8. Now I want to place 2 on top of 3, so I'll place 1 on A.
9. Then I'll take 2 from C, and place it from A to B.
10. And I'll take 1 and . . . place it from A to B.
11. So then, 4 will go from A to C.
12. And then . . . um . . . oh . . . um . . .

As you can see, there is a lot of information in these protocols. In conjunction with observing the actual behaviour of the participant, these protocols can give the experimenter a reasonably complete description of a psychological process. The task of the psychologist is to construct a computer program that will represent the procedures that the participant appears to be using. By studying a number of different problems, the hope is that the computer programs will reveal general principles that regulate human thought.

> The hypothesis that human thought processes are simple emerged from the information-processing research of the 1950s and 1960s. Most of that research employed puzzlelike tasks, similar to . . . the Tower of Hanoi puzzle, and problems of logical inference, all of which have been studied extensively in the psychological laboratory. . . . It is reasonable that research on human thinking should begin with relatively contentless tasks of these kinds, but not that it should end there. And so in the past decade research in both cognitive psychology and artificial intelligence has been turning more and more to . . . domains that have substantial, meaningful content, where skillful performance calls upon large amounts of specialized knowledge retrieved from memory. (Simon, 1981: 102)

Simon goes on to review computer simulations of such activities as medical diagnosis and solving physics problems, and concludes that the same simple principles regulate human thinking across a wide range of problems. One finds the same strategies, such as reducing the difference between one's current state and the goal to be achieved, no matter what the domain. This simplicity occurs in part because cognition, like good computer programs, has a *modular* construction. This means that cognitive processes can be decomposed into *modules*, or parts, that can be recombined in different ways to deal with changing circumstances. Each module solves a particular kind of problem, and by combining the appropriate modules, problems of great complexity can be solved using the same kinds of strategies that solve simple problems.

Simon (ibid., 200) illustrated the importance of modular construction by means of what has now become a famous **parable of the watchmakers**, Hora and Tempus. Tempus constructed watches piece by piece, but once he began to make a watch he had to finish it or it would fall apart. Since he was often interrupted, he made few watches. Hora, by contrast, built watches in modules, each one of which could exist on its own. Hora could then combine modules to make a completed watch. The virtue of Hora's procedure is that he could be interrupted and not lose his work.

Simon argues that any system able successfully to adapt to changing circumstances (such as interruptions) is likely to have a modular structure. Cognitive processes are just one example of an adaptive system. For example, the same modular principles that regulate cognition will be found in successfully adapting social systems as well. Rather than having a single structure in which one part cannot be changed without changing the whole thing, one should design modular systems that allow parts to be changed without disrupting the whole. Simon's concept of modularity had a large impact on those who are responsible for designing complex systems (e.g., Green, 1982).

Criticisms of Computer Simulation

It was common for computer simulation approaches to psychological processes to be criticized for what they appear to leave out. For example, even some cognitive psychologists (e.g., Neisser, 1964) suggested that the simulation of emotion by means of a computer program would not be a very meaningful exercise. Although Simon (1967) attempted to deal with this problem, most work in this area specialized in cognition (e.g., Simon, 1981: 65), and it is perhaps fair to say that the role of emotion in mental life was neglected (e.g., Simon, 1995: 508).

Another standard criticism is that computer programs do not show the kind of insightful behaviour that Gestalt psychologists such as

Köhler believed to be so characteristic of problem-solving. Newell and Simon (1972: 872) acknowledged that such phenomena were beyond the scope of their approach as it then existed. However, Simon never acknowledged that phenomena such as insight were beyond computer simulation approaches, and he continued to develop computer simulations of insight problems (e.g., Kaplan and Simon, 1990).

Yet another criticism comes from those who believe that explanations in psychology should come from neurophysiology. Since computer programs tell us little, if anything, about how the nervous system works, they are inadequate explanations of human behaviour. Simon refused to accept the validity of this argument, claiming that neurophysiological explanations are an inappropriate level of explanation for cognitive processes. 'Explanation of cognitive processes at the information processing (symbolic) level is largely independent of explanation at the physiological (neurological) level that shows how processes are implemented' (Simon, 1992: 153). Nevertheless, it is important to 'build the bridge theory' between neurophysiology and cognitive psychology 'that shows how the symbol structures and symbol-manipulating processes that handle information at a more aggregated level can be implemented by such neuronal structures and organizations' (ibid.).

Simon maintained that the relationship between cognitive psychology and social psychology was particularly close, since 'adaptive behavior is a function of strategies and knowledge, both largely acquired from the social environment' (ibid., 157). He particularly recommended the study of the history of science as a source of hypotheses concerning the way knowledge is acquired. Such 'histories do not draw a boundary around individual investigators, but encompass the sources of an investigator's knowledge and, more broadly, the social processes that direct the production of scientific knowledge and its communication' (ibid.).

Herbert Simon was awarded the National Medal of Science in 1986, as was Allen Newell in 1992.

IMPORTANT NAMES, WORKS, AND CONCEPTS

Names and Works

Bartlett, Sir Frederic

Broadbent, Donald E.

Bruner, Jerome

Chomsky, Noam

Cognitive Psychology

Gibson, James J.

Miller, George A.

Neisser, Ulric

Newell, Allen

Plans and the Structure of Behavior

Simon, Herbert A.

A Study of Thinking

Turing, Alan

Concepts

affordances

artificial intelligence

attention

channel capacity

cocktail party phenomenon

concept attainment

cybernetics

deep structure

dichotic listening

ecological validity

feedback loop

iconic storage

method of serial reproduction

minimax axiom

parable of the watchmakers

pattern recognition

perceptual readiness

reappearance hypothesis

schema

span of immediate memory

spurious correlation

Stroop task

subjective behaviorism

surface structure

thinking aloud

TOTE mechanisms

Turing's test

utilization hypothesis

RECOMMENDED READINGS

The Concept of 'Information'

For a useful review of early efforts, see F. Attneave, *Applications of Information Theory to Psychology* (New York: Holt, Rinehart and Winston, 1959). An excellent overview of information theory and its relation to information-processing theories in psychology is R. Duncan Luce, 'Whatever happened to information theory in psychology?', *Review of General Psychology* 7 (2003): 183–8.

Chomsky

A very readable account of Chomsky's impact on linguistics (and linguists) is D. Berreby, 'Figures of speech: The rise and fall and rise of Chomsky's linguistics', *The Sciences* 34 (Jan.–Feb. 1994): 44–9.

Miller

George Miller continued his pioneering work in the psychology of language: 'The place of language in a scientific psychology', *Psychological Science* 1 (1990): 7–14. For an informative debate concerning Miller's use of computer programs as models of mental processes, see H. Crowther-Heyck, 'George A. Miller, language, and the computer metaphor of the mind', *History of Psychology* 2 (1999): 37–64; Crowther-Heyck, 'Mystery and meaning: A reply to Green', *History of Psychology* 3 (2000): 67–70; C.D. Green, 'Dispelling the "mystery" of computational cognitive science', *History of Psychology* 3 (2000): 62–6.

Bruner

Bruner subsequently did extremely influential work on education (e.g., J.S. Bruner, *Toward a Theory of Instruction* [Cambridge, Mass.: Harvard University Press, 1966]) as well as cognitive development: Bruner, R.R. Olver, and P.M. Greenfield, *Studies in Cognitive Growth* (New York: Wiley, 1966). His work, such as *Actual Minds, Possible Worlds* (Cambridge, Mass.: Harvard University Press, 1986), also drew on a variety of disciplines to 'show how human minds and lives are reflections of culture and history as well as of biology and physical resources' (Bruner, 1990: 138). For a delightful collection of articles about play, see Bruner, A. Jolly, and K. Silva, eds, *Play* (New York: Penguin, 1976).

Bartlett

A useful review of the many studies evaluating Bartlett's memory theory is J.W. Alba and L. Hasher, 'Is memory schematic?', *Psychological Bulletin* 93 (1983): 203–31. The continuing relevance of Bartlett's theory of memory is well illustrated by K.J. Vicente and W.F. Brewer, 'Reconstructive remembering of the scientific literature', *Cognition* 46 (1993): 101–28. They found that the details of scientific experiments are often remembered in a more idealized form than was actually the case. Vicente and Brewer (1993) conclude that:

> Our study suggests that scientists also need to be aware of the power of schema-based memory processes so that they will not rely on memory as a replacement for careful re-reading of original sources. In fact, we have recently found an example of a writer attempting to make his readers aware of this problem in an introductory psychology text written in 1939! In that text, Lawrence Cole reviewed Bartlett's (1932) work on reconstructive remembering and then in a prophetic aside to his readers, states that Bartlett's research 'might well cause the student of psychology to do some reflecting, since the very textbook which he reads is a reproduction often many times removed from that source (human behavior) to which it professedly refers.' (Cole, 1939: 516)

E.B. Johnson, in 'The repeated reproduction of Bartlett's "Remembering"', *History of Psychology* 4 (2001): 341–66, makes the similar and highly relevant point that Bartlett's own work has been remembered in remarkably different ways by psychologists, depending on their own orientation.

Neisser

Neisser, 'The multiplicity of thought', *British Journal of Psychology* 54 (1964): 1–14, is an interesting anticipation of many of the themes he later developed in *Cognitive Psychology*. A collection of ecologically valid studies of memory is in Neisser, ed., *Memory Observed: Remembering Natural Contexts* (San Francisco: Freeman, 1982).

Simon

See J.R. Anderson, 'Herbert A. Simon (1916–2001)', *American Psychologist* 56 (2001): 516–18, who notes that Simon was not only interested in computer simulation, but also in other forms of simulation. '[H]e amused himself as a young man when he used to travel by train across America [by starting] a conversation with some fellow traveler, inquire about that person's profession, and carefully listen as they described what they did. When he was confident he understood the language of that profession, he would reveal to the traveler that he too shared that profession and then would try to maintain that deception for the rest of the trip' (p. 516). G. Kirkebøen, 'Descartes *Regulae*, mathematics and modern psychology', *History of Psychology* 3 (2000): 299–325, shows how Descartes may have anticipated Turing's approach to cognition. Charles Babbage (1791–1871) and Ada Lovelace (1815–52) are often credited with anticipating twentieth-century developments in computing. See C.D. Green, 'Charles Babbage, the analytical engine, and the possibility of a 19th-century cognitive science', in Green et al., eds, *The Transformation of Psychology* (Washington: American Psychological Association, 2001), 133–52.

For protocols, see A. Newell, 'On the analysis of human problem-solving protocols', in P.N. Johnson-Laird and P. Wason, eds, *Thinking: Readings in Cognitive Science* (Cambridge: Cambridge University Press, 1977). An interesting retrospective account of problem-solving research before the advent of the computer is Newell, 'Duncker on thinking: An inquiry into progress in cognition', in S. Koch and D. Leary, eds, *A Century of Psychology as Science* (New York: McGraw-Hill, 1985), 392–419. Simon's approach to problem-solving—'What is an "explanation" of behavior?', *Psychological Science* (1992): 150–61—presages the emerging discipline of cognitive psychology of science, which applies the methods of cognitive psychology to the study of scientific thought. See, e.g., R.D. Tweney, 'Toward a cognitive psychology of science: Recent research and its implications', *Current Directions in Psychological Science* 7 (1998): 150–4. For a thorough account of the development of artificial intelligence, see M.A. Boden, *Artificial Intelligence and Natural Man* (New York: Basic Books, 1987). Useful overviews of the history of the study of cognition are H. Gardner, *The Mind's New Science: A History of the Cognitive Revolution* (New York: Basic Books, 1985), and G. Mandler, 'Origins of the cognitive revolution', *Journal of the History of the Behavioral Sciences* 38 (2002): 339–53.

CHAPTER 15

THE FUTURE OF PSYCHOLOGY

Introduction

As the twentieth century drew to a close, several forces were reshaping the way psychologists thought about their discipline and its history. Rather than see psychology as necessarily progressive and objective, many began to draw attention to more subjective aspects of the discipline and to argue that important aspects of its history had been ignored. One of these neglected aspects was the contribution made by women. Feminists and others drew attention to the degree to which psychology had been at least partly determined by social forces. The pressure to include diverse interests within psychology led it to become more differentiated. Some saw this differentiation as hindering attempts to integrate psychology, while others welcomed it as leading to a more inclusive discipline.

At the same time as the humanistic and cognitive approaches were changing psychology, there were corresponding changes in the philosophy of science. The logical positivist methodology outlined in Chapter 10, which had been so hospitable to behaviourism, began to be challenged as an adequate description of the way science is actually done. Although logical positivism and operationism remained strong forces in academic psychology, their influence was muted somewhat by what **Laurel Furomoto** called the **new history of psychology**:

> Whereas traditional history portrayed the scientist as an objective fact finder and neutral observer, the new history emphasized the notion that scientists often operate in a subjective fashion, under the influence of a variety of extra-scientific factors. Also . . . the new history rejected the traditional view of scientific activity as a continuous

progression from error to truth, and opted instead for a model that depicts scientific change as a shift from one world view to another—world views that are linked to theoretical commitments involving esthetic as well as metaphysical considerations. (Furomoto, 1989: 11)

Furomoto (1989) drew attention to philosophers and historians of science whose work was responsible for a thoroughgoing reconsideration of the nature of these disciplines. In what follows we will consider the views of some of these 'new historians' who have proposed different ways of understanding the nature of psychology.

The New History of Science

Discussions of research methods towards the end of the twentieth century tended to emphasize the complexity of the research process more than had been the case in earlier discussions (e.g., Pedhazur, 1997). There was an acknowledgement that it is not always easy to specify the relations between independent and dependent variables in an unambiguous manner. The facts may not 'speak for themselves', but may need to be understood from within a particular theoretical framework. For example, Pedhazur (ibid., 769) pointed out that it is entirely possible for different theories all to be consistent with the same data. Being consistent with the data is no guarantee of the validity of a theory. In fact, an investigator's theory may, at least partially, determine how the data will be interpreted.

Many historians and philosophers of science have noted that the process of scientific inquiry inevitably contains a subjective aspect. **Thomas Kuhn** (1924–96) was among the most influential of these scholars. In *The Structure of Scientific Revolutions* (1970 [1962]), after reviewing the historical development of established sciences such as physics, Kuhn concluded that the development of these disciplines had not been smooth. It was *not* the case that they had simply grown and developed by accumulating data that guided the development of an adequate theory. On the contrary, scientific disciplines appeared to develop discontinuously—during long periods almost all workers in a discipline had the same beliefs about the methods, data, and theory that were appropriate for their discipline. However, at certain critical junctures, radical upheavals occurred and entire scientific communities changed their minds about what were the proper methods, data, and theory in their discipline. The set of fundamental beliefs that guide workers in a scientific discipline is called a **paradigm**. Revolutionary periods occur in which a new paradigm is emerging and an old paradigm is being overthrown. The controversy surrounding the emergence of Darwin's theory of evolution in the nineteenth century would be an example of such a revolution.

Kuhn argued that paradigms shape the scientist's view of the world. There can be *paradigm clashes* in which fundamentally different ways of interpreting the data exist. Kuhn likened this state of affairs to cases in which we can see different patterns in the same situation. A good example of the sort of thing Kuhn had in mind comes from the work of N.R. Hanson. Consider Figure 15.1A. What is it—a bird or an antelope? If we view Figure 15.1A in the context of Figure 15.1B, then we are able to see the similarity between it and a bird. As Hanson (1969: 13) pointed out, it is difficult to see it as an antelope when its similarities to all the other 'birds' in Figure 15.1B are so evident. However, if we view Figure 15.1A in the context of Figure 15.1C, then its similarity to an antelope becomes clear. Now it looks different. What was formerly the 'beak' of a bird is transformed into the 'horns' of an antelope. Hanson's demonstration is intended to make the following point. The two contexts are analogous to two different theories.

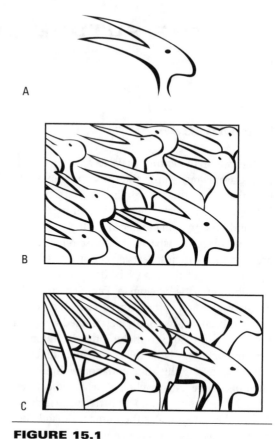

FIGURE 15.1
Is it a bird or an antelope?
Source: Hanson (1969: 13-14). Reprinted by permission of Cambridge University Press.

Each of the 'theories' suggests a different interpretation of the same fact. Each 'theory' is equally consistent with the data. In general, the theoretical context within which we interpret data may literally determine how those data are seen. Conflicting interpretations of the same data are entirely possible, perhaps even inevitable.

A related point can be made by adapting an example from the work of Paul Feyerabend (1970: 220). Consider Figure 15.2. Imagine that the horizontal line represents the range of data that psychologists have considered as relevant or potentially relevant. 'Data' here means any phenomenon that any psychologist has ever used to support his or her theory. Thus, this range includes introspectionist reports, psychotherapy sessions, case studies, psychophysical judgements, the behaviour of animals in mazes, computer simulations, and much else besides. In other words, it includes the entire gamut of phenomena we have considered as we have reviewed the various theoretical viewpoints in psychology. Obviously, what is legitimate data from the viewpoint of one theory is not necessarily legitimate data from the viewpoint of another theory. Thus, the various theories we have reviewed overlap somewhat with respect to the phenomena they attempt to explain, but each theory also tends to specialize in certain phenomena and to neglect others. This state of affairs is represented in Figure 15.2 by T_1 through T_4, which stand for four different psychological theories. Each theory attempts to explain a different range of data and no single theory explains all the data. T_1 through T_4 are not intended to represent any particular psychological theories, and we could have made the diagram more complex by adding additional overlapping points of view. The general idea is simply that no theory extends across the entire range, and different theories compete to explain some of the same data.

Another important feature of the history of psychology brought out by Figure 15.2 is that some theories (e.g., T_1 and T_4) do not overlap at all, meaning that what one theory explains is not regarded as data by the other theory and vice versa. This state of affairs has often existed in the history of psychology. For example, when behaviourism was taking over from introspectionism, introspectionist experiments were regarded as not yielding 'real' data, of which the observation of behaviour was seen as the sole source. This example points to what has been a recurrent problem in psychology, which is the specification of the boundaries of the discipline in terms of what is 'in' and what is 'out'. This was particularly clear during the period when humanistic psychologists were at the height of their influence and were arguing for the inclusion

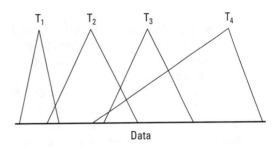

FIGURE 15.2
Different theoretical viewpoints in psychology.

of a wide range of 'subjective' phenomena that had earlier been ruled out of court by the then dominant behaviourist orientation.

It is, of course, not incumbent on psychology to explain everything that anyone who has ever imagined herself or himself to be a psychologist has wanted explained. From a Kuhnian perspective, the establishment of a single paradigm means that a discipline becomes a *normal science* in which the workers share a united view of what constitutes the proper problems and methods for their discipline. This inevitably means that certain data are regarded as illegitimate. An interesting question concerns whether psychology has ever had a paradigm. Another interesting question concerns whether psychology *should* have a paradigm (cf. ibid., 198).

Does Psychology Have Paradigms?

One issue that historians discussed was whether or not psychology has had paradigms that have unified the discipline at different times, or whether it is still *preparadigmatic* (Farrell, 1978). 'Kuhn (1962) himself initially considered psychology (as well as other social sciences) to be preparadigmatic, since there was no one single paradigm which was generally accepted within the discipline, and much debate and energy was still being spent on trying to resolve fundamentals' (Buss, 1978: 57). However, other historians argued that psychology has already moved through a succession of paradigms. For example, Kirsch suggested that Wundtian introspectionism exemplifies the first paradigm in psychology. Kirsch recommended that this paradigm be called **mentalism**. The distinguishing feature of this paradigm was that it defined psychology as 'the science of mind' (Kirsch, 1977: 322). Up until the behaviourist revolution, the mentalist paradigm united psychologists by providing them with a definition of their subject matter (mental events) and a method (introspection). Although individual groups working within the mentalist paradigm might disagree concerning the precise nature of mental events or the best form of introspection, there was still widespread agreement on these two fundamental points. Thus, as we saw in Chapter 4, Wundt and Kulpe could disagree over many particular things, and yet the mentalist paradigm still organized their efforts in a general way.

Those who accepted the notion that psychology is a paradigmatic discipline often claimed that cognitive psychology has been psychology's emerging paradigm since the 1970s (e.g., Neisser, 1972; Segal and Lachman, 1972). One implication of this view is that the competitors of cognitive psychology, such as psychoanalysis and behaviourism, must be declining in influence. To investigate this possibility, Friman, Allen, Kerwin, and Larzelere counted the frequency with which publications in cognitive psychology, psychoanalysis, and behavioural psychology were cited in journals during the period 1979–88. They found that citations to articles published in cognitive psychology journals did indeed increase during the period. Moreover, articles in cognitive psychology had more impact than articles from the other areas as measured by the average number of citations per article. However, the heightened influence of cognitive psychology was not reflected in 'corresponding decreases in citations to core journals in behavioral psychology. . . . In addition, classic source items in psychoanalysis appear to be cited more than classic source items in behavioral and cognitive psychology' (Friman et al., 1993: 661).

This study was amplified by Robins, Gosling, and Craik in 1999. They sampled the years from 1977 to 1996, and included neuroscience as well as cognitive psychology, psychoanalysis, and behavioural psychology. We have discussed neuroscience previously, most notably in relation to the work of Hebb in Chapter 11. Neuroscience was added to the mix by Robins et al. because of its increasing popularity in the 1990s. Several different measures of prominence were used, including frequency of citation in four 'flagship' American journals: *American Psychologist, Annual Review of Psychology, Psychological Bulletin*, and *Psychological Review*. Robins et al. found that research by psychoanalysts was not being cited very often by other psychologists. Moreover, it appeared that the prominence of behavioural psychology had also declined since the 1970s. Cognitive psychology was clearly the most prominent of the four approaches, rising steadily in terms of citations in the 'flagship' publications from the 1970s through the 1980s and then levelling off. However, an apparent anomaly was the poor showing of neuroscience, which did not demonstrate an increase in prominence during the period studied. This is despite the fact that 'membership in the Society for Neuroscience has increased dramatically since it was founded in 1970' to over 28,000 by the late 1990s (Robins et al., 1999: 125). The anomaly can be explained by noting that, although neuroscientists were not being cited extensively in 'flagship' psychology journals, they were being cited by prominent journals outside of psychology, such as *Nature* and *Science*. It could be that 'neuroscience may be located more centrally in the biological sciences than in psychology and in some ways may already constitute its own independent scientific discipline' (ibid., 126).

The evidence provided by Robins et al. suggests that if there is a paradigm in psychology, then it is the cognitive approach. However, even if we regard the emergence of cognitive psychology as 'revolutionary' in Kuhn's sense, it is still true that its emphasis on the study of mental events was not entirely original, but harked back to earlier schools such as the Würzburgers (Chapter 4) and the Gestalt psychologists (Chapter 9) (Greenwood, 1999; Murray, 1995). Thus, cognitive psychology illustrates the way in which historical change shows both 'revolutionary' or discontinuous developments and continuous developments.

Regardless of their relative dominance, the continued existence of various schools in psychology means that 'no single paradigm has yet prevailed' (Robins and Craik, 1994: 815). Some historians have questioned the usefulness of the paradigm concept itself, suggesting that scientific development in many disciplines does not actually involve 'sudden, drastic paradigm shifts' (Mayr, 1994: 333). Science may not inevitably lead to a single paradigm within a discipline, and it may not be necessary for different approaches to be mutually exclusive. Rather, it may be possible for different approaches in a discipline such as psychology to coexist and for 'fruitful exchange between rivals' to take place (e.g., Gholson and Barker, 1985: 766). Thus, one might expect the psychoanalytic, behavioural, cognitive, and neuroscientific orientations not only to survive, but also to continue to influence one another.

Feminism and the Psychology of Women

Feminism is not a single point of view but has many different aspects. Beginning with classic texts such as *The Second Sex* (1989 [1949]) by **Simone de Beauvoir** and Betty Friedan's *The Feminine Mystique* (1963), the perspectives of women were brought to bear on every aspect of contemporary culture, including psychology. There are several important ways in which feminism and the women's movement changed psychology. One of the most far-reaching contributions of feminist scholarship was to identify 'distortions and biases' in psychology (Banister et al., 1994: 122). One iconic figure in this regard was Naomi Weisstein:

a Harvard trained experimental psychologist who . . . had been intensely frustrated by her own educational and professional experience in psychology. . . . Denied the use of equipment she needed for her doctoral research (because she might break it), she somehow managed to finish first in her class in 1964. Prospective employers asked 'How can a little girl like you teach a great big class of men?' and 'Who did the research for you?' Even in a booming job market she received no job offers. Disappointed and outraged, she found support, and a feasible explanation for her own experience, in the emergence of feminism. She became a founding member of the Chicago Women's Liberation Movement. An organized women's movement, she came to believe, was more likely to 'change this man's world and this man's science' than were the empiricism and scientific reasoning she had cherished and nurtured for years. (Herman, 1995: 281)

Another landmark was the publication by Bernstein and Russo (1974) of 'The history of psychology revisited: Or, up with our foremothers'. In that article, Bernstein and Russo argued that 'male bias pervades the very essence of the profession—the historical definition of psychology itself' (ibid., 130). They went on to demonstrate that the contributions of women to psychology had not been acknowledged, and called for changes to the psychology curriculum so that students not only would be able to 'study the psychology of women, [but] also the women of psychology' (ibid., 133). Furomoto (1989) called this 'compensatory history', in the sense that it reminds us of the contributions of women that have been neglected by previous historians. For example, the contributions of Christine Ladd-Franklin (see Chapter 3) and Mary Calkins (see Chapter 4) have often been left out of older histories.

Furomoto (ibid., 24) noted that an extension of such research is the 'reconstruction of women's experiences' (e.g., Scarborough and Furomoto, 1987). Describing women's experiences as women was a central strand of feminist scholarship (Banister et al., 1994: 122). A recurrent theme was that the psychology of women has been presented from a masculine perspective, not from the perspective of women themselves. One response to this problem was an increase in the number of discussions of the psychology of women that were written by women (e.g., Dinnerstein, 1977; Matlin, 1987).

Kimball observed that feminist psychologists have worked within two different traditions. One tradition emphasized the similarities between the genders and discounted the importance of differences between them. The work of Letta Hollingworth, which we considered in Chapter 13, belongs to this tradition. The other tradition emphasized the 'positive human characteristics that have been undervalued because they are associated with women and with the symbolic feminine. Central to the concerns of this tradition are the sense of connectedness, concern with human relationships, and care giving that women, more than men, bring to human culture' (Kimball, 1994: 389).

The career of Evelyn Fox Keller (1985, 1995a, 1995b; Marder, 1993) is a good example of the second tradition in feminist scholarship that has influenced the history of science and of psychology. Keller received her Ph.D. in theoretical physics from Harvard at a time when it was extremely unusual for a woman to do so. She was not only struck by the relative absence of women in the sciences, but also by the fact that the style of thinking practised by scientists had a masculine origin. Keller began her analysis of the role of gender in science by quoting Simone de Beauvoir: 'Representation of the world, like the world itself, is the work of men; they describe it from their own point of view, which they confuse with the absolute truth' (Keller, 1985: 3).

The one-sidedness of masculine-oriented science is reflected in the view that science is an objective set of procedures that has the control of nature as its goal. Keller believed that traditional accounts of science tended to ignore the role played by factors such as intuition, empathy, and personal engagement. These qualities are not 'actually feminine attributes', but 'they have traditionally been seen as such' (Marder, 1993: 24). There is no necessity to the traditional view of the nature of science any more than there is a necessity to traditional views of the differences between genders.

> Both gender and science are socially constructed categories. Science is the name we give to a set of practices and a body of knowledge delineated by a community, not simply defined by the exigencies of logical proof and experimental verification. Similarly, masculine and feminine are categories defined by a culture, not by biological necessity. Women, men, and science are created, together, out of a complex dynamic of interwoven cognitive, emotional, and social forces. (Keller, 1985: 3–4)

Keller argued that we need to become aware of the **science-gender system** whereby our conception of gender and our conception of science mutually determine one another (ibid., 8). For example, a feminist analysis of science brings out the extent to which science is a personal as well as a social process—aspects of science that tend not to appear in traditional accounts of the history of science. Keller did not mean that the successes of 'masculine' science should be ignored, but that we need to acknowledge the degree to which the language and practices of science are 'fueled and elaborated, and sometimes also subverted, by the more parochial social, political, and emotional commitments (conscious or not) of particular individuals and groups' (ibid., 11). A feminist approach to the history of science insisted that these aspects of science be openly discussed, and not dismissed as irrelevant.

Psychology as a Social Construction

The notion that psychology, like other sciences, is a social construction is suggested by the approaches to history we have just considered. The paradigm concept and feminism both imply that psychology does not simply involve the objective accumulation of knowledge, but is also driven by social processes (e.g., Gergen, 1985). As a classic text in **social constructionism** put it:

> [People are] biologically predestined to construct and to inhabit a world with others. This world becomes for [them] the dominant and definite reality. Its limits are set by nature, but, once constructed, this world acts back upon nature. In the dialectic between nature and the socially constructed world the human organism is itself transformed. In this same dialectic [people] produce reality and thereby produce [themselves]. (Berger and Luckmann, 1967: 204)

In this context, a **dialectical process** is one in which opposing tendencies shape one another. The opposing tendencies of interest to social constructionists are the exogenic and the endogenic (Gergen, 1985: 269). '**Exogenic**' means 'coming from outside', and many psychologists have stressed the importance of factors external to the person as determinants of human experience. The classic example of the exogenic perspective is British empiricism. '**Endogenic**' means 'coming from inside', and refers to those psychologists who believe that 'humans harbor inherent tendencies . . . to think, categorize, or process information, and it is these tendencies (rather than features of the world in itself) that are of paramount importance in fashioning knowledge' (ibid.). Kant is the classic example of a theorist who takes an endogenic perspective.

Social constructionists acknowledged the limitations of both the endogenic and the exogenic perspectives. They attempted to avoid the problems inherent in each by moving to a new level of discourse in which knowledge is no longer seen as 'something people possess somewhere in their heads, but rather, something people do together' (ibid., 270). This means that psychological concepts are to be understood as the outcome of social processes. In particular, social constructionists focused on the way in which language shapes how we understand ourselves and others. The linguistic philosophy of Ludwig Wittgenstein was particularly influential in this regard.

Ludwig Wittgenstein (1889–1951)

Born in Austria, **Ludwig Wittgenstein** was a charismatic philosopher who deeply influenced many other philosophers, scientists, and social scientists throughout the twentieth century. Wittgenstein's work is usually thought of as falling into two distinct periods. It is customary to make a distinction between his early work, such as *Tractatus Logico-Philosophicus* (1974 [1922]) and his later work, such as *Philosophical Investigations* (1953). His early work shaped the logical positivist movement in the 1920s, a movement discussed in Chapter 10. However, Wittgenstein subsequently came to believe that approaches such as logical positivism were too simple. He turned to an examination of how concepts are used in ordinary language. This examination revealed a much more complex array of relationships between concepts than one might have expected. The complexity and philosophical nature of Wittgenstein's method is seen in his addressing of the question, What do all members of a category have in common? For example, what do all weapons have in common that makes them weapons? Or what do all vehicles have in common that makes them vehicles?

> Consider for example the proceedings we call 'games.' I mean board-games, card-games, ball-games, Olympic games, and so on. What is common to them all? Don't say: 'There must be something common, or they would not be called "games"'—but look and see whether there is anything common to all.— For if you look at them you will not see something that is common to all, but similarities, relationships, and a whole series of them at that. To repeat: don't think, but look!—Look for example at board-games, with their multifarious relationships. Now pass to card games; here you find many correspondences with the first group, but many common features drop

out, and others appear. When we pass next to ball-games, much that is common is retained, but much is lost.—Are they all 'amusing'? Compare chess with noughts and crosses [X's and O's]. Or is there always winning and losing, or competition between players? Think of patience. In ball games there is winning and losing; but when a child throws his ball at the wall and catches it again, this feature has disappeared. Look at the parts played by skill and luck; and at the difference between skill in chess and skill in tennis. Think now of games like ring-a-ring-a-roses; here is the element of amusement, but how many other characteristic features have disappeared! And we can go through the many, many other groups of games in the same way; can see how similarities crop up and disappear. (Wittgenstein, 1953: 31–2)

Wittgenstein pointed out that we do not place events together in a category because they all have something in common. Rather, we may give the same name to each member of a very heterogeneous set of events (e.g., 'games', 'furniture', 'weapons'). The concepts we ordinarily use do not admit of a very precise definition. It is impossible to define concepts such as these on the basis of what is common to all examples of the category without leaving out some members of the category. Thus, if we define games in terms of winning and losing, then some activities we normally call games will be left out. The same thing happens no matter how we choose to construct the definition. Any definition produces anomalous cases that do not fit the definition.

Psychological concepts can be analyzed in same way that Wittgenstein analyzed 'games'. Psychological concepts have their origin in ordinary language. For example, does the concept of 'emotion' admit of a precise definition, or will examples of what we ordinarily call emotion always resist a neat, logical classification? Moreover, is not our use of the word 'emotion' the result of the socialization practices in our culture? Might not different cultures have very different concepts of emotion, or even none at all?

Imagine that the people of a tribe were brought up from early youth to give no expression of feeling *of any kind*. They find it childish, something to be got rid of. Let the training be severe. 'Pain' is not spoken of; especially in the form of a conjecture 'Perhaps he has got . . .'. If anyone complains, he is ridiculed or punished. There is no such thing as the suspicion of shamming. Drilling someone to speak expressionlessly, in a monotone, to move mechanically.

I want to say: an education quite different from ours might also be the foundation for quite different concepts. (Wittgenstein, 1980: 118)

If we follow Wittgenstein's analyses, we are led to the conclusion that any theory based on precise definitions of concepts will fail to account for all cases. Even though precise definition is the hallmark of science as conceived of by some philosophers of science, such as the logical positivists, it turns out that precise definition leaves out many examples that could be of interest to us. As David Bloor (1983: 138; 1996) observed, Wittgenstein's analysis implies that everyone, including psychologists, will inevitably encounter events that do not fit nicely into one's favourite theory. Events that do not fit our theories are **anomalies**, and it appears that we have no shortage of them. Drawing on the work of the anthropologist Mary Douglas (1978, 1982), Bloor (1983) considered four ways in which we deal with anomalies: **indifference**, **exclusion**, **accommodation**, and **opportunism**.

Indifference. One can argue that the anomaly is trivial and not worth bothering with. Thus, events that cannot be accommodated easily within a particular theory may be discounted as unimportant. This is the easiest strategy to adopt, and if it works then the theory will be preserved. There is no end to the examples in psychology that illustrate this pattern. Virtually all the major schools, from introspectionism to Gestalt psychology, from psychoanalysis to humanistic psychology, and from behaviourism to cognitive psychology, have argued that the phenomena with which they were dealing were the really important ones, and that the phenomena with which they did not deal were either unimportant, or that a consideration of them could be postponed, perhaps indefinitely.

Exclusion. If an anomaly is acknowledged as important by enough people then it will threaten to force itself to be considered. At that point one may see the occurrence of another strategy that Lakatos (1976) called **monster barring**. Monster barring involves deliberately trying to exclude the anomalous phenomenon. Bloor (1983: 143) suggests that the controversy between Wundt and the Würzburg group illustrates this strategy. We considered this controversy in Chapter 4. The Würzburgers had insisted on the legitimacy of experimentally investigating 'higher mental processes', which Wundt maintained were outside of the scope of experimental psychology. Wundt was not indifferent to the Würzburgers' efforts, but actively tried to exclude them. Another example of this strategy that readily comes to mind is Freud's response to anyone who wanted to introduce major changes into psychoanalysis.

Accommodation. If forced to do so, the theorist may accept the importance of the anomaly and try to restructure the theory to accommodate to it. The behavioural theorists' reaction to the phenomenon of transposition, which we considered in Chapter 11, is an example of this possibility.

Opportunism. While accommodation may be the most sociable procedure for dealing with anomalies, it is far from the most common. A very common tactic in psychology is opportunism, which involves regarding anomalies as opportunities for introducing novel theoretical approaches. This leads to the proliferation of theories. Every time a new concept is introduced—whether it is the split brain or the inner child—there are many people who rush to generate theories that elaborate upon the new idea. This has both positive and

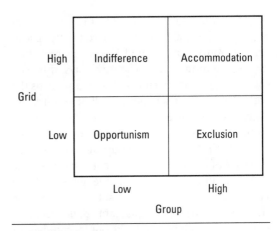

FIGURE 15.3
Responses to anomalies.

negative aspects. On the one hand, it ensures that the discipline remains active and engaged with contemporary concerns. Thus, psychology is a very popular discipline in America among undergraduates. On the other hand, it means that the discipline tends to be faddish and not to develop in a smooth and consistent way.

Figure 15.3 presents a classification scheme derived from the work of Bloor (1983) and Douglas (1978). The two dimensions in the figure have been labelled *grid* and *group*. By 'grid', Douglas (1982) meant the degree to which people occupy specific roles within a group. 'High grid' translates into a group with a clear hierarchical arrangement, with individual roles determined by definite rules. The 'group' dimension refers to the degree to which someone belongs to a particular group. 'Low group' translates into not belonging to a particular school or faction; high group translates into a strong commitment to a particular school or faction. Of course, the four quadrants of Figure 15.3 should not be seen as rigid categories, but only provide a rough guide to the possible social relations between psychologists and how these social relations influence their theorizing.

According to Bloor (1983: 141), the lower right-hand quadrant is characterized by strong feelings of group membership but low differentiation among group members. The early days of behaviourism must have been like this, and perhaps the early days of most schools are full of enthusiasm, with little internal discord. However, there is a corresponding tendency to exclude anyone who does not share the tenets of the group, again quite characteristic of a school in its early, enthusiastic stages. If there is little feeling of group membership, but a clear pecking order, then the situation is the one described by the top left quadrant. Under such circumstances, each person looks out for him/herself and is indifferent to the concerns of others. One would not expect to find people becoming outstanding figures in the history of psychology under conditions like these. People who are indifferent to others tend to find that others are indifferent to them. A more interesting case is the lower left quadrant in which one finds the entrepreneurs in psychology. These are people who are not concerned with group membership, or with status, but only with developing whatever new ideas come along. Many of the people we considered in Chapters 13 and 14, such as Maslow and Neisser, might be seen as belonging here. Neither one attempted to recruit followers, yet both were very aware of what were 'hot topics'. The top right quadrant is probably quite rare in psychology, because few if any approaches have developed to the point where there is not only a clear set of criteria for group membership, but also a clear set of criteria for 'progress through the ranks'. It will be interesting to see if any current approaches will reach such a state.

Psychological Research as a Social Construction

The idea that psychology is a social construction is disturbing to many people because it suggests that psychological research is not 'objective'. Although social constructionists vary in the extent to which they believe that psychological research is entirely a social construction, there is no doubt

that all of them believe that it is at least to some extent a social construction (Stam, 1990). Jill Morawski (1988; Morawski and Steele, 1991) described the situation:

> What actually occurs in the design and execution of an experiment includes complex negotiations about what is being observed and what counts as an observation. The written account of a laboratory event is itself the product of rhetorical deftness and artful editing. What kinds of experiments are conducted depends on the research community's customs, ethics, economics, policy interests, and even fads. What goes on in experimental laboratories is not limited solely by explicit methodological rules, but involves practical problem-solving by common-sense reasoners. Conventional histories of psychology recount none of these conditions of laboratory work. (Morawski, 1988: 73)

Other scholars point out that scientific research could both be a social construction and still be 'true' in some objective sense.

> The fact that scientific theories are themselves socially constructed is quite neutral with respect to the issue of . . . objectivity. Many theoretical concepts and models are of course socially constructed or created, in the sense that their meaning is not defined . . . by operational definitions in terms of observables. The concept of the double helical structure of DNA was not introduced by Watson and Crick to conventionally refer to something they could directly observe. This theoretical concept and its meaningful content were social in origin. Yet this does not preclude us from holding the view that Watson and Crick's theoretical account provides a more accurate description of the real dimensions of DNA than alternative theoretical accounts, nor does it oblige us to presuppose that DNA itself (as opposed to our theoretical concept of it) is socially constructed or created. (Greenwood, 1992: 139)

Thus, some social constructionist historians of psychology focus on the social processes that determine how psychological research is conducted without claiming that the products of this research necessarily have no empirical content. This is the spirit in which **Kurt Danziger** (1987, 1990, 1992, 1994, 1997) has contended that the psychological experiment is an elaborate social construction.

From Danziger's (1990) perspective, the psychological experiment came about as a part of psychology's overall strategy of claiming to have 'expert knowledge or knowledge different from everyday or common knowledge' (Stam, 1992: 630). A central feature of this strategy was the creation of a special setting—the psychological experiment—in which 'data' could be gathered and analyzed using the kinds of statistical methods we considered in Chapter 10. Thus, a central feature of psychological research in the twentieth century was that 'researchers moved away from their early emphasis on data ascribed to individual subjects and began to report their results in terms of groups, which were often analyzed statistically' (Capshew, 1992). As Danziger (1990: 85) put it, data gathered in the psychological laboratory 'points the way to a science that supplies its own categories for classifying people and is not dependent on the unreflected categories of everyday life. . . . [T]here is now the possibility that psychologically constituted collectivities will compete with and even replace some of the more traditional categories of social grouping. Categorizing children or recruits by intelligence quotient was an early example of such a process.' Thus, not only has psychological research itself been a social construction, but its results have led to a reconstruction of the social categories we now use.

> [T]he profound relevance of the history of a discipline for understanding the content of that discipline arises out of the recognition that *there is no such thing as a private science.* Any epistemic access to the world afforded by a science like psychology is a collective access, and the objects to which the practices of the science are directed cannot be other than social objects constructed through the interaction of real historical individuals. The norms which regulate psychological research practice are, of course, social norms and as such are the product of specific historical conditions. (Danziger, 1992: 256)

Far from detracting from the scientific content of psychology, 'a measure of historical sophistication about their field would work wonders for the ability of psychologists to enrich the cultural life of their own as well as other societies. And because they would be less dependent on current fads the quality of their more technical contributions might be expected to improve as well' (Danziger, 1994: 481).

Psychology, Modernism, and Postmodernism

Modernism

In many ways, the story of psychology in the twentieth century is the story of a typically modern discipline. That is, psychology defined itself and was defined by others in terms that are characteristic of twentieth-century modernism (Shore, 2001: 76–9). 'Modernism' is a term that is often used in connection with the arts, and Vitz and Glimcher (1984) showed numerous parallels between the development of art and psychology in the twentieth century. Sometimes the parallels reflect the attempts by a group of artists to apply a particular psychological theory to their work. An example of this kind of parallelism is the use of Gestalt theory by the Bauhaus school of architecture (ibid., 164). Other times the parallels are less specific, reflecting a mutuality of interest. An example of this kind of parallel is the mutual interest in dreams shared by psychoanalysis and the surrealist movement (ibid., 257). Although the relations between psychology and art are complex, the parallels between them are sufficient to demonstrate that both psychology and art respond to and illustrate similar cultural trends.

As Janik and Toulmin argued, twentieth-century **modernism** was in part a reaction against what was perceived as the excesses of the late nineteenth century. The nineteenth-century 'Victorian' style found expression in the kitsch art we often consider to be representative of the era. For examples of this decorative style, see any Sears catalogue from the 1890s. Every object, from stoves to watches, has elaborate ornamentation that is irrelevant to the function of the object. Thus, a pocket watch will have a complex but merely decorative backing, such as an engraving of a moose emerging from the forest at the edge of a lake. This is quite different from what one would find on the back of a twentieth-century watch, which is likely to be no decoration at all. The same point could be made by comparing objects, such as furniture and buildings, made then and made after a twentieth-century style established itself. Janik and Toulmin (1973: 43) describe how a typical parlour looked prior to the emergence of a twentieth-century style.

> Nowhere was the true nature of the era more apparent than in the lack of style which marked its design. Having no style of their own, they could only imitate the past; so they filled their homes with garish objets d'art in differing styles. Again and again, the complex was preferred to the simple, the decorative to the useful, resulting in rooms that were vulgar to look at and barely habitable.

Of course, many rooms still fit this description, but it is nonetheless true that many intellectuals in the twentieth century attempted to eliminate anything that might be merely decorative, and instead insisted that there should be no parts of structures that are merely decorative and serve no function. A pioneer of this way of thinking was the Viennese architect Adolf Loos (1870–1933), who said that 'Cultural evolution is equivalent to the removal of ornament from articles in use', and that 'The architect should follow the plumber as his model, not the sculptor' (ibid., 93). Loos was by no means the only person to hold such views. One only has to compare nineteenth-century buildings with the steel and glass slabs that came to dominate the centres of cities during the twentieth century to see how widespread this attitude was.

Gardner and Stevens (1992) have shown how much of psychology was closely tied to the rich cultural context of Vienna during the first few decades of the twentieth century. However, the modern attitude was also present in America, and one does not need to look further than John B. Watson for an example of how early twentieth-century psychologists saw nineteenth-century psychology as 'merely decorative'. Recall, for example, Watson's (1966 [1913]: 74) claim that 'The time seems to have come when psychology must discard all reference to consciousness; when it need no longer delude itself into thinking that it is making mental states the object of observation.' The next step in the evolution of psychology, for Watson, entailed the elimination of 'philosophical speculation', which 'need trouble the student of behavior as little as' it troubles 'the student of physics . . . I can state my position here no better than by saying that I should like to bring my students up in the same ignorance of such hypotheses as one finds among the students of branches of science.' Watson should not be singled out—his writing was only the clearest expression of the modern attitude towards the recent past. Earlier forms of psychology were largely worthless and could be safely ignored.

However, as the twentieth century progressed, the modern attitude towards the past began to wear a bit thin. Some cultural critics even argued that by eliminating so much of the past, we had thrown out much that had been of value. A good example of this development was Wolfe's *From Bauhaus to Our House* (1981: 7), a scathing critique of modern architecture.

> Every child goes to school in a building that looks like a duplicating-machine replacement parts wholesale distribution warehouse. . . . Every new $900,000 summer house in the north

woods or on the shore of Long Island has so many pipe railings, ramps, hob-tread metal spiral stairways, sheets of industrial plate glass, banks of tungsten-halogen lamps, and white cylindrical shapes, it looks like an insecticide refinery. I once saw the owners of such a place driven to the edge of sensory deprivation by the whiteness & lightness & leanness & cleanness & bareness & spareness of it all. They became desperate for an antidote, such as coziness and color.

Once the products of modernism began to be seen as not satisfying enough, then there was a tendency to turn and look back before modernism to see if there was not something in our earlier history that might improve the situation. The attempt to recycle the past and use it in a contemporary context is an essential part of the postmodern attitude.

Postmodernism

As Kvale (1992: 2) observed, 'the very term "postmodern" is controversial and ambiguous.' Christopher Jencks, a leading postmodern architect, noted that **postmodernism** was used by Arnold Toynbee (1888–1975) in his monumental *A Study of History* (1960 [1947]) to refer to 'a new historical cycle' signifying 'pluralism and a world culture' (Jencks, 1986: 2). Jencks noted as well that postmodernists did not reject the achievements of modernism, but hoped to appeal to a broader audience than did modernism. Thus, regardless of the discipline, postmodernists tended to argue for a more democratic and open system than may have existed previously.

As a part of broadening its appeal, postmodernism harked back to earlier forms that had been rejected by modernists. Of course, these earlier forms cannot be used in precisely the same way in which they were originally used. Consequently, a postmodern creation incorporates the past, but in a sophisticated way. Jencks uses an example from Umberto Eco (1984: 67–8) to illustrate this point:

I think of the postmodern attitude as that of a man who loves a very cultivated woman and knows he cannot say to her, 'I love you madly,' because he knows that she knows (and that she knows that he knows) that these words have already been written by Barbara Cartland. Still, there is a solution. He can say, 'As Barbara Cartland would put it, I love you madly.' At this point, having avoided false innocence, having said clearly that it is no longer possible to speak innocently, he will nevertheless have said what he wanted to say to the woman: that he loves her, but he loves her in an age of lost innocence. If the woman goes along with this, she will have received a declaration of love all the same. Neither of the two speakers will feel innocent, both will have accepted the challenge of the past, of the already said, which cannot be eliminated, both will consciously and with pleasure play the game of irony. . . . But both will have succeeded, once again, in speaking of love.

One of the signs of postmodernism is the reassertion of values that have previously been rejected. The person confronted with something postmodern 'is likely to have a shock of the old' (Jencks, 1986: 43). However, these values are not asserted in the same old way, but their historical status is acknowledged. One of the signs of a postmodern attitude is the revival of previously rejected forms of psychology. A good example is the rehabilitation of Wundt's approach to psychology, which we discussed in Chapter 3. It is not that Wundtian psychology was simply reasserted as the best approach, but rather that its value was being reassessed and used to enrich more recent approaches. One of the prospects of a postmodern psychology is the continuous re-evaluation of the past.

Postmodernism does not only mean an openness to the past. It also means an openness to those whose viewpoints may have been neglected. Postmodernism is pluralistic and multicultural (Gergen, 1991a, 1991b, 1994; Sampson, 1993). A postmodern psychology is open to the possibility that any approach to psychology might be legitimate. No approach to psychology necessarily has priority over any other approach. While some scholars, such as the postmodernist Kenneth Gergen (1994: 414), have seen postmodernism as an opportunity to 'live less aggressively, more tolerantly, and even more creatively with others in the world', others, such as M. Brewster Smith (1994), have lamented what they saw as the fragmentation of psychology that resulted from adopting a postmodern attitude.

The exchange between Gergen and Smith elicited a great deal of debate (e.g., Denner, 1995; Gergen, 1995, 2001; Mente, 1995; Russell and Gaubatz, 1995; Smith, 1995; White and Wang, 1995). There was clearly a tension between the *hedgehogs* and the *foxes*, to use the typology of Isaiah Berlin (1953). Hedgehogs 'try to relate everything to a single system or vision', while foxes 'pursue many different paths without trying to fit them together. . . . The distinction is based on the words of the Greek poet Archilochus, who said, "The fox knows many things, but the hedgehog knows one big thing"' (Sternberg and Grigorenko, 2001: 1069). Was psychology to be a discipline in which the proponents of a unified science (the hedgehogs) felt at home or was it to be one that suited the postmodern foxes?

The Differentiation of Psychology

One of the consequences of postmodernism has been that the previously dominant forms of psychology have found themselves competing for attention with any number of alternative approaches to psychology. There can be no doubt that psychology became more and more differentiated, increasing the number of factions within the discipline. Worldwide, there are a great many different national and international organizations to which psychologists belong, and one historically important example is given in Box 15.1. However, it is instructive at this point to examine the recent history of the American Psychological Association (APA), not only because it is the largest national association of psychologists, but also because its dynamics are probably similar to those elsewhere. One useful measure of differentiation within psychology is the number of divisions, or 'special interest groups', that were created within the APA. The APA had 20 divisions in 1960, representing very broad categories such as clinical psychology, developmental psychology, and experimental psychology. 'Since 1960, there has been a relatively steady increase, with the addition of 28 new divisions . . . in 35 years, for a rate of 0.8 divisions per year' (Dewsbury, 1997b: 733). The newer divisions tended to emphasize 'health, therapy, and assorted applied functions' (ibid., 736) with a corresponding decline in membership of 'basic science divisions' (ibid., 737).

As divisions proliferated, many American psychologists who had hoped for and worked towards a unified discipline believed that psychology had become too diversified. 'In my worst nightmares I foresee a decimation of institutional psychology as we know it. Human experimental psychologists desert to the emerging discipline of cognitive science; physiological psychologists go happily to departments of biology and neuroscience; industrial/organizational psychologists are snapped up by business schools; and psychopathologists find their home in medical schools' (Spence, 1987: 1053). Without a unifying paradigm to hold psychology together, what is to keep it from flying apart, with each aspect of psychology being assimilated by more established disciplines, such as biology, medicine, and economics?

As Dewsbury (1997b) observed, the growing influence of the non-academic sector was characteristic of the APA over the last few decades of the twentieth century. This was especially clear in the growth in membership of the APA since World War II.

> The number of health care providers has rapidly expanded to the point of rivaling or outstripping the number of those in academic specialties, and

| BOX 15.1 |

THE INTERNATIONAL UNION OF PSYCHOLOGICAL SCIENCE

Rozenzweig et al. (2000: xi) have traced the history of the **International Union of Psychological Science**, 'not only since its founding at the 14th International Congress of Psychology at Stockholm, 1951, but going back to 1881, when a young Polish psychologist' named Julian Ochorowicz (1850–1917) 'first proposed the ideas of an international Congress and of an international association of psychological societies.' Women, including Christine Ladd-Franklin, figure prominently in this history. Others are less well known, such as Jozefa Joteyko (1866–1928), a Polish scientist and the first woman appointed to the International Congress Committee. Many women attended the early congresses, and 'the announcements for the 3rd and 4th [1896 and 1900] congresses stated that women would be accorded the same rights and privileges as men' (ibid., 25).

Many of the great names in the history of psychology have played central roles in the history of the organization. A partial list of those who were active before 1950 includes: Baldwin, Bartlett, Bechterew, Binet, Boring, Bott, C. Bühler, Ebbinghaus, Ehrenfels, Galton, Hebb, James, Köhler, Pavlov, Spearman, Thorndike, Titchener, Tolman, Washburn, and Wundt. It is easy to see that the International Union of Psychological Science provided a context within which psychology could develop as an international discipline.

Rozenzweig et al. acknowledge that the development of the Union was not without controversy. Sometimes these controversies appear to have arisen mainly because of 'personal rivalries and piques' (ibid., 41). For example, the 13th Congress was cancelled because the organizers had difficulty agreeing on the committee memberships (Evans and Down Scott, 1978). However, other controversies appear to reflect some of the deeper schisms within psychology itself. For example, there was a discussion at the 1948 Edinburgh Congress concerning the proper name for the group. Some, including Jean Piaget, argued against calling it simply the 'International Union of Psychology' and insisted on the 'International Union of Scientific Psychology'. The intention was to distinguish the group from 'certain literary or philosophical forms of psychology' and 'certain therapeutic practices' (Rozenzweig et al., 2000: 60).

In general, however, the Union served to unite psychology rather than divide it. As Dumont and Louw (2001: 400) write, it 'has provided a major institutional forum for the internationalization of psychology, especially in its rapid growth since World War II. The formation and development of this organization demonstrated that psychologists, regardless of the country in which they lived and worked, belonged to one international psychological community.'

the resulting shift in the balance of power within APA has been well documented. . . . These changes have made it inevitable that attention to professional rather than scientific issues . . . has come to dominate APA activities. It was also inevitable that the greatest political and organizational conflicts within the Association would occur along the scientist-practitioner fracture line. (Spence, 1987: 1053)

Thus, by the end of the 1980s many academic psychologists were feeling alienated from the APA. Just as many other groups felt that their voices were not being heard by academic psychology (Sampson, 1993), so many academic psychologists felt that their voices were not being heard by the APA. The upshot of this discontent was the formation of the American Psychological Society (APS) in 1988, the goal of which was to 'advance the discipline of Psychology and preserve its scientific base; to promote public understanding of psychological science and its applications; and to encourage the "giving away" of psychology in the public interest' (Rodgers, 1990: 81).

Five years after its founding, the APS had 15,000 members. Interviews with individuals who had been central figures in the emergence of APS felt that it met:

> scientific psychologists' need for what many simply called 'identification' and 'a home.' . . . And several added that APS seemed to be reversing a trend that saw researchers casting aside the 'psychology' label of their core behavioral discipline and adopting the labels of other fields. Others found that APS was stimulating a deeper awareness of psychology's essentially scientific roots throughout the discipline. (Kent, 1993: 4)

Some members of the APS argued that by stressing the 'unity that exists in psychology', the APS represented a 'trend toward undifferentiation' (Hayes, 1993: 16). However, looking across American psychology as a whole, the picture was perhaps best described by Dewsbury. Looking back to the work of Herbert Spencer, Dewsbury (1997b: 737) likened the proliferation of divisions to the 'Spencerian pattern of progressive differentiation from homogeneity to heterogeneity'. However, it should be remembered that Spencer regarded development as consisting not simply of differentiation but also of integration between the different parts. While some were urging the integration of the modern and postmodern strands in psychology (e.g., Martin and Sugarman, 2000), others (e.g., Glassman, 2001; Greer, 2001) feared that such an integration could not do justice to either party.

The Future of the History of Psychology

For decades, academic psychologists subscribed to the version of the history of psychology that had been written by the discipline's best-known historian, **Edwin G. Boring** (1929, 1950b). Boring's history was originally written in the 1920s, when psychology in the United States was just as divided between 'scientists' and 'practitioners' as it was in the latter part of the century (O'Donnell, 1979). Boring realized that a history of psychology was not merely an objective recording of what had happened in the past. Rather, Boring's history was intended to persuade psychologists that academic, experimental psychology was the ideal form of psychology and should take priority over applied psychology. Boring's history was immensely scholarly, but it was also intentionally biased towards telling psychology's story from the point of view of an experimental psychologist (ibid.).

Many of the institutional problems that faced psychology as the twentieth century drew to a close were eerily similar to those that faced psychology in Boring's day. As a consequence, it is tempting to conclude that psychology as a discipline found itself on Ixion's wheel rather than climbing Jacob's ladder, to echo a theme we sounded in Chapter 1. However, the story of psychology does not admit of so simple a conclusion. This is partly true because the nature of storytelling itself changed since Boring told his story (e.g., O'Hara, 1992).

It was once conventional for stories to be told from a single point of view, with a single protagonist. Thus, Boring's history is from the viewpoint of an experimental psychologist, whose progress is synonymous with the progress of psychology itself. This is analogous to telling the story of evolution from the viewpoint of human beings, whose evolutionary triumph is the point of the story (ibid., 144). This way of telling the story of evolution seemed obvious to nineteenth-century thinkers such as Herbert Spencer, but it was much less obvious at the end of the twentieth century.

As the twentieth century drew to a close, it became more common to argue that history should not simply be told as 'the story of events which have been important in the history of us' (ibid., 154). History is not one story, but many.

When we come to realize that even among the vertebrates there are 50,000 different 'vertebrate stories', each one with a different ending and each one with a different narrative landscape; when we truly think in terms of the diverging tree, instead of the line; when we understand that it is absurd to talk of one animal being higher than another; only then will we see the full grandeur of the historical view of life. (Ibid., 157)

The history of psychology is but a tiny part of history as a whole. Nevertheless, within the history of psychology the same principles apply as apply to evolutionary history. There are many more stories that should be told than possibly can be told, and each story deserves as much respect as any other. No matter how inclusive a particular history of psychology may be, there will still be many parts of psychology that will not have been considered as fully as they might be. It is the task of future histories to continue to expand the range of viewpoints included and to do justice to the variety of psychologies and psychologists.

IMPORTANT NAMES, WORKS, AND CONCEPTS

Names and Works

Beauvoir, Simone de

Boring, Edwin G.

Danziger, Kurt

Furomoto, Laurel

Kuhn, Thomas

The Second Sex

The Structure of Scientific Revolutions

Wittgenstein, Ludwig

Concepts

accommodation

anomalies

dialectical process

endogenic

exclusion

exogenic

feminism

indifference

International Union of Psychological Science

mentalism

modernism

monster barring

new history of psychology

opportunism

paradigm

postmodernism

science-gender system

social constructionism

RECOMMENDED READINGS

New History of Science

I. Marková, *Paradigms, Thought, and Language* (Chichester, UK: Wiley, 1982), presents a scholarly analysis of the historical origins of the paradigm notion and its relation to a variety of psychological viewpoints. Another influential approach to the history of ideas grew out of Stephen C. Pepper's *contextualism*. See Pepper, 'The conceptual framework of Tolman's purposive behaviorism', *Psychological Review* 4 (1934): 108–33, and Pepper, *World Hypotheses* (Berkeley: University of California Press, 1970). Contextualism was made familiar to many American psychologists by James J. Jenkins, 'Remember that old theory of memory? Well, forget it', *American Psychologist* 29 (1974): 785–95. E.J. Capaldi and R.W. Proctor were highly critical of a contextualist approach to psychology and provided a thorough bibliography of contextualism. See their 'Contextualism: Is the act in context the adequate metaphor for scientific psychology?', *Psychonomic Bulletin & Review* 1 (1994): 239–49.

Feminism

For a review of the progress of women in American psychology in the final decades of the twentieth century, see M.E. Kite et al., 'Women psychologists in academe: Mixed progress, unwarranted complacency', *American Psychologist* 56 (2001): 1080–98. They concluded that, while the contributions of women had become more broadly recognized, 'barriers and obstacles persist, and their forms change as women move up the academic career ladder. Women need support at all points in their careers if they are to achieve their highest aspirations and fulfill their promise.' For a collection of papers on the development of feminist psychology and the psychology of women in Canada, see C. Storm and M. Gurevich, eds, 'Looking forward, looking back: Women in psychology', special issue of *Canadian Psychology* 42, 4 (2001). They observed that 'as long as women continue to be under-represented at levels where decisions are made, the interests and needs of feminist psychology and the psychology of women will not be adequately addressed' (p. 246).

Social Constructionism

Although we have been focusing on social constructionism as an approach to the history of psychology, K.J. Gergen and M.M. Gergen, eds, *Historical Social Psychology* (Hillsdale, NJ: Erlbaum, 1984), demonstrate how this approach can be applied to the study of psychological processes themselves. For an analysis and critique of the social constructionist approach to social psychology, see L. Wallach and M.A. Wallach, 'Gergen versus the mainstream', *Journal of Personality and Social Psychology* 67 (1994): 233–42. For thoughtful reviews of Danziger's *Constructing the Subject* (1990), see J.A. Mills, 'Deconstructing *Constructing the Subject*', *Theory and Psychology* 2 (1992): 248–50, and T.B. Rogers, 'Danziger and psychological testing', ibid., 251–4. Dorothy Ross, 'An historian's view of American Social Science', *Journal of the History of the Behavioral Sciences* 29 (1993): 99–111, provides an excellent overview of the history of social science from a perspective similar to the one we have been discussing in this section.

Modernism

Modernism is nowhere better illustrated than in the writings of the architect Le Corbusier. See his *The Modulor* (Cambridge, Mass.: Faber, 1954).

The Future of the History of Psychology

The history of psychology course has long been a fixture of psychology programs. However, some have expressed concern over its future, wondering whether it will retain its status as a mainstay of undergraduate and graduate education. See G. Bhatt and R. Tonks, 'What lies in the future of teaching the history of psychology?', *History and Philosophy of Psychology Bulletin* 14 (2002): 2–9. Others—e.g., A. Brock, 'Comment on Bhatt & Tonks: Reports of our death are greatly exaggerated', ibid., 10–16; A.H. Fuchs and W. Viney, 'The course in the history of psychology: present status and future concerns', *History of Psychology* 5 (2002): 3–15—are more sanguine, presenting evidence suggesting that 'individuals and programs appear to have a strong commitment to continuing the program into the future' (Fuchs and Viney, 2002: 12).

BIBLIOGRAPHY

Ach, N. 1951 [1905]. 'Determining tendencies and awareness', in Rapaport (1951: 15–38).

Adams-Webber, J.R. 1970. 'An analysis of the discriminant validity of several repertory grid indices', *British Journal of Psychology* 61: 83–90.

———. 1979. *Personal Construct Theory: Concepts and Research*. New York: Wiley.

Adler, H.E. 1992. 'William James and Gustav Fechner: From rejection to elective affinity', in Donnelly (1992: 253–62).

Alba, J.W., and L. Hasher. 1983. 'Is memory schematic?', *Psychological Bulletin* 93: 203–31.

Alcoholics Anonymous, 3rd edn. 1976. New York: Alcoholics Anonymous World Services.

Alexander, P. 1987. 'John Locke', in Gregory (1987: 438–9).

Allport, G. 1964. *Pattern and Growth in Personality*. New York: Holt, Rinehart and Winston.

———, P.E. Vernon, and G. Lindzey. 1960. *Manual: A Study of Values*. Boston: Houghton Mifflin.

Amacher, P. 1965. 'Freud's neurological education and its influence on psychoanalytic theory', *Psychological Issues* 4, 4: Monograph 16.

American Psychological Association. 1953 [1940]. *Psychoanalysis as Seen by Analyzed Psychologists*. Washington: APA.

Amundson, R. 1985. 'Psychology and epistemology: The place versus response controversy', *Cognition* 20: 127–53.

Anastasi, A., ed. 1965. *Individual Differences*. New York: Wiley.

Andersen, D.C., and L.J. Friedman. 1997. 'Erik Erikson on revolutionary leadership: Thematic trajectories', *Contemporary Psychology* 42: 1063–7.

Anderson, J.R. 2001. 'Herbert A. Simon (1916–2001)', *American Psychologist* 56: 516–18.

Anderson, K. 2001. 'Instincts and instruments', in Green et al. (2001: 153–74).

Angell, J.R. 1978 [1907]. 'The province of a functional psychology', in Hilgard (1978: 81–104).

Anglin, J. 1973. 'Editor's Preface', in Anglin, ed., *Beyond the Information Given*. New York: Norton, x–xii.

Ansbacher, H.L., and R.R. Ansbacher. 1964. *The Individual Psychology of Alfred Adler*. New York: Harper.

Anscombe, E., and P.T. Geach, eds. 1954. *Descartes: Philosophical Writings*. New York: Thomas Nelson.

Anzai, Y., and H.A. Simon. 1979. 'The theory of learning by doing', *Psychological Review* 86: 124–40.

Appignanesi, L., and J. Forrester. 1992. *Freud's Women*. New York: Basic Books.

Appleman, P., ed. 1979. *Darwin*. New York: Norton.

Archer, J., and B. Lloyd. 1982. *Sex and Gender*. Harmondsworth, UK: Penguin.

Arnheim, R. 1974. *Art and Visual Perception*. Berkeley: University of California Press.

———. 1986. 'The other Gustav Theodor Fechner', in Arnheim, ed., *New Essays on the Psychology of Art*. Berkeley: University of California Press, 39–49.

———. 1998. 'Wolfgang Köhler and Gestalt theory: an English translation of Köhler's introduction to "Die physischen Gestalten" for philosophers and biologists', *History of Psychology* 1: 21–6.

Aronson, L.R., E. Tobach, D.S. Lehrman, and J.S. Rosenblatt. 1970. *Development and Evolution of Behavior: Essays in Memory of T.C. Schneirla*. San Francisco: Freeman.

Asch, S.E. 1946. 'Forming impressions of personality', *Journal of Abnormal and Social Psychology* 41: 258–90.

———. 1952. *Social Psychology*. Englewood Cliffs, NJ: Prentice-Hall.

———. 1955. 'Opinions and social pressure', *Scientific American* 193: 31–5.

———. 1956. 'Studies of independence and conformity: I. A minority of one against a unanimous majority', *Psychological Monographs* 70: 1–70.

———. 1968a. 'Wolfgang Kohler: 1887–1967', *American Journal of Psychology* 81: 110–19.

———. 1968b. 'Gestalt theory', in *International Encyclopedia of the Social Sciences*. New York: Macmillan, 158–75.

—— and H.A. Witkin. 1948. 'Studies in space orientation. I. Perception of the upright with displaced visual fields', *Journal of Experimental Psychology: General* 38: 325–37.

—— and ——. 1992 [1948]. 'Studies in space orientation. II. Perception of the upright with displaced visual fields and with body tilted', *Journal of Experimental Psychology: General* 121: 407–18.

—— and H. Zukier. 1984. 'Thinking about persons', *Journal of Personality and Social Psychology* 6: 1230–40.

Ash, M.G. 1995. *Gestalt Psychology in German Culture 1890–1967: Holism and the Quest for Objectivity.* New York: Cambridge University Press.

—— and W.R. Woodward, eds. 1987. *Psychology in Twentieth-Century Thought and Society.* New York: Cambridge University Press.

Ashby, W.R. 1956. *Cybernetics.* London: Chapman & Hall.

Attneave, F. 1959. *Applications of Information Theory to Psychology.* New York: Holt, Rinehart and Winston.

Audley, R.J. 1980. Letter, *Bulletin of the British Psychological Society* 33: 135.

Augarde, T., ed. 1991. *The Oxford Dictionary of Modern Quotations.* Oxford: Oxford University Press.

Ausubel, D.P. 1968. *Educational Psychology: A Cognitive View.* New York: Holt, Rinehart and Winston.

Ayer, A.J. 1968. *The Origins of Pragmatism.* London: Macmillan.

Baars, B.J. 1986. *The Cognitive Revolution in Psychology.* New York: Guilford Press.

Backe, A. 2001. 'John Dewey and early Chicago functionalism', *History of Psychology* 4: 323–40.

Bakhurst, D. 2001. 'Review of Bekhterev's "Suggestion and its role in social life"', *Canadian Psychology* 42: 313–15.

Bahrick, H.P. 1984. 'Semantic memory in permastore: Fifty years of memory for Spanish learned in school', *Journal of Experimental Psychology: General* 113: 1–31.

—— and L.K. Hall. 1991. 'Lifetime maintenance of high school mathematics content', *Journal of Experimental Psychology: General* 120: 20–33.

Bakan, D. 1966. 'The test of significance in psychological research', *Psychological Bulletin* 66: 423–38.

Baldwin, J.M. 1897. *Mental Development of the Child and the Race*, 2nd edn. New York: Macmillan.

——. 1966 [1895]. 'Types of reaction', in Vanderplas (1966: 144–55).

——. 1966 [1896]. 'The "type theory" of reaction', in Vanderplas (1966: 164–73).

Baltes, P.B., and U.M. Staudinger. 1993. 'The search for a psychology of wisdom', *Current Directions in Psychological Science* 2: 75–80.

Bandura, A. 1965. 'Behavioral modifications through modeling procedures', in L. Krasner and L.P. Ullmann, eds, *Research in Behavior Modification.* New York: Holt, Rinehart and Winston, 310–40.

——. 1978. 'The self system in reciprocal determinism', *American Psychologist* 33: 344–58.

——. 1983. 'Temporal dynamics and decomposition of reciprocal determinism: A reply to Philips and Orton', *Psychological Review* 90: 166–70.

——. 1986. *Social Foundations of Thought and Action: A Social Cognitive Theory.* Englewood Cliffs, NJ: Prentice-Hall.

——, J.E. Grusec, and F.L. Menlove. 1967. 'Vicarious extinction of avoidance behavior', *Journal of Personality and Social Psychology* 5: 16–23.

——, D. Ross, and S. Ross. 1961. 'Transmission of aggression through imitation of aggressive models', *Journal of Abnormal and Social Psychology* 63: 575–82.

—— and R.H. Walters. 1963. *Social Learning and Personality Development.* New York: Holt, Rinehart and Winston.

Banister, P., E. Burman, I. Parker, M. Taylor, and C. Tindall. 1994. *Qualitative Methods in Psychology.* Buckingham, UK: Open University Press.

Bannister, D., and M. Bott. 1973. 'Evaluating the person', in P. Kline, ed., *New Approaches in Psychological Measurement.* London: Wiley, 157–77.

—— and F. Fransella. 1971. *Inquiring Man: The Theory of Personal Constructs.* Harmondsworth, UK: Penguin.

—— and J.M.M. Mair. 1968. *The Evaluation of Personal Constructs.* London: Academic Press.

Bantock, G.H. 1984. *Studies in the History of Educational Theory.* London: George Allen & Unwin.

Barnes, R.M. 1968. *Motion and Time Study: Design and Measurement of Work*, 6th edn. New York: Wiley.

Bartlett, F.C. 1932. *Remembering.* Cambridge: Cambridge University Press.

——. 1958. *Thinking: An Experimental and Social Study.* New York: Basic Books.

Bauer, R.A. 1952. *The New Man in Soviet Psychology.* Cambridge, Mass.: Harvard University Press.

Baumrin, J. 1975. 'Aristotle's empirical nativism', *American Psychologist* 30: 486–95.

Beatty, B. 1998. 'From laws of learning to a science of values: Efficiency and morality in Thorndike's educational psychology', *American Psychologist* 53: 1145–52.

Beauvoir, S. de. 1989 [1949]. *The Second Sex*. New York: Vintage.

Beck, J., ed. 1982. *Organization and Representation in Perception*. Hillsdale, NJ: Erlbaum.

Beck, L.W., ed. 'Introduction', in Kant (1950: vii–xx).

Beer, C.G. 1983. 'Darwin, instinct and ethology', *Journal of the History of the Behavioral Sciences* 19: 68–80.

Bekhterev, V.M. 2001 [1921]. *Collective Reflexology: The Complete Edition*, ed. L.H. Strickland, trans. E.L. Lockwood and A. Lockwood. New Brunswick, NJ: Transaction.

Bem, D.J., and C. Honorton. 1994. 'Does psi exist? Replicable evidence for an anomalous process of information transfer', *Psychological Bulletin* 115: 4–18.

Benedict, R. 1959. 'Mary Wollstonecraft', in M. Mead, ed., *Anthropologist at Work: Writings of Ruth Benedict*. Boston: Houghton Mifflin, 491–519.

———. 1989 [1935]. *Patterns of Culture*. Boston: Houghton Mifflin.

Benfari, R. 1991. *Understanding Your Management Style: Beyond the Myers-Briggs Type Indicators*. Lexington, Mass.: Lexington Books.

Benjafield, J. 1969a. 'Logical and empirical thinking in a problem solving task', *Psychonomic Science* 14: 285–6.

———. 1969b. 'Evidence that "thinking aloud" constitutes an externalization of inner speech', *Psychonomic Science* 15: 83–4.

———. 1983. 'Some psychological hypotheses concerning the evolution of constructs', *British Journal of Psychology* 74: 47–59.

———. 1985. 'A review of recent research on the Golden Section', *Empirical Studies of the Arts* 3: 117–34.

———. 1994. *Thinking Critically about Research Methods*. Boston: Allyn & Bacon.

———. 1997. *Cognition*, 2nd edn. Englewood Cliffs, NJ: Prentice-Hall.

———. 2001. 'The psychology of mathematical beauty in the nineteenth century', in Green et al. (2001: 87–105).

———. 2002a. 'Review of Bekhterev's *Collective Reflexology*', *Canadian Psychology* 43: 46–7.

———. 2002b. 'Research methods: A history of some important strands', *Archives of Suicide Research* 6: 5–14.

——— and T.R.G. Green. 1978. 'Golden section relations in interpersonal judgement', *British Journal of Psychology* 69: 25–35.

———, E. Pomeroy, and D. Jordan. 1976. 'Encounter groups: A return to the fundamental', *Psychotherapy: Theory, Research and Practice* 13: 387–9.

Benjamin, L.T. 1988. 'A history of teaching machines', *American Psychologist* 43: 703–12.

——— and D.N. Dixon. 1996. 'Dream analysis by mail: An American woman seeks Freud's advice', *American Psychologist* 51: 461–8.

———, M. Durkin, M. Link, M. Vestal, and J. Acord. 1992. 'Wundt's American doctoral students', *American Psychologist* 47: 123–31.

Benne, K.D. 1964. 'History of the T group in the laboratory setting', in L.P. Bradford, J.R. Gibb, and Benne, eds, *T-group Theory and Laboratory Method*. New York: Wiley, 80–135.

Bennett, J. 1971. *Locke, Berkeley, Hume*. Oxford: Clarendon Press.

Berger, P., and T. Luckmann. 1967. *The Social Construction of Reality*. Harmondsworth, UK: Penguin.

Bergman, G., and K.W. Spence. 1941. 'Operationism and theory in psychology', *Psychological Review* 48: 1–14.

Berkeley, G. 1910 [1709]. *A New Theory of Vision and Other Writings*. London: J.M. Dent.

Berlin, I. 1953. *The Hedgehog and the Fox*. New York: Simon & Schuster.

Berlyne, D.E. 1960. *Conflict, Arousal, and Curiosity*. New York: McGraw-Hill.

———. 1965. *Structure and Direction in Thinking*. New York: Wiley.

———. 1975. 'Behaviourism? Cognitive theory? Humanistic psychology—to Hull with them all!', *Canadian Psychological Review* 16: 69–80.

Bernstein, L. 1976. *The Unanswered Question*. Cambridge, Mass.: Harvard University Press.

Bernstein, M.D., and N.F. Russo. 1974. 'The history of psychology revisited: Or, up with our foremothers', *American Psychologist* 29: 130–4.

Berreby, D. 1994. 'Figures of speech: The rise and fall and rise of Chomsky's linguistics', *The Sciences* 34 (Jan.–Feb.): 44–9.

Bhatt, G., and R. Tonks. 2002. 'What lies in the future of teaching the history of psychology?', *History and Philosophy of Psychology Bulletin* 14: 2–9.

Bieri, J. 1955. 'Complexity-simplicity and predictive behavior', *Journal of Abnormal and Social Psychology* 51: 263–8.

———. 1961. 'Complexity-simplicity as a personality variable in cognitive and preferential behavior', in D.W. Fiske and S.R. Maddi, eds, *Functions of Varied Experience*. Homewood, Ill.: Dorsey, 355–79.

Bigelow, P. 1986. 'The indeterminability of time in "Sein und Zeit"', *Philosophy and Phenomenological Research* 46: 357–79.

Bilder, R.M., and F.F. LeFever, eds. 1998. 'Neuroscience of the mind on the centennial of Freud's "Project for a Scientific Psychology"', *Annals of the New York Academy of Sciences* 843.

Binet, A. 1969 [1903]. 'Imageless thought', in R.H. Pollack and M.J. Brenner, *The Experimental Psychology of Alfred Binet*. New York: Springer, 207–21.

——— and T. Simon. 1915 [1911]. *A Method of Measuring the Development of the Intelligence of Young Children*, trans. C.H. Town. Chicago: Chicago Medical Books.

——— and ———. 1965a [1905]. 'Upon the necessity of establishing a scientific diagnosis of inferior states of intelligence', in Anastasi (1965: 30–4).

——— and ———. 1965b [1905]. 'New methods for the diagnosis of the intellectual level of subnormals', in Anastasi (1965: 35–41).

——— and ———. 1965c [1908]. 'The development of intelligence in the child', in Anastasi (1965: 41–4).

Binswanger, L. 1975. *Being-in-the-World*. London: Souvenir Press.

Bitterman, M.E. 1967. 'Learning in animals', in H. Helson and W. Bevan, eds, *Contemporary Approaches to Psychology*. New York: Van Nostrand, 139–80.

Bjork, D.W. 1993. *B.F. Skinner: A Life*. New York: Basic Books.

———. 1997. *William James: The Center of His Vision*. Washington: American Psychological Association.

Blodgett, H.C. 1929. 'The effect of the introduction of reward upon the maze performance of rats', *University of California Publications in Psychology* 4.

Bloor, D. 1983. *Wittgenstein: A Social Theory of Knowledge*. New York: Columbia University Press.

———. 1996. 'The question of linguistic idealism revisited', in H. Sluga and D.G. Stern, eds, *The Cambridge Companion to Wittgenstein*. New York: Cambridge University Press, 354–82.

Blumenthal, A.L. 1970. *Language and Psychology: Historical Aspects of Psycholinguistics*. New York: Wiley.

———. 1975. 'A reappraisal of Wilhelm Wundt', *American Psychologist* 30: 1081–8.

———. 1977. *The Process of Cognition*. Englewood Cliffs, NJ: Prentice-Hall.

Boden, M.A. 1987. *Artificial Intelligence and Natural Man*. New York: Basic Books.

Bokun, Z. 1998. 'Daoist patterns of thought and the tradition of Chinese metaphysics', *Contemporary Chinese Thought* 29: 13–71.

Bond, M.H., and K.-H. Hwang. 1986. 'The social psychology of the Chinese people', in Bond, ed., *The Psychology of the Chinese People*. Hong Kong: Oxford University Press, 213–66.

Boneau, C.A. 1990. 'Psychological literacy: A first approximation', *American Psychologist* 45: 891–900.

Boring, E.G. 1929. *A History of Experimental Psychology*. New York: Century.

———. 1950a. 'Great men and scientific progress', *Proceedings of the American Philosophical Society* 94: 339–51.

———. 1950b. *A History of Experimental Psychology*, 2nd edn. New York: Appleton-Century-Crofts.

———. 1963a [1933]. *The Physical Dimensions of Consciousness*. New York: Dover.

———. 1963b [1961]. 'Fechner: Inadvertent founder of psychophysics', in R.I. Watson and D.T. Campbell, eds, *History, Psychology and Science: Selected Papers by E.G. Boring*. New York: Wiley, 126–31.

———. 1963c [1945]. 'The use of operational definitions in science', in Watson and Campbell, eds, *History, Psychology and Science*, 200–9.

———. 1963d [1921]. 'The stimulus-error', in Watson and Campbell, eds, *History, Psychology and Science*, 255–73.

———. 1969 [1923]. 'Intelligence as the tests test it', in L. Tyler, ed., *Intelligence: Some Recurring Issues*. New York: Van Nostrand, 25–8.

——— and G. Lindzey, eds. 1967. *A History of*

Psychology in Autobiography, vol. 5. New York: Appleton-Century-Crofts.

Bornstein, R.F. 1989. 'Exposure and affect: Overview and meta-analysis of research, 1968–1987', *Psychological Bulletin* 106: 265–89.

Boudewijnse, G.-J., D.J. Murray, and C.A. Bandomir. 1999. 'Herbart's mathematical psychology', *History of Psychology* 2: 163–93.

———, ———, and ———. 2001. 'The fate of Herbart's mathematical psychology', *History of Psychology* 4: 107–32.

Bower, G.H. 1970. 'Analysis of a mnemonic device', *American Scientist* 58: 496–510.

———. 1994. 'In appreciation of E.R. Hilgard's writings on learning theories', *Psychological Science* 5: 181–3.

——— and E.R. Hilgard. 1981. *Theories of Learning*, 5th edn. New York: Appleton-Century-Crofts.

Bowers, K.S. 1973. 'Situationism in psychology: An analysis and a critique', *Psychological Review* 80: 307–36.

Brainerd, C.J. 1996. 'Piaget: A centennial celebration', *Psychological Science* 7: 191–5.

Brentano, F. 1968 [1874]. 'Act psychology', in Sahakian (1968: 479–86).

———. 1973 [1874]. *Psychology from an Empirical Standpoint*, trans. A. Rancurello. New York: Humanities Press.

Bretherton, I. 1992. 'The origins of attachment theory: John Bowlby and Mary Ainsworth', *Developmental Psychology* 28: 759–75.

Breuer, J., and S. Freud. 1959 [1893]. 'On the psychical mechanism of hysterical phenomena', in Freud (1959a: I, 24–41).

Bridgman, P.W. 1927. *The Logic of Modern Physics*. New York: Macmillan.

———. 1940. 'Science: Public or private?', *Philosophy of Science* 7: 36.

Briggs, K.C., and I.B. Myers. 1976. *Myers-Briggs Type Indicator*. Palo Alto, Calif.: Consulting Psychologists Press.

Brigham, C.C. 1923. *A Study of American Intelligence*. Princeton, NJ: Princeton University Press.

Bringmann, W.G., M.W. Bringmann, and C.E. Early. 1992. 'G. Stanley Hall and the history of psychology', *American Psychologist* 47: 281–9.

———, A.N. DePace, and W.D.G. Balance. 1992. 'A brief, handwritten autobiography by Fechner', paper presented at the meeting of Cheiron

(International Society for the History of the Social and Behavioral Sciences), Windsor, Ont., June.

British Psychological Society. 1980. 'Monthly Report', *Bulletin of the British Psychological Society* 33: 71–2.

Broadbent, D.E. 1958. *Perception and Communication*. London: Pergamon.

———. 1980. 'Donald E. Broadbent', in Lindzey (1980: VII, 39–73).

———. 1992 [1952]. 'Listening to one of two synchronous messages', *Journal of Experimental Psychology, General* 121: 125–7.

Brock, A. 1992. 'Was Wundt a Nazi?', *Theory and Psychology* 2: 205–23.

———. 1993. 'Something old, something new: Wilhelm Wundt', *Theory and Psychology* 3: 235–42.

———. 2002. 'Comment on Bhatt & Tonks: Reports of our death are greatly exaggerated', *History and Philosophy of Psychology Bulletin* 14: 10–16.

Broughton, J.M., and D.J. Freeman-Moir, eds. 1982. *The Cognitive-Developmental Psychology of James Mark Baldwin: Current Theory and Research in Genetic Epistemology*. Norwood, NJ: Ablex.

Brown, J.A.C. 1954. *The Social Psychology of Industry*. Harmondsworth, UK: Penguin.

Brown, R. 1958. *Words and Things*. New York: Free Press.

——— and D. McNeill. 1966. 'The "tip of the tongue phenomenon"', *Journal of Verbal Learning and Verbal Behavior* 8: 325–37.

Bruce, D. 1986. 'Lashley's shift from bacteriology to neuropsychology, 1910–1917, and the influence of Jennings, Watson, and Franz', *Journal of the History of the Behavioral Sciences* 22: 27–43.

———. 1991. 'Integrations of Lashley', in Kimble et al. (1991: I, 306–23).

———. 1994. 'Lashley and the problem of serial order in behavior', *American Psychologist* 49: 93–103.

———. 1997. 'Lashley, Hebb, connections, and criticisms', *Canadian Psychology* 37: 129–36.

Brunberg, J.J., and N. Tomes. 1982. 'Women in the professions: A research agenda for American historians', *Reviews in American History* 10: 275–88.

Bruner, J.S. 1966. *Toward a Theory of Instruction*. Cambridge, Mass.: Harvard University Press.

———. 1973 [1957]. 'On perceptual readiness', in J. Anglin, ed., *Beyond the Information Given*. New York: Norton, 7–42.

———. 1980. 'Jerome S. Bruner', in Lindzey (1980: VII, 75–151).

———. 1986. *Actual Minds, Possible Worlds.* Cambridge, Mass.: Harvard University Press.

———. 1990. *Acts of Meaning.* Cambridge, Mass.: Harvard University Press.

———, J.J. Goodnow, and G.A. Austin. 1956. *A Study of Thinking.* New York: Wiley.

———, A. Jolly, and K. Silva, eds. 1976. *Play.* New York: Penguin.

——— and G. Klein. 1960. 'The functions of perceiving: New look retrospect', in B. Kaplan and S. Wapner, eds, *Perspectives in Psychological Theory.* New York: International Universities Press, 61–77.

———, R.R. Olver, and P.M. Greenfield. 1966. *Studies in Cognitive Growth.* New York: Wiley.

——— and L.J. Postman. 1973 [1949]. 'On the perception of incongruity', in J. Anglin, ed., *Beyond the Information Given.* New York: Norton, 68–83.

Brunswik, E. 1956. *Perception and the Representative Design of Experiments.* Berkeley: University of California Press.

Bryant, D.J., B. Tversky, and N. Franklin. 1992. 'Internal and external spatial frameworks for representing described scenes', *Journal of Memory and Language* 31: 74–98.

Brzezinski, E.J. 1984. 'Microcomputers and testing: Where are we and how did we get there?', *Educational Measurement: Issues and Practice* 3: 7–10.

Buckingham, H. 1984. 'Early development of associationist theory in psychology as a forerunner to connection theory', *Brain and Cognition* 3: 19–34.

Buckley, K.W. 1982. 'The selling of a psychologist: John Broadus Watson and the application of behavioral techniques to advertising', *Journal of the History of the Behavioral Sciences* 18: 207–21.

———. 1989. *Mechanical Man: John Broadus Watson and the Beginnings of Behaviorism.* New York: Guilford.

Bugental, J.F.T. 1964. 'The third force in psychology', *Journal of Humanistic Psychology* 4: 19–26.

Bühler, C. 1965. 'Some observations on the psychology of the third force', *Journal of Humanistic Psychology* 5: 54–5.

Bühler, K. 1951 [1907]. 'On thought connections', in Rapaport (1951: 39–57).

Bulmer, M. 1998. 'Galton's law of ancestral heredity', *Heredity* 81: 579-85.

Burnham, J.C. 1972. 'Thorndike's puzzle boxes', *Journal of the History of the Behavioral Sciences* 8: 159–67.

Burns, C. 1979. 'The role of emotion in the development of thought: The psychology of Mary Wollstonecraft', paper presented at the meeting of Cheiron (International Society for the History of the Social and Behavioral Sciences), Akron, Ohio, June.

Burt, C. 1972. 'Inheritance of general intelligence', *American Psychologist* 27: 175–90.

Buss, A.R. 1978. 'The structure of psychological revolutions', *Journal of the History of the Behavioral Sciences* 14: 57–64.

Butler, B.E., and J. Petrulis. 1999. 'Some further observations concerning Sir Cyril Burt', *British Journal of Psychology* 90: 155–60.

Cahan, E.D. 1992. 'John Dewey and human development', *Developmental Psychology* 28: 205–14.

Cairns, R.B. 1992. 'The making of a developmental science: The contributions and intellectual heritage of James Mark Baldwin', *Developmental Psychology* 28: 17–24.

Calkins, M.W. 1929. 'Introduction', in G. Berkeley, *Selections.* New York: Scribner's, ix–li.

———. 1966 [1896]. 'Association', in Herrnstein and Boring (1966: 530–4).

Campbell, D.T. 1960. 'Blind variation and selective retention in creative thought as in other knowledge processes', *Psychological Bulletin* 67: 380–400.

Campbell, J. 1964. *The Masks of God: Occidental Mythology.* New York: Viking.

Capaldi, E.J., and R.W. Proctor. 1994. 'Contextualism: Is the act in context the adequate metaphor for scientific psychology?', *Psychonomic Bulletin & Review* 1: 239–49.

Capshew, J.H. 1992. 'Constructing subjects, reconstructing psychology', *Theory and Psychology* 2: 243–7.

Carnap, R. 1959. 'Psychology in physical language', in A.J. Ayer, ed., *Logical Positivism.* Glencoe, Ill.: Free Press, 165–98.

Carnegie, A. 1979 [1900]. 'The gospel of wealth', in Appleman (1979: 399–405).

Carotenuto, A. 1982. *A Secret Symmetry: Sabina Spielrein between Freud and Jung.* New York: Pantheon Books.

Cartwright, D. 1959. 'Lewinian theory as a contemporary systematic framework', in Koch (1959: II, 7–91.

Cassirer, E. 1946. *Language and Myth*, trans. S.K. Langer. New York: Harper & Brothers.

———. 1963 [1945]. *Rousseau, Kant and Goethe*. New York: Harper & Row.

Cattell, J.M. 1886. 'The time it takes to see and name objects', *Mind* 11: 63–5.

———. 1903. 'Statistics of American Psychologists', *American Journal of Psychology* 14: 297–8.

———. 1948 [1890]. 'Mental tests and measurements', in Dennis (1948: 347–54).

Ceraso, J., H. Gruber, and I. Rock. 1990. 'On Solomon Asch', in Rock, ed., *The Legacy of Solomon Asch: Essays in Cognition and Social Psychology*. Hillsdale, NJ: Erlbaum, 3–22.

Chakerian, G.D. 1972. 'The golden ratio and a Greek crisis', *Fibonacci Quarterly* 11: 195–200.

Charlesworth, W.R. 1992. 'Darwin and developmental psychology: Past and present', *Developmental Psychology* 28: 5–16.

Cherfas, J., ed. 1983. *Darwin Up To Date*. London: IPC Magazines Ltd.

Cherry, E.C. 1953. 'Some experiments on the recognition of speech with one and with two ears', *Journal of the Acoustical Society of America* 25: 975–9.

Chomsky, N. 1957. *Syntactic Structures*. The Hague: Mouton.

———. 1959. 'Review of Skinner's verbal behavior', *Language* 35: 26–58.

———. 1966. *Cartesian Linguistics*. New York: Harper & Row.

———. 1967. 'The formal nature of language', in E. Lenneberg, *Biological Foundations of Language*. New York: Wiley, 397–442.

———. 1968. *Language and Mind*. New York: Harcourt, Brace & World.

———. 1972a. *Language and Mind*, enlarged edn. New York: Harcourt Brace Jovanovich.

———. 1972b. 'Psychology and ideology', *Cognition* 1: 11–46.

———. 1980. *Rules and Representations*. New York: Columbia University Press.

———. 1986. *Knowledge of Language: Its Nature, Origin and Use*. New York: Praeger.

———. 1995. 'Language and nature', *Mind* 104: 1–61.

Ciancia, F. 1980. 'Tolman and Honzik (1930) revisited or the mazes of psychology (1930–1980)', *Psychological Record* 41: 461–72.

Claparède, E. 1933. 'La genèse de l'hypothèse', *Archives de Psychologie* 24: 1–54.

Clifford, G.J. 1973 [1968]. 'E.L. Thorndike: The psychologist as professional man of science', in Henle et al. (1973: 230–45).

Cockburn, B. 1988. *Big Circumstance* (cassette recording). Hollywood, Calif.: Gold Castle Records.

Cohen, J. 1968. 'Multiple regression as a general data-analytic system', *Psychological Bulletin* 70: 426–43.

———. 1994. 'The earth is round (*p*<.05)', *American Psychologist* 49: 997–1003.

——— and P. Cohen. 1983. *Applied Multiple Regression-Correlation Analysis for the Behavioral Sciences*, 2nd edn. Hillsdale, NJ: Erlbaum.

Cole, L.E. 1939. *General Psychology*. New York: McGraw-Hill.

Cole, M., and S. Scribner. 1978. 'Introduction', in Vygotsky (1978: 1–16).

Coles, R. 1970. *Erik H. Erikson: The Growth of His Work*. Boston: Little, Brown.

Collingwood, R.G. 1946. *The Idea of History*. Oxford: Oxford University Press.

Conway, M.A., G. Cohen, and N. Stanhope. 1991. 'On the very long-term retention of knowledge acquired through formal education: Twelve years of cognitive psychology', *Journal of Experimental Psychology: General* 120: 395–412.

Coon, D.J. 1992. 'Testing the limits of sense and science: American experimental psychologists combat spiritualism, 1880–1920', *American Psychologist* 47: 143–51.

———. 2000. 'Salvaging the Self in a world without soul: William James' "The Principles of Psychology"', *History of Psychology* 3: 83–103.

Coren, S., and J.S. Girgus. 1980. 'Principles of perceptual organization and spatial distortion: The Gestalt illusions', *Journal of Experimental Psychology: Human Perception and Performance* 6: 404–12.

———, C. Porac, and L.M. Ward. 1984. *Sensation and Perception*, 2nd edn. New York: Academic Press.

Cornford, F.M. 1939. *Plato and Parmenides*. London: Routledge & Kegan Paul.

———. 1960 [1935]. *Plato's Theory of Knowledge.* London: Routledge & Kegan Paul.

———. 1967 [1950]. *The Unwritten Philosophy and Other Essays.* Cambridge: Cambridge University Press.

———. 1974 [1922]. 'Mysticism and science in the Pythagorean tradition', in P.D. Mourelatos, ed., *The Presocratics.* New York: Anchor Press/Doubleday, 135–60.

Costall, A. 1993. 'How Lloyd Morgan's Canon backfired', *Journal of the History of the Behavioral Sciences* 29: 113–22.

Crafts, L.W., T.C. Schneirla, E.E. Robinson, and R.W. Gilbert. 1950. *Recent Experiments in Psychology.* New York: McGraw-Hill.

Craik, F., and A. Baddeley. 1995. 'Donald E. Broadbent (1926–1993)', *American Psychologist* 50: 302–3.

Crews, F. 1996. 'The verdict on Freud', *Psychological Science* 7: 63–8.

———, ed. 1998. *Unauthorized Freud.* New York: Viking.

Cronbach, L.J. 1960. *Essentials of Psychological Testing,* 2nd edn. New York: Harper.

———. 1978 [1957]. 'The two disciplines of scientific psychology', in Hilgard (1978: 285–308).

Crovitz, H.F. 1970. *Galton's Walk.* New York: Harper & Row.

——— and H. Schiffman. 1974. 'Frequency of episodic memories as a function of their age', *Bulletin of the Psychonomic Society* 4: 517–18.

———, ———, and A. Apter. 1991. 'Galton's number', *Bulletin of the Psychonomic Society* 29: 331–2.

Crowther-Heyck, H. 1999. 'George A. Miller, language, and the computer metaphor of the mind', *History of Psychology* 2: 37–64.

———. 2000. 'Mystery and meaning: A reply to Green', *History of Psychology* 3: 67–70.

Dallenbach, K.M. 1959. 'Robert Morris Ogden: 1877–1959', *American Journal of Psychology* 72: 472–7.

Dallett, J. 1973. 'Theories of dream function', *Psychological Bulletin* 79: 408–16.

Danziger, K. 1980. 'The history of introspection reconsidered', *Journal of the History of the Behavioral Sciences* 16: 241–62.

———. 1983. 'Origins and basic principles of Wundt's *Volkerpsychologie*', *British Journal of Social Psychology* 22: 303–14.

———. 1987. 'Social context and investigative practice in early twentieth-century psychology', in Ash and Woodward (1987: 13–33).

———. 1990. *Constructing the Subject.* Cambridge: Cambridge University Press.

———. 1992. 'Ideas and constructions: Reply to reviewers', *Theory and Psychology* 2: 255–6.

———. 1994. 'Does the history of psychology have a future?', *Theory and Psychology* 4: 467–84.

———. 1997. *Naming the Mind: How Psychology Found Its Language.* London: Sage.

———. 2001. 'Sealing off the discipline: Wilhelm Wundt and the psychology of memory', in Green et al. (2001: 45–62).

Darwin, C. 1955 [1872]. *The Expression of the Emotions in Man and Animals.* New York: Philosophical Library.

———. 1958 [1892]. *The Autobiography of Charles Darwin and Selected Letters,* ed. F. Darwin. New York: Dover.

———. 1964 [1871]. *The Descent of Man.* New York: Modern Library.

———. 1964 [1859]. *The Origin of Species.* New York: Modern Library.

Darwin, F. 1958. Footnote, in C. Darwin (1958: 20).

Dawkins, R. 1983. 'The necessity of Darwinism', in Cherfas (1983: 61–3).

———. 1988. *The Blind Watchmaker.* London: Penguin.

Delbanco, A., and T. Delbanco. 1995. 'A.A. at the crossroads', *The New Yorker* 20, 3: 50–7.

Dember, W., ed. 1964. *Visual Perception: The Nineteenth Century.* New York: Wiley.

Denner, B. 1995. 'Stalked by the postmodern beast', *American Psychologist* 50: 390–1.

Dennis, W. 1948. *Readings in the History of Psychology.* New York: Appleton-Century-Crofts.

Dewey, J. 1930. *Individualism Old and New.* New York: Minton, Balch.

———. 1963 [1896]. 'The reflex arc concept in psychology', in J. Ratner, ed., *John Dewey: Philosophy, Psychology and Social Practice.* New York: Putnam, 252–66.

———. 1970 [1938]. 'Experience and education', in S.M. Cahn, ed., *The Philosophical Foundations of Education.* New York: Harper & Row, 221–61.

———. 1978 [1900]. 'Psychology and social practice', in Hilgard (1978: 65–79).

Dewsbury, D.A. 1992. 'Comparative psychology and ethology', *American Psychologist* 47: 208–15.

——. 1993. 'Contributions to the history of psychology: XCIV. The boys of summer at the end of summer: The Watson-Lashley correspondence of the 1950s', *Psychological Reports* 72: 263–9.

——. 1997a. 'Edward Bradford Titchener: Comparative psychologist?', *American Journal of Psychology* 110: 449–56.

——. 1997b. 'On the evolution of divisions', *American Psychologist* 52: 733–41.

——. 2000. 'Issues in comparative psychology at the dawn of the 20th century', *American Psychologist* 55: 750–3.

——. 2002a. 'Constructing representations of Karl Spencer Lashley', *Journal of the History of the Behavioral Sciences* 38: 225–45.

——. 2002b. 'The role of evidence in interpretations of the scientific work of Karl Lashley', *Journal of the History of the Behavioral Sciences* 38: 255–7.

Dinnerstein, D. 1977. *The Mermaid and the Minotaur.* New York: Harper & Row.

Dixon, T.R., and D.L. Horton, eds. 1968. *Verbal Behavior and General Behavior Theory.* Englewood Cliffs, NJ: Prentice-Hall.

Dollard, J., and N.E. Miller. 1950. *Personality and Psychotherapy.* New York: McGraw-Hill.

Donnelly, M. 1992. *Reinterpreting the Legacy of William James.* Washington: American Psychological Association.

Drob, S.L. 1999. 'Jung and the Kaballah', *History of Psychology* 2: 102–18.

Douglas, M. 1978. *Natural Symbols.* New York: Penguin.

——. 1982. 'Introduction to grid/group analysis', in Douglas, ed., *Essays in the Sociology of Perception.* London: Routledge & Kegan Paul.

Dowling, W.J., and D.L. Harwood. 1986. *Music Cognition.* Orlando, Fla: Academic Press.

Dumont, K., and J. Louw. 2001. 'The International Union of Psychological Science and the politics of membership: Psychological associations in South Africa and the German Democratic Republic', *History of Psychology* 4: 388–404.

Duncker, K. 1945. 'On problem solving', *Psychological Monographs* 58, 5: Whole No. 270.

Dunkel, H.B. 1969. *Herbart and Education.* New York: Random House.

——. 1970. *Herbart and Herbartianism: An Educational Ghost Story.* Chicago: University of Chicago Press.

Ebbinghaus, H. 1964 [1885]. *Memory: A Contribution to Experimental Psychology.* New York: Dover.

Eco, U. 1984. *Postscript to The Name of the Rose.* New York: Harcourt Brace Jovanovich.

——. 1989. *The Open Work*, trans. A. Cancogni. Cambridge, Mass.: Harvard University Press.

Edgerton, S. 1975. *The Renaissance Rediscovery of Linear Perspective.* New York: Basic Books.

Egeth, H. 1992. 'Dichotic listening: Long-lived echoes of Broadbent's early studies', *Journal of Experimental Psychology: General* 121: 124.

Einstein, A. 1952. 'Foreword', in Newton (1952: lix–lx).

Eiseley, L.C. 1987 [1956]. 'Charles Darwin', in O. Gingerich, ed., *Scientific Genius and Creativity.* New York: Freeman, 67–75.

El'konin, D.B. 1969. 'Some results of the study of the psychological development of preschool-age children', in M. Cole and I. Maltzman, eds, *A Handbook of Contemporary Soviet Psychology.* New York: Basic Books, 163–208.

Ellenberger, H.F. 1970. *The Discovery of the Unconscious.* New York: Basic Books.

Ellis, H.C. 1979 [1965]. 'Transfer and the educational process', in G.S. Belkin, ed., *Perspectives in the Educational Psychology.* Dubuque, Iowa: W.C. Brown, 71–82.

Ellis, W.D., ed. 1967. *A Source Book of Gestalt Psychology.* New York: Humanities Press.

Ellsworth, P.C. 1994. 'William James and emotion: Is a century of fame worth a century of misunderstanding?', *Psychological Review* 101: 222–9.

Epstein, R. 1991. 'Skinner, creativity, and the problem of spontaneous behavior', *Psychological Science* 2: 362–70.

Erdmann, E., and D. Stover. 2000 [1991]. *Beyond a World Divided: Human Values in the Brain-Mind Science of Roger Sperry.* San Jose, Calif.: Authors Choice Press.

Ericsson, K.A., and H.A. Simon. 1980. 'Verbal reports as data', *Psychological Review* 87: 215–51.

—— and ——. 1984. *Protocol Analysis.* Cambridge, Mass.: MIT Press.

Erikson, E.H. 1950. *Childhood and Society.* New York: Norton.

——. 1959. 'Identity and the life cycle', *Psychological Issues* 1, 1: Monograph 1.

——. 1962. *Young Man Luther.* New York: Norton.

———. 1963. *Childhood and Society*, 2nd edn. New York: Norton.

———. 1964. *Insight and Responsibility*. New York: Norton.

———. 1972. 'Play and actuality', in M.W. Piers, ed., *Play and Development*. New York: Norton, 127–67.

———, J. Erikson, and H.Q. Kivnick. 1986. *Vital Involvement in Old Age*. New York: Norton.

Esterson, A. 2002. 'The myth of Freud's ostracism by the medical community in 1896–1905: Jeffrey Masson's assault on truth', *History of Psychology* 5: 115–34.

Estes, W.K. 1960. 'Learning theory and the new mental chemistry', *Psychological Review* 67: 207–23.

———, ed. 1990. 'William James symposium', *Psychological Science* 1: 149–86.

Evans, R.B. 1973. 'E.B. Titchener and his lost system', in Henle et al. (1973: 83–97).

———. 2000. 'Psychological instruments at the turn of the century', *American Psychologist* 55: 322–5.

——— and F.J. Down Scott. 1978. 'The 1913 International Congress of Psychology: The American Congress that wasn't', *American Psychologist* 33: 711–23.

Evans, R.I. 1976. *The Making of Psychology*. New York: Knopf.

Falk, R. 1989. 'Judgement of coincidences: Mine versus yours', *American Journal of Psychology* 102: 477–93.

Fancher, R.E. 1983. 'Biographical origins of Francis Galton's psychology', *Isis* 74: 227–33.

———. 1985. *The Intelligence Men: Makers of the IQ Controversy*. New York: Norton.

———. 1989. 'Galton on examinations: An unpublished step in his invention of correlation', *Isis* 80: 446–55.

———. 1998. 'Biography and psychodynamic theory: Some lessons from the life of Francis Galton', *History of Psychology* 1: 99–115.

———. 2000. 'Snapshots of Freud in America, 1899–1999', *American Psychologist* 55: 1025–8.

———. 2001. 'Eugenics and other Victorian "secular religions"', in Green et al. (2001: 3–20).

Farr, R.M. 1983. 'Wilhelm Wundt (1832–1920) and the origins of psychology as an experimental and social science', *British Journal of Social Psychology* 22: 289–301.

Farrell, B.A. 1978. 'The progress of psychology', *British Journal of Psychology* 69: 1–8.

Farson, R. 1978. 'The technology of humanism', *Journal of Humanistic Psychology* 18: 5–35.

Fechner, G.T. 1871. *Zur experimentalen Aesthetik* [Toward an experimental aesthetic]. Leipzig: S. Hirzel.

———. 1876. *Vorschule der Aesthetik*. Leipzig: Breitkopf & Hartel.

———. 1966 [1860]. *Elements of Psychophysics*, vol. 1. New York: Holt, Rinehart and Winston.

Ferguson, J. 1970. *Socrates*. London: Macmillan.

Feyerabend, P.K. 1970. 'Consolations for the specialist', in I. Lakatos and A. Musgrave, eds, *Criticism and the Growth of Knowledge*. Cambridge: Cambridge University Press, 197–230.

Fisher, R.A. 1991 [1925]. *Statistical Methods, Experimental Design, and Scientific Inference*. Oxford: Oxford University Press.

Fiske, S.T., and S.E. Taylor. 1991. *Social Cognition*. New York: McGraw-Hill.

Fitzpatrick, F.J. 1987. 'Aquinas', in Gregory (1987: 36–8).

Flavell, J.H. 1963. *The Developmental Psychology of Jean Piaget*. New York: Van Nostrand.

———. 1985. *Cognitive Development*. Englewood Cliffs, NJ: Prentice-Hall.

——— and J.A. Draguns. 1957. 'A microgenetic approach to perception and thought', *Psychological Bulletin* 54: 197–217.

Fletcher, R. 1991. *Science, Ideology, and the Media: The Cyril Burt Scandal*. New Brunswick, NJ: Transaction.

Flowers, K.A. 1987. 'Parkinsonism', in Gregory (1987: 587–91).

Føllesdall, D. 1984. 'Brentano and Husserl on intentional objects and perception', in H.L. Dreyfus, ed., *Husserl, Intentionality and Cognitive Science*. Cambridge, Mass.: MIT Press, 31–42.

Franklin, M.B. 1990. 'Reshaping psychology at Clark: The Werner era', *Journal of the History of the Behavioral Sciences* 26: 176–89.

———. 1997. 'Constructing a developmental psychology: Heinz Werner's vision', *Contemporary Psychology* 42: 481–5.

Fransella, F. 1995. *George Kelly*. London: Sage.

——— and D. Bannister. 1977. *A Manual for Repertory Grid Technique*. London: Academic Press.

Franz, M.-L. von. 1974. *Number and Time*. London: Rider.

Franz, S.I. 1912. 'New phrenology', *Science* 35: 321–8.

Frazer, J.G. 1909. *Psyche's Task*. London: Macmillan.

———. 1959 [1911]. *The Golden Bough* (abridged), ed. T.H. Gaster, 1922. New York: Doubleday.

Freeman, L. 1980. 'Immortal Anna O.: From Freud to feminism', *New York Times Magazine* 30: 74, 78–83.

Freeman-Moir, D.J. 1982. 'The origin of intelligence', in Broughton and Freeman-Moir (1982: 127–68).

Freidan, B. 1963. *The Feminine Mystique*. New York: Dell.

Freud, A. 1946 [1936]. *The Ego and the Mechanisms of Defence*. London: Hogarth.

———. 1969. *Some Difficulties in the Path of Psychoanalysis*. New York: International Universities Press.

Freud, S. 1946 [1913]. *Totem and Taboo*, trans. A.A. Brill. New York: Random House.

———. 1950 [1935]. *An Autobiographical Study*, trans. J. Strachey. London: Hogarth Press.

———. 1953 [1927]. *The Future of an Illusion*, trans. W.D. Robson-Scott. New York: Doubleday.

———. 1957 [1920]. *Beyond the Pleasure Principle*. New York: Doubleday.

———. 1959a. *Collected Papers*, 5 vols. New York: Basic Books.

———. 1959b [1912]. 'A note on the unconscious in psychoanalysis', in Freud (1959a: IV, 22–9).

———. 1959c [1914]. 'On the history of the psychoanalytic movement', in Freud (1959a: I, 287–359).

———. 1959d [1893]. 'Some points in a comparative study of organic and hysterical paralyses', in Freud (1959a: IV, 42–58).

———. 1959e [1932]. 'Why war?', in Freud (1959a: V, 273–87).

———. 1959f [1896]. 'The ætiology of hysteria', in Freud (1959a: I, 183–219).

———. 1961 [1930]. *Civilization and Its Discontents*, trans. J. Strachey. New York: Norton.

———. 1964 [1933]. *New Introductory Lectures on Psychoanalysis*, trans. J. Strachey. New York: Norton.

———. 1965 [1900]. *The Interpretation of Dreams*, trans. J. Strachey. New York: Avon.

———. 1977 [1920]. *Introductory Lectures on Psychoanalysis*. New York: Norton.

Friedman, L.J. 1999. *Identity's Architect: A Biography of Erik H. Erikson*. New York: Scribner's.

Friedman, M. 1990. 'Kant and Newton: Why gravity is essential to matter', in P. Bricker and R.I.G. Hughes, eds, *Philosophical Perspectives on Newtonian Science*. Cambridge, Mass.: MIT Press, 185–202.

Friman, P.C., K.D. Allen, M.L.E. Kerwin, and R. Larzelere. 1993. 'Changes in modern psychology: A citation analysis of the Kuhnian displacement thesis', *American Psychologist* 48: 658–64.

Frye, N. 1966. 'Varieties of literary utopias', in Manuel (1966a: 25–49).

Fryer, D.M., and J.C. Marshall. 1979. 'The motives of Jacques de Vaucanson', *Technology & Culture* 20: 257–69.

Fuchs, A.H. 1997. 'The right text at the right time', *Contemporary Psychology* 42: 486–7.

——— and W. Viney. 2002. 'The course in the history of psychology: present status and future concerns', *History of Psychology* 5: 3–15.

Furomoto, L. 1987. 'On the margins: Women and the professionalization of psychology in the United States, 1890–1940', in Ash and Woodward (1987: 93–114).

———. 1989. 'The new history of psychology', in I.S. Cohen, ed., *The G. Stanley Hall Lecture Series*, vol. 9. Washington: American Psychological Association, 5–34.

———. 1991. 'From "paired associates" to a psychology of self: The intellectual odyssey of Mary Whiton Calkins', in Kimble et al. (1991: 57–74).

———. 1992. 'Joining separate spheres—Christine Ladd-Franklin, Woman-Scientist (1847–1930)', *American Psychologist* 47: 175–82.

Galton, F. 1886. 'Regression toward mediocrity in hereditary stature', *Journal of the Anthropological Institute* 15: 253.

———. 1965 [1869]. 'Hereditary genius: an inquiry into its laws and consequences', in Anastasi (1965: 239–48).

———. 1970 [1879]. 'Psychometric experiments', in Crovitz (1970).

———. 1973 [1883]. *Inquiries into Human Faculty and Its Development*. New York: AMS Press.

Gantt, W.H. 1928. 'Ivan P. Pavlov: A biographical sketch', in Pavlov (1928: 11–34).

Garcia, J. 1997. 'Tolman: Creative surges and dubious second thoughts', *Contemporary Psychology* 42: 285–91.

Gardner, H. 1974. *The Quest for Mind*. New York: Vintage.

——. 1982a. 'Ernst Cassirer and the symbolic approach to cognition', in Gardner, ed., *Art, Mind and Brain*. New York: Basic Books, 40–7.

——. 1982b. 'What we know (and do not know) about the two halves of the brain', in Gardner, ed., *Art, Mind and Brain*, 278–85.

——. 1983. *Frames of Mind*. New York: Basic Books.

——. 1985. *The Mind's New Science: A History of the Cognitive Revolution*. New York: Basic Books.

——. 1999. 'The enigma of Erik Erikson', *New York Review of Books*, 24 June, 51–6.

Gardner, S., and G. Stevens. 1992. *Red Vienna and the Golden Age of Psychology, 1918–1938*. New York: Praeger.

Garner, W.R. 1962. *Uncertainty and Structure as Psychological Concepts*. New York: Wiley.

Garrett, H.E. 1948. *Great Experiments in Psychology*. New York: Appleton-Century.

Gauld, A. 1992. *A History of Hypnotism*. Cambridge: Cambridge University Press.

Gay, P. 1988. *Freud: A Life for Our Time*. New York: Norton.

Geldard, F.A. 1972. *The Human Senses*, 2nd edn. New York: Wiley.

Gendlin, E.T. 1962. *Experiencing and the Creation of Meaning: A Philosophical and Psychological Approach to the Subjective*. Glencoe, Ill.: Free Press.

——. 1981. *Focusing*. New York: Bantam Books.

Gentner, D., and D.R. Gentner. 1983. 'Flowing waters or teeming crowds: Mental models of electricity', in Gentner and Stevens (1983: 99–129).

—— and J. Grudin. 1985. 'The evolution of mental metaphors in psychology: A 90-year retrospective', *American Psychologist* 40: 181–92.

—— and A.L. Stevens, eds. 1983. *Mental Models*. New York: Erlbaum.

Gergen, K.J. 1985. 'The social constructionist movement in modern psychology', *American Psychologist* 40: 266–75.

——. 1991a. 'Emerging challenges for theory and psychology', *Theory and Psychology* 1: 13–35.

——. 1991b. *The Saturated Self: Dilemmas of Identity in Contemporary Life*. New York: Basic Books.

——. 1994. 'Exploring the postmodern: Perils or potentials?', *American Psychologist* 49: 412–16.

——. 1995. 'Postmodern psychology: Resonance and reflection', *American Psychologist* 50: 394.

——. 2001. 'Psychological science in a postmodern context', *American Psychologist* 56: 803–13.

—— and M.M. Gergen, eds. 1984. *Historical Social Psychology*. Hillsdale, NJ: Erlbaum.

Ghiselin, M. 1966. *The Triumph of the Darwinian Method*. Berkeley: University of California Press.

——. 1983. 'The path to natural selection', in Cherfas (1983: 64–6).

Gholson, B., and P. Barker. 1985. 'Kuhn, Lakatos & Laudan: Applications in the history of physics and psychology', *American Psychologist* 40: 755–69.

Gibson, E.J. 1941. 'A critical review of the concept of set in contemporary experimental psychology', *Psychological Bulletin* 38: 781–817.

——. 1969. *Principles of Perceptual Learning and Development*. Englewood Cliffs, NJ: Prentice-Hall.

——. 1980. 'Eleanor J. Gibson', in Lindzey (1980: VII, 239–71).

——. 1991. 'Learning to read', in Gibson, ed., *An Odyssey in Learning and Perception*. Cambridge, Mass.: MIT Press, 393–412.

——. 1994. 'Has psychology a future?', *Psychological Science* 5: 69–76.

——. 2002. *Perceiving the Affordances: A Portrait of Two Psychologists*. Mahwah, NJ: Erlbaum.

—— and H. Levin. 1975. *The Psychology of Reading*. Cambridge, Mass.: MIT Press.

——, A. Pick, H. Osser, and M. Hammond. 1962. 'The role of grapheme phoneme correspondence in the perception of words', *American Journal of Psychology* 75: 554–70.

Gibson, J.J. 1950. *The Perception of the Visual World*. Boston: Houghton Mifflin.

——. 1960. 'The concept of the stimulus in psychology', *American Psychologist* 15: 694–703.

——. 1966. *The Senses Considered as Perceptual Systems*. Boston: Houghton Mifflin.

—— and E.J. Gibson. 1955. 'Perceptual learning—differentiation or enrichment?', *Psychological Review* 62: 32–41.

Gigerenzer, G. 1991. 'From tools to theories: A heuristic of discovery in cognitive psychology', *Psychological Review* 98: 254–67.

—— and D.J. Murray. 1987. *Cognition as Intuitive Statistics*. Hillsdale, NJ: Erlbaum.

——, Z. Swijtink, T. Porter, L. Daston, J. Beatty, and L. Kruger. 1989. *The Empire of Chance*. Cambridge: Cambridge University Press.

Gilbert, K.E., and H. Kuhn. 1972 [1953]. *A History of Esthetics*. New York: Dover.

Gillie, O. 1977. Letter, *Bulletin of the British Psychological Society* 30: 257–8.

Glassman, M. 2001. 'Where there is no middle ground', *American Psychologist* 56: 369–70.

Gleaves, D.H., and E. Hernandez. 1999. 'Recent reformulations of Freud's development and abandonment of his seduction theory: Historical/scientific clarification or a continued assault on truth?', *History of Psychology* 2: 324–54.

Gleaves, D.H., and E. Hernandez. 2002. 'Wethinks the author doth protest too much: A reply to Esterson (2002)', *History of Psychology* 5: 92–8.

Gleitman, H., P. Rozin, and J. Sabini. 1997. 'Solomon E. Asch (1907–1996)', *American Psychologist* 52: 984–5.

Glick, J. 1992. 'Werner's relevance for contemporary developmental psychology', *Developmental Psychology* 28: 558–65.

Goethe, J.W. von. 1970 [1840]. *Theory of Colors*, trans. C.L. Eastlake. Cambridge, Mass.: MIT Press.

Goffman, E. 1978. 'Response cries', *Language* 54: 787–815.

Goldie, P. 1997. *Darwin*, 2nd edn (CD-ROM). San Francisco: Lightbinders.

Goldstein, H., D.L. Krantz, and J.D. Rains. 1965. *Controversial Issues in Learning*. New York: Appleton-Century-Crofts.

Goldstein, K. 1963 [1940]. *Human Nature in the Light of Psychopathology*. New York: Schocken.

———. 1963 [1939]. *The Organism*. Boston: Beacon Press.

———. 1967. 'Kurt Goldstein', in Boring and Lindzey (1967: V, 147–66).

——— and M. Scheerer. 1941. 'Abstract and concrete behavior, an experimental study with special tests', *Psychological Monographs* 53, Whole No. 2.

Gombrich, E. 1965. 'The use of art for the study of symbols', *American Psychologist* 20: 34–50.

Gorfein, D.S., and R.R. Hoffman. 1987. *Memory and Learning: The Ebbinghaus Centennial Conference*. Hillsdale, NJ: Erlbaum.

Gorman, P. 1979. *Pythagoras: A Life*. London: Routledge & Kegan Paul.

Gottschaldt, K. 1967 [1926]. 'Gestalt factors and repetition', in Ellis (1967: 109–22).

Gould, S.J. 1977. *Ontogeny and Phylogeny*. Cambridge, Mass.: Harvard University Press.

———. 1982. 'A nation of morons', *New Scientist*, 6 May, 349–52.

———. 1996. *The Mismeasure of Man*, rev. edn. New York: Norton.

Gray, P. 1996. 'Evolution by natural selection as an integrative theme in psychology courses', *APS Observer* (May–June): 26, 27, 37.

———. 2002. *Psychology*, 4th edn. New York: Worth.

Green, B.F. 1992. 'Exposé or smear?', *Psychological Science* 6: 328–31.

Green, C.D. 1992. 'Operationism in psychology', *Theory and Psychology* 2: 291–320.

———. 1995. 'All that glitters: A review of psychological research on the aesthetics of the golden section', *Perception* 24: 937–68.

———. 1996. 'Where did the word "cognitive" come from anyway?', *Canadian Psychology* 37: 31–9.

———. 1998. 'The thoroughly modern Aristotle: Was he really a functionalist?', *History of Psychology* 1: 8–20.

———. 2000. 'Dispelling the "mystery" of computational cognitive science', *History of Psychology* 3: 62–6.

———. 2001. 'Charles Babbage, the analytical engine, and the possibility of a 19th-century cognitive science', in Green et al. (2001: 133–52).

———, M. Shore, and T. Teo, eds. 2001. *The Transformation of Psychology: The Influences of 19th-Century Natural Science, Technology, and Philosophy*. Washington: American Psychological Association.

Green, T.R.G. 1982. 'Pictures of programs and other processes, or how to do things with lines', *Behaviour and Information Technology* 1: 3–36.

Greene, J. 1972. *Psycholinguistics: Chomsky and Psychology*. Baltimore: Penguin.

Greenglass, E. 1982. *A World of Difference: Gender Roles in Perspective*. Toronto: Wiley.

Greenwald, A.G., E.R. Spangenberg, A.R. Pratkanis, and J. Eskanazi. 1991. 'Double-blind tests of subliminal self-help audiotapes', *Psychological Science* 2: 119–22.

Greenwood, J.D. 1992. 'Realism, empiricism and social construction', *Theory and Psychology* 2: 131–52.

———. 1999. 'Understanding the "cognitive revolution" in psychology', *Journal of the History of the Behavioral Sciences* 35: 1–22.

Greer, S. 1997. 'Nietzsche and social construction: Directions for a post-modern historiography', *Theory and Psychology* 7: 83–100.

————. 2001. 'Falling off the edge of the modern world?', *American Psychologist* 56: 367–8.

Gregory, R.L. 1970. *The Intelligent Eye*. London: Weidenfeld & Nicholson.

————, ed. 1987. *The Oxford Companion to the Mind*. Oxford: Oxford University Press.

Grinder, R.E., ed. 1967. *A History of Genetic Psychology*. New York: Wiley.

Gruber, H.E. 1981. *Darwin on Man: A Psychological Study of Scientific Creativity*, 2nd edn. Chicago: University of Chicago Press.

————. 1998. 'Bärbel Inhelder (1913–1997)', *American Psychologist* 53: 1221–2.

Grusec, J.E. 1992. 'Social learning theory and developmental psychology: The legacies of Robert Sears and Albert Bandura', *Developmental Psychology* 28: 776–86.

Gunderson, K. 1964. 'The imitation game', in A.R. Anderson, ed. *Minds and Machines*. Englewood Cliffs, NJ: Prentice-Hall, 60–71.

Guthrie, E.R. 1938. *The Psychology of Human Conflict*. New York: Harper & Row.

————. 1959. 'Association by contiguity', in Koch (1959: II, 158–95).

————. 1960 [1952]. *The Psychology of Learning*, rev. edn. Gloucester, Mass.: Peter Smith.

————. 1961 [1930]. 'Conditioning as a principle of learning', in R.C. Birney and R.C. Teevan, eds, *Reinforcement*. New York: Van Nostrand, 16–32.

Guthrie, K.S. 1987 [1920]. *The Pythagorean Sourcebook and Library*. Grand Rapids, Mich.: Phanes Press.

Guthrie, R.V. 1976. *Even the Rat Was White: A Historical View of Psychology*. New York: Harper & Row.

Haggbloom, S.J., R. Warnick, J.E. Warnick, V.K. Jones, G.L. Yarbrough, T.M. Russell, C.M. Boreckey, R. McGahhey, J.L. Powell, J. Beavers, and E. Monte. 2002. 'The 100 most eminent psychologists of the 20th century', *Review of General Psychology* 6: 139–52.

Hall, G.S. 1948 [1883]. 'The contents of children's minds', in Dennis (1948: 255–76).

————. 1967 [1904]. 'The psychology of adolescence', in Grinder (1967: 213–36).

————. 1968 [1904]. 'Adolescent psychology from a genetic standpoint', in Sahakian (1968: 195–9).

Hamilton, E., and H. Cairns. 1961. *Plato: The Collected Dialogues, Including the Letters*. Princeton, NJ: Princeton University Press.

Hamlyn, D.W. 1962 [1953]. 'Behavior', in V.C. Chappell, ed., *The Philosophy of Mind*. Englewood Cliffs, NJ: Prentice-Hall, 60–73.

Hanfmann, E., M. Rickers-Ovsiankina, and K. Goldstein. 1944. 'Case Ianuti: Extreme concretization of behavior due to damage of the brain cortex', *Psychological Monographs* 57, 4 (Whole No. 264).

Hannush, M.J. 1987. 'John B. Watson remembered: An interview with James B. Watson', *Journal of the History of the Behavioral Sciences* 23: 137–52.

Hanson, N.R. 1969. *Patterns of Discovery*. Cambridge: Cambridge University Press.

Hardin, G. 1968. 'The tragedy of the commons', *Science* 162: 1243–8.

Harlow, H. 1958. 'The nature of love', *American Psychologist* 13: 673–85.

Harrington, D.M., J.H. Block, and J. Block. 1987. 'Carl Rogers' theory of creative environments: Child-rearing antecedents of creative potential in young adoloescents', *Journal of Personality and Social Psychology* 52: 851–6.

Harrower, M. 1983. *Kurt Koffka: An Unwitting Self-Portrait*. Gainesville: University of Florida Press.

Hartmann, H. 1976. 'The historical roots of occupational segregation: Capitalism, patriarchy, and job segregation by sex', *Signs* 1: 137–69.

Hassard, J. 1990. 'The AHP Soviet exchange project: 1983–1990', *Journal of Humanistic Psychology* 30: 5–51.

Hatfield, G. 1998. 'Kant and empirical psychology in the 18th century', *Psychological Science* 9: 423–8.

———— and W. Epstein. 1987. 'The status of the minimum principle in the theoretical analysis of visual perception', *Psychological Bulletin* 97: 155–86.

Hayes, S.C. 1993. 'Balancing unity and diversity: Reflections on the five year history of APS', *APS Observer* 6: 2, 16, 22.

Hearnshaw, L.S. 1979. *Cyril Burt, Psychologist*. Ithaca, NY: Cornell University Press.

Hebb, D.O. 1949. *The Organization of Behavior*. New York: Wiley.

————. 1955. 'Drives and the C.N.S. (Conceptual Nervous System)', *Psychological Review* 62: 243–354.

————. 1958. *A Textbook of Psychology*. Philadelphia: Saunders.

————. 1959. 'A neuropsychological theory', in Koch (1959: I, 622–43).

————. 1960. 'The American revolution', *American Psychologist* 15: 735–45.

————. 1968. 'Concerning imagery', *Psychological Review* 75: 466–78.

————. 1980a. *An Essay on Mind*. Hillsdale, NJ: Erlbaum.

————. 1980b. 'D.O. Hebb', in Lindzey (1980: VII, 275–303).

Heidbreder, E. 1933. *Seven Psychologies*. New York: Appleton-Century-Crofts.

————. 1969. 'Functionalism', in Krantz (1969a: 35–50).

Heidegger, M. 1962. *Being and Time*. London: SCM.

Heider, F. 1958. *The Psychology of Interpersonal Relations*. New York: Wiley.

————. 1983. *The Life of a Psychologist: An Autobiography*. Lawrence: University of Kansas Press.

Hein, S.F., and W.J. Austin. 2001. 'Empirical and hermeneutic approaches to phenomenological research in psychology: A comparison', *Psychological Methods* 6: 3–17.

Helmholtz, H. von. 1954 [1885]. *On the Sensations of Tone*. New York: Dover.

————. 1961 [1909]. 'The sensations of vision', in R.C. Teevan and R.C. Birney, eds, *Color Vision*. New York: Van Nostrand, 10–27.

————. 1962 [1881]. *Popular Scientific Lectures*. New York: Dover.

Henle, M. 1968 [1962]. 'Deductive reasoning', in P.C. Wason and P.N. Johnson-Laird, eds, *Deductive Reasoning*. Baltimore: Penguin, 93–107.

————. 1978. 'Gestalt psychology and Gestalt therapy', *Journal of the History of the Behavioral Sciences* 14: 23–32.

————. 1986 [1978]. 'One man against the Nazis— Wolfgang Kohler', in Henle, ed., *1879 and All That: Essays in the Theory and History of Psychology*. New York: Columbia University Press, 225–37.

————. 1986 [1957]. 'Some problems of eclecticism', in Henle, ed., *1879 and All That*, 81–92.

————. 1986 [1977]. 'The influence of Gestalt psychology in America', in Henle, ed., *1879 and All That*, 118–32.

————. 1987. 'Koffka's "Principles" after fifty years', *Journal of the History of the Behavioral Sciences* 23: 14–21.

————, J. Jaynes, and J.J. Sullivan, eds. 1973. *Historical Conceptions of Psychology*. New York: Springer.

Herbart, J.F. 1966 [1891]. 'A text book in psychology', trans. M.K. Smith, in B. Rand, ed., *The Classical Psychologists*. Gloucester, Mass.: Peter Smith, 395–415.

Hering, E. 1961 [1878]. 'Principles of a new theory of the color sense', in R.C. Teevan and R.C. Birney, eds, *Color Vision*. New York: Van Nostrand, 28–31.

Herman, E. 1995. *The Romance of American Psychology: Political Culture in the Age of Experts*. Berkeley: University of California Press.

Heron, W. 1957. 'The pathology of boredom', *Scientific American* 196: 52–6.

Herrnstein, R.J. 1967. 'Introduction', in J.B. Watson, *Behavior: An Introduction to Comparative Psychology*. New York: Holt, Rinehart and Winston, xi–xxi.

————. 1977. 'The evolution of behaviorism', *American Psychologist* 32: 593–603.

———— and E.G. Boring. 1966. *A Source Book in the History of Psychology*. Cambridge, Mass.: Harvard University Press.

———— and C. Murray. 1994. *The Bell Curve: Intelligence and Class Structure in American Life*. New York: Free Press.

Herz-Fischler, R. 1998. *A Mathematical History of the Golden Number*. New York: Dover.

Hilgard, E.R. 1948. *Theories of Learning*. New York: Appleton-Century-Crofts.

————. 1953. *Introduction to Psychology*. New York: Harcourt, Brace, and Co.

————. 1956. *Theories of Learning*, 2nd edn. New York: Appleton-Century-Crofts.

————. 1964. 'Introduction', in Ebbinghaus (1964: vii–x).

————. 1969. 'Levels of awareness: Second thoughts on some of William James' ideas', in MacLeod (1969a: 45–58).

————, ed. 1978. *American Psychology in Historical Perspective*. Washington: American Psychological Association.

————. 1980. 'The trilogy of mind: Cognition, affection and conation', *Journal of the History of the Behavioral Sciences* 16: 107–17.

————. 1987. *Psychology in America: An Historical Survey*. New York: Harcourt Brace Jovanovich.

————. 1993. 'Which psychologists prominent in the second half of this century made lasting contributions to psychological theory?', *Psychological Science* 4: 70–80.

———— and G.H. Bower. 1966. *Theories of Learning*, 3rd edn. New York: Appleton-Century-Crofts.

———— and ————. 1975. *Theories of Learning*, 4th edn. New York: Appleton-Century-Crofts.

———— and D.G. Marquis. 1940. *Conditioning and Learning*. New York: Appleton-Century.

Hillman, J. 1972. *The Myth of Analysis*. Evanston, Ill.: Northwestern University Press.

Hindle, E. 1983. 'Darwin's greatest work', in Cherfas (1983: 67–8).

Hirst, W., U. Neisser, and E. Spelke. 1978. 'Divided attention', *Human Nature* 1: 54–61.

————, E.S. Spelke, C.C. Reaves, G. Caharack, and U. Neisser. 1980. 'Dividing attention without alternation or automaticity', *Journal of Experimental Psychology: General* 109: 98–117.

Hochberg, J. 1988. 'Perception in space', in E.R. Hilgard, ed., *Fifty Years of Psychology: Essays in Honor of Floyd Ruch*. Glenview, Ill.: Scott, Foresman, 57–73.

Hodos, W., and C.B.G. Campbell. 1969. '*Scala naturae*: Why there is no theory in comparative psychology', *Psychological Review* 76: 337–50.

Hoff, E.T. 1992. 'Psychology in Canada one hundred years ago: James Mark Baldwin at the University of Toronto', *Canadian Psychology* 33: 683–94.

Hoffding, H. 1955 [1900]. *A History of Modern Philosophy*, vol. 2. New York: Dover.

Hoffman, E. 1988. *The Right To Be Human: A Biography of Abraham Maslow*. Los Angeles: Tarcher.

Hofstadter, T. 1979 [1955]. 'The vogue of Spencer', in Appleman (1979: 389–99).

Holland, J.G. 1962. 'Teaching machines: An application of principles from the laboratory', in Smith and Moore (1962: 34–48).

Hollingworth, L.S. 1914a. 'Variability as related to sex differences in achievement', *American Journal of Sociology* 19: 510–30.

————. 1914b. *Functional Periodicity: An Experimental Study of the Mental and Motor Abilities of Women during Menstruation*. New York: Teachers College, Columbia University.

Holzman, P.S. 1994. 'Hilgard on psychoanalysis as science', *Psychological Science* 5: 190–1.

Horley, J. 2001. 'After "The Baltimore Affair": James Mark Baldwin's life and work, 1908–1934', *History of Psychology* 4: 24–33.

Horney, K. 1950. *Neurosis and Human Growth*. New York: Norton.

Hornstein, G.A. 1992. 'The return of the repressed: Psychology's problematic relations with psychoanalysis, 1909–1960', *American Psychologist* 47: 254–63.

Horton, D.L., and T.R. Dixon. 1968. 'Traditions, trends, and innovations', in Dixon and Horton (1968: 572–80).

Hsueh, Y. 2002. 'The Hawthorne experiments and the introduction of Jean Piaget in American industrial psychology, 1929–1932', *History of Psychology* 5: 163–89.

Hull, C.L. 1943. *Principles of Behavior*. New York: Appleton-Century.

————. 1952. *A Behavior System*. New Haven: Yale University Press.

Hume, D. 1927 [1757]. 'The natural history of religion', in C.W. Hendel, ed., *Hume Selections*. New York: Scribner's, 253–82.

————. 1951 [1748]. 'An enquiry concerning human understanding', in D.C. Yalden-Thomson, ed., *Hume: Theory of Knowledge*. Edinburgh: Thomas Nelson, 2–176.

Humphrey, G. 1951. *Thinking: An Introduction to Its Experimental Psychology*. London: Methuen.

Hunt, E. 1992. 'Editor's statement', *Journal of Experimental Psychology* 121: 403.

Hunt, R.R. 1995. 'The subtlety of distinctiveness: What von Restorff really did', *Psychonomic Bulletin and Review* 2: 105–12.

Huntley, H.E. 1970. *The Divine Proportion*. New York: Dover.

Hurvich, L.M., and D. Jameson. 1949. 'Helmholtz and the three color theory: An historical note', *American Journal of Psychology* 62: 111–14.

———— and ————. 1957. 'An opponent-process theory of color vision', *Psychological Review* 64: 384–90.

Husserl, E. 1965. *Phenomenology and the Crisis of Philosophy*. New York: Harper.

I Ching, or Book of Changes. 1967. Trans. Cary F. Baynes, from the German version of R. Wilhelm. Princeton, NJ: Princeton University Press.

Innis, N.K. 1998. 'David Krech: Social activist', in Kimble and Wertheimer (1998: III, 295–306).

Izard, C.E. 1977. *Human Emotions*. New York: Plenum.

Jacobi, J. 1968. *The Psychology of C.G. Jung*. London: Routledge & Kegan Paul.

———. 1971. *Complex/Archetype/Symbol*. Princeton, NJ: Princeton University Press.

Jacobson, E. 1925. 'Progressive relaxation', *American Journal of Psychology* 36: 73–87.

———. 1938. *Progressive Relaxation*, 2nd edn. Chicago: University of Chicago Press.

———. 1977. *You Must Relax*, 5th edn. London: Unwin.

Jacobson, R. 1967. *Selected Writings*. The Hague: Mouton.

James, W. 1890. *The Principles of Psychology*, 2 vols. New York: Holt.

———. 1950 [1890]. *The Principles of Psychology*, 2 vols. New York: Dover.

———. 1958 [1902]. *The Varieties of Religious Experience*. New York: New American Library.

———. 1962 [1892]. *Psychology: Briefer Course*. New York: Collier.

———. 1968 [1908]. 'Psychological types', in Sahakian (1968: 216–17).

———. 1983 [1890]. *The Principles of Psychology*. Cambridge, Mass.: Harvard University Press.

Janik, A., and S. Toulmin. 1973. *Wittgenstein's Vienna*. New York: Simon & Schuster.

Jankowicz, A.D. 1987. 'Whatever became of George Kelly?', *American Psychologist* 42: 481–7.

Jaynes, J. 1973. 'Animate motion in the 17th century', in Henle et al. (1973: 166–79).

———. 1977. *The Origins of Consciousness in the Breakdown of the Bicameral Mind*. Boston: Houghton Mifflin.

Jencks, C. 1986. *What Is Postmodernism?* New York: St Martin's Press.

Jenkins, J.J. 1974. 'Remember that old theory of memory? Well, forget it', *American Psychologist* 29: 785–95.

Jensen, A.R. 1972. *Genetics and Education*. New York: Harper & Row.

Johnson, D. 1990. 'Animal rights and human lives: Time for scientists to right the balance', *Psychological Science* 1: 213–14.

Johnson, E.B. 2001. 'The repeated reproduction of Bartlett's "Remembering"', *History of Psychology* 4: 341–66.

Johnson, R.C., G.E. MacClearn, S. Yuen, C.T. Nagoshi, F.M. Ahern, and R.E. Cole. 1985. 'Galton's data a century later', *American Psychologist* 40: 875–92.

Jones, E. 1963. *The Life and Work of Sigmund Freud*. New York: Anchor.

Jones, M.C. 1924a. 'The elimination of children's fears', *Journal of Experimental Psychology* 7: 383–90.

———. 1924b. 'A laboratory study of fear: The case of Peter', *Journal of Genetic Psychology* 31: 308–15.

Joynson, R.B. 1989. *The Burt Affair*. London: Routledge.

———. 2003. 'Selective interest and psychological practice: A new interpretation of the Burt affair', *British Journal of Psychology* 94: 409–26.

Judd, D.B. 1970. 'Introduction', in J.W. von Goethe, *Theory of Colors*, trans. C.L. Eastlake. Cambridge, Mass.: MIT Press.

Jung, C.G. 1933. *Modern Man in Search of a Soul*. New York: Harcourt Brace.

———. 1950. 'Foreword', in *The I Ching, or Book of Changes*. Princeton, NJ: Princeton University Press, xxi–xxxix.

———. 1956 [1943]. *Two Essays on Analytical Psychology*. New York: World Publishing.

———. 1965. *Memories, Dreams and Reflections*. New York: Vintage.

———. 1969. *Analytical Psychology: Its Theory and Practice*. New York: Pantheon.

———. 1973. *Synchronicity: An Acausal Connecting Principle*. Princeton, NJ: Princeton University Press.

———. 1974 [1904]. 'Psychoanalysis and association experiments', in Jung, *The Psychoanalytic Years*. Princeton, NJ: Princeton University Press, 3–32.

———. 1976 [1921]. *Psychological Types* (A revision by R.F.C. Hull of the translation by H.G. Baynes). Princeton, NJ: Princeton University Press.

———. 1977. *The Symbolic Life*. Princeton, NJ: Princeton University Press.

Kahneman, D. 1968. 'Method, findings, and theory in studies of visual masking', *Psychological Bulletin* 69: 404–25.

Kaltenmark, M. 1969. *Lao Tzu and Taoism*. Stanford, Calif.: Stanford University Press

Kamin, L.J. 1974. *The Science and Politics of IQ*. New York: Wiley.

———. 1977. Letter, *Bulletin of the British Psychological Society* 30: 259.

Kanigel, R. 1997. *The One Best Way: Frederick Winslow Taylor and the Enigma of Efficiency*. New York: Viking.

Kant, I. 1950 [1783]. *Prolegomena to Any Future Metaphysics*. Indianapolis: Bobbs-Merrill.

————. 1960 [1763]. *Observations on the Beautiful and Sublime*, trans. J.T. Goldthwait. Berkeley: University of California Press.

————. 1965 [1787]. *Critique of Pure Reason*, trans. N.K. Smith. New York: St Martin's Press.

————. 1968 [1768]. *Selective Pre-critical Writings and Correspondence with Beck*, trans. G.B. Kerferd and D.E. Walford. Manchester: Manchester University Press.

Kaplan, B. 1992. 'Strife of systems: tension between organismic and developmental points of view', *Theory and Psychology* 2: 431–43.

———— and S. Wapner. 1960. 'Introductory remarks', in Kaplan and Wapner, eds, *Perspectives in Psychological Theory*. New York: International Universities Press, 13–19.

Kaplan, C.A., and H.A. Simon. 1990. 'In search of insight', *Cognitive Psychology* 22: 374–419.

Kaplan, E. 1983. 'Process and achievement revisited', in S. Wapner and B. Kaplan, eds, *Toward a Holistic Developmental Psychology*. Hillsdale, NJ: Erlbaum.

Katona, G. 1967 [1940]. *Organizing and Memorizing*. New York: Hafner.

Keegan, R.T., and H.E. Gruber. 1983. 'Love, death, and continuity in Darwin's thinking', *Journal of the History of the Behavioral Sciences* 19: 15–30.

Keenan, T. 2002. *An Introduction to Child Development*. London: Sage.

Keller, E.F. 1985. *Reflections on Gender and Science*. New Haven: Yale University Press.

————. 1995a. 'Gender and science: origin, history and politics', *Osiris* 10: 27–38.

————. 1995b. *Refiguring Life*. New York: Columbia University Press.

Keller, F.S. 1991. 'Burrhus Frederic Skinner (1904–1990)', *Journal of the History of the Behavioral Sciences* 27: 3–6.

Kellman, P., and E.S. Spelke. 1983. 'Perception of partly occluded objects in infancy', *Cognitive Psychology* 15: 483–524.

Kelly, G.A. 1955. *The Psychology of Personal Constructs*. New York: Norton.

————. 1965. 'The threat of aggression', *Journal of Humanistic Psychology* 5: 195–201.

————. 1969a. 'Humanistic methodology in psychological research', in B. Maher, ed., *Clinical Psychology and Personality: The Selected Papers of George Kelly*. New York: Wiley, 133–46.

————. 1969b. 'The autobiography of a theory', in Maher, ed., *Clinical Psychology and Personality*, 46–65.

Kennedy, J.M. 1997. 'How the blind draw', *Scientific American* 276: 60–5.

Kent, D. 1992. 'E. Gibson, A. Newell receive National Medal of Science', *APS Observer* 5 (Sept.): 1, 14–15.

————. 1993. 'Accomplished at 5, APS remains on track', *APS Observer* 6: 1, 4, 14, 28–31.

Kepler, J. 1966 [1611]. *The Six-Cornered Snowflake*. Oxford: Oxford University Press.

Kevles, D.J. 1985. *In the Name of Eugenics*. New York: Knopf.

Keynes, J.M. 1956. 'Newton, the man', in J.R. Newman, ed., *The World of Mathematics*. New York: Simon & Schuster, 277–85.

Kierkegaard, S. 1954 [1843, 1849]. *Fear and Trembling and The Sickness unto Death*. New York: Anchor Books.

————. 1959 [1843]. *Either/Or*. New York: Anchor Books.

Kiesler, D.J. 1983. 'The 1982 interpersonal circle: A taxonomy for complementarity in human transactions', *Psychological Review* 90: 185–214.

Kihlstrom, J.F. 1987. 'The cognitive unconscious', *Science* 237: 1445–52.

————. 1994. 'Ernest R. Hilgard: A life in psychology', *Psychological Science* 5: 179–80.

———— and K.M. McConkey. 1990. 'William James and hypnosis: A centennial reflection', *Psychological Science* 1: 174–8.

Kimball, M.M. 1994. 'The worlds we live in: Gender similarities and differences', *Canadian Psychology* 35: 388–404.

————. 1998. 'Bertha Pappenheim's blessed phantasy: Transforming private pain into public action', *History and Philosophy of Psychology Bulletin* 10: 21–5.

Kimble, G.A. 1961. *Hilgard and Marquis' Conditioning and Learning*, 2nd edn. New York: Appleton-Century-Crofts.

————. 1990. 'Mother Nature's bag of tricks is small', *Psychological Science* 1: 36–41.

————. 1993. 'A modest proposal for a minor revolution in the language of psychology', *Psychological Science* 4: 253–5.

———— and M. Wertheimer, eds. 1998. *Portraits of Pioneers in Psychology*, vol. 3. Hillsdale, NJ: Erlbaum.

————, ————, and C.L. White, eds. 1991. *Portraits of Pioneers in Psychology*, vol. 1. Hillsdale, NJ: Erlbaum.

Kingsley, P. 1995. *Ancient Philosophy, Mystery, and Magic: Empedocles and Pythagorean Tradition*. Oxford: Clarendon Press.

Kirk, G.S., and J.E. Raven. 1957. *The Presocratic Philosophers*. London: Cambridge University Press.

Kirkebøen, G. 2000. 'Descartes *Regulae*, mathematics and modern psychology', *History of Psychology* 3: 299–325.

Kirsch, I. 1977. 'Psychology's first paradigm', *Journal of the History of the Behavioral Sciences* 13: 317–25.

Kite, M.E., N.F. Russo, S.S. Brehm, N.A. Fouad, C.C.I. Hall, J.S. Hyde, and G.P. Keita. 2001. 'Women psychologists in academe: Mixed progress, unwarranted complacency', *American Psychologist* 56: 1080–98.

Klein, P., and M.R. Westcott. 1994. 'The changing character of phenomenological psychology', *Canadian Psychology* 35: 133–56.

Kline, M. 1962. 'Introduction', in Helmholtz (1962: vii–xii).

————. 1985. *Mathematics and the Search for Knowledge*. New York: Oxford University Press.

Knight, I.F. 1984. 'Freud's "Project": A theory for *Studies on Hysteria*', *Journal of the History of the Behavioral Sciences* 20: 340–58.

Knox, B. 1993. *The Oldest Dead White European Males*. New York: Norton.

Koch, S., ed. 1959. *Psychology: A Study of a Science*, 3 vols. New York: McGraw-Hill.

————. 1992. 'Psychology's Bridgman vs Bridgman's Bridgman', *Theory and Psychology* 2: 261–90.

Koestler, A. 1974. *The Roots of Coincidence*. Bungay, UK: Picador.

Koffka, K. 1935. *Principles of Gestalt Psychology*. New York: Harcourt, Brace & World.

————. 1959 [1928]. *The Growth of the Mind*. Paterson, NJ: Littlefield Adams.

Kohlberg, L. 1982. 'Moral development', in Broughton and Freeman-Moir (1982: 277–325).

Köhler, W. 1956 [1925]. *The Mentality of Apes*. New York: Vintage.

————. 1959 [1947]. *Gestalt Psychology*. New York: Mentor.

————. 1960 [1940]. *Dynamics in Psychology*. New York: Grove.

————. 1967 [1920]. 'Physical gestalten', in Ellis (1967: 17–53).

————. 1967 [1918]. 'Simple structural functions in the chimpanzee and the chicken', in Ellis (1967: 217–27).

————. 1969 [1967]. 'Gestalt psychology', in Krantz (1969a).

————. 1969. *The Task of Gestalt Psychology*. Princeton, NJ: Princeton University Press.

————. 1971 [1965]. 'Unsolved problems in the field of figural aftereffects', in M. Henle, ed., *The Selected Papers of Wolfgang Köhler*. New York: Liveright, 274–302.

———— and H. Wallach. 1944. 'Figural after-effects: An investigation of visual processes', *Proceedings of the American Philosophical Society* 88: 269–357.

Korn, J.H., R. Davis, and S.F. Davis. 1991. 'Historians' and Chairpersons' judgments of eminence among psychologists', *American Psychologist* 46: 789–92.

Koutstaal, W. 1992. 'Skirting the abyss: A history of experimental explorations of automatic writing in psychology', *Journal of the History of the Behavioral Sciences* 28: 5–27.

Koyré, A. 1954. 'Introduction', in Anscombe and Geach (1954: vii–xliv).

Krantz, D.L., ed. 1969a. *Schools of Psychology*. New York: Appleton-Century-Crofts.

————. 1969b. 'The Baldwin-Titchener controversy: A case study in the functioning and malfunctioning of schools', in Krantz (1969a: 1–19).

Krasnick, C.L. 1982. '"In charge of the loons": A portrait of the London, Ontario Asylum for the Insane in the Nineteenth Century', *Ontario History* 74: 138–84.

Kraus, O. 1976 [1926]. 'Biographical sketch of Franz Brentano', in L.L. McAlister, ed., *The Philosophy of Brentano*. Atlantic Highlands, NJ: Humanities Press, 1–9.

Krech, D. 1962. 'Cortical localization of function', in L. Postman, ed., *Psychology in the Making*. New York: Knopf, 31–72.

Krecz, C.A. 1986. 'Parts and pieces', *Philosophy and Phenomenological Research* 46: 381–400.

Kreitler, H., and S. Kreitler. 1972. *The Psychology of the Arts*. Durham, NC: Duke University Press.

Kubie, L. 1961. *Neurotic Distortion of the Creative Process*. New York: Noonday Press.

Kubovy, M. 1986. *The Psychology of Perspective and Renaissance Art*. New York: Cambridge University Press.

Kuhn, T.S. 1962. *The Structure of Scientific Revolutions*. Chicago: University of Chicago Press.

———. 1970. *The Structure of Scientific Revolutions*, 2nd edn. Chicago: University of Chicago Press.

Kulpe, O. 1964 [1912]. 'The modern psychology of thinking', in Mandler and Mandler (1964: 208–16).

Kvale, S., ed. 1992. *Psychology and Postmodernism*. London: Sage.

Laberge, D.L. 1990. 'Attention', *Psychological Science* 1: 156–62.

———. 1994. 'Hilgard's *Introduction to psychology*', *Psychological Science* 5: 184–5.

Ladd-Franklin, C. 1929. *Color and Color Theories*. New York: Harcourt, Brace.

Lagerwey, J. 1987. *Taoist Ritual in Chinese Society and History*. New York: Macmillan.

Lakatos, I. 1976. 'Proofs and refutations', in J. Worral and E. Zahar, eds, *Proofs and Refutations: The Logic of Mathematical Discovery*. Cambridge: Cambridge University Press, 6–105.

Lakin, M. 1998. 'Carl Rogers and the culture of psychotherapy', in Kimble and Wertheimer (1998: III, 245–58).

Lamarck, J.B. 1914 [1809]. *Zoological Philosophy*, trans. H. Elliot. London: Macmillan.

Landsberger, H.A. 1958. *Hawthorne Revisited: Management and Worker, Its Critics and Developments in Human Relations in Industry*. Ithaca, NY: Cornell University Press.

Lane, M. 1970. *Introduction to Structuralism*. New York: Basic Books.

Lashley, K.S. 1929. *Brain Mechanisms and Intelligence*. Chicago: University of Chicago Press.

———. 1951. 'The problem of serial order in behavior', in L.A. Jeffress, ed., *Cerebral Mechanisms in Behavior: The Hixon Symposium*. New York: Wiley, 112–46.

———. 1978 [1930]. 'Basic neural mechanisms in behavior', in Hilgard (1978: 265–83).

———, K.L. Chow, and J. Semmes. 1951. 'An examination of electrical field theory of cerebral integration', *Psychological Review* 58: 123–36.

Lau, D.C., ed. and trans. 1963. *Lao Tsu/Tao Te Ching*. Baltimore: Penguin Books.

Laughlin, P., R. Lange, and J. Adamopoulos. 1982.

'Selection strategies for "Master-mind" problems', *Journal of Experimental Psychology: Learning, Memory and Cognition* 8: 475–83.

Lavie, P., and J.A. Hobson. 1986. 'Origin of dreams: Anticipation of modern theories in the philosophy and physiology of the eighteenth and nineteenth centuries', *Psychological Bulletin* 100: 229–40.

Lazarus, R.S. 1984. 'On the primacy of cognition', *American Psychologist* 39: 124–9.

Leary, D.E. 1980. 'The historical foundation of Herbart's mathematicization of psychology', *Journal of the History of the Behavioral Sciences* 16: 150–63.

———. 2002. 'Ernest R. Hilgard (1904–2001)', *History of Psychology* 5: 310–14.

———, F. Kessel, and W. Bevan. 1998. 'Sigmund Koch (1917–1996)', *American Psychologist* 53: 316–17.

Le Corbusier [C.E. Jeanneret]. 1954. *The Modulor*. Cambridge, Mass.: Faber.

Lederer, S.E. 1985. 'Hideo Noguchi's luetin experiment and the antivivisectionists', *Isis* 76: 31–48.

Leeuwenberg, E., and F. Boselie. 1988. 'Against the likelihood principle in visual form perception', *Psychological Review* 95: 485–91.

Lefcourt, H.M. 1966. 'Internal versus external control of reinforcement: A review', *Psychological Bulletin* 65: 206–20.

———. 1992. 'Durability and impact of the locus of control construct', *Psychological Bulletin* 112: 411–14.

Le Ny, J.F. 1964. 'Conditioned reactions', in P. Fraisse and J. Piaget, eds, *Experimental Psychology: Its Scope and Method*, vol. 4. London: Routledge & Kegan Paul.

Leonard, G. 1983. 'Abraham Maslow and the new self', *Esquire* (Dec.): 326–8, 331–2, 335–6.

Lerner, R.M., ed. 1982. *Developmental Psychology: Historical and Philosophical Perspectives*. Hillsdale, NJ: Erlbaum.

———. 1986. *Concepts and Theories of Human Development*. New York: Random House.

Levi-Straus, C. 1967. *The Savage Mind*. London: Weidenfeld & Nicholson.

Lewin, K. 1936. *Principles of Topological Psychology*, trans. F. Heider and G.M. Heider. New York: McGraw-Hill.

———. 1946. 'Action research and minority problems', *Journal of Social Issues* 2: 34–46.

———. 1951. *Field Theory in Social Science*, ed. D. Cartwright. New York: Harper & Row.

———— and P. Grabbe. 1945. 'Conduct, knowledge and the acceptance of new values', *Journal of Social Issues* 1: 53–63.

Ley, R. 1990. *A Whisper of Espionage: Wolfgang Köhler and the Apes of Tenerife*. Garden City Park, NY: Avery.

Lindsley, O. 1969. 'The secret life of William James', in MacLeod (1969a: 35–43).

Lindzey, G., ed. 1980. *A History of Psychology in Autobiography*, vol. 7. San Francisco: Freeman.

Link, S. 1994. 'Rediscovering the past: Gustav Fechner and signal detection theory', *Psychological Science* 5: 335–40.

Livingstone, M.S. 1988. 'Art, illusion and the visual system', *Scientific American* 258: 78–85.

Locke, J. 1964 [1690]. *An Essay Concerning Human Understanding*. London: Fontana/Collins.

————. 1965 [1699]. 'Rewards, reputation and curiosity', in W. Kessen, ed., *The Child*. New York: Wiley, 60–71.

Loehlin, J.C. 1989. 'Partitioning environmental and genetic contributions to behavioral development', *American Psychologist* 44: 1285–92.

————. 1992. *Latent Variable Models*, 2nd edn. Hillsdale, NJ: Lawrence Erlbaum.

Loftus, E.F. 1991. 'The glitter of everyday memory . . . and the gold', *American Psychologist* 46: 16–18.

———— and G.R. Loftus. 1980. 'On the permanence of stored information in the human brain', *American Psychologist* 35: 409–20.

———— and J.C. Palmer. 1974. 'Reconstruction of automobile destruction: An example of the interaction between language and memory', *Journal of Verbal Learning and Verbal Behavior* 13: 585–9.

Logan, F.A. 1959. 'The Hull-Spence approach', in Koch (1959: II, 293–358).

Lovejoy, A.O. 1971 [1936]. *The Great Chain of Being*. Cambridge, Mass.: Harvard University Press.

Lovelock, J.E. 1987. *Gaia: A New Look at Life on Earth*. New York: Oxford University Press.

Lovie, A.D., and P. Lovie. 1993. 'Charles Spearman, Cyril Burt, and the origins of factor analysis', *Journal of the History of the Behavioral Sciences* 29: 308–21.

Lubek, I., and E. Apfelbaum. 1987. 'Neo-behaviorism and the Garcia effect: A social psychological approach to the history of a paradigm clash', in Ash and Woodward (1987: 59–91).

Luria, A.R. 1978. 'Biographical note on L.S. Vygotsky', in Vygotsky (1978: 15–16).

Lyell, C. 1969 [1830–3]. *Principles of Geology*, 3 vols. New York: Johnson Reprint.

————. 1979 [1853]. 'Principles of geology', in Appleman (1979: 10–15).

Lyons, W. 1983. 'The transformation of introspection', *British Journal of Social Psychology* 22: 327–42.

————. 1986. *The Disappearance of Introspection*. Cambridge, Mass.: MIT Press.

McCarley, R.W., and J.A. Hobson. 1977. 'The neurobiological origins of psychoanalytic dream theory', *American Journal of Psychiatry* 134: 1211–21.

McClearn, G.E. 1991. 'A trans-time visit with Francis Galton', in Kimble et al. (1991: I, 1–11).

McClelland, J.L., D.E. Rumelhart, and G.E. Hinton. 1986. 'The appeal of parallel distributed processing', in Rumelhart and McClelland, eds, *Parallel Distributed Processing: Explorations in the Micro structure of Cognition*, vol. 1: *Foundations*. Cambridge, Mass.: MIT Press, 3–44.

McCrae, R.R., P.T. Costa, and R.L. Piedmont. 1993. 'Folk concepts, natural language, and psychological constructs: The California Psychological Inventory and the five-factor model', *Journal of Personality* 61: 1–26.

McCrary, J.W., and W.S. Hunter. 1953. 'Serial position curves in verbal learning', *Science* 117: 131–4.

McGuire, W., ed. 1974. *The Freud/Jung Letters*. Princeton, NJ: Princeton University Press.

MacIntyre, A.C. 1958. *The Unconscious*. London: Routledge & Kegan Paul.

Mackavey, W.R., J.E. Malley, and A.J. Stewart. 1991. 'Remembering autobiographically consequential experiences: Content analysis of psychologists' accounts of their lives', *Psychology and Aging* 6: 50–9.

McKeon, R., ed. 1941. *The Basic Works of Aristotle*. Oxford: Oxford University Press.

McLaren, A. 1990. *Our Own Master Race*. Toronto: McClelland & Stewart.

MacLennan, J.H. 1945. *Two Solitudes*. New York: Duell, Sloan & Pearce.

MacLeod, C.M. 1992. 'The Stroop Task: The "Gold Standard" of attentional measures', *Journal of Experimental Psychology: General* 121: 12–15.

MacLeod, R.B., ed. 1969a. *William James: Unfinished Business*. Washington: American Psychological Association.

————. 1969b. 'James as a phenomenologist', in MacLeod (1969a: v–ix).

————. 1975. *The Persistent Problems of Psychology.* Pittsburgh: Duquesne University Press.

McReynolds, P. 1996. 'Lightner Witmer: A centennial tribute', *American Psychologist* 51: 237–40.

Madigan, S., and R. O'Hara. 1992. 'Short-term memory at the turn of the century: Mary Whiton Calkins's memory research', *American Psychologist* 47: 170–4.

Mahrer, A.R. 1996. 'The existential megabomb is still ticking', *Contemporary Psychology* 41: 870–2.

Maier, N.R.F., and T.C. Schneirla. 1964 [1935]. *Principles of Animal Psychology.* New York: Dover.

Malthus, T.R. 1956 [1798]. 'Mathematics of population and food', in J.R. Newman, ed., *The World of Mathematics.* New York: Simon & Schuster, 1192–1202.

Mancuso, J.C. 1970. *Readings for a Cognitive Theory of Personality.* New York: Holt, Rinehart and Winston.

Mandler, G. 1975. *Mind and Emotion.* New York: Wiley.

————. 1990. 'William James and the construction of the emotions', *Psychological Science* 1: 179–80.

————. 2002. 'Origins of the cognitive revolution', *Journal of the History of the Behavioral Sciences* 38: 339–53.

Mandler, J.M., and G. Mandler, eds. 1964. *Thinking: From Association to Gestalt.* New York: Wiley.

Manuel, F.E. 1965. *Shapes of Philosophical History.* Stanford, Calif.: Stanford University Press.

————, ed. 1966a. *Utopias and Utopian Thought.* Boston: Houghton Mifflin.

————. 1966b. 'Toward a psychological history of Utopias', in Manuel (1966a: 69–98).

————. 1968. *A Portrait of Isaac Newton.* Cambridge, Mass.: Harvard University Press.

————. 1974. *The Religion of Isaac Newton.* Oxford: Oxford University Press.

Marcel, A.J. 1983a. 'Conscious and unconscious perception: Experiments on visual masking and word recognition', *Cognitive Psychology* 15: 197–237.

————. 1983b. 'Conscious and unconscious perception: An approach to the relations between phenomenal experience and perceptual processes', *Cognitive Psychology* 15: 238–300.

————, L. Katz, and M. Smith. 1974. 'Laterality and reading proficiency', *Neuropsychologia* 12: 131–9.

Marder, B. 1993. 'Evelyn Fox Keller '57 reflects on gender and science', *Brandeis Review* 12: 22–5.

Margenau, H. 1954 [1885]. 'Introduction', in Helmholtz (1954: i–xi).

Marková, I. 1982. *Paradigms, Thought, and Language.* Chichester, UK: Wiley.

Marks, L.E. 1984. 'Psychology and physics: An historical perspective', in M.H. Bornstein, ed., *Psychology and Its Allied Disciplines*, vol. 3: *The Natural Sciences.* Hillsdale, NJ: Erlbaum, 229–64.

Markus, H. 1990. 'On splitting the universe', *Psychological Science* 1: 181–4.

Marrow, A.J. 1969. *The Practical Theorist: The Life and Work of Kurt Lewin.* New York: Basic Books.

Marshall, M. 1990. 'The theme of quantification and the hidden Weber in the early work of Gustav Theodor Fechner', *Canadian Psychology* 31: 45–53.

Martin, J., and J. Sugarman. 2000. 'Between the modern and the postmodern: The possibility of self and progressive understanding in psychology', *American Psychologist* 55: 397–406.

Martindale, A.E., and C. Martindale. 1988. 'Metaphorical equivalence of elements and temperaments: Empirical studies of Bachelard's theory of imagination', *Journal of Personality and Social Psychology* 55: 836–48.

Martindale, C. 1981. *Cognition and Consciousness.* Homewood, Ill.: Dorsey Press.

————. 1984. 'The pleasures of thought: A theory of cognitive hedonics', *Journal of Mind and Behavior* 5: 49–80.

———— and K. Moore. 1988. 'Priming, prototypicality, and preference', *Journal of Experimental Psychology: Human Perception and Performance* 14: 661–70.

Maslow, A.H. 1954. *Motivation and Personality.* New York: Harper & Row.

————. 1961. 'Existential psychology: What's in it for us?', in May (1961: 52–60).

————. 1962. *Toward a Psychology of Being.* New York: Van Nostrand.

————. 1964a. 'Synergy in the society and in the individual', *Journal of Individual Psychology* 20: 153–64.

————. 1964b. *Religions, Values and Peak-Experiences.* Columbus: Ohio State University Press.

————. 1965a. 'Humanistic psychology and transcendent experiences', *Journal of Humanistic Psychology* 5: 219–28.

————. 1965b. *Eupsychian Management.* Homewood, Ill.: Dorsey.

————. 1966. *The Psychology of Science: A Reconnaissance*. New York: Harper & Row.

————. 1971. *The Farther Reaches of Human Nature*. New York: Viking.

Masson, J.M. 1992 [1984]. *The Assault on Truth*. New York: HarperCollins.

Matlin, M.W. 1987. *The Psychology of Women*. New York: Holt, Rinehart and Winston.

May, R. 1950. *The Meaning of Anxiety*. New York: Ronald Press.

————. 1953. *Man's Search for Himself*. New York: Norton.

————. 1958. 'Existential psychotherapy', in May et al. (1958: 37–91).

————, ed. 1961. *Existential Psychology*. New York: Random House.

————. 1965. 'Intentionality, the heart of human will', *Journal of Humanistic Psychology* 5: 202–9.

————. 1969a. 'William James, humanism and the problem of the will', in MacLeod (1969a: 73–92).

————. 1969b. *Love and Will*. New York: Norton.

————, E. Angel, and H.F. Ellenberger. 1958. *Existence: A New Dimension in Psychiatry and Psychology*. New York: Basic Books.

Mayer, R.E. 1983. *Thinking, Problem Solving, Cognition*. New York: Freeman.

Mayer, R.W. 1997. 'Review of Benjafield, *A History of Psychology*', *Contemporary Psychology* 42: 841–2.

Mayo, E.B. 1960 [1933]. *The Human Problems of an Industrial Civilization*. New York: Viking Press.

Mayr, E. 1991. 'The ideological resistance to Darwin's theory of natural selection', *Proceedings of the American Philosophical Society* 135: 123–39.

————. 1994. 'The advance of science and scientific revolutions', *Journal of the History of the Behavioral Sciences* 30: 328–34.

Mazur, J.E. 1990. *Learning and Behavior*, 2nd edn. Englewood Cliffs, NJ: Prentice-Hall.

Mednick, S.A. 1962. 'The associative basis of the creative process', *Psychological Review* 69: 220–7.

Mente, D. 1995. 'Whose truth? Whose goodness? Whose beauty?', *American Psychologist* 50: 391.

Metcalfe, J., and D. Wiebe. 1987. 'Intuition in insight and non-insight problem solving', *Memory and Cognition* 15: 238–46.

Meyer, A., and J. Orth. 1964 [1901]. 'The qualitative investigation of associations', in Mandler and Mandler (1964: 135–43).

Meyer, A.E. 1975. *Grandmasters of Educational Thought*. New York: McGraw-Hill.

Meyer, G.E., and K. Hilterbrand. 1984. 'Does it pay to be "Bashful"? The seven dwarfs and long term memory', *American Journal of Psychology* 97: 47–55.

Michotte, A. 1963. *The Perception of Causality*, trans. T.R. Miles and E. Miles. New York: Basic Books.

Mill, J. 1948 [1829]. 'Analysis of the phenomena of the human mind', in Dennis (1948: 140–54).

Mill, J.S. 1948 [1843]. 'Psychology and ethology', in Dennis (1948: 169–77).

————. 1973 [1846]. 'A system of logic, ratiocinative and inductive', in J.M. Robson, ed., *Collected Works of John Stuart Mill*, vol. 7. Toronto: University of Toronto Press.

————. 1986 [1861]. *The Subjection of Women*. Buffalo, NY: Prometheus Books.

Miller, A. 1988. 'Toward a typology of personality styles', *Canadian Psychology* 29: 263–83.

Miller, G.A. 1953. 'What is information measurement?', *American Psychologist* 8: 3–11.

————. 1964. *Mathematics and Psychology*. New York: Wiley.

————. 1967 [1956]. 'The magical number seven, plus or minus two', in Miller, ed., *The Psychology of Communication: Seven Essays*. New York: Basic Books, 14–44.

————. 1970 [1969]. 'Psychology as a means of promoting human welfare', in F.F. Korten, S.W. Wood, and J.I. Lacey, eds, *Psychology and the Problems of Society*. Washington: American Psychological Association, 5–21.

————. 1979. 'A very personal history', talk given to Cognitive Science Workshop, MIT, Boston, Mass., June.

————. 1990. 'The place of language in a scientific psychology', *Psychological Science* 1: 7–14.

————. 2003. 'The cognitive revolution: a historical perspective', *Trends in Cognitive Science* 7: 141–4.

————, E. Galanter, and K. Pribram. 1960. *Plans and the Structure of Behavior*. New York: Holt, Rinehart and Winston.

Mills, J.A. 1988. 'The genesis of Hull's *Principles of Behavior*', *Journal of the History of the Behavioral Sciences* 24: 392–401.

————. 1992. 'Deconstructing *Constructing the Subject*', *Theory and Psychology* 2: 248–50.

Milner, P.M. 1993. 'The mind and Donald O. Hebb', *Scientific American* 268 (Jan.): 124–9.

Mischel, T. 1967. 'Kant and the possibility of a science of psychology', *The Monist* 51: 599–622.

————. 1969. 'Scientific and philosophical psychology: An historical introduction', in Mischel, ed., *Human Action*. New York: Academic Press, 1–40.

Mischel, W. 1968. *Personality and Assessment*. New York: Wiley.

Morawski, J.G. 1982. 'Assessing psychology's moral heritage through our neglected Utopias', *American Psychologist* 37: 1082–95.

————. 1988. 'Impossible experiments and practical constructions: The social bases of psychologists' work', in J.G. Morawski, ed., *The Rise of Experimentation in American Psychology*. New Haven: Yale University Press, 72–93.

————. 1992. 'There is more to our history of giving: The place of introductory textbooks in American psychology', *American Psychologist* 47: 161–9.

———— and R.S. Steele. 1991. 'The one or the other? Textual analysis of masculine power and feminist empowerment', *Theory and Psychology* 1: 107–31.

Morgan, C.L. 1966 [1894]. 'Lloyd Morgan's canon', in Herrnstein and Boring (1966: 462–8).

————. 1979 [1894]. 'The canon of interpretation of animal activity', in Watson (1979: 184–6).

Moruzzi, G., and H.W. Magoun. 1949. 'Brain stem reticular formation and activation of the EEG', *EEG Clinical Neurophysiology* 1: 455–73.

Muller, J. 1964 [1838]. 'Of the senses', in Dember (1964: 35–70).

Mumford, L. 1966. 'Utopia, the city and the machine', in Manuel (1966a: 3–24).

Mungello, D.E. 1977. *Leibniz and Confucianism, The Search for an Accord*. Honolulu: University of Hawaii Press.

Murphy, G., and L.B. Murphy. 1968. *Asian Psychology*. New York: Basic Books.

Murray, D.J. 1993. 'A perspective for viewing the history of psychophysics', *Behavioral and Brain Sciences* 16: 115–86.

————. 1995. *Gestalt Psychology and the Cognitive Revolution*. London: Harvester Wheatsheaf.

Myers, C.R. 1982. 'Psychology at Toronto', in M.J. Wright and Myers, eds, *A History of Academic Psychology in Canada*. Toronto: Hogrefe, 68–89.

Nagel, E. 1960. 'Methodological issues in psychoanalytic theory', in S. Hook, ed., *Psychoanalysis: Scientific Method and Philosophy*. New York: Grove Press, 38–56.

Natsoulas, T. 1978. 'Consciousness', *American Psychologist* 33: 906–14.

Necker, L.A. 1964 [1832]. 'On an apparent change of position in a drawing or engraved figure of a crystal', in Dember (1964: 78–83).

Needham, J. 1962. *Science and Civilization in China*, vol. 2. Cambridge: Cambridge University Press.

Neimeyer, R.A. 1985. *The Development of Personal Construct Psychology*. Lincoln: University of Nebraska Press.

Neisser, U. 1964. 'The multiplicity of thought', *British Journal of Psychology* 54: 1–14.

————. 1967. *Cognitive Psychology*. New York: Appleton-Century-Crofts.

————. 1972. 'A paradigm shift in psychology', *Science* 176: 628–30.

————. 1976. *Cognition and Reality*. San Francisco: Freeman.

————. 1978. 'Memory: What are the important questions?', in M.M. Gruneberg, P.M. Morris, and R.N. Sykes, eds, *Practical Aspects of Memory*. London: Academic Press, 3–24.

————. 1981. 'Obituary: James J. Gibson (1904–1979)', *American Psychologist* 36: 214–15.

————, ed. 1982. *Memory Observed: Remembering in Natural Contexts*. San Francisco: Freeman.

————, G. Boodoo, T.J. Bouchard, A.W. Boykin, N. Brody, S.J. Ceci, D.F. Halpern, J.C. Loehlin, R. Perloff, R.J. Sternberg, and S. Urbina. 1996. 'Intelligence: Knowns and unknowns', *American Psychologist* 51: 77–101.

Nerlich, D., and D.D. Clarke. 1998. 'The linguistic repudiation of Wundt', *History of Psychology* 1: 179–204.

Newell, A. 1977. 'On the analysis of human problem solving protocols', in P.N. Johnson-Laird and P. Wason, eds, *Thinking: Readings in Cognitive Science*. Cambridge: Cambridge University Press.

————. 1985. 'Duncker on thinking: An inquiry into progress in cognition', in S. Koch and D. Leary, eds, *A Century of Psychology as Science: Retrospections and Assessments*. New York: McGraw-Hill, 392–419.

———— and H.A. Simon. 1972. *Human Problem Solving*. Englewood Cliffs, NJ: Prentice-Hall.

————, J.C. Shaw, and H.A. Simon. 1958. 'Chess-playing programs and the problem of complexity', *IBM Journal of Research and Development* 2: 320–35.

Newton, I. 1952 [1730]. *Opticks: Or a Treatise of the Reflections, Refractions, Inflections & Colours of Light*. New York: Dover.

Nicholson, I.A.M. 1998. 'Gordon Allport, character, and the "Culture of Personality", 1897–1937', *History of Psychology* 1: 52–68.

———. 2001. '"Giving up maleness": Abraham Maslow, masculinity, and the boundaries of psychology', *History of Psychology* 4: 79–91.

Nicolas, S., and L. Ferrand. 1999. 'Wundt's laboratory at Leipzig in 1891', *History of Psychology* 2: 194–203.

——— and ———. 2002. 'Alfred Binet and higher education', *History of Psychology* 5: 264–83.

Nietzsche, F. 1967 [1901]. *The Will to Power*, trans. W. Kaufmann and R.J. Hollingdale. New York: Random House.

Noll, R. 1997. *The Aryan Christ: The Secret Life of Carl Jung*. New York: Random House.

O'Donnell, J.M. 1979. 'The crisis of experimentalism in the 1920s: E.G. Boring and his uses of history', *American Psychologist* 34: 289–95.

O'Hara, R.J. 1992. 'Telling the tree: Narrative representation and the study of evolutionary history', *Biology and Philosophy* 7: 135–60.

Olton, D.S. 1992. 'Tolman's cognitive analyses: Predecessors of current approaches in psychology', *Journal of Experimental Psychology: General* 121: 427–8.

O'Meara, D.J. 1987. *Pythagoras Revived: Mathematics and Philosophy in Late Antiquity*. Oxford: Clarendon Press.

Osgood, C.E. 1952. 'The nature and measurement of meaning', *Psychological Bulletin* 49: 197–237.

———. 1980. 'Charles E. Osgood', in Lindzey (1980: VII, 335–93).

——— and M.M. Richards. 1973. 'From Yang and Yin to "and" or "but"', *Language* 49: 380–412.

———, W.H. May, and M.S. Miron. 1975. *Cross-Cultural Universals of Affective Meaning*. Urbana: University of Illinois Press.

———, G.J. Suci, and P. Tannenbaum. 1957. *The Measurement of Meaning*. Urbana: University of Illinois Press.

Oxford English Dictionary. 1989. Oxford: Oxford University Press.

Oxford English Dictionary (CD). 1992. Oxford: Oxford University Press.

Paivio, A. 1971. *Imagery and Verbal Processes*. New York: Holt, Rinehart and Winston.

———. 1986. *Mental Representations*. Oxford: Oxford University Press.

Palmer, S.E. 1990. 'Modern theories of Gestalt perception', *Mind & Language* 5: 290–323.

———. 1992. 'Common region: A new principle of perceptual grouping', *Cognitive Psychology* 24: 436–47.

Pastore, N. 1971. *Selective History of Visual Perception*. New York: Oxford University Press.

Pauli, W. 1955. *The Influence of Archetypal Ideas on the Scientific Theories of Kepler*. New York: Pantheon.

Pauly, P.J. 1979. 'Psychology at Hopkins: Its rise and fall and rise and fall and . . .', *Johns Hopkins Magazine* (Dec.): 36–41.

Pavlov, I.P. 1928. *Lectures on Conditioned Reflexes*, trans. W.H. Gantt. New York: International Publishers.

———. 1960 [1927]. *Conditioned Reflexes*, ed. and trans. G.V. Anrep. New York: Dover.

———. 1997 [1897]. 'Excerpts from "The work of the digestive glands"', *American Psychologist* 52: 936–40.

Payne, D. 1986. 'The dirty legacy of brainwashing', *New Scientist* (6 Nov.): 28–9.

Pears, D. 1990. *Hume's System: An Examination of the First Book of the Treatise*. Oxford: Oxford University Press.

Pedhazur, E.J. 1997. *Multiple Regression in Behavioral Research*, 2nd edn. New York: Harcourt Brace.

——— and L.P. Schmelkin. 1991. *Measurement, Design and Analysis: An Integrated Approach*. Hillsdale, NJ: Erlbaum.

Pegis, A.C., ed. 1948. *Introduction to Saint Thomas Aquinas*. New York: Modern Library.

Pepper, S.C. 1934. 'The conceptual framework of Tolman's purposive behaviorism', *Psychological Review* 4: 108–33.

———. 1970. *World Hypotheses*. Berkeley: University of California Press.

Petrinovich, L., and J.L. McGaugh, eds. 1976. *Knowing, Thinking, and Believing: Festschrift for Professor David Krech*. New York: Plenum.

Pfungst, O. 1911. *Clever Hans (the Horse of Mr. von Osten): A Contribution to Experimental Animal, and Human Psychology*. New York: Holt.

Philip, J.A. 1966. *Pythagoras and Early Pythagoreanism*. Toronto: University of Toronto Press.

Philips, D.C., and R. Orton. 1983. 'The new causal principle of cognitive learning theory: perspectives on Bandura's "reciprocal determinism"', *Psychological Review* 90: 158–65.

Piaget, J. 1951 [1936]. 'The biological problem of intelligence', in Rapaport (1951: 176–92).

———. 1957. *Logic and Psychology.* New York: Basic Books.

———. 1959 [1923]. *The Language and Thought of the Child.* London: Routledge & Kegan Paul.

———. 1962. *Play, Dreams and Imitation in Childhood,* trans. G. Gattegno and F.M. Hodgson. London: Routledge & Kegan Paul.

———. 1963. *The Origins of Intelligence in Children,* trans. M. Cook. New York: Norton.

———. 1966. *Psychology of Intelligence.* Totawa, NJ: Littlefield, Adams.

———. 1968a. *Genetic Epistemology,* trans. E. Duckworth. New York: Columbia University Press.

———. 1968b. *On the Development of Memory and Identity,* trans. E. Duckworth. Worcester, Mass.: Clark University Press.

———. 1971. *Structuralism.* New York: Harper.

———. 1973. *Main Trends in Psychology.* New York: Harper.

———. 1976 [1965]. 'The rules of the game of marbles', in J.S. Bruner, A. Jolly, and K. Sylva, eds, *Play.* New York: Penguin, 413–41.

——— and B. Inhelder. 1969. *The Psychology of the Child.* New York: Basic Books.

——— and ———. 1973. *Memory and Intelligence,* trans. A.J. Pomerans. New York: Basic Books.

Pick, A., ed. 1979. *Perception and Its Development: A Tribute to Eleanor J. Gibson.* Hillsdale, NJ: Erlbaum.

Pick, H.L. 1992. 'Eleanor J. Gibson: Learning to perceive and perceiving to learn', *Developmental Psychology* 28: 787–94.

Platt, J. 1973. 'Social traps', *American Psychologist* 28: 641–51.

Plous, S. 1996. 'Attitudes toward the use of animals in psychological research and education', *American Psychologist* 51: 1167–80.

Pols, H. 2001. 'Between the laboratory, the school, and the community: The psychology of human development, Toronto, 1916–1956', *Canadian Journal of Community Mental Health* 19: 13–30.

———. 2002. 'Between the laboratory and life: Child development research in Toronto, 1919–1956', *History of Psychology* 5: 135–62.

Popper, K.R. 1965. *The Logic of Scientific Discovery.* New York: Harper.

Postman, L. 1962. 'Repetition and paired-associate learning', *American Journal of Psychology* 75: 372–89.

——— and G. Keppel, eds. 1969. *Verbal Learning and Memory.* Baltimore: Penguin.

Pötzl, O. 1960 [1917]. 'The relationship between experimentally induced dream images and indirect vision', *Psychological Issues* 2: 41–120.

Pressey, S.L. 1926. 'Simple apparatus which gives test and scores and teaches', *School and Society* 23: 373–6.

———. 1962. 'Development and appraisal of devices providing immediate automatic scoring of objective tests and concomitant self-instruction', in Smith and Moore (1962: 111–49).

Pribram, K. 1981. 'The brain, the telephone, the thermostat, the computer, and the hologram', *Cognition and Brain Theory* 4: 105–22.

——— and M. Gill. 1976. *Freud's Project Re-assessed.* London: Hutchinson.

Pritchard, R.M., W. Heron, and D.O. Hebb. 1960. 'Visual perception approached by the method of stabilized images', *Canadian Journal of Psychology* 14: 67–77.

Prochner, L., and P. Doyon. 1997. 'Researchers and their subjects in the history of child study: William Blatz and the Dionne quintuplets', *Canadian Psychology* 38: 103–10.

Puente, A.E. 1995. 'Roger Wolcott Sperry (1913–1994)', *American Psychologist* 50: 940–1.

Pyke, S., and N.M. Agnew. 1991. *The Science Game,* 5th edn. Englewood Cliffs, NJ: Prentice-Hall.

Quinn, S. 1987. *A Mind of Her Own: The Life of Karen Horney.* New York: Summit Books.

Rancurello, A.C. 1968. *A Study of Franz Brentano.* New York: Academic Press.

Randall, J.H. 1953. 'Introduction', in H.S. Thayer, ed., *Newton's Philosophy of Nature: Selections from His Writings.* New York: Hafner Press, ix–xvi.

Rao, C.R. 1992. 'R.A. Fisher: The founder of modern statistics', *Statistical Science* 7, 34–48.

Rapaport, D., ed. 1951. *Organization and Pathology of Thought.* New York: Columbia University Press.

———. 1959a. 'The structure of psychoanalytic theory', in Koch (1959: III, 55–183).

———. 1959b. 'Introduction', *Psychological Issues* 1, 1 (Monograph 1): 5–17.

Raphelson, A.C. 1982. 'The history course as the capstone of the psychology curriculum', *Journal of the History of the Behavioral Sciences* 18: 279–85.

Rawson, P., and L. Legeza. 1973. *Tao: The Chinese Philosophy of Time and Change.* London: Thames & Hudson.

Reber, A.S. 1985. *Dictionary of Psychology*. New York: Penguin.

Reichenbach, H. 1938. *Experience and Prediction*. Chicago: University of Chicago Press.

Reisman, J.M. 1991. *A History of Clinical Psychology*. New York: Hemisphere.

Richards, R.J. 1983. 'Why Darwin delayed, or interesting problems and models in the history of science', *Journal of the History of the Behavioral Sciences* 19: 45–53.

Rilling, M. 2000. 'John Watson's paradoxical struggle to explain Freud', *American Psychologist* 55: 301–12.

Robins, R.W., and K.H. Craik. 1994. 'A more appropriate test of the Kuhnian displacement thesis', *American Psychologist* 49: 815–916.

———, S.D. Gosling, and K.H. Craik. 1999. 'An empirical analysis of trends in psychology', *American Psychologist* 54: 117–28.

Robinson, D.N. 1977. 'Preface', in Romanes (1977: xxi–xxxv).

———. 1989. *Aristotle's Psychology*. New York: Columbia University Press.

Robinson, E.S. 1964 [1932]. *Association Theory Today*. New York: Hafner.

Rock, I. 1957. 'The role of repetition in associative learning', *American Journal of Psychology* 70: 186–93.

———. 1983. *The Logic of Perception*. Cambridge, Mass.: MIT Press.

———. 1992. 'Comment on Asch & Witkin's "Studies in Space Orientation II"', *Journal of Experimental Psychology: General* 121: 404–6.

——— and W. Heimer. 1959. 'Further evidence of one-trial associative learning', *American Journal of Psychology* 72: 1–16.

——— and S.E. Palmer. 1990. 'The legacy of Gestalt psychology', *Scientific American* 236 (Dec.): 84–90.

Rodgers, J.L. 1990. 'About APS: Structural models of the American Psychological Society at birth', *Psychological Science* 1: 85–96.

Roediger, H.L., ed. 1985. 'Ebbinghaus centennial', *Journal of Experimental Psychology: Learning, Memory and Cognition* 11: 414–35.

——— and R.G. Crowder. 1982. 'A serial position effect in recall of United States Presidents', in Neisser (1982: 230–7).

Rogers, C.R. 1951. *Client-Centered Therapy*. Boston: Houghton Mifflin.

———. 1952. '"Client-centered" psychotherapy', *Scientific American* 187: 66–74.

———. 1959. 'A theory of therapy, personality, and interpersonal relationships, as developed in the client-centered framework', in Koch (1959: III, 184–256).

———. 1961a. 'Two divergent trends', in May (1961: 85–93).

———. 1961b. *On Becoming a Person*. Boston: Houghton Mifflin.

———. 1964a. 'Some questions and challenges facing a humanistic psychology', *Journal of Humanistic Psychology* 5: 1–5.

———. 1964b. 'Toward a science of the person', in T.W. Wann, ed., *Behaviorism and Phenomenology: Contrasting Bases for Modern Psychology*. Chicago: University of Chicago Press, 109–40.

———. 1965. 'Some thoughts regarding the current philosophy of the behavioral sciences', *Journal of Humanistic Psychology* 5: 182–94.

———. 1967. 'Carl R. Rogers', in Boring and Lindzey (1967: V, 343–84).

———. 1970. *On Encounter Groups*. New York: Harper & Row.

———. 1970 [1954]. 'Towards a theory of creativity', in P.E. Vernon, ed., *Creativity*. Harmondsworth, UK: Penguin, 137–51.

———. 1978 [1947]. 'Some observations on the organization of personality', in Hilgard (1978: 417–34).

———. 1980. *A Way of Being*. Boston: Houghton Mifflin.

Rogers, T.B. 1989. 'Operationism in psychology: A discussion of contextual antecedents and an historical interpretation of its longevity', *Journal of the History of the Behavioral Sciences* 25: 139–53.

———. 1992. 'Danziger and psychological testing', *Theory and Psychology* 2: 251–4.

Rogoff, B., and J. Wertsch. 1984. *Children's Learning in the Zone of Proximal Development*. San Francisco: Jossey-Bass.

Romanes, G.J. 1977 [1883]. *Animal Intelligence*. New York: University Publications.

Ronan, C.A., and J. Needham. 1978. *The Shorter Science and Civilization in China*. New York: Cambridge University Press.

Rosch, E.H. 1978. 'Principles of categorization', in Rosch and B. Lloyd, eds, *Cognition and Categorization*. Hillsdale, NJ: Erlbaum, 27–48.

———. 1999. 'Is wisdom in the brain?', *Psychological Science* 10: 222–4.

Rosen, R.D. 1977. *Psychobabble: Fast Talk and Quick Cure in the Era of Feeling*. New York: Atheneum.

Rosenberg, S. 1993. 'Chomsky's theory of language: Some recent observations', *Psychological Science* 4: 15–19.

Rosenblith, J.F. 1992. 'A singular career: Nancy Bayley', *Developmental Psychology* 28: 747–58.

Rosenthal, R. 1966. *Experimenter Effects in Behavioral Research*. New York: Appleton-Century-Crofts.

———. 1967. 'Covert communication in the psychological experiment', *Psychological Bulletin* 67: 356–67.

Rosnow, R.L., and R. Rosenthal. 1989. 'Statistical procedures and the justification of knowledge in psychological science', *American Psychologist* 44: 1276–84.

Ross, B. 1991. 'William James: Spoiled child of American psychology', in Kimble et al. (1991: I, 13–26).

Ross, D. 1993. 'An historian's view of American Social Science', *Journal of the History of the Behavioral Sciences* 29: 99–111.

Ross, D.G. 1972. *Stanley Hall: The Psychologist as Prophet*. Chicago: University of Chicago Press.

Rossotti, H. 1983. *Colour*. Harmondsworth, UK: Penguin.

Roth, N. 1962. 'Freud and Galton', *Comprehensive Psychiatry* 3: 77–83.

Rotter, J. 1954. *Social Learning and Clinical Psychology*. Englewood Cliffs, NJ: Prentice-Hall.

———. 1966. 'Generalized expectancies for internal versus external control of reinforcement', *Psychological Monographs* 80, 1 (Whole No. 609).

Rozenzweig, M.R., W.H. Holzman, M. Sabourin, and D. Bélanger. 2000. *History of the International Union of Psychological Science (IUPsyS)*. Hove, UK: Psychology Press.

Rozin, P. 1990. 'Social and moral aspects of food and eating', in I. Rock, ed., *Legacy of Solomon Asch: Essays in Cognition and Social Psychology*. Hillsdale, NJ: Erlbaum, 97–110.

——— and A.E. Fallon. 1987. 'A perspective on disgust', *Psychological Review* 94: 23–41.

———, ———, and M. Augostoni-Ziskind. 1985. 'The child's conception of food: The development of contamination sensitivity to "disgusting" substances', *Developmental Psychology* 21: 1075–9.

———, L. Millman, and C. Nemeroff. 1986. 'Operation of the laws of sympathetic magic in disgust and other domains', *Journal of Personality and Social Psychology* 50: 703–12.

Rubin, D.C., S.E. Wetzler, and R.D. Nebes. 1986. 'Autobiographical memory across the lifespan', in Rubin, ed., *Autobiographical Memory*. Cambridge: Cambridge University Press, 202–21.

Rubin, E. 1958 [1915]. 'Figure and ground', in D.C. Beardslee and M. Wertheimer, eds., *Readings in Perception*. Princeton, NJ: Van Nostrand, 194–203.

Rumbaugh, D.M. 1996. 'In search of Red Oktober's psychology', *Contemporary Psychology* 41: 639–41.

Russell, B. 1945. *A History of Western Philosophy*. New York: Simon & Schuster.

Russell, J.A. 1980. 'A circumplex model of affect', *Journal of Personality and Social Psychology* 39: 1161–78.

Russell, R.L., and M.D. Gaubatz. 1995. 'Contested affinities: Reactions to Gergen's (1994) and Smith's (1994) postmodernisms', *American Psychologist* 50: 389–90.

Rutherford, A. 2000. 'Radical behaviorism and psychology's public: B.F. Skinner in the popular press, 1934–1990', *History of Psychology* 3: 371–95.

———. 2003. 'B.F. Skinner's technology of behavior in American life: from consumer culture to counterculture', *Journal of the History of the Behavioral Sciences* 39: 1–23.

Rycroft, C. 1969. 'All in the mind', *New York Review of Books* (16 Jan.): 4.

Ryle, A. 1975. *Frames and Cages*. Sussex: Sussex University Press.

Ryle, G. 1949. *The Concept of Mind*. New York: Barnes & Noble.

Sacks, O. 1974. *Awakenings*. Garden City, NY: Doubleday.

Sahakian, W.S., ed. 1968. *History of Psychology: A Source Book in Systematic Psychology*. Itaska, Ill.: Peacock.

Sambursky, S. 1956. *The Physical World of the Greeks*. London: Routledge & Kegan Paul.

Samelson, F. 1992. 'Rescuing the reputation of Sir Cyril [Burt]', *Journal of the History of the Behavioral Sciences* 28: 221–3.

———. 1993. 'Grappling with fraud charges in science, or: will the Burt Affair ever end?', paper presented at the meeting of Cheiron (International Society for the History of the Social and Behavioral Sciences), Durham, NH, June.

————. 1996. 'He didn't? yes, he did (probably)!', *Contemporary Psychology* 41: 1177–9.

Sampson, E.E. 1993. 'Identity politics', *American Psychologist* 48: 1219–30.

Sapiro, V. 1992. *A Vindication of Political Virtue: The Political Theory of Mary Wollstonecraft*. Chicago: University of Chicago Press.

Sappington, A.A. 1990. 'Recent psychological approaches to the free will versus determinism issue', *Psychological Bulletin* 108: 19–29.

Sarter, M., G.G. Berntson, and J.T. Cacioppo. 1996. 'Brain imaging and cognitive neuroscience: Toward strong inference in attributing function to structure', *American Psychologist* 51: 13–21.

Sartre, J.-P. 1957. *Existentialism and Human Emotions*. New York: Philosophical Library.

————. 1962 [1939]. *Sketch for a Theory of the Emotions*. London: Methuen.

————. 1966. *Being and Nothingness*. New York: Washington Square Press.

Sawyer, T.F. 2000. 'Francis Cecil Sumner: His views and influence on African American higher education', *History of Psychology* 3: 122–41.

Sayers, J. 1991. *Mothers of Psychoanalysis*. New York: Norton.

Scarborough, E., and L. Furomoto. 1987. *Untold Lives: The First Generation of American Women Psychologists*. New York: Columbia University Press.

Schachter, S. 1959. *The Psychology of Affiliation*. Stanford, Calif.: Stanford University Press.

Schlick, M. 1962 [1938]. 'Meaning and verification', in W. Barrett and H.D. Aiken, eds, *Philosophy in the Twentieth Century*, vol. 3. New York: Random House, 28–51.

Schlosberg, H. 1952. 'The description of facial expressions in terms of two dimensions', *Journal of Experimental Psychology* 44: 229–37.

Schmeidler, G. 1992. 'William James: Pioneering ancestor of modern parapsychology', in Donnelly (1992: 339–52).

Schmidgen, H., and R.B. Evans. 2003. 'The virtual laboratory: A new on-line resource for the history of psychology', *History of Psychology* 6: 208–13.

Schneirla, T.C. 1957. 'The concept of development in comparative psychology', in D.B. Harris, ed., *The Concept of Development*. Minneapolis: University of Minnesota Press, 78–108.

Schrag, C.O. 1967. 'Phenomenology, ontology, and history in the philosophy of Heidegger', in J.J. Kockelmans, ed., *Phenomenology*. New York: Anchor, 277–93.

Schull, J. 1992. 'Selection—James's principal principle', in Donnelly (1992: 139–52).

Seaman, J.D. 1984. 'On phi-phenomena', *Journal of the History of the Behavioral Sciences* 20: 3–8.

Sears, F.W., and M.W. Zemansky. 1970. *University Physics*. Reading, Mass.: Addison-Wesley.

Sedgwick, H.A. 1980. 'The geometry of spatial layout in pictorial representation', in M.A. Hagen, ed., *The Perception of Pictures*. New York: Academic Press, 33–90.

Segal, I., and R. Lachman. 1972. 'Complex behavior or higher mental process: Is there a paradigm shift', *American Psychologist* 27: 46–55.

Senders, V.L. 1958. *Measurement and Statistics*. New York: Oxford.

Shakow, D. 1969. 'Psychoanalysis', in Krantz (1969a: 87–122).

Shakow, D., and D. Rapaport. 1964. 'The influence of Freud on American psychology', *Psychological Issues* 4, 1 (Monograph 13).

Shannon, C., and W. Weaver. 1949. *The Mathematical Theory of Communication*. Urbana: University of Illinois Press.

Shapiro, K.J., and I.E. Alexander. 1975. *The Experience of Introversion*. Durham, NC: Duke University Press.

Shelley, M. 1963 [1818]. *Frankenstein*. New York: NAL Penguin.

Shepard, R. 1978. 'The mental image', *American Psychologist* 33: 125–37.

Shiffrin, R.M., and W. Schneider. 1977. 'Controlled and automatic human information processing: II. Perceptual learning, automatic attending, and a general theory', *Psychological Review* 84: 155–71.

Shore, M. 2001. 'Psychology and memory in the midst of change: The social concerns of late 19th-century North American psychologists', in Green et al. (2001: 63–86).

Shortt, S.E.D. 1986. *Victorian Lunacy: Richard M. Bucke and the Practice of Late Nineteenth-Century Psychiatry*. Cambridge: Cambridge University Press

Siegler, R.S. 1986. *Children's Thinking*. Englewood Cliffs, NJ: Prentice-Hall.

Simmel, M.L. 1956. 'Phantoms in patients with leprosy and in elderly digital amputees', *American Journal of Psychology* 69: 529–45.

————. 1968. 'Kurt Goldstein 1878–1965', in M.L. Simmel, ed., *The Reach of Mind*. New York: Springer, 3–12.

Simon, H.A. 1954. 'Spurious correlation: A causal interpretation', *Journal of the American Statistical Association* 49: 467–79.

————. 1967. 'Motivational and emotional controls of cognition', *Psychological Review* 74: 29–39.

————. 1975. 'The functional equivalence of problem solving skills', *Cognitive Psychology* 7: 268–88.

————. 1980. 'Herbert A. Simon', in Lindzey (1980: VII, 435–72).

————. 1981. *The Sciences of the Artificial*, 2nd edn. Cambridge, Mass.: MIT Press.

————. 1991. *Models of My Life*. New York: Basic Books.

————. 1992. 'What is an "explanation" of behavior?', *Psychological Science* 3: 150–61.

————. 1995. 'The information-processing theory of mind', *American Psychologist* 50: 507–8.

Simon, L. 1992. 'Reform starts at the dinner table', *Brandeis Review* 11: 34–9.

Simonton, D.K. 1984. *Genius, Creativity and Leadership*. Cambridge, Mass.: Harvard University Press.

————. 1988. *Scientific Genius*. New York: Cambridge University Press.

Skinner, B.F. 1938. *The Behavior of Organisms*. New York: Appleton-Century-Crofts.

————. 1945a. 'The operational analysis of psychological terms', *Psychological Review* 52: 270–7.

————. 1945b. 'Baby in a box', *Ladies Home Journal* 62 (Oct.): 30–1, 135–6, 138.

————. 1948. *Walden Two*. New York: Macmillan.

————. 1956. 'A case history in scientific method', *American Psychologist* 11: 221–33.

————. 1957. *Verbal Behavior*. New York: Appleton-Century.

————. 1961 [1953]. 'Freud's psychoanalytic theory', in P.K. Frank, ed., *The Validation of Psychoanalytic Theory*. New York: Collier, 110–21.

————. 1962. 'The science of learning and the art of teaching', in Smith and Moore (1962: 19–33).

————. 1964. 'Behaviorism at fifty', in T.W. Wann, ed., *Behaviorism and Phenomenology: Contrasting Bases for Modern Psychology*. Chicago: University of Chicago Press, 79–97.

————. 1971. *Beyond Freedom and Dignity*. New York: Knopf.

————. 1979. *The Shaping of a Behaviorist*. New York: Knopf.

————. 1980. *Notebooks*. Englewood Cliffs, NJ: Prentice-Hall.

————. 1984. 'Selection by consequences', *Behavioral and Brain Sciences* 7: 477–81.

————. 1986. 'What is wrong with daily life in the Western world?', *American Psychologist* 41: 568–74.

————. 1987. *Upon Further Reflection*. Englewood Cliffs, NJ: Prentice-Hall.

Slamecka, N.J., ed. 1967. *Human Learning and Memory*. Oxford: Oxford University Press.

————. 1985. 'Ebbinghaus: Some associations', *Journal of Experimental Psychology* 11: 414–35.

Smith, C.U.M. 1987. 'David Hartley's Newtonian neuropsychology', *Journal of the History of the Behavioral Sciences* 23: 123–38.

Smith, H.C. 1973. *Sensitivity Training: The Scientific Understanding of Individuals*. New York: McGraw-Hill.

Smith, L.D., L.A. Best, V.A. Cylke, and D.A. Stubbes. 2000. 'Psychology without *p* values: Data analysis at the turn of the 20th century', *American Psychologist* 55: 260–3.

Smith, M.B. 1994. 'Selfhood at risk: Postmodern perils and the perils of postmodernism', *American Psychologist* 49: 405–11.

————. 1995. 'About postmodernism: Reply to Gergen and others', *American Psychologist* 50: 393.

————. 1998. 'Review of Benjafield, *A History of Psychology*', *Journal of the History of the Behavioral Sciences* 34: 90–4.

Smith, W.I., and J.W. Moore, eds. 1962. *Programmed Learning: Theory and Research*. New York: Van Nostrand.

Snyderman, M., and R.J. Herrnstein. 1983. 'Intelligence tests and the Immigration Act of 1924', *American Psychologist* 38: 986–95.

Sokal, M.M. 1984. 'The Gestalt psychologists in behaviorist America', *American Historical Review* 89: 1240–63.

————. 1990. 'G. Stanley Hall and the institutional character of Clark University', *Journal of the History of the Behavioral Sciences* 26: 114–24.

————. 2001. 'Practical phrenology as psychological counseling in the 19th-century United States', in Green et al. (2001: 21–44).

Soyland, A.J. 1994. 'After Lashley: Neuropsychology, metaphors, promissory notes', *Theory and Psychology* 4: 227–44.

Spearman, C. 1904. '"General intelligence" objectively determined and measured', *American Journal of Psychology* 15: 201–92.

———. 1970 [1932]. *The Abilities of Man: Their Nature and Measurement.* New York: AMS Press.

Spelke, E., W. Hirst, and U. Neisser. 1976. 'Skills of divided attention', *Cognition* 4: 215–30.

Spence, J.T. 1987. 'Centrifugal versus centripetal tendencies in psychology: Will the center hold?', *American Psychologist* 42: 1052–4.

Spence, K.W. 1937. 'The differential response in animals to stimuli varying within a single dimension', *Psychological Review* 44: 430–44.

———. 1944. 'The nature of theory construction in contemporary psychology', *Psychological Review* 51: 47–68.

———. 1956. *Behavior Theory and Conditioning.* New Haven: Yale University Press.

———. 1960. *Behavior Theory and Learning: Selected Papers.* Englewood Cliffs, NJ: Prentice-Hall.

Spencer, H. 1880 [1862]. *First Principles*, 5th edn. New York: A.L. Burt.

———. 1897. *Principles of Psychology.* New York: Appleton.

———. 1968 [1855]. 'Life as a continuous adjustment', in Sahakian (1968: 181–2).

Sperber, D., and D. Wilson. 1986. *Relevance: Communication and Cognition.* Cambridge, Mass.: Harvard University Press.

Sperling, G. 1960. 'The information available in brief visual presentations', *Psychological Monographs* 74, 11.

Sperry, R.W. 1961. 'Cerebral organization and behaviour', *Science* 133 (June): 1750.

———. 1964. 'The great cerebral commissure', *Scientific American* 210 (Jan.): 42–52.

———. 1987. 'Consciousness and causality', in Gregory (1987: 164–6).

———. 1988. 'Psychology's mentalist paradigm and the religion/science tension', *American Psychologist* 43: 607–13.

———. 1995. 'The future of psychology', *American Psychologist* 50: 505–6.

——— and N. Milner. 1955. 'Pattern perception following the insertion of mica plates into visual cortex', *Journal of Comparative and Physiological Psychology* 48: 463–9.

Stam, H.J. 1990. 'Rebuilding the ship at sea: The historical and theoretical problems of constructionist epistemologies in psychology', *Canadian Psychology* 31: 239–61.

———. 1992. 'Deconstructing the subject: Banishing the ghost of Boring', *Contemporary Psychology* 37: 629–32.

——— and T. Kalmanovich. 1998. 'E.L. Thorndike and the origins of animal psychology', *American Psychologist* 53: 1135–44.

Steinem, G. 1994. 'What if Freud were Phyllis? or, The Watergate of the Western World', in Steinem, *Moving Beyond Words.* New York: Knopf, 32–92.

Steinfeld, G.J., and I. Rock. 1968. 'Control for item selection and familiarization in the formation of associations', *American Journal of Psychology* 61: 42–6.

Stern, W. 1966 [1912]. 'On the mental quotient', in Herrnstein and Boring (1966: 450–3).

Sternberg, R.J. 1984. 'Preface', in Sternberg, ed., *Mechanisms of Cognitive Development.* New York: Freeman, vii–ix.

———. 1988. *The Triarchic Mind: A New Theory of Human Intelligence.* New York: Viking.

———. 1992. 'Ability tests, measurements, and markets', *Journal of Educational Psychology* 84: 134–40.

———. 2000. 'Cross-disciplinary verification of theories: The case of the triarchic theory', *History of Psychology* 3: 177–9

——— and E.L. Grigorenko. 2001. 'Unified psychology', *American Psychologist* 56: 1069–79.

Stevens, G., and S. Gardner. 1982. *The Women of Psychology*, vol. 1. Cambridge, Mass.: Schenkman.

Stevens, P.S. 1974. *Patterns in Nature.* Boston: Little, Brown.

Stevenson, L. 1974. *Seven Theories of Human Nature.* New York: Oxford University Press.

Stigler, S.M. 1986. *The History of Statistics: The Measurement of Uncertainty before 1900.* Cambridge, Mass.: Harvard University Press.

Stillings, N.A., M.H. Feinstein, J.L. Garfield, E.L. Rissland, D.A. Rosenbaum, S.E. Weisler, and L. Baker-Ward. 1987. *Cognitive Science: An Introduction.* Cambridge, Mass.: MIT Press.

Stone, I. 1983. 'The death of Darwin', in Cherfas (1983: 68–9).

Storm, C., and M. Gurevich. 2001. 'Looking forward, looking back: Women in psychology', *Canadian Psychology* 42, 4 (special issue).

Stover, D., and E. Erdmann. 2000. *A Mind for Tomorrow: Facts, Values, and the Future*. Westport, Conn.: Praeger.

Stratton, G.M. 1964 [1897]. 'Vision without inversion of the retinal image', in Dember (1964: 143–54).

Strauss, S., ed. 1988. *Ontogeny, Phylogeny and Historical Development*. Norwood, NJ: Ablex.

Street, W.R. 1994. *A Chronology of Noteworthy Events in American Psychology*. Washington: American Psychological Association.

Stricker, L.J., and J. Ross. 1964. An assessment of some structural properties of the Jungian personality typology', *Journal of Abnormal and Social Psychology* 68: 62–71.

Stroop, J.R. 1992 [1935]. 'Studies of interference in serial verbal reactions', *Journal of Experimental Psychology: General* 121: 15–23.

Suedfeld, P., and S. Coren. 1989. 'Perceptual isolation, sensory deprivation, and rest: Moving introductory psychology texts out of the 1950s', *Canadian Psychology* 30: 17–29.

Sulloway, F.J. 1979. *Freud: Biologist of the Mind*. New York: Basic Books.

Suls, J.M., and R.L. Rosnow. 1988. 'Concerns about artifacts in psychological experiments', in J. Morawski, ed., *The Rise of Experimentation in American Psychology*. New Haven: Yale University Press, 163–87.

Suzuki, D.T. 1956. *Zen Buddhism: Selected writings of D.T. Suzuki*, ed. W. Barrett. Garden City, NY: Doubleday.

Tanner, N.M. 1983. 'Hunters, gatherers and sex roles in space and time', *American Anthropologist* 85: 335–41.

Tart, C.T. 1975. *Transpersonal Psychologies*. New York: Harper & Row.

Tavolga, W.N. 1969. *Principles of Animal Behavior*. New York: Harper & Row.

Taylor, E. 1999a. 'William James and Sigmund Freud: "The future of psychology belongs to your work"', *Psychological Science* 10: 465–9.

———. 1999b. *Shadow Culture: Psychology and Spirituality in America*. Washington: Counterpoint.

Taylor, F.W. 1967 [1911]. *The Principles of Scientific Management*. New York: Norton.

Teo, T. 2001. 'Karl Marx and Wilhelm Dilthey on the socio-historical conception of the mind', in Green et al. (2001: 195–218).

Terman, L.M. 1948 [1916]. 'The measurement of intelligence', in Dennis (1948: 485–96).

Thelen, E., and K.E. Adolph. 1992. 'Arnold L. Gesell: The paradox of Nature and nurture', *Developmental Psychology* 28: 368–80.

Thomson, K.S. 1998. '1798: Darwin and Malthus', *American Scientist* 86: 226–9.

Thompson, D.W. 1929. 'Excess and defect: or the little more and the little less', *Mind* 38: 43–55.

———. 1942. *On Growth and Form*. Cambridge: Cambridge University Press.

Thompson, E.P. 1994. *Making History: Writings on History and Culture*. New York: Norton.

Thorndike, E.L. 1917. 'Individual differences in judgements of the beauty of simple forms', *Psychological Review* 24: 147–53.

———. 1948 [1898]. 'Animal intelligence', in Dennis (1948: 377–87).

———. 1949a. *Selected Writings from a Connectionist's Psychology*. New York: Appleton-Century-Crofts.

———. 1949b [1936]. 'Edward Lee Thorndike', in Thorndike (1949a: 1-11).

———. 1949c [1922]. 'The constitution of arithmetic abilities', in Thorndike (1949a: 165–75).

———. 1949d [1933]. 'The law of effect', in Thorndike (1949a: 13-26). New York: Appleton-Century-Crofts.

———. 1966 [1931]. *Human Learning*. Cambridge, Mass.: MIT Press.

———. 1979 [1898]. 'Animal and human learning by trial and error', in Watson (1979: 255–62).

———. 1998 [1898]. 'Animal intelligence: An experimental study of the associative process in animals', *American Psychologist* 53: 1125–7.

——— and I. Lorge. 1944. *The Teacher's Word Book of 30,000 Words*. New York: Columbia University Press.

——— and R.S. Woodworth. 1948 [1901]. 'The influence of improvement in one mental function upon the efficiency of other functions', in Dennis (1948: 388–98).

Thorndike, R.L. 1954. 'The psychological value system of psychologists', *American Psychologist* 9: 787–90.

Thurstone, L.L. 1938. *Primary Mental Abilities*. Chicago: University of Chicago Press.

———. 1944. *A Factorial Study of Perception*. Chicago: University of Chicago Press.

———. 1965 [1948]. 'Psychological implications of factor analysis', in Anastasi (1965: 58–64).

———. 1978 [1934]. 'The vectors of mind', in Hilgard (1978: 285–308).

Tigner, R.B., and S.S. Tigner. 2000. 'Triarchic theories of intelligence: Aristotle and Sternberg', *History of Psychology* 3: 168–76.

Titchener, E.B. 1966a [1910]. 'From "A text-book of psychology"', in Herrnstein and Boring (1966: 599–605).

———. 1966b [1896]. 'The "type theory" of the simple reaction', in Vanderplas (1966: 173–9).

———. 1966c [1898]. 'The postulates of a structural psychology', in Vanderplas (1966: 35–47).

———. 1966d [1895]. 'The type theory of the simple reaction', in Vanderplas (1966: 155–64).

———. 1968 [1921]. 'Brentano and Wundt: Empirical and experimental psychology', in L.L. McAlister, ed., *The Philosophy of Brentano*. Atlantic Highlands, NJ: Humanities Press, 80–90.

———. 1971a [1902]. *Experimental Psychology: A Manual of Laboratory Practice*, vol. 1. New York: Johnson Reprint.

———. 1971b [1905]. *Experimental Psychology: A Manual of Laboratory Practice*, vol. 2, parts 1 and 2. New York: Johnson Reprint.

———. 1972 [1929]. *Systematic Psychology: Prolegomena*. Ithaca, NY: Cornell University Press.

Todes, D.P. 1997. 'From the machine to the ghost within: Pavlov's transition from digestive physiology to conditional reflexes', *American Psychologist* 52: 947–55.

Tolman, C.W. 2001. 'Philosophical doubts about psychology as a natural science', in Green et al. (2001: 175–93).

Tolman, E.C. 1948. 'Cognitive maps in rats and men', *Psychological Review* 55.

———. 1951a. *Behavior and Psychological Man*. Berkeley: University of California Press.

———. 1951b [1935]. 'Psychology versus immediate experience', in Tolman (1951a: 94–114).

———. 1959. 'Principles of purposive behavior', in Koch (1959: II, 92–157).

———. 1967 [1932]. *Purposive Behavior in Animals and Men*. New York: Appleton-Century-Crofts.

——— and C.H. Honzik. 1930. 'Degrees of hunger, reward and non-reward, and maze learning in rats', *University of California Publications in Psychology* 4: 241–56.

———, B.F. Ritchie, and D. Kalish. 1992 [1946]. 'Studies in spatial learning: I. Orientation and the short cut', *Journal of Experimental Psychology: General* 121: 429–34.

Toman, W. 1960. *An Introduction to the Psychoanalytic Theory of Motivation*. New York: Pergamon.

———. 1971. 'The duplication theorem of social relationships as tested in the general population', *Psychological Review* 78: 380–90.

Toulmin, S. 1972. *Human Understanding: The Collective Use and Evolution of Concepts*. Princeton, NJ: Princeton University Press.

Toynbee, A.J. 1960 [1947]. *A Study of History*. Oxford: Oxford University Press.

Tracy, T.J. 1969. *Physiological Theory and the Doctrine of the Mean in Plato and Aristotle*. The Hague: Mouton.

Trilling, L. 1972. *Sincerity and Authenticity*. Cambridge, Mass.: Harvard University Press.

Tryon, W.W. 2001. 'Evaluating statistical difference, equivalence, and indeterminacy using confidence intervals: An integrated alternative method of conducting null hypothesis statistical tests', *Psychological Methods* 6: 371–86.

Tucker, W.H. 1997. 'Re-reconsidering Burt: Beyond a reasonable doubt', *Journal of the History of the Behavioral Sciences* 33: 145–62.

Turing, A. 1950. 'Computing machinery and intelligence', *Mind* 59: 433–50.

Tweney, R.D. 1987. 'Programmatic research in experimental psychology: E.B. Titchener's laboratory investigations, 1891–1927', in Ash and Woodward (1987: 35–58).

———. 1998. 'Toward a cognitive psychology of science: Recent research and its implications', *Current Directions in Psychological Science* 7: 150–4.

Underwood, B.J. 1964. 'The representativeness of rote verbal learning', in A.W. Melton, ed., *Categories of Verbal Learning*. New York: Academic Press, 48–78.

———, R. Rehula, and G. Keppel. 1962. 'Item-selection on paired associate learning', *American Journal of Psychology* 75: 353–71.

Urban, W.J. 1989. 'The black scholar and intelligence testing: The case of Horace Mann Bond', *Journal of the History of the Behavioral Sciences* 25: 323–34.

Vande Kemp, H. 1992. 'G. Stanley Hall and the Clark school of religious psychology', *American Psychologist* 47: 290–8.

Vanderplas, J.M., ed. 1966. *Controversial Issues in Psychology*. Boston: Houghton Mifflin.

van Elteren, M. 1992. 'Kurt Lewin as filmmaker and methodologist', *Canadian Psychologist* 33: 599–608.

Varela, F.J., E. Thompson, and E. Rosch. 1991. *The Embodied Mind*. Cambridge, Mass.: MIT Press.

Vicente, K.J., and W.F. Brewer. 1993. 'Reconstructive remembering of the scientific literature', *Cognition* 46: 101–28.

Vickery, J.B. 1973. *The Literary Impact of the Golden Bough*. Princeton, NJ: Princeton University Press.

Vidal, F., M. Buscaglia, and J.J. Voneche. 1983. 'Darwinism and developmental psychology', *Journal of the History of the Behavioral Sciences* 19: 81–94.

Vitz, P.C., and A.B. Glimcher. 1984. *Modern Art and Modern Science*. New York: Praeger.

Vonèche, J.J. 1982. 'Evolution, development, and knowledge', in Broughton and Freeman-Moir (1982: 51–79).

Von Mayrhauser, R.T. 1989. 'Making intelligence functional: Walter Dill Scott and Applied psychological testing in World War I', *Journal of the History of the Behavioral Sciences* 25: 60–72.

———. 1992. 'The mental testing community and validity', *American Psychologist* 47: 244–53.

von Restorff, H. 1933. 'Über die Wirkung von Bereichsbildungen im Spurenfeld', *Psychologische Forschung* 18: 299–342.

Vygotsky, L.S. 1962 [1934]. *Thought and Language*, trans. E. Hanfmann and G. Vakar. Cambridge, Mass.: MIT Press.

———. 1971. *The Psychology of Art*. Cambridge, Mass.: MIT Press.

———. 1978 [1935]. *Mind in Society*. Cambridge, Mass.: Harvard University Press.

———. 1986 [1934]. *Thought and Language*, trans. A. Kozulin. Cambridge, Mass.: MIT Press.

Walk, R.D., and E.J. Gibson. 1961. 'A comparative and analytic study of visual depth perception', *Psychological Monographs* 75, 15 (Whole No. 519).

Wallach, L., and M.A. Wallach. 1994. 'Gergen versus the mainstream', *Journal of Personality and Social Psychology* 67: 233–42.

Wallach, M.A., and L. Wallach. 1983. *Psychology's Sanction for Selfishness: The Error of Egoism in Theory and Therapy*. San Francisco: Freeman.

Wallas, G. 1926. *The Art of Thought*. London: Cape.

Wapner, S. 1964. 'Some aspects of a research program based on an organismic-developmental approach to cognition: Experiments and theory', *Journal of the American Academy of Child Psychiatry* 3: 193–230.

Ward, J. 1910. 'Herbart, Johann Friedrich', in *Encyclopedia Britannica*, 11th edn., vol. 13. New York: Encyclopedia Britannica Company, 335–8.

Warden, C.J., T.N. Jenkins, and L.H. Warner. 1934. *Introduction to Comparative Psychology*. New York: Ronald.

Warnock, G.J. 1987. 'George Berkeley', in Gregory (1987: 82–3).

Warnock, M. 1970. *Existentialism*. London: Oxford University Press.

Warr, P.B. 1970. *Thought and Personality*. Harmondsworth, UK: Penguin.

Warren, D.H. 1978. 'Perception by the blind', in E.C. Carterette and M.P. Friedman, eds, *Handbook of Perception*, vol. 10: *Perceptual Ecology*. New York: Academic Press, 65–90.

Watson, J.B. 1962 [1930]. *Behaviorism*, rev. edn. Chicago: University of Chicago Press.

———. 1966 [1913]. 'Psychology as the behaviorist views it', in Vanderplas (1966: 70–84).

———. 1970 [1916]. 'The place of the conditioned reflex in psychology', in W.H. Gantt, L. Pickenhain, and C. Zwingmann, eds, *Pavlovian Approach to Psychopathology*. Oxford: Pergamon, 35–46.

——— and R. Rayner. 2000 [1920]. 'Conditioned emotional reactions', *American Psychologist* 55: 313–17.

Watson, R.I. 1979. *Basic Writings in the History of Psychology*. New York: Oxford University Press.

Weidman, N. 1994. 'Mental testing and machine intelligence: The Lashley-Hull debate', *Journal of the History of the Behavioral Sciences* 30: 162–80.

———. 1997. 'Review of Benjafield, A History of Psychology', *Isis* 88, 1: 127–8.

———. 1999. *Constructing Scientific Psychology: Karl Lashley's Mind-Brain Debates*. New York: Cambridge University Press

———. 2002. 'The depoliticization of Karl Lashley: A response to Dewsbury', *Journal of the History of the Behavioral Sciences* 38: 247–53.

Weikart, R. 1995. 'A recently discovered Darwin letter on Social Darwinism', *Isis* 86: 609–11.

Weimer, W.B. 1973. 'Psycholinguistics and Plato's paradoxes of the *Meno*', *American Psychologist* 28: 15–32.

Weisberg, R.W., and J.W.A. Alba. 1981. 'An examination of the role of fixation in the solution of several insight problems', *Journal of Experimental Psychology: General* 110: 169–92.

Weizmann, F. 2001. 'Early development and psychology: Genetic and embryological influences, 1880–1920', in Green et al. (2001: 219–35).

Wentworth, P.A. 1999. 'The moral of her story: Exploring the philosophical and religious commitments in Mary Whiton Calkins' self-psychology', *History of Psychology* 2: 119–31.

Werner, H. 1935. 'Studies on contour: I. Qualitative analyses', *American Journal of Psychology* 47: 40–64.

———. 1937. 'Process and achievement: A basic problem of education and developmental psychology', *Harvard Educational Review* 7: 353–68.

———. 1957. 'The concept of development from a comparative and organismic point of view', in D.B. Harris, ed., *The Concept of Development*. Minneapolis: University of Minnesota Press, 125–48.

———. 1961. *Comparative Psychology of Mental Development*. New York: Science Editions.

——— and B. Kaplan. 1963. *Symbol Formation*. New York: Wiley.

——— and E. Kaplan. 1952. 'The acquisition of word meanings: A developmental study', *Monographs of the Society for Research in Child Development* 15, 1 (Serial No. 51).

Wertheimer, Max. 1912. 'Experimentelle Studien über das Sehen von Bewegung', *Psychologische Forschung* 61: 161–265.

———. 1958. 'Principles of perceptual organization', in D.C. Beardslee and Michael Wertheimer, eds, *Readings in Perception*. Princeton, NJ: Van Nostrand, 115–35.

———. 1959. *Productive Thinking*. New York: Harper.

———. 1961 [1934]. 'On truth', in M. Henle, ed., *Documents of Gestalt Psychology*. Berkeley: University of California Press, 19–28.

———. 1961 [1935]. 'Some problems in the theory of ethics', in Henle, ed., *Documents of Gestalt Psychology*, 29–41.

———. 1967a [1925]. 'Gestalt theory', in Ellis (1967: 1–16).

———. 1967b [1923]. 'Laws of organization in perceptual forms', in Ellis (1967: 71–88).

Wertheimer, Michael. 1978. 'Humanistic psychology and the humane but tough-minded psychologist', *American Psychologist* 33: 739–45.

———, D.B. King, M.A. Peckler, S. Raney, and R.W. Schaef. 1992. 'Carl Jung and Max Wertheimer on a priority issue', *Journal of the History of the Behavioral Sciences* 28: 45–56.

Wertsch, J.V., ed. 1985. *Vygotsky and the Social Function of Mind*. Cambridge, Mass.: Harvard University Press.

——— and P. Tulviste. 1992. 'L.S. Vygotsky and contemporary developmental psychology', *Developmental Psychology* 28: 548–57.

Wertz, F.J. 1994. 'Of rats and psychologists: A study of the history and meaning of science', *Theory and Psychology* 4: 165–97.

———. 1998. 'The role of the humanistic movement in the history of psychology', *Journal of Humanistic Psychology* 38: 42–70.

Westen, D. 1998. 'The scientific legacy of Sigmund Freud: Toward a psychodynamically informed psychological science', *Psychological Bulletin* 124: 333–71.

Westkott, M. 1986. *The Feminist Legacy of Karen Horney*. New Haven: Yale University Press.

Wheelwright, P. 1966. *The Presocratics*. New York: Odyssey Press.

White, D.R., and A.Y. Wang. 1995. 'Universalism, humanism, and postmodernism', *American Psychologist* 50: 392–3.

White, G.S. 1992. 'G. Stanley Hall: From philosophy to developmental psychology', *Developmental Psychology* 28: 25–34.

Whorf, B.L. 1956. *Language, Thought and Reality*. Cambridge, Mass.: MIT Press.

Wilhelm, H. 1975. *Change*, trans. Cary F. Baynes. London: Routledge & Kegan Paul.

Wilhelm, R. 1967. 'Introduction', in *The I Ching, or Book of Changes*, trans. Cary F. Baynes. Princeton, NJ: Princeton University Press, xii–lxii.

Windholz, G. 1990. 'Pavlov and the Pavlovians in the laboratory', *Journal of the History of the Behavioral Sciences* 26: 64–74.

———. 1996. 'Pavlov's conceptualization of the dynamic stereotype in the theory of nervous activity', *American Journal of Psychology* 109: 287–95.

———. 1997. 'Ivan P. Pavlov: An overview of his life and psychological work', *American Psychologist* 52: 941–6.

Winner, E. 1982. *Invented Worlds*. Cambridge, Mass.: Harvard University Press.

Winston, A.S. 1990. 'R.S. Woodworth and the "Columbia Bible": How the psychological experiment was redefined', *American Journal of Psychology* 103: 391–401.

———. 1996. 'R.S. Woodworth's letters of reference and employment for Jewish psychologists in the 1930s', *Journal of the History of the Behavioral Sciences* 32: 30–43.

———. 2001. 'Cause into function: Ernst Mach and the reconstruction of explanation in psychology', in Green et al. (2001: 107–31).

Winter, A. 1998. *Mesmerized: Powers of Mind in Victorian Britain*. Chicago: University of Chicago Press.

Wisdom, J. 1957. *Philosophy and Psychoanalysis*. Cambridge: Basil Blackwell.

Witkin, H.A., H.B. Lewis, M. Hertzman, K. Machover, P.B. Meissner, and S. Wapner. 1954. *Personality through Perception*. New York: Harper.

Witmer, L. 1894. 'Zur experimentellen Aesthetik einfacher räumlicher Formverhältnisse [Toward an experimental aesthetic of simple spatial proportions]', *Philosophische Studien* 9: 96–144, 209–63.

Wittgenstein, L. 1953. *Philosophical Investigations*. Oxford: Basil Blackwell.

———. 1974 [1922]. *Tractatus Logico-philosophicus*. London: Routledge & Kegan Paul.

———. 1980. *Remarks on the Philosophy of Psychology*, vol. 2. Chicago: University of Chicago Press.

Wolfe, T. 1982. *From Bauhaus to Our House*. New York: Pocket Books.

Wolff, P. 1960. 'The developmental psychologies of Jean Piaget and psychoanalysis', *Psychological Issues* 2, 1 (Monograph 5).

Wollstonecraft, M. 1988 [1792]. 'A vindication of the rights of woman', in C.H. Poston, ed., *A Vindication of the Rights of Woman, an Authoritative Text, Backgrounds, the Wollstonecraft Debate, Criticism*. New York: Norton, 1–194.

Wolman, B.B. 1968. 'Immanuel Kant and his impact on psychology', in Wolman, ed., *Historical Roots of Contemporary Psychology*. New York: Harper & Row, 229–47.

Wolpe, J. 1958. *Psychotherapy by Reciprocal Inhibition*. Stanford, Calif.: Stanford University Press.

Woodworth, R.S. 1931. *Schools of Psychology*. New York: Ronald.

———. 1938. *Experimental Psychology*. New York: Holt.

———. 1940. *Psychology*, 4th edn. New York: Holt.

——— and H. Schlosberg. 1954. *Experimental Psychology*, 2nd edn. New York: Holt.

Wozniak, R. 1982. 'Metaphysics and science, reason and reality: The intellectual origins of genetic epistemology', in Broughton and Freeman-Moir (1982: 13–45).

———, ed. 1993a. *Theoretical Roots of Early Behaviorism: Functionalism, the Critique of Introspection, and the Nature and Evolution of Consciousness*. London: Routledge/Thomes Press.

———, ed. 1993b. *Experimental and Comparative Roots of Early Behaviorism: Studies of Animal and Infant Behavior*. London: Routledge/Thomes Press.

Wulf, M.D. 1959 [1922]. *The System of Thomas Aquinas*. New York: Dover.

Wulff, D.M. 1985. 'Experimental introspection and religious experience', *Journal of the History of the Behavioral Sciences* 21: 131–50.

Wundt, W. 1970 [1912]. 'The psychology of the sentence', in Blumenthal (1970: 20–31).

———. 1973 [1912]. *An Introduction to Psychology*. New York: Arno Press.

Yates, F.A. 1966. *The Art of Memory*. Chicago: University of Chicago Press.

Yerkes, R.M. 1948 [1921]. 'Psychological examining in the United States Army', in Dennis (1948: 528–40).

——— and S. Morgulis. 1909. 'The method of Pavlov in animal psychology', *Psychological Bulletin* 6: 264.

Young-Bruehl, E. 1988. *Anna Freud: A Biography*. New York: Summit.

Zangwill, O.L. 1972. 'Remembering revisited', *Quarterly Journal of Experimental Psychology* 24: 123–38.

Zaretsky, E. 1994. 'The attack on Freud', *Tikkun* 9: 65–70.

Zederland, L. 1988. 'The child-study legacy', *Journal of the History of the Behavioral Sciences* 24: 152–65.

Zeigarnik, B. 1967 [1927]. 'On finished and unfinished tasks', in Ellis (1967: 300–14).

INDEX